THE ART OF FEMINISM

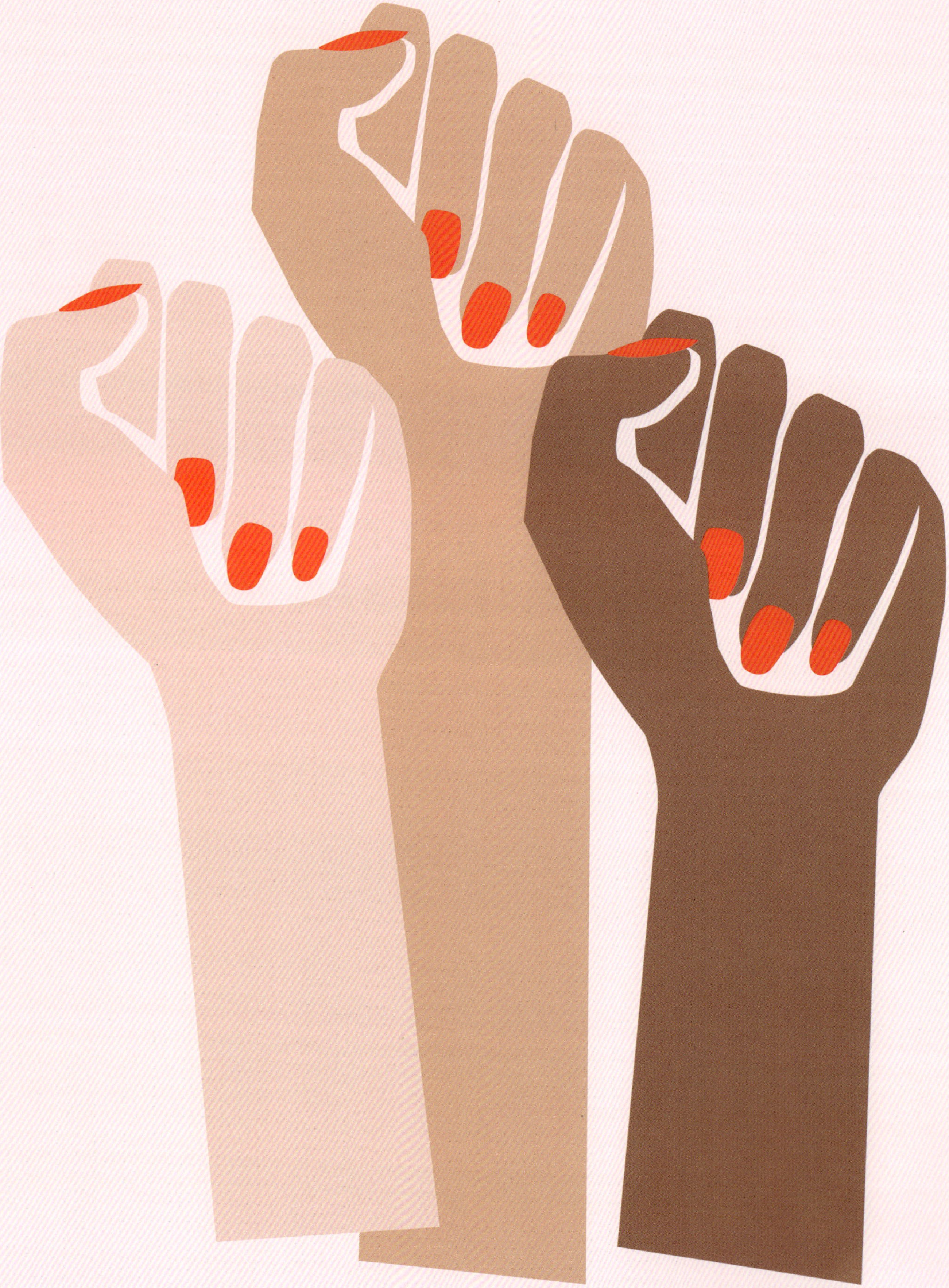

THE ART OF FEMINISM

Images that Shaped the Fight for Equality, 1857–2017

Helena Reckitt, Consultant Editor

Written by Lucinda Gosling, Hilary Robinson, and Amy Tobin

Preface by Maria Balshaw • Foreword by Xabier Arakistain

CHRONICLE BOOKS

SAN FRANCISCO

This 2018 edition published by Chronicle Books by arrangement with Elephant Book Company Limited, Southbank House, Black Prince Road, London SE1 7SJ, United Kingdom

Pages 264–265 constitute a continuation of the copyright page.

ISBN: 978-1-4521-6992-7

Manufactured in China

Cover: Femme Fists illustration copyright © by Deva Pardue,
For All Womankind, www.forallwomankind.com
Cover design by Kristen Hewitt

Editorial Director: Will Steeds
Executive Editor: Joanna de Vries
Project Editor: Anna Southgate
Book Design: Paul Palmer-Edwards
Picture Research: Sally Claxton; Katie Greenwood
Proofreader: Marion Dent
Indexer: Cheryl Hunston

For Chronicle Books: Natalie Butterfield

10 9 8 7 6 5 4 3 2 1

Chronicle Books LLC
680 Second Street
San Francisco, California 94107

www.chroniclebooks.com

Contents

Preface

Maria Balshaw, Director of Tate

I write this preface after a weekend where the United Kingdom witnessed a feminist performance on an epic scale. Many tens of thousands of women, in London, Glasgow, Newcastle, and from across the whole country, became *Processions*—a mass-movement art performance marking 100 years since partial suffrage was granted in the United Kingdom.

This collective performance, with women carrying and wearing banners and costumes in the purple, white, and green of the suffragette movement, created a feminist spectacle that closed the center of London as both protest and celebration. This two-fold orientation speaks of the gender conflicts of the past one hundred years, and the issues and challenges that are still part of our now. A more than one-hundred-year view is the admirable aspiration of this important text. This book reminds us, as *Processions* does, how feminism has always been a plural and intersectional movement, even if this has not always been acknowledged or properly addressed. The United Kingdom's 1918 suffrage victory was, of course, a limited emancipation of some white women and too many decades passed with change being felt in unequal measure across the differences of race, ethnicity, sexuality, and class.

The optimism of our now is that art and social mores are moving in nonbinary directions and, as this book vividly documents, we see an ever more plural feminist art practice meeting an engaged activism that seeks to shape an intersectional world view beyond gender and other hierarchies. In seeking to represent over a century of change, this collectively authored text allows us to see the long history of this kind of thinking in the practice of artists and to notice the ellisions and omissions we now also need to own. In taking us from the art of the original suffrage banners to the gender fluid activism of the present day, *The Art of Feminism* sets out in plain language the, as yet, incomplete story of feminist emancipation. We are all on that procession and there is still some way to go. As a feminist Director of Tate, I salute the multiple and contested practices of artists working within the wide variety of feminist paradigms traced by the authors and I commend the authors for their determination to encompass many world views.

Foreword

Xabier Arakistain, feminist curator, Bilbao, Spain

It was only fifty years ago that, lifted by the feminist activism of the 1960s and 1970s, women became permanently and centrally involved in art theory and practice. It was in that context, echoing Virginia Woolf's proposition about women and literature in *A Room of One's Own*, that American art historian Linda Nochlin first applied the renewed feminist perspective to art history with her now legendary article "Why Have There Been No Great Women Artists?," published in *Artnews* in 1971.

Nochlin's article revealed that art is one of the institutions that reproduce the enduring sociosexual order that maintains and perpetuates masculine hierarchy, which in those years came to be designated by a new term: the patriarchy. Nochlin's article inspired a series of studies, publications, and exhibitions devoted to recovering female artists who had been ignored or undervalued by official art history. It also provided the basis for a new paradigm of historiographical and curatorial practice that, at the risk of oversimplification, aims to include women and their work in the discipline.

Some felt this approach was insufficiently transformative because it would fail to incorporate the knowledge and political and social agenda of feminism. A decade later, in 1981, British art historians Griselda Pollock and Rozsika Parker published *Old Mistresses: Women, Art and Ideology*, in which they affirm that, contrary to popular belief at the time, women have always made art, and had not been systematically erased from the history of art until the twentieth century. They add that art made by women has been categorized as minor under the negative stereotype that they lacked creativity and were therefore unable to contribute to or influence the course of art. They stress that rather than merely being a means of excluding women, such stereotypes are absolutely foundational in the current construction of the discipline of art history and its canons. Therefore, they object to presenting the history of women in art merely as a struggle for inclusion in institutions such as art academies. In their view, this approach conceals the ways in which women have succeeded in making art in different contexts, despite being constrained as much by their sex as their class. Moreover, they emphasize that if we only see women's history as a progressive struggle for inclusion against great odds, we are falling into the trap of reaffirming the assumed, established, and often unconscious norms of the field as it has been shaped by men and male dominance. Finally, Parker and Pollock openly question the belief that women should fight for recognition in the current status quo, rather than focusing on dismantling it. In *Old Mistresses*, they establish the basis for the question that Pollock would ask in 1994, namely: "Can art history survive feminism?" She argues that, in her attempt to understand the nature and effects of feminist intervention, she cannot confine herself to the strict domain of the history of art and its discourse in the context of art history: to understand the effect of feminism she has to go far beyond art historical critical and interpretative schemas. In turn, Pollock's perspective has also inspired another historiographical and curatorial practice, focused on exhibiting and explaining the work of women artists from positions and terms different from those of dominant art criticism—a practice that Pollock herself has continuously explored. A valid objection to this approach is that the process of reevaluating artworks made by women may in some instances lead to a lack of critical appraisal of such works as a product of a specific patriarchal power relations.

Those of us who work in the field of art from feminist perspectives have witnessed how the crucial work of Nochlin and Pollock is periodically reactivated. *The Art of Feminism* contains numerous echoes of the debate alongside an extremely rich roster of thinkers and artists who worked, or are still working, in the intersections between art and feminism. The first section of the book demonstrates how the two positions are prefigured in the work of women prior to the women's liberation movement of the 1960s: On the one hand are those who appear simply to want to add women into the art world, while on the other, are those such as Sylvia Pankhurst, Claude Cahun, and Frida Kahlo, who appear to believe that the whole way of thinking that has produced this exclusion must be fundamentally altered. The debates come into sharp focus in the second section of the book, from the displacing of Jesus and his disciples with Georgia O'Keeffe and other American women artists in Mary Beth Edelson's work to the fragmentation of femininity by Polish artist Alina Szapocznikow or Austrian Renate Bertlmann, and the need to intersect structures of race and class with those of sex, as in the work of The Hackney Flashers and Carrie Mae Weems. This intersectionality increases in the third section of the book, after the fall of the Berlin Wall (1989) and 9/11 (2001), to highlight similar rifts between the assimilation of women into existing structures and the demand for fundamental shifts in culture. In conclusion, I would like to stress that, in the twenty-first century, we have learnt that both Nochlin's perspective and that of Pollock continue to posit two entirely relevant models for feminist intervention in the art world, and can even complement each other in different projects for art institutions.

Introduction

Helena Reckitt

This is the first book to present feminist interventions in art and visual culture from the nineteenth century to the current era. By no means an exhaustive history, and focusing primarily on the Western tradition, it nonetheless shows how women moved from the art world's margins to its centers. While claiming the visibility and space that had long been denied them, female artists demanded the transformation of the terms under which they had been excluded.

We see women assert their right to become subjects, and not just objects, of the gaze. The portraits created by female modernists have an almost performative ambition, as if by depicting confident, dynamic female subjects they might help bring about this longed-for liberation. Returning the gaze with a vengeance, women imbued images of themselves and one another with curiosity and desire. They experimented with masquerade and self-fashioning. "Masculine? Feminine? But it depends on the situation. Neuter is the only gender that always suits me," wrote Claude Cahun of her and Marcel Moore's staged photographs. "I will never finish removing all these masks."

Suffragettes understood the contagious power of spectacle. Their dramatic processions incorporated embroidered banners depicting allegorical figures of female heroism and grace. Protestors were urged to dress elegantly, to wear white dresses, accessorized in the suffrage color schemes: purple, white, and green in the United Kingdom; purple, white, and gold in the United States. Designed to win hearts and minds, and to counter stereotypes of feminist dowdiness, their campaigns were reproduced widely in newspapers. Half a century later, women's liberation activists also used mass media to disseminate their message. The 1970 anti-Miss World protest in London, during which Angry Brigade members pelted flour bombs at the contestants, was broadcast live, reaching almost twenty-four million viewers. Feminists drew sustenance from seeing, and being seen, together. Asked why she attended a women's liberation demonstration in 1971, one participant replied, "we wanted to come together and look at each other."

Throughout the periods surveyed here artists have critiqued the degrading, stereotyped, and fetishistic depictions of women that appear in art and popular culture. Combining image and text in their work, they have experimented with strategies of estrangement to highlight the constructed nature of gender. Some artists refuse to represent women altogether. Hélène Cixous's argument that women must write from the self and the body resonated within feminist art circles. Evoking bodily experience, they made artworks that disrupt deep-seated patriarchal divisions between reason and passion, mind and matter. Filmmaker Laura Mulvey urged feminists to create "a new language of desire," a call that artists from Mary Kelly to Theresa Hak Kyung Cha have taken up. The psychoanalytical concept of jouissance, an experimental practice that ruptures the male symbolic order, has been generative for feminist art. That jouissance relates to the culturally feminine, rather than biologically female, chimes with current understandings of gender fluidity. Contemporary artist Heather Phillipson devises haptic installations that celebrate bodily functions, creating a state of heightened excitement. Operating almost synaesthetically, tropes echo and rhyme across screens, objects, and soundscapes. Like artists Carolee Schneemann and Joan Jonas before her, Phillipson frequently explores relationships between human and nonhuman animals, and is alert to the agency of objects and matter.

Feminists have given symbolic value to denigrated realms of female creativity and experience, from eroticism and sex work to friendship, conversation, childbirth, and housework. By staging acts associated with domestic and parental labor in the museum, artists such as Mierle Laderman Ukeles, Lea Lublin, and Lenka Clayton highlight society's reliance on this under-seen, undervalued work. Yet feminists have contested the idea that women are inherently more nurturing, domestically inclined, or peaceful than men. They recognize that naturalizing feminine activities, and suggesting that they are performed as labors of love, only perpetuates feminized subjects' exploitation and their work's devaluation.

Where some feminist artists invent fictional and mythic characters with whom to identify, others scour the past for evidence of creative women and female relationships. Intergenerational calls-and-responses play out across artworks. Mary Cassatt's 1893 mural for The Women's Building imagines female exchanges over the eras. Decades later, Miriam Schapiro includes a reproduction of one of Cassatt's portraits in *Mary Cassatt and Me*, 1975. Maud Sulter pays homage to nine black female muses, including novelist Alice Walker and Ysaye Maria Barnwell from Sweet Honey in the Rock, in her 1989 Zabat series, its title referencing forms of embodied knowledge including ritual and dance.

The use of female subjects and bodies has taken on new contours in online contexts. While feminist artists were among those to criticize the internet's military/industrial origins, many, including SubRosa, VNS Matrix, and Lucy Kimbell, were key particpants in the Netart movement of the 1990s in which art was circulated, and often made, online. They responded to the internet's potential for initiating more expansive forms of communication and collaboration, intimacy, and identity. Recently, however, Net optimism has given way to Net cynicism. Feminists have critiqued the internet's commodification of all aspects of life and subjectivity, highlighting its increasingly predictive and preemptive operations. Hito Steyerl is among artists who explore how to withdraw from the internet's regime of surveillance, as well as how to inhabit it critically and

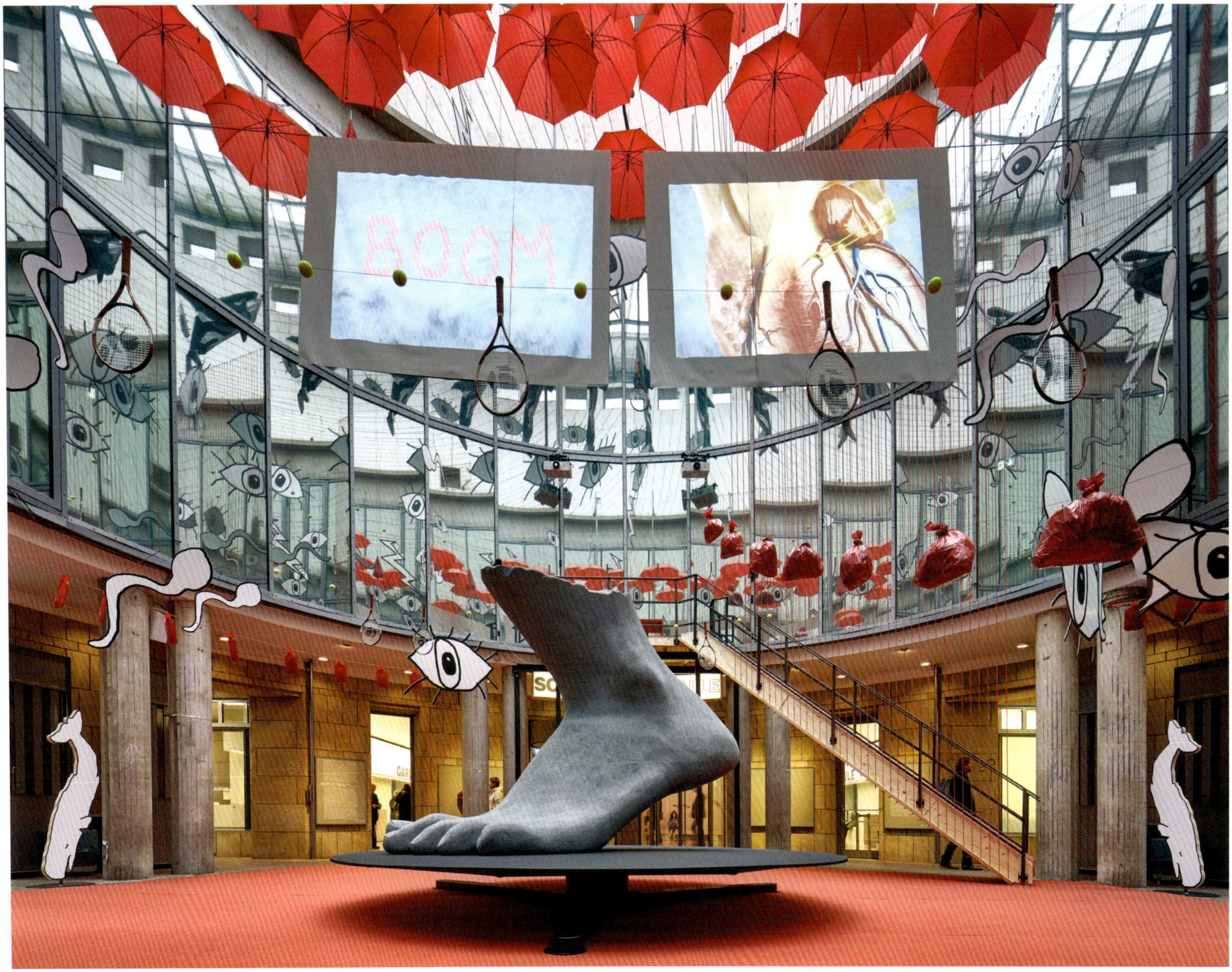

Above: **Heather Phillipson, *EAT HERE*, 2015–16**

Animated with objects that evoke the intensive effects of activities ranging from tennis, sex, and excessive consumption, to being caught in the rain, the rotunda of the Schirn Kunsthalle Frankfurt becomes a circulatory system in Heather Phillipson's *EAT HERE*. *COMMISERATIONS!*, a looped video at the installation's center, depicts a beating heart, underlining the mood of sensory overload, vulnerability, and risk. Sampling the languages of poetry, experimental film, pop art, hip-hop, and social media, Phillipson's work generates haptic responses that surpass the cognitive.

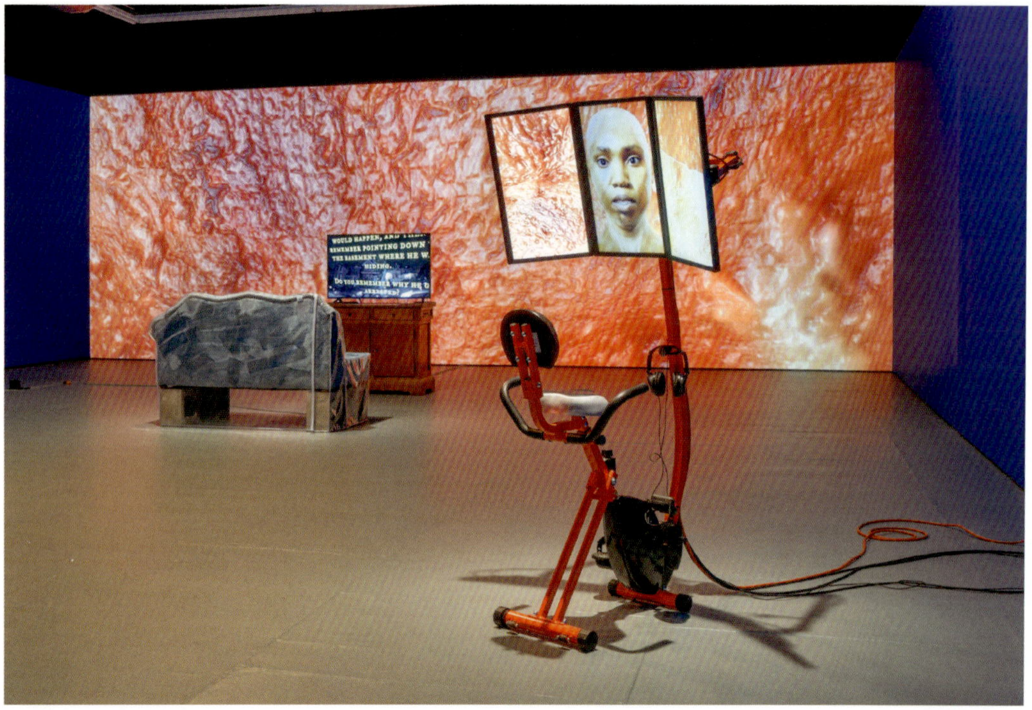

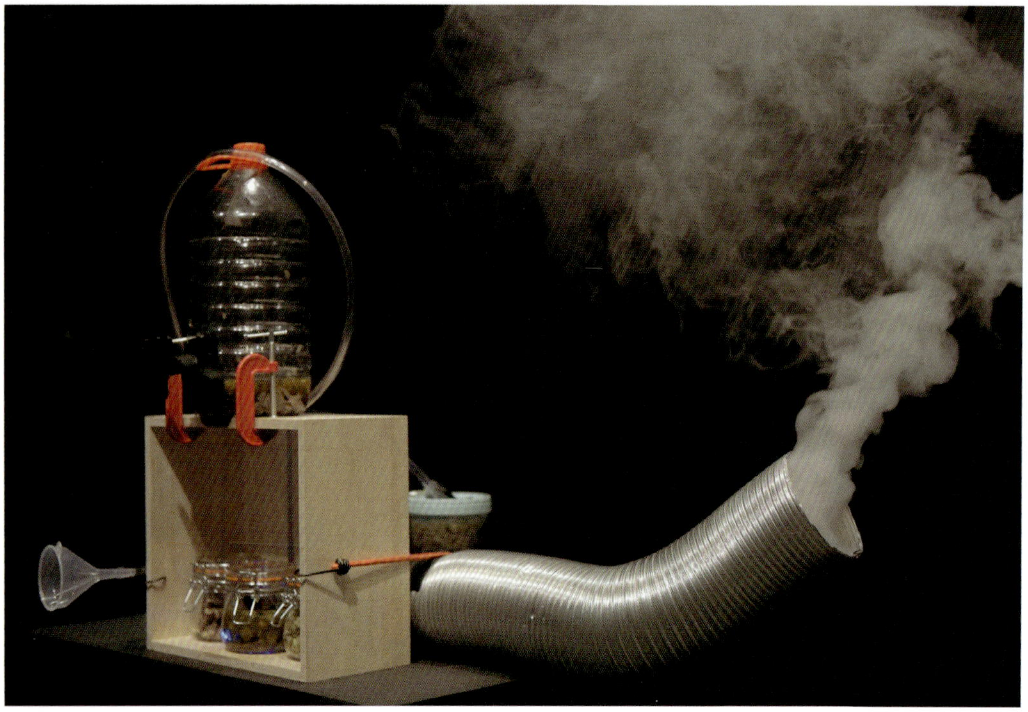

Top: **Sondra Perry, *Resident Evil*, 2016**

Microscopic projections of the artist's skin cells, pulsating like lava or flames, form a backdrop to Sondra Perry's exhibition. LCD monitors mounted on bicycle workstations encourage visitors to exercise while they watch, contrasting the wellness industry's insistence on productivity and self-management with the vulnerability of the black lives evoked. Videos incorporating found footage, including smartphone videos taken by witnesses of police brutality, underscore how social media is haunted by images of black death. A 3D avatar based on Perry's features suggests a more resistant response to AI capture that exceeds the flattening produced by existing formats: "We're the second version of ourselves that we know of," it intones, "rendered to her fullest ability," with limits, as she "could not replicate her fatness in the software that was used to make us."

Bottom: **Candice Lin and Patrick Staff, *Hormonal Fog*, 2016**

Vapor made from extracts of licorice and black cohosh, plants known to suppress the body's production of testosterone, creates a slow-forming cloud in *Hormonal Fog*. Installed in the exhibition *LESBIAN GULLS, DEAD ZONES, SWEAT AND T*, within a hexagonal frame mimicking benzene's chemical compound, the work alludes to contemporary practices of biohacking and gendered self-determination. Incorporating unofficial genealogies of botanical knowledge, the work evokes the permeability of bodies and subjectivities, and the transmissibility of affects across human and nonhuman agents.

disruptively. Meanwhile, artists such as E. Jane and Sondra Perry deploy fictional personae and avatars both to play with and disrupt assumptions about gendered and racial identities.

Reflecting how business profits from human data trails, and mimicking venture capitalist practices, in 2014 Jennifer Lyn Monroe incorporated herself as JLM Inc. She evaluated and issued shares in her material and intangible assets and raised capital based on her potential success. Similarly, Erica Scourti attempts to repurpose platforms of networked capitalism. Her "live twitter bot with feelings," *Empathy Deck*, responds to its followers' tweets by sending them one-of-a-kind empathy cards that combine images and inspirational text. For her 2014 book *The Outage*, Scourti gave a writer access to her online passwords and accounts, on which he then drew to ghostwrite her memoir. We see related tactics of hyperbolic mimicry in the work of other artists, including Andrea Fraser and Tanja Ostojić.

Scourti likens her approach to Paul B. Preciado's account of self-administering testosterone as a form of overidentifying with "pharmacopornographic capital." Preciado's understanding of bodies as a locus of chemical, hormonal, and cosmetic modification finds resonance in Candice Lin and Patrick Staff's *Hormonal Fog*, 2016, in which testosterone-reducing, plant-based tinctures are pumped into the gallery foyer. Transgender politics are nonetheless a lightning rod for contemporary feminist debate. Faultlines have emerged between trans-exclusionary radical feminists (TERFS) who insist that only people born as women can lay claim to that gender, and other feminists who see claiming trans or nonbinary gender identity as a central tenet of the feminist struggle for self-determination.

For the 2016 online curatorial project *URL IRL* members of the black female collective sorryyoufeeluncomfortable collaborated with curator Francesca Altamura to ask where the internet ends and the real world begins. Discussing the program, artist and cocurator Deborah Findalter highlighted the unequal ways that black female bodies circulate online. Where content generated by black women often goes viral, those women rarely receive recognition or pay for their meme-ified images and words. In Zarina Muhammad's *Digjihad*, 2015, a work included in the program, leotard-clad women dance over videos of military and terrorist actions—stitched together from a compilation including iPhone footage, CCTV, computer games, and state and terrorist propaganda. Mischievously jamming viral tropes, including GIFs, emojis, and bhangra dance moves, Muhammad calls out the contagious nature of macho glamorizations of violence.

While hypersexualized representations of black female bodies circulate as commodities online and off, the perspectives of women of color are often sidelined. "White feminism has failed the true test of feminist solidarity," Myriam François-Cerrah wrote in 2014, treating non-Western critiques as "quaint contributions permitted to confirm the eternal truth of Western supremacy." Meanwhile, the goal of female liberation is used to justify imperialist wars and occupations, with women from the Arab world stereotyped as passive victims and grateful recipients of Western aid. Some artists have developed strategies that aim to challenge white supremacy. Trinh T. Minh-ha makes experimental films in proximity to, rather than on behalf of, subaltern individuals and groups. Using the hypervisibility of Hollywood, in *Love Story* (2016), Candice Breitz cast celebrity actors to narrate the accounts of people who had fled their homes due to sexual and gender prejudice and violence. On an institutional level, resonating with Flavia Dzodan's mantra, "My feminism will be intersectional or it will be bullshit," arts organizations have initiated activities that foreground global feminist struggles. The Showroom has developed its artist commission program in collaboration with community groups in London, including a woman's shelter and Justice for Domestic Workers. In 2017, basis voor actuele kunst (BAK) in Utrecht launched *Propositions for Non-Fascist Living*, a research itinerary designed to contest the normalization and internalization of fascisms, and to institute new realities.

The sustainability of an art world that relies on feminized labor—care, passion, flexibility, communication—while making it hard for many workers in the sector to support themselves, is of increasing feminist concern. While continuing to pressurize institutions into giving fairer representation to artists from diverse backgrounds, feminists also question the logic of participating in a system that undermines their ability to care for themselves and others. Céline Condorelli, Park McArthur, Raju Rage, and A.L. Steiner are among artists who highlight the networks of kinship and mutual aid that enable cultural and social survival. Curators and organizational directors are realizing that it is not enough to exhibit feminist art and program feminist content if the host institution's values contradict the politics on show. Binna Choi, Director of Utrecht's CASCO, argues that the "back" of purportedly radical institutions needs to reflect more accurately their public "front." For *Site for Unlearning (Art Organisation*; 2014–ongoing), Choi and her coworkers collaborated with artist Annette Krauss to interrogate ingrained institutional behaviors. They concluded that their preoccupation with being busy and productive had created exploitative conditions for themselves and those they worked with that emphasized productivity over collective care. Through "unlearning exercises" they sought to make the maintenance activities that supported the organization more visible, valued, and equitably distributed.

Feminism can be adapted and diluted to mean different things to different people. To rediscover feminism's radicalism and relevance, artists today revisit feminist art, thinking, and activism history. Sharon Hayes describes her artworks, which often restage events from queer feminist history, as "placeholders" that try to keep earlier moments of political promise alive. Alex Martinis Roe, whose art establishes feminist genealogies and forges intergenerational feminist networks, works in a spirit of "dutifully undutiful" feminism. "Fans of feminism" is art historian Catherine Grant's term for the combined playfulness, reverence, and critique with which artists revisit feminism's past. By creating feminist cultures and awakening feminist subjectivities, their art helps us to understand and imagine the world differently.

Suffrage and Beyond

1857–1949

Part 1

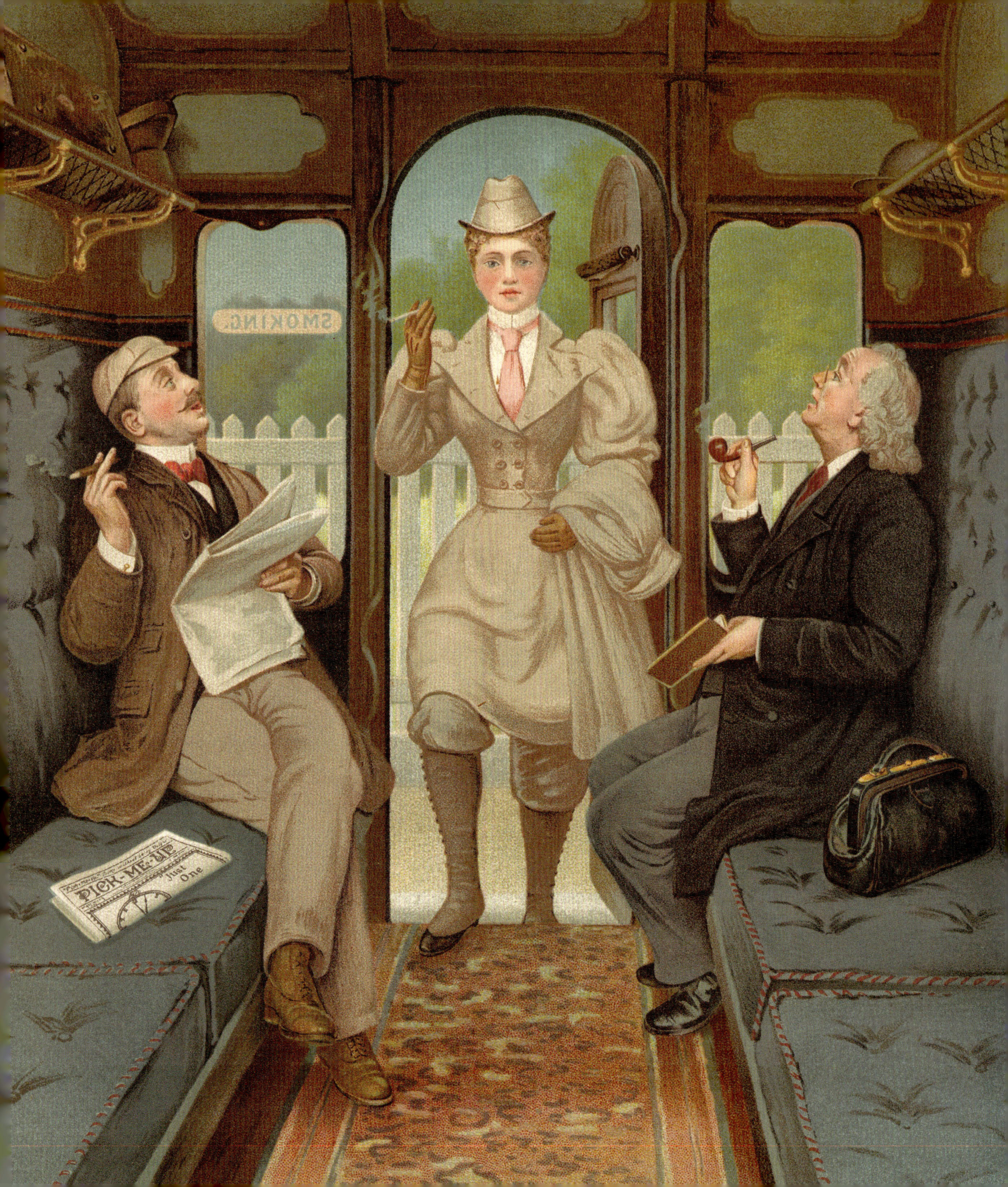
SMOKING
PICK-ME-UP
Just One

Femininity and Freedom

From Being Seen to Being Heard

1

"To really excel in Art one should live for that alone, is her opinion, though unfortunately this is rarely, if ever possible to a woman, who has many calls upon her time and energy and is not often able to give herself up entirely to her career."

Mary Ellen Edwards, in an interview in *The Girl's Own Paper*, 1907

When a group of avant-garde artists exhibited for the first time in Paris, in 1874, and under the name The Anonymous Society of Painters, Sculptors, Engravers, etc., the art world was bewildered. The unnatural colors were baffling, the stippling and unfinished daubing surely a mistake? Two years later, at another of the group's exhibitions, art critic Louis Leroy derided Claude Monet's *Impression, Sunrise*, as inferior to wallpaper, while French newspaper *Le Figaro* wrote dismissively of "an exhibition of what is said to be painting . . . Five or six lunatics, of whom one is a woman, have chosen to exhibit their works. There are people who burst into laughter in front of these objects. Personally I am saddened by them."

The female "lunatic" was Berthe Morisot, who had grown up in a bourgeois family where she had received private art lessons. Showing conspicuous talent, she studied under the Barbizon painter Jean-Baptiste-Camille Corot, became a copyist at the Louvre, and began to exhibit her work, eventually attracting the attention of the art dealer Paul Durand-Ruel, whose championing of the impressionists—as this group of artists came to be known—would be the driving factor in their eventual success. Another prominent female member of the group was the American Mary Cassatt, responsible, through her high-society connections, for introducing impressionist art to an enthusiastic American audience. These women were exceptional, not just because of their artistic talent, but because of their status as professional artists.

Until this time, art was simply part of an arsenal of feminine accomplishments women were expected to learn, not a skill with which to build a career and gain public recognition. Women's magazines and instruction manuals regularly suggested drawing as a hobby to their readers. *Godey's Lady's Book*, with a circulation of 150,000 in the United States during the 1860s and 1870s, featured "A Course of Lessons in Drawing," though more pages focused on needlework and decorative art for the household. In 1842, British writer Sarah Stickney Ellis addressed the subject of art and its benefits to young women in *Daughters of England*, one of four popular advice manuals she authored: "Amongst these advantages" she wrote "I will begin with the least—it is quiet. It disturbs no one; for however defective the performance may be, it does not necessarily, like music, jar upon the sense. It is true, it may when seen offend the practised eye; but we can always draw in private, and keep our productions to ourselves."

Underpinning each of Ellis's books was the firm belief that, as a wife and mother, a woman's prime purpose in life was to instill strong moral values and Christian beliefs into the next generation and, consequently, any learning or cultivation of talents was exercised purely within the framework of family obligations. In her previous manual, *Women of England*, Ellis had suggested that women might earn money from such dainty pastimes as engraving or drawing embroidery patterns. It was clear from such periodicals that women's innate creativity was in no doubt. For generations, across the globe, women had been makers of tapestries, quilts, samplers, rugs, and clothes. But there is no suggestion that a woman might practice what was considered "fine art," or that she could seek formal training and perhaps exhibit her paintings in public. While women continued to practice art without tuition or professional encouragement, they remained invisible with little opportunity to improve or to challenge the status quo of the male-dominated art world. But the following decades would see persistent attempts to challenge this monopoly, a movement that, unsurprisingly, was to dovetail with a growing political activism culminating in the very visible campaign for female suffrage at the end of the nineteenth century.

Around the same time Sarah Stickney Ellis was disseminating her vision of the Victorian feminine ideal in Britain, a young woman in Paris was frequenting abattoirs and veterinary schools, in order to pursue her own creative ambitions. Rosa Bonheur, who specialized in animal painting, became one of the most famous artists of the nineteenth century. She began to exhibit in 1840 and, by 1855, had produced her best-known work, *The Horse Fair*. Bonheur subverted all traditional preconceptions of the "feminine" artist. With a permit to do so from the French government, she wore trousers, boots, and a smock while out sketching, claiming they were practical and allowed her some camouflage in such a male environment. She remained unmarried, living instead with two women—her childhood friend Nathalie Micas until Nathalie's death in 1889, and in her latter years, another artist, Anna Klumpke. Bonheur had no qualms over earning a substantial income, commenting, "I mean to earn a good deal of 'filthy lucre' for it is only with that you can do what you like." Clearly understanding the relationship between financial security, independence, and creative freedom, hers was a declaration that bore particular resonance at the time. In the 1850s, married women, regardless of their wealth prior to marriage or of any subsequent earnings or inheritance, legally owned nothing, with all money subsumed under their husbands' names.

Page 14: Entering the male domain. From the masculine attire to the lit cigarette, this unattributed illustration from the British *Pick-Me-Up* magazine ca. 1900, plays to the frequent visual stereotypes associated with the "New Woman" of the late nineteenth century. Regardless of the consternation of her male traveling companions, it is an image that reflects a growing desire among many women to challenge the proscribed Victorian feminine ideal of the "angel of the home" and to seek out the same opportunities and spaces as men.

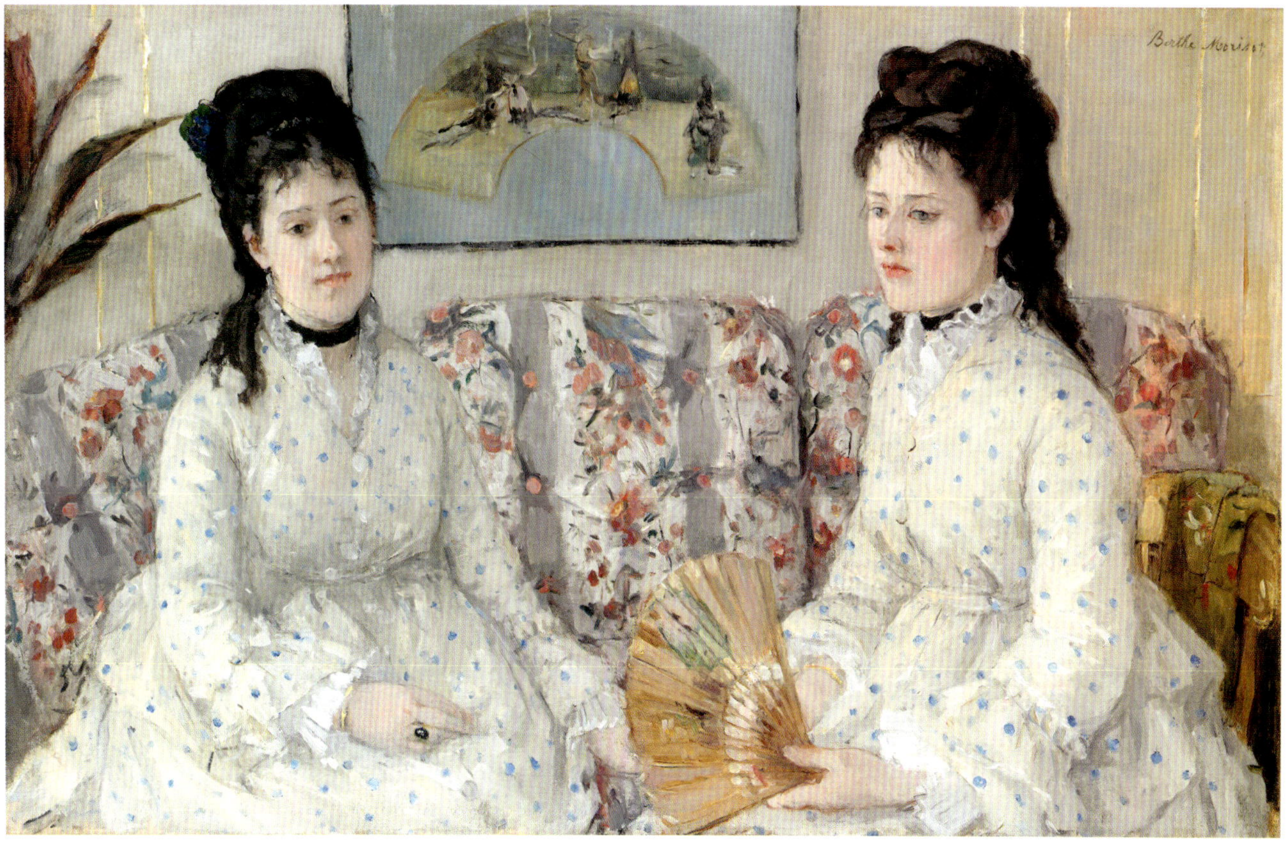

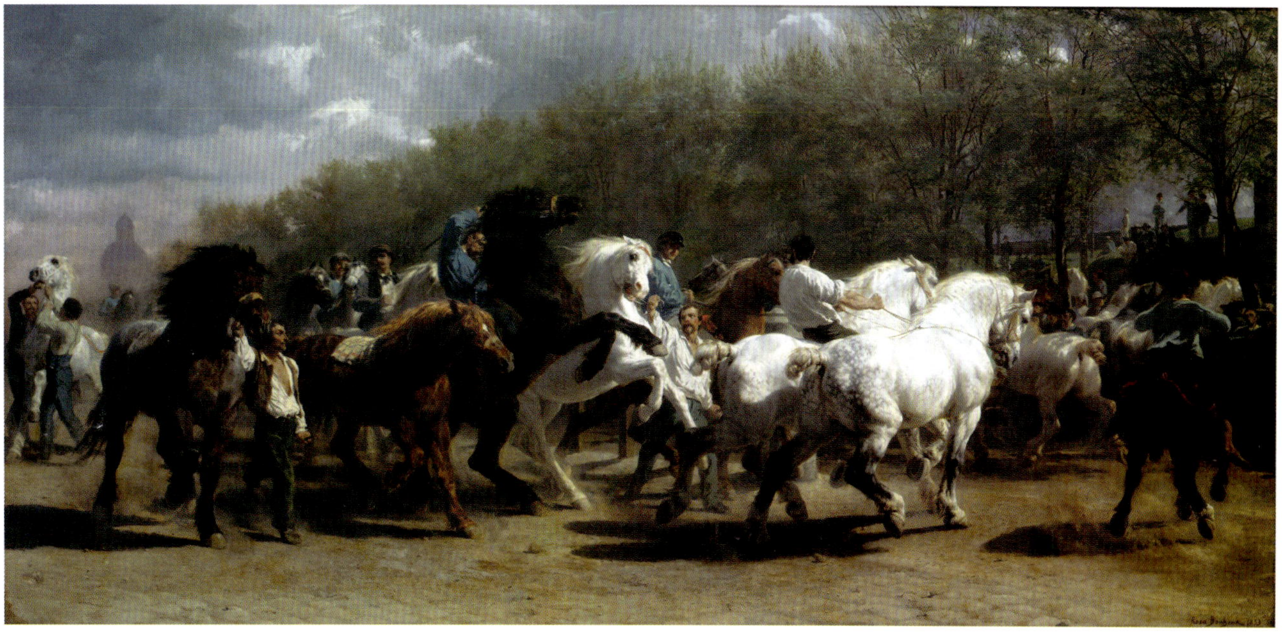

Top: Berthe Morisot, *The Sisters*, 1869

Morisot, at the center of the impressionist circle, and with a successful career lasting thirty years, frequently used family members as sitters, visiting themes of domesticity, motherhood, familial ties, and contemporary fashions, rendered in a loose and spontaneous style. The color white featured prominently in many paintings, including this one, in which her sisters Yves and Edma, in matching dresses, are pictured with a Japanese fan and framed fan design, hinting at the fashionable, bourgeois tastes of the period.

Bottom: Rosa Bonheur, *The Horse Fair*, 1855

Rosa Bonheur's status as one of the nineteenth-century's greatest painters was sealed with this immense canvas. Measuring a vast 16 x 8 ft (4.9 x 2.4 m), it caused an artistic sensation when exhibited at the Paris Salon in 1855. Later that year, the art dealer Ernest Gambart bought the painting and toured it around Britain, including a private viewing at Windsor Castle at the request of Queen Victoria. The painting's ambitious size and muscular dynamism proved there need be no limitations on the subjects women chose to portray.

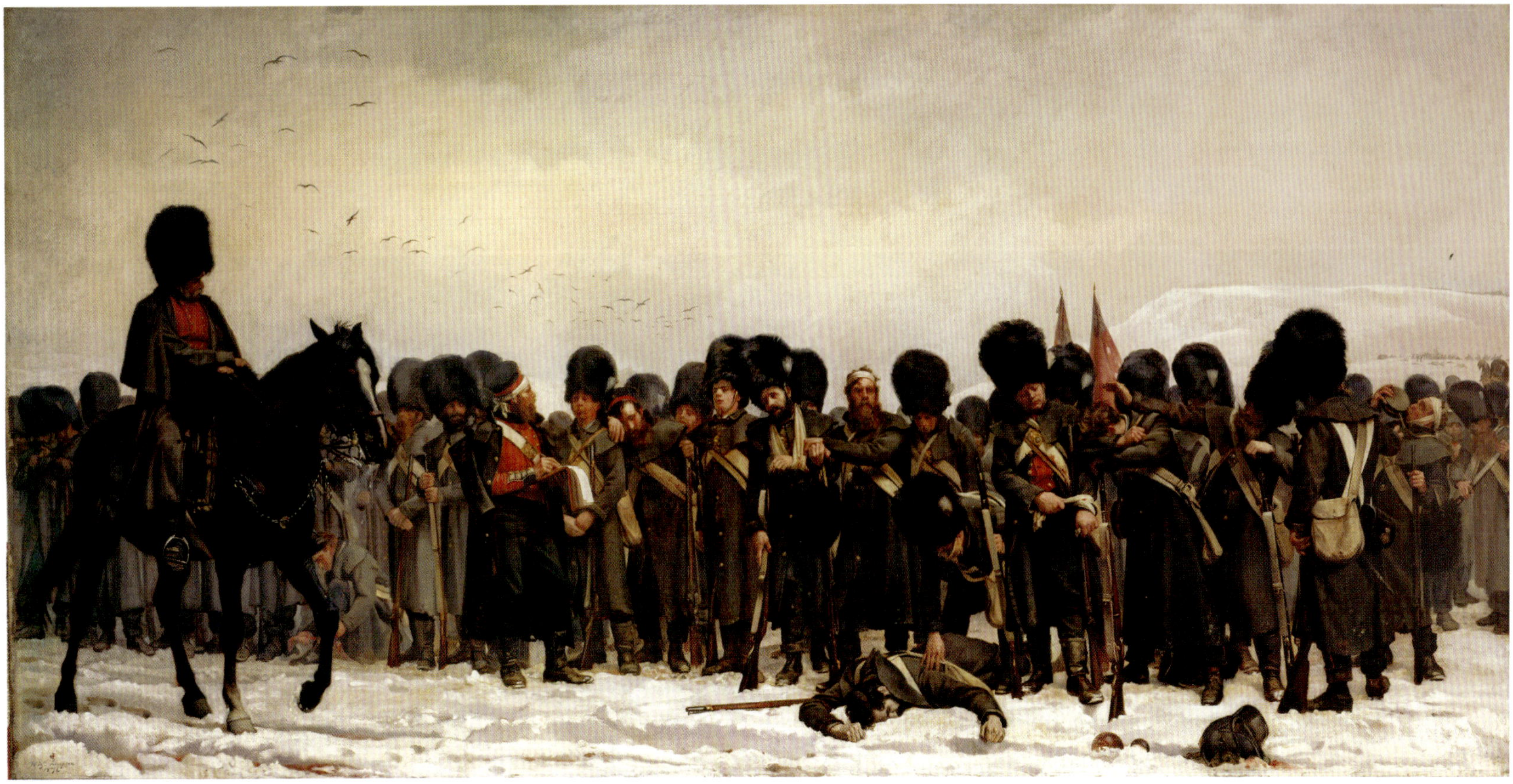

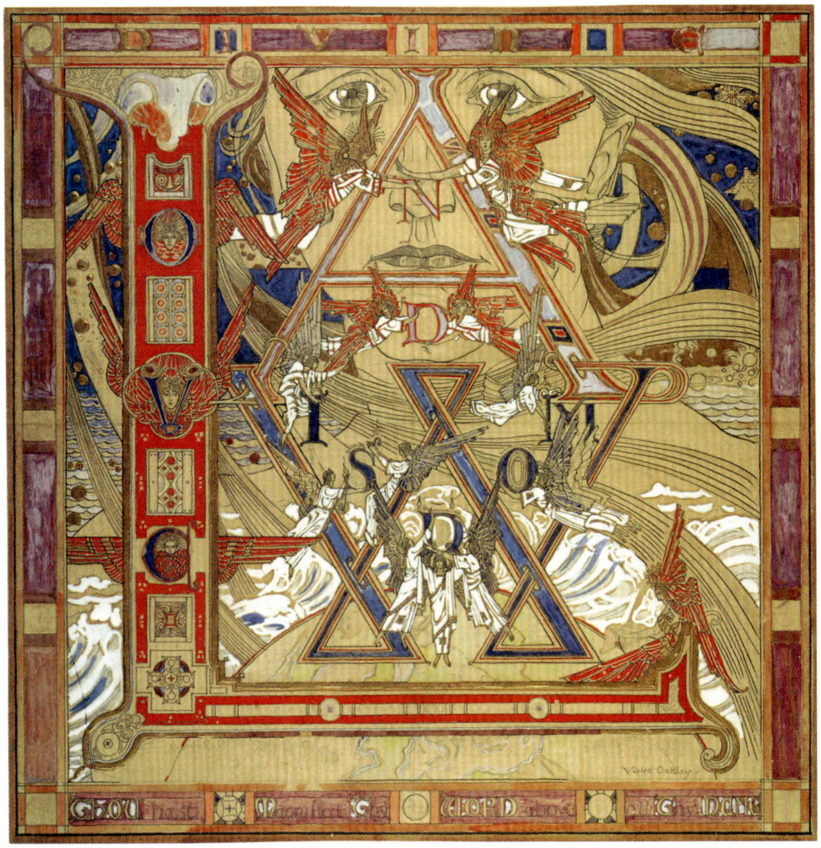

Top: Elizabeth Thompson, Lady Butler, *The Roll Call*, 1874

When *The Roll Call* was exhibited at the Royal Academy in 1874, a policeman was engaged to control the crowds desperate to see this new kind of military painting, which gave a sympathetic portrayal of the suffering of the ordinary soldier. Despite her popularity, Lady Butler had endured the challenges facing many women painters during this period. As an art student, she had felt such frustration at the endless drawing of plaster casts at the Female School that she paid for a private life class complete with an "undraped female." She was rejected as a member of the academy three times between 1879 and 1881.

Bottom: Violet Oakley, Study for "*Divine Law*," ca. 1917

Oakley studied art under Cecilia Beaux at the Pennsylvania Academy of the Fine Arts and then under the tutorship of illustrator Howard Pyle at Drexel University. Pyle, recognizing her strong graphic talent, encouraged her to take up mural painting. This design, interweaving celtic style lettering and art nouveau figures, was one of a series of murals she painted for the Supreme Court Room in the Pennsylvania State Capitol in Harrisburg, the first public commission of its kind carried out by a woman.

In July 1848, in the United States, Elizabeth Cady Stanton and a group of female Quakers organized a convention at Seneca Falls in New York, which served as the first public discussion of women's rights. Debating a number of issues concerning women's moral, social, and political rights, the meeting ended with one hundred signatories to a Declaration of Sentiments in which women's right to vote was a central argument. In 1855, Massachusetts became the first state in America to pass its own Married Women's Property Act, allowing married women to own and sell real and personal property, to control their earnings, to sue, and to make wills. A few months later, a parliamentary petition in Britain gathered 26,000 signatures in support of reform of married women's property laws. Prominent among the organizers of this campaign was Barbara Leigh Smith (later Bodichon), an artist herself, and Bessie Rayner Parkes, founder of the feminist *English Woman's Journal* in 1858. The petition failed to make an impact, but was the beginning of a growing tide of political challenge. However, married women in Britain would have to wait until 1870 for the first women's property act to be made law, and a further twelve years before an act that gave them parity with their husbands.

It is significant that so many women artists, such as Barbara Leigh Smith, were at the vanguard of agitation for this change, and natural that they should also campaign for equality within their profession. Here were women who had left the notion of the lady amateur behind and who were exhibiting and selling their work, carving out a rightful place within the art world. To hone their craft, more affluent aspiring women artists would travel, often in pairs or groups, to Europe—to Paris, Rome, or Munich—where they might study with private tutors and absorb the culture. In Britain, the schools of the Royal Academy (RA) were considered the pinnacle of art training but even though two women, Angelica Kauffman and Mary Moser, had been foundation members, no female members had been elected since, nor could women enroll to study there. In 1860, Laura Herford gained admission, simply because the drawings she submitted for the entrance exam were signed with only her initials. With her gender cloaked, and judged on her art alone, her application was a success, much to the bemusement of the male academicians who could find no rules to deny her entry. What should have been a trailblazing moment stuttered to a halt in 1863, however, when it was voted by the academy that no further female students should be admitted. To keep quotas up, a further handful of women were admitted in 1867, but it was not until 1922 that another woman, Annie Swynnerton, was elected as an associate member, while Dame Laura Knight became the first woman to be elected a full member in 1936. Women wishing to study in Paris, considered the epicenter of the artistic world, fared little better; they were not allowed to attend the École des Beaux-Arts, the country's leading art academy, until 1897. In comparison, women artists in the United States found their art schools more receptive. The portraitist Sarah Peale and her sister Anna Claypoole were the first women to become members of the prestigious Pennsylvania Academy of the Fine Arts (PAFA) as early as 1824, though it would be another two decades before female students were welcomed through its doors.

By the end of the century, art was becoming a legitimate vocation for women. The 1891 census in Britain had 3,032 women listing their occupations as painters or engravers. This represented just one-third of the number of men defining themselves in the same way, but it was more than double the number recorded in the previous decade. In the United States, many mixed-sex art schools had, at times, a ratio of 80 percent female students to 20 percent male.

Progress did not solve the challenge of combining a career with marriage and motherhood, a dilemma that rarely troubled male artists. The English artist Mary Ellen Edwards forged a successful career as a magazine illustrator during the 1860s and 1870s, contributing to titles such as *Good Words*, *The Cornhill Magazine*, and *The Graphic*. The last, particularly prestigious, would eventually employ her as a paid member of staff. It was a fruitful time for the illustrated periodical, with work aplenty for talented illustrators and engravers. But it was also a fiercely competitive male arena, making Edwards's success all the more remarkable. Some women gave up art after marrying, others had their careers cut tragically short when they died in childbirth, the fate of both American artist May Alcott Nieriker and the German Paula Modersohn-Becker. There were also women who made a success of being working mothers, such as Helen Allingham, Laura Herford's niece. One of the most popular British artists of the nineteenth century, Allingham often painted her three children in her idyllic scenes of rural life, an art genre that may have been easier to combine with motherhood than the military subjects that were the specialization of fellow British artist Elizabeth Thompson. For some, art was a financial necessity, as in the case of Louise Jopling, who separated from her first husband in 1871 and, with two sons to raise, took to painting professionally, eventually founding her own art school. Other women chose relationships beyond the boundaries of contemporary convention. The American muralist Violet Oakley, the first woman to receive the Gold Medal of Honor from the PAFA, lived openly with her life partner, Edith Emerson, for forty years.

Acceptance and access to an art education were the defining themes in the late nineteenth century, allowing women to claim their position as artists with talent and ability to equal that of men. There was still much ground to cover—black or working-class women artists are significant by their absence during this period—but those who did blaze a trail did so in parallel with the women's rights movement of the 1850s, and the power of the visual image to further this cause would be fully exploited in time. English novelist George Eliot (Mary Anne Evans), after viewing Rosa Bonheur's *Bocairus Crossing the Pyrenees* at the French Gallery in 1857, wrote to a friend exclaiming, "What Power! This is the way women should assert their rights." The first decade of the twentieth century would see women do exactly that.

Below: **Mary Cassatt, *In the Loge*, 1878**

Philadelphia-born Mary Cassatt spent three years in Paris building her reputation as an artist before she was invited by Edgar Degas to exhibit at the fourth impressionist exhibition. *In the Loge*, showing a scene at a matinee at the Théâtre-Français, is typical of Cassatt's subject matter, which drew on her own experiences as an unmarried woman in the French capital. Ignoring the impudent, yet impotent, gaze of a male admirer in the distance, Cassatt's independent theater-goer confidently surveys the auditorium through her opera glasses, casting her as bold onlooker rather than vulnerable object.

Opposite: **Lilly Martin Spencer, *Young Husband: First Marketing*, 1854**

Lilly Spencer used her own husband as the model for this lighthearted commentary on married life, in which a young man, sent grocery shopping by his wife, feels the sting of public humiliation as the contents of his basket tumble to the ground. This role switch, though carried out in the naive romantic flush of early marriage, is an unusual subject and offers an alternative to the conventional nuclear family traditionally depicted in most mid-nineteenth century art.

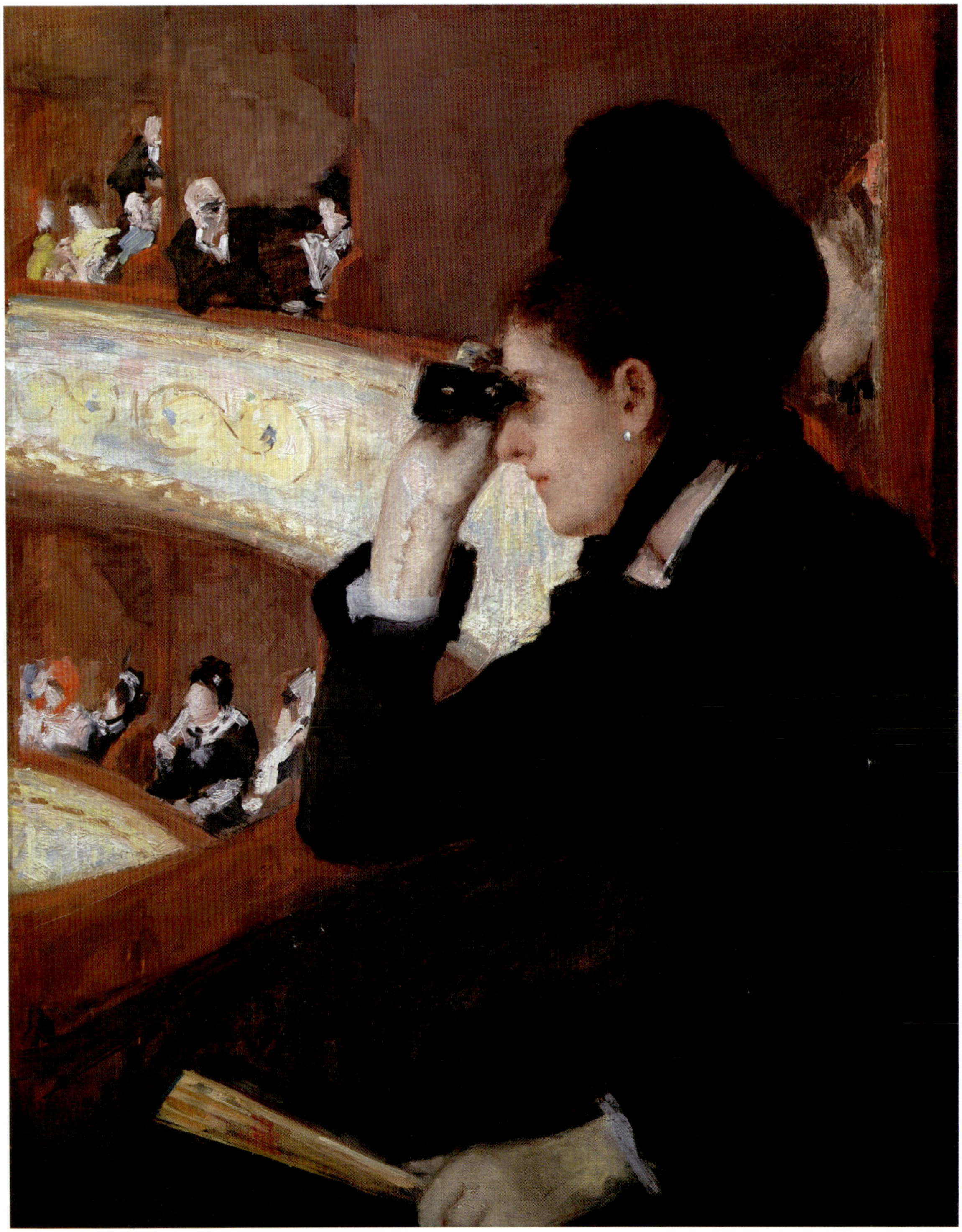

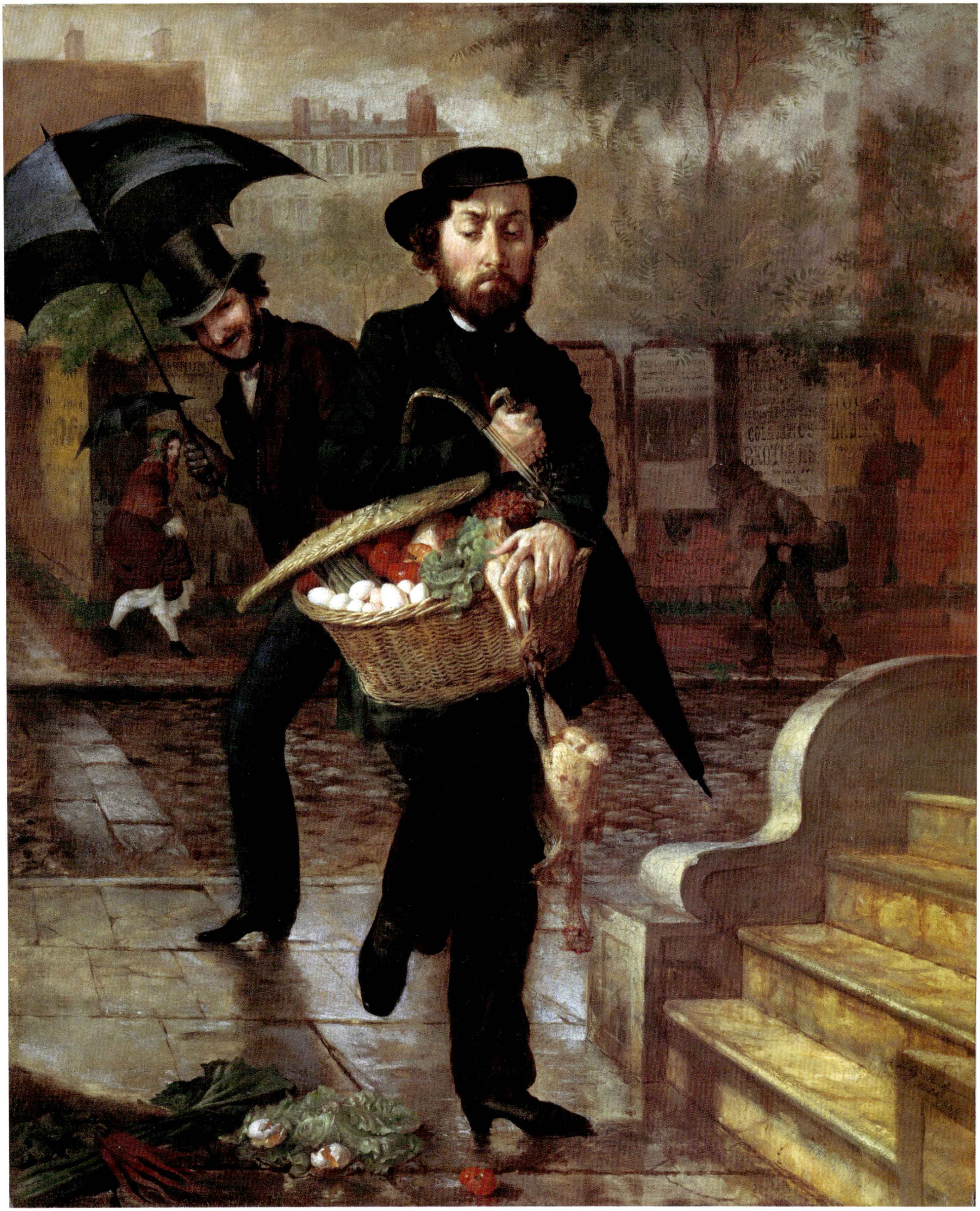

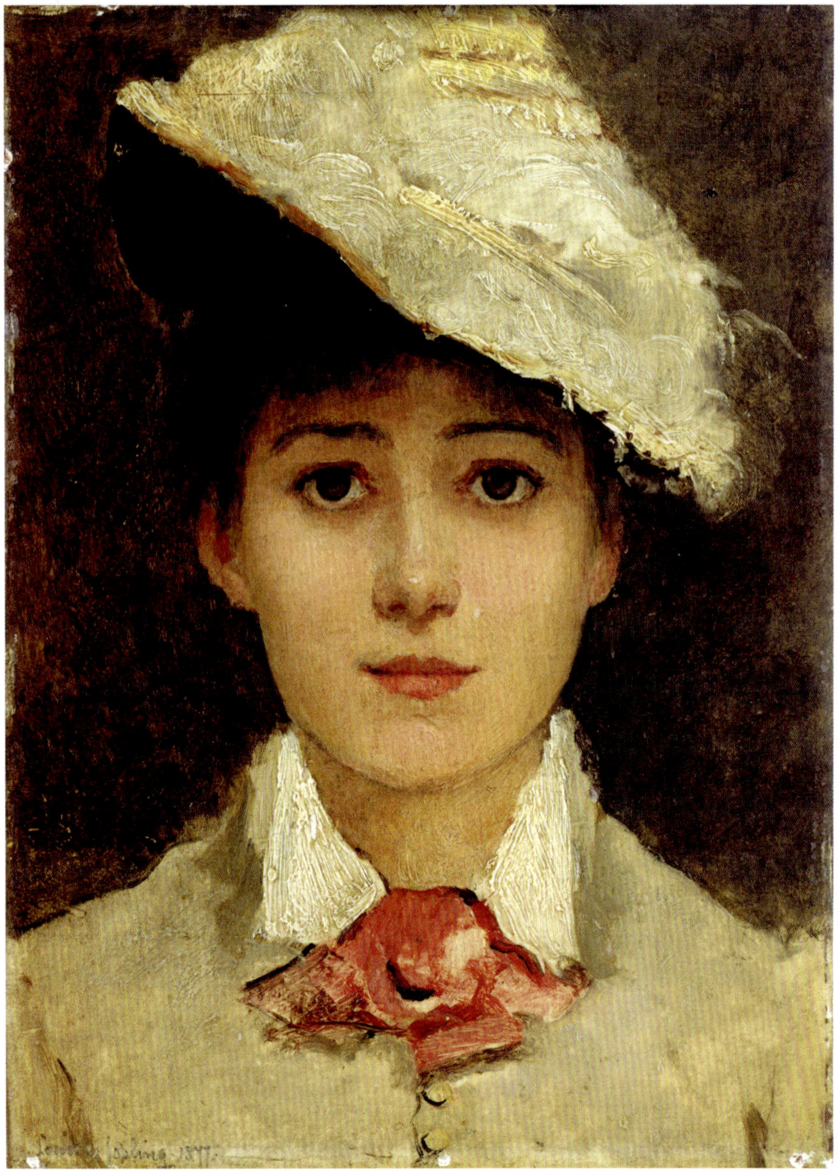

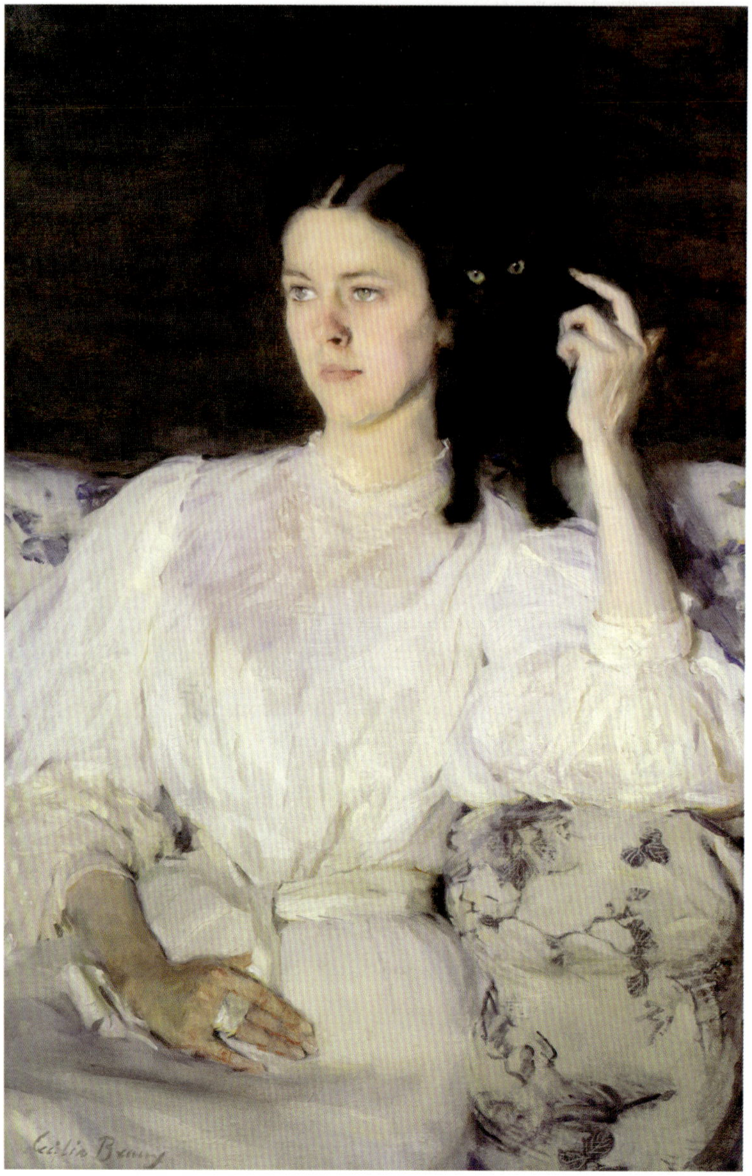

Above left: **Louise Jopling, *Self-Portrait*, 1877**

Louise Jopling Rowe studied in Paris under Charles Chaplin and, during a long career, achieved revered professional status and public celebrity, which she used to benefit the women's rights movement. She established her own art school in Kensington, London, in 1890, where she made her studio available for meetings of the Women's Franchise League, Women's Suffrage Society, and the Women's Freedom League. She also attended suffrage demonstrations and was an active supporter of the Suffrage Atelier (see page 46).

Above right: **Cecilia Beaux, *Sita and Sarita, or Young Girl with a Cat*, 1893–94**

Best known for society portraiture in the grand manner, Beaux's mesmerizing painting of her cousin's wife, Sarah Allibone Leavitt, with her jet-black cat perched on her shoulder and their green eyes aligned, reflects an artist of undeniable skill, but also of wit and modern sensibilities. Fiercely ambitious, Beaux never married, believing it would limit her career. In 1895, she became the first woman to have a regular teaching position at the Pennsylvania Academy of the Fine Arts.

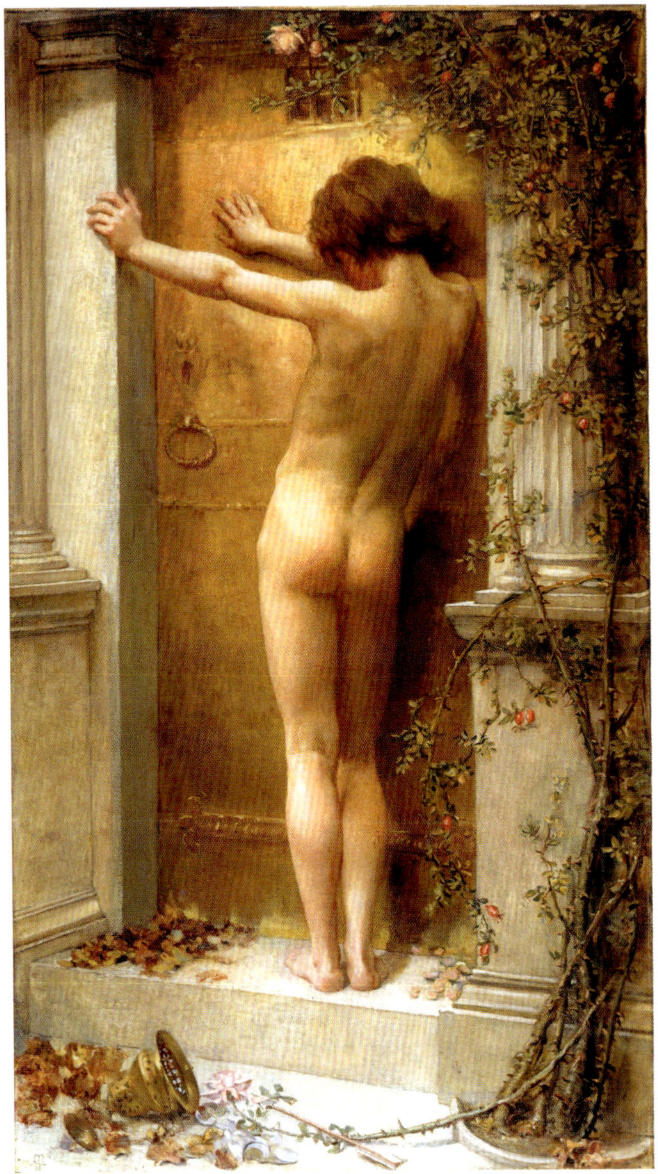

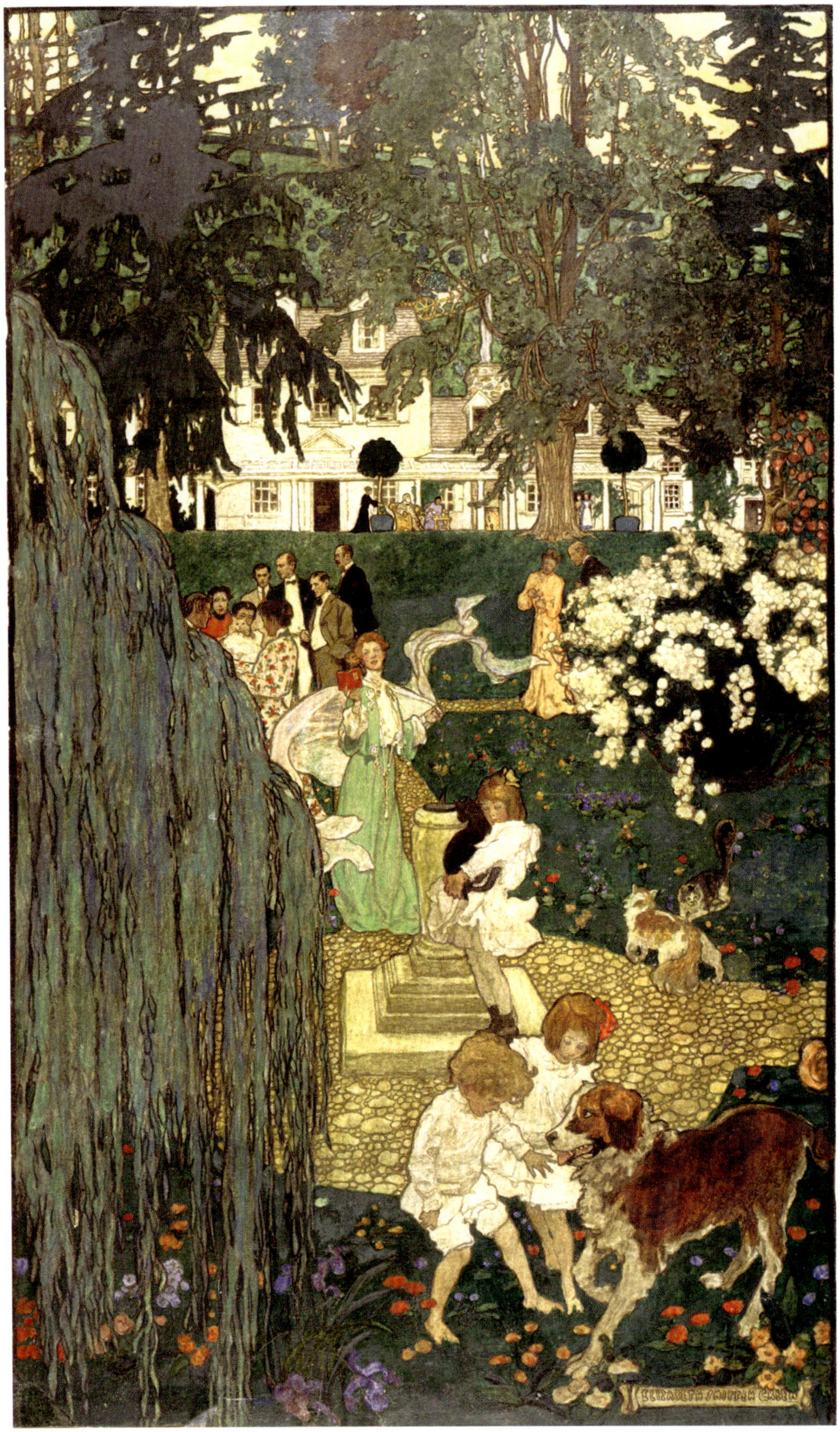

Above left: **Anna Lea Merritt, *Love Locked Out*, 1890**

Love Locked Out was painted as a tribute to the artist's late husband, but for a woman to paint a male nude was contentious. As Merritt's painting showed an unclothed child it was favorably received when exhibited at the Royal Academy in 1890, and was subsequently the first picture by a woman purchased for the British nation by the Chantrey Bequest. Female nudes as subjects were almost exclusively the preserve of male artists and when Merritt exhibited her own female nude painting, *Eve*, five years earlier, the *Athenaeum* magazine's critic described it as "dull and incompetent."

Above right: **Elizabeth Shippen Green, *Life was made for love and cheer*, from *Harper's* magazine, 1904**

Green met artists Violet Oakley and Jessie Willcox Smith while studying at the Drexel Institute under Howard Pyle. They formed a personal and professional friendship and, from 1901 to 1906, lived and worked together at the Red Rose Inn, a 200-acre estate in Villanova, Pennsylvania. Shippen Green was one of the leading lights in American illustration and was the first woman to have an exclusive contract with *Harper's* magazine. This picture depicts the "Red Rose Girls" in the grounds of their home and suggests an idyllic community.

Art Schools and the Women's Art Education Boom

Prior to the 1860s, most women with an ambition to make a career as an artist were obliged to build a patchwork program of training that might include instruction by a family member or acquaintance, trips to study in Europe, and private art classes.

Even as late as the 1830s, art schools for women were practically nonexistent. In the United Kingdom at this time, Henry Sass opened an art school in London's Charlotte Street to which he admitted some women; Eliza Fox and Anna Mary Howitt studied there in the 1840s, but opportunities were scarce. Instead, women might travel to Paris, where it was commonplace to study in the well-run ateliers of established artists such as Charles Chaplin, whose pupils included Louise Jopling and the impressionists Eva Gonzales and Mary Cassatt. The studio system was also in place in the United States; William Morris Hunt, who had studied in Paris alongside Millet, was a vigorous exponent of European art. He became one of the leading teachers in Boston, with May Alcott Nieriker among his students.

The opening of the Female School of Art in London, in 1842, not only met a growing demand among women for an art education but, as a single-sex school, addressed the concerns of a society obsessed with propriety. The National Art Training School at South Kensington, founded in 1843, spawned 130 free, government-funded art-training schools around Britain. Both schools emphasized art for manufacturing and industry, and formed a blueprint for the establishment of similar schools in the United States, specifically the Philadelphia School of Design for Women, opened in 1848 by Sarah Peter, the wife of the city's British consul. The school's aim was to provide a practical, employment-oriented approach to an art and design education, while equipping women with the skills they needed to earn an income, in turn allowing them to seek independence and self-sufficiency. Philadelphia's industrialization meant demand was high for skilled designers, and the school focused on salable skills, such as wood engraving and textile and wallpaper design. Other schools, such as Boston's Cowles Art School, proliferated in the wake of the Centennial Exposition in Philadelphia in 1876, where it became clear from the exhibits displayed by British companies that a marriage of industry and the aesthetic was a desirable alliance within the accelerating consumer economy.

Schools in the United States had the most progressive attitude toward women with an ambition to study "fine" art. In its 1810 charter, the Pennsylvania Academy of the Fine Arts (PAFA) stated that it should be organized for "the youth of both sexes." Women were invited to exhibit in its inaugural exhibition and, in 1844, the school opened its antiquity classes to women. Twelve years later, segregation of these classes was abolished, though fig leaves were applied to all the male statues to preserve the minds of the female students. By 1860, a group of women headed by Eliza Haldeman and Mary Cassatt had organized their own life class, and were offered a room in the school for their group; by 1868, women had successfully petitioned to be given life classes organized by the PAFA. Other U.S. art schools were liberal enough to admit women—New York's Cooper Union, founded by Peter Cooper, welcomed not only women, but also black students, as did Oberlin College in Ohio, where the sculptor Edmonia Lewis's artistic talent first came to notice in the 1850s.

For much of the nineteenth century, many American female art students had their sights set on Europe, aided by the PAFA, who introduced a traveling scholarship of $800 in 1891. Thousands of women made their way to Paris each year to pursue art. Such were their numbers by the end of the century that an American Girls' Art Club was founded. Situated in the city's Latin Quarter, it provided a base for the women to meet, network, and take part in dances, concerts, sketch clubs, and exhibitions.

In the United Kingdom, the opening of London's Slade School of Fine Art, in 1871, at last presented a serious alternative to Royal Academy schools, which had only reluctantly opened their doors to female students in the 1860s. Offering an education on equal terms with men, The Slade's alumni included some of the most successful British artists of the period: Kate Greenaway, Helen Allingham, Evelyn de Morgan, Constance Markievicz, Gwen John, and Winifred Knights. Women and men studied together, except in life classes, where women had to be satisfied with a model who was modestly draped—a compromise, but at least an improvement on classical statuary.

The Académie Julian in Paris, which opened in 1868, offered a highly regarded alternative to the Académie des Beaux-Arts (which did not admit women until 1897) and taught both men and women, though classes were segregated. The *académie* experience was intense. Life classes took place in crowded rooms from 8 am in the morning, with only short breaks until lunchtime. Those who were particularly dedicated, and there were many, might carry on with additional classes until 10 pm in the evening.

Other Parisian establishments, the Académie Colarossi and the Académie de la Grande Chaumière, also taught men and women together in classes, though there was still systemic inequality in that women were charged around 30 percent more in fees than their male counterparts. In Germany, the academies of Berlin, Dusseldorf, and Munich did not admit women until well into the twentieth century. Though choices and opportunities for women in art education had expanded enormously, in some quarters, deep-rooted prejudices remained.

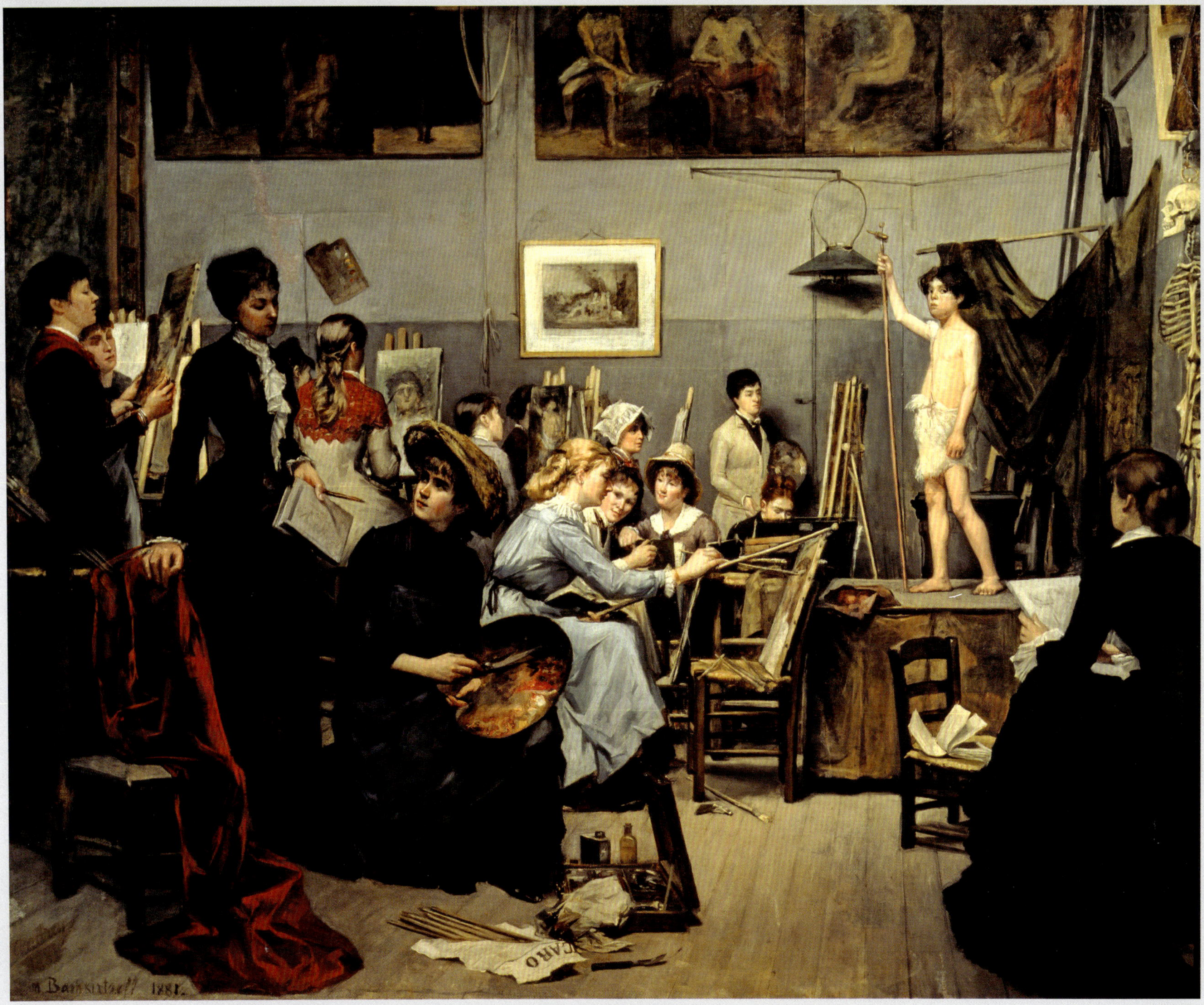

"People often say that, with only one or two exceptions, no woman has made a great name in art; but they were given none of the opportunities which each male artist claimed as his right."

Rodolphe Julian, founder of Académie Julian, interviewed in *The Sketch* magazine, 1893

Above: Marie Bashkirtseff, *In the Académie Julian in Paris*, 1881

Founded in 1868, the Académie Julian admitted women, taught in classes separate to men and without access to life models. Marie Bashkirtseff began her studies in 1877, and reveled in the independence of art-student life, writing: "One feels so happy, so free, so proud." She organized anatomy lessons for herself before successfully lobbying for women students to be taught using life models. Her busy scene depicting such a class nevertheless has a male youth partially draped rather than fully nude.

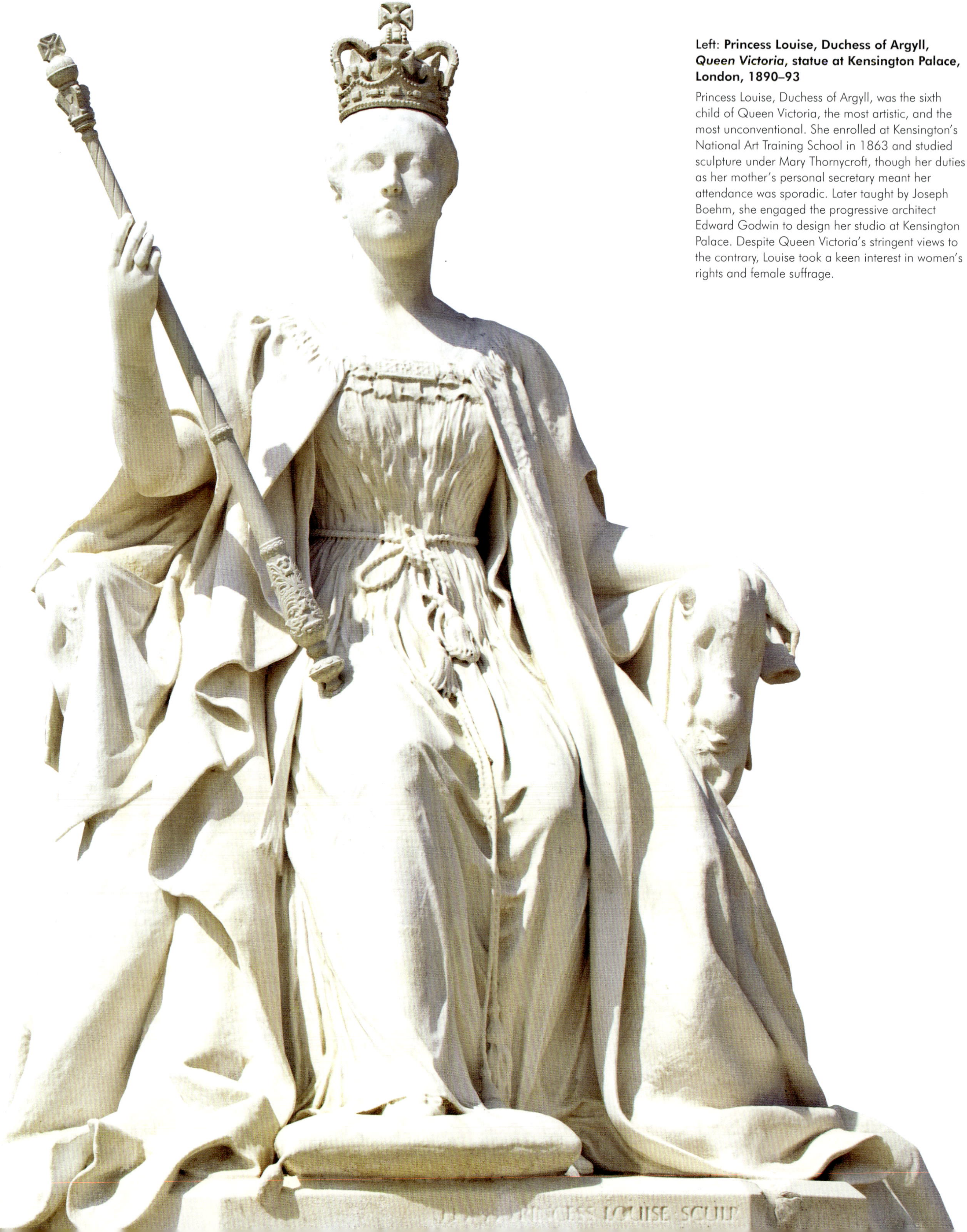

Left: **Princess Louise, Duchess of Argyll, *Queen Victoria*, statue at Kensington Palace, London, 1890–93**

Princess Louise, Duchess of Argyll, was the sixth child of Queen Victoria, the most artistic, and the most unconventional. She enrolled at Kensington's National Art Training School in 1863 and studied sculpture under Mary Thornycroft, though her duties as her mother's personal secretary meant her attendance was sporadic. Later taught by Joseph Boehm, she engaged the progressive architect Edward Godwin to design her studio at Kensington Palace. Despite Queen Victoria's stringent views to the contrary, Louise took a keen interest in women's rights and female suffrage.

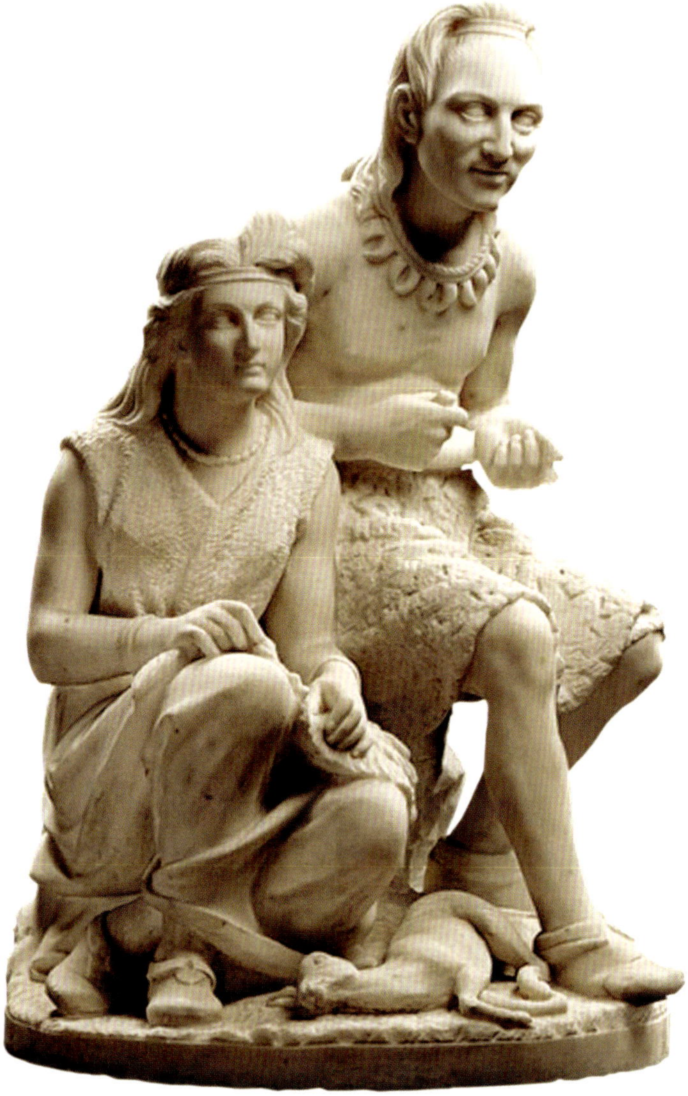

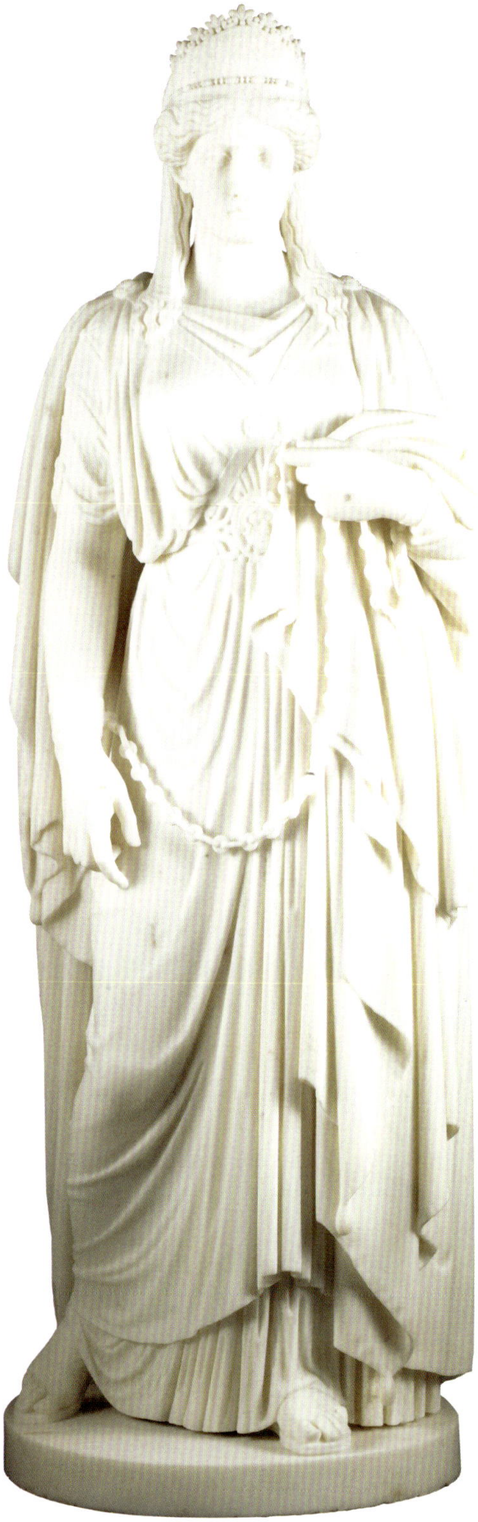

Above left: **Edmonia Lewis, *Old Arrow Maker*, 1872**

The daughter of a Chippewa mother and black father, Edmonia Lewis's career is all the more remarkable for succeeding in a climate of racial, as well as gender, prejudice. She studied at Oberlin College in Ohio, the first American college to admit women of all races, and later moved to Rome in 1865, joining the group of American expatriate female sculptors based there. A number of her works reference her ethnic heritage, such as this marble composition.

Above right: **Harriet Goodhue Hosmer, *Zenobia in Chains*, ca. 1859**

Hosmer chose Zenobia as the subject of her most celebrated sculpture for "her womanly modesty, her manly courage, and her intellectual tastes." The 6.5 ft (2 m) marble figure, which eloquently conveys the dignity of the captured queen, was displayed at the International Exhibition in London in 1862, where it drew crowds. But it was suggested by two British publications, *The Queen* and *The Crayon*, that the bulk of the work had been carried out by Hosmer's male assistant in Rome. Outraged by such an accusation, Hosmer engaged lawyers who extracted an apology from the journals.

Early Women Photographers

To take up the art of photography in the 1850s required no small amount of commitment. It was often a case of trial, error, patience, and tenacity; an artistic eye counted for very little if the practical science of photography could not be navigated.

Early women photographers were undaunted by the technical challenges they faced and their photographs, consciously or not, form a remarkable body of work that frequently veers into experimental and imaginative territory. Most photography from this time is the work of amateurs, intended purely for distribution among friends and family. Untrammeled by the tastes and expectations of patron or public (which frequently influenced the choice of subject matter for women painters), they redefined the preordained vision of early twentieth-century womanhood. Women photographers often used their sisters, friends, or daughters as sitters, and took photographs in their homes—both factors that helped incubate the intimate and uninhibited nature of the images.

Photography required space to work, money to buy equipment, and time to practice. Consequently, in these early years, it was almost exclusively a pastime of the wealthy, which makes the activities of Sarah Louise Judd, a school teacher in Minnesota, all the more remarkable. County history records show she began working at producing daguerreotypes in a professional capacity in Stillwater in 1848, though none of her photographs survive.

In Britain, Clementina, Lady Hawarden, a mother of ten, was an upper-class British woman who turned the first floor of her London home into a large studio, where, in the early 1860s, she photographed her adolescent daughters in a series of enigmatic studies. Using a freestanding mirror to play with light and reflection, she created compositions with an evocative elegance. In her otherwise stark studio, she framed her sitters wearing extravagant, fashionable clothes against a backdrop of furniture, hangings, and star-patterned wallpaper. She gained a degree of recognition in her lifetime and was awarded a silver medal on the two occasions she exhibited at the Photographic Society in 1863 and 1864.

Julia Margaret Cameron, also British, came to photography comparatively late in life, when her daughter presented her with a camera at the age of 48. A complete novice, Cameron wrote of her first attempts, "I did not know where to place my dark box, how to focus my sitter and my first picture I effaced to my consternation by rubbing my hand over the filmy side of the glass." It was not long before she had become proficient, adapting early mistakes to create a deliberate hazy focus that became the hallmark of her work. Boasting a starry circle of acquaintances, she captured some of the era's most eminent figures at the height of their celebrity, including John Herschel and Scottish philosopher Thomas Carlyle. While almost all of her well-known sitters were male, her portrayals of women drew on themes from history, literature, and mythology, and show the marked influence of the aesthetic and later Pre-Raphaelite movements. Her work benefited from greater exposure in her lifetime and after her death, due in part to her network of high-profile connections.

Both Cameron and Hawarden exhibited an idiosyncratic talent for creative experimentation at a time when photography was in its infancy. They tamed and transformed this new artistic medium and used it to construct a fresh, more complex image of woman reimagined through the female gaze. They also blazed a trail for the next generation of female photographers.

The later years of the nineteenth century also witnessed a number of women photographers come to prominence in the United States. Clover Adams, wife of the writer Henry Adams, took up photography in 1883, and showed an instinct for capturing women's lives. Catharine Weed Barnes began to take photographs around the same time and, by 1890, had become editor of *American Amateur Photographer* magazine, which she used as a platform to champion other women photographers. Frances Benjamin Johnston, one of America's first female photojournalists, was an energetic advocate of women photographers. She traveled countrywide on a broad range of assignments, mainly for Bain News Service, and, in 1900, organized an exhibition of artistic photographs by women for the International Congress of Photography, held in Paris, France, during the International Exposition. Among those whose work was included in the exhibition was Sarah Choate Sears, a prominent art patron in Boston, who had studied at the city's Cowles Art School in the 1870s and had taken up photography around 1890. The interest and participation of women such as Sears and another of Johnston's friends, Gertrude Käsebier, who was a member of the Photo-Secession, helped to elevate photography as an art form. Anne Brigman, also a member of the Photo-Secession, pushed this concept further, producing provocative, countercultural images suggestive of paganism and female liberation. Whether pictorial or documentary, by the end of the nineteenth century, it was clear photography was an oeuvre in which women could excel and compete on equal terms with men.

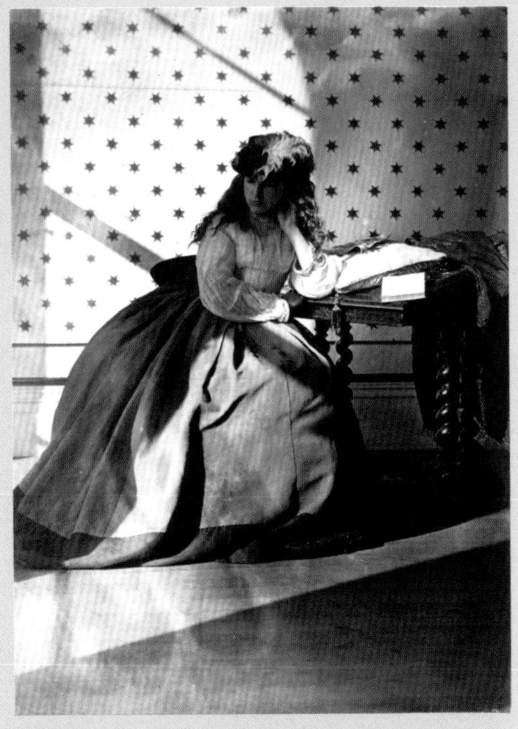

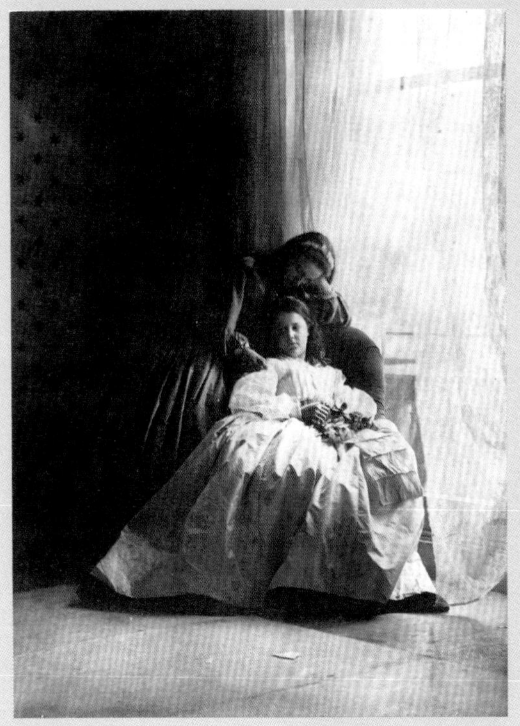

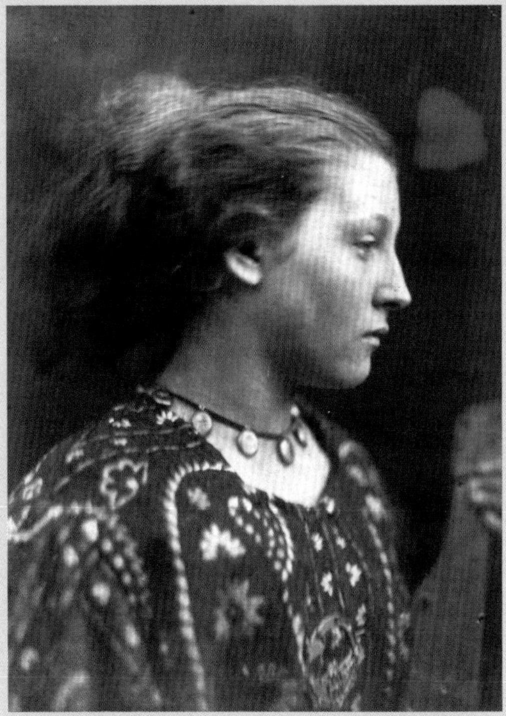

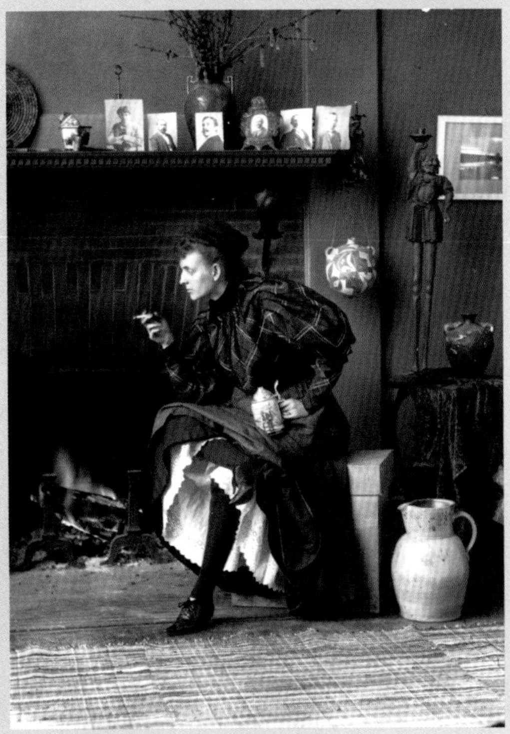

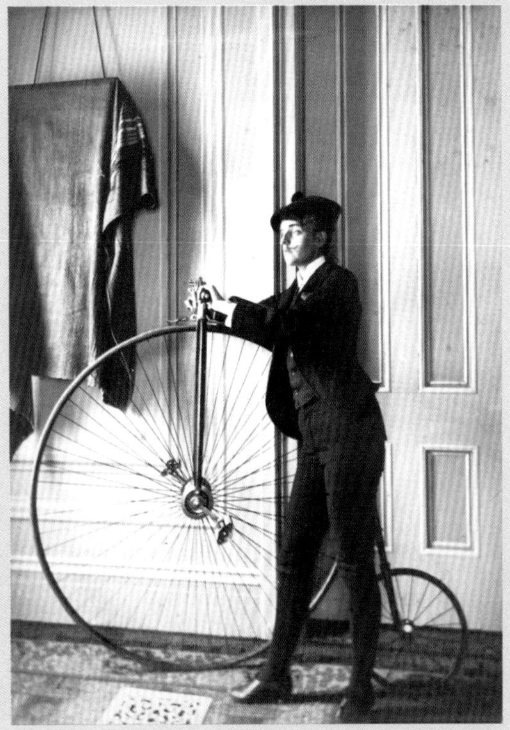

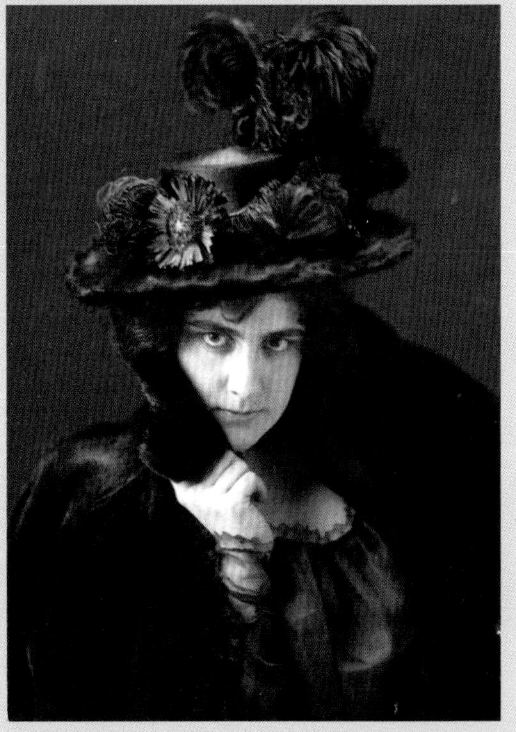

"To an energetic, ambitious woman with even ordinary opportunities, success is always possible . . . hard, intelligent and conscientious work seldom fails to develop small beginnings into large results."

Frances Benjamin Johnston in an article recommending photography as a career, *Ladies' Home Journal*, 1897

This page: From the dreamy experimentalism of Clementina Hawarden (top left and center) and Julia Margaret Cameron (top right), to the artful wit of Frances Benjamin Johnston (bottom), the work of early women photographers fell somewhere between art and reality. The results of their endeavors are often intimate, compelling, and disarming portraits of private lives.

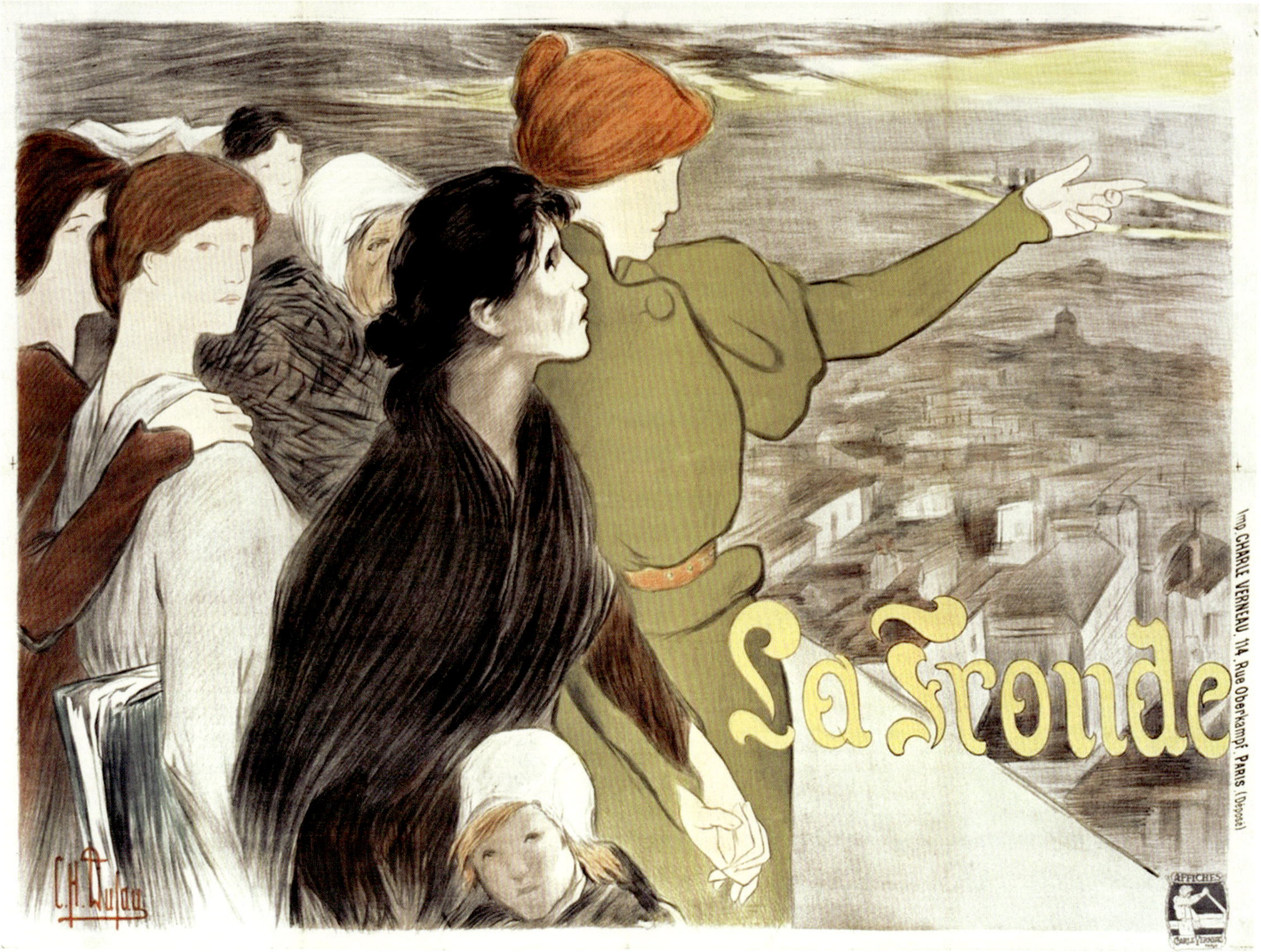

Above: Poster for *La Fronde* feminist newspaper, 1898

Founded by actress and journalist Marguerite Durand in 1897, *La Fronde* was financed by Jewish banker Gustave de Rothschild and took its name from the sling used to hurl stones by antimonarchists, or *"frondeurs,"* of seventeenth-century France. Inspired to found the paper by the matchgirls' strike in East London, Durand was passionate about equal rights and pay for women workers. The paper was staffed entirely by women who were all paid according to levels for male employees set by trade unions.

Top row: American graphic artist Ethel Reed's striking poster designs, made mainly for the publisher Lamson, Wolff & Co., combined various influences from art nouveau to Japanese art, and wove together striking color palettes, boldly outlined figures, and stylized flowers or plants. She spent time in London, where she contributed a cover to the avant-garde *Yellow Book*, edited by Aubrey Beardsley. *The Boston Sunday Herald* poster (center) was her first published commission.

Bottom row: Artistic dress, which eschewed tight corseting in favor of looser styles in a palette of tasteful colors, was popular with artists and within bohemian circles, allowing women freedom of movement as well as artistic expression. The Healthy and Artistic Dress Union promoted this philosophy and published three issues of *Aglaia* (left) between 1893 and 1894, named for the "grace of adornment" in Greek mythology. Edited by the stained-glass designer Henry Holiday, who also designed the cover featuring the three graces, contributors included G.F. Watts, Walter Crane, and Arthur Liberty, founder of the department store in London. Similar dress reform movements were founded in Germany and Austria and the two illustrations (center and right) are taken from the German magazine *Jugend*, 1903.

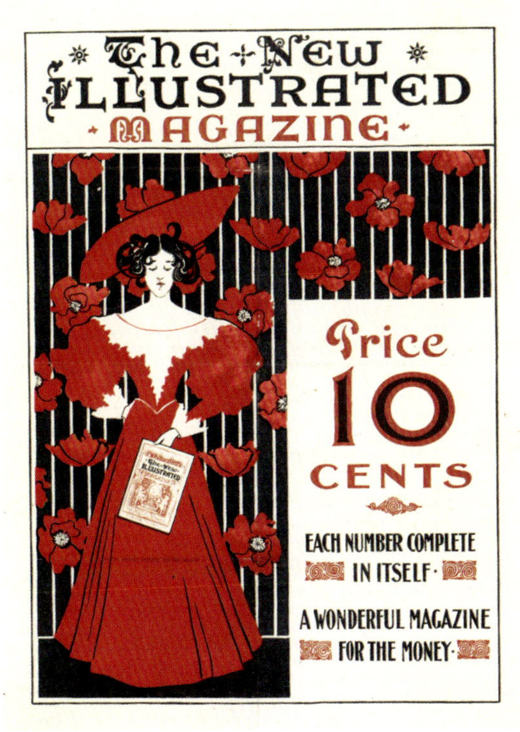

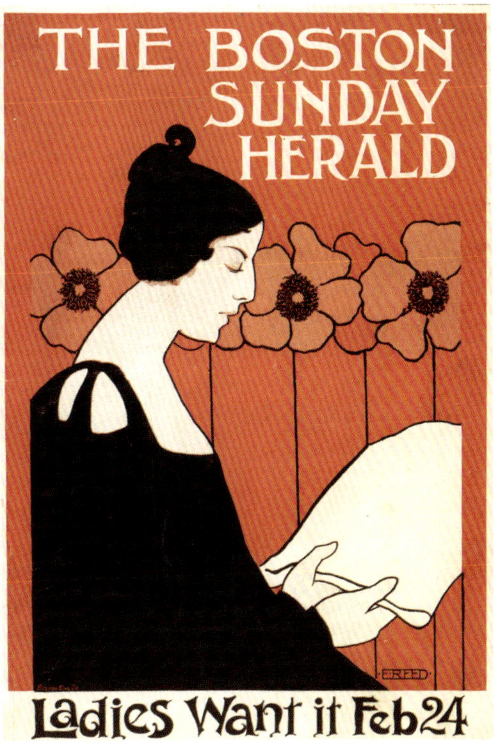

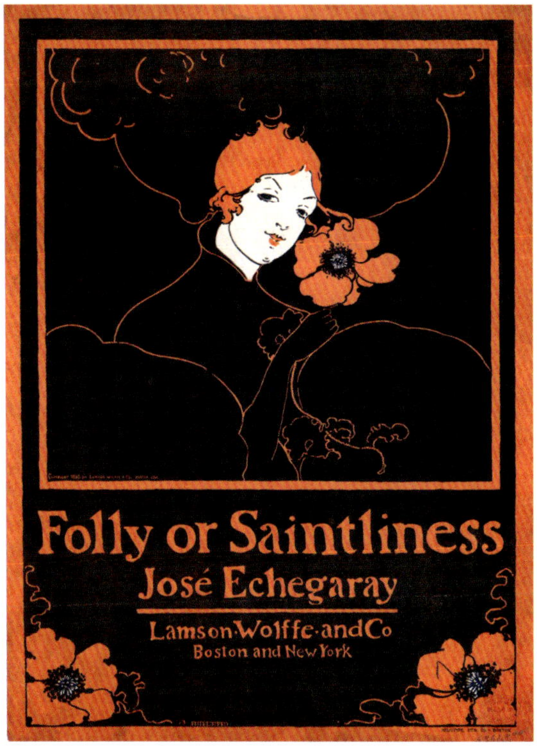

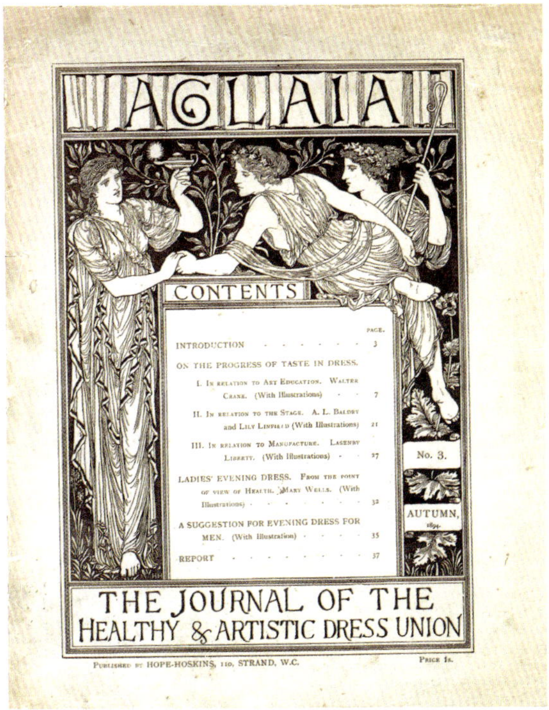

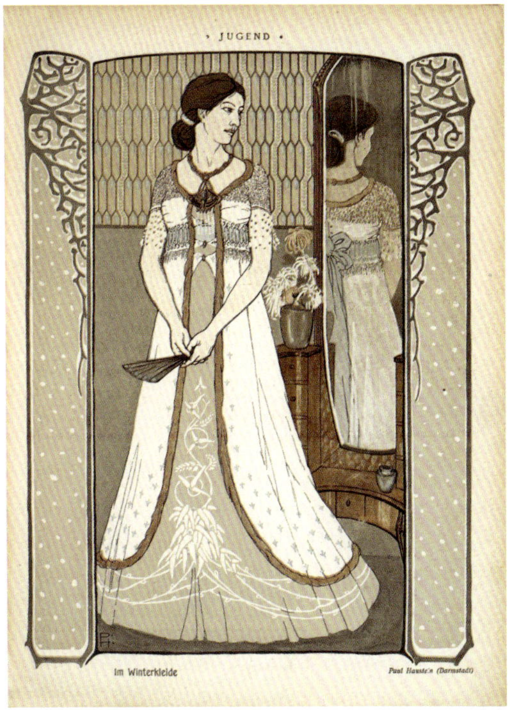

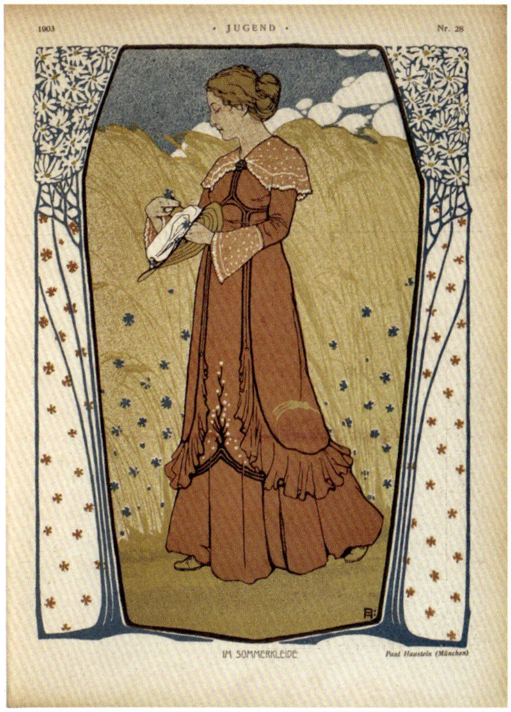

The Woman Artist: Dressing the Part and Self-Image

Women's emergence and growing visibility in the art world during the nineteenth century was fortified by an increasing confidence in how women promoted their own image.

As women transitioned from amateur to professional status in the art world, they also moved into the public arena, where success and recognition elided with being seen. Women painted themselves and each other, presenting in many cases a more truthful expression of how they saw themselves and how they wished to be perceived. Though these depictions varied greatly in style, they were significant in that the artists took control of their self-image, contesting the visual assumptions of womanhood that had long been the output of the male artist.

When Italian-born Emma Richards painted her self-portrait in 1853, she adopted the contrapposto posture favored by great artists of the past, such as Van Dyck and Rembrandt, adopting a businesslike appearance of practical black dress, neatly parted hair, and the tools of her trade—her brushes and palette. Regarding the viewer with an expression of solemnity and determination, there is no doubt that this is an artist of serious intent. In later decades, women's portrayals of themselves in work clothes became more prevalent. Anna Bilinska's *Self-Portrait with Apron and Brushes*, painted in 1887, depicts the working artist as she sits against a stark canvas backdrop, her apron crumpled and stained, her hair escaping from its pins. This new, assertive self-presentation indicated a leap of confidence among women artists. While women's place in art through the centuries had been largely as muse and subject, these portraits have more in common with the poses and attitudes of female painters of the Renaissance. Artemisia Gentileschi's self-portrait of 1638–39, in which her arm confidently sweeps across a canvas, might well have served as inspiration to artists such as Bilinska, Marie Bashkirtseff, and Elizabeth Nourse, all of whom painted themselves as resolute and capable.

Many women artists cultivated a bohemian appearance, in particular adopting the principles of dress reform advocated by organizations such as the Healthy and Artistic Dress Union. Disciples of dress reform advocated loose, flowing gowns in harmonious colors, echoing the medieval tastes of the Pre-Raphaelites and in tune with the aesthetic movement of the 1870s. The aesthetic movement was a cult of beauty, of which paintings by its leading exponents (G.F. Watts and James Whistler, among others) were just one element. The style cascaded from the walls of art galleries into public buildings, the home, and clothing, announcing followers as people of discernment, individuality, and taste. Liberty, the London department store opened in 1875, offered "art fabrics" and gowns with a historic flavor with which fans of aestheticism could emulate the Pre-Raphaelite look. The artist Marie Spartali, who modeled for Edward Burne-Jones, developed a personal style that saw her wear similar costumes both on canvas and in real life. Emilie Flöge, the partner of Gustav Klimt, designed striking dresses that fell from the shoulders with wide sleeves, specifically for a small artistic customer base in Austria. Elisabeth Winterwerber was active in Germany in the 1890s working in a similar oeuvre. Women of the Glasgow School of Art, such as Jessie Newbery and Ann Macbeth, designed and embroidered their own dresses. For women artists, it was a style that was comfortable and practical, but also a statement of creative individuality. Furthermore, artistic dress was unrestricted in contrast to the tightly corseted conventions of nineteenth-century fashion and so expressed a freedom of spirit and creativity beyond its aesthetic appeal.

The new medium of photography offered women artists an inexpensive method of distributing their image to a wide audience at a time when the collecting of *cartes-des-visites* was popular. Such images show how women artists chose to present themselves, often projecting a style that denoted their profession, modeled on the self-presentation of male artists through the centuries. Photography was also a tool to verify and prove female ability. The American sculptor Harriet Hosmer was photographed in her studio, dressed in short skirts and bloomers, standing on a scaffold, dwarfed by her looming statue of Missouri senator Thomas Benton. For Hosmer, dissemination of this image was vital after she had been accused of leaving work to craftsmen rather than executing it herself.

Rosa Bonheur posed for photographs not in the smock, breeches, and boots she wore when sketching in the abbatoirs, markets, and stables of Paris, but in a skirt paired with a military jacket, her hair chopped to her ears. Her fame may have been enhanced by stories of her unconventional appearance but she believed in dressing up smartly for visitors and patrons.

Elizabeth Thompson, Lady Butler, presented a different image, but one that, in its own way, subverted preconceived expectations. Forging a place in the masculine stronghold of military painting, Thompson's 1874 breakthrough painting, *The Roll Call*, was all the more intriguing to the public for having been painted by a young, twenty-seven-year-old woman, stylishly dressed but with no eccentric affectations.

In this respect, artists such as Bonheur and Thompson may have been diametrically opposed in terms of their personal style, but they each projected an individuality that did much to disrupt the notion of women artists as one homogenous and indiscriminate group. Here, instead, were creators of serious work—individuals with taste, whether consciously bohemian, practically garbed, or more conventionally corseted. Instead of conforming to a standard type, women artists proved that femininity came in as many varieties as the works they produced.

This page: Self-portraiture and photography allowed women to take control of their professional image, molding how they wished to be perceived by the public. Rosa Bonheur (top left, ca. 1870) is businesslike in a tailored tunic and full-length skirt, the breeches she famously wore relegated to research trips to abbatoirs and stables. Edmonia Lewis (top right, ca. 1870) cultivated a bohemian look with her smoking cap and cloak. Emma Richards (bottom left, 1853) paints herself as the consummate professional, the tools of her trade visibly part of the picture, and the tense set of her jaw suggesting a faint irritation at being interrupted in her work. Anna Bilinska's self-portrait (1887, bottom right) does not seek to glamorize her profession but is, instead, a truthful presentation of an artist first, and a woman second.

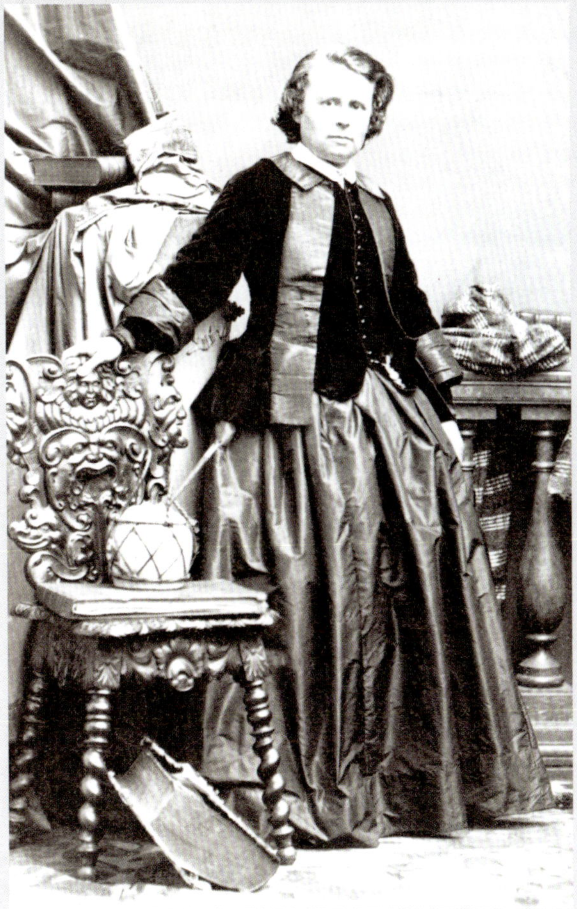

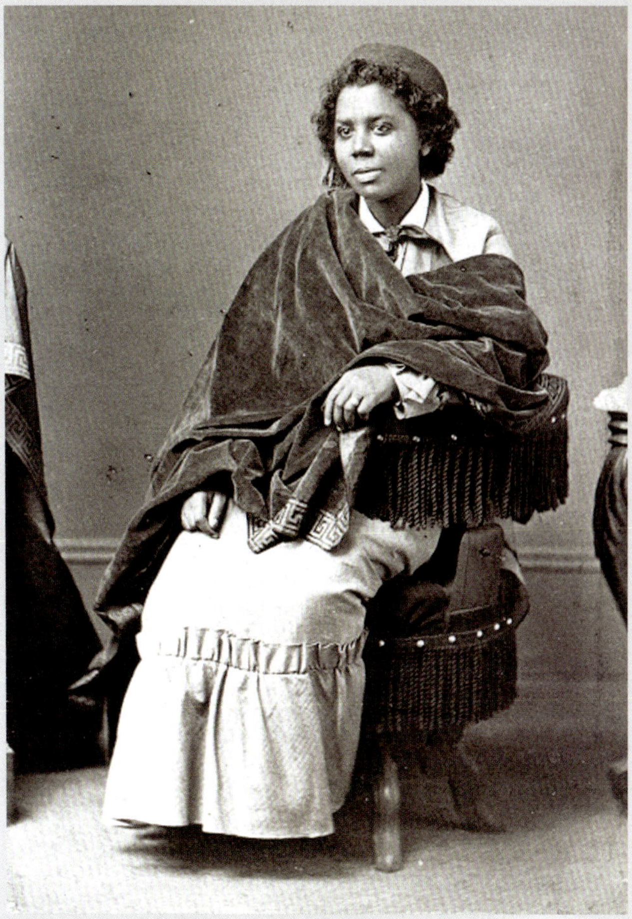

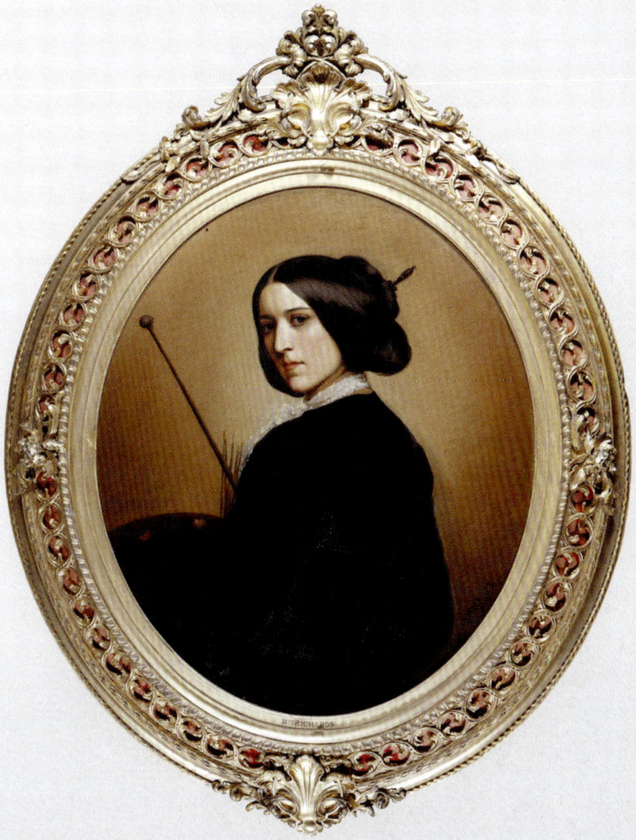

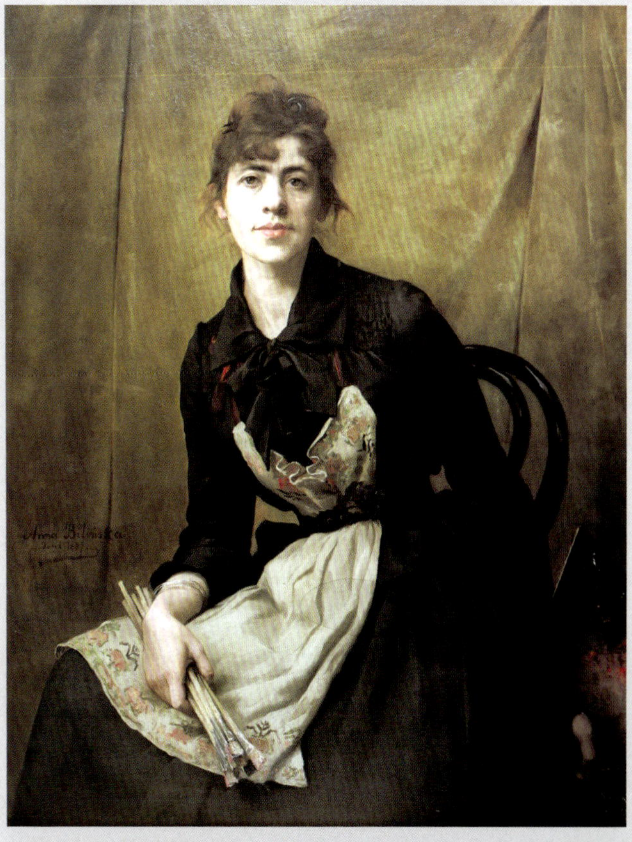

Below: **John Leech, *The Parliamentary Female*, *Punch* magazine, 1853**
Role reversal, and the disruption of the marital status quo, provided fertile material for comic papers of the period. As lighthearted as Leech's cartoon for the English satirical maagzine appears, the neglect and disintegration of home life that would be the direct result of a working wife and mother was a persistent argument used by anti-suffrage campaigners.

Bottom left: **Bertha Newcombe, *An Incident in Connection with a Presentation of the First Women's Suffrage Petition to Parliament in 1866*, 1910 (detail)**
Newcombe's painting of a key moment in suffrage history, when Elizabeth Garrett Anderson and Emily Davies presented a petition containing 1,499 signatures to John Stuart Mill at Westminster, has a cosy quality to it. The suffrage art historian Elizabeth Crawford suggests the unthreatening tone may have been to emphasize the constitutional roots of the movement at a time when militancy was dominating the public's perception of the suffrage campaign.

Bottom right: **Matt Morgan, *The Girl of the Period* in *Tomahawk*, 1868**
In March 1868, British weekly magazine *The Saturday Review* published an article by Eliza Lynn Linton attacking modern women as lacking the grace, purity, and propriety of previous generations. Linton's comments provoked a media storm and satirical ripostes such as this cartoon published by *Tomahawk* the following month, in which a perfectly pleasant young woman is painted as wicked and demonic by *The Saturday Review*.

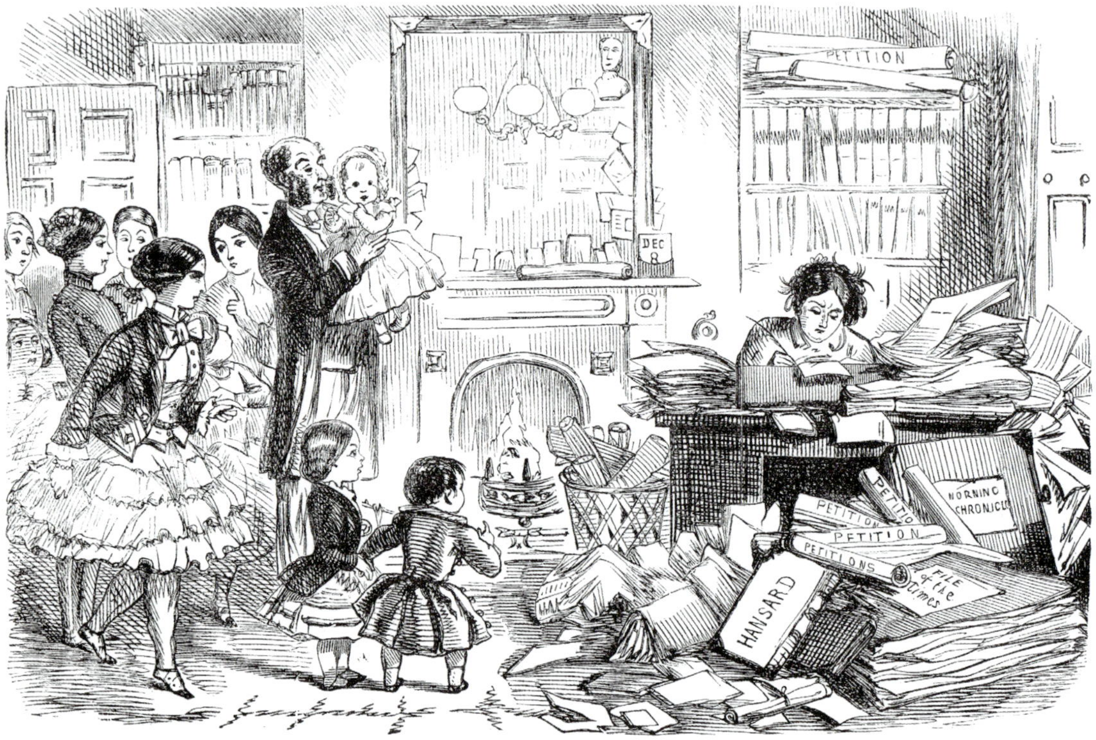

THE PARLIAMENTARY FEMALE.

Father of the Family. "COME, DEAR; WE SO SELDOM GO OUT TOGETHER NOW—CAN'T YOU TAKE US ALL TO THE PLAY TO-NIGHT?"
Mistress of the House, and M.P. "HOW YOU TALK, CHARLES! DON'T YOU SEE THAT I AM TOO BUSY. I HAVE A COMMITTEE TO-MORROW MORNING, AND I HAVE MY SPEECH ON THE GREAT CROCHET QUESTION TO PREPARE FOR THE EVENING."

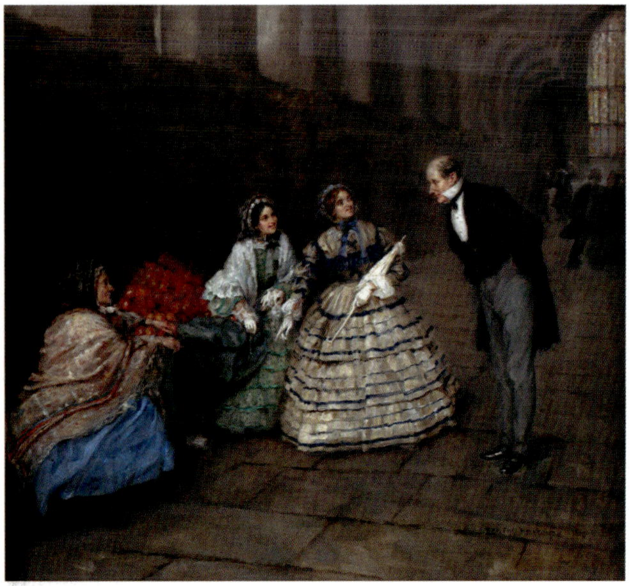

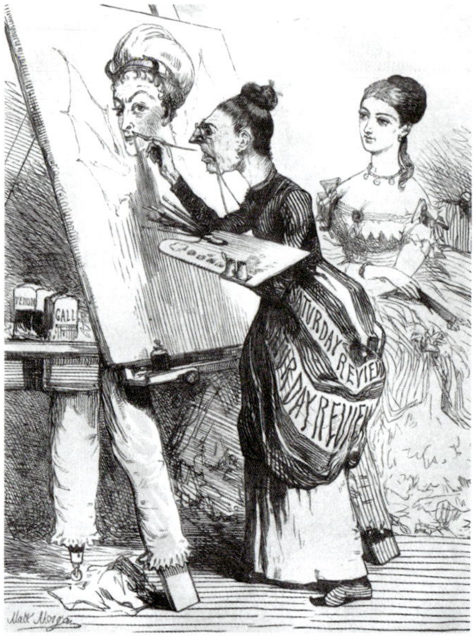

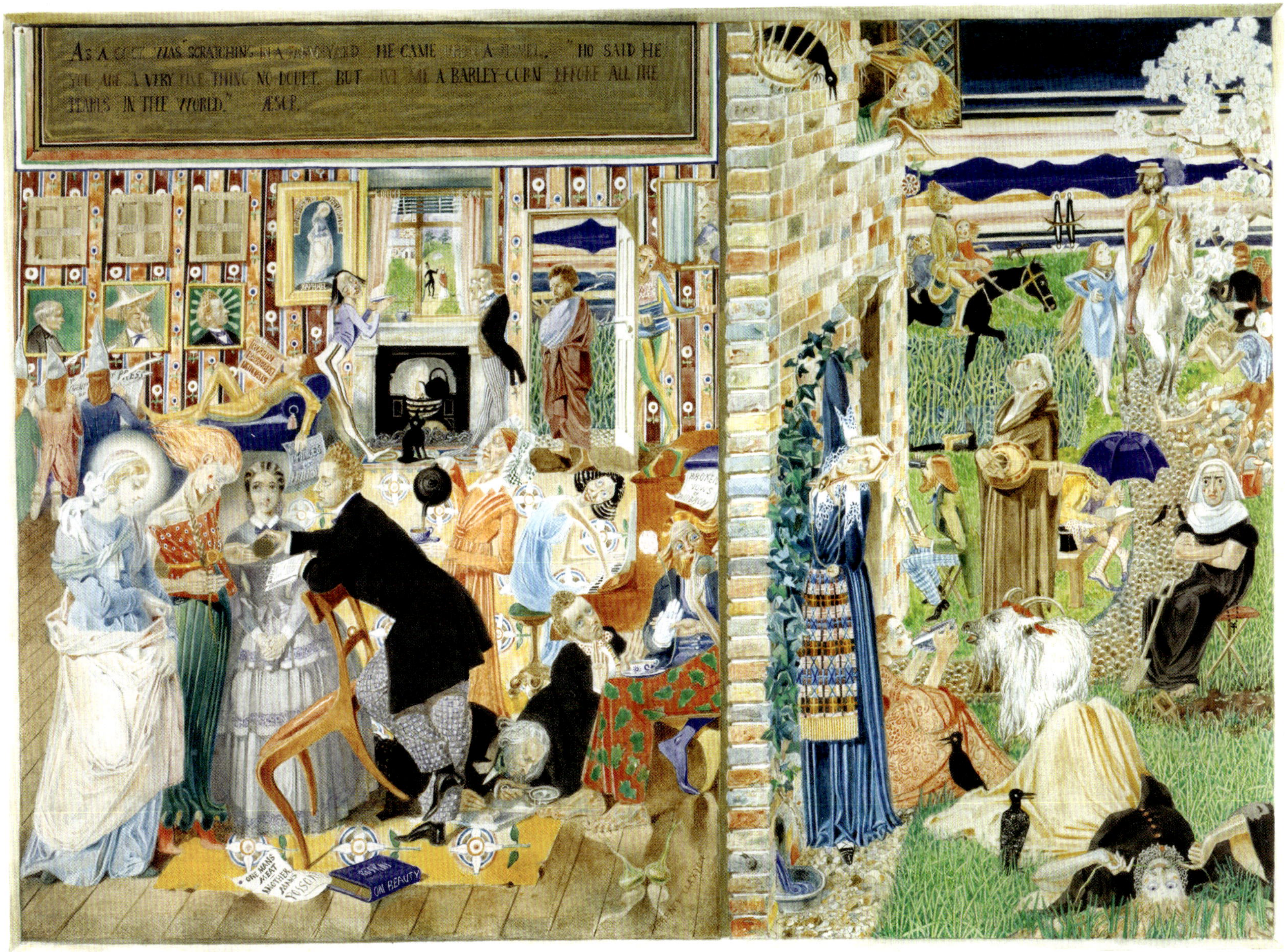

Above: **Florence Claxton, *The Choice of Paris, An Idyll,* 1860**

Florence Claxton worked primarily as a comic illustrator for the periodical press during the mid-nineteenth century, with several of her pictures engraved in the era's leading publication, *The Illustrated London News*. This, her most famous picture, was a parody of the Pre-Raphaelite Brotherhood, with many elements recognizable to those who had been exposed to the satirical backlash against the movement's audacious ideas. In the foreground stands a founder of the movement, Sir John Millais, making his "choice" of a slender, medieval maiden over the Renaissance Madonna and conventional, crinoline-garbed Victorian. Another of Claxton's paintings, *Women's Work: A Medley* (1861), was a witty riposte to *Work* by Pre-Raphaelite artist Ford Madox Brown. Satire was not unusual in the nineteenth century, but such self-assured satire by a woman was.

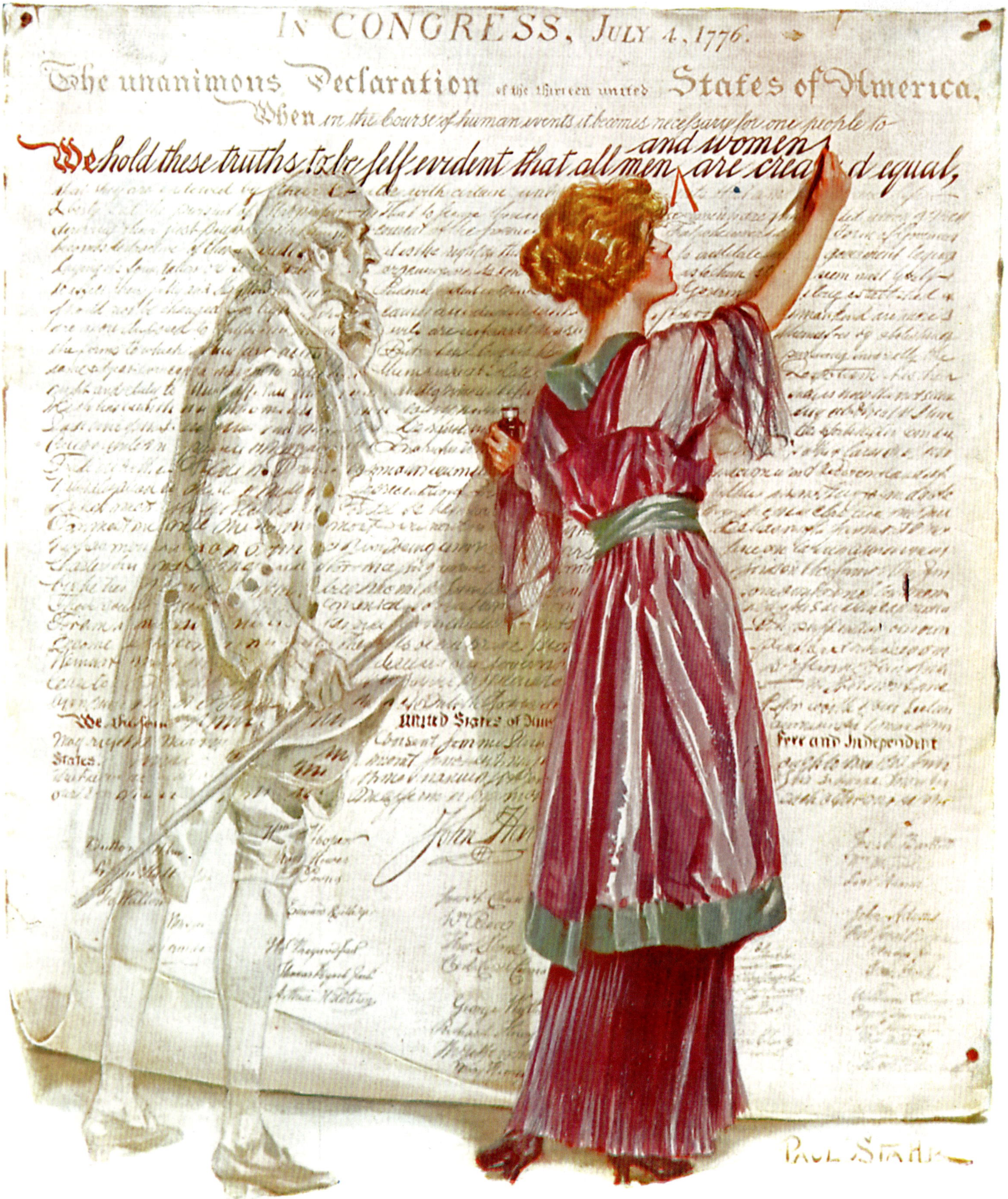

1776—RETOUCHING AN OLD MASTERPIECE—1915

The March of the Women

Visualizing Suffrage

2

"... of all the many demonstrators who have tramped the same route, the women have by far the greatest sense of the picturesque."

The Sphere **magazine, reporting on the banners that accompanied the suffragists' march from London's Embankment to the Albert Hall on June 13, 1908**

By 1900, access to art education had greatly improved, with the result that women were a growing presence in a variety of artistic disciplines—as exhibiting artists, as book and magazine illustrators, as jewelry designers, muralists, and sculptors. The fight for educational opportunities during the previous century had run in parallel to a wider demand for political equality and the 1900s would witness an acceleration of organized agitation focused on women achieving one fundamental aim—the right to vote.

In the United States, suffrage campaigners formed the National American Woman Suffrage Association (NAWSA) in 1890 out of two separate organizations, with Susan B. Anthony, a campaigner since the 1860s, at its head. By 1916, Alice Paul had formed a splinter organization from this group, the National Woman's Party. It had a single focus: achieving national enfranchisement, using violent methods if necessary.

In Britain, the suffrage movement gained a tangible identity in 1897, with the formation of the National Union of Women's Suffrage Societies (NUWSS) under the leadership of Millicent Fawcett. The suffragist members of the NUWSS employed patience and persuasion, believing that reasoned debate and lobbying were key to eventually winning the vote. A separate organization, the Women's Social and Political Union (WSPU), emerged in 1903, led by Manchester suffragist Emmeline Pankhurst, who conceived a more militant strategy summarized by its motto, "Deeds not Words." Derisively dubbed "suffragettes" by the *Daily Mail*, the term was quickly adopted by the WSPU, who named the organization's paper *The Suffragette*.

This rise in suffrage activity in the decade leading up to World War I saw art and design become a dominant tool in communicating the movement's message. In January 1907, professional artists, illustrators, and engravers (mostly female) formed the Artists' Suffrage League (ASL) in Britain, expressly to assist with preparations for the first large-scale procession organized by the NUWSS on February 7. Later known as the "Mud March," owing to unfortunate weather, the rally nevertheless attracted three thousand participants, notable for their red-and-white rosettes and numerous ASL-designed banners. Most of the banner designs were the work of Mary Lowndes, whose ideas were sketched out on paper, filled in with watercolor, and often accompanied by swatches of fabric. Lowndes, who had trained at The Slade, worked as a stained-glass artist. She used the principles of stained-glass design to good effect in her banners, which were a marriage of the bold and the beautiful. Suffrage banners inevitably drew comparisons with those of the burgeoning trade union movement, the earliest examples of which had been hand-stitched and embroidered by women. Most trade union banners were now manufactured, but Lowndes insisted on reviving needlework skills to produce hers, thus utilizing what was increasingly considered a lowly, feminine skill to create powerful messages, enshrined in the socialist principles of arts and crafts.

On June 13, 1908, the ASL's skills were employed at a far larger event comprising various branches of the nonmilitant "suffragists" on a march from London's Embankment to a meeting at the Albert Hall. Again, the visual impact created by the sea of banners was impressed upon witnesses. Reared on a diet of romantic and medieval themes in art, they recognized distinct similarities between the spectacle before them and the pageantry and crusades of the Middle Ages. A total of 770 banners were created—70 large and 700 in a smaller size—and were considered of sufficient popular interest and artistic merit to be displayed at Caxton Hall the previous week. Sylvia Pankhurst, artist and daughter of the WSPU leader Emmeline Pankhurst, described it as "a striking pageant with its many gorgeous banners, richly embroidered and fashioned of velvets, silks and every kind of beautiful material and the small bannerettes serving as innumerable patches of brilliant and lovely colour, each one varying both in shape and hue." Sylvia herself, who had trained at the Manchester School of Art and the Royal College of Art, had been busy preparing for the WSPU's own demonstration a week later, on June 21. She produced various heraldic and border designs that were then sent to a manufacturer of banners and bunting to be mass-produced for the event.

The adoption that year of purple, white, and green as the colors of the WSPU provided the suffrage movement with the foundations of an unmistakable and widely recognized visual identity. Emmeline Pethick-Lawrence, writing as editor

Page 36: **Paul Stahr, *1776—Retouching an Old Masterpiece—1915*, front cover of *Life* magazine, 1915**

Watched by the ghost of Thomas Jefferson, a woman wearing the purple, green, and white colors adopted by the American Women's Political Union "retouches" the Declaration of Independence, by editing its most-famous line to read: "We hold these truths to be self evident, that all men and women are created equal."

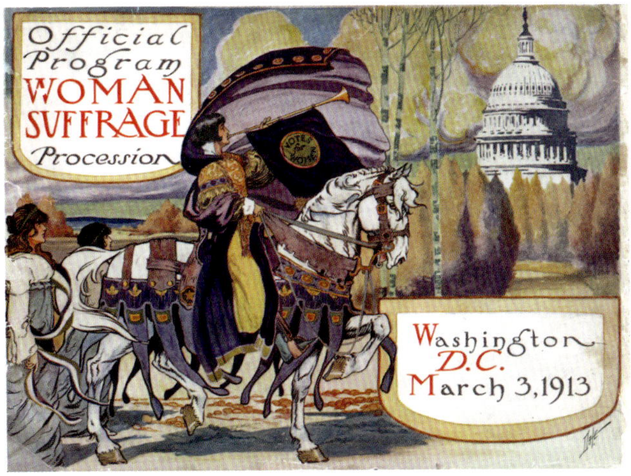

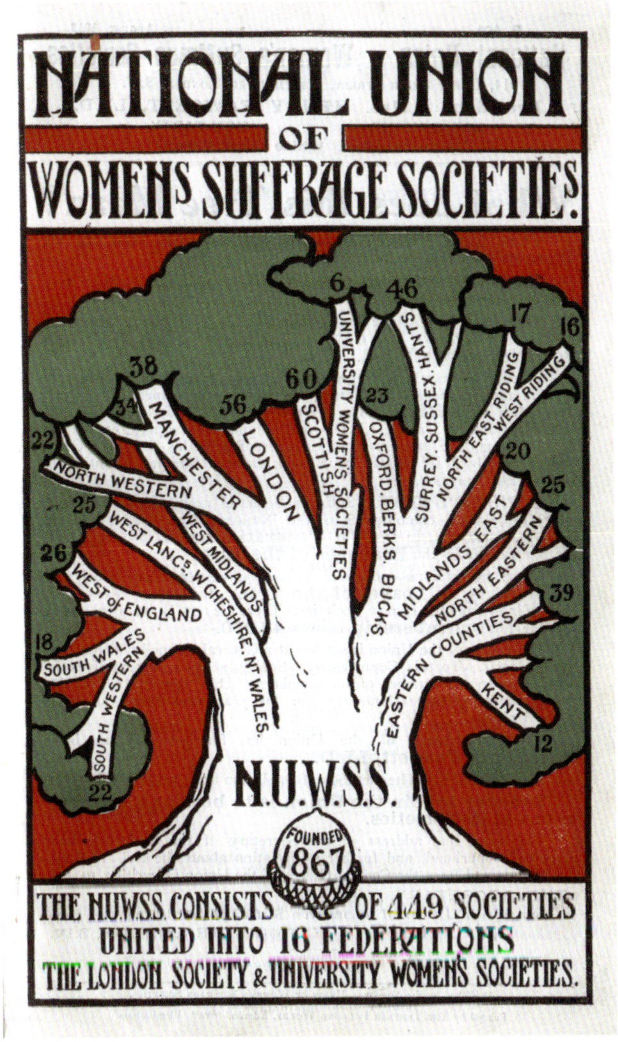

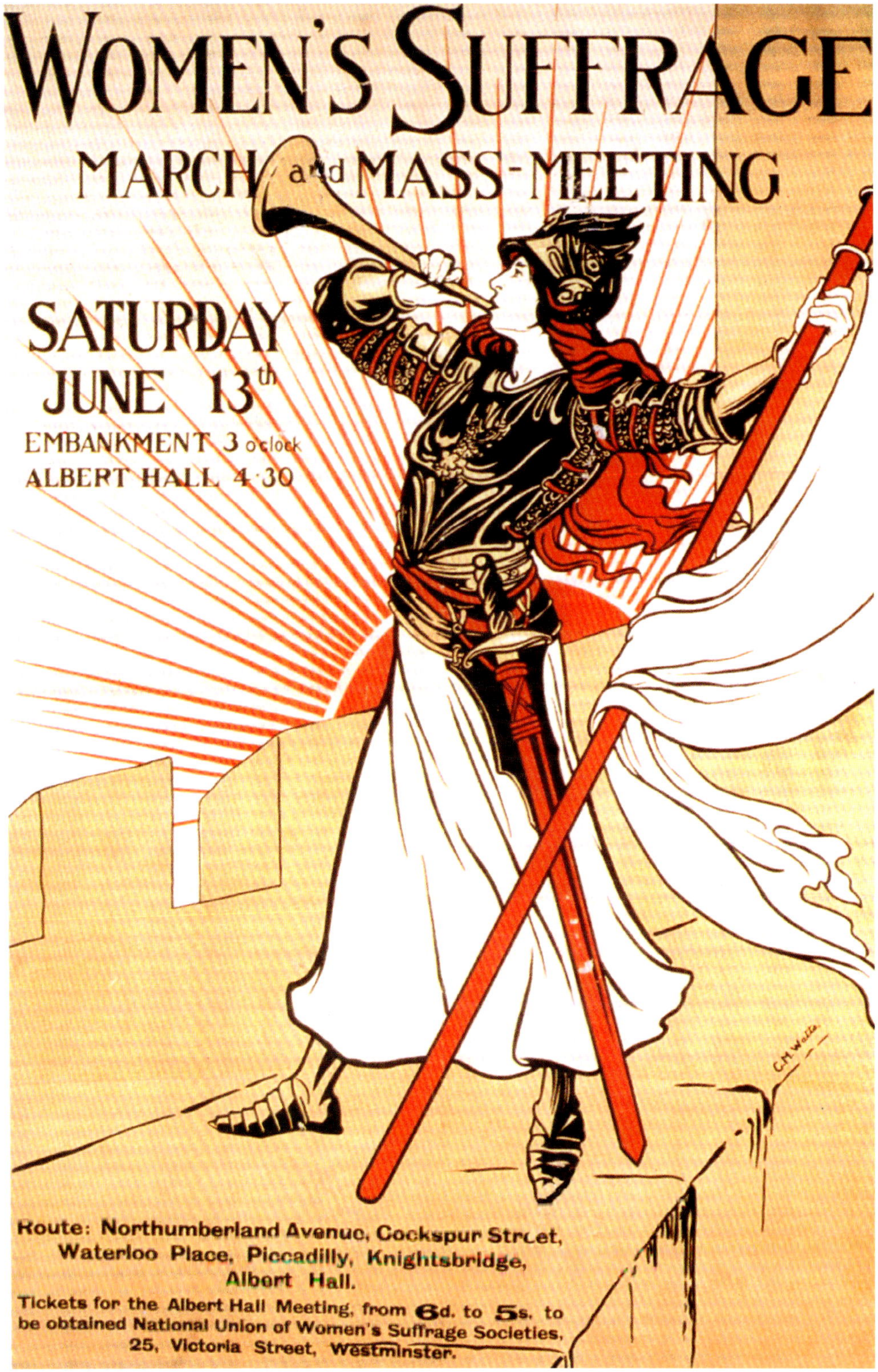

Top left: **Benjamin M. Dale, Woman Suffrage Procession program, 1913**

Dale studied at the Pennsylvania Museum and School of Industrial Art. His cover for the Woman Suffrage Procession program employs the romantic imagery of the medieval crusade with a woman on horseback acting as a herald or Joan of Arc figure.

Bottom left: **NUWSS pamphlet, 1909–14**

The National Union of Women's Suffrage Societies (NUWSS), founded by Millicent Fawcett, sought to ally suffrage societies around the United Kingdom under one banner and to campaign for the vote using peaceful means. The society adopted the colors of red, white, and green.

Above right: **Caroline Watts, *Bugler Girl*, 1908**

Caroline Watts studied at The Slade in London and worked as a magazine and book illustrator before becoming a designer for the Artists' Suffrage League (ASL). Her "Bugler Girl" was borrowed by the American women's suffrage movement, where it was recolored purple, white, and green.

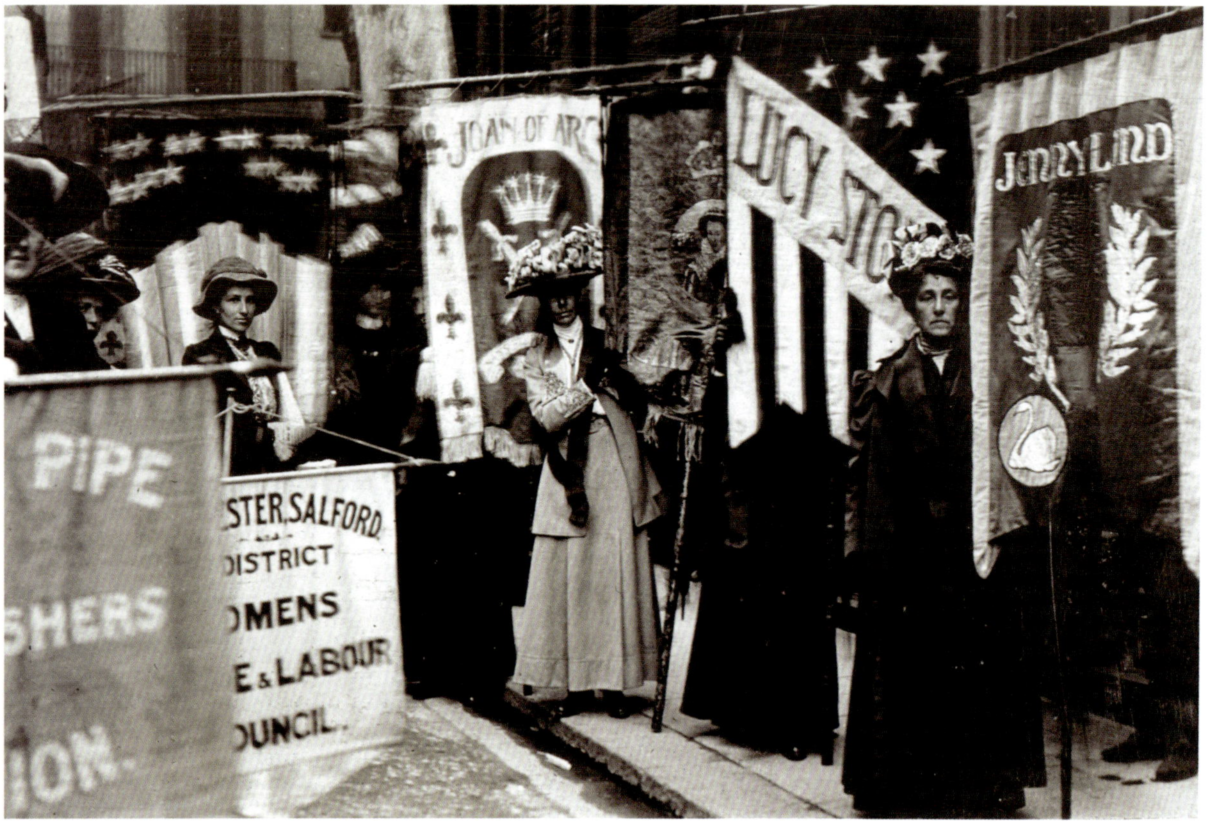

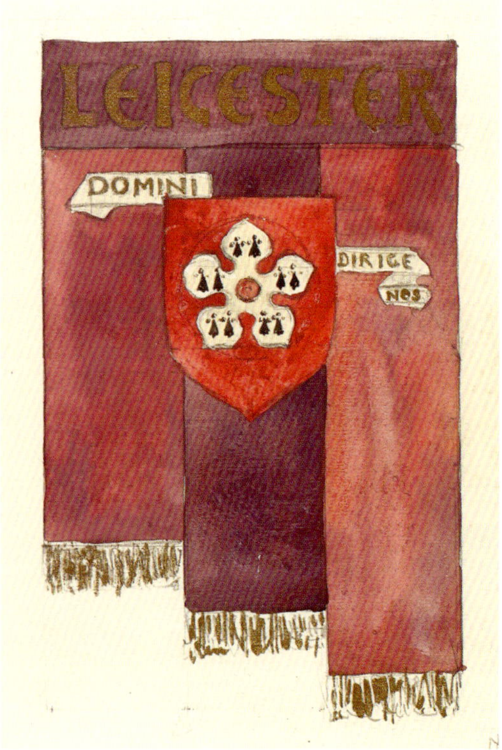

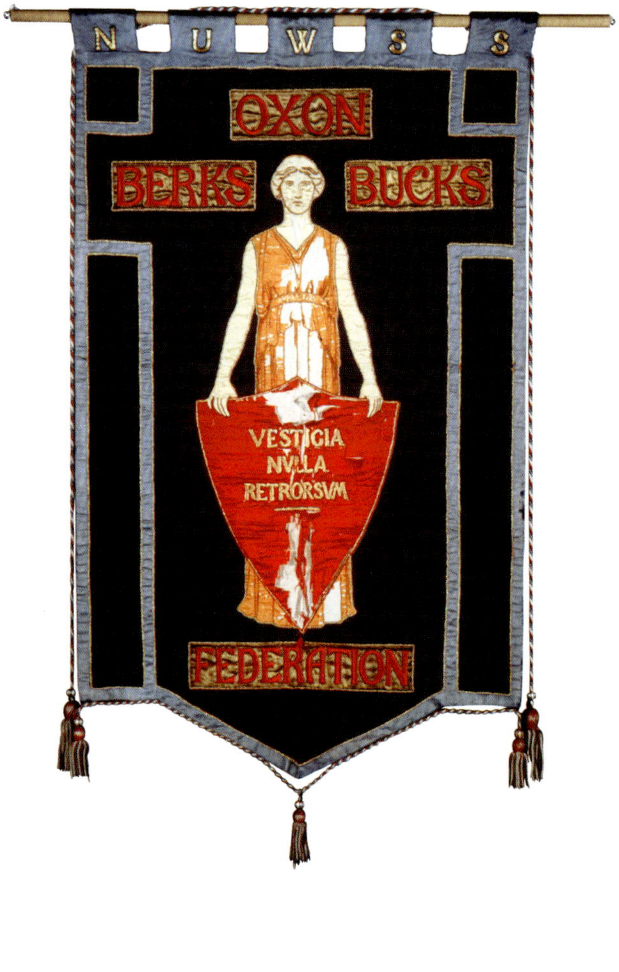

This page: **Mary Lowndes, banner designs**

Mary Lowndes ran a successful stained-glass workshop, and her innate feel for color and contrast transferred well to banner design. The NUWSS procession of June 13, 1908, was the first to employ colorful banners on a large scale, the majority of which were designed by Lowndes. The photograph shows members of the ASL with their banners on the day. Lowndes composed ideas in watercolor on paper before they were sewn, and an album of her original designs is now held at the Women's Library at the London School of Economics.

of *Votes for Women*, explained the choice of colors: "Purple as everyone knows is the royal colour, it stands for the royal blood that flows in the veins of every suffragette, the instinct of freedom and dignity . . . white stands for purity in private and public life . . . green is the colour of hope and the emblem of spring."

The June 21 demonstration saw pamphlets, leaflets, programs, and badges, official and otherwise, distributed in the distinctive color scheme. Introduced at the height of the WSPU's popularity and notoriety, the colors came to dominate the overall appearance of literature, propaganda, and merchandise, recognized not only by supporters of the movement, but by its opponents, too. Pethick-Lawrence wrote, "the colours enable us to make that appeal to the eye which is so irresistible. The result of our processions is that this movement becomes identified in the mind of the onlooker with colour, gay sound, movement, and beauty." A network of WSPU stores across the country not only dispensed advice and pamphlets, but also sold a wide range of paraphernalia in the organization's colors.

The WSPU brand colors were exported to the suffragette movement in the United States, where they were utilized, initially, by the Women's Political Union, whose founder, Harriet Stanton Blatch, had spent twenty years in the United Kingdom. More widely used in America by the NAWSA was a tricolor of purple, white, and gold, the gold symbolizing "the color of light and life, is as the torch that guides our purpose, pure and unswerving." (*The Suffragist*, 1913) Gold and yellow also had associations with the sunflower, the state flower of Kansas, the first state to have a referendum on women's suffrage, in 1867. While the Women's Political Union borrowed colors from the British WSPU, its emblem echoed another British suffragette motif, the Bugler Girl designed by Caroline Watts for the NUWSS Albert Hall meeting in 1908. In 1913, when the Woman's Suffrage Parade took place in Washington, D.C., the eight thousand marchers, mounted brigades, and floats took inspiration from the mass demonstrations of suffrage campaigners across the Atlantic. At the head of the march was campaigner, lawyer, and journalist Inez Milholland, a striking allegorical vision made flesh, riding on a white horse with her white cape billowing behind her.

Allegorical and historical figures such as the Bugler Girl or Joan of Arc proved effective devices for replicating across a range of promotional literature and merchandise. Sylvia Pankhurst designed a number of versions for the WSPU, including a heraldic "angel of freedom," a woman emerging from prison gates, and another of a woman sowing a field. American artist Bertha M. Boye's quasi-religious figure clad in Native American draperies was the winning design in the San Francisco College Equal Suffrage League poster competition and exhibited the same graphic impact as the motifs used in Britain. All the images were simple and easy to reproduce in the now-familiar color scheme. But they were also rife with symbolism and in keeping with tastes of the period, drawing on the styles of arts and crafts and art nouveau—Sylvia was a particular admirer of Walter Crane and William Morris. They were used to give a cohesive look across albums, programs, cards, and pamphlets; the angel of freedom even decorated a suffragette tea set.

Contrary to the stereotype peddled by anti-suffrage supporters—who typically portrayed the suffragette as an ugly, masculine, shrieking termagant—women were encouraged to take an interest in fashion and to dress stylishly. "Suffragettes should not be dowdy," declared Christabel Pankhurst, Sylvia's elder sister and the driving force behind the increasingly militant WSPU. As a poster girl for the movement, Christabel's image graced millions of postcards distributed by the WSPU. Many suffragettes wore delicate white dresses of lace and cotton muslin, embellished with sashes, scarves, and ribbons in the colors. By the end of 1908, Mappin & Webb, jewelers by royal appointment, had produced a catalog of suffragette jewelry. Made with semiprecious stones such as amethyst and peridot to replicate the suffragette colors, here was a more subtle way to express support for the movement. Annie Steen was a jewelry designer and member of another artist collective, the Suffrage Atelier, associated closely with the WSPU. Advertisements for her suffragette jewelry were placed in the organization's magazine, *Votes for Women* (later renamed *The Suffragette*). The magazine in turn carried cover designs in the color scheme, as did its advertising posters, some of the most memorable designed by Hilda Dallas. Many major London department stores, including Selfridges, supported the suffragettes by advertising in the magazine and stocking suggested outfits for upcoming rallies and demonstrations. Macy's in New York catered similarly to suffrage campaigners in the United States. It was an expedient alignment, a brand affiliation whereby support of, and association with, the movement created commercial benefit for both parties.

As an early example of brand marketing, the suffragette movement, and particularly the designs and schemes of the WSPU, are an impressive example of how artistic focus and energetic promotion could create a clear, compelling visual statement for followers to adopt with ease. It is worth remembering that even within the progressive social milieu of the suffrage movement, the women involved in shaping this brand came predominantly from white, middle-, or upper-class backgrounds and were privileged enough to have received some kind of art education. Nevertheless, it was significant in drawing upon the rich pool of talent available, with much work carried out by women artists and designers. Here was a platform from which to prove their skills and where standards were equal to those of their male counterparts. The output from this enormous marketing drive is no less significant today, with suffragette objects and ephemera highly collectable not only for their historical significance, but also for their distinctive design and appeal, more than a century on.

Below left: **Emily J. Harding Andrews, *Convicts, Lunatics and Women! Have No Vote in Parliament*, 1908**

Published by the ASL, this poster was probably the design entered into an annual poster competition organized by the ASL and the NUWSS. Given second prize, the poster echoed Frances Power Cobbe's article, "Criminals, Idiots, Women, Minors, is the classification sound?" published in *Fraser's* Magazine in 1868. The contrast of the dignified and physically perfect woman with the degeneracy of disenfranchised males hammers the message home.

Below right: ***A Suffragette in Holloway Prison*, sketch in *The Lady's Realm*, 1908**

Signed E.R., this sketch was one of several accompanying an article in *Lady's Realm* by Dr. Helen Bourchier, recounting her experiences of imprisonment in London's Holloway Prison as an "educated woman." Bourchier, a member of the Women's Freedom League, was arrested on January 31, 1908, after taking part in an impromptu rally on the steps of Prime Minister Herbert Asquith's house.

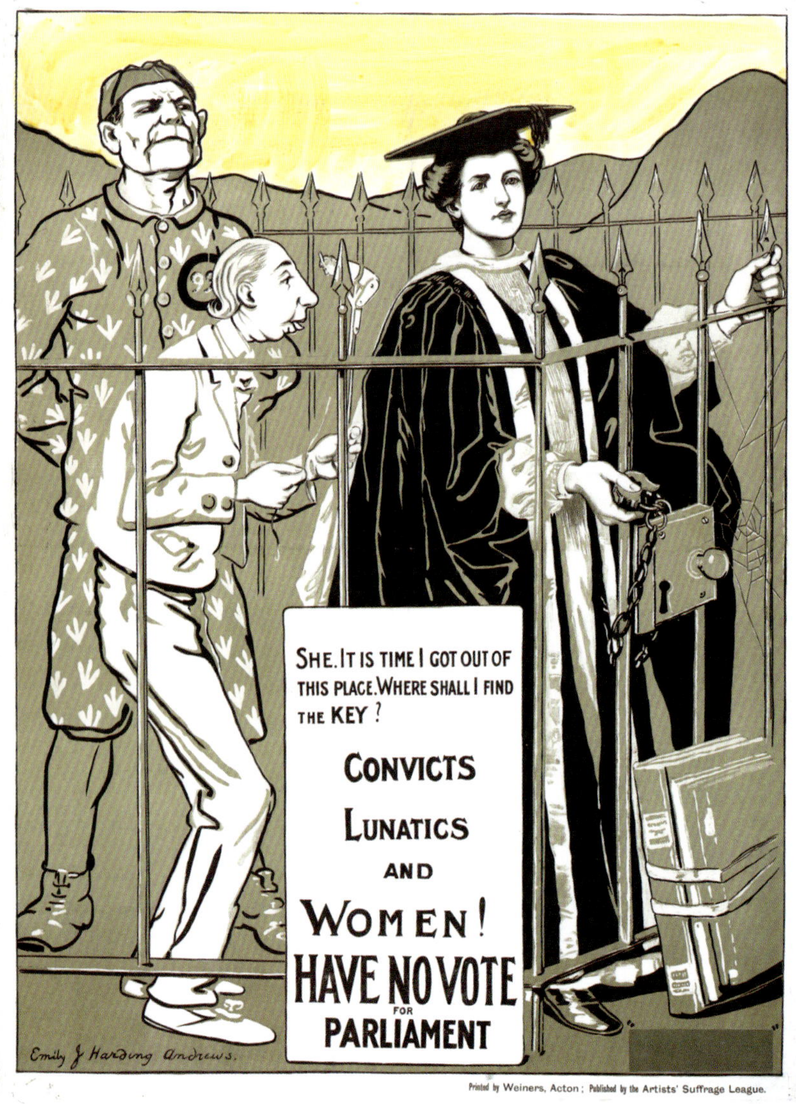

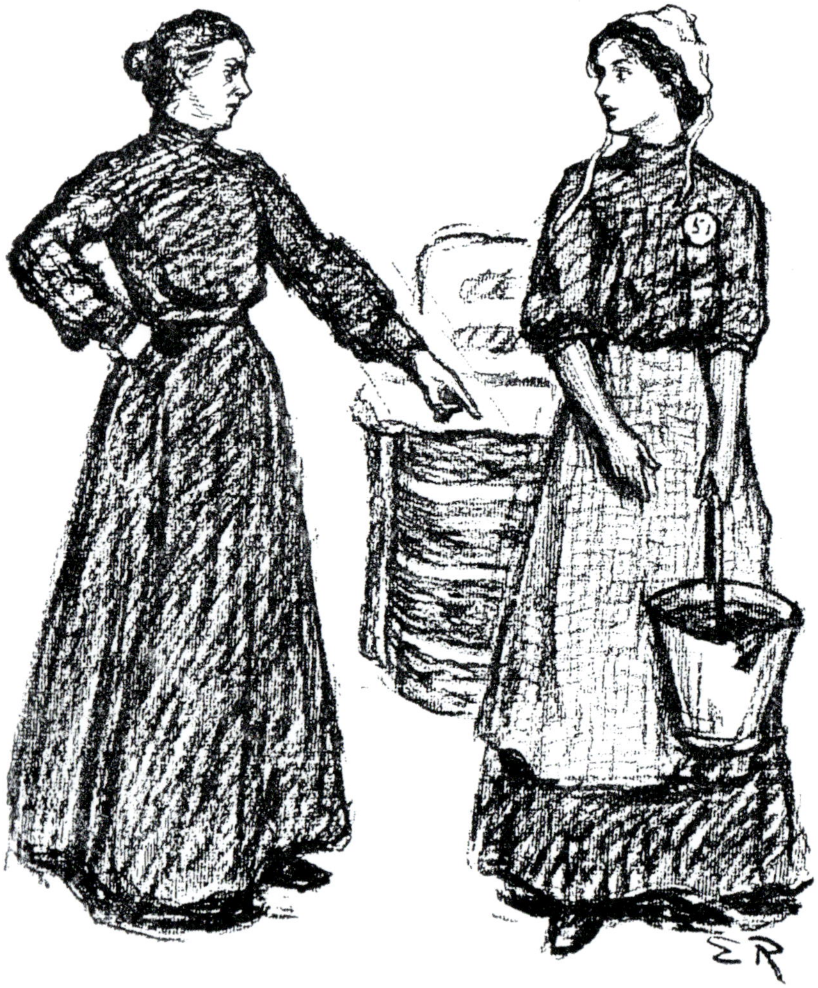

"She had a commanding personality."

Right: **Artist unknown, Women's Social and Political Union (WSPU) poster, ca. 1910**

Between 1909 and 1914 in Britain, women prisoners who went on hunger strike were subjected to the brutal procedure of forcible feeding, a painful and humiliating violation described as an "outrage" by those who experienced it. The practice was considered government-sponsored torture by the WSPU. The brutality of forced feeding endured by suffrage prisoners, seen through this poster and others, has become one of the defining images of the movement.

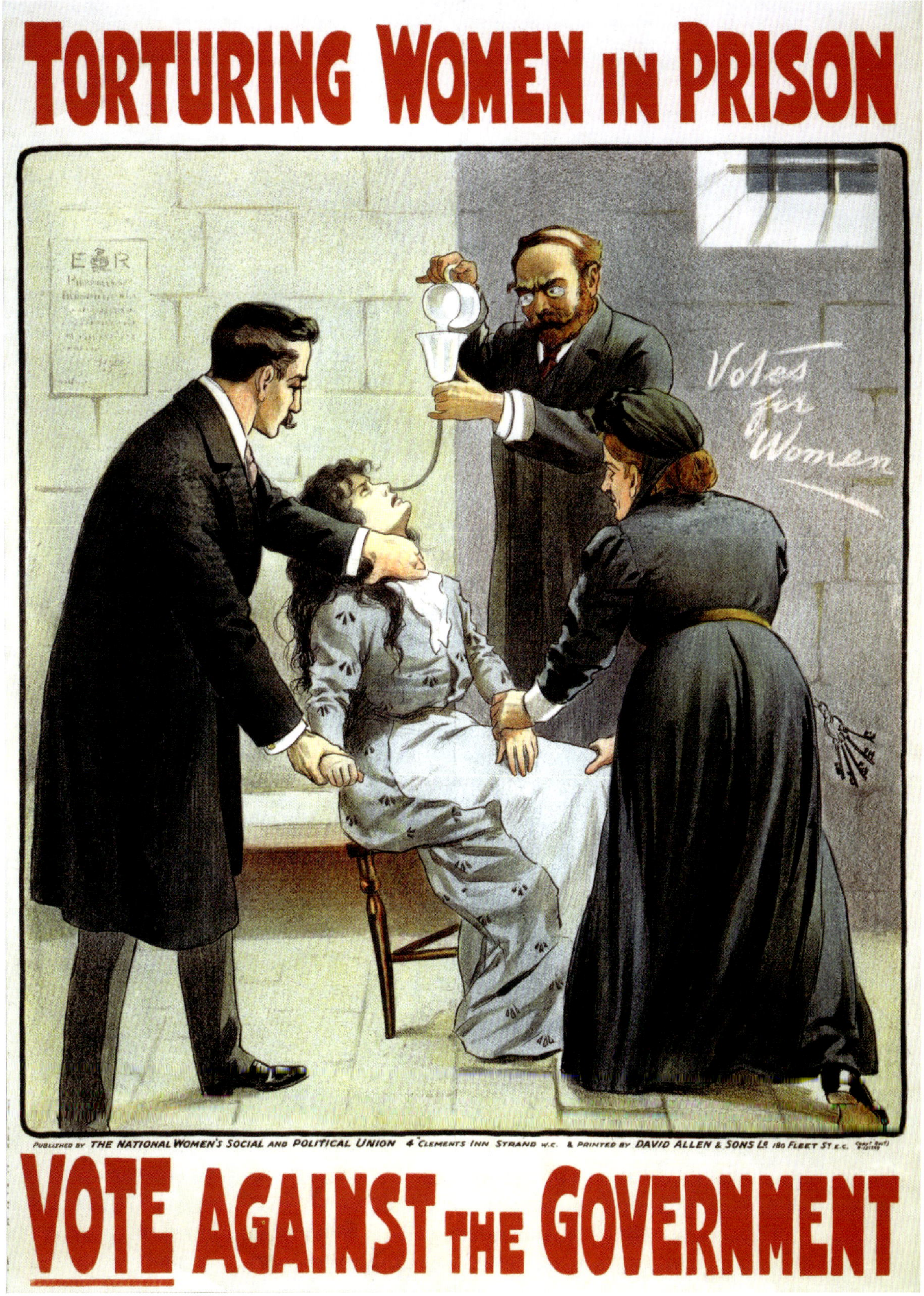

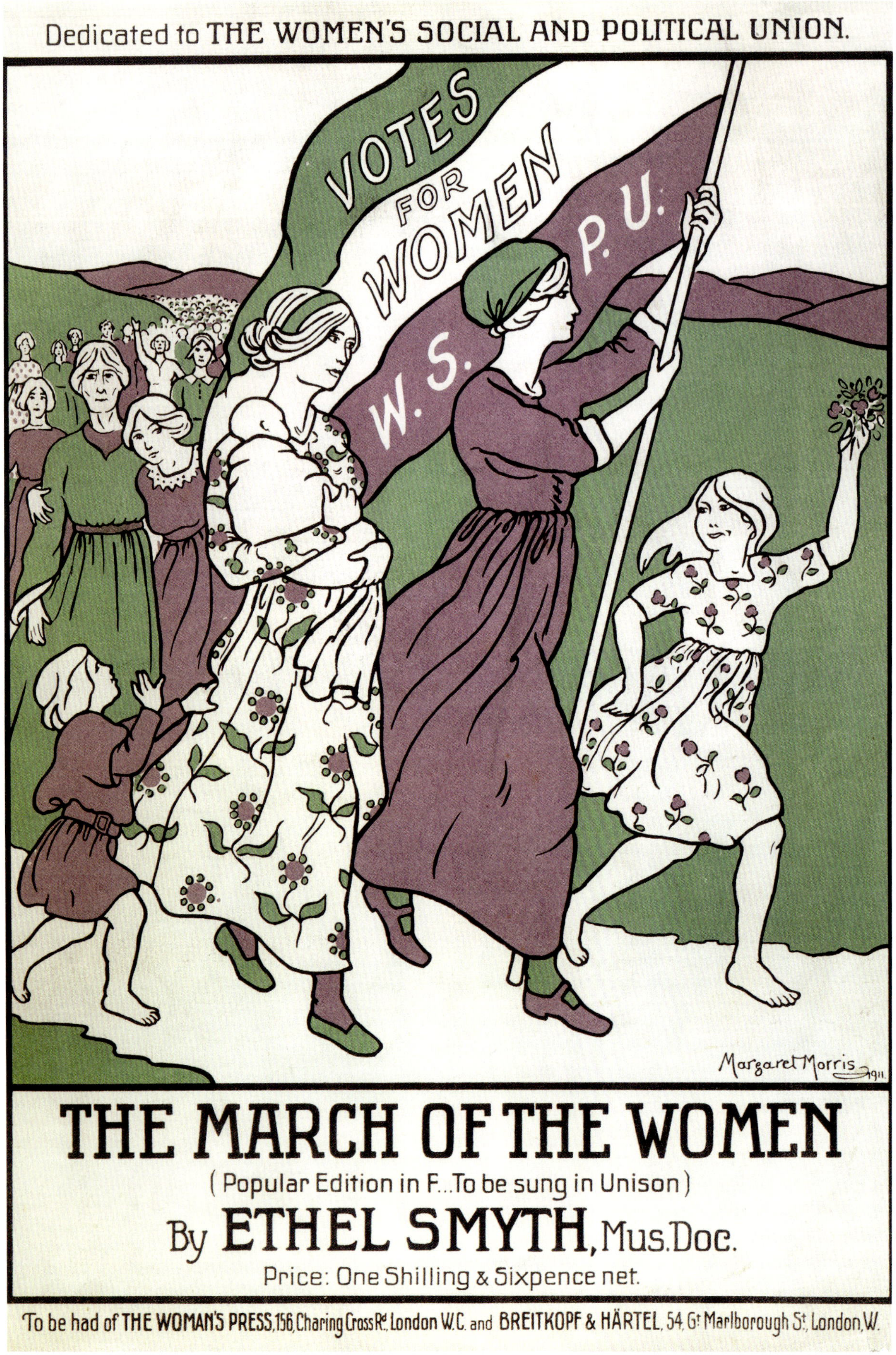

Left: Margaret Morris, *The March of the Women*, song sheet, 1911

Margaret Morris is better known as a dance pioneer and founder of the "Margaret Morris Movement" network of schools in Britain, but she was also an artist and, through family connections and friendships, naturally drawn to the suffrage cause. This gentle design, reminiscent of Walter Crane's socialist illustrations, accompanies the Women's Social and Political Union (WSPU) anthem composed by Ethel Smyth and Cicely Hamilton and suggests the cause mattered to all generations of women, including young mothers.

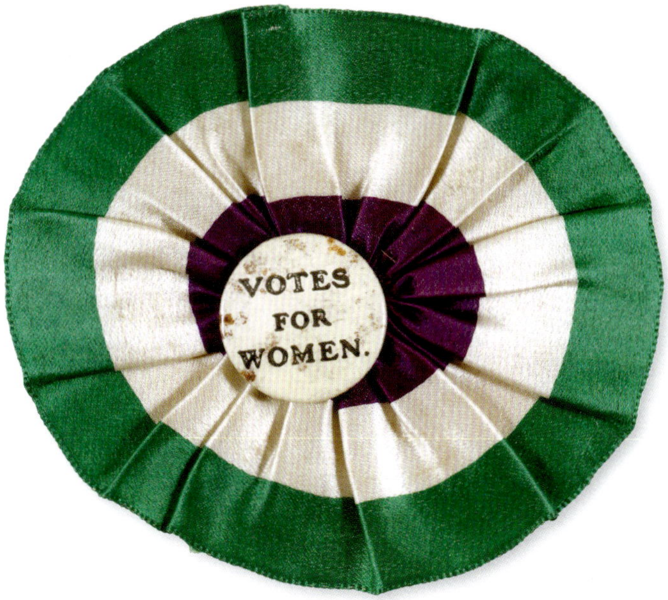

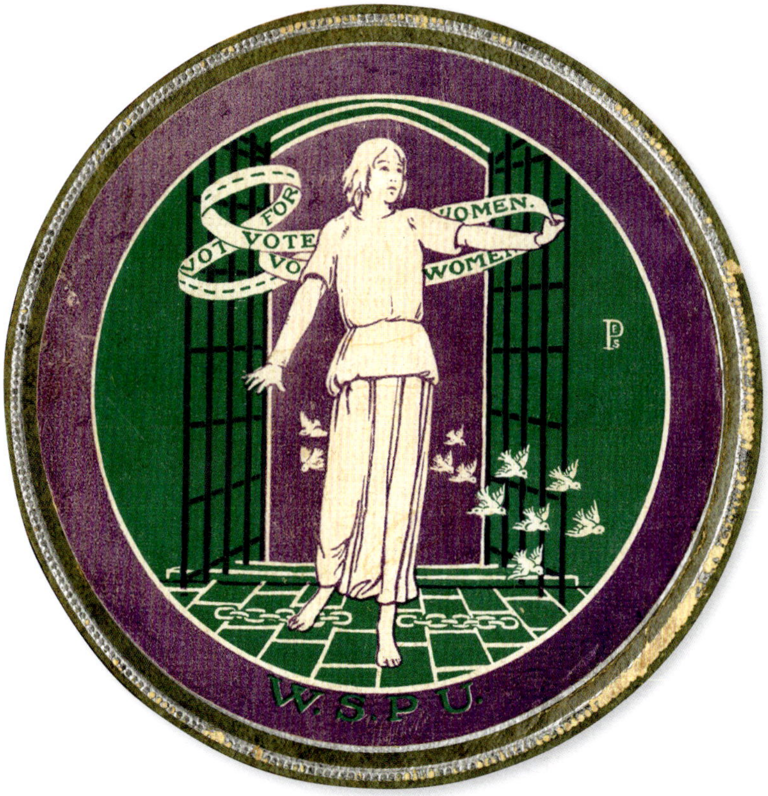

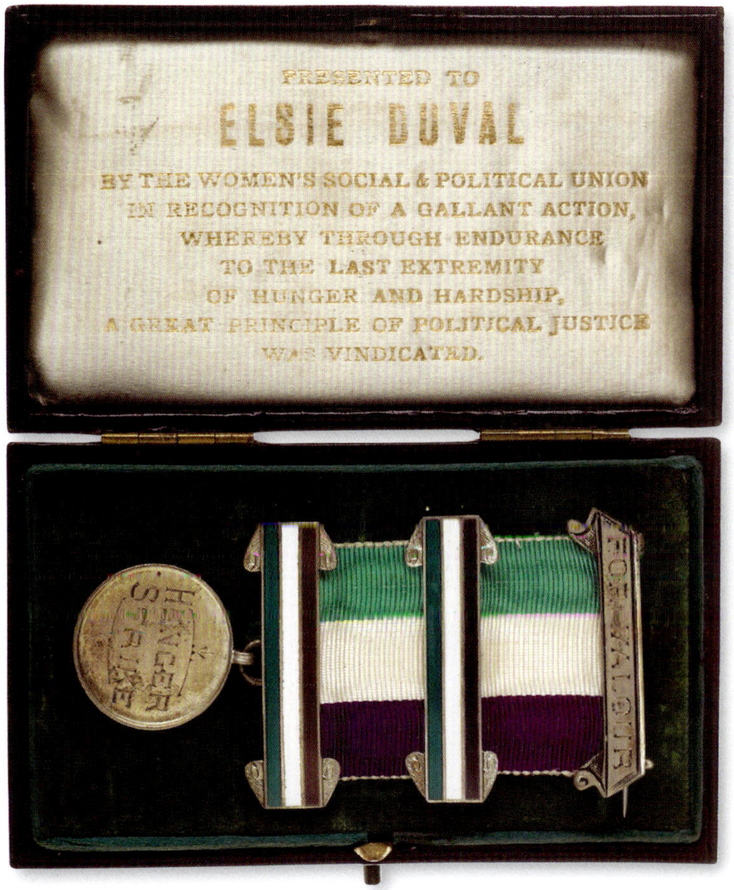

This page: Purple, white, and green, the colors of the WSPU became synonymous with the cause in Britain and were adopted by thousands nationwide who were implored to "wear the colors" as a public declaration of their support. From the livery of a campaigning Austin car used by the Pankhursts to ribbons, rosettes, and badges, the layering and repetition of the tricolor identified supporters and created a cohesive and unified appearance, regardless of the widening chasm of disagreement between separate factions.

The Suffrage Atelier

In February 1909, the Suffrage Atelier held its first public meeting in London, England. Formed by a group of like-minded artists and writers, the group sought to use the various skills and crafts of its members to support women's suffrage.

The Suffrage Atelier styled itself as "an Arts and Crafts Society Working for the Enfranchisement of Women." It was not the first suffrage organization formed with the aim of producing art to support the cause—the Artists' Suffrage League (ASL), founded two years earlier, was already designing banners and posters for the National Union of Women's Suffrage Societies (NUWSS). But, while the ASL comprised largely established, professional artists, the Suffrage Atelier took a more holistic approach, encouraging amateurs to submit designs, paying them a small percentage of any designs sold, and offering women opportunities to develop as artists and designers.

The atelier held exhibitions of its work and established a schedule of workshops and classes where members could train in a number of arts and crafts disciplines with a dual objective of not only increasing the effectiveness of its suffrage propaganda, but also of equipping women with skills that would make them employable. A typical timetable at the Suffrage Atelier's headquarters might include instruction on printing processes, banner-making, drawing methods, stenciling, and life drawing; designs were regularly critiqued and there were even classes in public speaking.

Utilizing cheap, if rather crude, block-printing techniques, often by hand, from either wood or linocuts, artists had the agility to respond at speed to current events and to produce posters and pamphlets at short notice. This advantage was discussed at the Suffrage Atelier's first public meeting in June 1909 and reported in the NUWSS paper, *The Common Cause*, which wrote, "fresh cartoons could be got out at a very short notice and very little expense. This should be particularly valuable at election times, when something topical is needed at once." It was an unorthodox approach, but one that proved effective as the Suffrage Atelier produced three times as many designs as the ASL, whose posters were limited by the cost and techniques of lithographic printing.

Key figures in the Suffrage Atelier were two of its cofounders, Laurence and Clemence Housman, the brother and sister of the poet A.E. Housman. Laurence was already a leading illustrator in pen and ink, providing drawings from his "freakish imagination" for Christina Rossetti's "Goblin Market," as well as illustrating volumes of self-penned poetry. Clemence worked as an engraver for leading weekly periodicals *The Graphic* and *The Illustrated London News* during the 1880s but, as photomechanical processes began to eclipse engraving, she turned to publishers who were actively preserving the art of fine printing, such as Grant Richards and the Pear Tree Press. Though the atelier's designs are more rough-and-ready than the Housmans' illustration work, their influence is clear. The resulting designs are also refreshingly modern, despite their derivative, primitive style, due in part to the fashionable revival of woodblocking at the time.

Laurence was a founding member of the Men's League for Women's Suffrage and, as his eyesight began to fail, became a prolific author of over one hundred books and plays, many of them tackling controversial topics. He claimed his political awakening came after hearing Emmeline Pankhurst speak and, despite being born into a typically conservative middle-class family, would remain a socialist and pacifist for the rest of his life. Clemence, meanwhile, became "chief worker" at the atelier, according to Laurence, who lent his studio in the garden of their London home at 1 Pembroke Cottages, Edwardes Square, in Kensington for its activities. Clemence's illustrious, if waning, career as an engraver may be echoed in the monochrome style of the atelier, but the organization also recognized the need to embrace new technology alongside the preservation of historic craftsmanship.

Although it was originally founded to "work as far as possible for all the Women's Suffrage Societies impartially," in 1912, the atelier allied itself with the Women's Freedom League (WFL), at which time it began to produce a color supplement to be inserted into the organization's magazine, *Vote*. In introducing this pictorial content, its editor, Charlotte Despard, underlined the importance of learning new techniques in line with modern reproduction processes. Hers was a robust and unsentimental strategy, focused on giving supporters of suffrage, particularly women, a foothold in the rapidly changing landscape of commercial art. The Suffrage Atelier safeguarded traditional skills while promoting the acquisition of new ones, but it is also a case study in enlightened reciprocity, where artists and designers could support a political cause while reaping practical benefits, valuable experience, and lifelong skills.

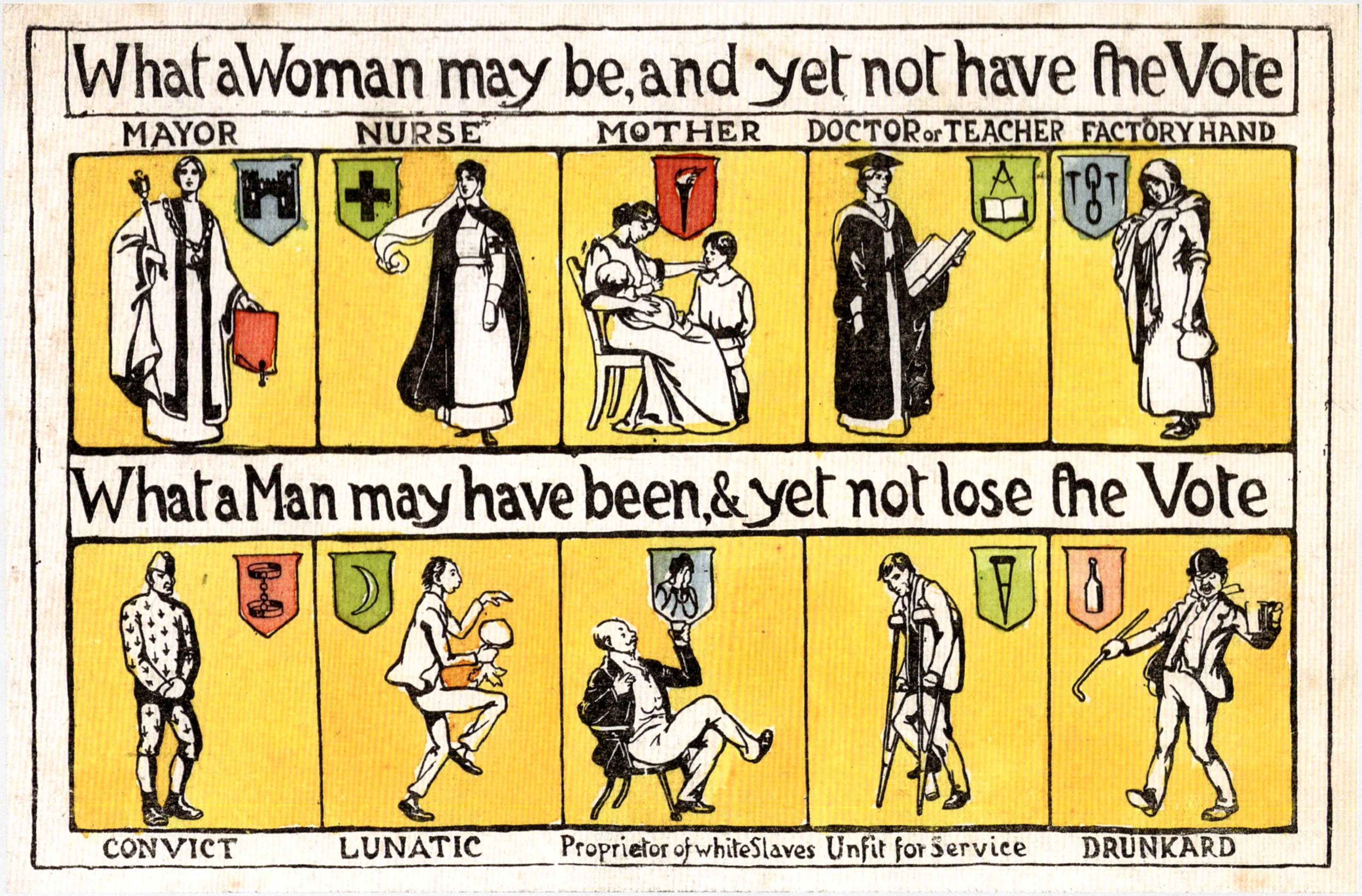

"It is common knowledge that in journalistic, advertising, and poster illustrative work, the artist, on leaving the schools, frequently has so little real knowledge of the style and subject lending itself most effectively to printing work . . . Too little attention is paid to the practical side of the training, viz., the consideration of the market value of certain forms of work, so as to provide art pupils not only with an art training, but with a working career which will have a definite commercial value."

Charlotte Despard, *Vote* magazine color supplement, 1912

Above: **Suffrage Atelier, *What a Woman May be and yet not have the Vote*, ca. 1912**

Design for poster and postcard.

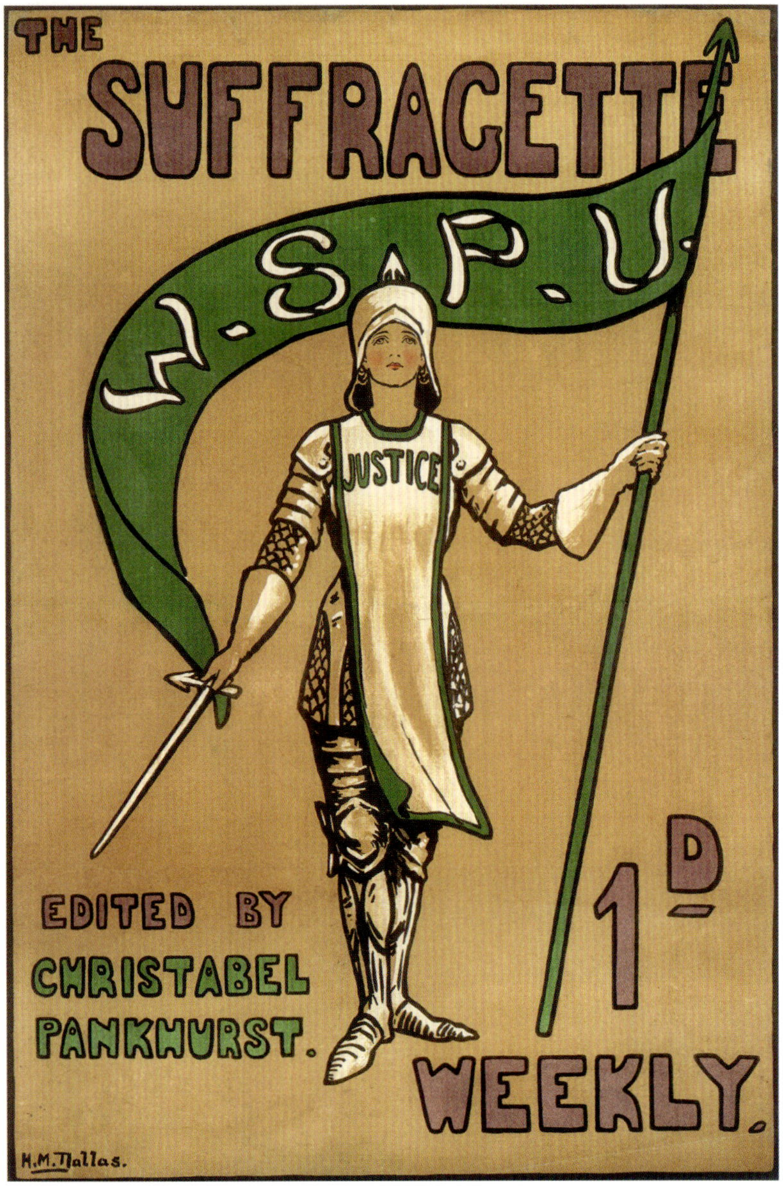

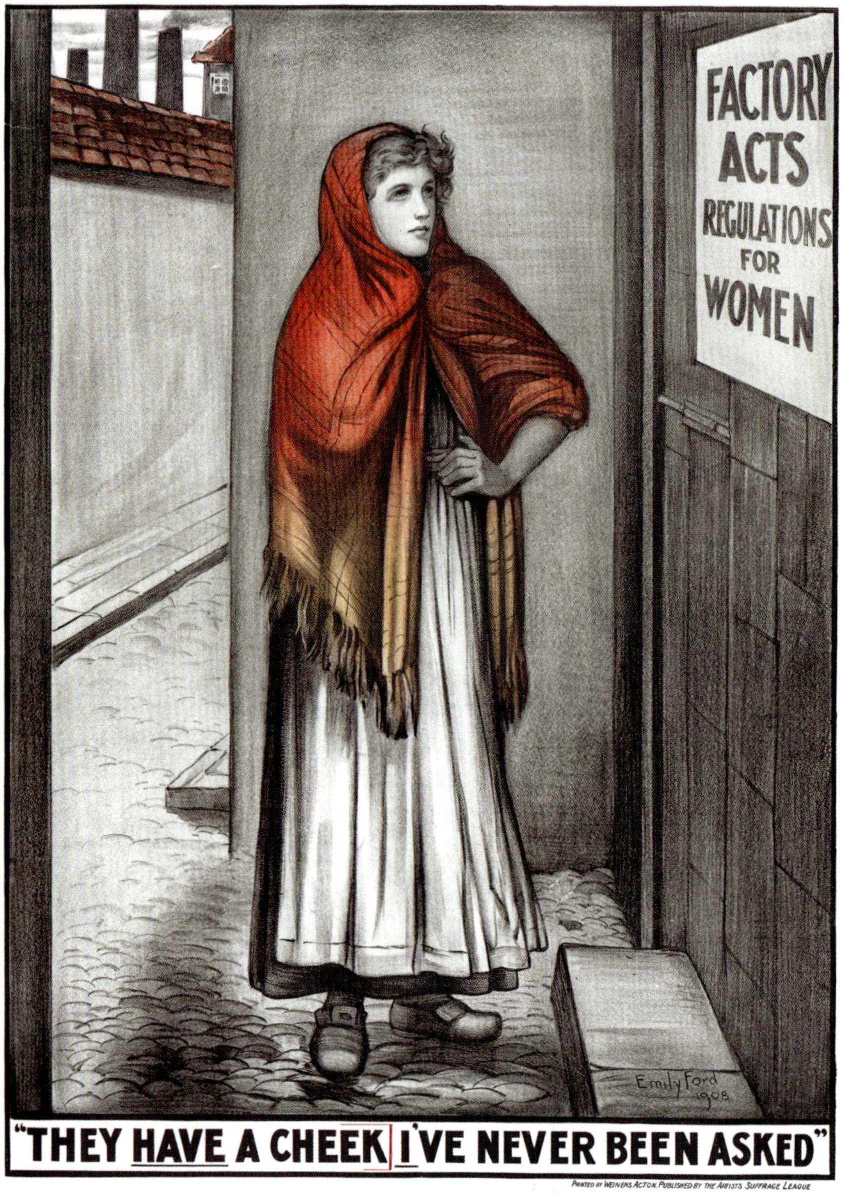

Above left: **Hilda Dallas, poster for *The Suffragette*, 1912**

Hilda Dallas's designs for the WSPU echo the bold outlines and spare composition of contemporary commercial poster designers such as John Hassall and Will Owen, and are highly effective as a result. An ally of the Pankhursts, Dallas designed posters for *Votes for Women* and, later, for *The Suffragette*, edited by Christabel Pankhurst. The knightly figure with the fluttering pennant was the type increasingly used by the WSPU and likened the cause to a holy crusade, suffusing the militancy of the movement with a sense of justice.

Above right: **Emily Ford, *They Have a Cheek*, poster for the Artists' Suffrage League, 1908**

Emily Ford was a founding member and vice chairman of the ASL. Her poster criticizing the passing of factory acts features a mill girl of the north of England, one of the thousands of women workers who had no say in the legislation affecting them directly.

Right: **Duncan Grant, *Handicapped*, poster, 1909**

Duncan Grant, whose introduction to the suffrage cause was through his cousin, Philippa Strachey, was joint winner of the ASL and NUWSS annual poster competition with this design, which uses an effective visual metaphor for the disadvantages faced by women without the vote.

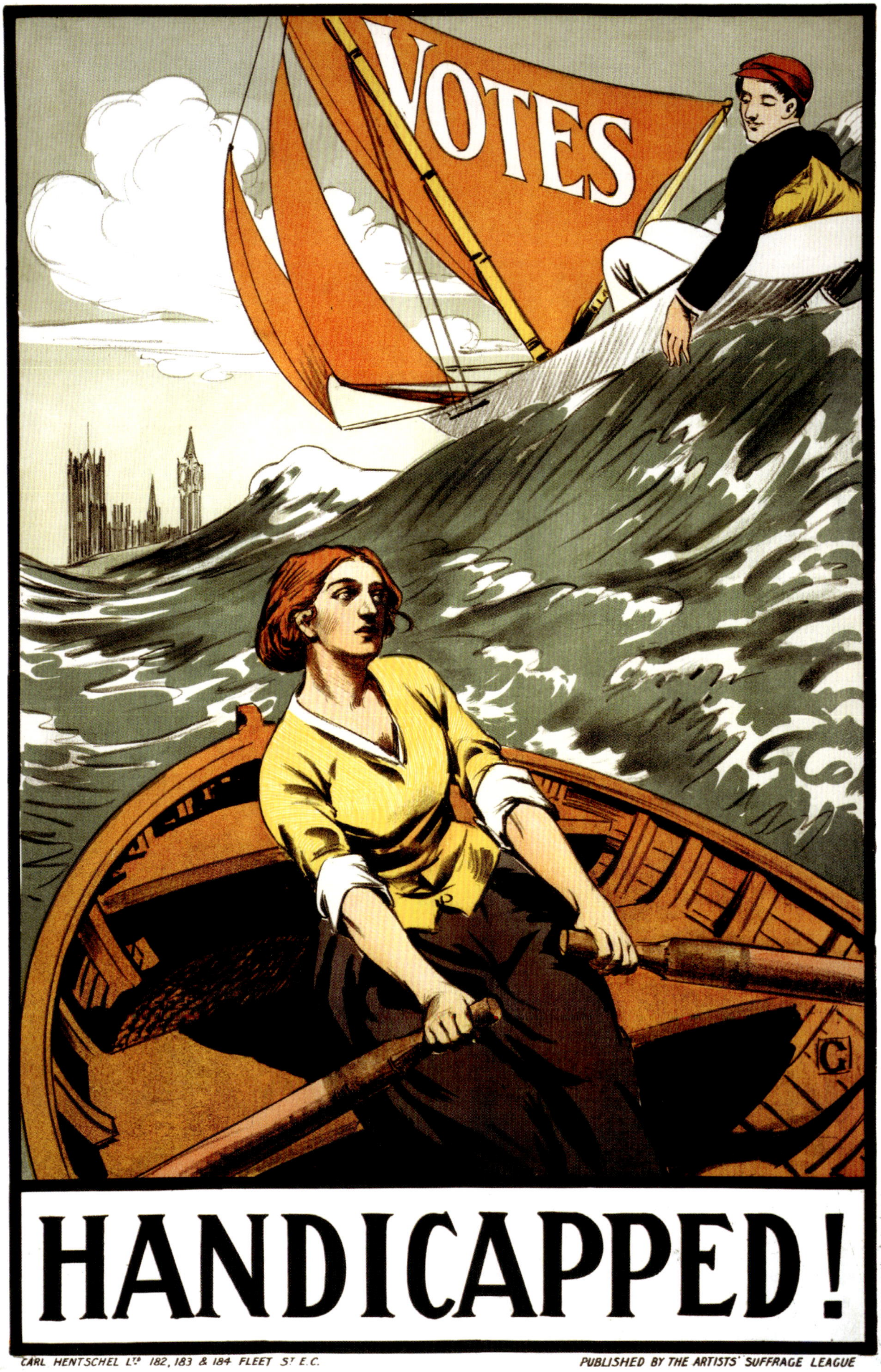

Exhibiting Feminism

At 2 pm, on May 1, 1893, the World's Columbian Exposition, better known as the Chicago World's Fair, opened to visitors—bigger and better than any exhibition yet mounted in a century that showed a particular enthusiasm for such things. A similar model was later adopted by suffrage campaigners in Britain.

Chicago was notable for including a Woman's Building, dedicated to showcasing the achievements of the female sex through a mix of art, crafts, and culture. It was the first of its kind. Even the building itself, measuring an enormous 76,000 sq ft (7,000 sq m), was designed by a young twenty-one-year-old female architect, Sophia C. Hayden. Inside, exhibits and displays that included embroidery, carvings, sculpture, jewelry, and a library were exclusively the creation of women. Of particular significance were two 58 x 12 ft (17.5 x 3.5 m) mural canvases located at the north and south points of the building's Gallery of Honor. One, on the theme of "Primitive Woman," was by Mary Fairchild Macmonnies and showed women from the past engaged in various industries. The other was executed by America's greatest impressionist artist, Mary Cassatt, who at the time, having spent years studying and living in Paris, was relatively unknown. Perhaps the predominantly male critics were bemused by the subject matter of Cassatt's work, which symbolized women as ambitious knowledge seekers and creators of more than just children, while the large central panel implied the passing of knowledge from one female generation to the next—all independent of male influence. Though both murals were lost after the dismantling of the exhibition, photographs survived. The Woman's Building and its exhibits did not carry a specific suffrage message, but it was nevertheless a resounding fanfare for the accomplishments and abilities of women.

In Britain, in 1909, Sylvia Pankhurst was tasked with providing murals to decorate the walls of Prince's Skating Rink in Knightsbridge, the setting for the Women's Exhibition. Remembered as a suffragette and feminist, Sylvia's early ambitions were to be an artist. She was raised in a radical middle-class household where books illustrated by the socialist artists Walter Crane and William Morris were her inspiration. The exhibition was organized by the Women's Social and Political Union (WSPU) led by her mother and sister, Emmeline and Christabel, and was to be a two-week-long fundraiser in May. It was an ambitious event energetically advertised around London with banner parades, the WSPU's own girl drum and fife band, and a festooned boat sailing down the Thames River.

Prince's Skating Rink was a vast space, measuring 250 x 150 ft (76 x 46 m), for which Sylvia created a series of mammoth canvases. She enlisted the help of acquaintances from her time as a student at the Royal College of Art, all of whom were paid a modest fee, and worked around the clock using paint and stencils to recreate her designs on 20 ft (6 m) canvas sheets. The completed decorations, rendered in WSPU colors of purple, white, and green, used the words of the Psalms, "They that sow in sorrow, reap in joy," as a thread running through the deeply symbolic motifs, clearly reflecting the influence of Walter Crane's work. The female sower, a design of Sylvia's already being used across WSPU literature and merchandise, loomed over the entrance, flanked on either side by blossoming almond trees. At the opposite end of the hall, a trio of similarly colossal figures—two angels with a woman bearing a sheath of grain—stood triumphant. All along the walls, twining leaves, trees, birds, and floral patterns formed a backdrop of imposing grandeur to the event. The canvases, only ever meant to be temporary, were destroyed during one of Sylvia's periods of imprisonment for suffrage protests. Nevertheless, they remained symbolic of the militant women's movement and were frequently reproduced in suffragette publications in subsequent years.

Elsewhere, the exhibition combined customary elements of the traditional bazaar, a distinctly feminine phenomenon and familiar territory of the Victorian woman, with awareness-raising exhibits and speakers. Stalls selling cakes, floral buttonholes, and handicrafts joined a host of interactive events and activities designed to push the *Votes for Women* message. It was an engaging mix calculated to demonstrate that enfranchisement did not necessarily mean an abandonment of those activities that were considered natural and "womanly," nor that suffrage campaigners lacked femininity. Every visitor, male or female, was given a ballot paper as they entered and were encouraged to vote on a different issue each day, using a mock polling booth. A replica second-class prison cell, inhabited by women who had personally experienced conditions at Holloway, demonstrated the conditions endured by the imprisoned suffragette. To provide context, an example of the type of first-class cell given to male political prisoners was displayed alongside. Dioramas showed wax cartoon figures of leading members of the cabinet, including Prime Minister Asquith and minister Lloyd George, in a variety of satirical scrapes.

Merchandise for sale included a stylish Staffordshire tea set, as well as a variety of badges, scarves, and ribbons, all bearing the WSPU colors and the angel herald symbol created by Sylvia. One stall offered portrait sketches to visitors done by suffragette artists, and a portrait of Emmeline Pankhurst by Ethel Wright was on display in the art gallery with a £100 price tag destined for WSPU coffers. Purchases intended as gifts could be taken to a special parcel area where they would be wrapped using ribbons in the color scheme. By the end of the fortnight, the Women's Exhibition had raised over £5,000, the equivalent of around £600,000 ($830,000) today. Having attracted thousands of visitors and recruited more supporters, much of the exhibition's success could be attributed to the organizers' shrewd employment of art and design.

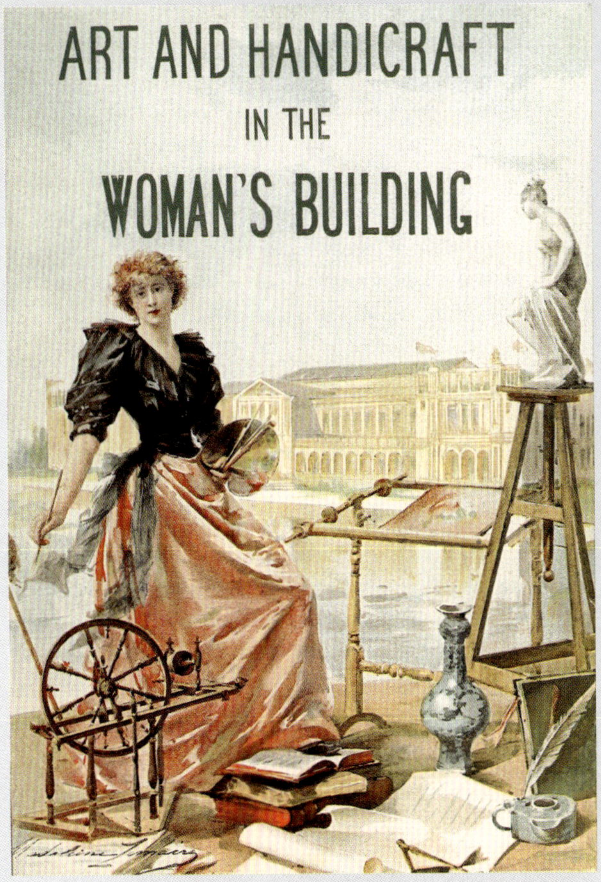

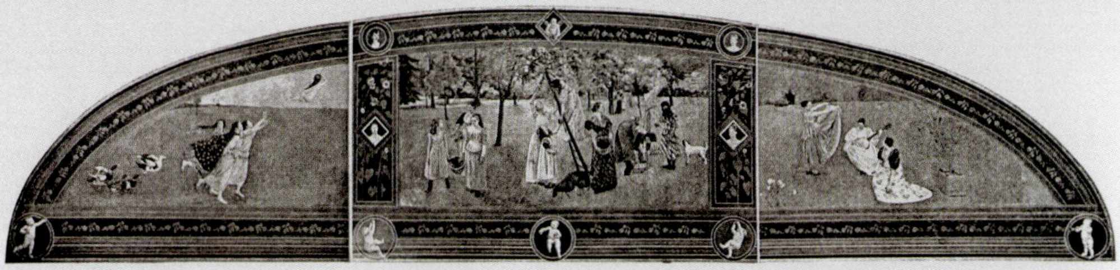

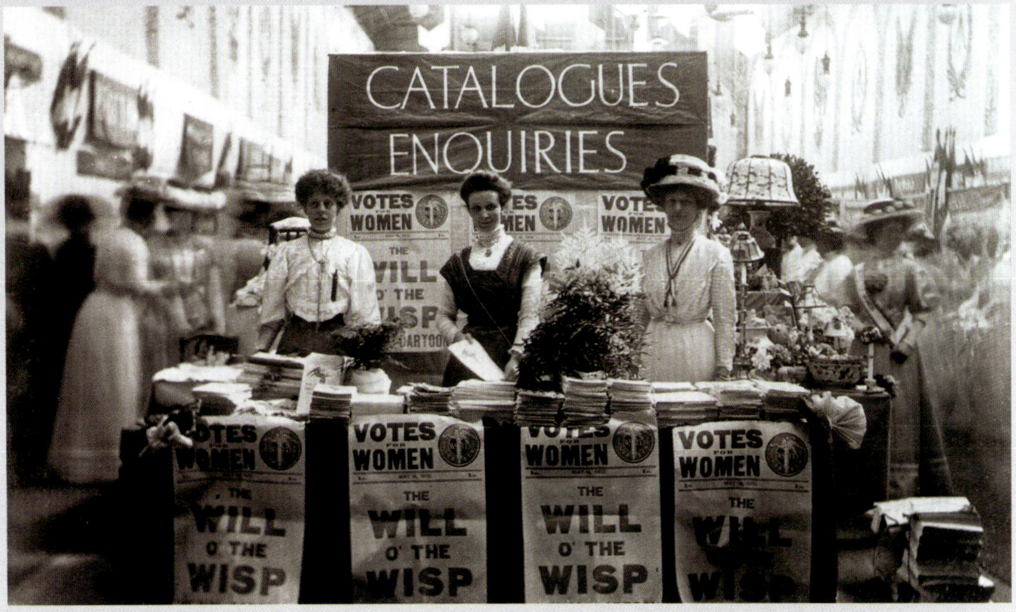

"The hall has never looked better. The scheme of decoration in the Suffragette colours—purple, green and white—was most clever and effective."

The Illustrated Sporting & Dramatic News, on the Women's Exhibition in London, 1909

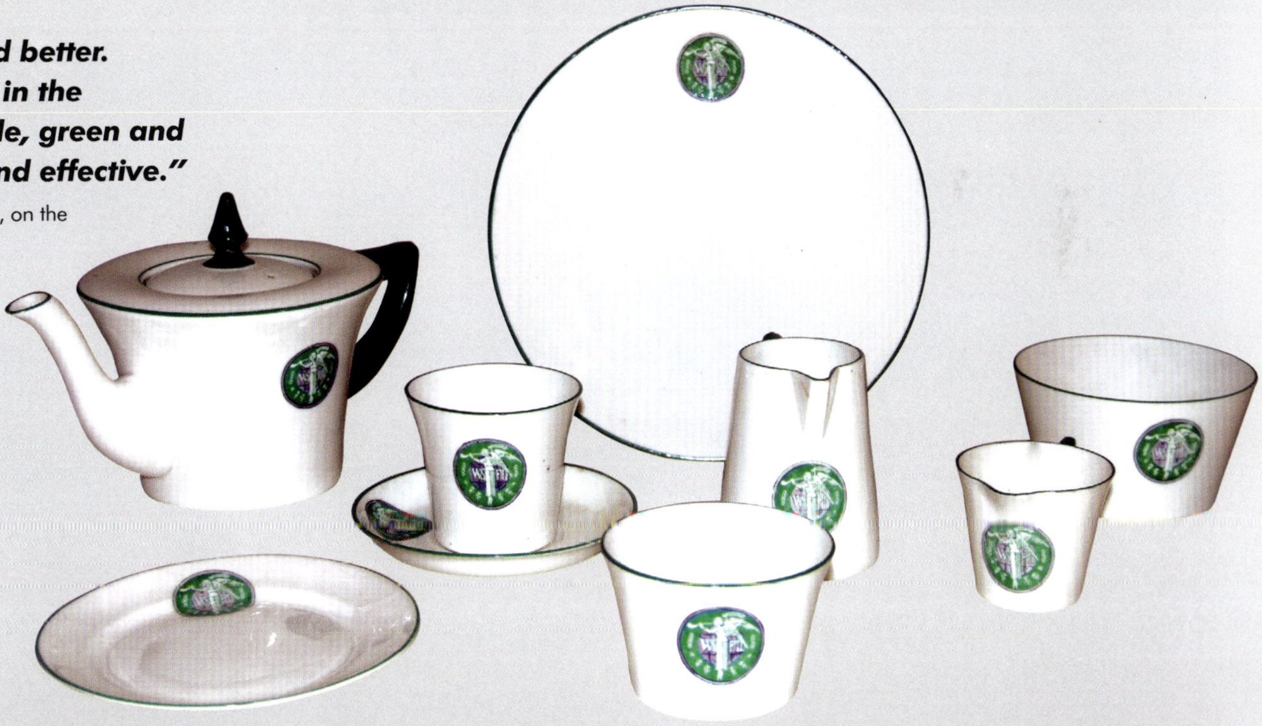

Above left: Woman's Building, Chicago World's Fair.

Middle right: The Women's Exhibition, Prince's Skating Rink, 1911. Sylvia Pankhurst's glorious canvases decorating the wall of the hall can just be seen in the background.

Bottom right: WSPU tea set with emblem designed by Sylvia Pankhurst.

Top right: Mary Cassatt's mural for the Women's Building at the Chicago World's Fair celebrated the advancement of "Modern Woman" with an allegorical triptych: "Young Girls Pursuing Fame," "Young Women Plucking the Fruits of Knowledge or Science," and "The Arts, Music, Dancing." Displaying the artistic influences of Renaissance and Pre-Raphaelite imagery, the impressionist color palette was a choice that jarred with some critics, who grumbled about the "impudent greens" and "brutal blues."

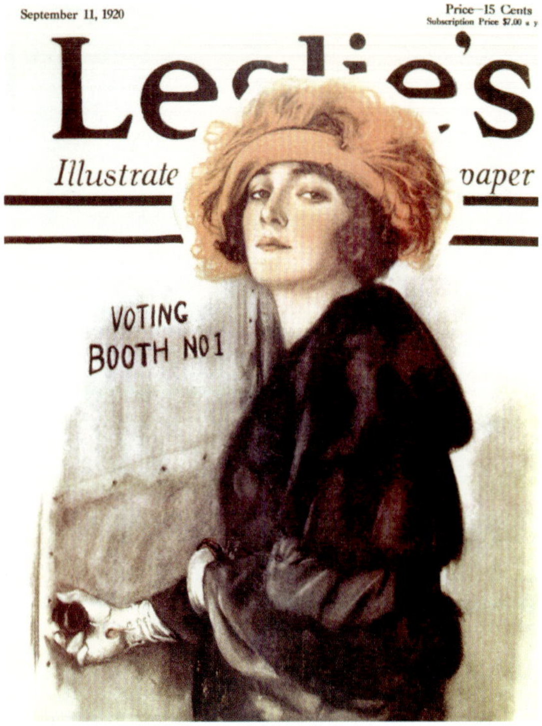

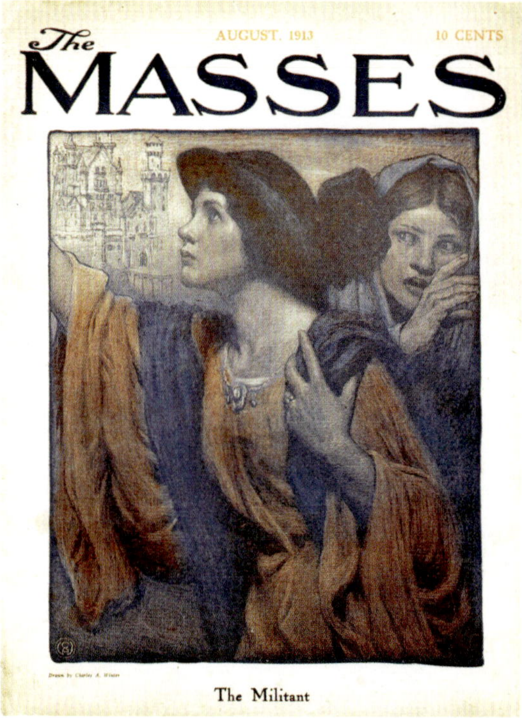

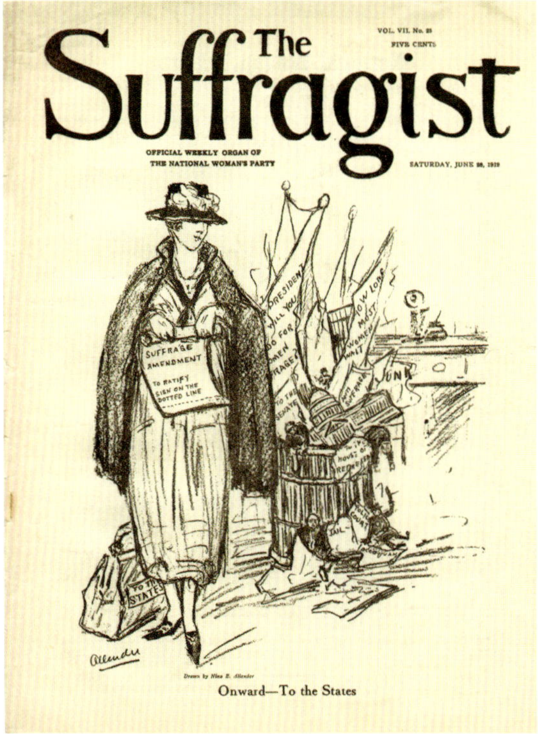

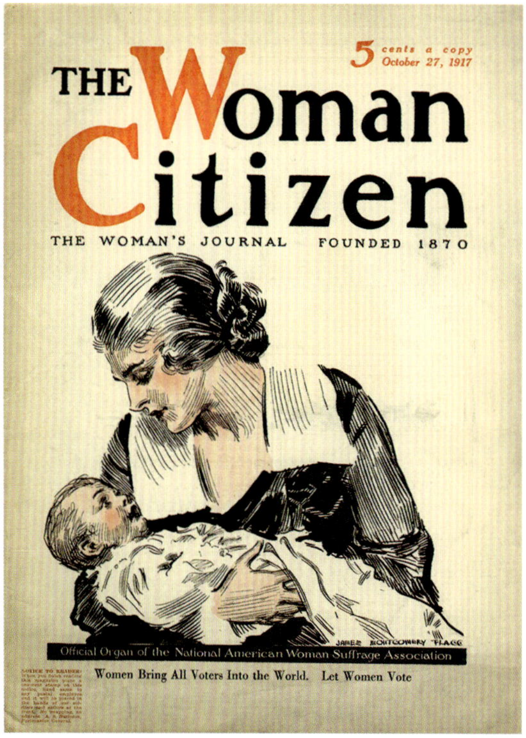

Top left: Following the ratification of the 19th Amendment in August 1920, the presidential election of September that year was the first in which women in every state were able to vote. The landmark was celebrated by this cover of *Leslie's Illustrated Newspaper*, published on September 11, 1920.

Bottom left: Cover for *The Suffragist*, 1919, by Nina Allender, president of the Washington, D.C., branch of the National American Woman's Suffrage Association from 1910. Her cartoons provided a positive image of suffragists that was critical to shaping public opinion.

Top right: *The Masses* was an American socialist magazine published from 1911 to 1917, when it was suppressed due to its anti-government and anti-war views. Its editor, Max Eastman, was founding secretary of the Men's League for Woman Suffrage in the state of New York.

Bottom right: *The Woman Citizen* magazine supported women's suffrage and addressed such issues as child labor and education for women. James Montgomery Flagg's 1917 illustration, *Women Bring All Voters into the World. Let Women Vote*, argues that women's status as mothers was a fundamental qualification for enfranchisement.

Right: *Sunday Magazine*, Chicago, 1912.

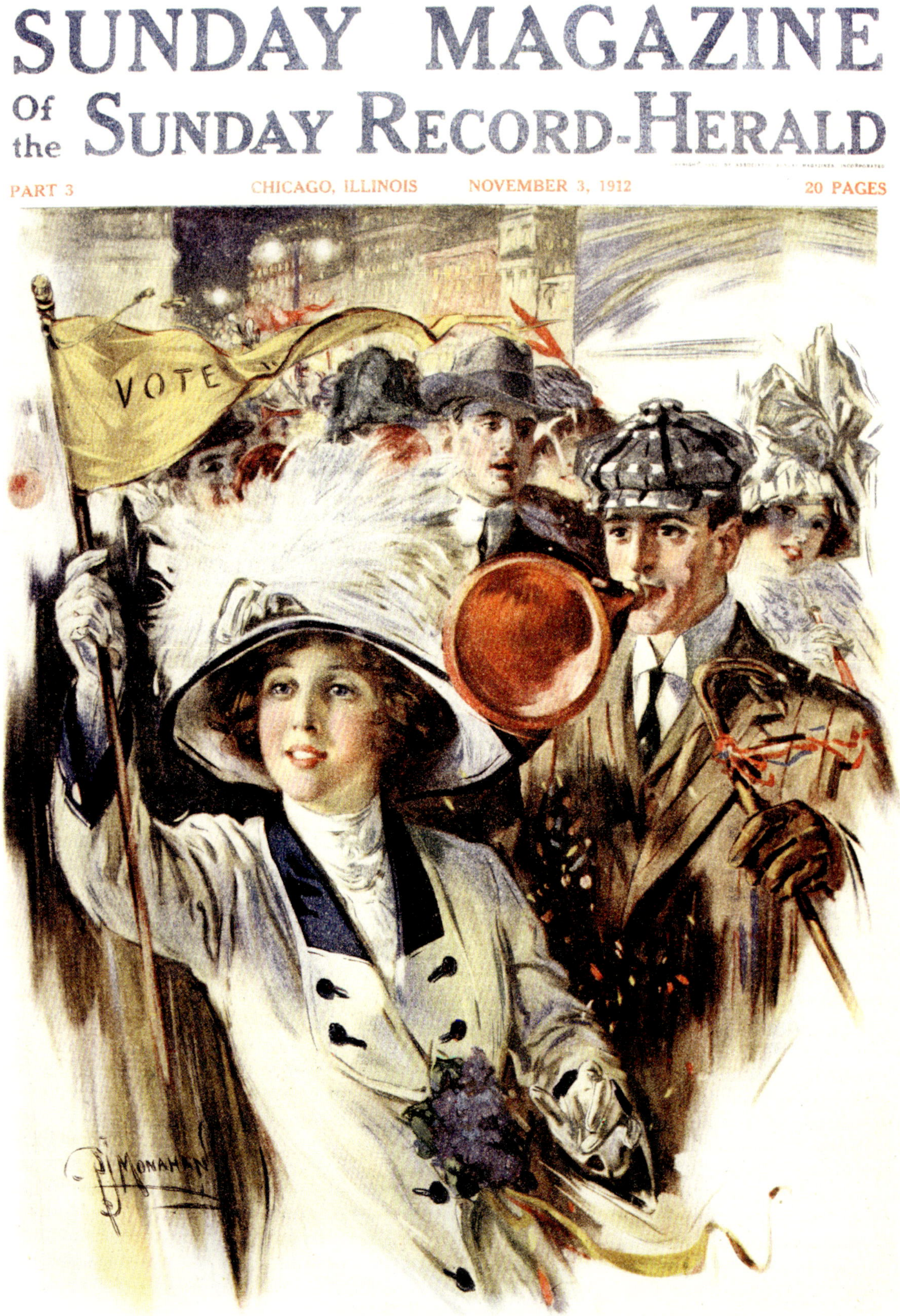

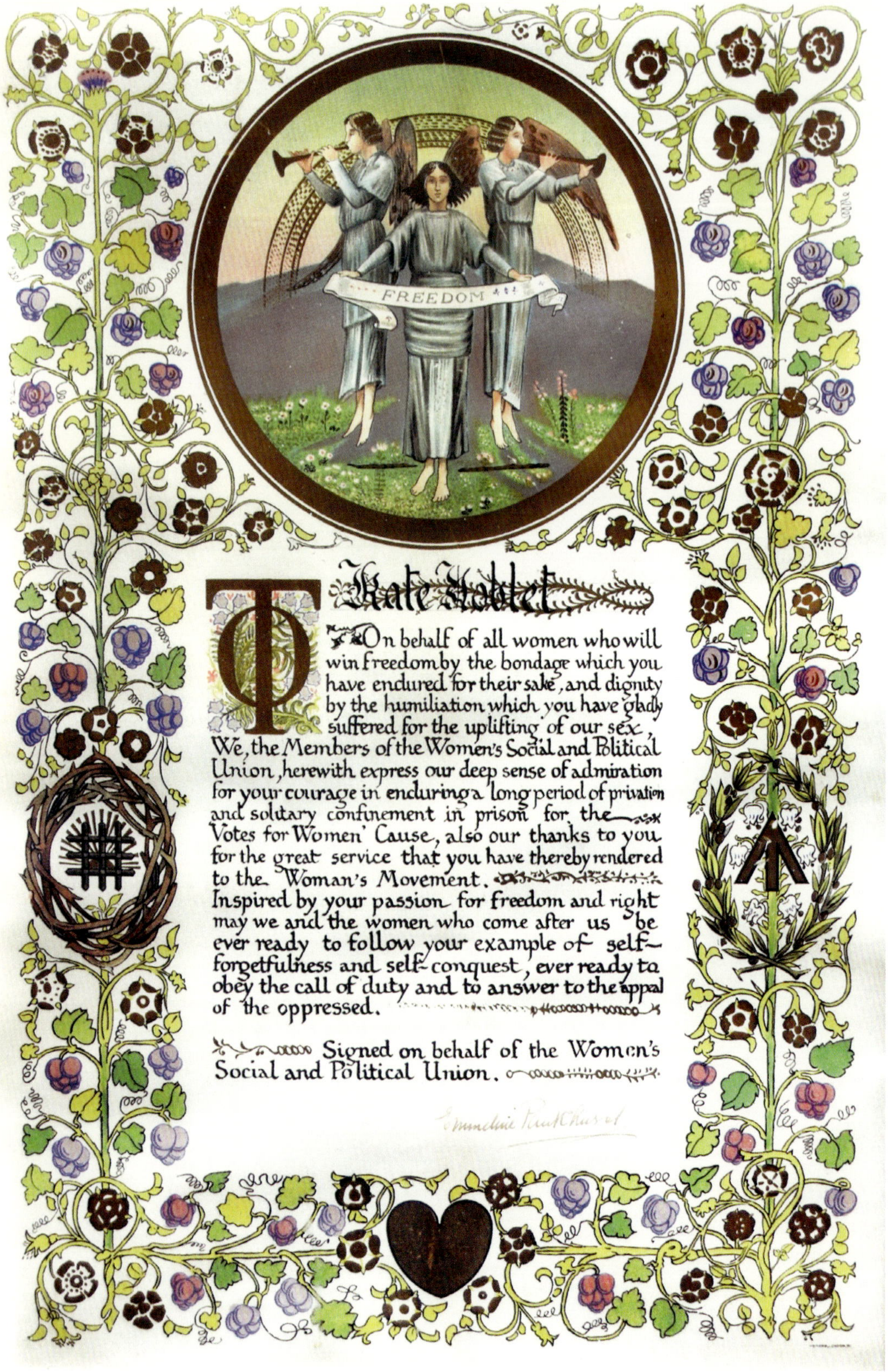

Above: **Sylvia Pankhurst, WSPU certificate**

This exquisitely decorated certificate, with its medieval, illuminated border and medallion featuring three angels, was presented to women who had served time in a British prison for the cause. The certificate was an official record of the WSPU's appreciation.

Below left: Alice Kaub-Casalonga, *La Française*, poster, 1906

La Française was founded in 1906 by Jane Misme, a journalist who had been drama critic for *La Fronde*. Intended to fill the gap left by the closure of *La Fronde*, *La Française* was adopted as the publication of the Conseil National des Femmes (National Union of French Women). Alice Kaub-Casalonga was a painter whose subjects included some provocative nudes, but this poster follows the classic art nouveau style of the period.

Below right: Charles Gesmar, *La Baïonnette*, magazine cover, "Looking forward to when women get to vote," July 31, 1919

Gesmar was a renowned designer of costumes during the Paris jazz age. He drew this modern woman, rendered patriotically in the colors of the *tricoleur*, for the cover of satirical magazine *La Baïonnette*, aged just nineteen. Its meaning is ambiguous, but whether satirical or optimistic, it would be another quarter of a century before women in France finally gained the vote in 1945.

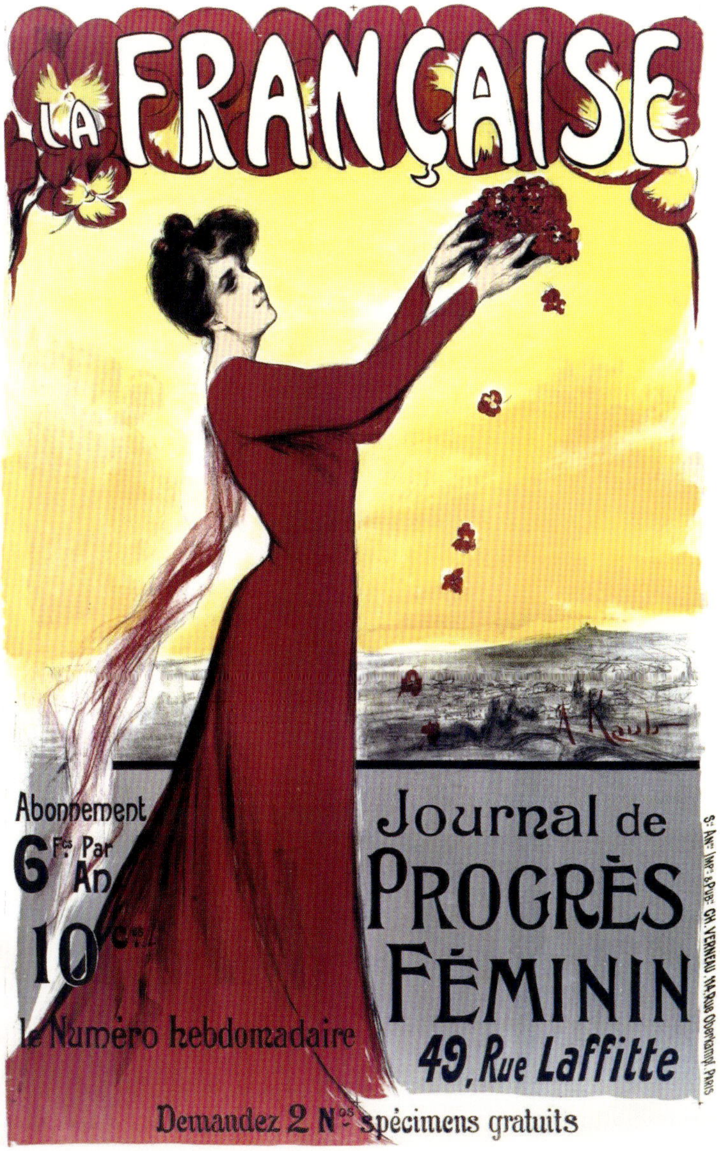

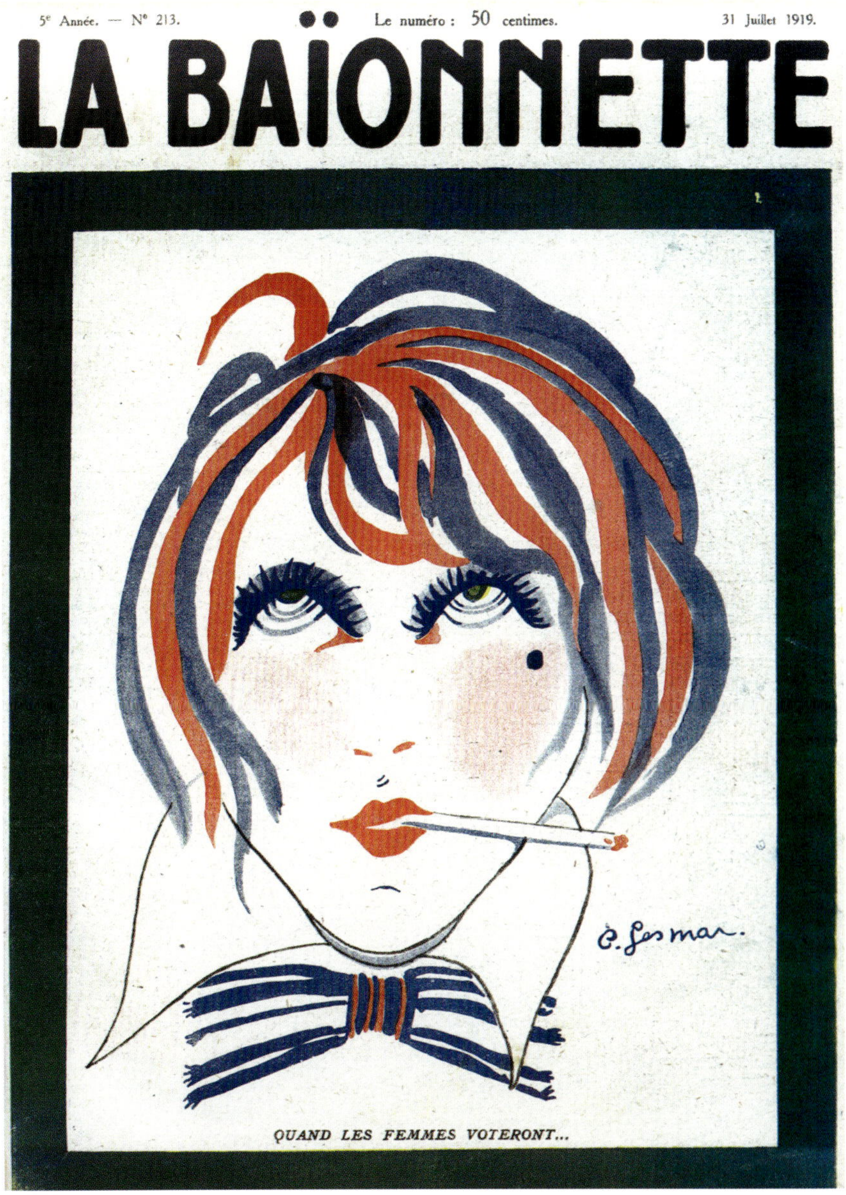

Suffragist versus Anti-Suffragist—Visual Conflict

While the support of artists and designers helped the growing suffrage movement of the 1900s gain visibility and traction, there was also vigorous activity from anti-suffrage campaigners, who harnessed the power of the image to force their own agenda.

In Britain, the Women's National Anti-Suffrage League was formed in 1908 and merged with the Men's League for Opposing Woman Suffrage in 1910, to form the National League for Opposing Women's Suffrage (NLOWS). There had also been challenges to female suffrage in different American states dating back to the 1870s, but the formation of a national organization in 1911 (claiming the same title as its British counterpart) galvanized and strengthened a movement that could boast 350,000 members during World War I.

Anti-suffragists claimed that women did not have the intellectual capacity to use their vote wisely and that, more ominously, it was a threat to the traditional family unit, with the woman—"the angel of the home"—at its heart. Seeking political equality disrupted and upset the traditional roles of men as workers, fighters, and leaders, and women as homemakers and mothers. It was an argument with its roots in the nineteenth century, when John Leech in the satirical *Punch* magazine lampooned the idea of a Parliamentary Female, busy and absorbed at her office desk, while her hapless husband is left holding the baby and the household falls into disarray. Leech's vision was lighthearted satire, flipping gender stereotypes in a scenario that seemed, at the time, unlikely to happen. But as pressure by suffrage organizations intensified, the enfranchised female began to be portrayed as a serious threat. English illustrator John Hassall's poster, *A Suffragette's Home*, designed for the NLOWS in around 1910, speaks to the working man, portraying one of his kind arriving home after a hard day's work only to find no meal awaiting him, his house untidy, and his children neglected. It is one of the strongest and simplest images produced in support of the anti-suffrage cause—Hassall was the leading poster artist of his day—but a large proportion of anti-suffrage propaganda lacked his design flair and exhibited far less subtlety.

During this period, two diametrically opposed representations of female suffrage emerged. The anti-suffrage vision of the suffragette ranged from merely unflattering to painfully grotesque—a dangerous mutation of the "New Woman" who had been satirized in the nineteenth-century press. Campaigners were portrayed as shrieking, hysterical harridans, wizened and pinched, or else comically stout and bullish. Dressed in masculine tailormades, brandishing umbrellas and axes, they are often toothless, middle-aged, spinsterish types to be pitied and ridiculed. These stereotypes, repeated time and again in anti-suffrage propaganda, validated women according to their sexual attractiveness and the suggestive captions accompanying "comic" postcards depicting suffragettes and police officers seem particularly distasteful considering the abuse suffered by some suffrage campaigners at the hands of the police.

There was also the ambiguity of the middle ground, where depictions of women avoided the savagery of anti-suffrage designs, but still accentuated stereotypes with gentle mockery. The Gibson Girl, the sporty and sophisticated creation of Charles Dana Gibson, whose illustrations appeared in *LIFE* as well as many other leading magazines, had introduced a new kind of woman to America and Britain—one who flirted and golfed her way into peoples' hearts. In comparison to her predecessors, she was a self-assured, modern woman and considered a popular representation of feminism. And yet Gibson also drew cartoons poking fun at the idea of women voters. In one such cartoon, he imagines the after-dinner talk if women got the vote, choosing to portray the two women who are interested in politics as middle-aged, stout, and bespectacled, while the rest of the table—Gibson Girl types—yawn and look visibly bored.

One British anti-suffrage poster, by Harold Bird, appropriated a wholesome, allegorical female figure, more typical of suffrage designs, and drew her holding a banner politely stating, "No Votes Thank You," while a militant suffragette wreaks havoc in Westminster behind her. In riposte, the artist Louise Jacobs produced a poster using the same iconography and the same tagline—The Appeal of Womanhood—but instead her banner declared, "We want the vote to stop the white slave traffic, sweated labour, and to save the children."

While the suffrage movement pioneered a visual strategy that was optimistic and aesthetically pleasing, the anti-suffrage propaganda can rarely be commended on its artistic quality—posters and postcards by the likes of John Hassall were the exception rather than the rule. Even *The Anti-Suffragist* paper, edited by Mrs. Humphrey Ward, looked dull next to the lively and professionally illustrated *Votes for Women*. Where suffrage design really excelled was in its inherent ability to signal values and aspirations regardless of factious tensions and differences. With the outbreak of war in 1914, and the suspension of suffrage activities, the British anti-suffragist movement became redundant. But in America, the anti-suffragists continued their fight until the 19th Amendment finally gave women across the nation the right to vote in August 1920.

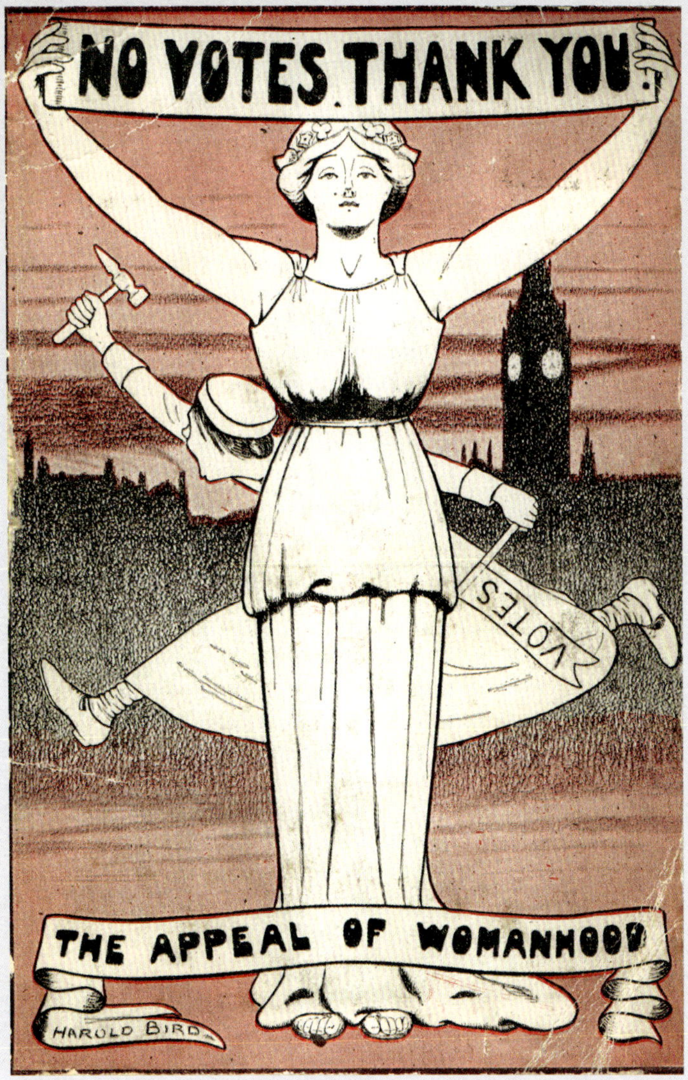

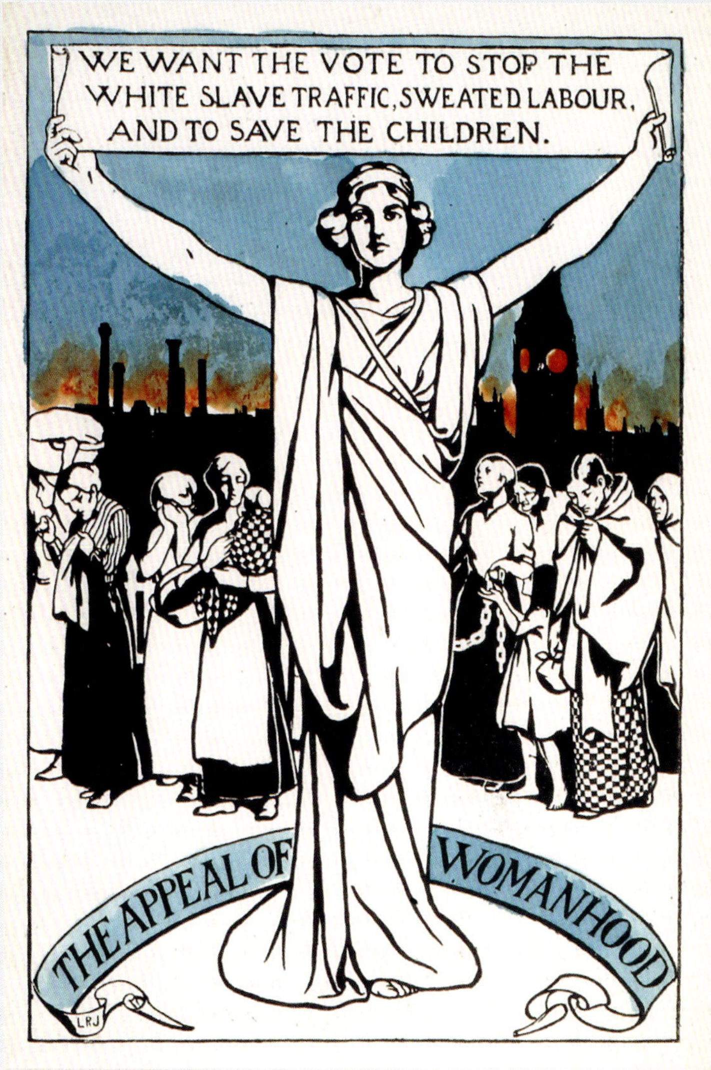

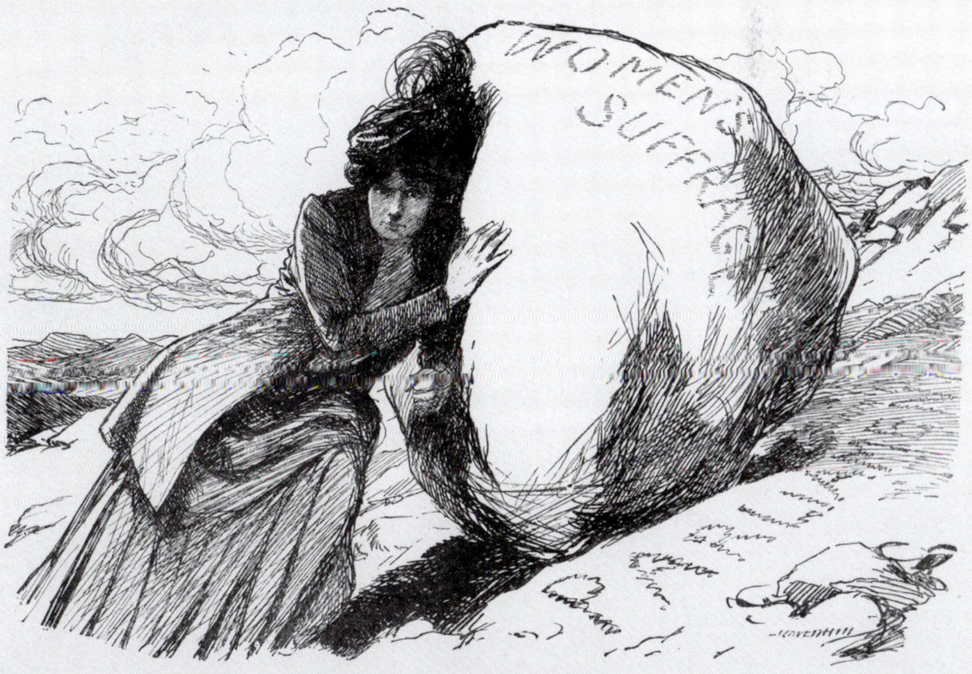

Top left: **Harold Bird, *The Appeal of Womanhood: "No Votes Thank You,"* 1912**

Top right: **Louise Jacobs, *The Appeal of Womanhood: "We Want the Vote,"* 1912**

Bottom right: **Leonard Raven-Hill, *Excelsior!: "It's no good talking to me about Sisyphus; he was only a man!" in Punch* magazine, 1910**

In Greek mythology, Sisyphus was condemned to a life of rolling a heavy boulder up a hill, only to watch it roll back down again—a story used here as a metaphor by Leonard Raven-Hill to reflect the suffragists' frustrating struggle to have their demands recognized by Parliament.

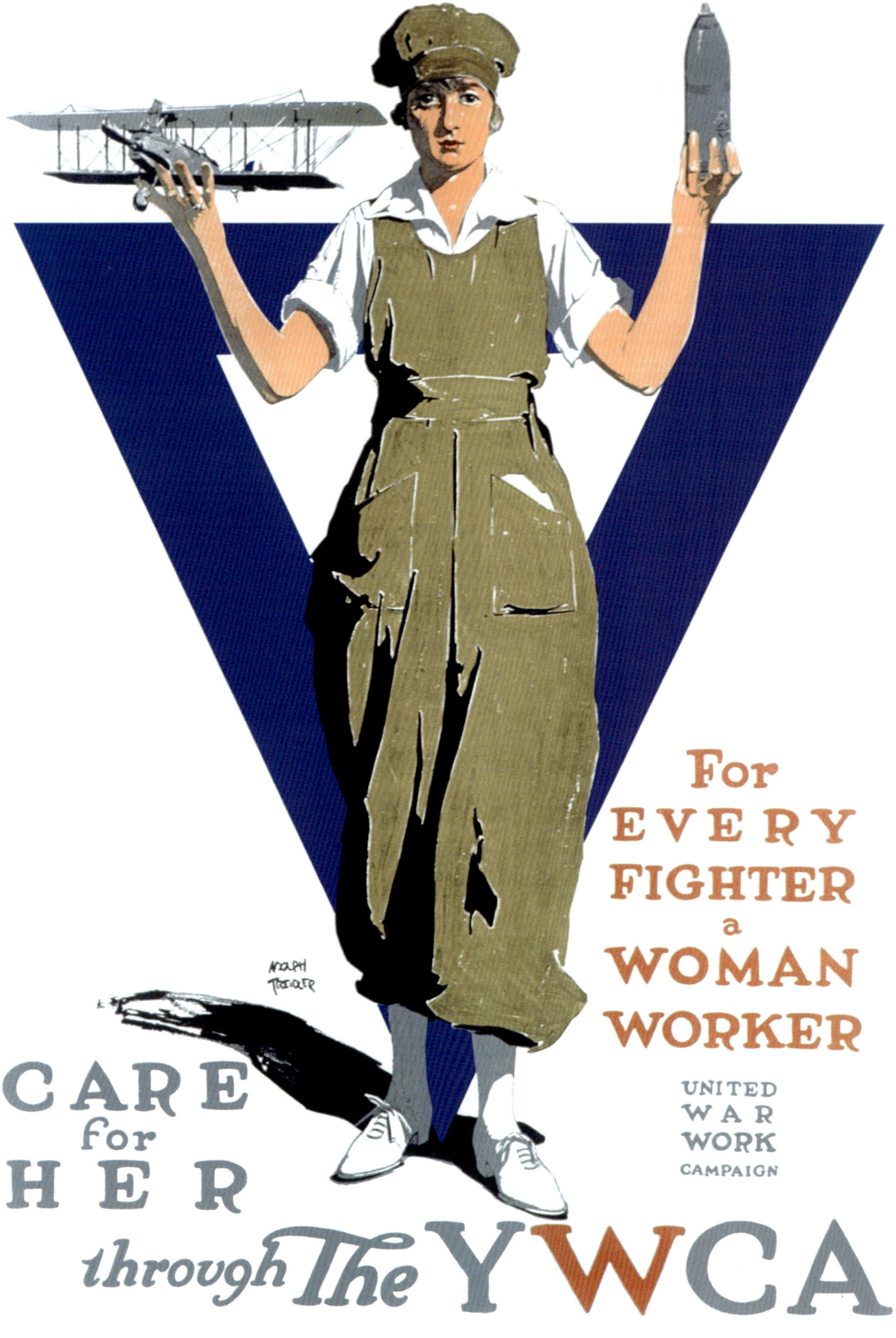

For
EVERY
FIGHTER
a
WOMAN
WORKER
UNITED
WAR
WORK
CAMPAIGN
CARE
for
HER
through The YWCA

3

To War and To Work

On the Battlefield and in the Factory

"So ends, for the present, the war of women against men. As of old the women become the nurturing mothers of men, their sisters and uncomplaining helpmates."

Emmeline Pankhurst, August 1914

Emmeline Pankhurst wrote these words just a few days after Britain's declaration of war against Germany on August 4, 1914, so suspending the campaign for women's suffrage. The Pankhursts knew that continuing militancy was futile when the country was at war, and many women recognized the conflict could offer opportunities that would further their cause in the long term. The *Votes for Women* paper moved quickly to stress the part women could play. Its August 14, 1914, issue carried an illustration by Alfred Pearse of women carrying stretchers of wounded men to be administered by nurses, accompanied by the lyrics to a popular suffrage song, "Women This and Women That."

Pankhurst's nurturing mothers and uncomplaining helpmates never quite materialized (though poster artists frequently adopted them as a device to aid recruitment). Eclipsing them, instead, was an army of willing and able female volunteers and workers, and though many had moral reservations, most were anxious to help the war effort in any way they could. This collective desire was demonstrated by the Women's Right to Serve March in July 1915, organized by Pankhurst, with the support of the minister of munitions, David Lloyd George. In visual terms, the march echoed the suffrage parades of previous years, with its use of costumes and banners to create a spectacle. Its message—that women wanted to work, but for a living wage—was firmly entrenched in feminist principles.

As the war progressed and increasing numbers of men left their employment to join up, women stepped into myriad different roles. In addition to supporting the armed forces, they served as nurses and ambulance drivers, they ran canteens, worked the land, felled trees, and filled civil service roles. They became chauffeurs, window cleaners, bus conductors, or elevator attendants, and carried out essential work in the munitions factories that were multiplying across the country. Ironically, for women artists, professional opportunities were fewer. When the British government set up an official war artists' scheme in 1916, only four of the forty-seven artists selected were women. Three had their work rejected and the fourth did not accept the commission. Some of the best-known pictures by women artists from this period were undertaken at the request of the Women's War Work Subcommittee (WWWC) of London's Imperial War Museum, which felt that women's activities could be best captured by women artists. No female artists made it close to the frontline, and even those paintings that record women's war work were made in 1919 or 1920, after the armistice.

In terms of style and influence, these women painters largely confined themselves to pure representational realism. There is no hint of the experimental movements of expressionism and abstraction that were rocking the art world in the years leading up to the war—or any sign of the simplified forms and blazing color of the fauvists. Cubism and futurism, as embodied in the work of Russian modernist Liubov Popova, who was working around this time, bore no relation to the growing cache of art compiled by the WWWC. Male official war artists, such as Paul Nash, Percy Wyndham Lewis, and Christopher Nevinson, were producing dark, abstract visions of war that bore the hallmarks of European avant-garde art movements. In Germany, Otto Dix gave an unflinching, apocalyptic view of the conflict.

In contrast, the paintings produced by the commissioned artists of the WWWC seem unchallenging, but this does not diminish their value as a record of women's achievements in wartime. Clare Atwood's *Christmas Day in London Bridge YMCA Canteen; Red Cross Work Room, 5th Avenue, NYC* by Jane Peterson; the impressionistic *Women Making Shells* by Canadian Henrietta Mabel May; or Lucy Kemp-Welch's majestic panel *Women's War Work* on the walls of the Royal Exchange in London—these, and many more, reflect a broadening definition of conflict. This was a war being fought at home and abroad, by all sections of society, regardless of gender.

Early war posters used formulaic stereotypes, such as the selfless and stoic woman of Edgar James Kealey's 1914 poster *Women of Britain Say GO!,* waving her menfolk off to war. There was also the patriotic outrage of Justice, a virtue always personified as a woman, in Bernard Partridge's *Take Up the Sword of Justice*, which was published after the sinking of the British ocean liner RMS *Lusitania* in 1915. The allegorical militancy of Justice is frequently invoked in World

Page 58: Adolph Treidler, *For Every Fighter, a Woman Worker*, ca. 1918

Treidler was a high-profile American commercial illustrator whose long career saw him design posters during World Wars I and II. This design for the YWCA, with its satisfying sense of equilibrium, was carried out for the United War Work Campaign. The female figure adopts the pose of a classical beauty, masking the dirty, dangerous reality of war work, and conveying a higher sense of purpose.

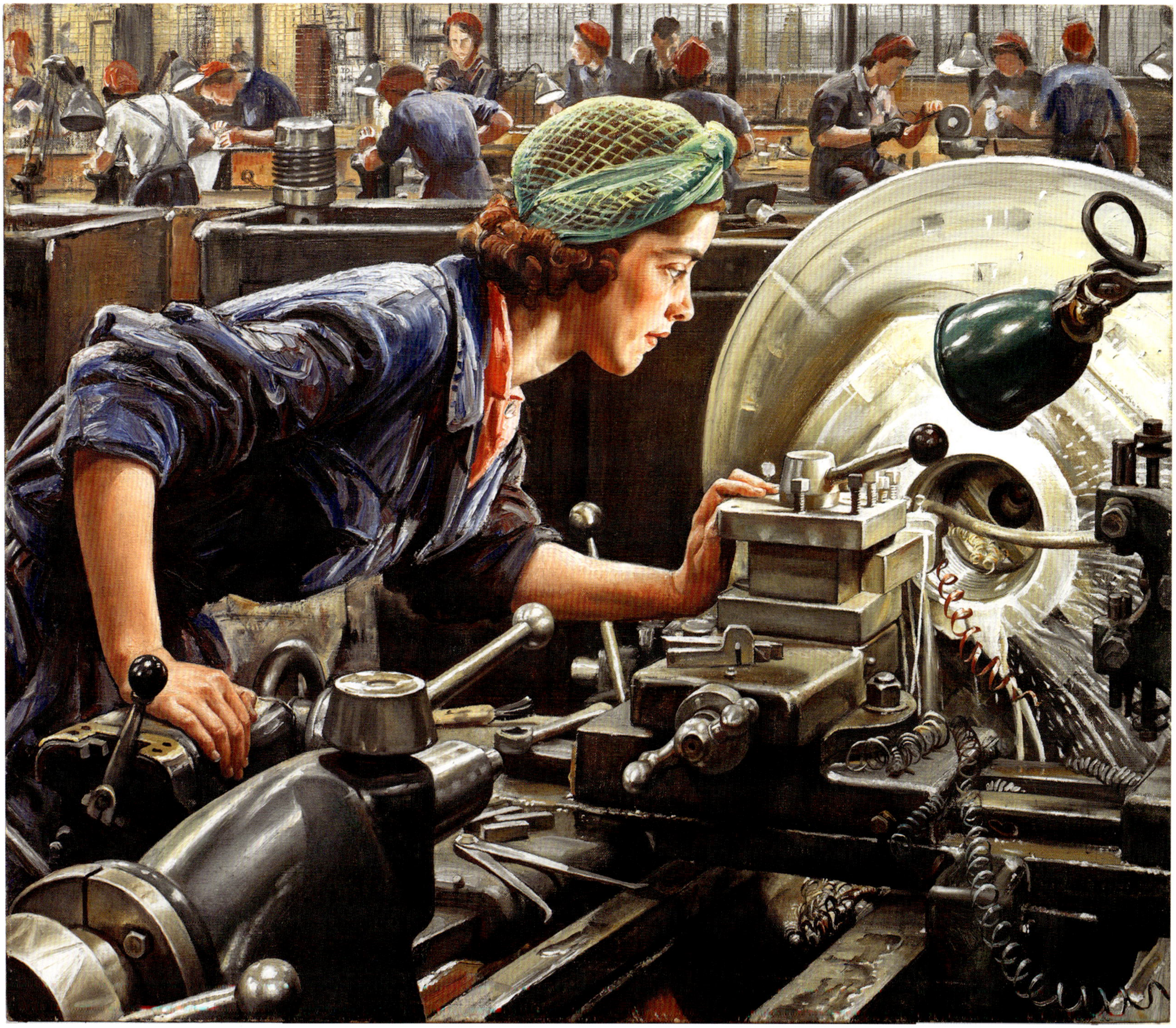

Above: **Laura Knight, *Ruby Loftus Screwing the Breech Ring*, 1942**

Knight was commissioned by the Ministry of Supply to paint an ordnance factory worker, Ruby Loftus, who combined glossy good looks with a particular skill at screwing the Bofors breech ring onto automatic antiaircraft guns, a technique that often took qualified engineers eight or nine years to perfect. The painting was part of a drive to encourage recruitment in factories and was reproduced on a Women's Army Auxiliary Corps (WAAC) poster.

Below left: ***J. Howard Miller, We Can Do It, poster for the War Production Coordinating Committee, 1943***

Although the distribution of Miller's poster was originally limited to just forty-two copies for Westinghouse Electric and Manufacturing companies in Pennsylvania, the image of "Rosie the Riveter"—powerful, feminine, patriotic—became a cultural phenomenon. The *We Can Do It* poster, representing the working woman as the empowered woman, has been reinterpreted over the years, and remains a potent symbol of female strength over seventy-five years later.

Bottom left: **Artist unknown, front cover of *Women and War Work* by Helen Fraser, 1918**

Helen Fraser was a Scottish suffragist and a close friend of Adela Pankhurst. Due to the increasing militancy of the WSPU, she transferred her allegiance to the NUWSS, and during World War I toured the United States speaking about Britain's female war workers. This book was written to urge American women to join the war effort, with the cover image reflecting the rousing words of Fraser in her introduction: "The women of all the allies are one in this great struggle."

Bottom right: **Helen McKie, *Birmingham puts her back into it*, in *The Bystander*, 1918**

During World War I, the role of artist correspondent in the British illustrated press was almost exclusively the preserve of male artists. However, Helen McKie, who was employed as a staff member by *The Graphic* and *The Bystander*, was the quintessential roving reporter. She was in Russia when war broke out in 1914, and spent time near the front in France and Belgium, later recording scenes around the United Kingdom, such as this image of Birmingham as a hive of industry, in which female munitions workers are the central focus.

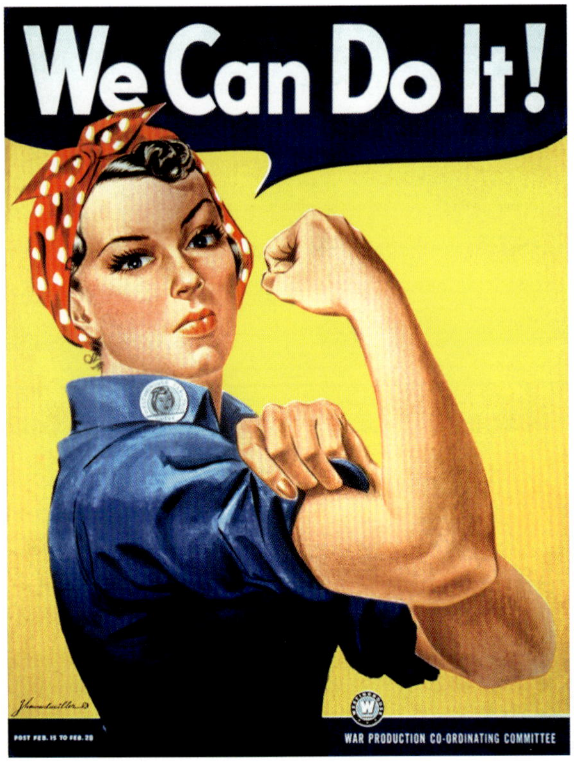

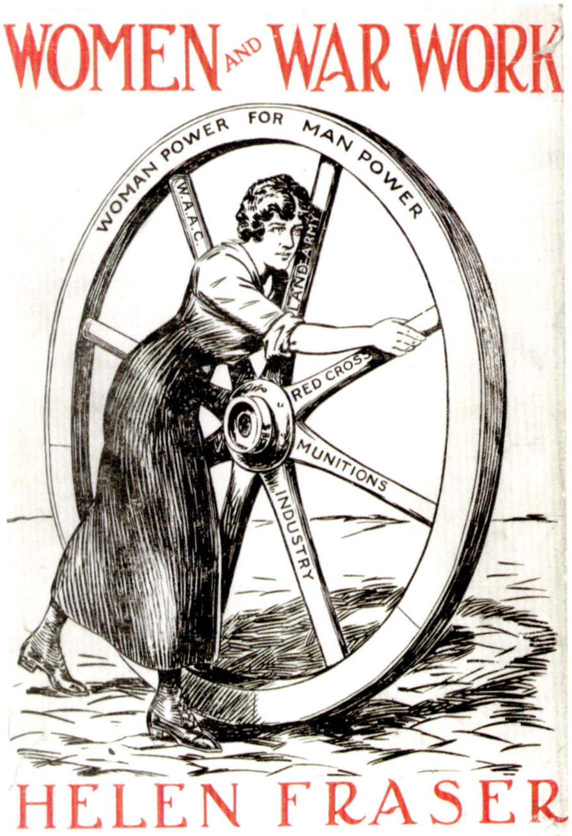

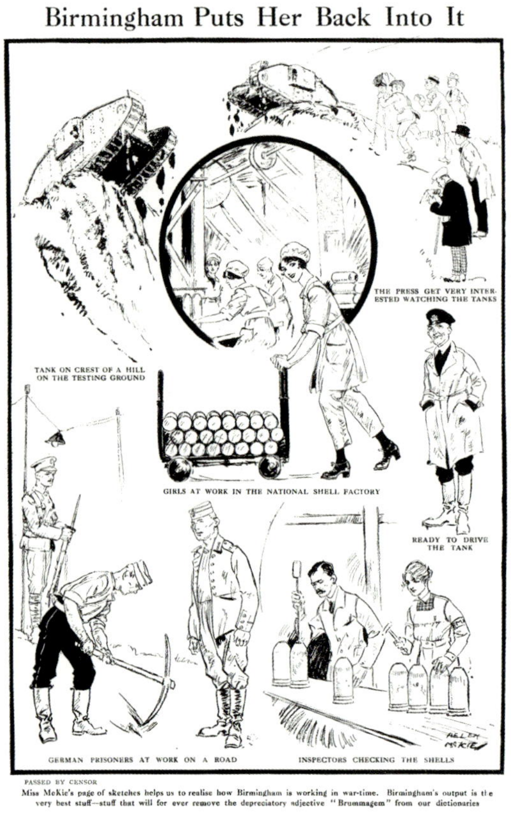

War I propaganda; not long after it became a popular emblem of the suffrage movement. As the war progressed and women's participation grew, uniformed female figures, cheery and upbeat, wave encouragement and beckon the viewer to join them.

There were also those who fully supported pacifism. Artists of the Bloomsbury Group were ardent pacifists: Vanessa Bell and Duncan Grant repaired to a farmhouse in Sussex, Charleston, for the duration of the war. Bell's 1914 painting of a mantelpiece, on which stand handmade flowers from the Omega workshop, suggests a complete disinterest in the jingoism and hubris of war. Instead, Bell concentrates on a tiny piece of home, though the picture itself also exhibits the influence of French fauvism and cubism.

In general, magazines published a swelling tide of positive imagery in which women's roles were taken seriously and traditional notions of femininity shifted. One magazine illustrator was Helen McKie, who worked as a staff artist for British weeklies *The Graphic* and *The Bystander*. She traveled around war-torn Europe drawing refugees, women workers, and soldiers behind the lines. When at home in Britain, she sketched topical subjects ranging from the Eagle Hut for American servicemen in London to the munitions workers at the National Ordnance Factory in Birmingham. *The Bystander* chose to highlight their roving reporter's gender as an asset, with illustrations such as *Battle-Areas—A Woman's Point of View* drawn in France at the end of the war. Helen McKie differs from the women painters commissioned by the WWWC. Her employment as a magazine illustrator not only gave her more freedom and independence to travel, but also her style of illustration (pen-and-ink sketches) allowed her to cover a wider range of subjects. In this she followed in the tradition of Victorian "specials" transported around the globe to send back pictures to the papers from the seat of war. However, restricted by gender, her body of work stopped short of battle scenes and frontline action. Nevertheless, she represented a new breed of independent working women who would become more prominent in the next war, particularly in the field of photography.

A new breed of intrepid female photojournalist emerged during World War II. By this time, photography was becoming a democratic art form, accessible to all—from the amateur with their box Brownie to the professional who welcomed the advent of the Leica camera of the 1920s, which was light, easy to handle, and produced high-quality "snapshots" on 35-mm film. A handful of women, among them American documentary photographers Margaret Bourke-White, Elizabeth "Lee" Miller, and Dickey Chapelle, produced extraordinary work and frequently showed remarkable grit and resolve in difficult circumstances.

Women artists were given more scope during World War II, but similar patterns of inequality remained. Out of the four hundred artists engaged by the War Artists' Advisory Committee (WAAC) in Britain, one-quarter were women, but most of those were paid less and given fewer commissions than men. In other Allied nations, women artists were few and far between. Canadian Molly Lamb Bobak was the only woman appointed an official war artist in her country. The Australian war artists' scheme appointed three female artists including Stella Bowen, an expatriate who was based in Britain and painted scenes of the Blitz. On painting members of the Royal Australian Air Force based in Britain, Bowen remembered how the airmen she had been painting often failed to return from a bombing mission, "It was terrible having to finish the picture after the men were lost. Like painting ghosts." Another, Nora Heyson, traveled to New Guinea, where she was determined to get as close to the war as possible, despite resistance from male officialdom. The only salaried female artist painting for the Women's Army Auxiliary Corps (WAAC) was Evelyn Dunbar. She recorded the activities of land girls, women who replaced men in agricultural work who had joined the military.

In 1936, Laura Knight had been made the first female academician since the Royal Academy's foundation and was Britain's highest-profile woman artist. Many of her wartime paintings feature female participation in the war effort, most notably *Ruby Loftus Screwing the Breech Ring*, which is infused with a luminous glamour. But Knight also branched out into other subjects. One painting shows the interior of a Stirling Mk. III bomber with the crew preparing for takeoff; and in 1946 she traveled to Germany to record the Nuremberg trials. Doris Zinkeisen traveled around northwestern Europe in 1945, attached to the Red Cross. Her paintings from Bergen-Belsen, shortly after its liberation, present a stark and uncompromising record of what she encountered. Another British artist, Mary Kessell, also traveled to Germany and, through a series of bleak charcoal sketches, recorded the devastating effects of war on refugees, particularly women and children. Although Laura Knight, Mary Kessell, and Doris Zinkeisen never saw or recorded the heat of battle, their work in Nuremberg and Belsen is proof that women could bear witness to the horrors of war and produce works of power and integrity in response.

The poster was more likely to portray women as a powerful force in wartime. The female image became a repeated and potent symbol in war propaganda, vacillating between the victim, the mother, the symbol, and the worker. J. Howard Miller's *We Can Do It!* poster, distributed by the War Production Coordinating Committee in the United States, has become enshrined in feminist iconography as a classic symbol of women's power and capability.

Working in the most masculine of arenas, women war artists were frequently limited by the constraints imposed upon them. At the same time, the nature of modern warfare offered opportunities where previous conflicts had offered none. From oil paintings, through photography and poster design to the picture postcard, art was a powerful indicator of a marked and pivotal change in the narrative of feminist history.

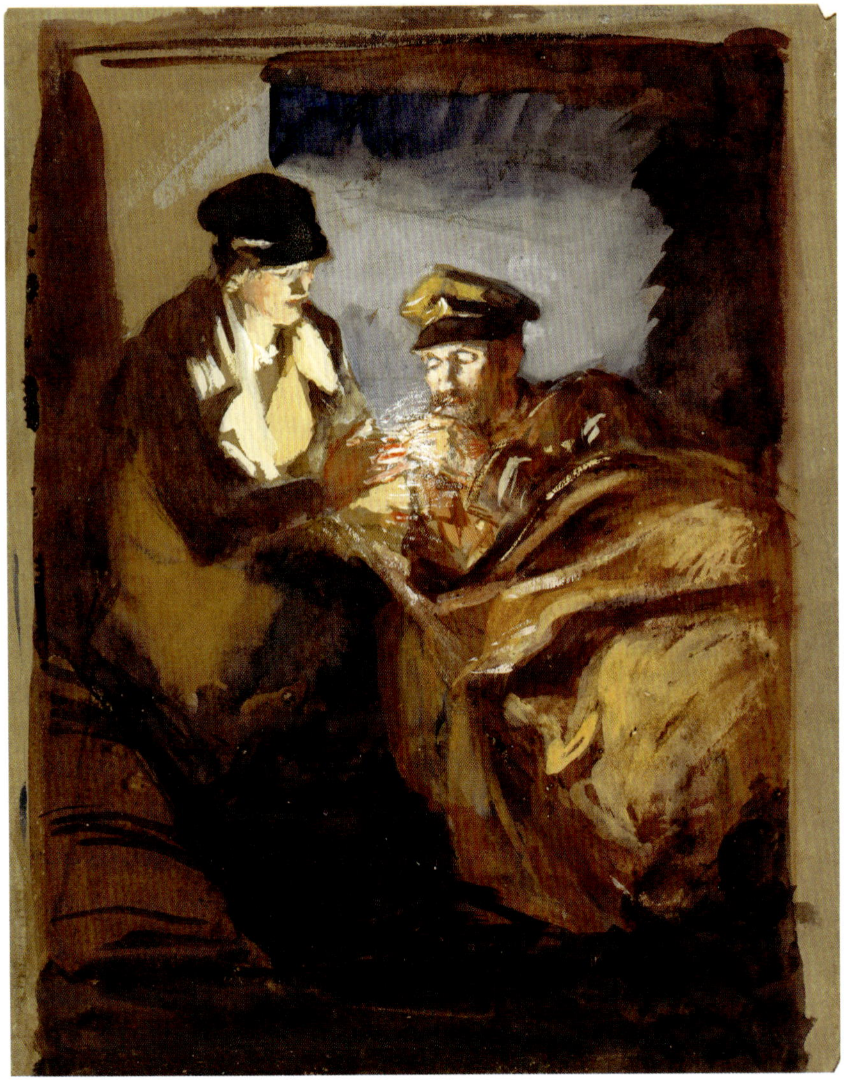

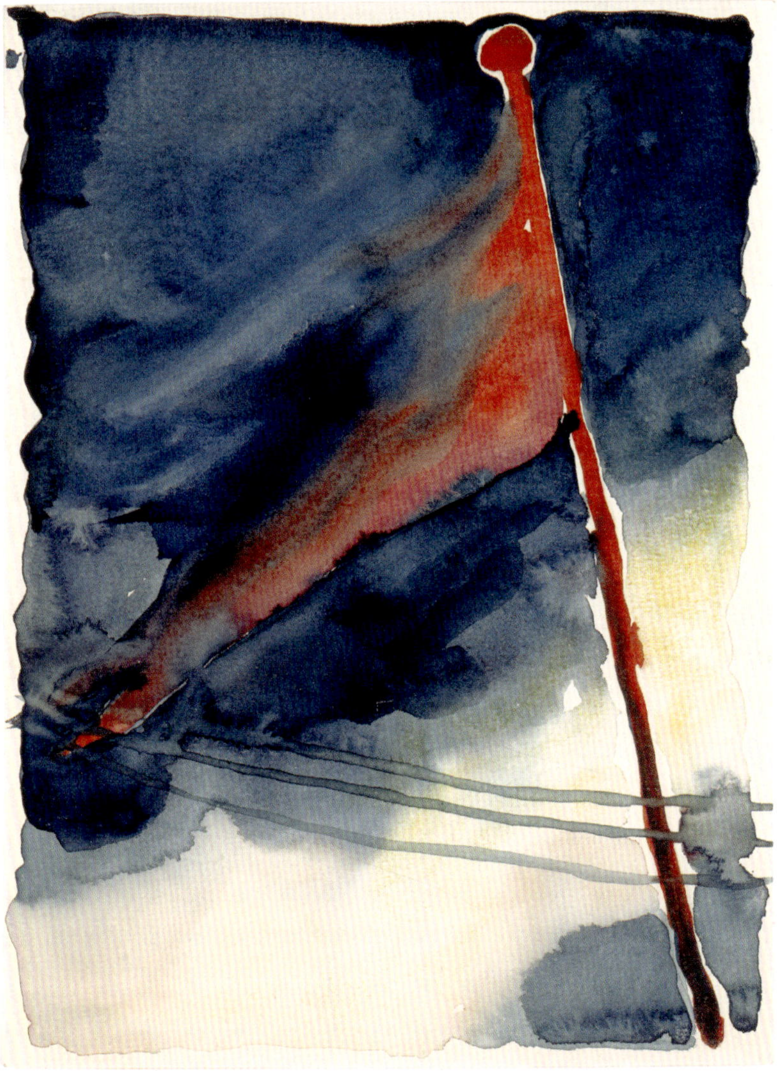

Above left: **Olive Mudie-Cooke, *In an Ambulance, a VAD Lighting a Cigarette for a Patient*, 1919**

Olive Mudie-Cooke had served in the British Voluntary Aid Detachment (VAD) and the First Aid Nursing Yeomanry (FANY), and many of her paintings, commissioned by the Women's War Work Subcommittee (WWWC), have an autobiographical feel. Cigarettes, or "smokes," powered many men through the war, and this intimate scene of a VAD and patient, illuminated by the strike of a match, demonstrates a companionable and equitable understanding between them.

Above right: **Georgia O'Keeffe, *The Flag*, 1918**

Georgia O'Keeffe's painting articulates the conflicted emotions she felt when her younger brother Alexis joined up to fight after America entered World War I in 1917. It is a simple but haunting picture. A limp red flag, with its connotations of communism, fades into a blue sky representing her brother's unquestioning patriotism. O'Keeffe's fears were realized when Alexis died in France due to the effects of mustard gas.

Opposite: **Hilda Rix Nicholas, *A Man*, 1921**

An Australian artist working in France, Hilda Rix Nicholas lost her husband of just five weeks after he was killed at Flers on the Somme. Grief-stricken, her painting acted as a coping mechanism. This work is not of her husband, but an anonymous Australian soldier, yet the care and love taken by the artist make the painting a remarkably sensitive military portrait.

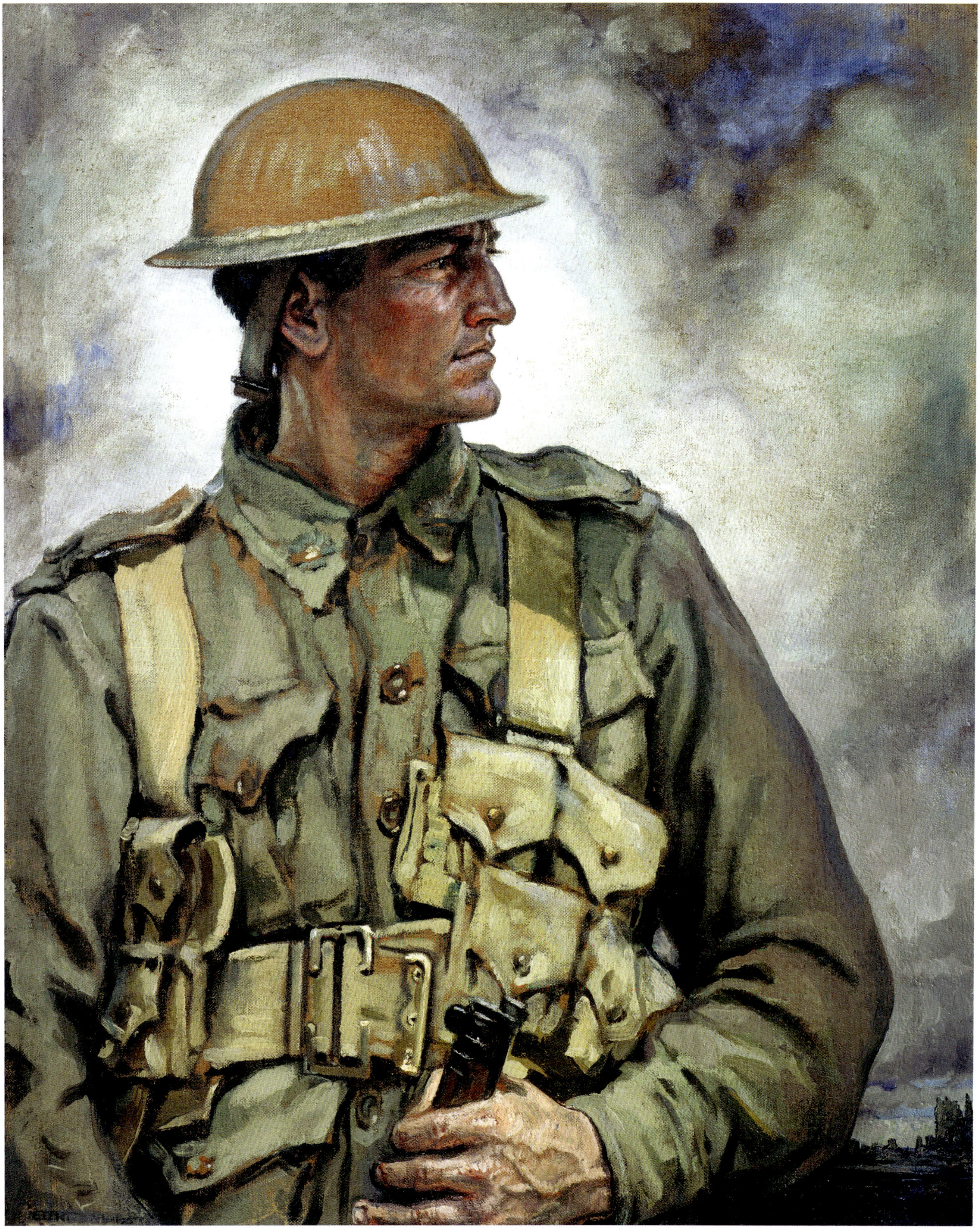

This page: *Women on War Work*, Black Cat cigarette cards for Carreras Ltd., 1916

In a short space of time, the slew of postcards and cartoons ridiculing suffragettes in the previous decade were replaced by those celebrating the woman war worker. These cigarette cards, part of a set of more than fifty, demonstrate just some of the myriad roles taken on by British women during World War I.

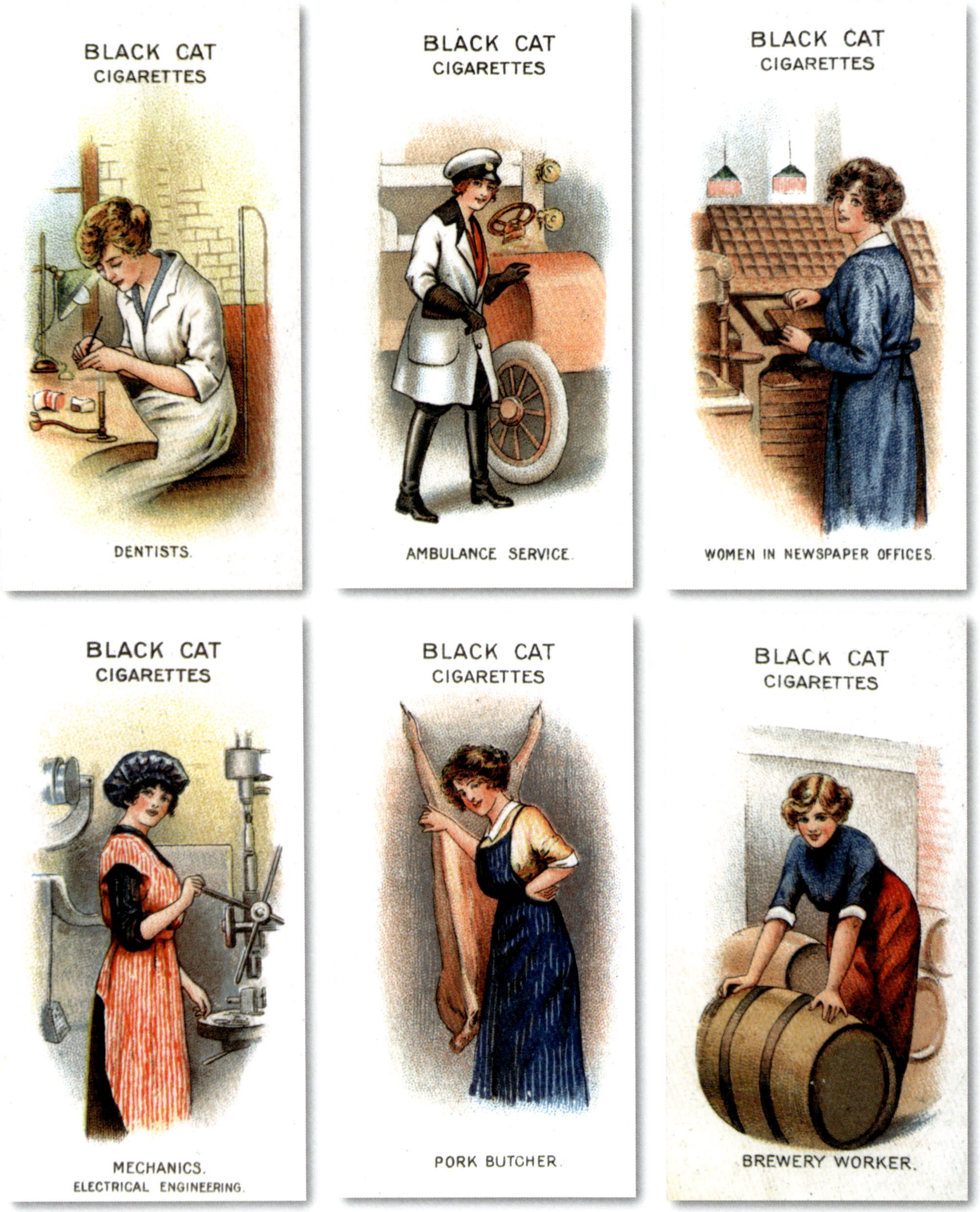

Right: **Molly Lamb Bobak, *Private Roy, CWAC*, 1946**

The only Canadian woman appointed as an official war artist in her country (after serving for three years with the Canadian Women's Auxiliary Corps), Molly Lamb Bobak made several sketches of Private Roy at a canteen in Halifax, Nova Scotia, before completing this painting. The portrait is typical of her vibrant style and gives a uniquely female perspective on the war experience.

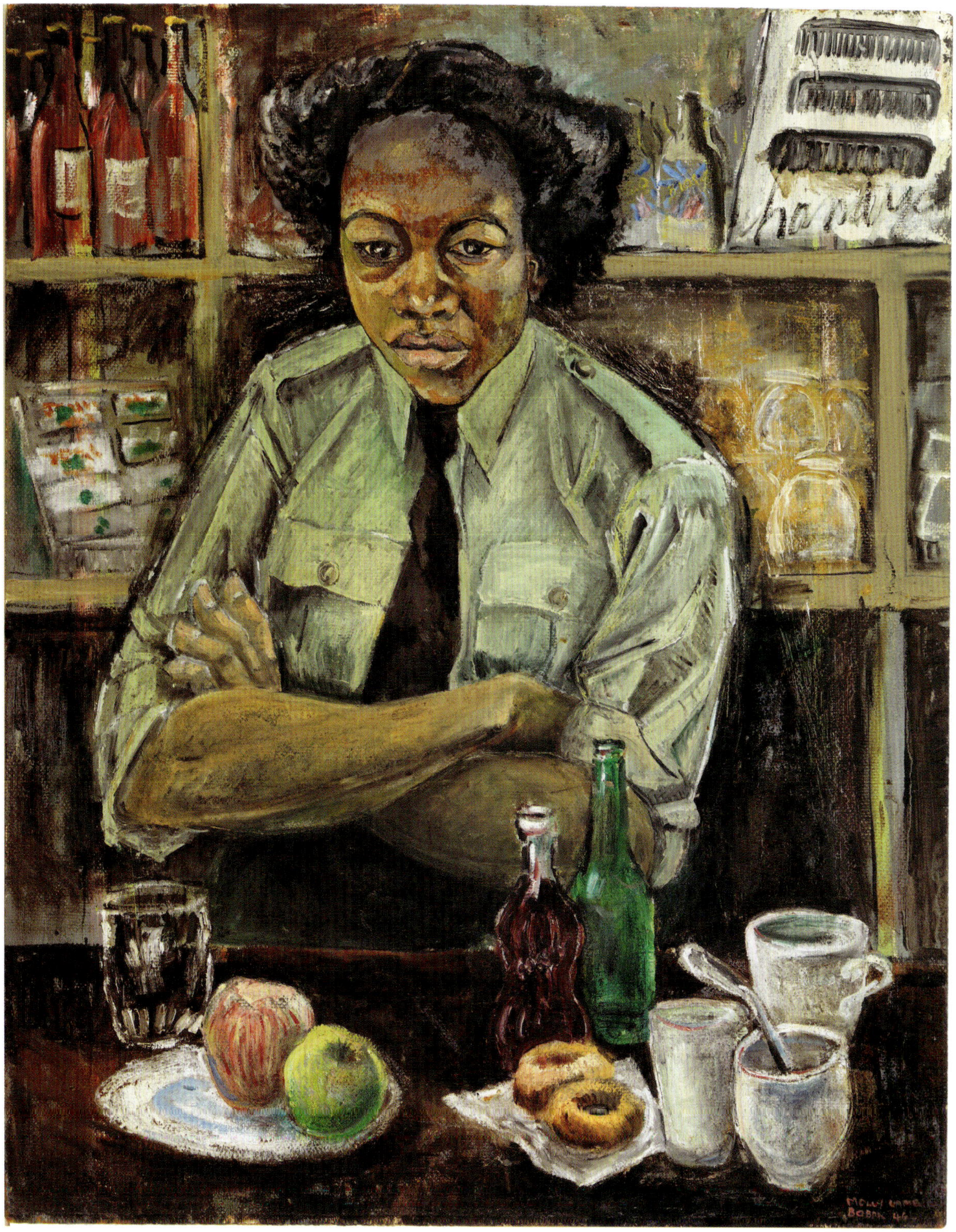

The Power of the Poster

Pasted on walls, hoardings, store windows, buses, trolleys, and railroad stations, recruitment and propaganda posters formed a backdrop to everyday life on the home front during the two world wars.

By June 1915, after ten months of war, ninety separate poster designs were already in circulation in Britain, through the Parliamentary Recruiting Committee (PRC), with a collective print run of approximately 2.5 million. Combining sheer volume with a variety of persuasive designs, posters waged their own war on the consciences of the male population.

Britain's east coast had been subjected to a bombardment by German warships in December 1914 and among the initial poster designs was *Remember Scarborough*, in which an enraged Britannia rouses an army of male civilians to fight, pointing out the towns of Scarborough and Hartlepool ablaze. The artist was Edith Kemp-Welch, better known as a miniatures painter and sister of the more famous Lucy Kemp-Welch, a leading equine artist. Lucy, the first president of the Society of Animal Painters, ran her own art school in Bushey, Hertfordshire. She also designed a poster for the PRC, *Forward! Forward to Victory Enlist Now,* for which she drew on her expertise by depicting a gallant, mounted officer charging toward the viewer.

The Kemp-Welch sisters were unusual in designing posters at a time when men created most commissioned war posters. Less unusual was Edith's depiction of Britannia, a powerful national symbol, widely recognized and strongly associated with the concept of empire. In America, from 1917, Charles Dana Gibson, creator of the "Gibson Girl" of the prewar era, was appointed head of the Division of Pictorial Publicity and was responsible for recruiting the country's finest illustrators. Recognizing the power of art and design, he implored those he commissioned to "Draw 'til it hurts." As in Britain, numerous American artists chose national personification to perform this function. Columbia, who wears a Phrygian cap to represent freedom and liberty, appears in James Montgomery Flagg's *Wake Up* design, slumbering even though civilization requires her intervention. She is also summoned in *Columbia Calls*, designed by Frances Adams Halstead and painted by Vincent Aderente, holding the American flag aloft in a direct appeal to the patriotism of her countrymen. Consciences were also pricked by the depiction of women as helpless victims abducted by German brutes, or as ragged and hungry refugees from "Brave Little Belgium."

When conscription was introduced in Britain in 1916, posters remained essential in a new recruitment drive, to encourage women to step into the shoes of departing men and work toward victory. The working woman was a novelty and her image on posters helped to reappraise and reframe the role of women within society. Such posters were careful to ensure girls employed in military or civilian service looked wholesome, pretty, and fulfilled in their jobs.

This new idea of femininity had evolved further by the time of World War II. The essential contribution of women to the war effort had already been proven, and many poster designs sought to reinforce the image of the skilled and resolute, but *feminine* woman worker. Posters tend to cast her as glossy and glamorous; even when undertaking heavy, dirty, or dangerous work she wears lipstick and her hair (when not hidden under a headscarf) is beautifully coiffured. Uniforms are stylish; work overalls are worn with panache. These were compelling images that served to encourage women and mollify public expectations. The addition of positive slogans, such as "I'm in This War Too" or "She Serves So That Men Might Fly," have ambiguous meaning. They suggest that, while women are essential, they are also subordinate, working to enable fighting men.

Posters signaled contradictory messages in other countries, too. The propaganda posters encouraging women to serve in Nazi Germany were at odds with those sanctifying the role of the mother, yet artists were careful to give women a different type of attractiveness than that of the cosmetically enhanced film-star glamour of the American poster girl. Instead, they were wholesome and typically "Aryan."

Russia's political climate in the 1930s and 1940s produced a distinctive and striking style of poster, some of the best by Nina Vatolina, who had studied art at the Moscow State Institute. The strident confrontation of the Russian mother in Vatolina's 1941 design, *Fascism—The Most Evil Enemy of Women*, and *Keep Your Mouth Shut!* of the same year, were modeled on Vatolina's neighbor, a woman who had seen two sons go off to fight in the war. Prior to the 1917 revolution, Russian artists, including women such as Natalia Goncharova and Liubov Popova, had been at the forefront of modern abstract art movements. Art in postrevolutionary Russia could not exist for its own sake, but was harnessed for political purposes and for the good of the people. Social realism—reproduced in posters, pamphlets, and monolithic sculpture—exalted leaders and Soviet workers, and replaced expressionism, constructivism, and futurism, which were considered elitist by the regime. Some of Vatolina's posters, such as *Long Live the Equal Woman of the USSR*, strongly adhere to the state ideology of Stalinist Russia. But her most effective designs, in which women take center stage, signal a move away from the cult of Stalin to focus on Russia as the "motherland." The Stalinist regime's equal opportunities policy, implemented in the 1930s, proved to fall short of its utopian aims in reality. Combining powerful imagery with persuasive messages, the woman of the war poster was not always what she seemed.

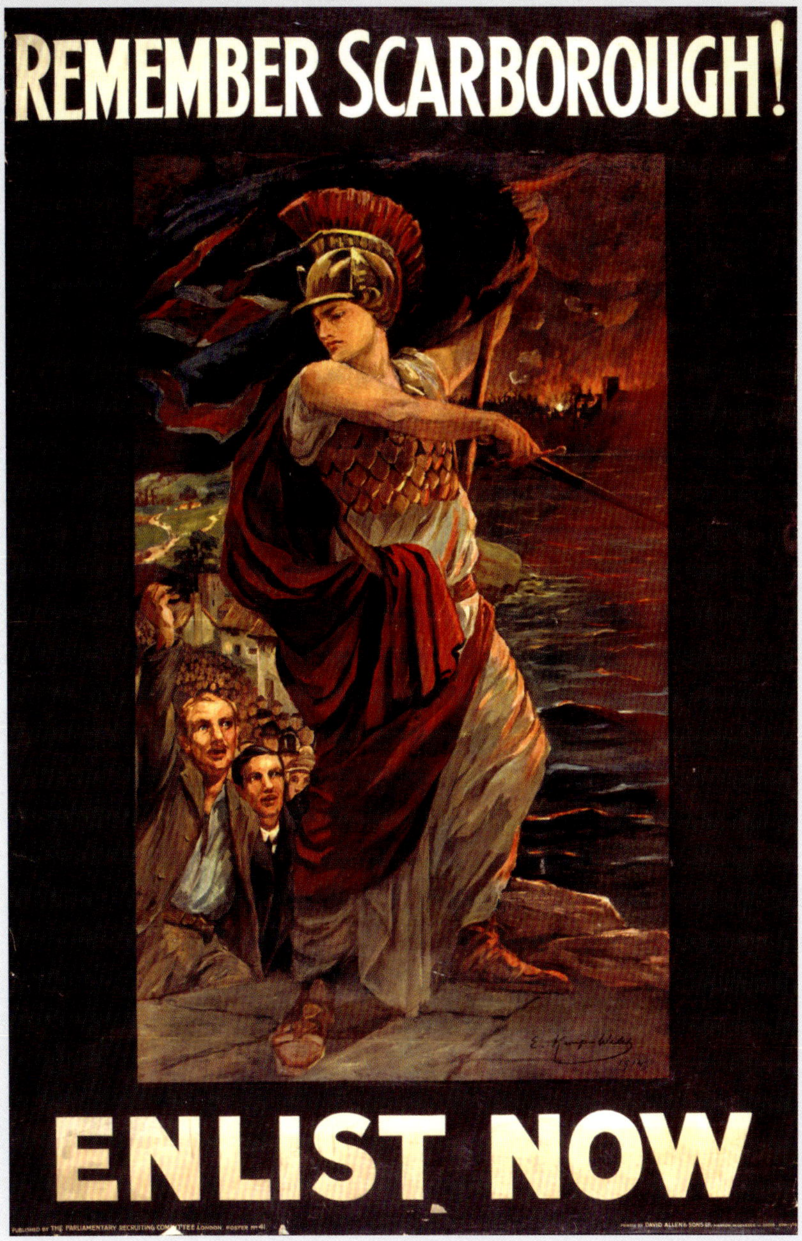

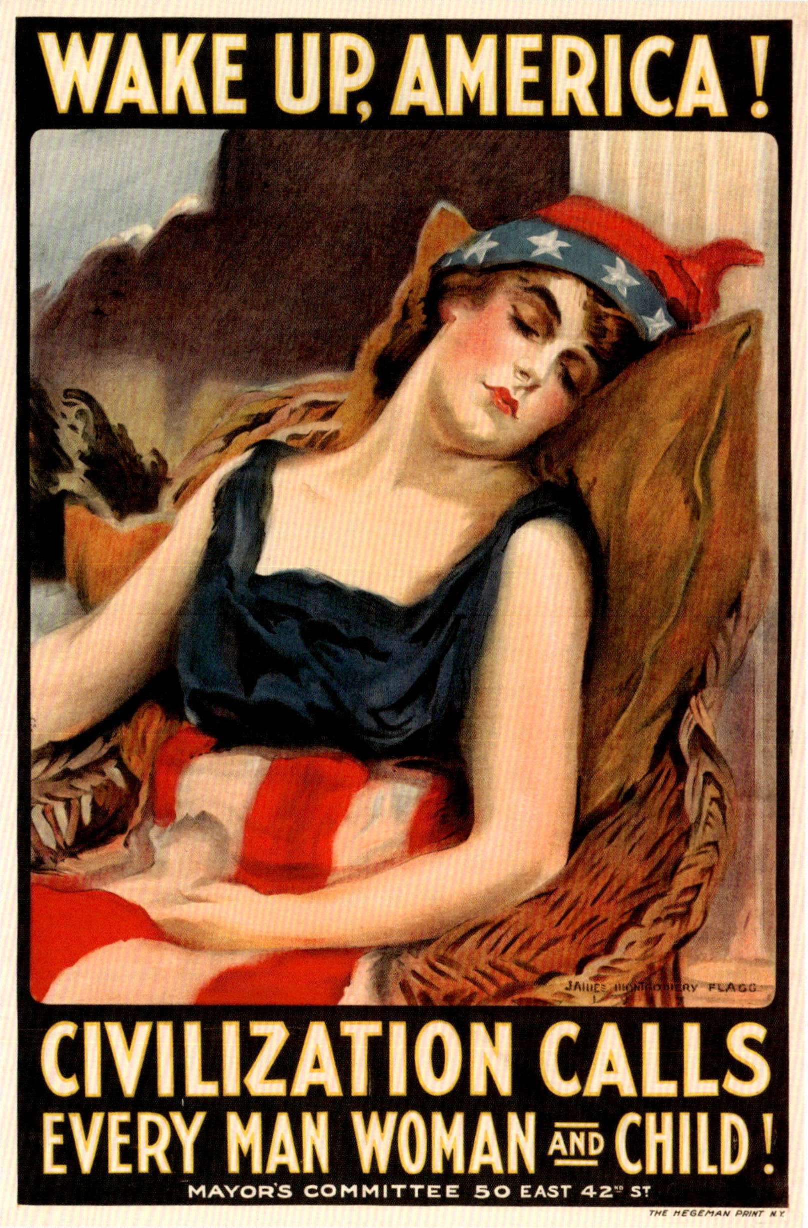

"It is difficult to understand how any young man of military age, who has the patriotic fire within him, can resist such a strong call upon his manhood."

The Windsor Magazine, in an article on recruiting posters, 1915

Above left: **Edith Kemp-Welch, *Remember Scarborough!*, 1914**

The German bombardment of Scarborough and the other East Coast towns of Whitby and Hartlepool in December 1914 caused widespread outrage in Britain, inspiring Edith Kemp-Welch to invoke the powerful image of Britannia for her poster. Symbols of patriotism and nationalism were almost exclusively personified by women, their militancy presented as righteous.

Above right: **James Montgomery Flagg, *Wake Up, America!*, 1917**

While Britannia had already roused men to battle in Britain, a version of Columbia, the national symbol of America, was created by James Montgomery Flagg to stir similar patriotic feelings in his home country.

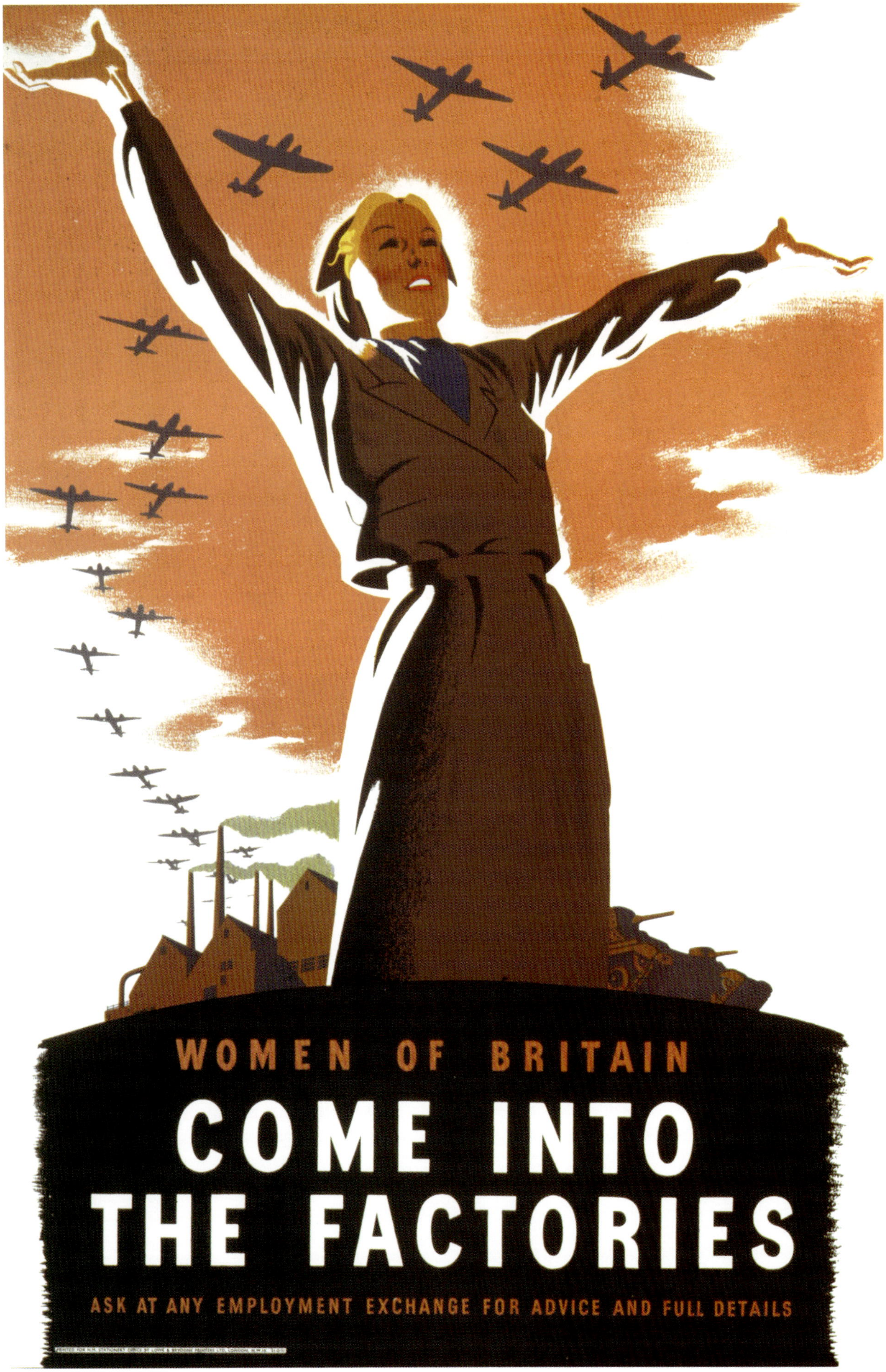

Left: **Donald Zec, *Women of Britain, Come into the Factories*, poster, 1941**

Willing and fulfilled, Donald Zec's poster depicting a munitions worker strikes visual parallels with the practical and purposeful women populating Soviet propaganda posters of the period.

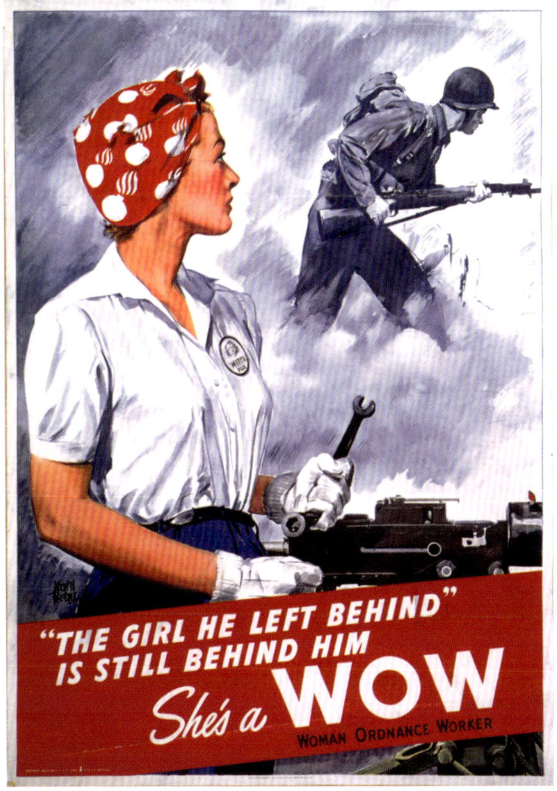

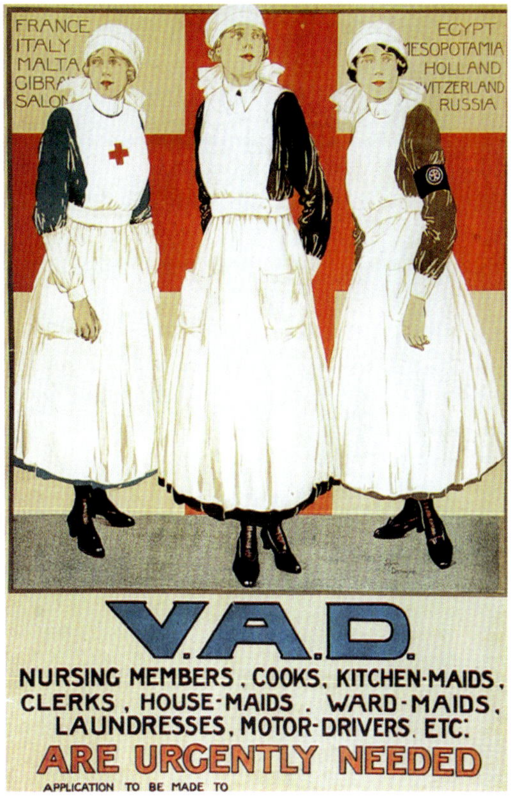

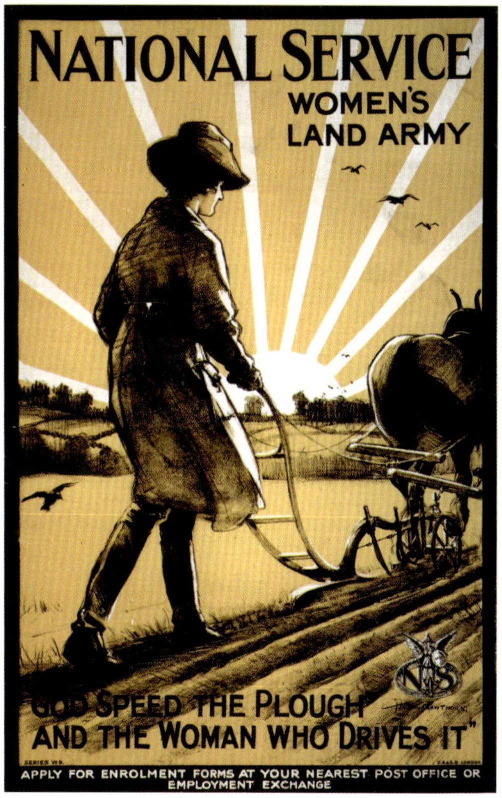

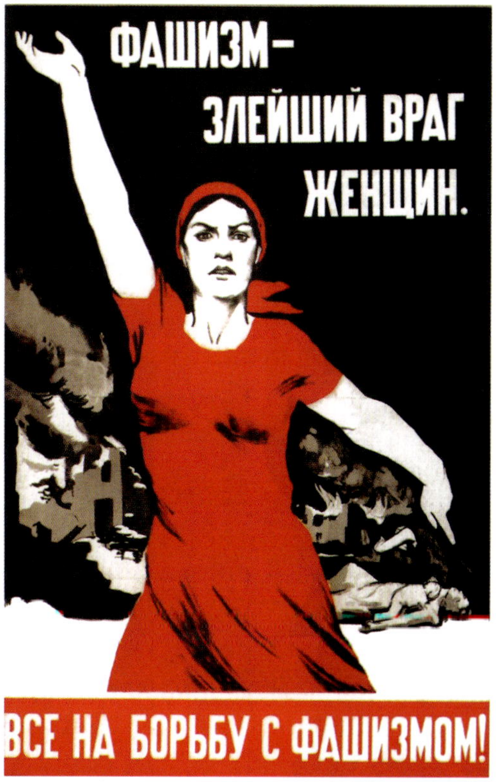

Top left: **Adolph Treidler, *She's a WOW*, poster, 1942**

American artist Adolph Treidler designed seven separate posters for the Women Ordnance Workers (WOW). The headscarf his women were pictured wearing, complete with exploding cannonball motif pattern, was officially part of the WOW uniform.

Top middle: **Joyce Dennys, *Voluntary Aid Detachment*, poster, 1914–18**

British artist Joyce Dennys, whose natural genre was humor, designed two World War I posters aimed at women, one for the Voluntary Aid Detachment (VAD; pictured), and the other for the Women's Royal Naval Service (WRNS). The designs are strong, but graceful, her uniformed women combining an air of competence with a feminine appearance.

Top right: **Henry George Gawthorn, *Women's Land Army*, poster, 1917**

The British Women's Land Army (WLA) was formed in 1917, and posters such as this one depicted the experience as wholesome and idyllic. The reality could be far removed from this, but the rays of the rising sun in Gawthorn's design suggest a godliness in agricultural work.

Bottom right: **Nina Vatolina, *Fascism—The Most Evil Enemy of Women*, poster, 1941**

The model for Russian Nina Vitolina's poster was her neighbor, a woman who had seen her two sons leave to fight in the war. The woman's attitude and stance echo the furious rage of Britannia in Edith Kemp-Welch's World War I poster.

Women Behind the Lens

Women were not necessarily found at the frontline with their cameras, yet their images show a side of war that demands attention and commands empathy in a way that broke the boundaries set by male photojournalists.

Christina Broom made the unlikeliest of wartime photographers. Aged fifty-one at the outbreak of hostilities in 1914, and measuring just 5 ft (1.5 m), she did not set out to be a war photographer, nor would she have considered herself one. But she could lay claim to being Britain's first female press photographer. Broom became a professional photographer in 1903, in order to support her invalid husband, Albert, and their daughter Winifred. Working at the height of the picture-postcard craze, she built a business selling "snapshot" postcards of scenes and events around London. Armed with a cumbersome tripod and medium-format camera, she became a familiar sight around the capital. In 1904, she was appointed official photographer to the prestigious Queen's Guards. She was therefore uniquely placed to capture on camera the mobilization of the Guards regiments when war broke out a decade later.

Broom's style was devoid of trickery or artistic pretensions. Usually, she photographed her subjects outdoors at their barracks. What emerges from her simple formula is a series of spontaneous, natural photographs, resonant with atmosphere and clearly demonstrating the trust that had grown between Broom and the men of the division during a decade-long relationship. Were her portraits obviously the work of a woman? They are certainly unlike anything else from that period; they lack the formal production-line feel of studio portraits, eschew the sensationalism or clichéd military focus of press photographs, and are disarming in their simplicity and sheer ordinariness. They have the spontaneity and intimacy of a family snap, but are technically far superior. Broom's photographs urge us to see the men before we see the uniforms, and it is rare to find images of soldiers that feel quite so intimate. We study their faces; we care about what happened to them.

While Broom took her wartime photographs in a professional capacity, Florence Farmborough combined photography with her work as a Red Cross nurse on the Eastern Front, having been a governess in Russia before the war. Unlike nurses on the Western Front, who worked in hospitals behind the lines, Florence was part of a "flying column," moving with the Russian army as it advanced, witnessing combat firsthand, and triaging and treating the wounded on the frontline. Her photographs, which were used by *The Times* newspaper, were opportunistic, taken when her nursing duties allowed, yet form an unflinching record of the reality of war. Not only do they serve as proof of her own experience, but her work acted as documentary evidence of the scenes she witnessed. In this, her work can be considered an early example of documentary photojournalism. Similarly, the American Helen Johns Kirtland photographed the Austro-Italian front for Frank Leslie's *Illustrated Weekly*, one of the most popular papers in the United States at the time.

By the outbreak of World War II, a growing number of women had established successful careers across Europe, in a range of different photographic disciplines. In the United States, movements such as New York's Photo-Secession, spearheaded by Alfred Stieglitz, had welcomed female members, including Gertrude Käsebier. The influx of European émigré photographers brought new ideas and fresh talent. Alfred Eisenstaedt, a German Jew, moved to America in 1935, just before the reinvention of *LIFE* magazine in 1936, under publisher Henry Luce. Repositioning itself as a picture magazine, *LIFE* made photojournalism its driving force. While Eisenstaedt became the magazine's most prolific photographer during this period, a woman shot its first cover. Margaret Bourke-White had been the first female staff photographer for the magazine *Fortune* at just twenty-five and then became the first female photographer on the staff at *LIFE*. In a hat trick of firsts, she was also the first woman accredited by the United States military as an official war correspondent during World War II. She survived bombardments and a torpedo attack on a U.S. Navy ship, but told the press she was never afraid with a camera in her hand.

Elizabeth "Lee" Miller's background was artistic rather than journalistic, having first worked as a model. She studied under, and then collaborated with, Man Ray in Paris, becoming a leading exponent of surrealist photography. Commissioned by British *Vogue* in 1940, her images of Blitz-ravaged London clearly channeled this surrealist mindset. As the war progressed, Miller traveled through Europe, where her artistic sensibilities were eclipsed by a stronger journalistic focus, and she began to accompany her combat photographs with written reports. Her images of a Normandy field hospital were unsparing and searing documents of war, all the more resonant following their incongruous positioning in *Vogue* alongside images of fashion and beauty.

Female photojournalists did not follow a set technique or pattern of behavior. Experience, interests, training, circumstance, and personality all intervened to map out a photographer's individual style, and many women working during World War II were keen to prove themselves equal to men. A subtle feminine sensibility is present in the intense human experiences captured by Miller. This sensibility is also alive in Thérèse Bonney's work, which focused specifically on the plight of the displaced people she witnessed in Europe, particularly children. Dickey Chapelle, who had studied engineering before taking up photography, was renowned for her intrepid frontline work, having been present at the Battle of Iwo Jima in 1945 in Japan. She would later be killed while working in Vietnam in 1965.

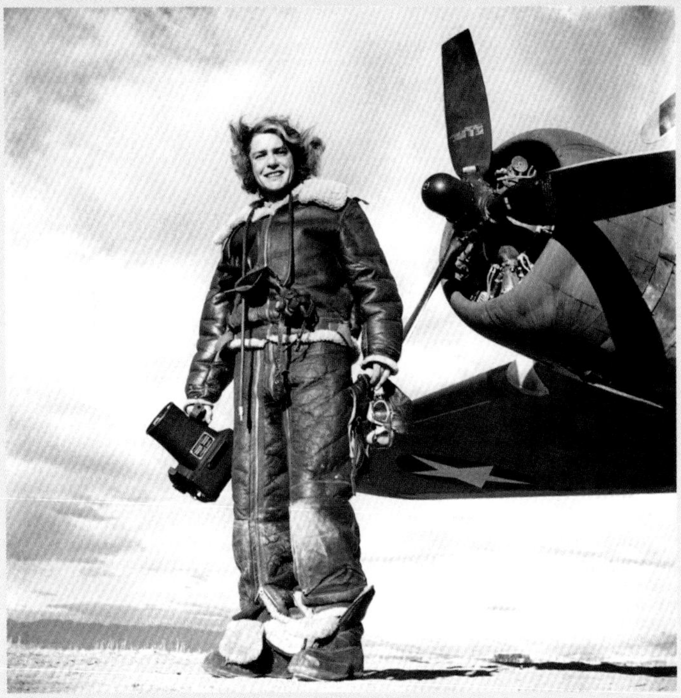

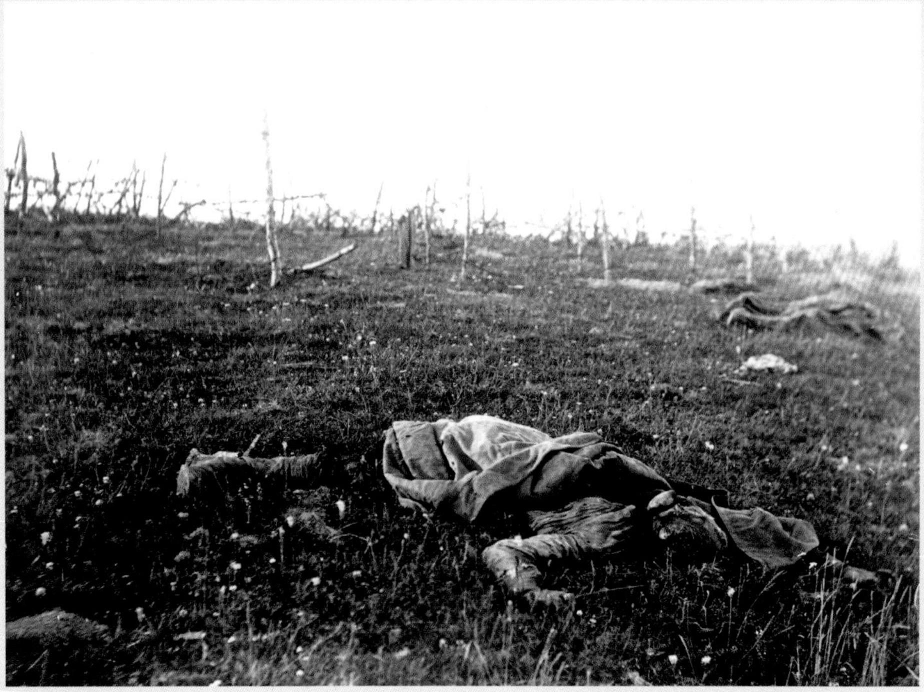

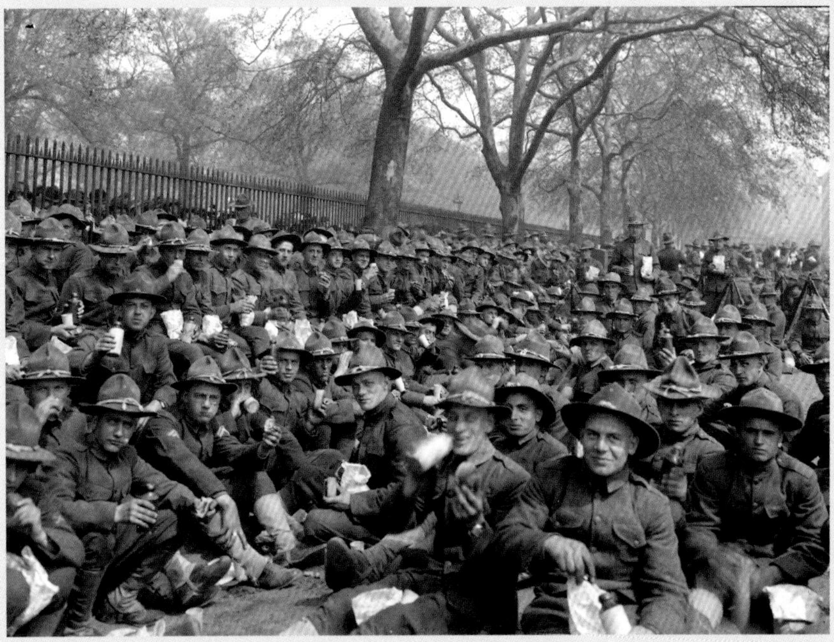

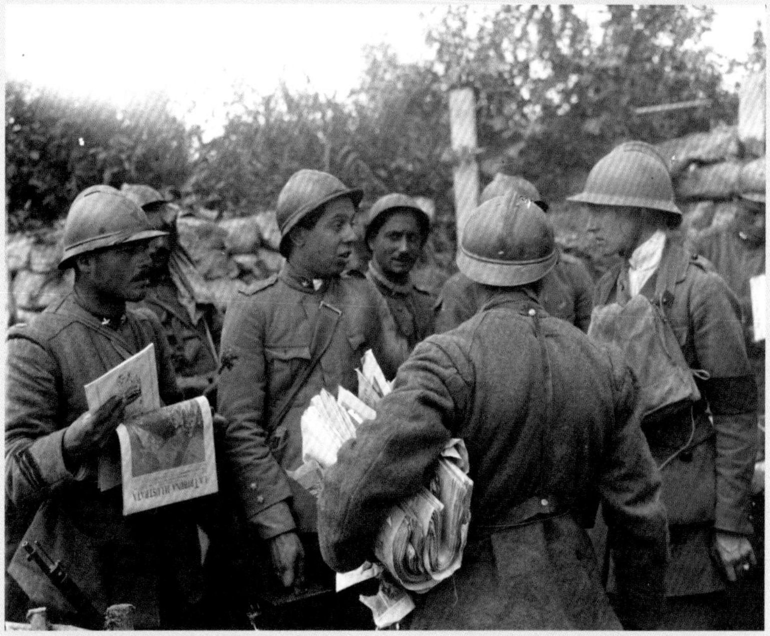

"It is not a woman's place. There's no question about it. There's only one other species on earth for whom a war zone is no place, and that's men. But as long as men continue to fight wars, I think observers of both sexes will be sent to see what happens."

Dickey Chapelle, 1962

Counterclockwise from top left: Margaret Bourke-White was the first woman accredited by the U.S. military as a war correspondent and in appearance and attitude embodied the intrepid photojournalist. But female war photographers came in many different guises. Christina Broom's decade-long relationship with the Guards regiments she photographed left us with some of the most natural and spontaneous images of Word War I soldiers. Helen Johns Kirtland had traveled to Europe in 1917 just days after her marriage to fellow photojournalist Lucian Swift Kirtland and witnessed hand-to-hand fighting and the retreat of Italian troops after Caporetto. The photographs of Florence Farmborough, a Red Cross nurse on the Eastern Front, were an unflinching record of the suffering she was there to help relieve.

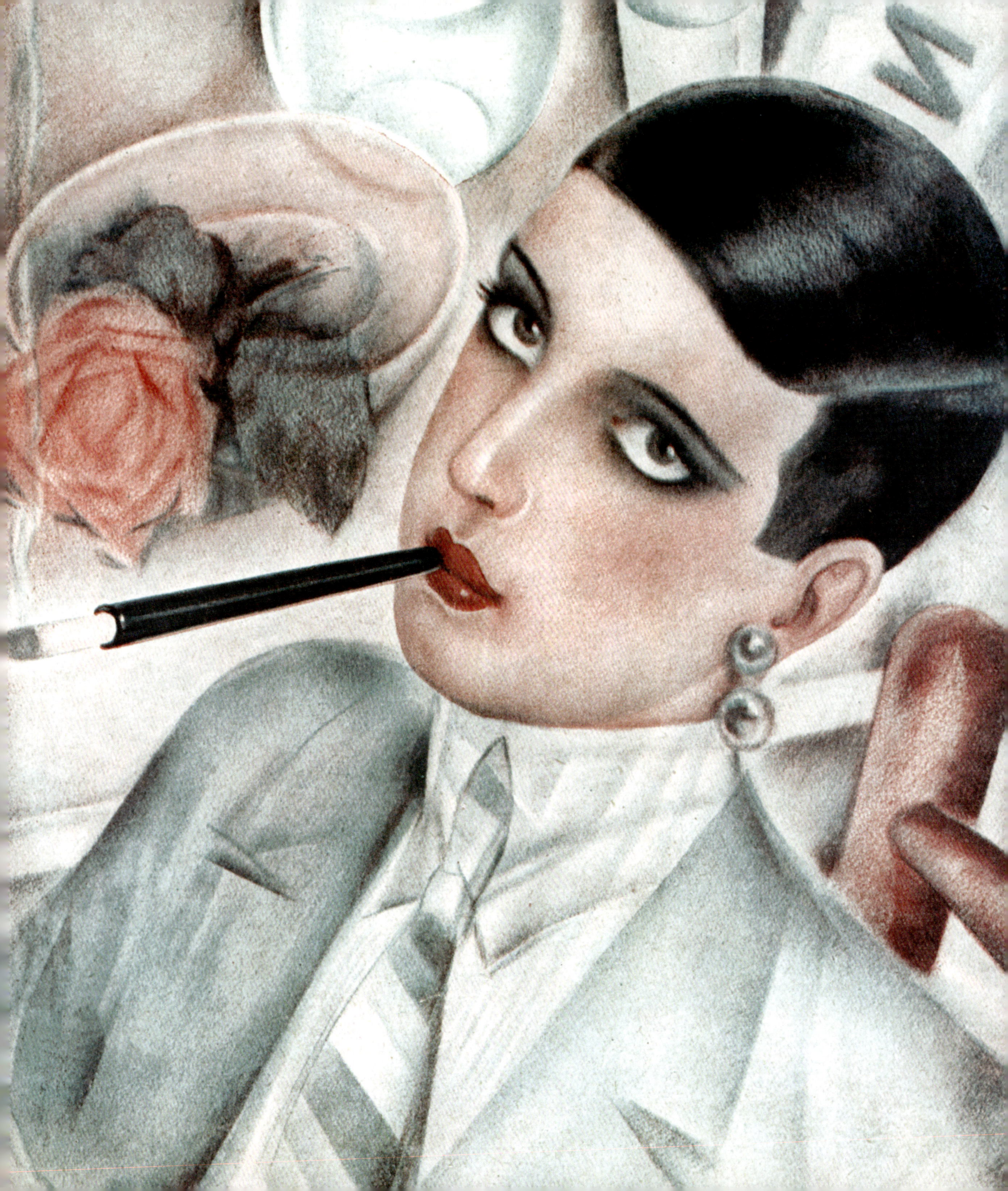

4

A New Woman Emerges

Pushing Boundaries, Celebrating Difference

"They were smart and sophisticated, with an air of independence about them . . . they represented the wave of the future, [and] I was drawn to them."

American actress Colleen Moore (1899–1988) on the New Woman, ca. 1980

Page 74: Sacha Zaliouk, *Eve Adamized, Fantasio* magazine, 1927

The new woman of a liberated age as imagined by Zaliouk wears a suit and tie and her hair in a sleek Eton crop, but signals her gender with makeup, earrings, and a cigarette holder. Zaliouk was a Russian immigrant painter, at the center of the artistic Montparnasse community in Paris, where such style statements and gender ambiguity would have been a more familiar sight than elsewhere.

The twenty years book-ended by the end of one war and the beginning of another was a period of contrasts. In America, the Great Depression, triggered by the stock-market crash of 1929, brought rising unemployment, bread lines, soup kitchens, and homelessness. Yet the response to this economic crisis— Franklin D. Roosevelt's New Deal—was to give birth to a program of federal-funded art initiatives. Recognizing that the downturn affected artists as much as any other workers, the project offered employment while setting on course a production line of creativity designed to adorn public spaces. Art was used not only for economic benefit, but also for the greater good and as an antidote to low national morale. The Federal Art Project, part of the Works Progress Administration (WPA), hired 3,749 artists who in a ten-year period from 1933 to 1943, produced 15,663 paintings, murals, prints, crafts, and sculptures to be displayed in public buildings across the country. Most art revolved around the themes of American life and followed the principles of social realism, and although women artists were in the minority, the employment of minority groups and female artists was encouraged.

The years between the wars were also a time of growing home ownership and mass consumerism, where paid time off work meant that leisure time became a phenomenon enjoyed by the many rather than the few. Car ownership, developing coastal resorts, and the advent of civil aviation opened up the concept of travel, broadening people's horizons, both literally and cerebrally. In the home, labor-saving devices such as washing machines, electric ovens, and vacuum cleaners reduced the hours of chores endured by generations of wives and mothers, although, arguably, they also raised expectations of domestic perfection.

Birth-control pioneers such as Margaret Sanger and Marie Stopes advocated contraception that would allow increasing numbers of women to take control of their fertility. Women's fashionable silhouette changed radically as hemlines rose, restrictive corsets were cast aside, and hair was chopped into boyish crops. This dawning postwar age also brought with it a taste for cocktails, nightclubs, and new, modern dances inspired by the exciting sound of jazz—a more permissive entertainment landscape in which women were participants. In the press, women were pictured smoking, driving cars, and playing golf—it was not necessarily an image that accurately reflected all of society, but this confident, modern Miss became the symbol of the 1920s. It seemed as if the new woman that had so intrigued and appalled Victorian society in equal measure had metamorphosed into her less serious, thrill-seeking younger sister and had finally found an era in which she could flourish.

How did women artists fit into this apparent new order? The female students who had flocked to The Slade and other progressive art colleges since the boom of the 1890s were the first of many, and women continued to fill art school places, frequently outnumbering male students. Studying art in order to become accomplished was supplanted by the concept of education as an essential stepping-stone to a career. What that career was, and how long it might last, posed more of a problem. Many women who studied art progressed to become art teachers. Others used their art training to gain employment as designers in textiles, ceramics, theater, or fashion; as poster artists, photographers, or book and magazine illustrators—all areas that had variously encouraged women since the establishment of colleges specializing in applied arts for women in the nineteenth century. Yet, despite what may be viewed as progress, women artists continued to be defined by their sex or by their relationships to men. Their employment as teachers tended to be restricted to girls' secondary schools rather than higher education, which meant they had no opportunity to shape and influence the artists of tomorrow as their male peers did. The marriage bar, ruling that women in professional and clerical roles were obliged to give up employment after their marriage, was enforced during these years in response to high unemployment and economic depression.

In 1935, a flurry of publicity surrounded the interior decoration of the magnificent Cunard liner RMS *Queen Mary*. A number of women were given the prestigious commission to provide designs, including Scottish sisters Anna and Doris Zinkeisen, British artist Angela Pinder Davis, and the English muralist Mary Adshead. A photograph of the latter working on her mural appeared in *The Sketch* magazine with the caption "Stephen Bone, son of the famous artist, Muirhead Bone, watching his wife working on a giant canvas which will form part of the interior scheme of the giant liner." Mary Adshead, standing on a scaffold by her canvas, is clearly the focus of the photograph and the story, and yet is entirely eclipsed by her husband's celebrity, her name not even deemed worthy of mention. An editorial blunder, perhaps, but it is symptomatic of a more widespread inequality beyond the art world, in which it was proving difficult to dislodge centuries of female subordination and entrenched chauvinism, despite the veneer of sophistication and freedom associated with this period.

Women artists repeatedly suffered from prejudiced judgments about their abilities, based on endemic assumptions about male and female artists stretching back through the centuries. This was clear in contemporary

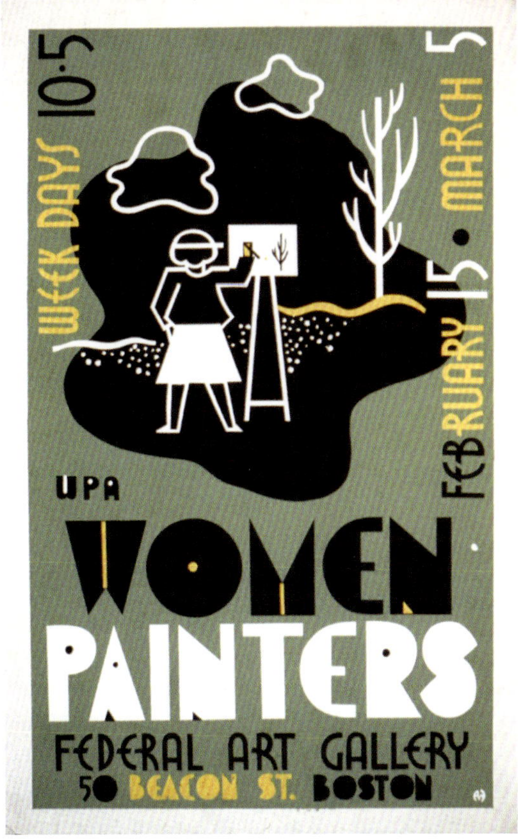

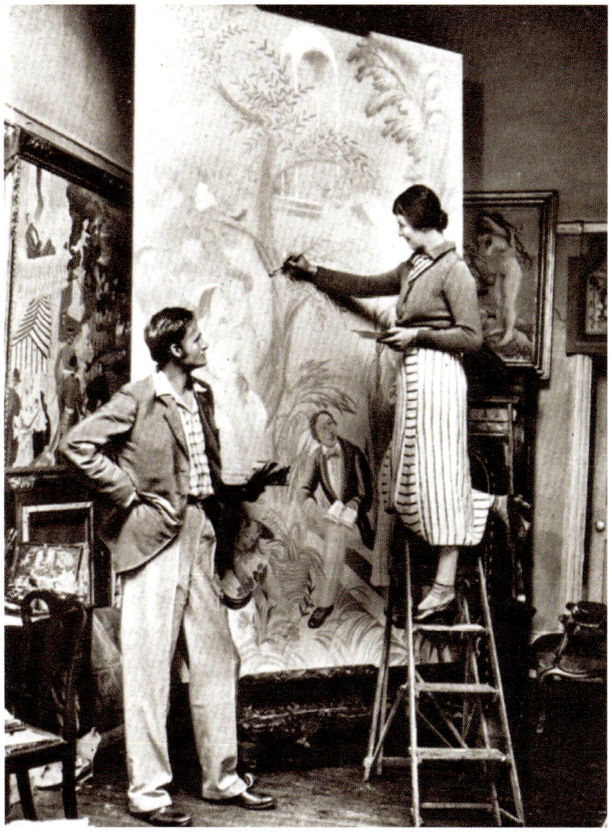

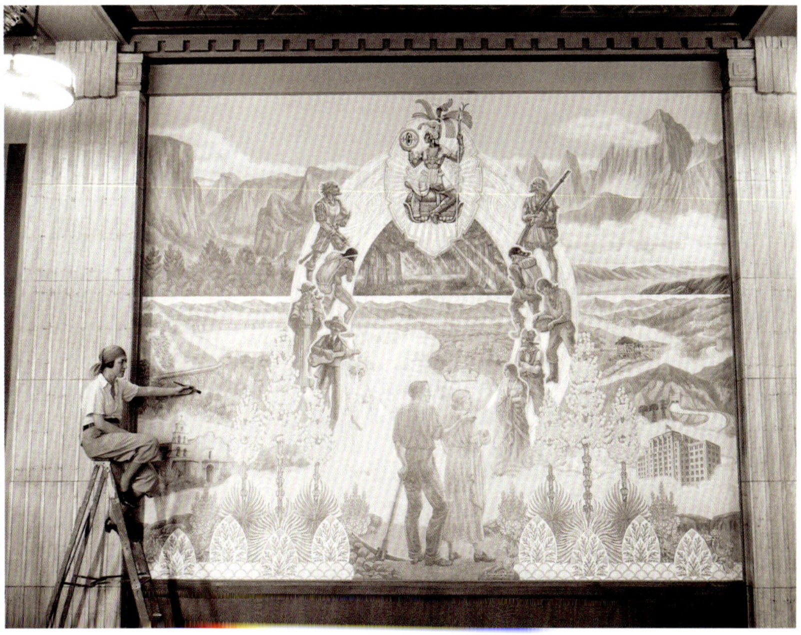

Top left: **Poster for the Works Progress Administration (WPA) women painters' exhibition, 1936**

The Federal Art Project, where artists were employed by the government to decorate public spaces, was one of the most progressive aspects of Roosevelt's New Deal policy. The scheme gave employment to impoverished artists while using art to improve the lives and environment of the population. Women and artists of color were encouraged to take part in the scheme, offering opportunities previously monopolized by male artists.

Top right: **Mary Adshead, mural for the RMS *Queen Mary*, 1936**

British mural artist Mary Adshead, watched by her husband and collaborator Stephen Bone, was one of several women, including Anna and Doris Zinkeisen, commissioned to provide murals for Cunard's RMS *Queen Mary* ocean liner. Adshead's *Queen Mary* murals were never installed, but during her long career she carried out numerous public and private commissions including work for London Underground stations, the Commonwealth Institute, and Selfridges restaurant.

Bottom right: **Lucile Lloyd, mural for the California State Building in Los Angeles, WPA, 1936**

Lucile Lloyd, a muralist who studied at the Art Students League and Cooper Union, was the first woman artist in California to receive a commission from the WPA. Considered professional and efficient by her clients, media profiles focused unnecessarily on how her gender affected her chosen discipline, marveling for instance at how she was able to climb scaffolding "without handicap."

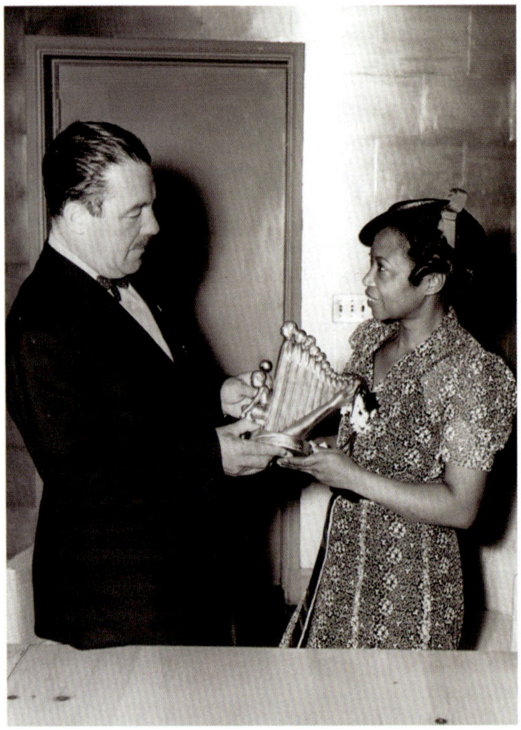

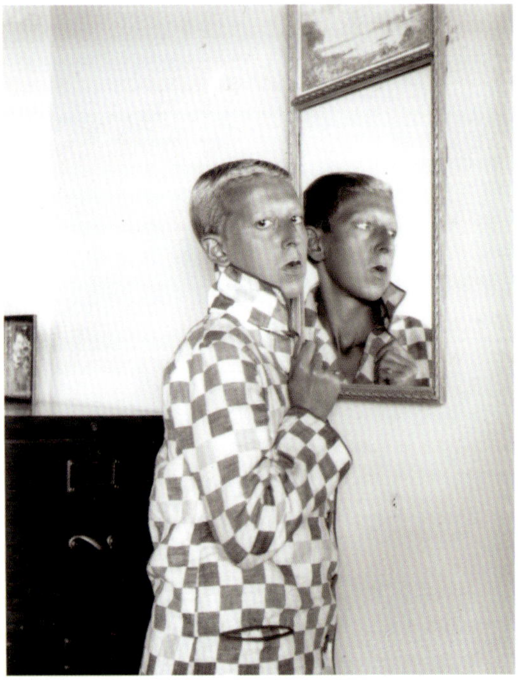

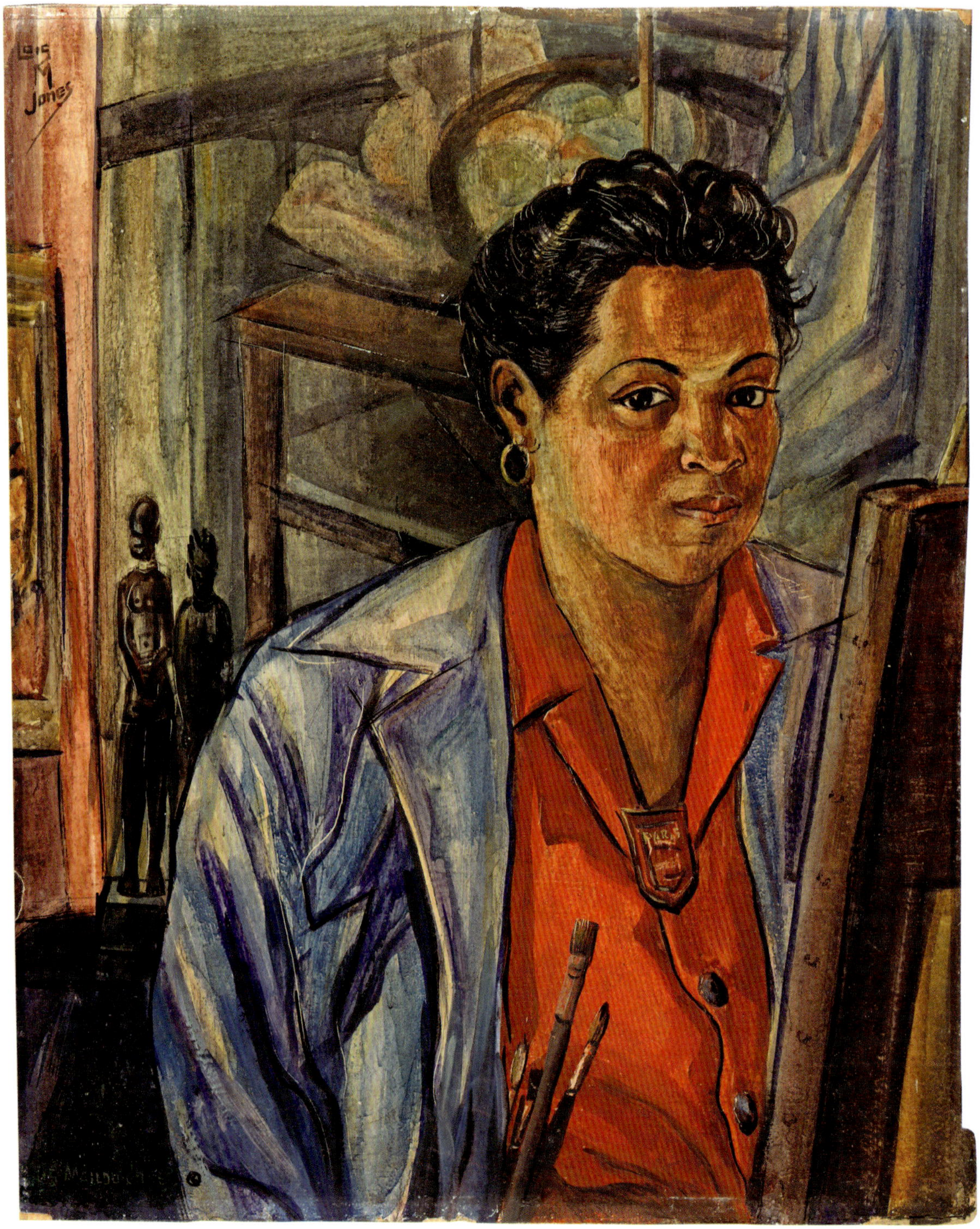

Top left: **Augusta Savage presents a model of her sculpture, to Grover Whelan, organizer of the 1939 New York World's Fair**

Augusta Savage was the first African American to be elected to the Association of American Women Painters and Sculptors. Her sculpture *The Harp* was inspired by "Lift Every Voice and Sing," a song often regarded as the black national anthem, and depicted black singers as the harp's ascending strings.

Above right: **Lois Mailou Jones, self-portrait, 1940**

During a long career, Lois Mailou Jones explored a variety of artistic styles using different media, many evolving to reflect her African heritage. In this self-portrait from 1940, she presents herself according to the conventions of a serious, working artist, yet the African carved figures in the background are a strong indicator of her identity as an African-American woman.

Bottom left: **Claude Cahun, *Self-portrait (reflected image in mirror with checkered jacket)*, 1928**

Born Lucy Schwob into a French-Jewish, middle-class family, Claude Cahun did not identify with any gender, describing herself as "neuter." Her body of work is a thought-provoking series of self-portraits in which she used costume and props to explore identity beyond conventional definitions. In this photograph of Cahun, in which she appears tanned, crop-headed, and genderless, consciously theatrical, the artist uses a mirror to suggest the dual aspects of her personality.

America, too, where black women artists of the Harlem Renaissance faced racial as well as sexual prejudice. One of its most successful artists, Lois Mailou Jones, won countless prizes while studying, but entered competitions anonymously and did not collect her prizes in person until her growing cluster of awards had cemented her reputation. After four years of study at the School of the Museum of Fine Arts in Boston, she was refused a teaching position, but was eventually recruited by the art department of Howard University in Washington, D.C. In 1937 she received a fellowship to study at the Académie Julian in Paris, a more accepting environment, in which she flourished. The African-American sculptor Augusta Savage, who attended Cooper Union, had her application to study in France in 1923 refused due to her race. It was an experience that was to galvanize her into action, lobbying against discrimination and actively supporting the rights of black artists to be involved in the WPA program during the 1930s.

Leading British women artists, such as Laura Knight, Gwen John, and Ethel Walker, are frequently described as exceptional in both contemporary and latter-day accounts, implying that the majority of female artists were unexceptional, and that those who were preeminent were unusual. The subjects frequently favored by women artists, such as still-life and genre paintings, were often considered "safe" during a period that saw male artists dominate wave after wave of avant-garde art movements. Furthermore, compared to the potent genius naturally associated with the male artist, there was an insidious and complicit belief that women were not similarly endowed with such a creative spark. Linda Nochlin, in her groundbreaking essay of 1971, "Why Have There Been No Great Women Artists?" called out this invocation of male genius, this radiation of "mysterious, holy effulgence," as a systemically created myth, arguing that compared to women, male artists had access to opportunities and institutions that were denied to women. She also points out that throughout history, male artists from the seventeenth-century Dutch school to the impressionists also chose still-life and genre subjects without attracting disdain.

In many instances, women artists moved to find their own niches either within particular art movements, or by forming groups and networks within which they could delve into areas of experimentation and expression. It is here that we find some of the most unconventional and thought-provoking work. Consider Claude Cahun, alter ego of French artist Lucie Schwob, who challenged notions of gender and identity through a series of costumed self-portraits, experimenting with mercurial image changes and photomontage in a body of work that shows the influence of dadaism and surrealism. There was the British artist Hannah Gluckstein, who, wishing to distance herself from her wealthy family—cofounders of the J. Lyons catering empire—used the name Gluck and painted for a cosmopolitan, high-society clientele who were accepting of her masculine attire and pipe-smoking habit. Frida Kahlo's intensive exploration of her body, her relationships, and her sense of self through her paintings began in 1926, and while her compelling self-portraits have much in common with the surrealist movement, she would claim, "I never painted dreams. I painted my own reality."

The interwar years witnessed women illustrators and designers finding popular and commercial success with work in the applied arts. Although traditionally perceived as inferior to fine art, a burgeoning consumer market meant that good design was in demand. Ceramics designers such as Susie Cooper and Clarice Cliff created ranges of china that allowed people to own a piece of art deco style in an affordable and usable form. Women were also making their mark in theater and costume design. The American Gordon Conway, discovered by *Vanity Fair* art director Hepworth Campbell, was in great demand during the late 1920s and early 1930s, designing womenswear as well as costumes for stage and screen. Gladys Calthrop's partnership with Noel Coward resulted in some of the most stylish backdrops to the most talked-about plays in London and New York.

Many other women successfully managed a multidisciplinary career across a range of media. Jessie Willcox Smith was a book illustrator who also designed advertisements and posters. She was an early member of the Philadelphia women-only art group The Plastic Club, formed in reaction to the Philadelphia Sketch Club, which was exclusively male. Helen Dryden applied her design skills not only to the covers of American *Vogue* and, subsequently, *Delineator*, but also to theater design, packaging, and wallpaper patterns. In the 1930s, she branched out into industrial design when she was invited to style the 1937 Studebaker car, a collaboration that was made much of in the company's advertisements. It was rumored that Studebaker paid her $35,000 per year at one point, which, along with other design and consultancy work, made her the highest-paid female designer in America. Ukrainian-born Sonia Delaunay began her career in France as a painter, but replicated her abstract images in dress and textile designs with great success. She worked with couturiers such as Jacques Heim and Jacques Doucet, on designs that gained a following among well-heeled socialites, in a move that was to form an innovative marriage between modernist, avant-garde ideas and commercial success.

This idea of artistic alliances for profit was successfully carried out in Britain by a number of highly popular female illustrators including Mabel Lucie Attwell, Gladys Peto, and Hilda Cowham. All had their book and magazine illustrations of whimsical children licensed and syndicated widely, for postcards, handkerchiefs, china, soft toys, cookie tins, or in advertising. All three designed London Transport posters, in a style that had charm and catered to popular tastes. Unchallenging and sentimental, this may have been a type of women's art that was diametrically opposed to the avant-garde high art of this period, but even across genres, it was proof that creative and innovative women could wield considerable economic agency through their artistic talent.

Below left: **Gwen John, *Nude Girl*, 1909–10**

During time spent studying art in Paris, where she took life classes at Académie Colarossi, British artist Gwen John posed as a life model herself for artists including Auguste Rodin (the pair became lovers for a time). Her nude portrait of Fenella Lovell, who she also painted in the same pose clothed, is typical of John's spare composition and muted color palette. The faintly reproachful gaze and awkward stance of the model, far removed from the traditional nubile sensuality of the female nude, may draw on her own uncomfortable experiences as a model.

Below right: **Isabel Bishop, *Tidying Up*, 1941**

Born in Cincinnati, Isabel Bishop arrived in New York in 1918, at the age of sixteen, to study illustration. She eventually set up her studio in Union Square. From 1936–37 she taught at the Art Students League where she was the only female instructor. A member of the Fourteenth Street School, she was influenced by her immediate urban environment and its inhabitants. This candid painting of a New Yorker captures her in the act of making up, oblivious to public scrutiny as she appears to check her teeth for lipstick marks. Only two decades earlier, women applying lipstick in public were considered "fast," but Bishop's subject, one of the city's growing population of female workers, suggests this ritual of beautifying as a natural statement of feminine confidence.

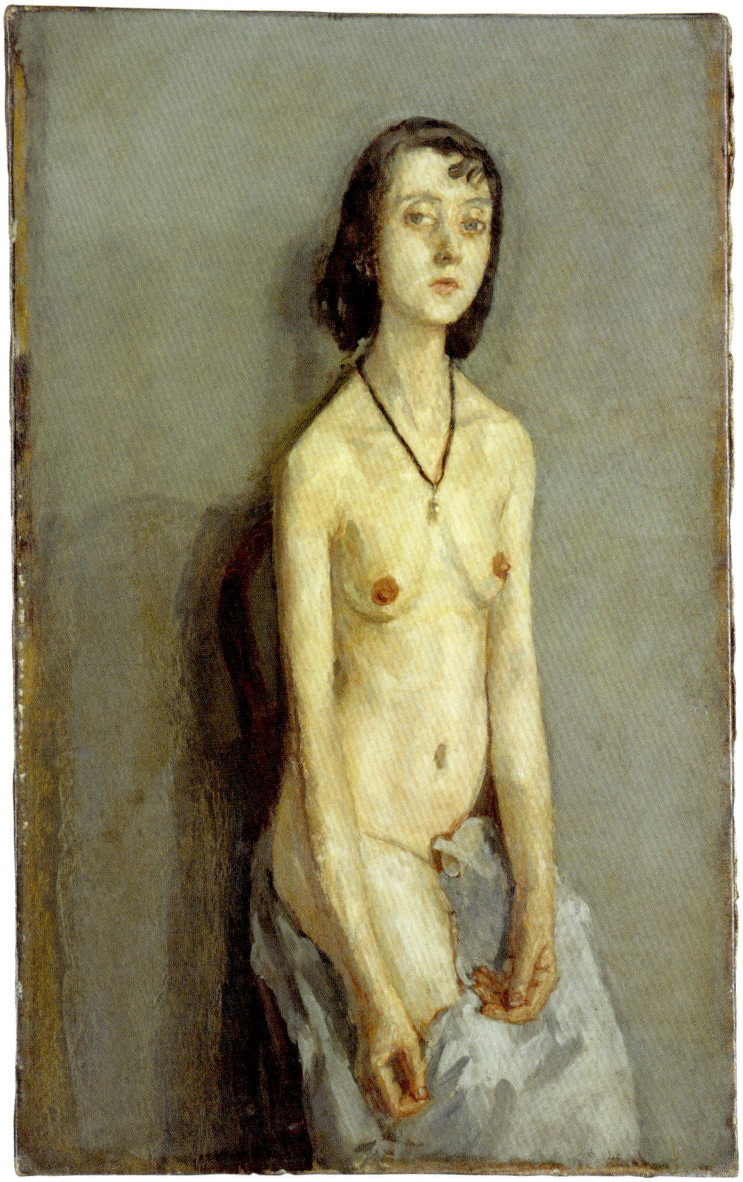

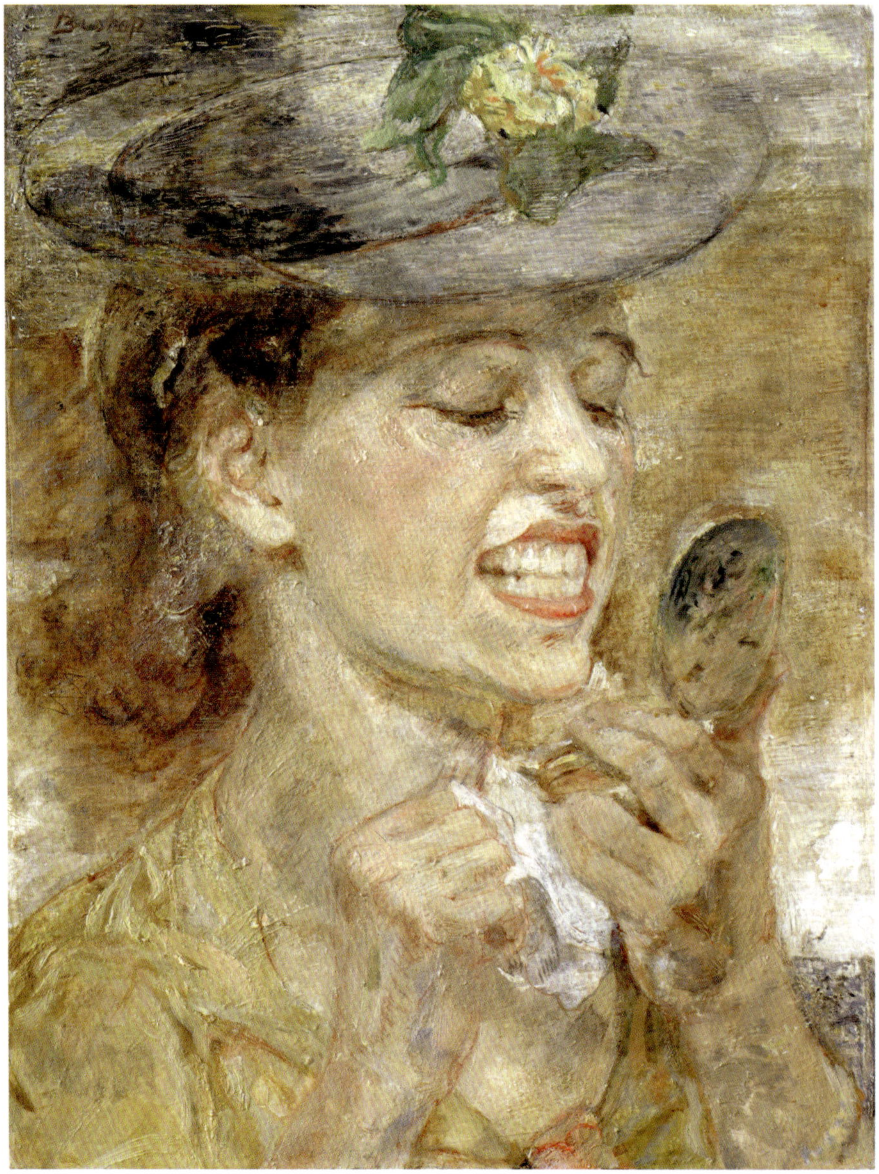

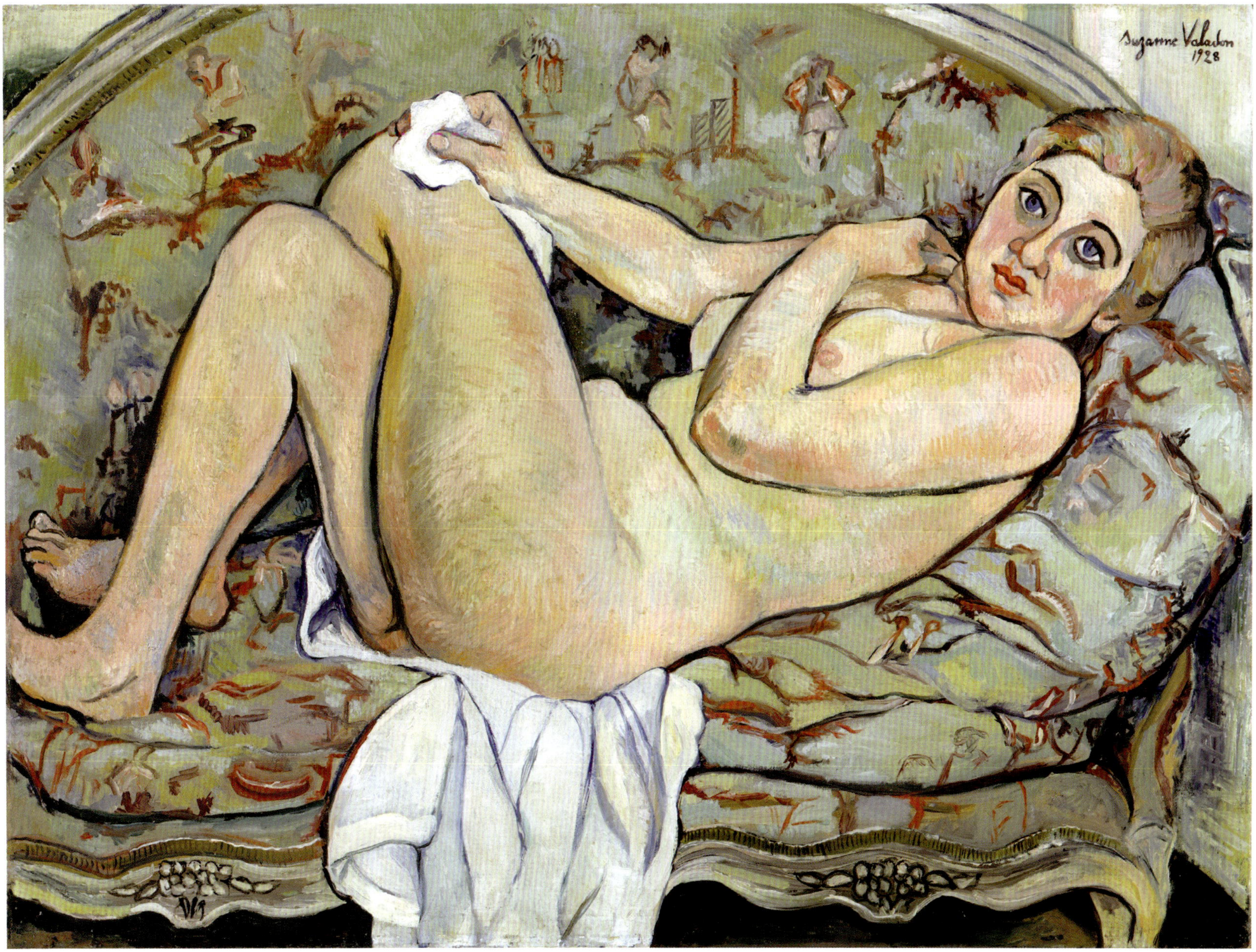

Above: **Suzanne Valadon, *Reclining Nude*, 1928**

Like Gwen John, French artist Suzanne Valadon also worked as an artist's model before pursuing her own artistic career. And as with John's painting (opposite) her subject does not conform to the conventions of nude painting carried out by generations of male painters since the Renaissance. Though the fleshy contours are there, the woman in this picture seems uncertain and partially covers herself while meeting the viewer's gaze directly. By subverting the idealized classical nude, Valadon presents us with an image that is relatable and familiar.

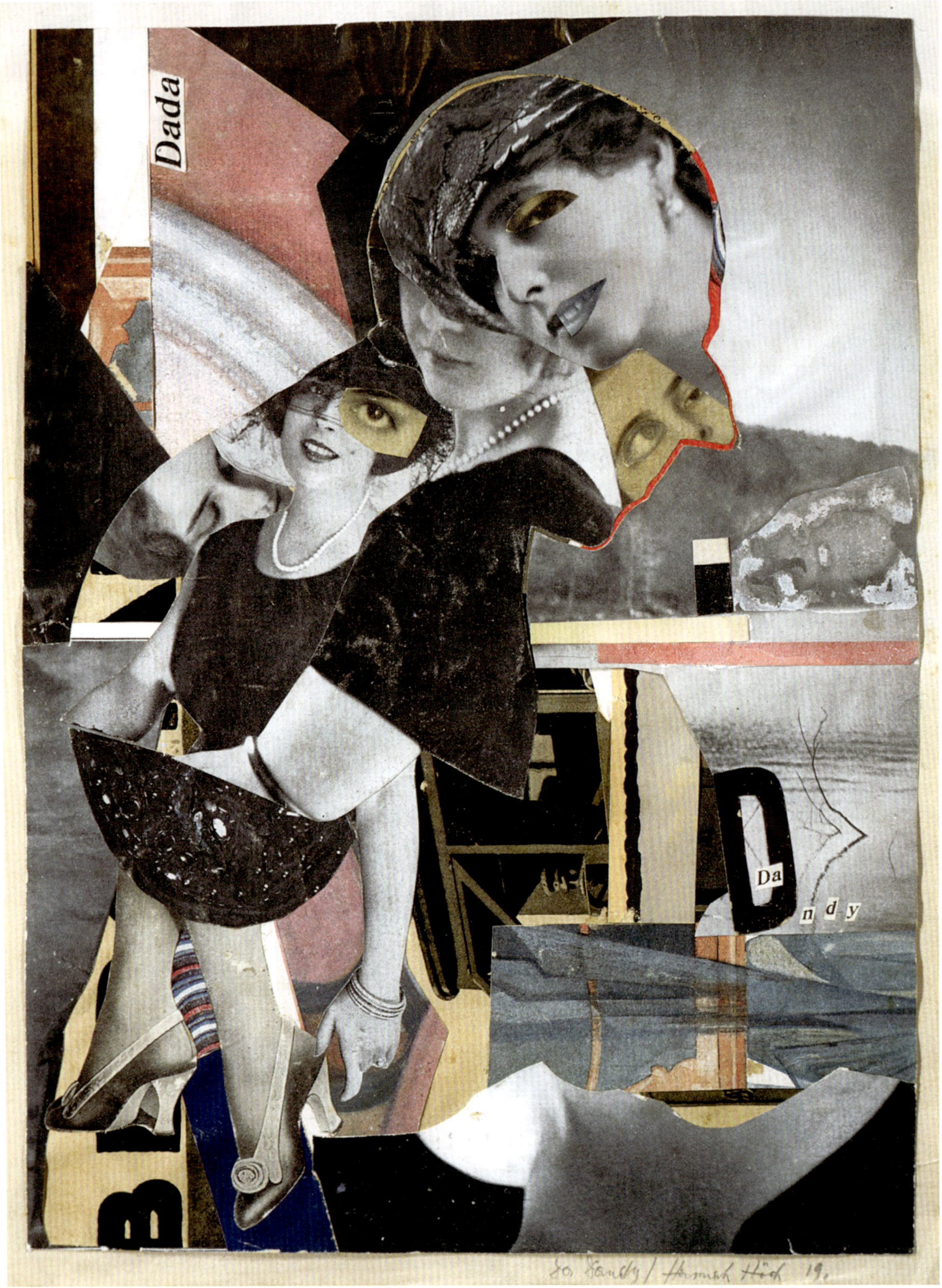

Left: **Hannah Höch, *Da-Dandy*, 1919**

Dadaism originated in Austria and sought to explore new forms of creativity in reaction to the unfolding chaos in society brought about by World War I. German artist Hannah Höch, the only woman member of the Berlin dadaists, was an early pioneer of photomontage, and through layering and juxtaposing images from women's magazines explored and challenged prevailing attitudes about women, their appearance, and their place in society. Through her pictures, Höch questioned whether the media's vision of an emancipated and androgynous "new woman" was a contrived conceit rather than the reality for most members of her sex.

Below: **Liubov Popova, *Painterly Architectonic*, 1917**

Popova was at the center of the dynamic avant-garde movement active in Russia in the decade leading up to the Russian Revolution of 1917. After working in cubo-futurist style, she began to develop a bold, abstract visual language in response to Kazimir Malevich's suprematist paintings in which she took a constructivist approach, layering shape and color and intersecting angular shapes to create powerful, nonobjective compositions. After the revolution, when the Soviet government ruled all art should serve the state, she worked particularly in textiles, where her explorations in geometric form and limited color palettes reflected the rise of industrialized manufacture and the rejection of individual artistry and craftsmanship.

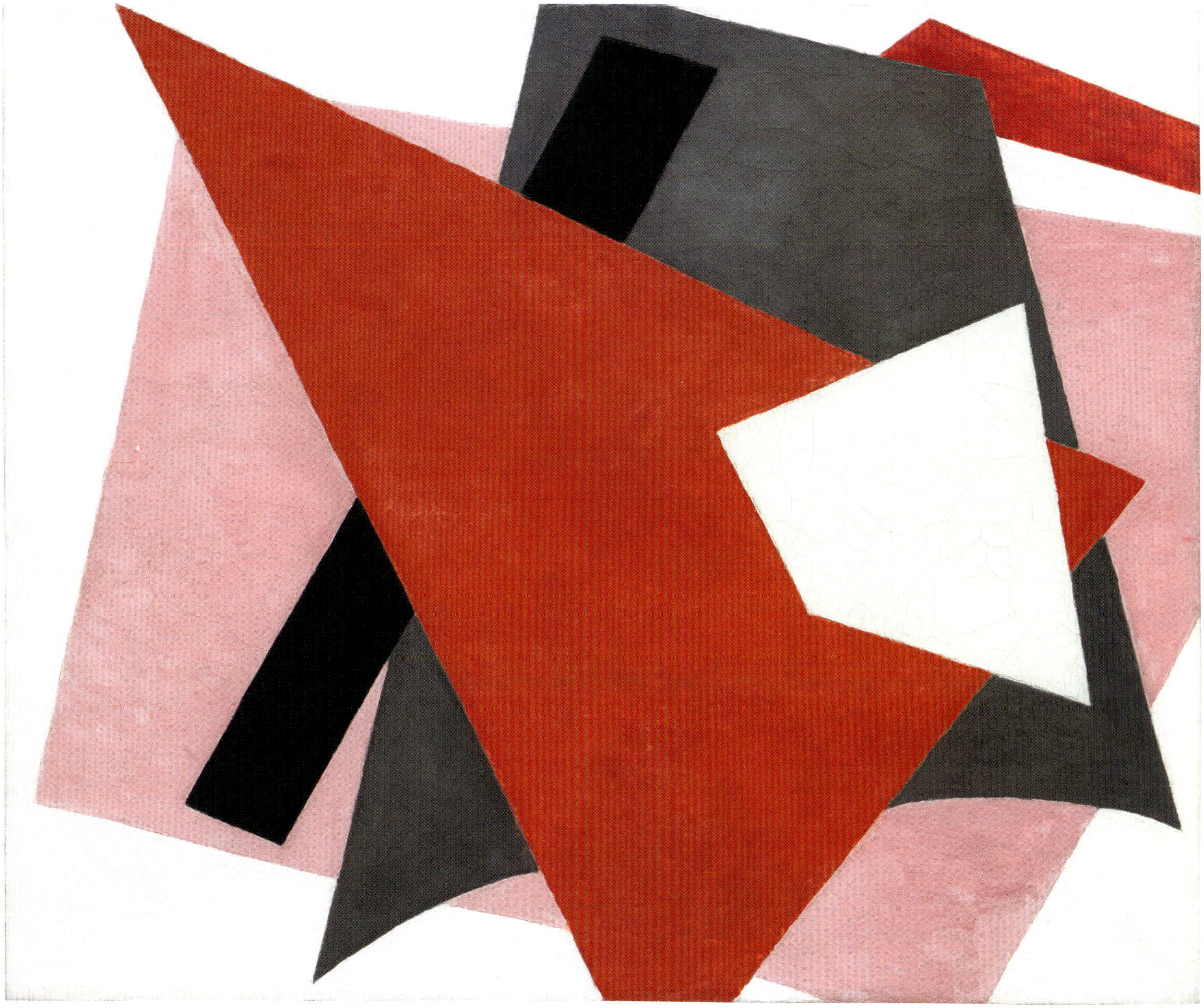

Tamara de Lempicka—Style and Substance

With her blonde waves, aquiline nose, and chic sense of personal style, Tamara de Lempicka could have stepped right out of one of her own paintings. As an artist, her work defined the decadent glamour and bold assertiveness of the 1920s and 1930s. As a woman, she was no mere observer, but the personification of the liberated, independent female her paintings celebrated.

Born Maria Gorska in Warsaw, in 1898, to a Russian merchant father and wealthy Polish mother, Lempicka's interest in art was ignited by a trip to Italy as a young girl, where she admired the Renaissance masters, particularly Bronzino. She married young and gave birth to a daughter in St. Petersburg but fled Russia in 1918 following the Bolshevik Revolution. Like many Russian artists, the de Lempickas settled in Paris, where Tamara studied at the Académie de la Grande Chaumière under the post-symbolist painter Maurice Denis, who taught her the principles of Les Nabis, a group of postimpressionists who advocated the importance of graphic design elements in paintings. She also took lessons from André Lhote, whose technique of "synthetic cubism" recommended a more palatable version of cubism in tune with bourgeois tastes. Tamara took elements of Lhote's teaching and applied them to the classical iconography of Renaissance figurative art. She injected her images with high contrast color and a heightened sense of light and shade. Formed from small, geometric planes, her figures, set against granite-like cityscapes, loom large on the canvas in a sensual riot of multifaceted voluptuousness.

Having developed an individual painting style that chimed in perfect tune with the art deco aesthetic, Tamara cultivated a lifestyle that imitated and almost outshone her art. Paris in the 1920s was an intoxicating and glittering magnet for bohemians, philosophers, musicians, writers, and artists, who flocked to the bars and nightclubs where morals were loose and behavior lascivious. Moving effortlessly within this milieu, Tamara de Lempicka cut an elegant and remarkable figure. She had a penchant for designer hats by the likes of Rose Descat and, as fashion designers became clients, was the recipient of clothes as a mark of their appreciation. She attended the Friday afternoon salons of expat American and high-profile lesbian Natalie Barney, to which she was invited initially owing to her resemblance to film actress Greta Garbo, of whom Barney was a fan. An expert networker who was able to combine business with pleasure, attending Barney's salons and cultivating a circle of acquaintances that included the filmmaker Jean Cocteau and the Italian poet Gabriele D'Annunzio placed her at the center of the Parisian social elite and gained her an increasing number of portrait commissions. Always driven by work, she sent her daughter to boarding school, conveniently omitting to mention her to friends. Disregarding her husband, she embarked on a series of affairs, some fleeting, some intense, with both men and women. The model for the 1927 painting *La Belle Raphaela*, a sprawling, sensual nude, was a prostitute Tamara had met in the street and with whom she would embark on an affair. Unaware of this backstory, *The Graphic* magazine in its review of an exhibition at the Salon des Indépendants declared the painting a "powerful nude in oils . . . remarkable for its combination of plastic form and sound construction. This, and the clever use of light and shade, makes the picture one of the most effective. . . ."

Many other examples of Lempicka's work display the same audacious sexual charge. Her female nudes are ripe and uninhibited, with generous curves and protruding nipples—nudity was standard in art deco imagery, but Tamara's nudes are flamboyant and verge on the sexually explicit. They suggest an artist who took pleasure in the spectacle of the female body and whose pictures were produced in an exploratory atmosphere of sexual permissiveness. Arsène Alexandre, the art critic of leading French newspaper *Le Figaro*, called her nudes "perverse Ingrism," refashioning, as they did, the sweep and curve of French neoclassical painter Jean-Auguste-Dominique Ingres's *Odalisque* or *Turkish Bath*. A portrait of Suzy Solidor, chanteuse and Parisian nightclub owner, is similarly provocative. Solidor had embarked on a well-publicized project to be painted by a succession of artists. Tamara de Lempicka's portrait of her captures the singer's lithe athleticism best. The pair went on to be lovers for a time.

Tamara de Lempicka's most fêted picture is her self-portrait, *Autoportrait*, in which she pictures herself at the wheel of a green Bugatti as a goddess of the modern age, harnessing the power of machinery to speed her toward freedom. Originally commissioned as a cover by the female editor of *Die Dame* magazine, it was intended as a celebration of female emancipation. De Lempicka adjusted details of the picture, promoting her own yellow Renault to the luxurious Bugatti while her face, with its vibrant red lips, pencil brows, and cool gaze has the smooth detachment of a mannequin. It is an exhilarating love letter to modernism.

In later years, the increasing domination of abstract art would cause Tamara de Lempicka's distinctive art to fall out of favor and she would fade into obscurity. *Autoportrait*, however, shows her at the height of her powers. Sexually confident, defiantly provocative, and financially self-sufficient, Tamara de Lempicka was the new woman of the 1920s made flesh.

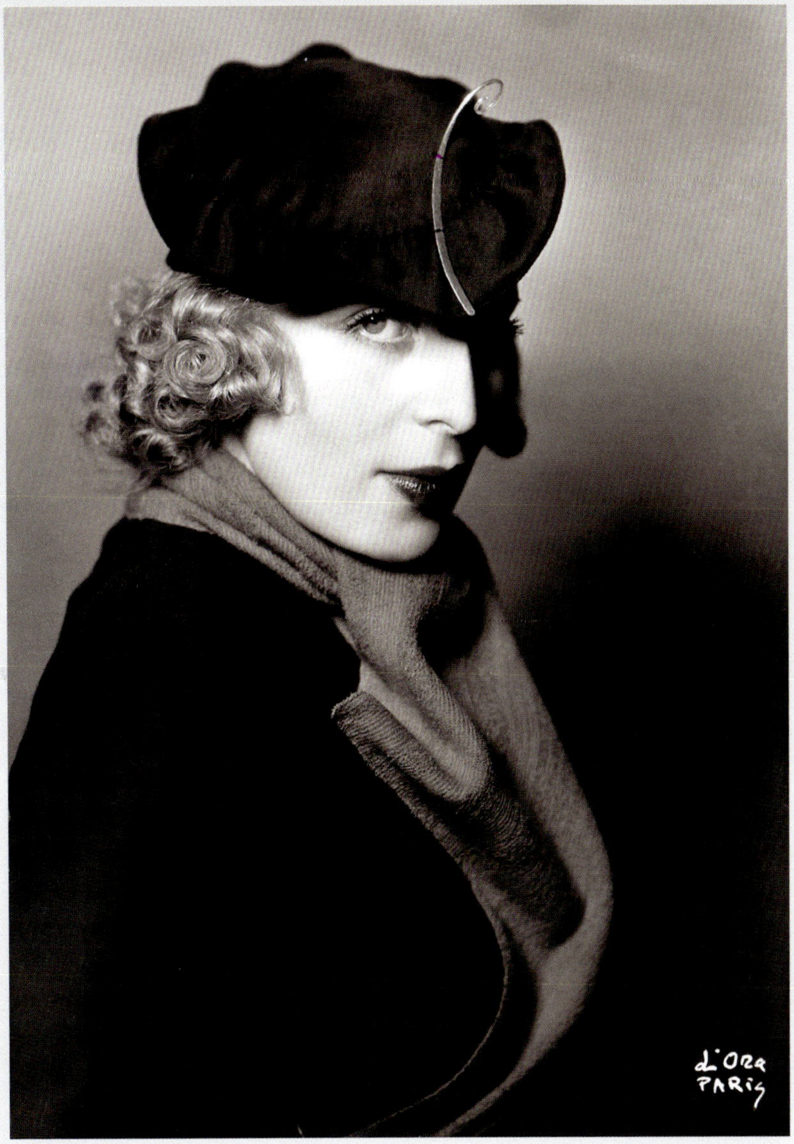

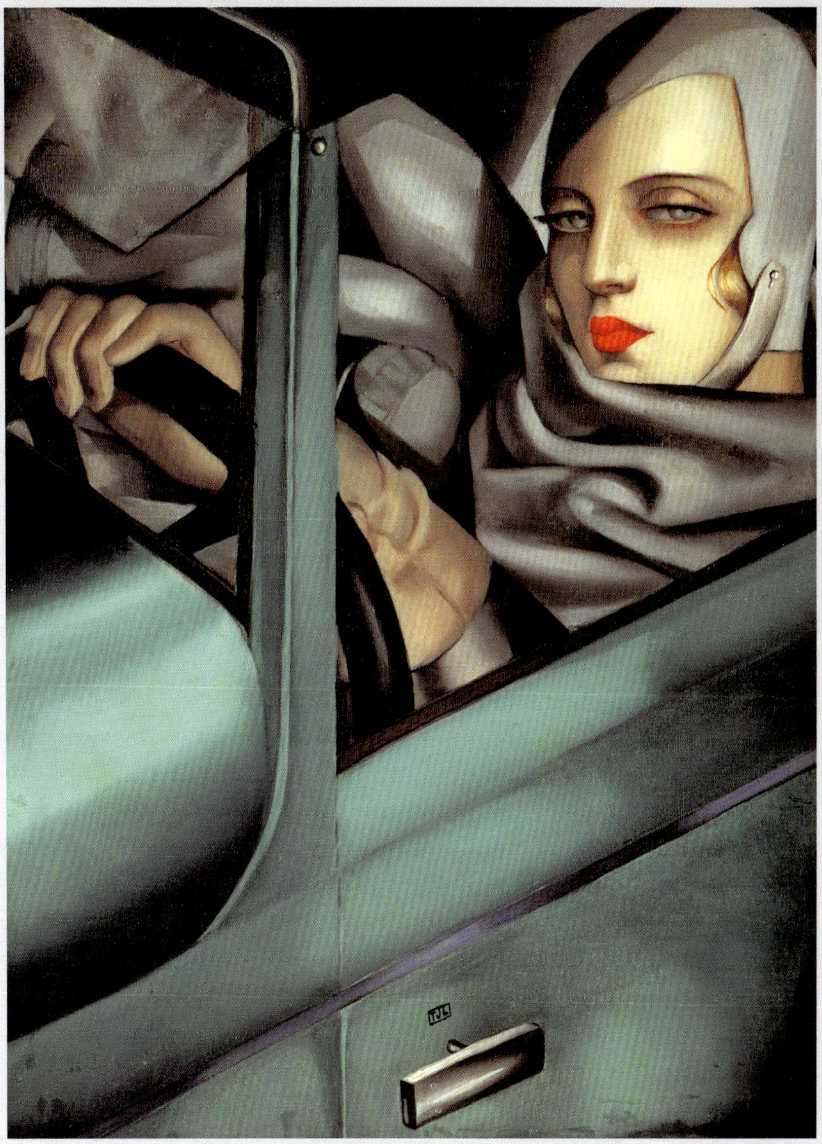

"My goal was never to copy, but to create a new style, in bright luminous colors and to scent out elegance in my models."

Tamara de Lempicka

Above left: **Dora Kallmus, *Tamara de Lempicka*, 1932**

A seasoned publicist, de Lempicka chose Dora Kallmus to take this dashing portrait of her wearing a hat by the fashionable French milliner Rose Descat. It was one of many photographs in which she consciously created and controlled a sophisticated image mirroring the sharp glamour of her paintings. Kallmus was the first woman to be admitted to Vienna's influential Graphische Lehr und Versuchsanstalt in 1907.

Above right: **Tamara de Lempicka, *Self-portrait in the Green Bugatti*, 1929**

This confident assertion of female liberation, in which de Lempicka pictures herself behind the wheel of a green Bugatti, was commissioned for the cover of *Die Dame*, a German magazine concerned with the modern woman. Its publication increased her celebrity, leading to further commissions. During a trip to Germany in 1934, she was questioned for traveling without a permit, but when the German officer realized her identity, he released her, explaining that he and his wife were enthusiastic collectors of *Die Dame* covers featuring her work.

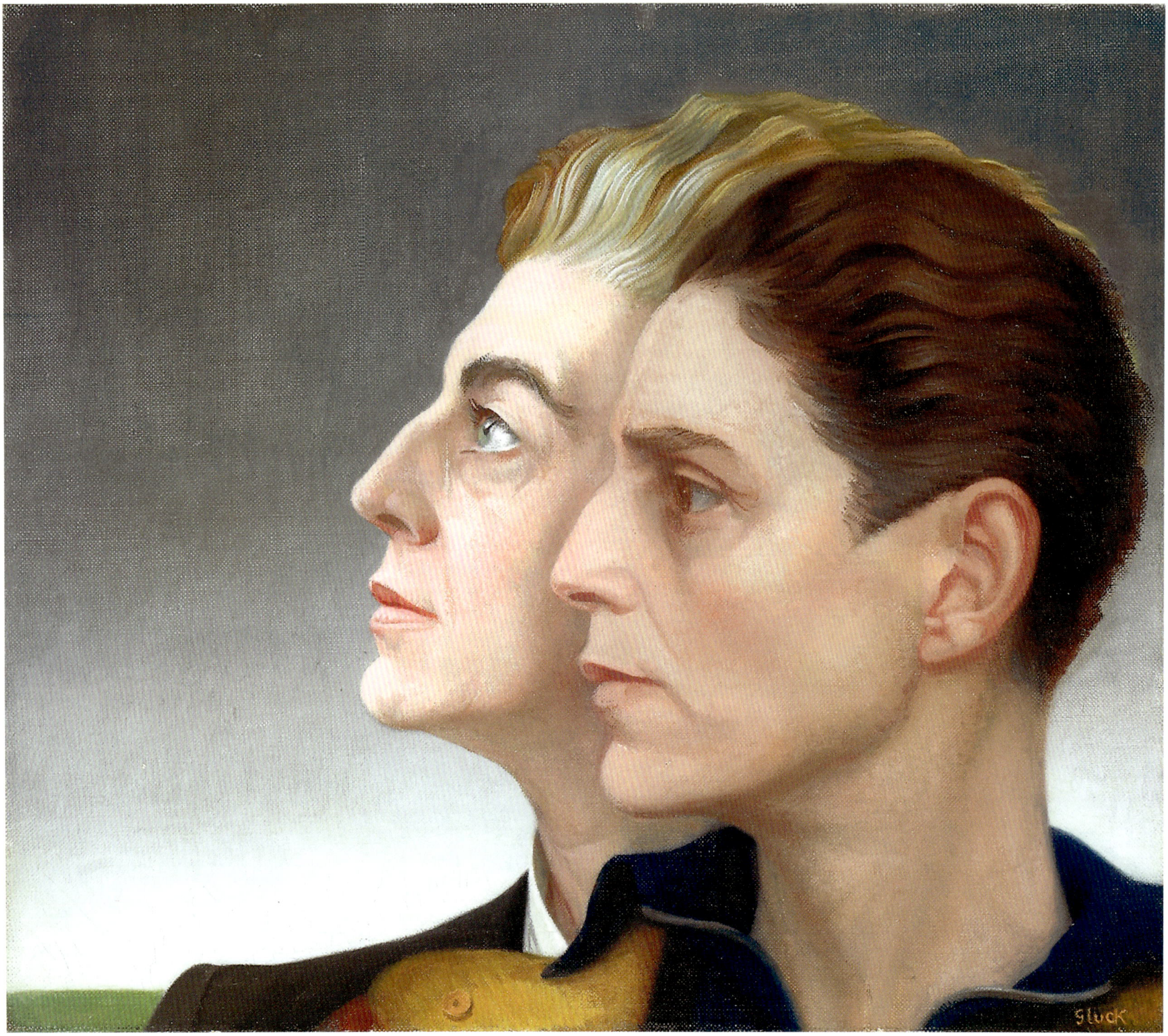

Above: **Gluck, *Medallion (You/We)*, 1936**

Hannah Gluckstein adopted the name of Gluck, which not only distanced her professionally from her wealthy family, but also underlined her gender-fluid status; she once resigned from an art society that insisted on calling her "Miss Gluck." This portrait shows Gluck with her lover, the American socialite Nesta Obermer, who she called "my darling own wife," despite Nesta remaining married to her husband. Radical for its depiction of a same-sex relationship, the painting was inspired by an intense evening the pair spent at the Glyndeborne opera. When the painting was finished, Gluck wrote to Nesta triumphantly declaring, "Now it is out."

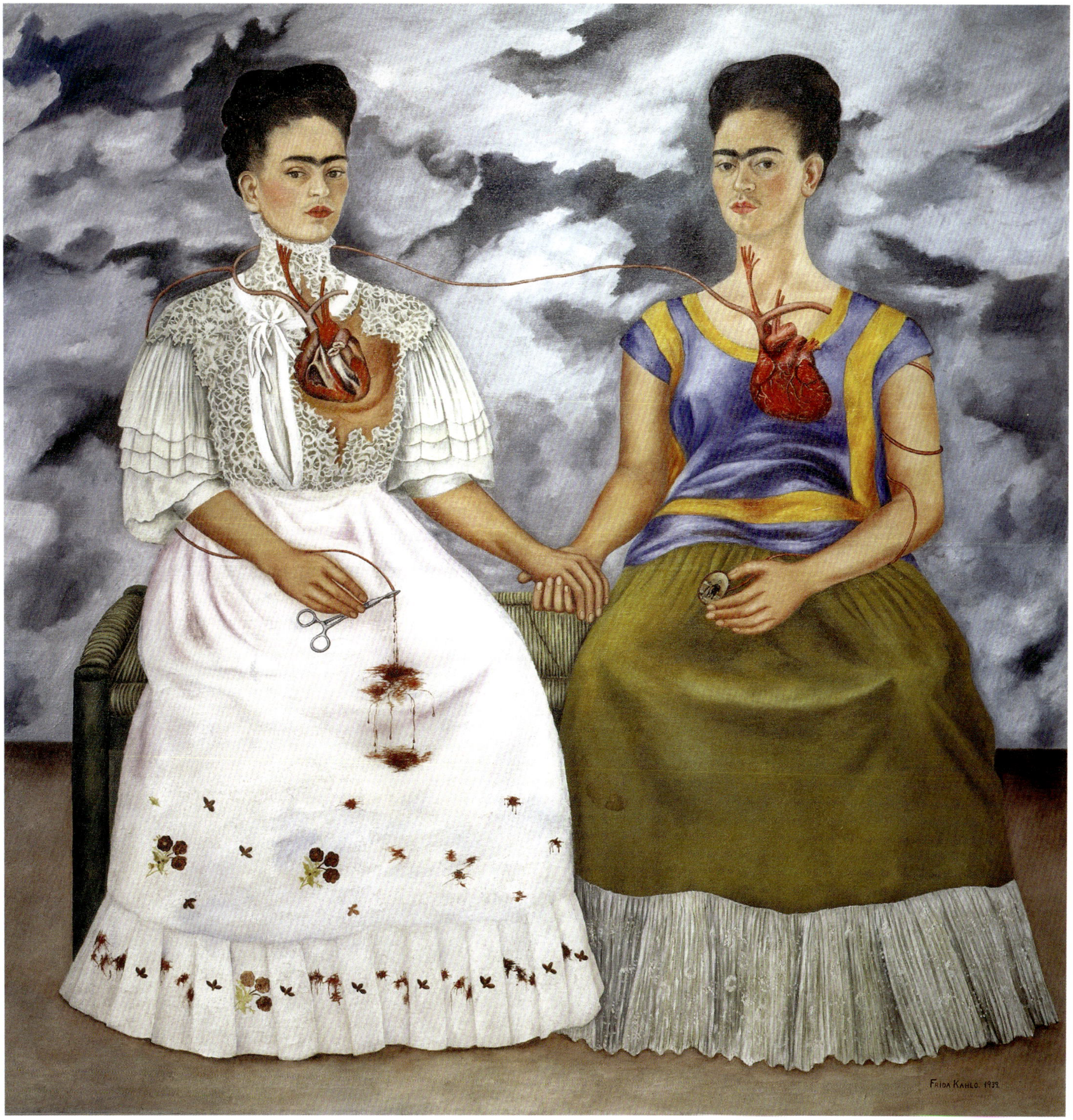

Above: **Frida Kahlo, *The Two Fridas*, 1939**

Frida Kahlo's German-Jewish and Spanish-Mexican heritage was a frequent theme in her art and her self-presentation. In her rich series of exploratory self-portraits, costume plays a significant role and here she depicts herself as two; on the left in a European wedding dress and on the right wearing the traditional costume of the Tehuana region of Mexico. Painted after her divorce from Diego Rivera, *The Two Fridas*, linked by blood, support one another in a sorority of strength eclipsing the superficial relationship of marriage.

The Modern Woman in Magazines

High-quality fashion magazines of the interwar period acknowledged the agency of the newly enfranchised woman, providing plentiful female role models, both real and imagined.

In October 1929, American women's fashion magazine *Harper's Bazaar* launched in the United Kingdom. Hitting the newsstands at the height of the art deco period, its first issue carried a sensational cover by the artist Léon Benigni. It featured two highly stylized women—one in an elegant helmet-style hat, the other in a simple, but striking, red dress, with slicked, short hair, and exotic bangles adorning her slim wrists. The two women epitomized late-1920s chic—they were stylish, androgynous, and aloof.

Benigni's design for *Harper's Bazaar* set the tone. This was a confident, modern magazine for the confident, modern woman. For several years, Benigni's covers alternated with designs by another great art deco illustrator, Romain de Tirtoff, familiarly known as Erté, who had already been providing covers for American *Harper's Bazaar*. Together, the two artists established an immaculately conceived house style for the magazine that fired a warning shot to its rival, the high-fashion bible *Vogue*. Meanwhile, *Vanity Fair*, out to catch the discerning, cosmopolitan woman in search of intellectual stimulation, used the witty cartoonish style of British artist Annie Fish on its covers.

This was a period of great synergy between art and fashion. Italian surrealist provocateur Leonor Fini not only designed magazine covers for *Harper's Bazaar*, but also collaborated with the fashion designer Elsa Schiaparelli, a fellow Italian, to create the iconic bottle for the designer's scent, Shocking, reputedly inspired by the hourglass figure of Mae West. In turn, socialite Daisy Fellowes, Paris fashion editor for American *Harper's Bazaar*, wore Schiaparelli's irreverent and flamboyant surrealist designs with aplomb. The cross-pollination between art, fashion, and female influencers reveals an industry in which women were taking inspiration from each other, and the male-artist-female-muse dynamic was no longer typical.

For women with talent, magazines also provided a source of employment, with many working across a number of different titles. Helen Dryden's cover designs for the *Delineator* magazine in the United States used a flat, angular technique to depict women in fashionable hats, tennis gear, or behind the wheel of a sports car. She also provided covers for *Vogue* during the 1920s and 1930s. Along with Irma Campbell, Lee Creelman, and Claire Avery, she was one of a number of female artists employed by the magazine across their London, Paris, and New York offices.

Male magazine artists were just as dedicated to promoting this new vision of the modern woman. Vienna-born Ernst Dryden took over art direction of the German *Die Dame* magazine in 1925, and conceived a series of covers over which stalked a cast of insouciant, elegantly dressed women. In France, along with *Vogue* and *Gazette du Bon Ton*—which had trailblazed the new woman fashion plate—*La Femina* also used Benigni's spare, linear style for its covers. Gordon Conway, a designer from Texas, drew similarly stylized women for British magazines *The Tatler* and *Britannia and Eve*—picturing them in neat suits for daytime, beach pyjamas for the French Riviera, or sinuous, embellished evening dresses. Matching clutch bags and shoes featured in the corners or borders of the pictures, lending a pleasing symmetry to Conway's drawings and offering readers a sophisticated piece of art to enjoy for its own sake as well as style guidance. Tall, red-haired, and well dressed, Conway mirrored the svelte chic of the women she created on the printed page. She courted publicity, alongside her famous pet cat Mr. Fing, as part of an effective marketing drive that was to lead to multiple commissions in magazines, theater, and film during the 1920s and 1930s.

The confident vision of style and independence presented by high-fashion magazines of this period, though unattainable for most women, nevertheless confronted and supplanted the old notions of femininity. American magazines aiming at the mass market, such as *Good Housekeeping*, *Home Chat*, or *Ladies' Home Journal*, chose more approachable subjects for their covers. Both *Good Housekeeping* and *Woman's Pictorial* used illustrations of children throughout the 1920s, 1930s, and 1940s; Jessie Willcox Smith was a frequent contributor to the former, while in Britain, Muriel Dawson was regularly employed by the latter. Though these magazines underlined domesticity as women's prime interests, they are, again, notable in employing women artists. Fashion drawing was a career in which women had been encouraged for some time. As far back as 1907, *The Lady's Realm* in its "Careers for Women" series named it as one of the "less-considered but better-paid branches of art."

In marked contrast to the homely femininity preferred by high-circulation, mass-market titles, another type of woman began to emerge from the drawing boards of female illustrators, a figure in control of her own sexuality, and an active participant rather than an object of the male gaze. The homes of such erotic woman included the risqué French magazines *La Sourire* and *La Vie Parisienne*, which frequently featured the work of Suzanne Meunier on their covers. Danish artist Gerda Wegener found fame and fortune with her swirling, elegant, erotically charged compositions in *La Vie Parisienne* and *La Baionette*. Her provocative illustrations echoed not only a more liberal society, but also her own unconventional personal life. Her husband Einar had begun to cross-dress in order to model for her, and eventually identified as transgender, a decision fully supported by Gerda, who continued to live with Lilli—as Einar had become—until her premature death as the result of a fifth gender-reassignment operation in 1931.

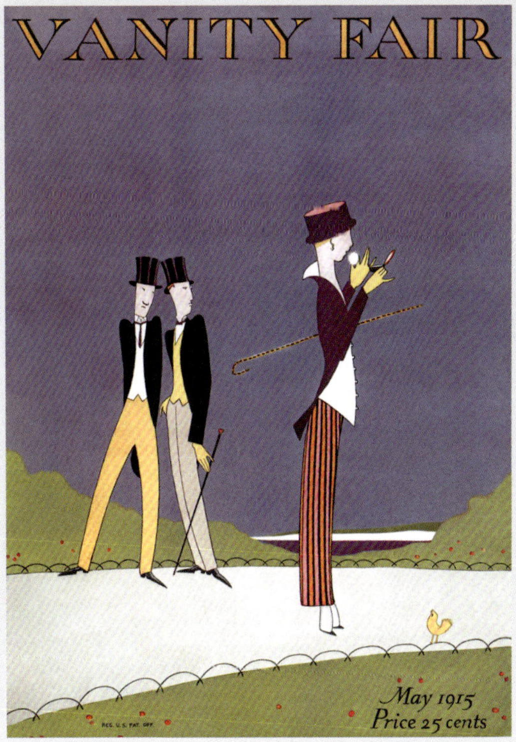

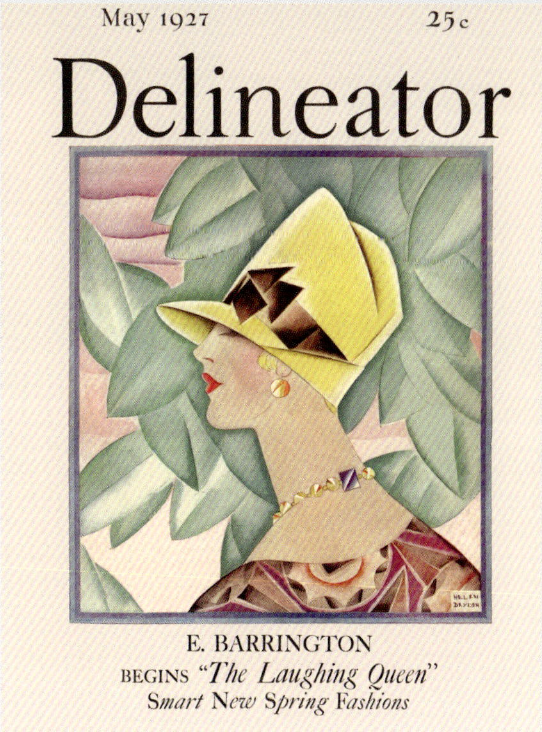

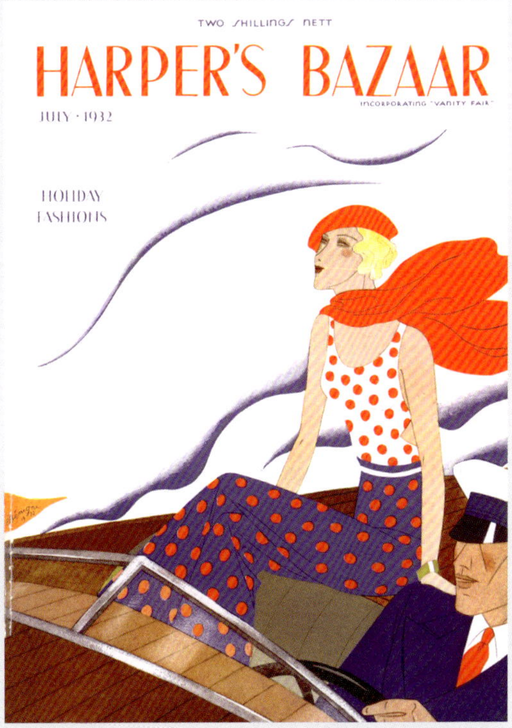

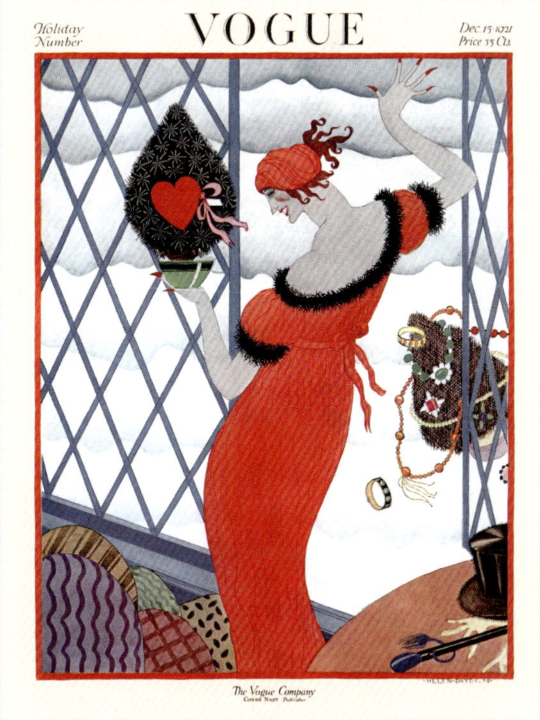

Clockwise from top left: *Vanity Fair* cover by Annie Fish, 1915. World War I lent a militarism and masculinity to women's fashion, a development gently mocked here by Annie Fish. Fish's linear, cartoonish style originated during the war and heralded a coming era of optimism. She had studied at the art school founded by poster artist John Hassall, and the bold color contrasts of her magazine cover art show his influence; *Delineator* cover by Helen Dryden, 1927; *Vogue* cover by Helen Dryden; *Harper's Bazaar* cover by Leon Benigni, July 1932. Benigni was a leading illustrator for a selection of high-profile women's magazines during the 1920s and 1930s, including *Femina*, *Modes et Travaux*, and *Harper's Bazaar*. Benigni's elegant woman, at ease in her surroundings, exudes an aura of glamour, sophistication, and independence as she shops, visits restaurants, or enjoys the mechanized possibilities of the modern age. Unfettered by domestic concerns, here was the aspirational modern woman, diametrically opposed to the previous century's "angel of the home."

"We hereby announce ourselves as determined and bigoted feminists."

Declaration in the March 1914 issue of *Vanity Fair*

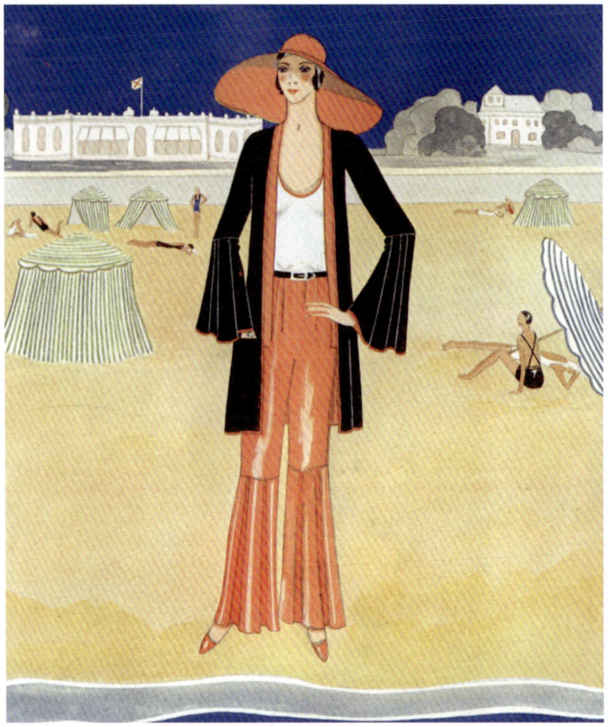

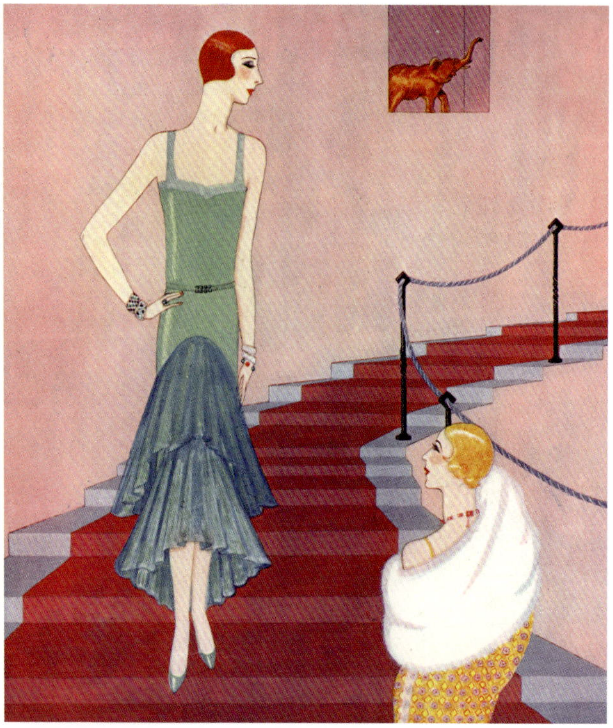

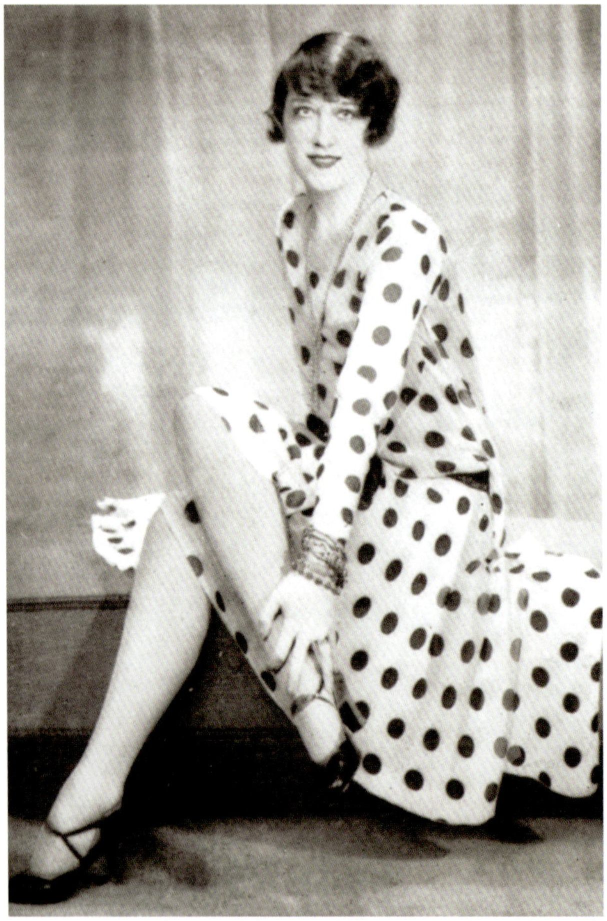

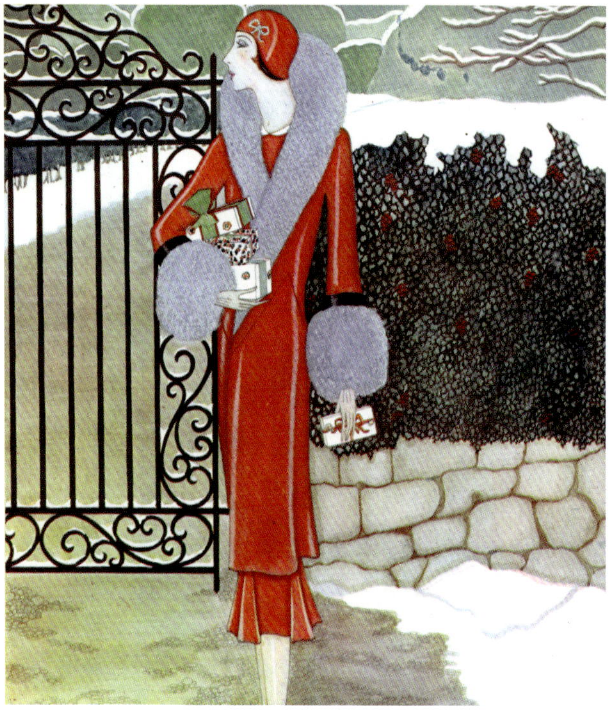

This page: **Gordon Conway, fashion illustrations for *The Tatler* magazine, 1920s/30s**

Texas-born Gordon Conway (bottom left) worked as a theater and fashion designer in London and Paris during the 1920s, establishing the first autonomous film costume department at Gaumont-British Picture Corporation. Talented, high profile, and stylish, the "redheaded gal," as she was known, epitomized the successful woman of the modern age.

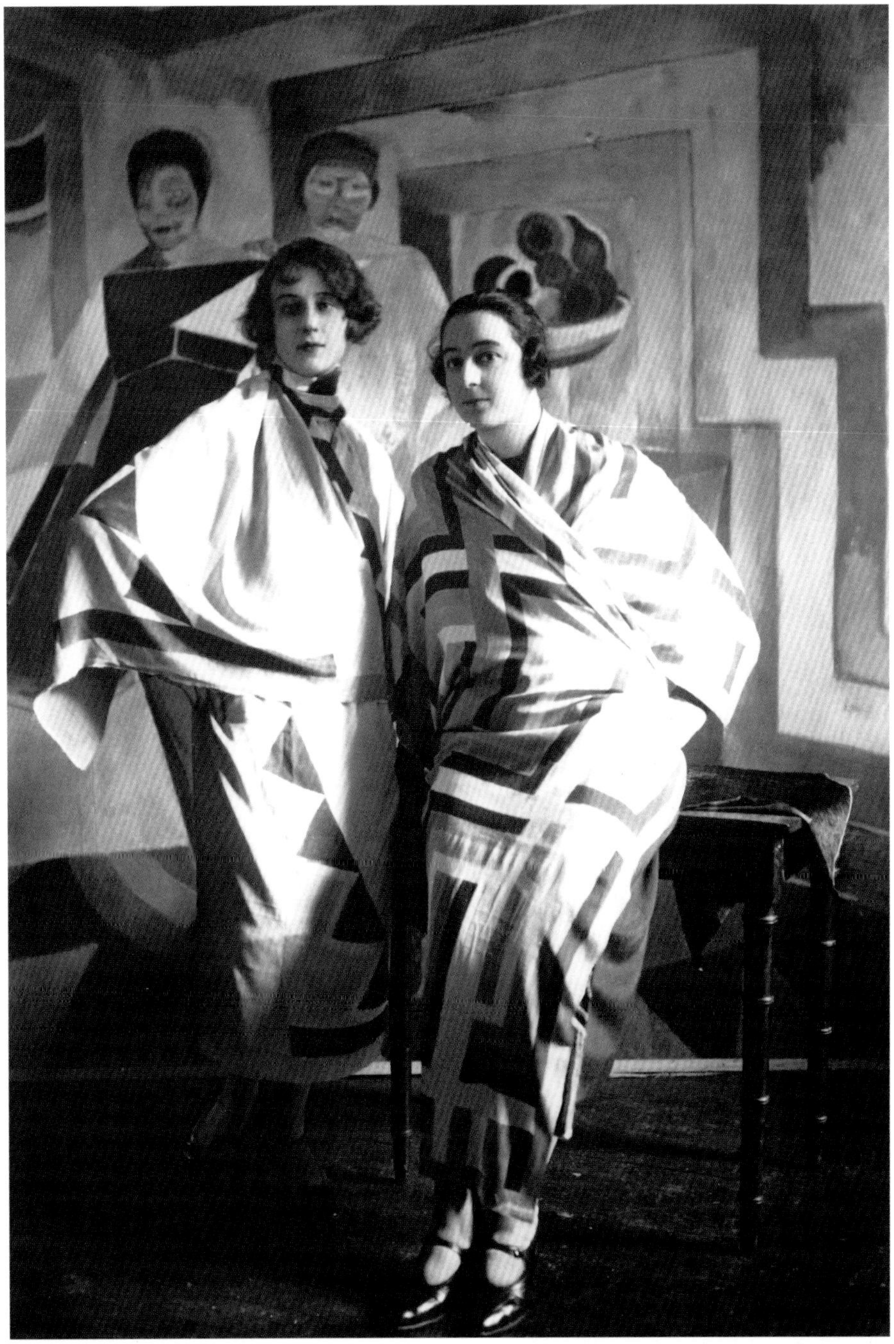

Below: Synergy between art and life was an underlying principle in Sonia Delaunay's career. Having originally studied art in Germany, she moved to Paris in 1905 where she came into the orbit of influential avant-garde artists and began to experiment with color and shape. She followed a new branch of cubist painting known as "orphism," named for the fact the abstract color formations sang with movement and music. Later, after sewing a colorful, patchwork blanket for her newborn son, she and her husband developed a style that focused on the rhythmic arrangement of color known as "simultaneity." Simultaneity lent itself to a range of decorative applications. Delaunay used the concept to create dazzling designs for theater and film costume work, *Vogue* covers, bookbindings, and clothing in collaboration with couturiers such as Jacques Haim and Jacques Doucet. She set up Casa Sonia, a fashion and interiors boutique in 1918, and her company, Tissus Delaunay, sold her textile designs worldwide. The nineteenth century had seen women art students steered toward the perceived inferior disciplines of decorative and applied art, but Delaunay successfully blurred the distinction between painting and design, claiming the latter was "noble work, as much as a still life or a self-portrait."

Defining Feminism

1960–1988

Part 2

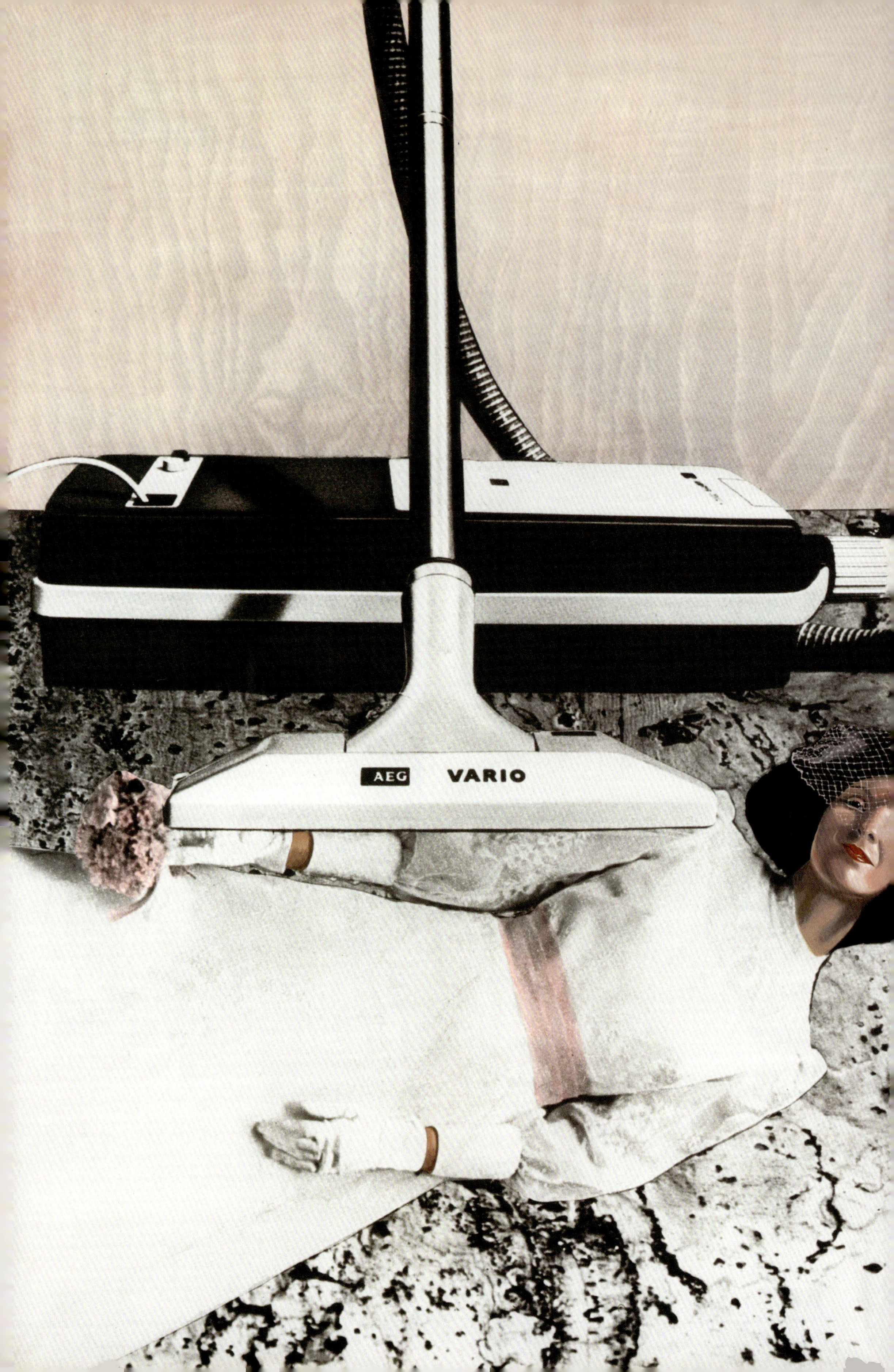
AEG
VARIO

Homesickness

Domestic Politics

5

"I am an artist. I am a woman. I am a wife. I am a mother (random order). I do a hell of a lot of washing, cleaning, cooking, renewing, supporting, preserving, etc. Also, (up to now separately) I 'do' Art. Now, I will simply do these maintenance everyday things, and flush them up to consciousness, exhibit them, as Art."

Mierle Laderman Ukeles, in her manifesto on Maintenance Art, 1969

In 1969, a year after the birth of her first child, the American artist Mierle Laderman Ukeles wrote a manifesto for what she called Maintenance Art. She proposed that maintenance is the stuff of life, the stuff that takes all the time, and the stuff that is most poorly remunerated. It is how artworks are kept looking fresh and avant-garde in a museum, and it is the work that still has to be done after the revolution. But for Ukeles, "maintenance" also became a new way to make her artwork. In 1973, when invited by the writer and feminist Lucy R. Lippard to take part in Lippard's touring exhibition *c. 7,500*, which originated at CalArts, Valencia, California, Ukeles proposed to live in a museum and do as she would at home for the duration of the show. Lippard had to ring Ukeles to ask if she was "for real," so surprised was she that an artist should propose that her housework be her artwork. Ukeles's work is now renowned in the history of feminist-influenced art, and demonstrates how women artists began to explore the idea of home, domesticity, and family between 1960 and 1988.

Inspired by feminist critiques of domesticity, many women expressed their frustration with family life in this period. In an article about a project entitled the Women's Postal Art Event (1975–77), art historian Alexandra Kokoli discusses home "as a site of crisis and violence" for women. Following the French theorist Luce Irigaray, Kokoli argues that, when at home, the woman is in "internal exile." In other words, the home might not be a place of belonging and safety for women, but a place of work and responsibility that is endlessly repeating and therefore inescapable. Kokoli also points out that it is the presence of a woman in the home that makes it a place of safety and belonging for others. "Home" does not simply refer to the architectural structure of the house, but the work of maintaining that structure and its inhabitants, as well as the familial roles played out inside it. These physical limits were circumscribed by moral, ideological, and psychic boundaries that also served to keep women in place and prevent them from accessing the wider world. In this context, "homesickness" does not refer to a longing for the home, but a desire to escape its confining bounds. From the 1960s, women artists began to take a critical approach to the home as a site of enclosure, boredom, labor, and depression.

Not all artists strove to represent domesticity as some form of confinement. Some reflected on motherhood, on craft, and on housework and began to reimagine the house as a place of creativity. In doing so, they also rearticulated what might constitute an artwork. This is particularly notable in the work produced in the Women's Postal Art Event, which comprised a multitude of small objects made by numerous women that were mailed to each other across the United Kingdom. These objects were usually made from cheap materials, gleaned from the detritus of the house, or from what was available on the weekly shop. Exhibited as a collection at the Institute of Contemporary Art in London in 1977, they not only represented a catalog of perspectives on domestic life, but a set of conversations that provided support for women who were otherwise isolated and alone.

Other works engaged with the idea of movement and mobility beyond and between the home. Barbara T. Smith's *Xerox* (1965) works represent a kind of feminist home industry. Unable to do much beyond her Pasadena home while her three children were young, Smith rented a commercial photocopier—the Xerox 914—and produced an impressive range of bound artist's books and framed works. Smith's experiments with the possibilities of image production, including exposure, as well as toner and paper type, resulted in portraits of her children, and explorations of her own body, which she pressed directly on to the glass plate to create almost abstracted forms. Smith is just one example of an artist who transformed her home and home life into a studio.

Page 94: **Eulàlia Grau, *Aspiradora (Vacuum Cleaner)*, 1973**

Grau studied fine art and cinema in Barcelona and Milan. She made many silk screens, collages, and paintings during the 1970s. Her subjects were wide ranging, with discrimination against women one among several critical themes in her work. *Aspiradora* is from Grau's series *Ethnografia* (Ethnographies,1972–74), a series that juxtaposed images found in advertisements and pop culture, critically representing the bourgeois aspiration celebrated in Franco's Spain.

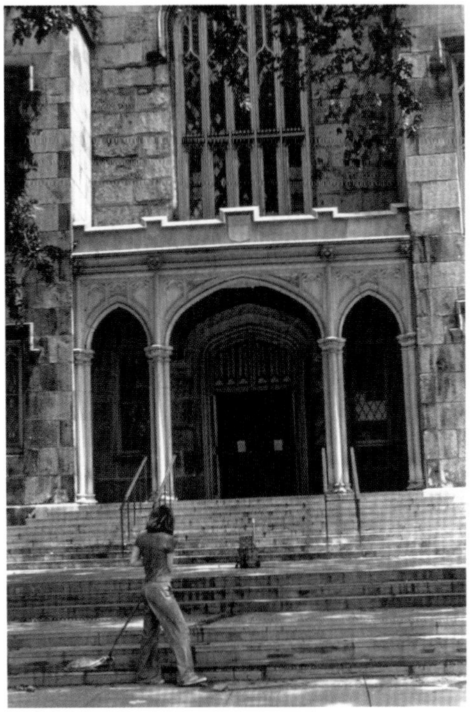

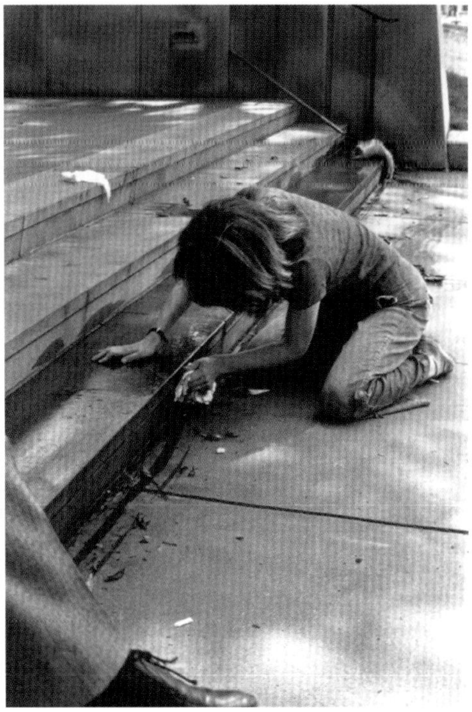

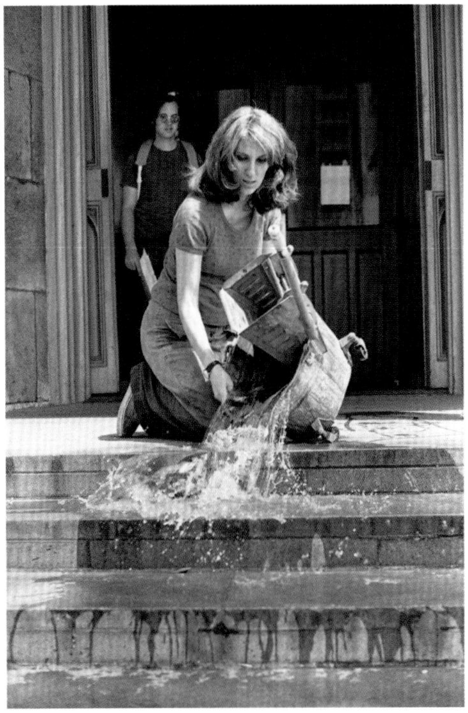

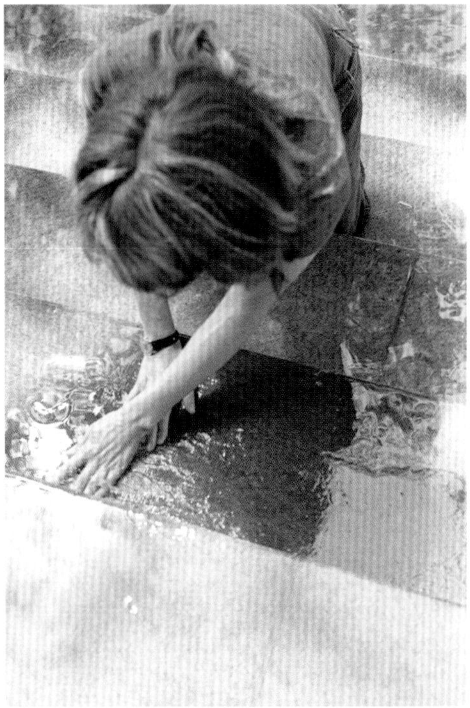

This page: **Mierle Laderman Ukeles, *Washing/Tracks/ Maintenance: Outside*, 1973**

These images document one of Ukeles's Maintenance Art performances at the Wadsworth Atheneum Museum of Art, Hartford, Connecticut, in 1973. The cycle of four performances was carried out when the museum was open, over eight hours—the duration of a working day—and all related to tasks associated with low-paid or free domestic work. In addition to cleaning the building's front steps, Ukeles scrubbed the interior floor with diaper cloths, cleaned the case of the museum's Egyptian mummy, and locked the doors of the museum offices at irregular periods.

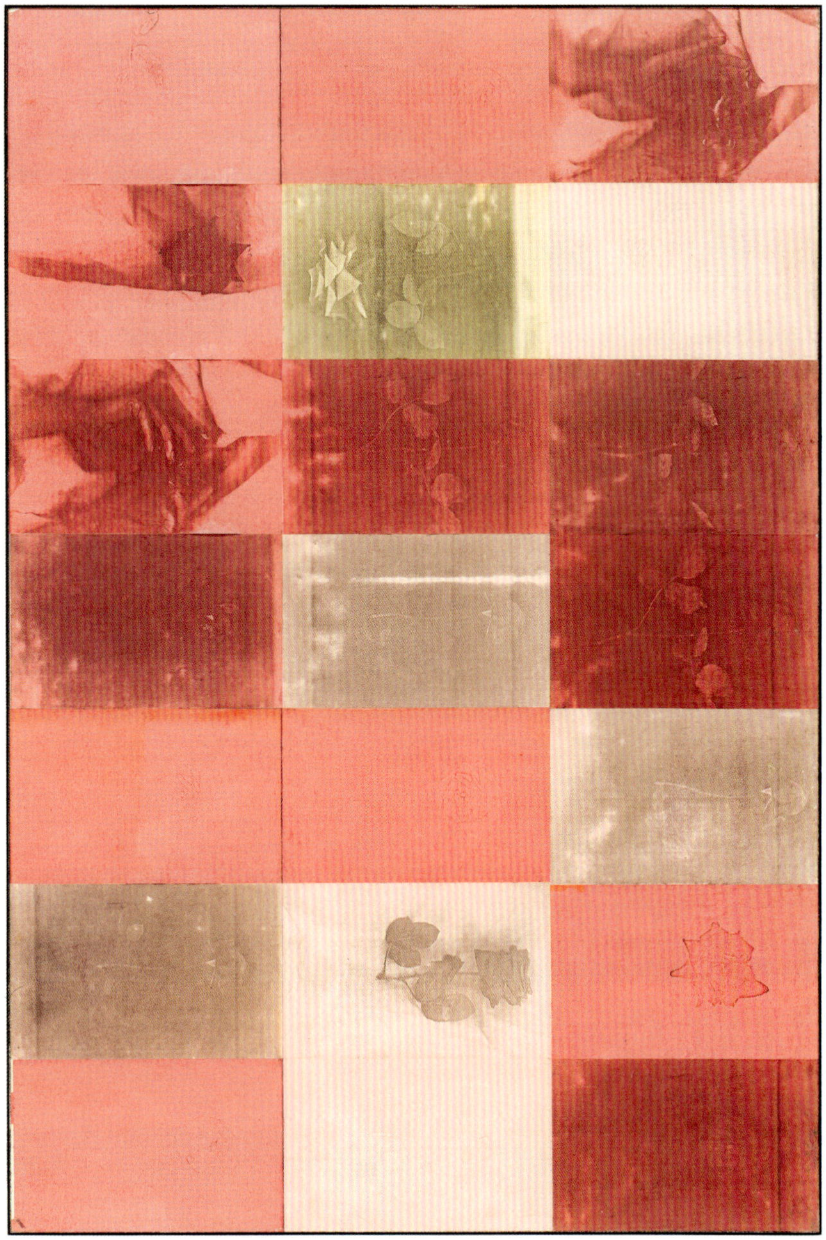

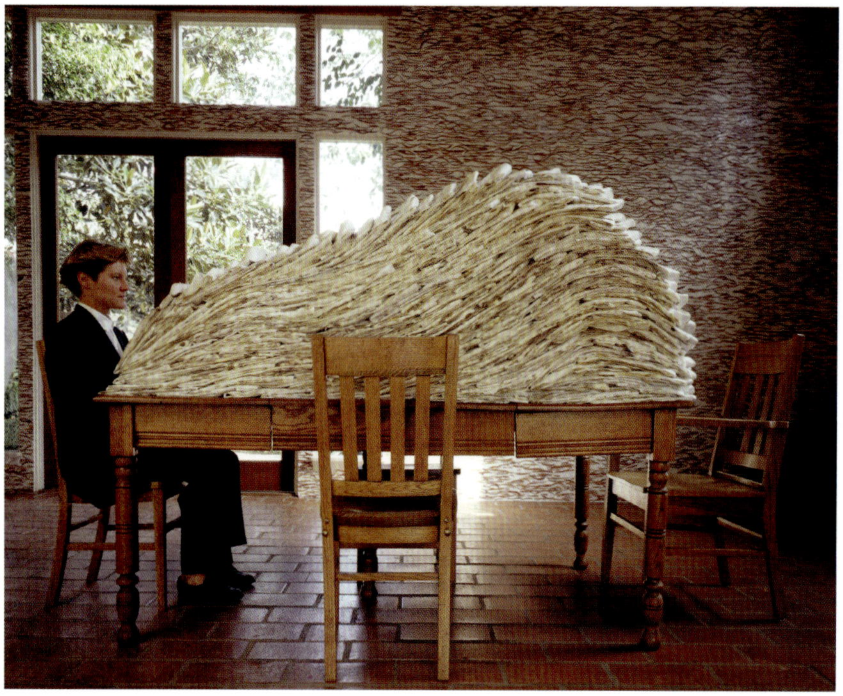

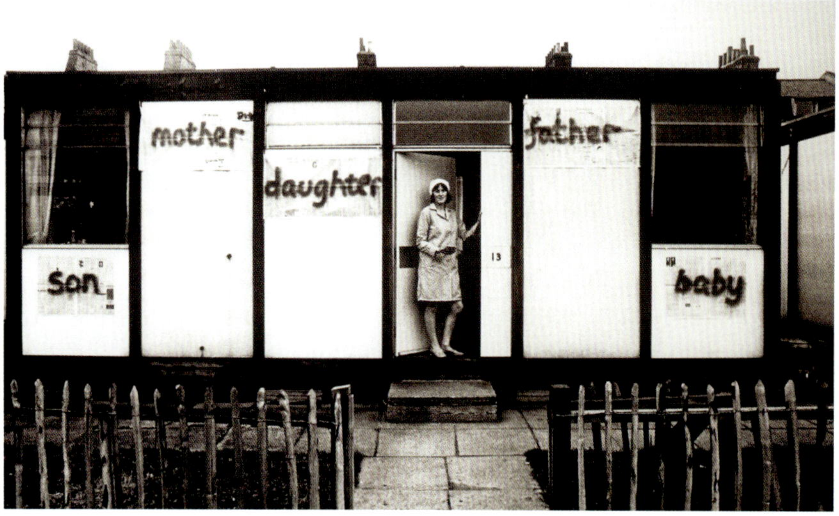

Above left: Barbara T. Smith, *Pink*, from the Xerox series, 1965

Pink is a twenty-one panel grid that Smith made using the Xerox 914 photocopier. Some of the windows contain photocopy prints made on various shades of pink paper, others appear as if they have been passed through the copier with a blank glass. Others show foliage and leaves, and three appear to be images of a woman's body, the artist's body. The juxtaposition of natural motifs, the artist's body, and the color pink evokes and subverts gender conventions—the body shown in a confused entanglement, the images of the foliage repeated and banal, and the pink is kitsch and bright.

Top right: Ann Hamilton, *still life*, 1988

still life was originally shown in an exhibition, also entitled *Still Life*, during the 1988 Home Show in Santa Barbara, California. The installation took place in a domestic environment, emptied of furnishings. A table at the center of the room was piled with a stack of eight hundred white men's shirts that had been laundered, then singed and gilded at the edges. For most of the exhibition an attendant sat at the table, facing the slope of shirts. Hamilton covered the walls of the room with preserved eucalyptus leaves taken from the garden outside, scented the room with eucalyptus oil, and played music. This total environment is characteristic of her interest in the harmony and discord between fiber, fabric, and architecture.

Bottom right: Bobby Baker, *Edible Family in a Mobile Home*, 1976

Bobby Baker's *Edible Family in a Mobile Home* staged a breakdown of the family home. Baker made use of her recently acquired Acme studio—a prefabricated building in Hackney, London—as a site for a public installation. The formerly domestic rooms were papered in newsprint, and occupied by sculptures of mother, father, son, daughter, and baby. The figures were made of cake baked by the artist, except the daughter, who was composed of spindly wire, and the mother, whose body was made from a dressmaker's dummy with a teapot for a head. Visitors to the exhibition could explore the installation, eat the sculptures, and have tea served straight from the mother figure's spout. As the days went on, the cake was eaten and left to molder, while the brittle daughter and mother remained.

Many artists and artist groups reflected on the home as a site of entrapment. Works such as Bobby Baker's *Edible Family in a Mobile Home* (1977), the Kanonklubben's *Damebilleder* (1970), and *Womanhouse* (1971) by the students and teachers of the California Institute of Art's Feminist Art Program used the space of the artwork to create immersive environments that recreated the suburban home as a nightmare. Baker's mother figure had a teapot for a head, from which tea was served for the span of the work's short duration. The performance length was itself determined by the availability of the cake that made up the bodies of the father, son, and baby, which Baker served with the tea. *Womanhouse* featured mannequins quartered by linen closet shelves and buried in bathtubs of sand. In the Danish *Damebilleder*, members of the all-woman art group Kanonklubben set up tableaux exploring washing up, beauty, and sex. These living images moved from oppressive situations to empowering ones and included a self-defense class, a celebration, and a camp during which members of the group lived together and talked to visitors.

If many artists explored either the limits or the creative potential of the home, others reflected on the uneven access many women had to stable and secure places in which to live or work. These works show the diversity and critical acuity of defining feminism during this period, and include Faith Ringgold's painting *For The Woman's House* (1971), made for the women's prison at Rikers Island, New York. Ringgold's oil painting in eight segments shows women doing things in the world—from directing traffic to playing basketball to giving a political address. The painting gave the women inmates a window on a world that hadn't yet come into fruition. Nil Yalter, Judy Blum, and Nicole Croiset's *La Roquette Prison de Femmes* (1974) depicts a different view of prison life. The installation pictures an often invisible constituency of women, even in the context of feminist activism, and shows the vulnerability they face both inside and outside the cell, as well as the solidarity and community formed in the woman-only space. In this context, confinement takes on a very different meaning.

The works of Carrie Mae Weems and Sonia Boyce also describe a more complex idea of home and belonging. Weems's Family Pictures and Stories (1978–84) is a photographic series documenting the artist's family. The series depicts family members in detail and with realism, showing middle-class African-American family life in contrast to the negative conclusions of the Moynihan Report (1965), which controversially argued that single-mother families hindered racial equality. The black British artist Sonia Boyce's painting *Lay back, keep quiet and think of what made Britain so great* (1986) considers the experience of migration and diaspora. The work's four panels combine the Victorian wallpaper prints of William Morris—a famous exponent of domestic socialism—with scenes of imperialist print culture framed by missionary crucifixes—two signifiers of British colonial power. The artist's self-portrait in the fourth panel looks out to the viewer from a background of gentility bound with struggle. Boyce's work powerfully communicates the violent foundations that supported colonial homemaking, and that remained embedded in silence.

Other themes that arose during this period include the politicization of the home as a site of consumption. This is clear in the exploration of products, in the reproduction of the home, and in the maintenance of the housewife herself. Such issues are evident in a number of works made beyond the context of the women's liberation movement—before the first protests in the United States, Great Britain, and Europe—but also in a global context. Sometimes associated with pop art, the works of Maria Pinińiska-Beres, Isabel Oliver, Eulàlia Grau, and many others show the home as a consumer battleground.

A number of artists sought to reenvisage the home as a site for new kinds of life and different kinds of relationships. Italian artist Carla Accardi's *Triplice Tenda* (*Triple Tent*, 1969) is a painted plastic tent, described by the art historian Teresa Kittler as a reflection of Accardi's interest in a utopian mode of flexible living, resistant to the closed spaces of Catholic family life. Meanwhile *Berlin* (1976), by Rose English and Sally Potter, recast a grand family home in London, along with a local ice rink and swimming pool, as the site for a somber performance. With a chorus of suited dancers on the fireplace, the home and its fixtures were transformed into a place of uncanny familiarity. Likewise Penny Slinger's photo-collage series An Exorcism (1970–71) used a near-derelict stately home in Northamptonshire, United Kingdom, as a backdrop to a melodrama of self-discovery, including sequences of erotic acts between two women. This work, like Louise Nevelson's *Black Wall* (1959), imagines the traditional home broken down and rearranged, able to hold what we might now call a queer feminist domesticity.

Below: **Sonia Boyce, *Lay back, keep quiet and think of what made Britain so great*, 1986**

This is a quadriptych in charcoal, pastel, and watercolor on paper by the British artist Sonia Boyce. The four panels are united by the same speckled red background and twisting, thorny black rose. The first three panels include monochrome pencil drawings of scenes within cross-shaped windows. These scenes are caricatures of colonial propaganda posters advertising South Africa, India, and Australia. The crosses invoke colonial missionary zeal, the gravestone, and maritime tattoos, while the dense thicket on the wallpaper is somewhere between William Morris's designs and Charlotte Perkins Gilman's pulsating wall coverings in her novella, *The Yellow Wallpaper*. The figure looking out from the canvas in the fourth panel is the artist herself. She stands in the foreground, but looks perilously close to being folded into the background whorl.

Opposite, top: **Trinh T. Minh-Ha, *Naked Spaces—Living is Round*, 1985, still**

Born in Vietnam, Trinh T. Minh-Ha is a filmmaker, writer, and composer. She has made eight feature-length films, of which *Naked Spaces—Living is Round* is the second. This film records life in Mauritania, Mali, Burkina Faso, Togo, Benin, and Senegal. Breaking with linear narrative and earlier ethnographic filmmaking, *Naked Spaces—Living is Round* explores the different domestic rituals and rhythms in the six West African countries.

Opposite, bottom: **Carrie Mae Weems, *Family Reunion*, Family Pictures and Stories, 1978–84**

This image is from a large series of photographs entitled Family Pictures and Stories by the American artist Carrie Mae Weems. This series was her first major body of work, and it documents Weems's large family in many different settings: at home and work, celebrating events, and getting on with everyday life. The images were accompanied by short captions and audio recordings contributed by family members, to create a multivocal context around the scenes depicted in the photographs.

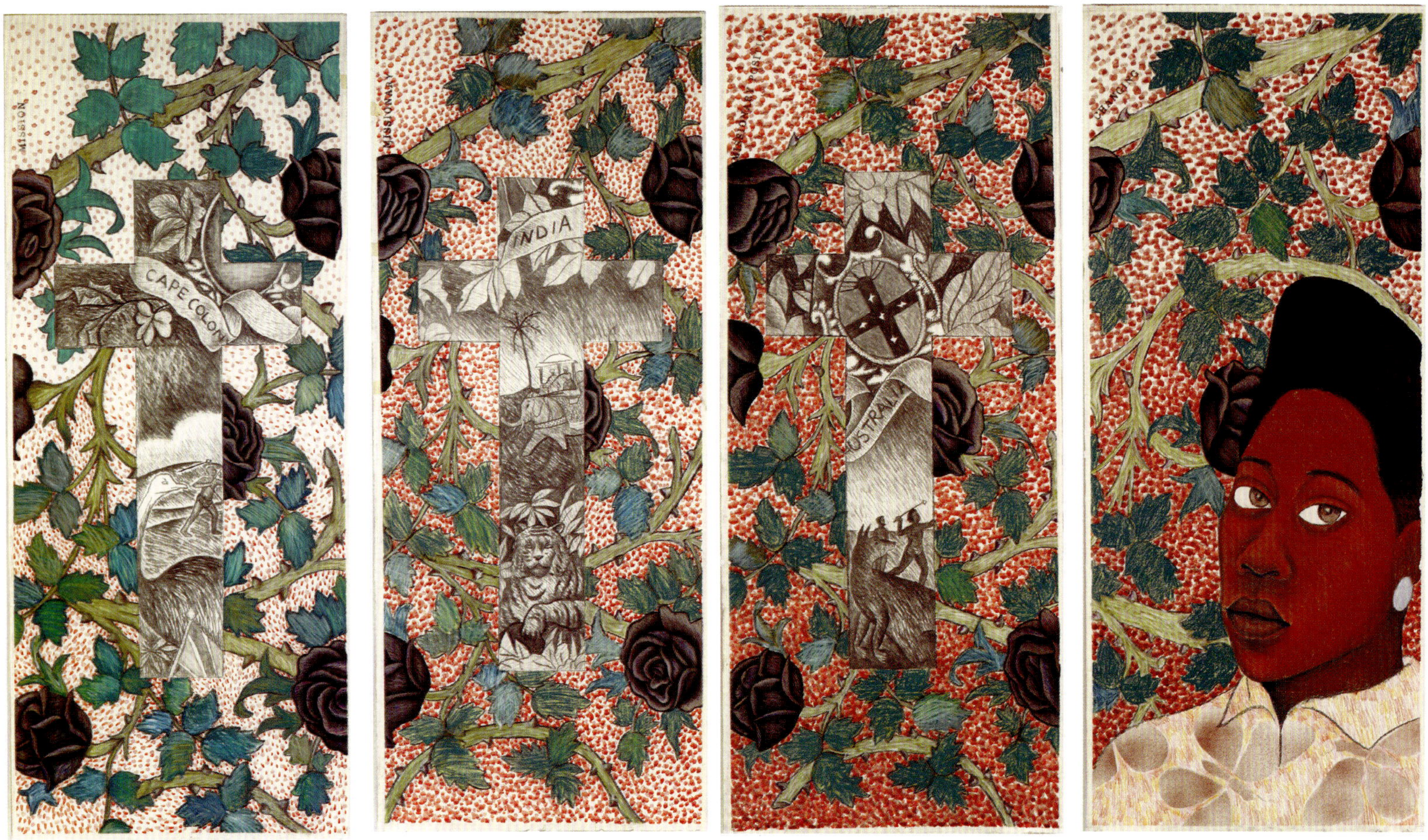

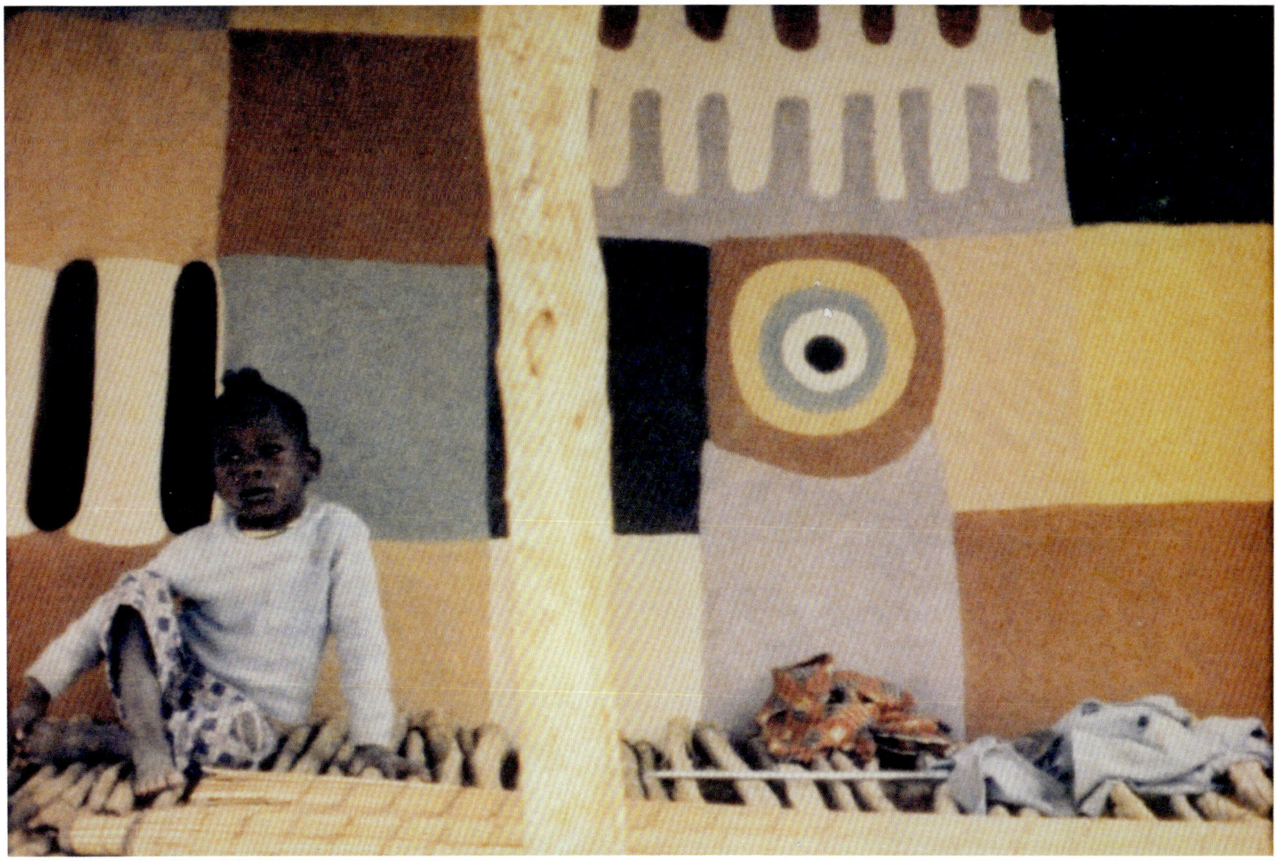

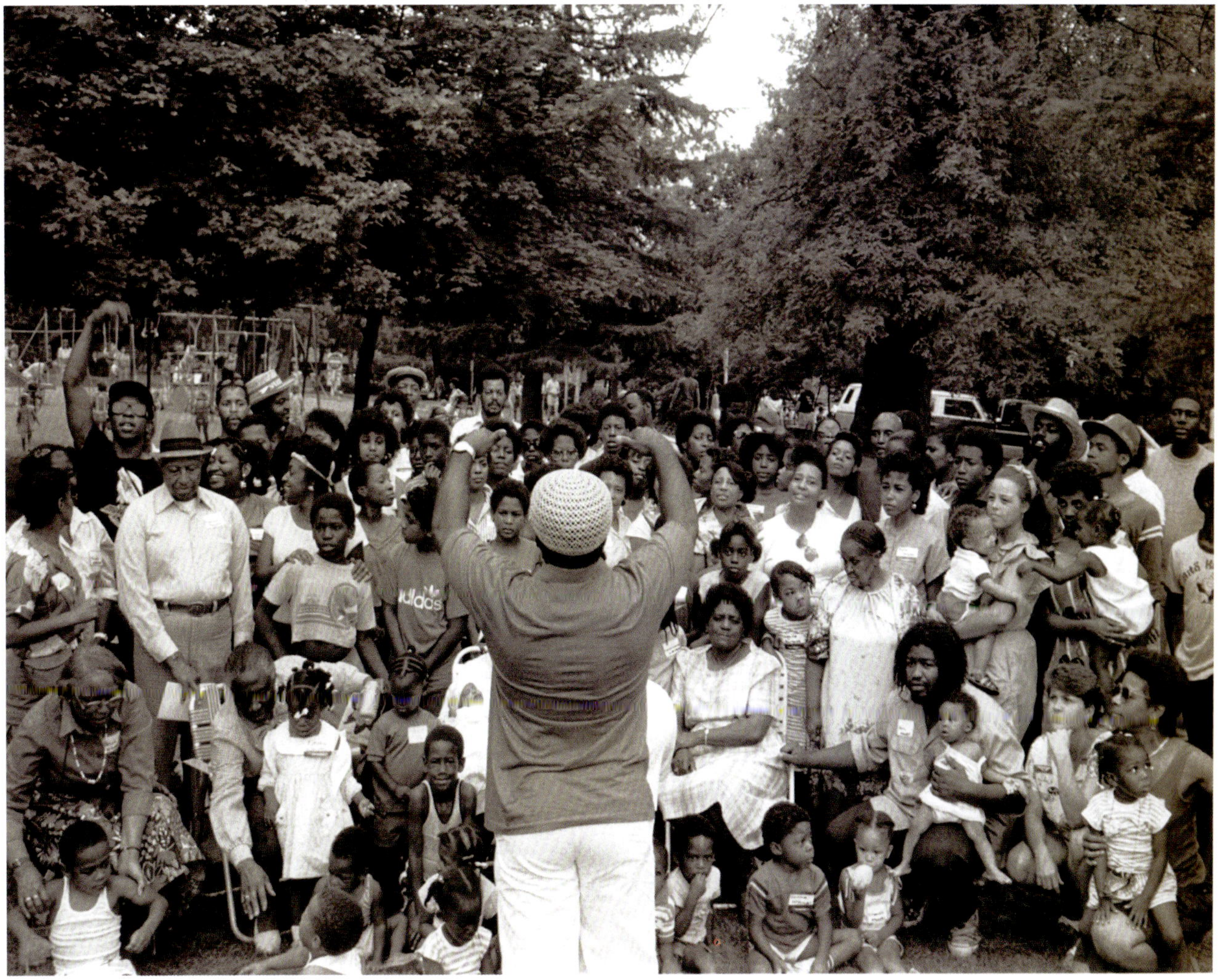

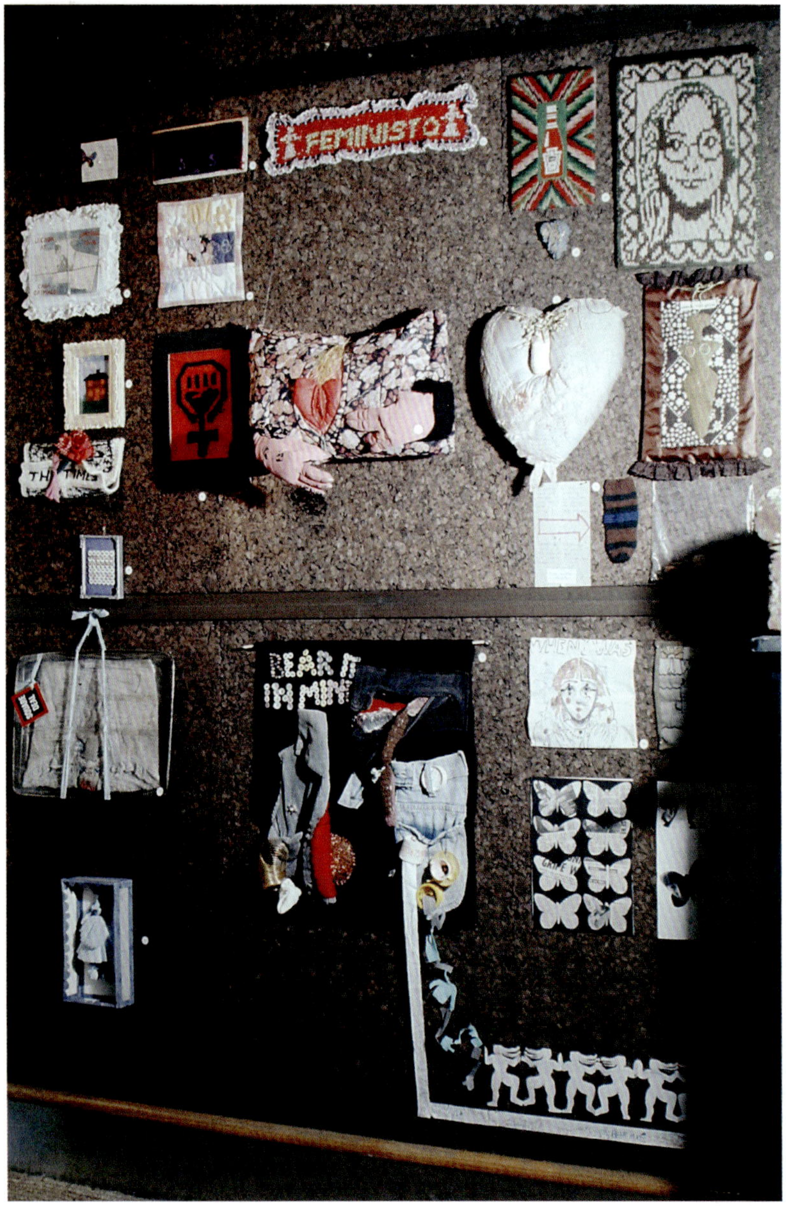

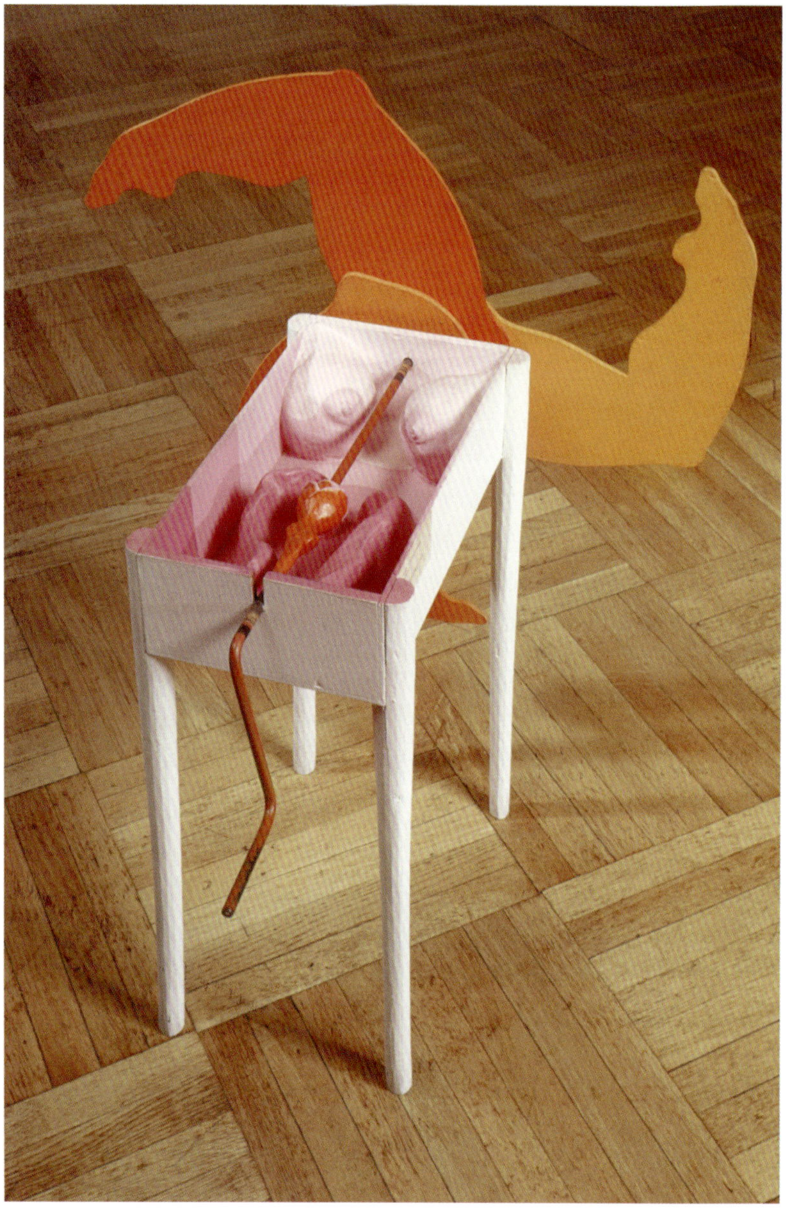

Above left: **Su Richardson and Kate Walker, *Feministo: Portrait of the Artist as a Housewife*, 1977**

The Women's Postal Art Event of the mid-1970s was initiated by Kate Walker and Sally Gallop in an attempt to keep in contact and to encourage each other to make work. The network expanded after a gathering at the Women's Art History Conference in 1975 and included the artists Angela Amesbury, Lyn Austin, Penny Booth, Lyn Foulkes, Tricia Davis, Phil Goodall, Chick Hull, Su Richardson, Monica Ross, and Suzy Varty among others. It continued to attract new members as the group exhibited the objects they received in group exhibitions in Manchester, Birmingham, Liverpool, Edinburgh, and London. The work produced was incredibly diverse, although each was small enough to post and made inexpensively from materials found around the home. Ross commented that the Women's Postal Art Event was "a nonstop process, new work constantly emerges as a visual conversation develops. The aim is communication, not perfect aesthetics."

Above right: **Maria Pinińska-Bereś, *Love Machine*, 1969**

Pinińska-Bereś studied and worked in Kraków, Poland. Although she distanced herself from feminism, she began exploring gender politics in 1965, with a series of sculptural installations using soft materials. *Love Machine* was included in a body of work titled Psycho Furniture, which Pinińska-Bereś began in 1968. The sculpture seems to invite the viewer to turn the handle and manipulate the brightly colored body machine, creating a frightening, if playful, image of dehumanization.

Below: **Ree Morton, *Signs of Love*, 1976**

Ree Morton's *Signs of Love* was made in the fall of 1976, after the New York–based artist had spent time in a studio in the Woman's Building in Los Angeles. The installation comprises multiple parts, including numerous words made of felt letters, as well as portraits, ladders, swags, roses, and an overflowing laundry basket made of the material Celastic, often used to make stage props. Morton's Celastic objects make reference to high romance and the domestic everyday, showing the interconnection of love and care.

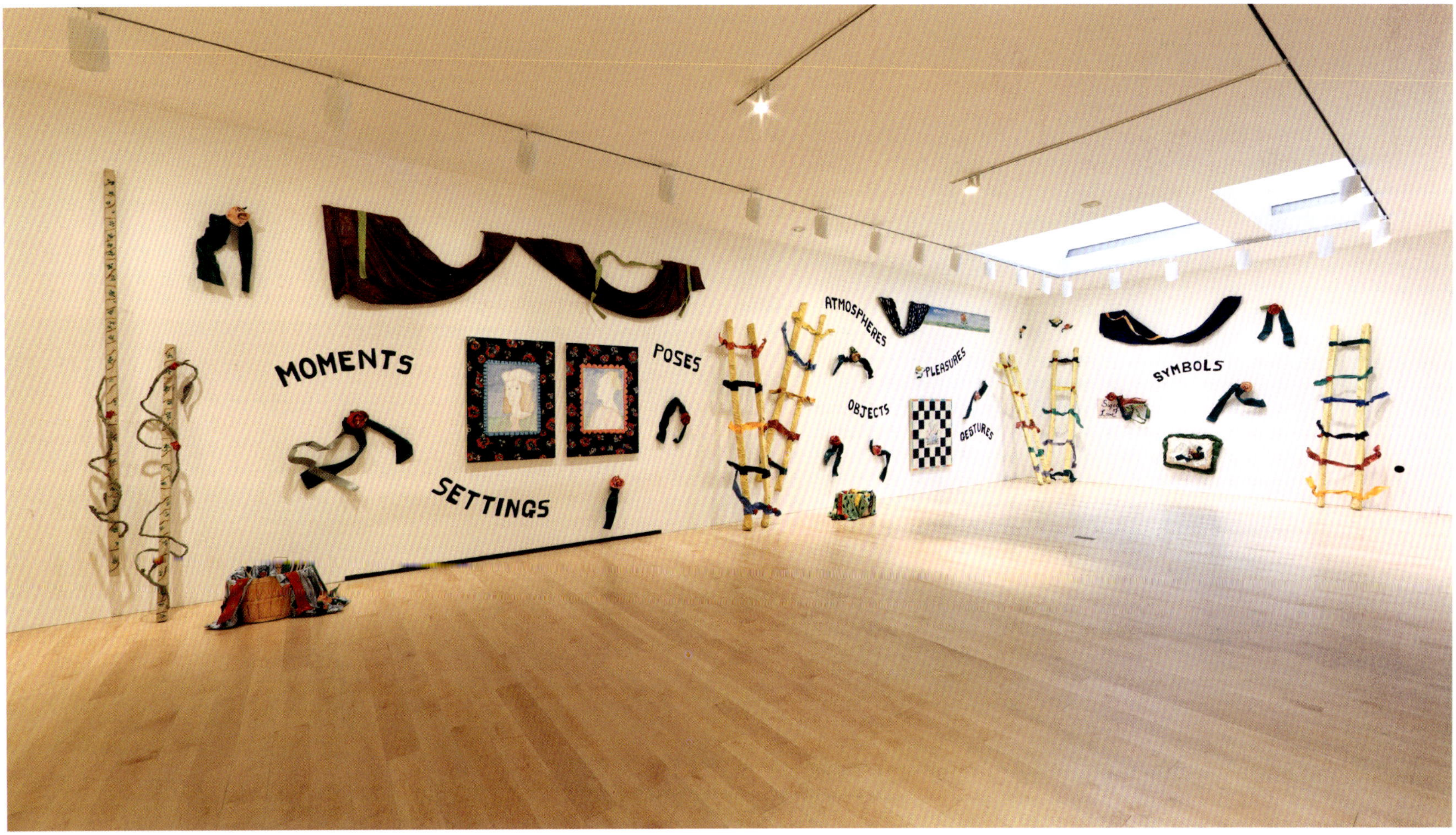

Alienation and Dislocation

by Catherine Spencer

Many artists explored the claustrophobia of traditional domestic arrangements, using their art to evoke feelings of alienation and dislocation. This marked a departure from associations of safety and security, and instead, revealed a place that could be both boring and disturbing. Marta Minujín's *Colchones* emphasize these contradictory feelings: Being both soft and heavy, they represent both refuge and threat.

During the 1960s, the Argentine artist Marta Minujín made several extended trips to Paris, enabling her to forge networks with artists working in assemblage and performance. The city provided the stage for her first performance work, or "happening," *La Destrucción* (*The Destruction*), in 1963. In Paris, Minujín experimented with domestic materials including cardboard boxes and mattresses, and began to flex the formidable skills for performance art that would become central to her artistic persona. The works that ensued from this period explored the dynamics of alienation and dislocation generated by a move away from home, as well as testing the shifting relationships between physicality, eroticism, and subjectivity.

The works using mattresses (often referred to as the *Colchones*, from *colchón*, the Spanish word for "mattress") began before Minujín traveled to Paris, and have been framed by the artist as an avant-garde move born out of frustration with traditional materials: "One day I punched a hole in the middle of my painting, took the mattress off my bed and said 'I'm going to work with mattresses' [. . .] I had almost no money, slept three years on the floor and made a kind of plastic house." Minujín's description of the mattress work as a "plastic house" is highly evocative, and one to which she would return when discussing the mattress assemblages that she made in Paris between 1962 and 1963, in a large rented studio "without water or heat" on the rue Delambre. By this point, Minujín had begun altering and adapting the mattresses, combining them with stuffed sacks of material to form immersive structures emblazoned with bright stripes of paint.

The houselike qualities of Minujín's *Colchones* are vividly performed in a photograph from her Paris studio that shows her sequestered bodily inside the padded sections, supported by the frame of one assemblage. It becomes a movable shelter to protect against the difficulties of relocation and living in a foreign city. Equally, the imprisoning effect of the *colchón*, and the barrier erected between the individual and the outside world by its soft, bulbous protrusions, resonate with the existentialist thinking that Minujín imbibed in France. A common theme of existentialism was its focus on the personal experience of the individual within the context of the wider world.

There are correlations in this respect with the transfigured furniture sculptures bristling with phallic protrusions that Yayoi Kusama made in New York after relocating there from Japan, and, in particular, with a staged photograph that shows Kusama curled up on the squishy bed provided by the entrails of a red assemblage made from rubber gloves and wadding. Yet the apparent offer made by Minujín and Kusama's structures of space for physical respite is complicated by their connection with the erotic and with violence. The photograph from Minujín's Paris studio equates the body of the artist with the soft, fleshy sections of mattress, a material metaphorically connected with sex and desire. In an influential 1961 exhibition in Buenos Aires entitled *Arte Destructivo* (*Destructive Art*) organized by the artist Kenneth Kemble, one work consisted of an armchair with a vaginal rent torn in the seat. The erotic violence embedded in Minujín's manipulation of domestic materials was signaled explicitly by her 1963 collaboration with the French artist Max Brusse on *Chambre d'amour* (*Chamber of Love*), an installation that combined psychedelically fluorescent sections of mattresses with a structure of sadomasochistic metal spikes and chains.

Yet there is a discernible difference between the dizzying color spectrum of Minujín's mattresses with their invitation to play, hide, and experiment, and the abject reference to women's bodies in *Arte Destructivo*. At the same time, art historian Nadja Rottner argues that Minujín's "notion of soft sculpture departs from a normative craft-based aesthetic of sewing and stuffing associated with the territory of women; as her fabric sculptures, large-scale environments, and performative media interventions are situated tactically at the intersection of the body and technology." The violence in Minujín's work is of a more delirious, destabilizing kind, as demonstrated by her immolation of several mattress works in *La Destrucción*.

After exhibiting the works she had made in Paris during a show with Lourdes Castro and Miguel Otero, she took them to an empty lot on the Impasse Ronsin and invited other artists first to modify her sculptures, and then to destroy them, before releasing birds and rabbits. This gesture might be construed as both the culmination and rejection of the existentialist concerns that had initially engaged Minujín in Paris; it can also be read as a powerful reversal of both geopolitical norms and gender roles, in which Minujín assumed the position of director over a group of predominantly male European artists. Yet it should also perhaps be interpreted as an embrace of dissolution, an erasure of markers of difference between inside and outside, which the *Colchones*, even before they were consigned to the flames, had signaled through their intestinal forms and enveloping structures.

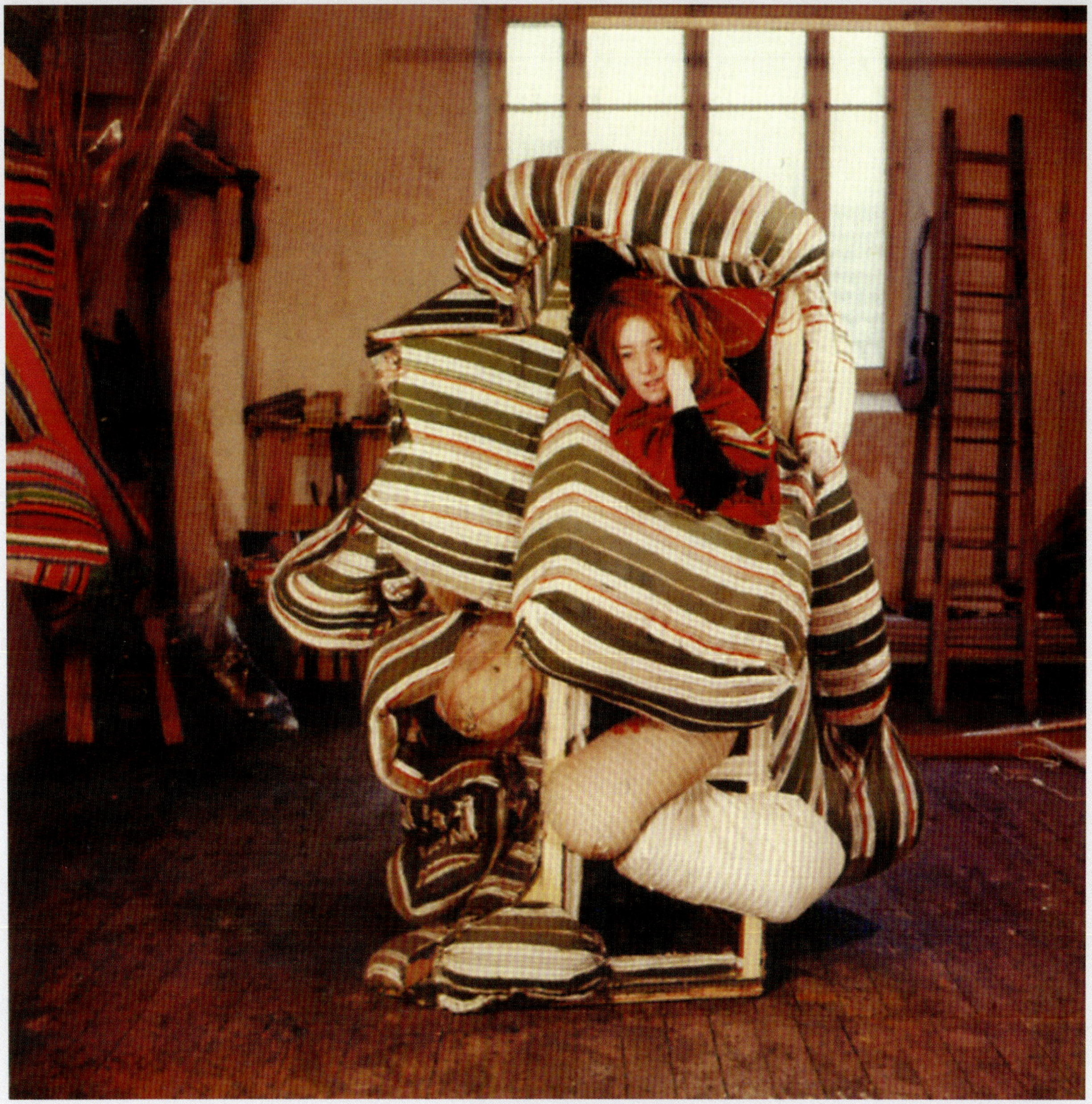

"I bought fabric and a glue pen and managed to borrow a sewing machine and the first one I created was my first environment. It was a kind of mattress house, a construction of about three square meters of wood covered with overlapping, twisted-up embracing mattresses."

Marta Minujín, 2000

Above: Marta Minujín in her studio in Paris, 1962.

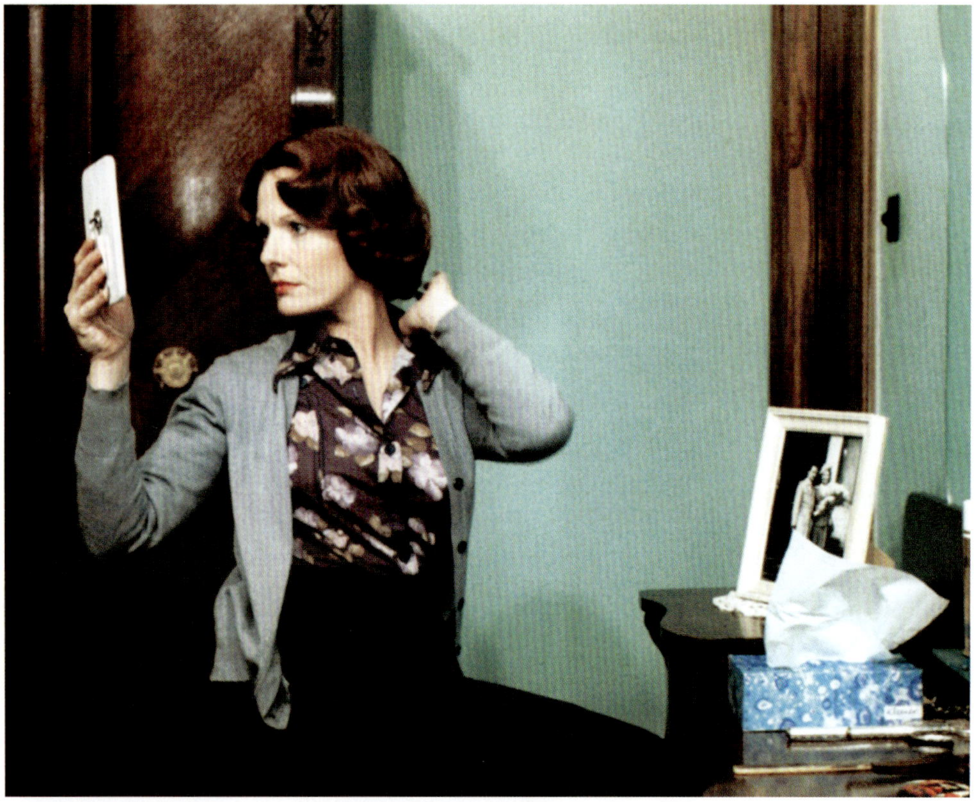

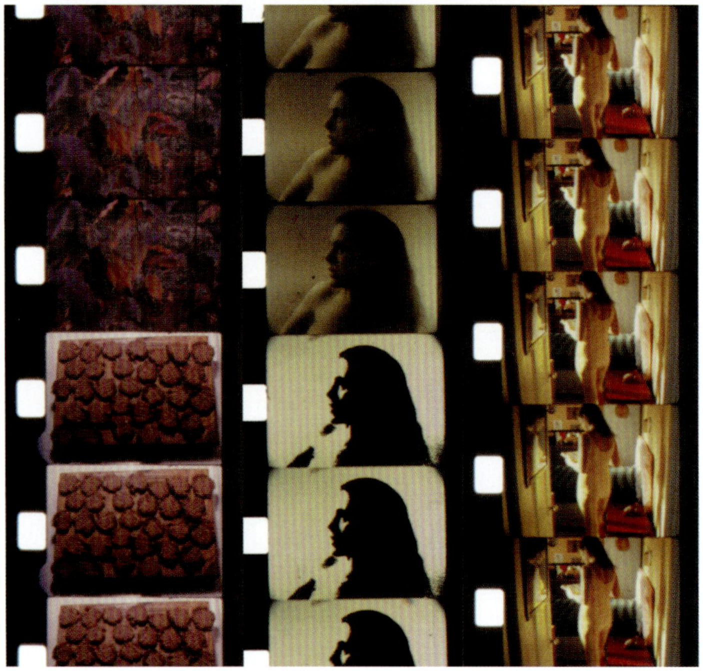

Top: **Chantal Akerman, *Jeanne Dielman, 23 quai du Commerce, 1080 Bruxelles*, 1975, still**

In the film *Jeanne Dielman*, the viewer follows the title character over a period of three days. The camera patiently records Jeanne, played by Delphine Seyrig, as she makes coffee, washes up, tidies, and bathes her son, among other things, for almost entirely the film's long two-hundred-minute duration. Akerman made the film in parallel with discussions around new women's cinema in the United States, but *Jeanne Dielman* breaks with both the avant-garde and the documentary, to represent the profound solitude of her title character, who, in turn, symbolized and politicized the figure of the housewife.

Bottom: **Anne Charlotte Robertson, *Five Year Diary*, 1981–87**

Robertson was a filmmaker who lived in Framingham, Massachusetts. She began making films during her studies at the University of Massachusetts, Boston. *Five Year Diary* is a thirty-eight-hour documentary of Robertson's life, her domestic environment, her cats, her garden, her mental illness, and her addictions. The diary comprises a number of episodes that span different lengths of time, and includes multilayered soundtracks Robertson made on audio cassettes, sometimes further layered with dialogue recorded directly on film. When Robertson screened the *Five Year Diary* she frequently added live commentary during the event as well.

Top: **Robin Schiff, *Nightmare Bathroom*, from *Womanhouse*, California Institute of Art, 1971–72**

The *Womanhouse* project was part of the Feminist Art Program established first at Fresno State College, and then at Cal Arts, by Judy Chicago and Miriam Schapiro in the early 1970s. It involved a series of installations created within an abandoned home in Los Angeles. In addition to Schiff's *Nightmare Bathroom*, exhibits included Chicago's *Menstruation Bathroom*, Sandra Orgel's *Linen Closet*, and Faith Wilding's *Womb Room*.

Bottom: **Martha Rosler, *Semiotics of the Kitchen*, 1975**

Rosler made *Semiotics of the Kitchen* in New York, after she had moved back to the city in 1974, following her MFA at the University of California, San Diego. The video is a parody of television cookery shows that feature demonstrations. Rosler appears in an apron, in the borrowed loft kitchen of the artist Ida Applebroog, and proceeds to run through an alphabet of cooking utensils. With each object's name, Rosler demonstrates an action. As the video goes on, the actions become more angry. In this way Rosler described both the limitations placed on women's voices, and the frustration of such restriction.

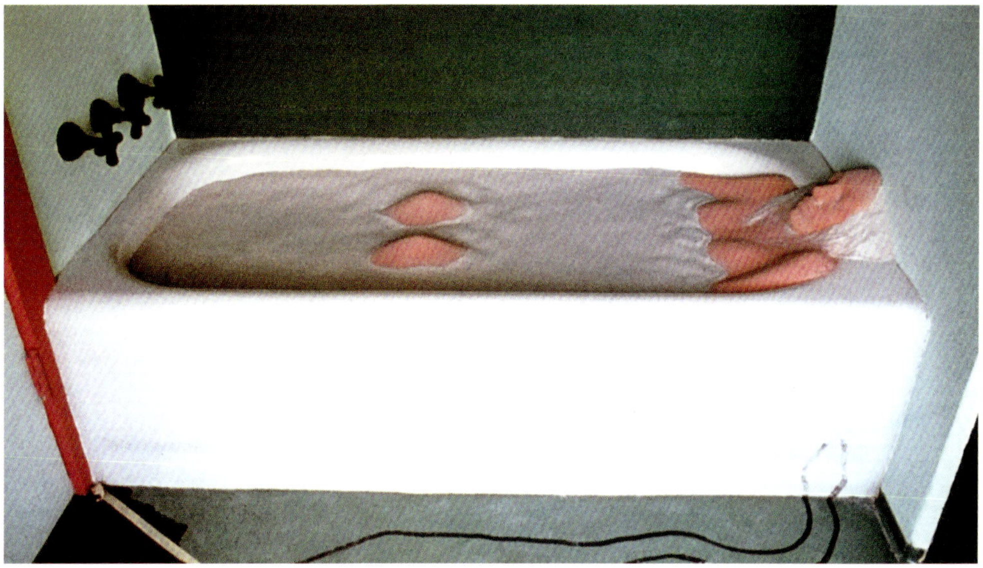

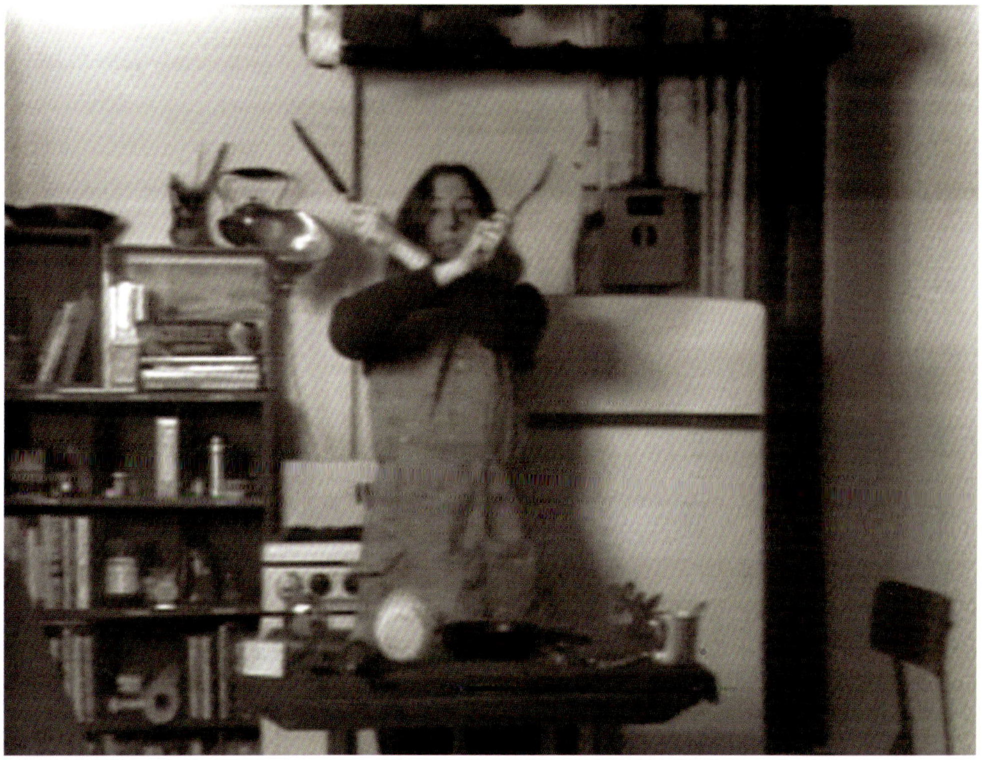

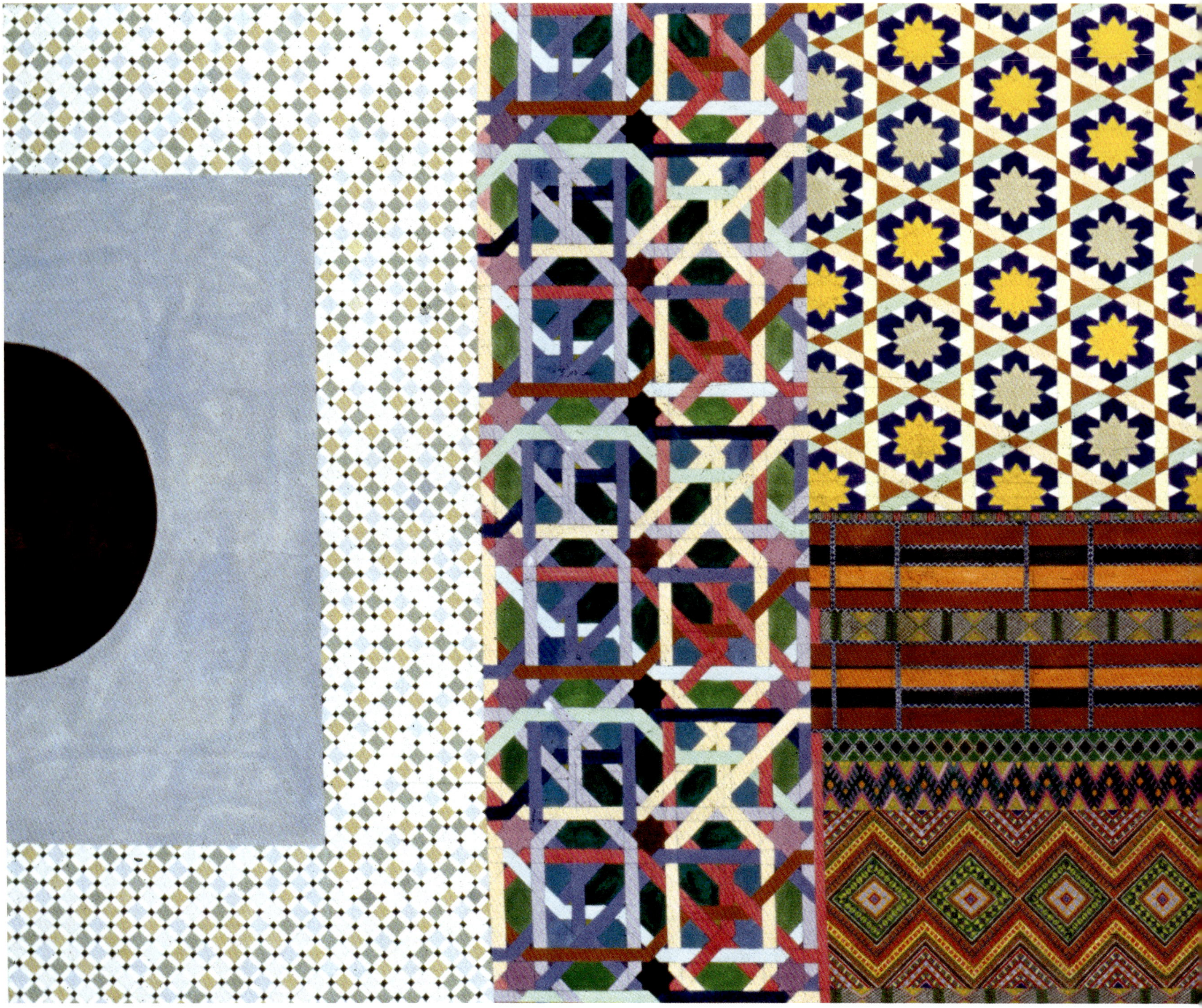

Above: Joyce Kozloff, *Three Portals . . . Pink Triangle*, 1977

Although Kozloff was largely based in New York, her art and politics were shaped by travel. In 1971, during a one-year stint in Los Angeles, she protested the lack of women on display at the Los Angles County Museum of Art. In 1973 she traveled to Mexico, and in 1975 to Morocco to study different decorative traditions. Kozloff brought these motifs into her paintings, often juxtaposing cultural references from a variety of origins. She saw this practice as political, because it challenged the hierarchal relation between fine art and craft, which Kozloff also saw as betraying cultural and gendered distinctions.

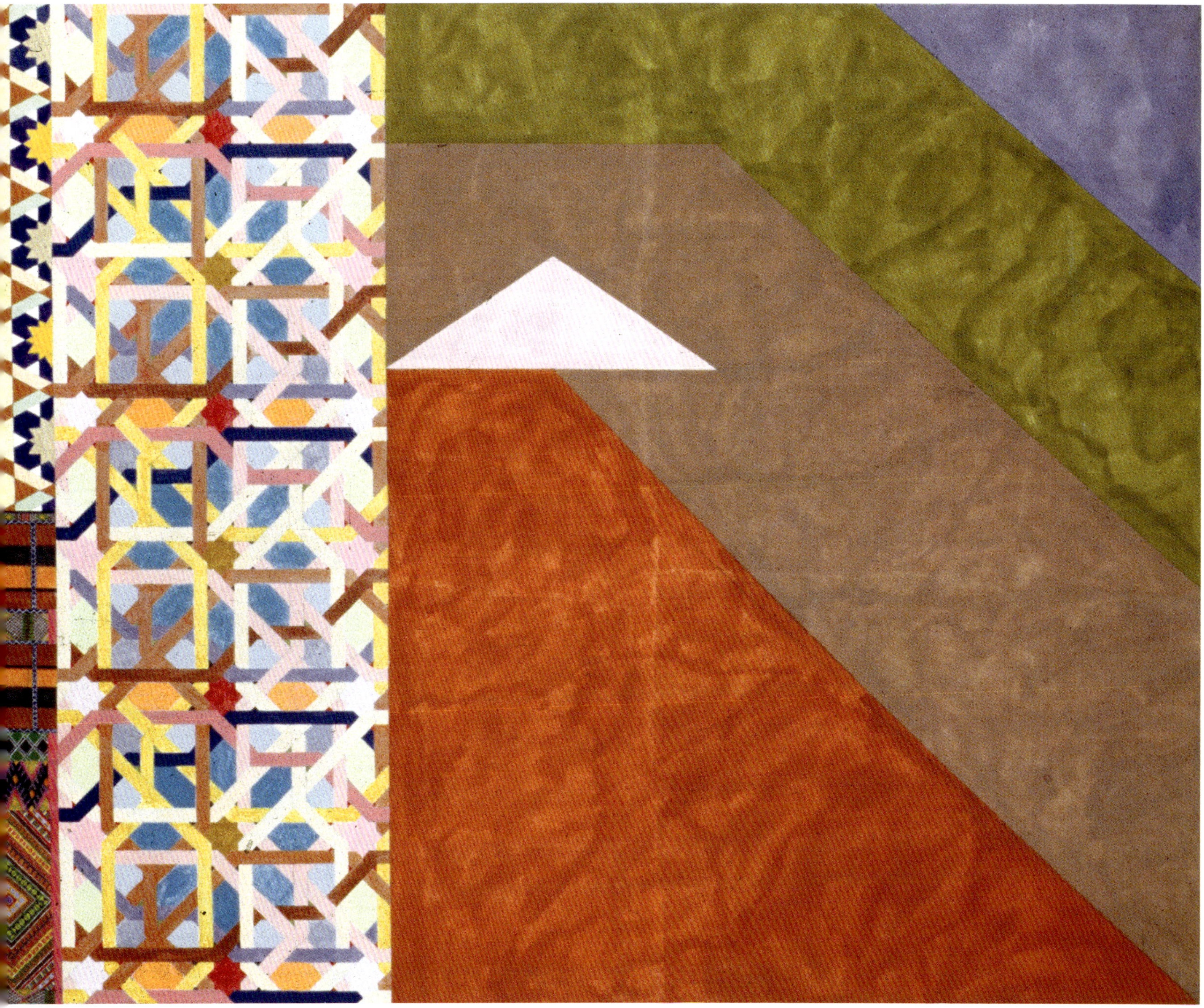

For The Woman's House

In January 1972, a mural dedicated to inmates was unveiled in the Women's House of Detention on Rikers Island, New York. The work of New York–based artist Faith Ringgold, the mural presented a society formed around, and by, women.

The Creative Artists Public Service Program commissioned the mural in March 1971. Before setting about making the painting, Ringgold interviewed the inmates at the Women's House of Detention (now New York City Correctional Institution for Women), inquiring about what they wanted to see each day of their sentence. Ringgold reported their answer as: "justice, freedom, a groovy mural on peace, a long road leading out of here, the rehabilitation of all prisoners." Ringgold's response was an inspiring scene of women's community. The mural was divided into eight sections, each filled with a vignette of women working together. It represented a multicultural community, with images of public service, teaching, policing, and childcare.

This, Ringgold's first commission, followed a body of work that included two series: American People and America Black, both of which documented tensions between people of different races following the 1960s civil-rights struggle. *For The Woman's House* makes use of the same figurative style as Ringgold's earlier paintings and features boldly rendered figures evocative of pop art and post-cubism. These are not portraits of particular people, but characters for Ringgold's investigation of social discord.

Ringgold's interest in making a public work coincided with a moment of heightened political activism in the New York art world, and criticism of museum and gallery displays. In the early 1970s, Ringgold had attended the meetings of the New York–based Art Workers' Coalition (AWC) and participated in the infamous collective action *Flag Show* (1970) at Judson Church, in protest of American involvement in the Vietnam War. The AWC issued thirteen demands to address both inequity in the New York art world, and the American wars in Vietnam and Cambodia. One of the demands was directed toward art-world racism, however the practice did not always meet policy in AWC activism. When AWC members Robert Morris and Poppy Johnson called the New York Art Strike Against Racism, Sexism, and War, the companion fundraising exhibition included only prominent, white male artists. In response Ringgold, along with Michele Wallace (Ringgold's daughter), walked out of the AWC and formed a new organization: Women Students and Artists for Black Art Liberation. Later both Ringgold and Wallace contributed to the protests of the Ad Hoc Women Artists' Committee at the yearly exhibition of contemporary art held at the Whitney Museum of American Art in New York.

Ringgold's commitment to the commission for the prison was shaped by her political activism and her awareness of an art world inhospitable to women artists and artists of color. A public commission allowed her to work in large scale, on a project that would be seen by many, but that was not integrated into a corrupted institutional scene.

The commission also offered Ringgold the opportunity to focus, for the first time, on the situation of women and to make a "feminist mural." While the scenes in *For The Woman's House* undoubtedly represented a positive future, especially for its inmate viewers, the women depicted are also mainly shown hard at work rather than enjoying their freedom and leisure. A traffic cop stops a woman builder wearing a hard hat emblazoned with the words "Build Baby Build" in one segment; in another, a doctor wearing a lab coat labeled with the name of the fictional "Rosa Parks Hospital" teaches a class on drug rehabilitation. In the next panel, a woman drives a bus heading to Sojourner Truth Square, and in the diagonally opposite panel, a white mother reads her mixed-heritage daughter the words of Parks and Coretta Scott King.

The mural not only depicts women at work in jobs that were rare for women to hold in America during the early 1970s, but also imagines a world in which women's achievements are commemorated in civic spaces and written in history books. While the work doesn't represent a separatist community—Ringgold has implied that there is a husband for the wife, and a father of the child—it does show a society remade, complete with a cadre of women politicians in the upper right.

Ringgold's acts of transformation are evident in other panels, too. On the right side of the composition, a panel shows a woman wearing the jersey of the New York basketball team, the Knicks, while shooting for the hoop. On the bottom left, another woman plays a drum, traditionally, as Ringgold has described, an instrument associated with masculinity. Above that, the next panel shows one side of a wedding party, with a mother giving her daughter away, and the hint of woman priest in the manicured hand on the bible lectern.

For The Woman's House offered a window of a very different world for the inmates of the detention center. But more than just inspiration for rehabilitation—after all, the women are all "working within the system," as Wallace argues—the mural depicts an image of equality and hope from both race and gender oppression. That this message was located in the women's prison emphasized the need to bring all women together to break more than chains on the long road ahead.

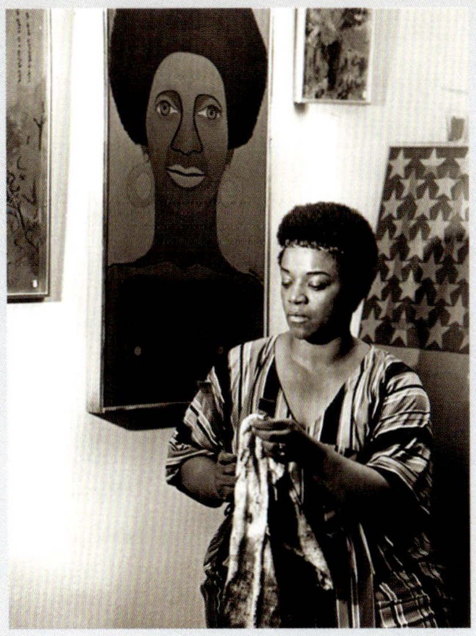

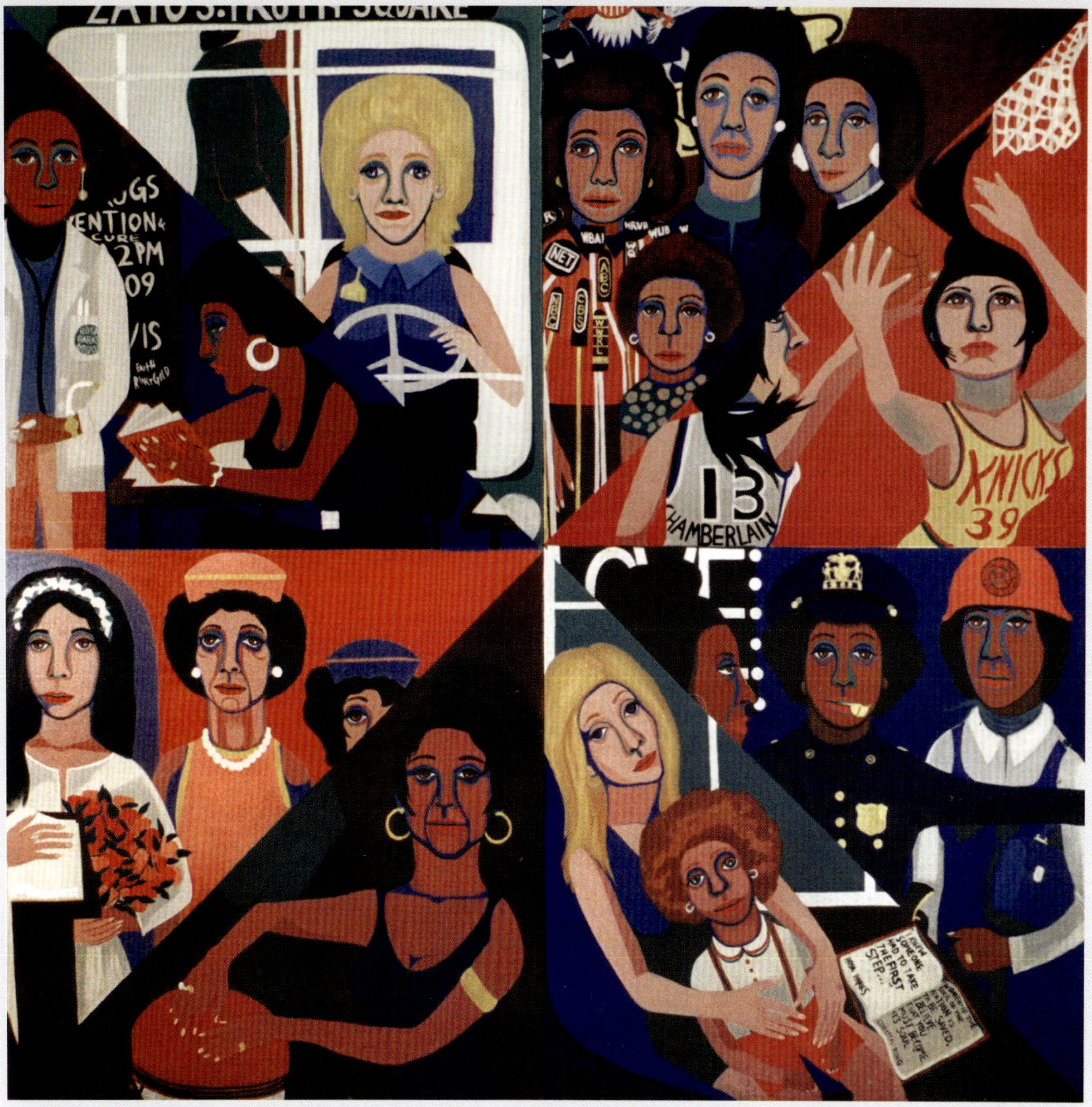

"[My art intends] . . . to confront the viewer and get the viewer involved . . . my art is something to be dealt with . . . my art is all about you the viewer."

Ringgold to Wallace, on the tight focus on the characters in her work

Above left: Faith Ringgold in her studio, 1969.

Above right: **Faith Ringgold, *For The Woman's House*, 1971**

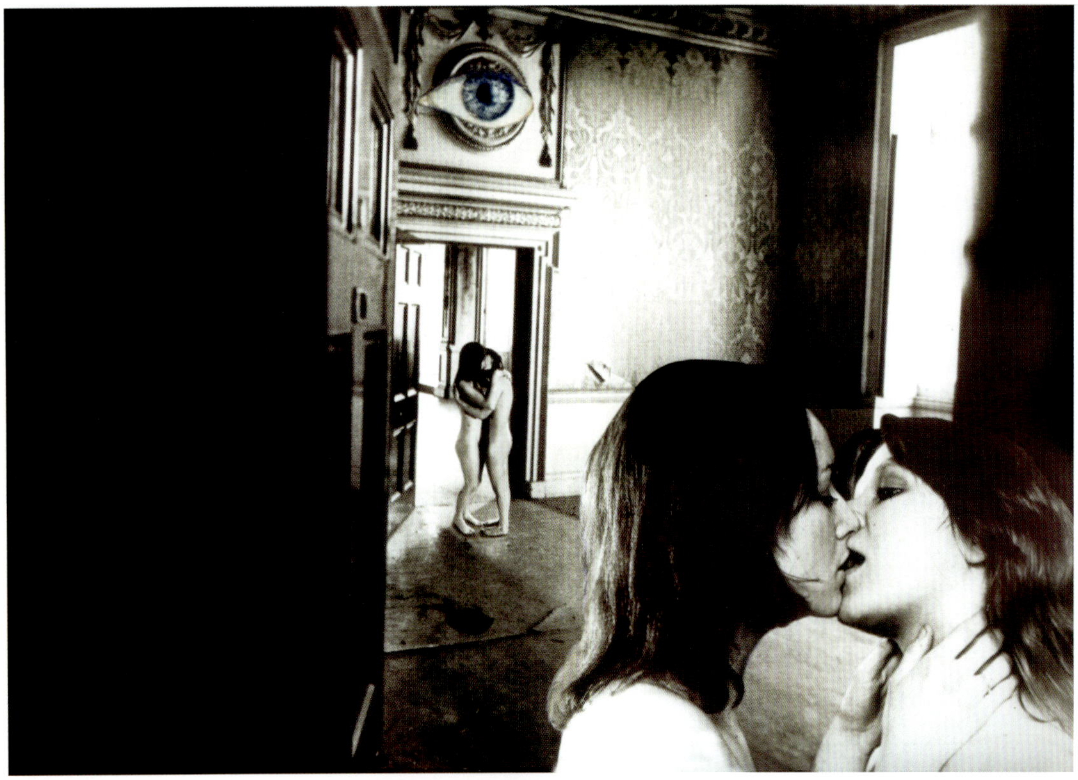

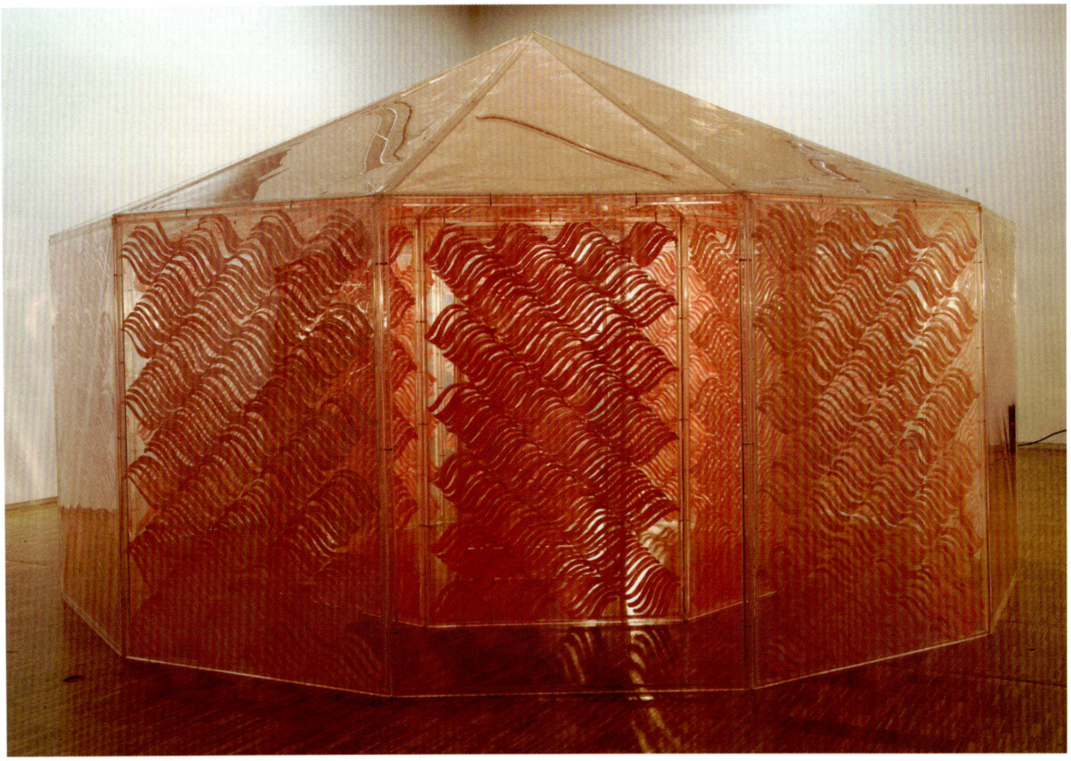

Top: Penny Slinger, *On Her Lips, You Kiss Your Own*, from An Exorcism, 1970–77, still

Penny Slinger developed the series titled An Exorcism over seven years, a period that coincided with the raising of her political consciousness. The series started life as a film, made in collaboration with her partner, the filmmaker Peter Whitehead, at a near-derelict stately home in Northamptonshire. After pausing to return to London and work with a women's theater group, Slinger renewed the project, this time working through, or exorcizing, gendered social conventions. Slinger acted out the scenes herself, working with her girlfriend Suzanka Fraey.

Bottom: Carla Accardi, *Triplice Tenda*, 1969

Carla Accardi studied painting in Florence, but lived and worked in Rome. In the early 1960s she gave up painting on canvas and began using the transparent *sicofoil* (plastic wrap). By the mid-1960s Accardi had developed a sculptural practice. *Triplice Tenda* (*Triple Tent*) is an important example of this practice, which seems to combine object and environment, place and space. In 1970, Accardi formed the feminist group Rivolta Femminile (Feminine Revolt), with Carla Lonzi and Elvira Banotti.

Below: Louise Nevelson, *Black Wall*, 1959

Black Wall is an early example of the sculptural assemblages American artist Louise Nevelson became well known for. The work comprises fragments found and collected by the artist on the New York streets around her studio apartment. These assemblages evoke both the domestic and the social. They are made from bits and pieces cast aside in New York's redevelopment in the 1950s and 1960s, as well as the worlds that Nevelson created for herself and her partner.

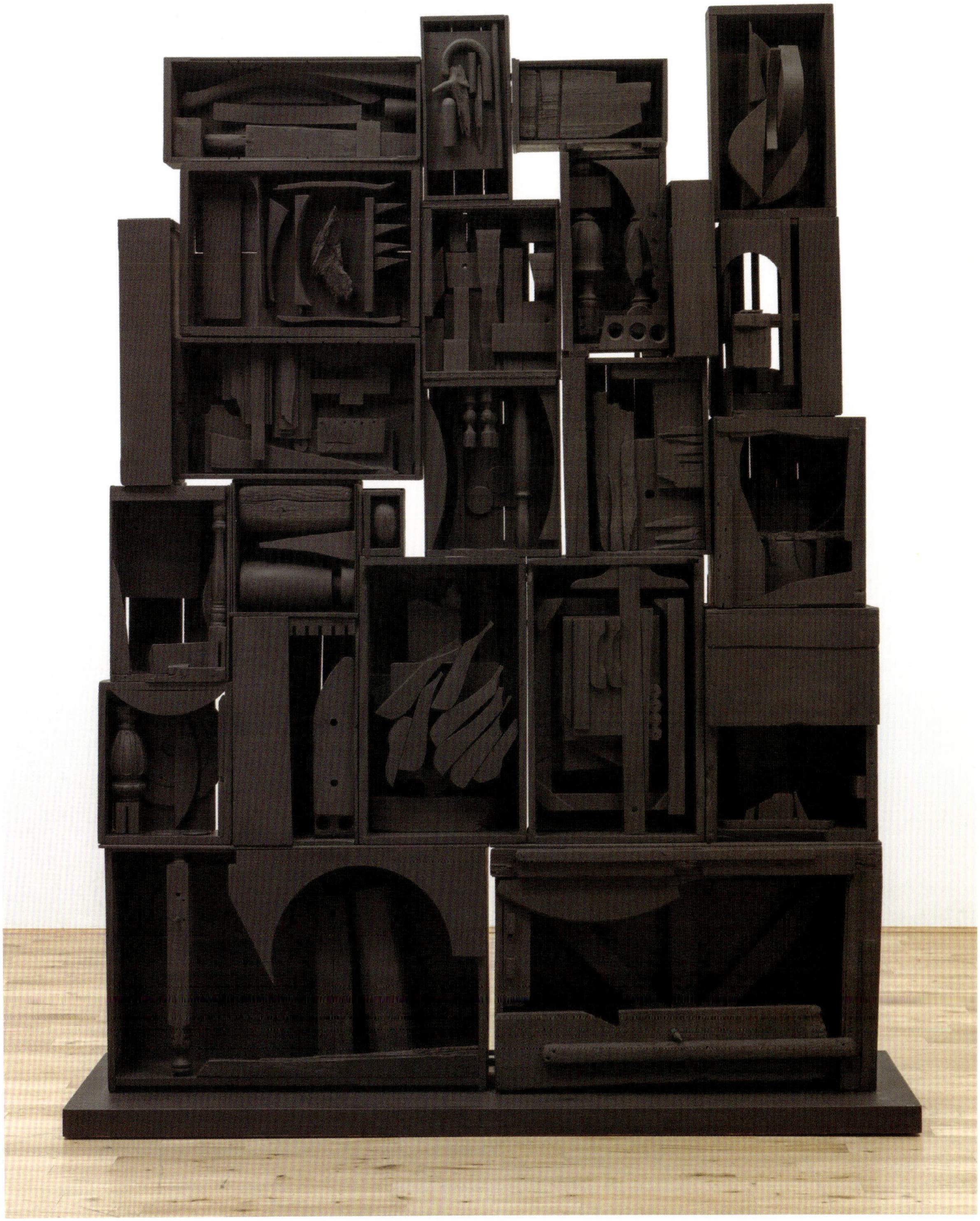

("QUOTE"): SOUND OF "DAISY" FADING IN BACKGROUND FOLLOWED BY SOUND OF "ALSO SPRACH ZARATHUSTRA" (R. STRAUSS) FOLLOWED BY SOUND OF "THE BLUE DANUBE" (J. STRAUSS) — SOUNDTRACK, 2001 (S. KUBRICK)

GENERAL STRIKE PIECE (STARTED FEB. 8, '69)*

GRADUALLY BUT DETERMINEDLY AVOID BEING PRESENT AT OFFICIAL OR PUBLIC "UPTOWN" FUNCTIONS OR GATHERINGS† RELATED TO THE "ART WORLD" IN ORDER TO PURSUE INVESTIGATION OF TOTAL PERSONAL & PUBLIC REVOLUTION.° EXHIBIT IN PUBLIC ONLY PIECES WHICH FURTHER SHARING OF IDEAS & INFORMATION RELATED TO TOTAL PERSONAL & PUBLIC REVOLUTION.♄

IN PROCESS AT LEAST THROUGH SUMMER, '69.

*WITHDRAWAL FROM 3-MAN SHOW COMPILED BY RICHARD BELLAMY, GOLDOWSKY GALLERY, 1078 MADISON AVE.

†DATE OF LAST VISIT TO UPTOWN GALLERIES FOR PERUSAL OF ART — FEB. 13 OR 14, 69
" " " " " A MUSEUM — MARCH 24, 69
" " " " " UPTOWN GALLERY OPENING — MARCH 15, 69
" " " " " A BAR — APRIL 5, 69
" " " ATTENDANCE AT A CONCERT — APRIL 18, 69
" " " " " " FILM SHOWING — APRIL 4, 69
" " " " " AN "EVENT" — APRIL 18, 69
" " " " " A BIG PARTY — MARCH 15, 69

°TERMS OF TOTAL PERSONAL & PUBLIC REVOLUTION SET FORTH IN BRIEF STATEMENT READ AT OPEN PUBLIC HEARING, ART WORKERS COALITION, SCHOOL OF VISUAL ARTS, APRIL 10, 69. FURTHER PARTICIPATION IN ART WORKERS COALITION OR ANY OTHER GROUP DECLINED AS PART OF GENERAL STRIKE PIECE. THIS INCLUDES ARTISTS AGAINST THE EXPRESSWAY GROUP & OTHERS.

♄FIRST PIECE EXHIBITED AT ART/PEACE EVENT, N.Y. SHAKESPEARE FESTIVAL PUBLIC THEATER, MARCH 5, 69. GRASS PIECE & NO-GRASS PIECE EXHIBITED IN NUMBER 7 SHOW COMPILED BY LUCY LIPPARD, PAULA COOPER, MAY 18, 69. INVESTMENT PIECE & CASH PIECE EXHIBITED IN LANGUAGE III SHOW, DWAN GALLERY, MAY 24, 69.

LEE LOZANO, JUNE 12, 69.

Resistance and Rage

Raising Consciousness and Fighting Back

"Demonstrating against Miss World, Women's Liberation struck a blow . . . against the physical confines of the way women are seen and the way they fit into society. Most of all, it was a blow against passivity, not only the forced passivity of the girls on the stage, but the passivity we all felt within ourselves."

Margarita Jimenez, in her account of the Miss World demonstration in London, 1970, published in the Women's Liberation Workshop journal, *Shrew*

Like the campaign for suffrage before it, the women's liberation movement brought women out onto the streets across countries and continents. Some of the earliest and most controversial campaigns involved protests against the Miss World competitions. Women in cities across the United States and in London organized demonstrations outside the competition venues. In Los Angeles protestors encouraged women to throw their "instruments of oppression" into a bin labeled "the freedom trashcan." The symbolic trashing of lipsticks, high heels, and, of course, bras, led to the mainstream press's favorite misnomer for a politicized woman—the bra burner—even though the trashcan was never set alight. Meanwhile in London's Royal Albert Hall, protesters entered the event posing as audience members. Midway through the show, they threw rotten tomatoes, flour, and stink bombs, before running away to evade arrest.

The protesters' attacks on the Miss World pageant, along with the marches held in many cities across the world, were important public demonstrations of women's discontent and of their rage and resistance. In the film documentation of the London Women's Liberation demonstration in March 1971, one woman describes her reason for attending as a chance "to see some other women who have been active and that we know nothing about. No one tells us about women organizing in this country and we wanted to come together and look at each other." That women wanted to come together to "look at each other" indicates how important vision and recognition were for the movement. It also gives some sense of the integral role visual art, as well as graphic design, played for women's liberation. Not only did feminist-influenced fine art, film, photography, and illustration open up new avenues for representation, women also began to critique the spectacle of femininity and the sexualization of images of women in the public sphere—from art to film and advertising.

One thing that characterized the otherwise disparate women's liberation and feminist politics of the 1970s was small-group organizing, and consciousness-raising (CR) in particular. Gathered together in small groups, women would share stories on a particular theme, uninterrupted. The idea was that, in this uninterrupted speech, they could each explore how the themes discussed related to their own lives. They might recognize the story of another member of the group and discuss their own experience of the same situation. It was in this way that an awareness of shared oppression between women emerged. In Italy a slightly different version of this practice, named *autocoscienza* ("self-consciousness") emerged within the practices of feminist collectives that included Rivolta Femminile (Feminine Revolt) in Rome, Libreria delle Donne di Milano (Milan Women's Bookstore Collective), Diotima in Verona, and Cooperativa Beato Angelico in Rome. This separatist process later developed into *affidamento*, or "entrustment," which sought to name differences between women and treat them as a source of collective strength, rather than weakness—this formalized approach was not evident in the Anglo-American or other European movements.

Consciousness-raising impacted on art and image-making, too; for the American artist Suzanne Lacy, the stories of sexual violence she heard in CR led to her making a series of visceral installations—and later participatory works—that broke the social silence on rape and sexual violence. In *Three Weeks in May*, Lacy organized a three-week program of events in Los Angeles that encouraged discussion of sexual violence, gave women access to workshops in self-defense, and literally mapped instances of sexual violence, gathered through a police radio, onto a map of the city.

Other women used CR as a model for experiments in art and graphic design. Shelia Levrant de Bretteville, also based in Los Angeles, designed an issue of the feminist magazine *Everywoman* (1970) around the idea of sharing stories in a similar approach to CR. The issue focused on the feminist art program established by Judy Chicago at Fresno State College of Art. Rather than report on Chicago—the charismatic leader of the course—Levrant de Bretteville dedicated a double-page spread to each participant in the program. These pages featured sections of text printed in different configurations and close-up profile portraits of the women. Levrant de Bretteville went on to expand this design concept beyond the publication—which circulated widely—to an urban installation called *Pink* (1973).

Page 114: **Lee Lozano, *General Strike Piece*, 1969**

General Strike Piece is one of Lozano's "Language Pieces," which she began in 1968, after moving away from painting. *General Strike Piece* announced Lozano's withdrawal from the New York art world and coincided with her fraught participation in the Art Workers' Coalition. In 1971, Lozano withdrew more fully with her *Dropout Piece* and announced her "boycott of women" in the face of feminist organizing. Although these works indicate Lozano's resistance to collective politics, they also resist the art world status quo.

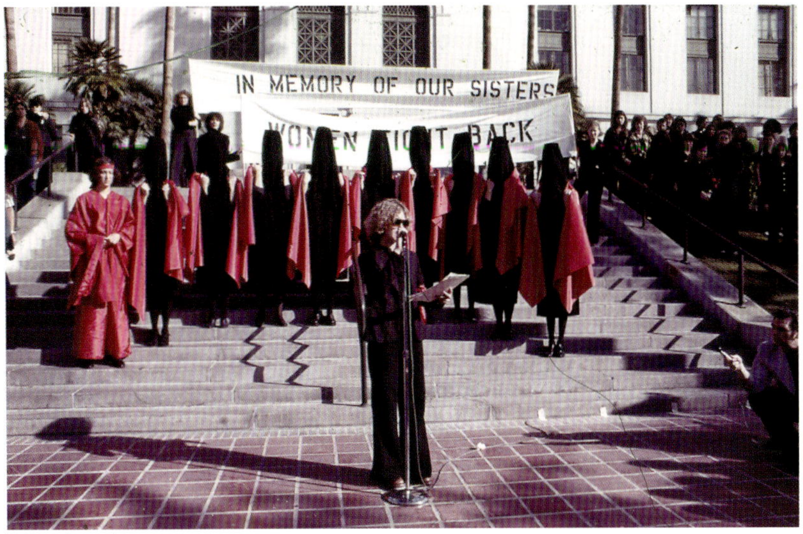

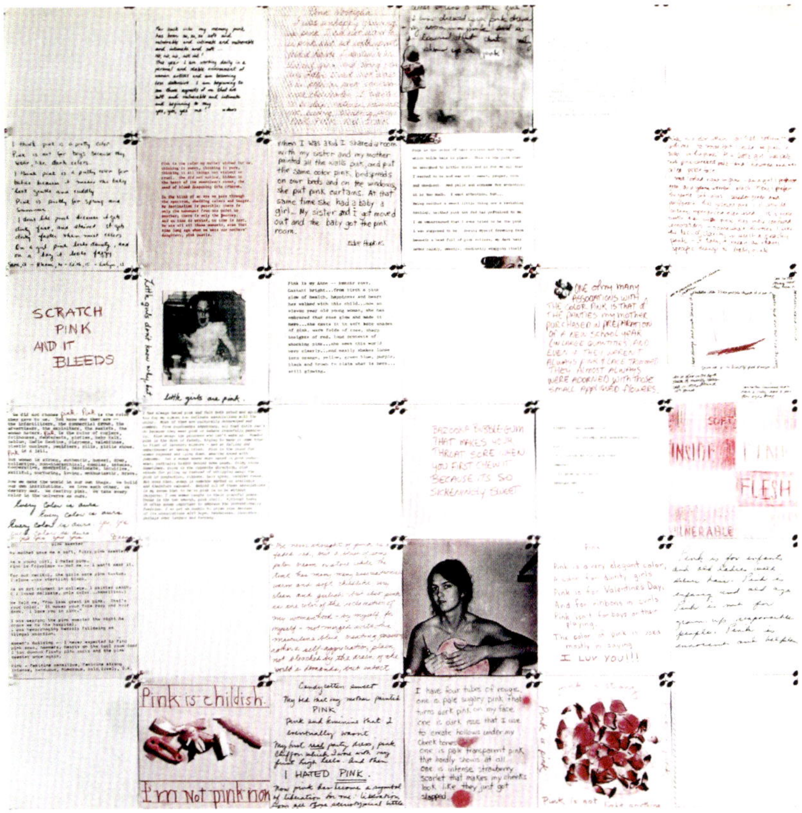

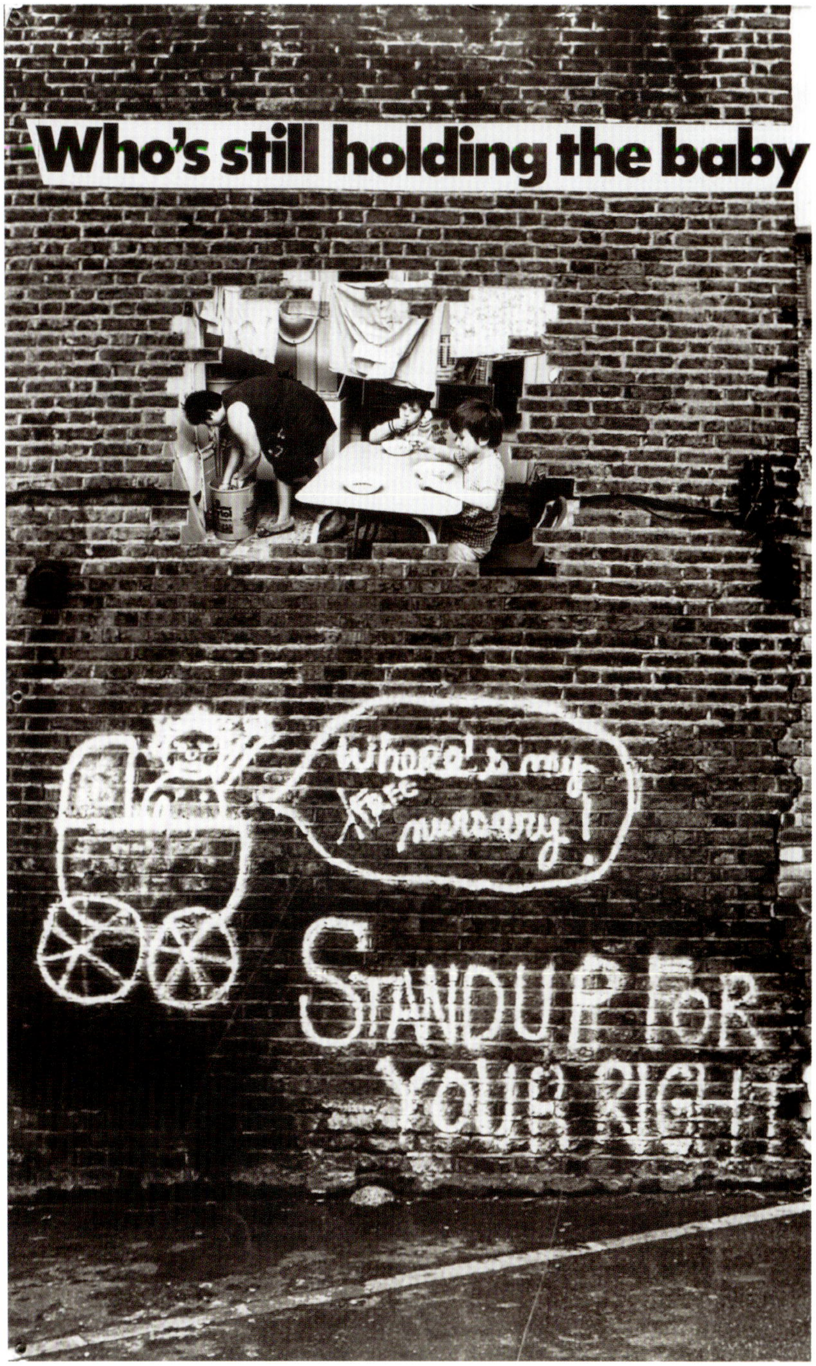

Top left: Ariadne, *In Mourning and In Rage*, 1977

In Mourning and In Rage was a public ritual jointly conceived by the Los Angeles–based artists Suzanne Lacy and Leslie Labowitz, working under the name Ariadne. The performance responded to a spate of violent murders of young women, known as the "Hillside Strangler" case. The performance took place on the steps of City Hall in Los Angeles, to an audience that included the local press. Nine women, dressed in mourners' black and wearing headdresses that extended their height, each named a form of violence against women, before joining together in a chant. The tenth woman, dressed in red represented women's collective rage.

Bottom left: Sheila Levrant de Bretteville, *Pink*, 1973

This poster was commissioned by the American Institute of Graphic Arts for an exhibition about color; it was displayed in the Whitney exhibition in New York. Levrant de Bretteville, who was based in Los Angeles, then printed a run of five hundred at the Woman's Building, LA, an organization she cofounded with Judy Chicago and Arlene Raven. The poster is made of up squares, some filled in by different women, recounting what the color pink means to them; others are left empty, prompting the viewer to add a response of their own. *Pink* is an early example of Levrant de Bretteville's feminist, poly-vocal approach to graphic design.

Above right: Hackney Flashers, *Who's Still Holding the Baby?*, 1978

The Hackney Flashers were a collective of photographers, illustrators, and designers based in East London. The group emerged from the radical Photography Workshop at Half Moon Gallery run by Terry Dennett and Jo Spence. *Who's Still Holding the Baby?* was the Flashers' second project. It sought to document the lives of mothers in Hackney. The twenty-four panels that make up the project meditate on numerous subjects including drugs, nursery places, and domestic isolation. The panels were made to be shown easily in different surroundings from political meetings to libraries and community centers.

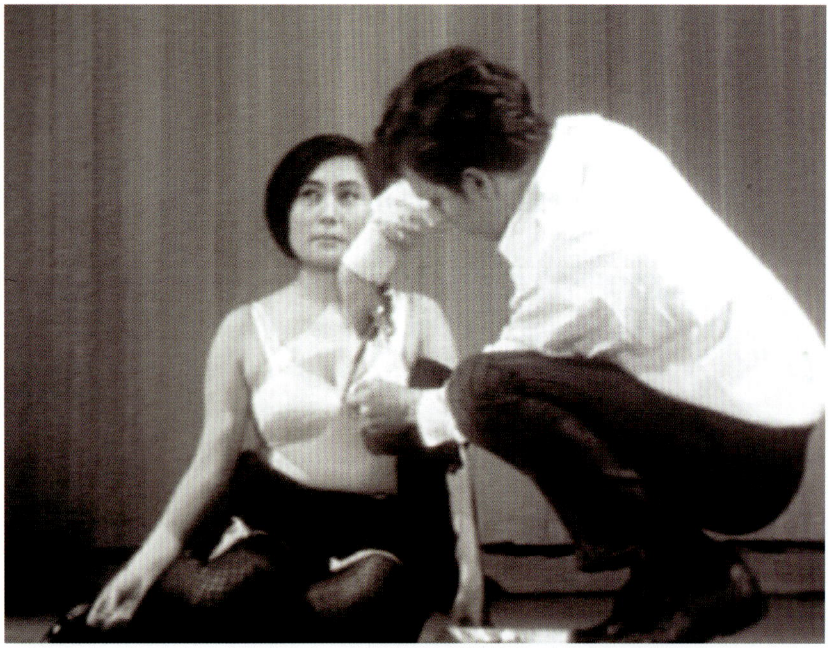

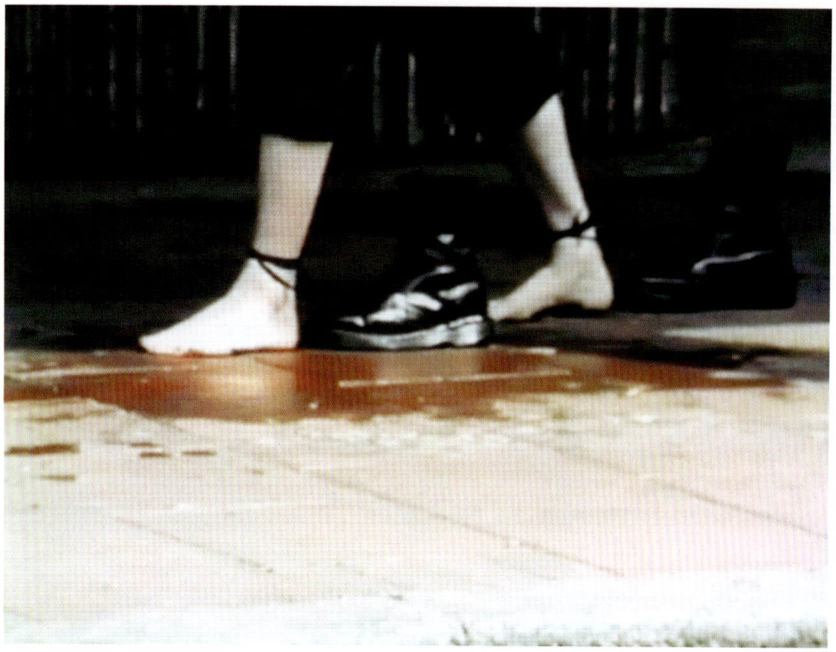

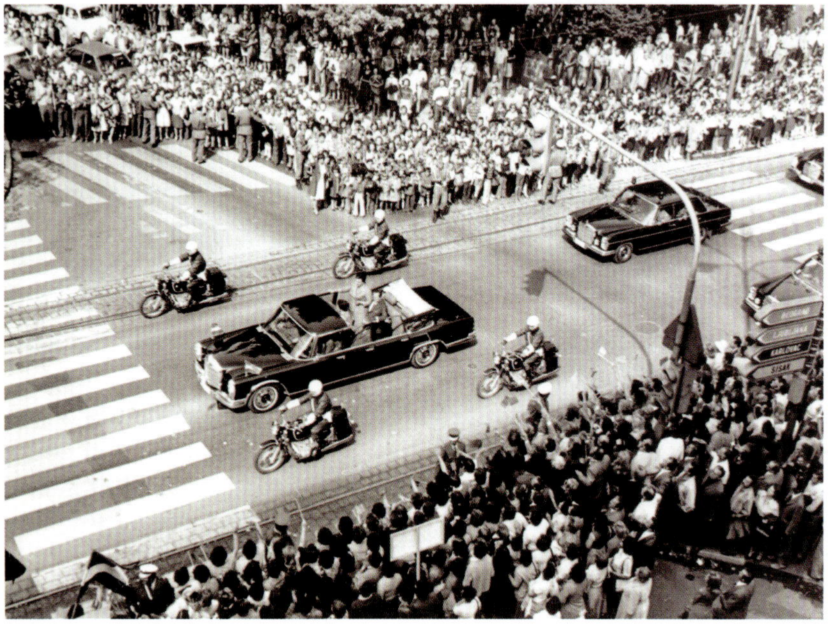

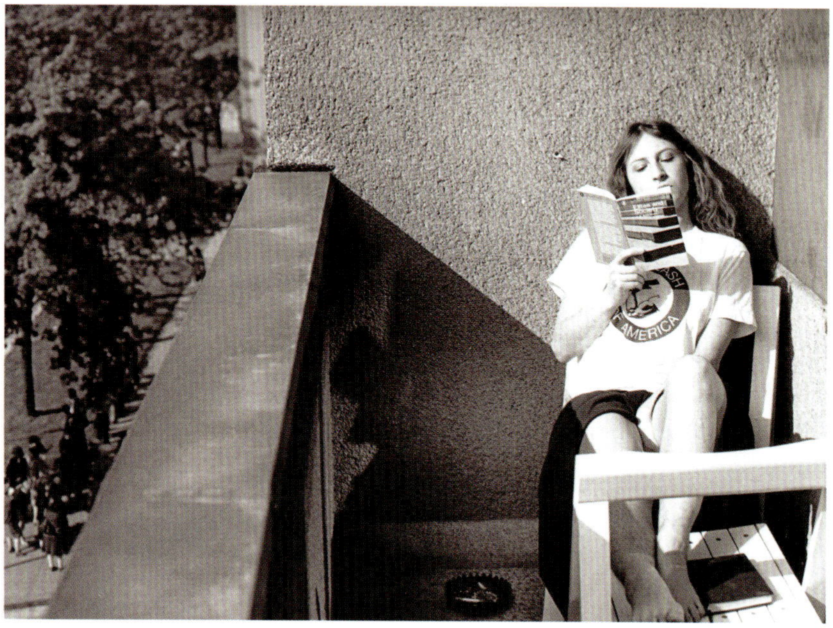

Top left: **Yoko Ono, *Cut Piece*, 1965**

Ono's *Cut Piece*, recently revived in Paris, is structured by a score that reads: "Cut Piece. First version for single performer: Performer sits on stage with a pair of scissors in front of him. It is announced that members of the audience may come on stage—one at a time—to cut a small piece of the performer's clothing to take with them. Performer remains motionless throughout the piece. Piece ends at the performer's option." In the 1965 performance, while some participants carefully cut small sections from a sleeve or skirt, others, sometimes aggressively, cut to expose Ono's body. For the duration of the work she remained motionless, opening herself up to the participants' will.

Top right: **Mona Hatoum, *Roadworks*, 1985**

In Mona Hatoum's *Roadworks*, the artist walks the streets of Brixton with Doc Marten boots tied to her ankles by their laces. The boots reference the footwear of the racist National Front, the police, and the army. On a local scale, the boots relate to the history of this South London area—in 1981, Brixton had been the site of demonstrations against racism that developed into violent skirmishes involving the police. The boots could also invoke the army and, on a global scale, the conflict in Lebanon, where Hatoum was born, and which had been split since 1975 by civil war between Muslims and Christians. Hatoum became a resident in London because of the conflict. It had begun while she was visiting the city and prevented her return.

Bottom left & right: **Sanja Iveković, *Trokut (Triangle)*, 1979**

Iveković's *Trokut* comprises four silver-gelatin photographs, and a text documenting an action from May 10, 1979. The text reads: "The action begins when I walk out onto the balcony and sit on a chair, I sip whiskey, read a book, and make gestures as if I perform masturbation. After a period of time, the policeman rings my doorbell and orders the 'persons and objects are to be removed from the balcony'." Occupying her balcony, at the threshold of public and private space, Iveković appears to masturbate, aware that, to the watching state surveillance, this intimate, private act would appear disruptive on the day of President Tito's parade through the city.

During this period, some works sought to make a definitive break from the rarefied arena of fine art. Collectives such as London-based See Red Women's Workshop and the Hackney Flashers, distanced themselves from the art world and, in particular, from the associations and values of both the museum and commercial sectors. See Red Women's Workshop wanted to challenge the notion of the individual Artist with a capital "A" by setting up a collective to produce posters for the women's liberation movement. The collective shared all skills and tasks—from design to printing to cleaning screens—teaching each other, and other women at conferences, meetings, and on their apprenticeship scheme. See Red Women's Workshop also provided service printing for women's, LGBTQ, black, and community groups. The collective was active in seeking change within the movement and worked to empower many women and to picture a women's liberation that was diverse. The Hackney Flashers were also organized around sharing skills and resources, although they worked in photography and illustration. Based in the East London borough of Hackney, the group sought to document and describe the lives of women that had so far remained invisible. The group's second work, *Who's Still Holding the Baby?* (1978), represented the conditions for mothers and children in the borough, in support of their campaign for better nurseries. The panels were openly available to booking for political organizations, women's centers, and campaign meetings, but when the work was slated for inclusion in a photography exhibition at London's Hayward Gallery, the group split apart.

Some women were happier to work across different media, and to different ends. The Pakistani artist Lala Rukh, for example, designed work for the Women's Action Forum, Pakistan, but was also a painter. Faith Ringgold, who was also primarily a painter, designed a reproducible poster titled *Women, Freedom, Now* for the Feminist Poster Series.

If some women moved away from the mainstream art world, others sought to transform it. One way in which women artists found a means to make art was by exploring performance and new media. The history of women's demonstrative resistance extends beyond that of women's liberation. Artists such as Yoko Ono, Mona Hatoum, and Sanja Iveković used their bodies to explore the biopolitics of gendered and state oppression. Ono's important *Cut Piece* (1965), in which the artist sits on stage while audience members cut away her clothes, staged feminine vulnerability and defiance in, and through, spectacle. In Iveković's *Triangle* (1979) and Hatoum's *Roadworks* (1985), the artist's body is caught in a circuit of surveillance. Both artists acted outside of expectations, Hatoum performing a somber march through a busy Brixton street, London, with military boots tied to her ankles, and Iveković on the balcony of her apartment in Zagreb, Croatia, during a state ceremonial parade. Hatoum's surveillance was a construction, and her performance a commentary on state antagonism in London. Iveković pretended to masturbate while reading a copy of Tom Bottomore's *Elites and Society* (1964) in order to aggravate a response from the secret police monitoring the parade; they eventually demanded that she stop. *Triangle* exposed the extent of surveillance in the Croatian state, even in the semiprivacy of the artist's balcony. The performance and the documentation not only highlighted the oppressive conditions of life under Josip Tito, they also described the disruptive character of the sexualized woman's body.

Despite the solidarity that emerged through small-group activism, the women's liberation movement was also subject to discord and division. In her 1971 article "What the Black Woman Thinks About Women's Lib," the American author Toni Morrison writes:

". . . there is not only the question of color, there is the question of the color of experience. Black women are not convinced that Women's Lib serves their best interests or that it can cope with the uniqueness of their experience, which is itself an alienating factor. The early image of Women's Lib was of an elitist organization made up of upper-middle-class women with the concerns of that class and not paying attention to the problems of most black women . . . not in how to exercise freedom from the 'head of the house,' but in how to be head of the household."

Morrison's text names the difficulty white women had in taking account of the different experiences of women of color. In response to this resistance, women formed alternate organizations, such as the New York–based National Black Feminist Organization, a parallel to the National Organization for Women (NOW). Black women artists also came together to form support groups, organize exhibitions, and publish written works. This is evident in the Where We At collective formed by Kay Brown, Jerrolyn Crooks, Pat Davis, Mai Mai Leabua, Dindga McCannon, and Faith Ringgold in 1971, to organize an exhibition of black women's art in New York. The exhibition at Acts of Art Gallery was arranged to show "the community we did exist." Artists such as Brown and McCannon, as well as Elizabeth Catlett, Jae Jarrell, and Barbara Jones-Hogu, all contributed to imaging black women's empowerment, from picturing a revolutionary sister or calling on black men to show solidarity with the women's cause.

Other significant exhibitions from this time include the Where We At exhibition *Cookin' and Smokin'* (1972), held at the Weusi-Nyumba Ya Sanaa Gallery (later the Weusi Academy of Art), and Ana Mendieta, Kazuko Miyamoto, and Zarina's landmark show *Dialectics of Isolation: An Exhibition of Third World Women Artists in the United States*, held at the predominantly white cooperative A.I.R. Gallery (Artists in Residence) in September 1980. While the title of the latter, specifically the term "dialectics," highlighted the friction between the event and the gallery in which it took place, the work included did not present a united agenda. Among the pieces shown, Howardena Pindell's *Free, White and 21* (1980) exposed the privilege and antagonistic behavior of the predominantly white, A.I.R. audience.

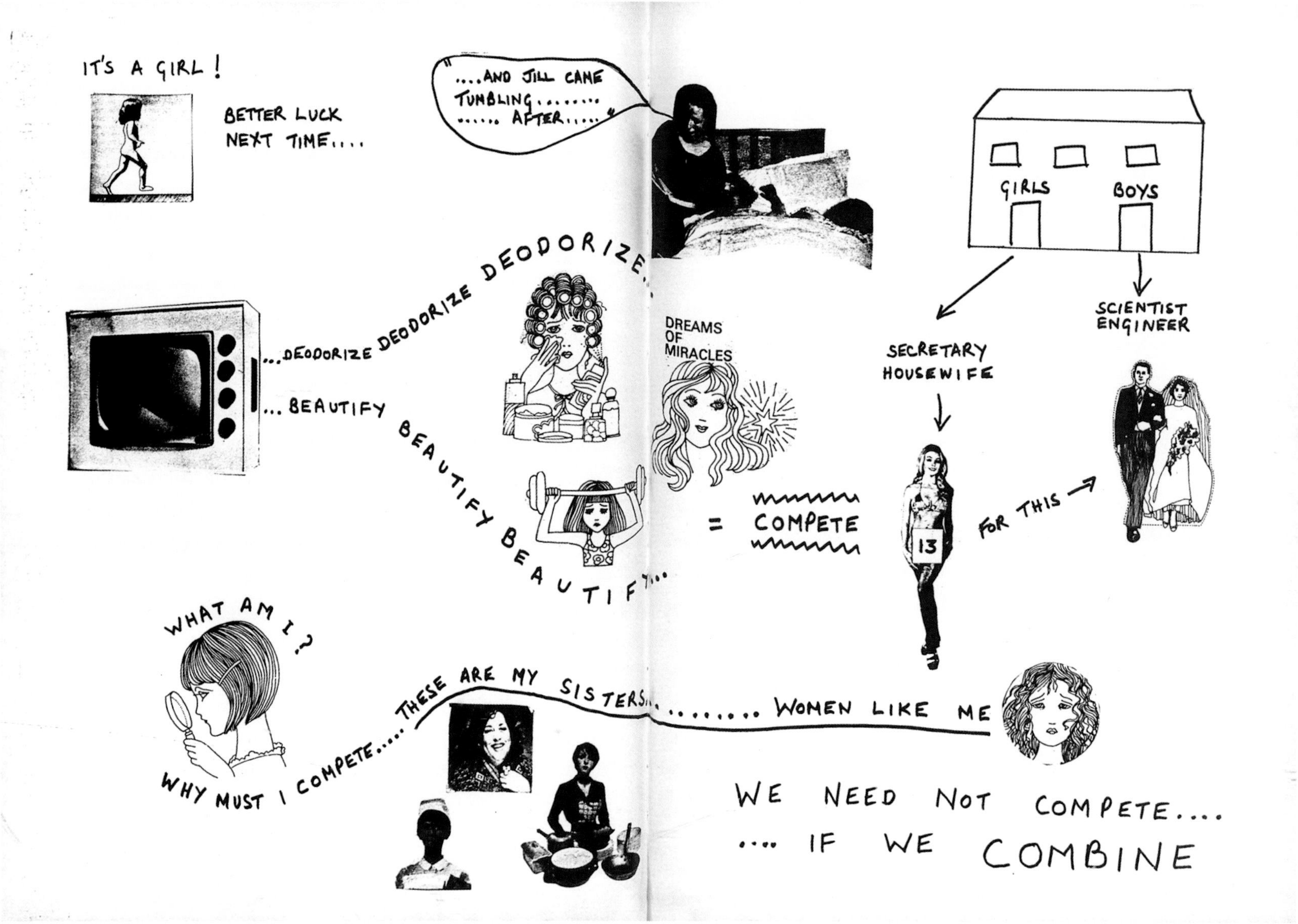

Above and opposite, bottom left: *Shrew* magazine

Shrew ran between 1969 and 1978. It was not focused on art and had no central editorial collective. Each issue was compiled by groups within the London Women's Liberation Workshop and represented the interests of those groups. Content ranged from political—often socialist—analysis, health advice, journalism, and reportage, as well as including much illustration and photo-collage. Because of the fluctuating production it varied in size, font, and paper stock. Unlike *Lip* and *Heresies*, it was not professionally printed. The History Group produced an issue of *Shrew* in 1970 that reflected on the Miss World protests they had been part of. The issue includes Laura Mulvey's first published text written with Margarita Jimenez "The Spectacle is Vulnerable: Miss World, 1970" and provided Mary Kelly with experience of magazine layout design.

Top left: *Lip* magazine

Lip was published from 1976–84 by a collective of women based in Carlton, Victoria, Australia. The journal was interdisciplinary in scope. Its content ranged from commentaries on film, visual arts, theater, and dance, and encompassed a range of political affiliations. The title punned on the multiple meanings of the word "lip," referring to impudent speech, to singing, and to the "stiff upper lip" that suggests strength and self-reliance. The front cover of the first issue presented these definitions as a manifesto.

Top right: *Heresies: A Feminist Publication on Art and Politics*

Heresies ran from 1977 to 1993. Each issue was thematic, and edited by a guest collective overseen by a consistent editorial Mother Collective. *Heresies* was an open-call journal, which meant that content was both received and solicited—up-and-coming themes were advertised in advance. The journal published a wide range of writers and artists on diverse topics. Contributions included poems, stories, journalistic interviews and reports, manifestos, scholarly articles, and artworks. *Heresies* attempted to bring together different voices in, and beyond, the women's liberation movement, but this was not without mistakes, antagonisms, and collective reflection. Like *Lip* magazine, the title invoked dissidence.

Bottom right: *le torchon brûle!*

le torchon brûle! was published from May 1971 to June 1973, although the first issue (pictured) appeared in December 1970, inset in Jean-Edern Hallier's *L'idiot liberté*. The magazine was founded by Marie Dedieu after one of the regular meetings of the *Mouvement de liberation des femmes* (MLF) at the School of Fine Arts in Paris. It was produced collectively and published irregularly. Unlike many feminist publications, its contents were sometimes published without credited authors in an attempt to assuage authorial responsibility. The title translates as "the tea towel burns."

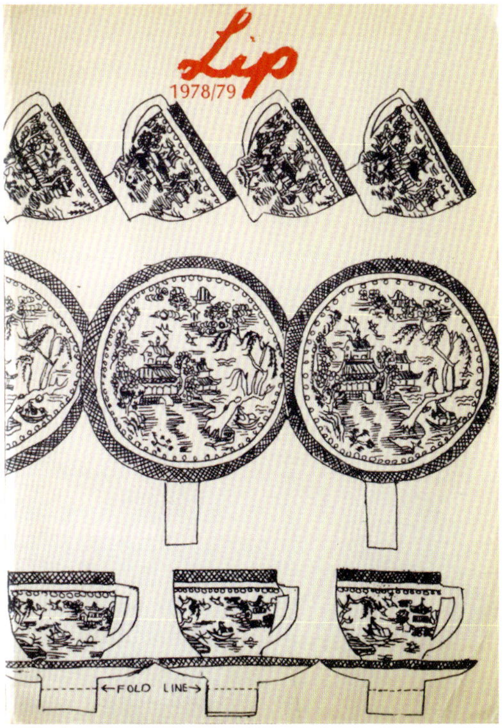

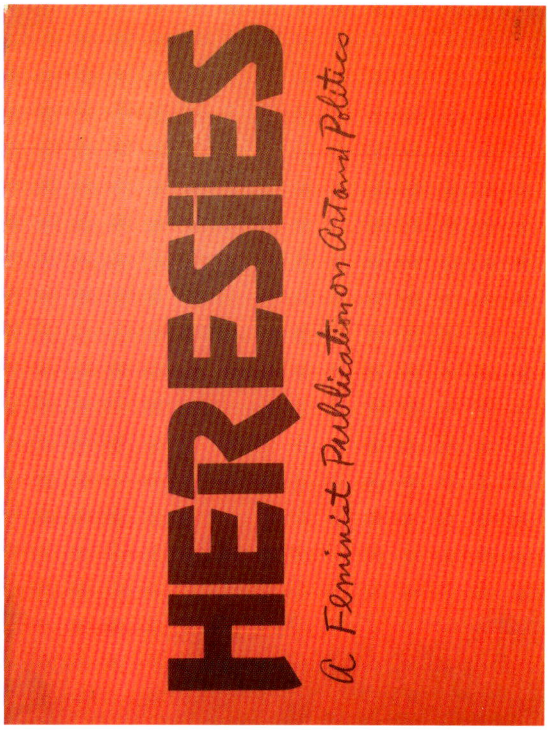

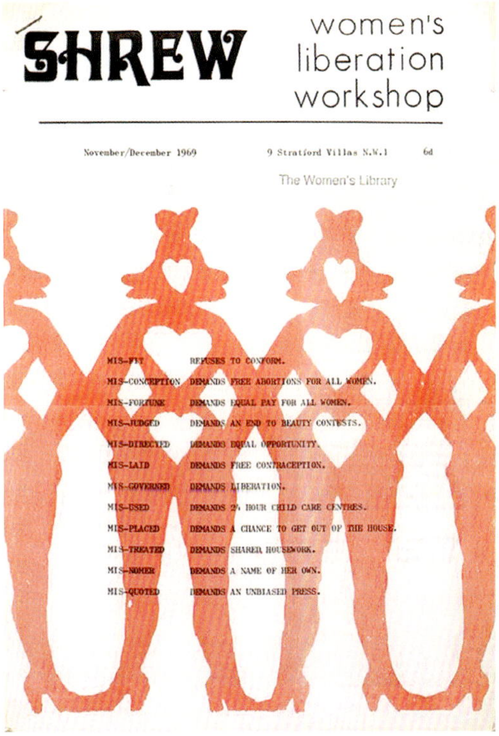

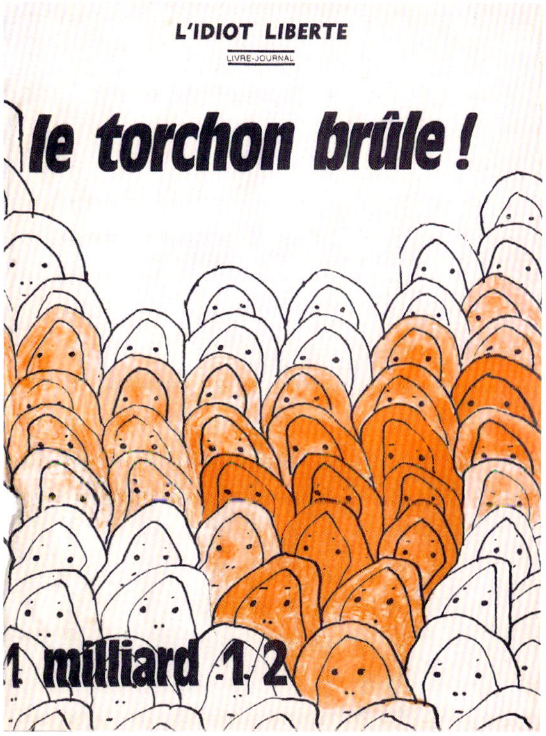

Below left and right: See Red Women's Workshop, *Organise Against the National Front*, 1978–79; *Alone We Are Powerless, Together We Are Strong*, 1976

See Red Women's Workshop was a silk-screen printing collective formed by three ex-art students in 1974. The group expanded through the 1970s and stopped making original designs in 1983, although it continued doing service printing and design for women's and LGBTQ groups until 1990. See Red Women's Workshop sought to counter negative images of women in the media and to challenge women's role in society. They worked together, with more than forty women joining the collective in sixteen years, sharing stories of their lives, as well as sharing skills and working collaboratively on designs. See Red Women's Workshop posters aimed to be both radical and accessible and were distributed widely in Britain, and internationally. As well as making their own designs, the collective also ran an apprenticeship scheme from the 1980s.

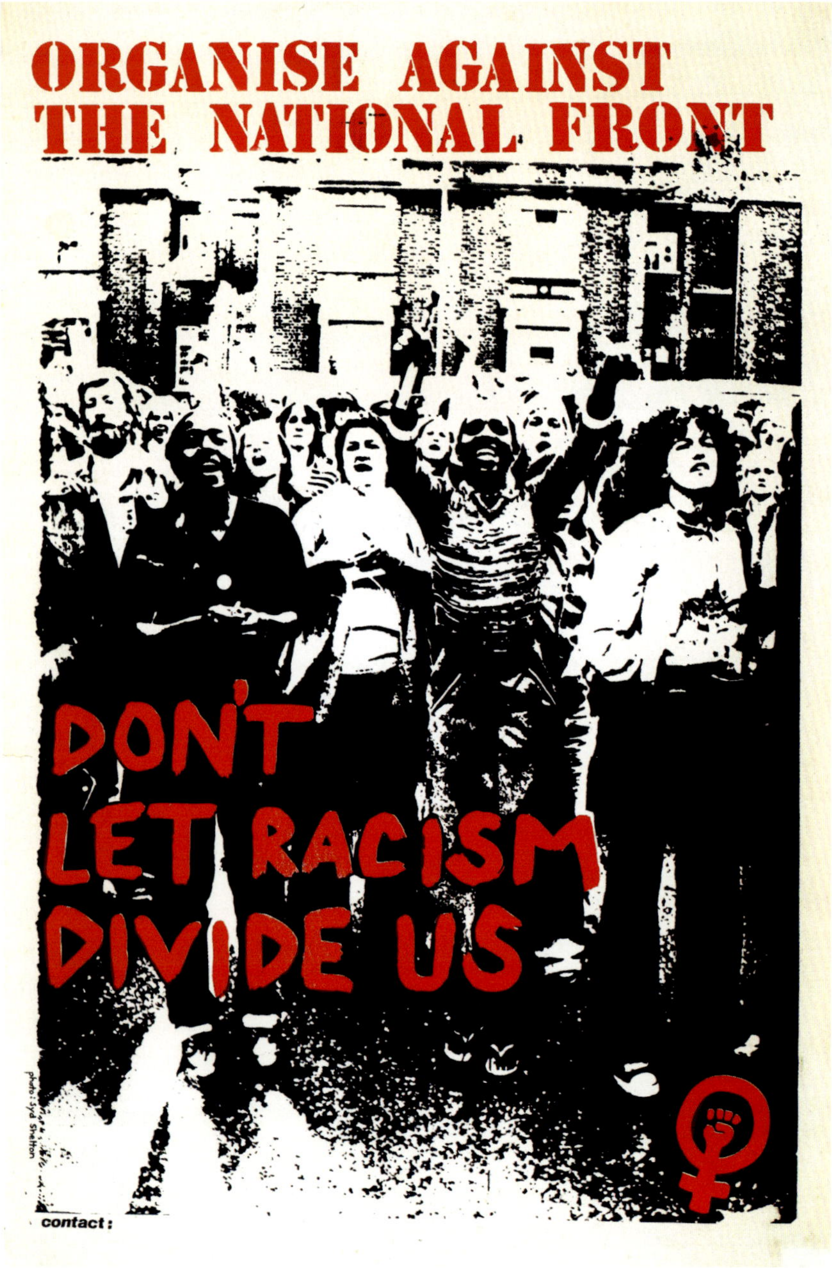

Below left and right: Lala Rukh, *Masawi Huqooq* poster for Women's Action Forum, Lahore, 1983–84; *Crimes Against Women*, poster for Women's Action Forum, Lahore, ca. 1985–87

Lala Rukh was a founding member of the Women's Action Forum (WAF), a women's rights organization that spanned Karachi, Lahore, and Islamabad in Pakistan. She was also an artist, with a degree in fine arts from Punjab University, where she later taught. These posters date from her work with the WAF, which was originally formed to protest the Hudood Ordinances installed by the Muhammad Zia-ul-Haq regime. These ordinances sought violent punishments for minor indiscretions, often focused on curbing women's freedom. Rukh produced many visual materials for WAF. She also established a screen-printing workshop in her garden and ran educational programs alongside her WAF activism.

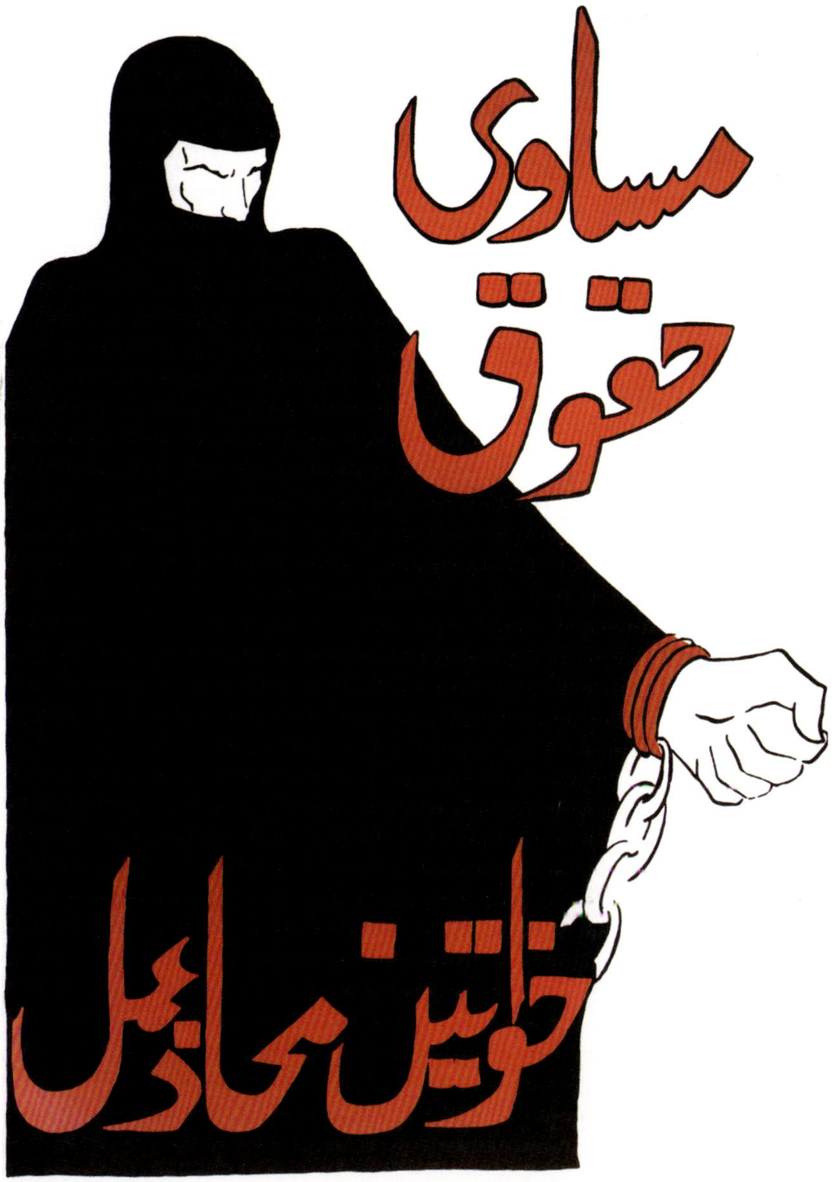

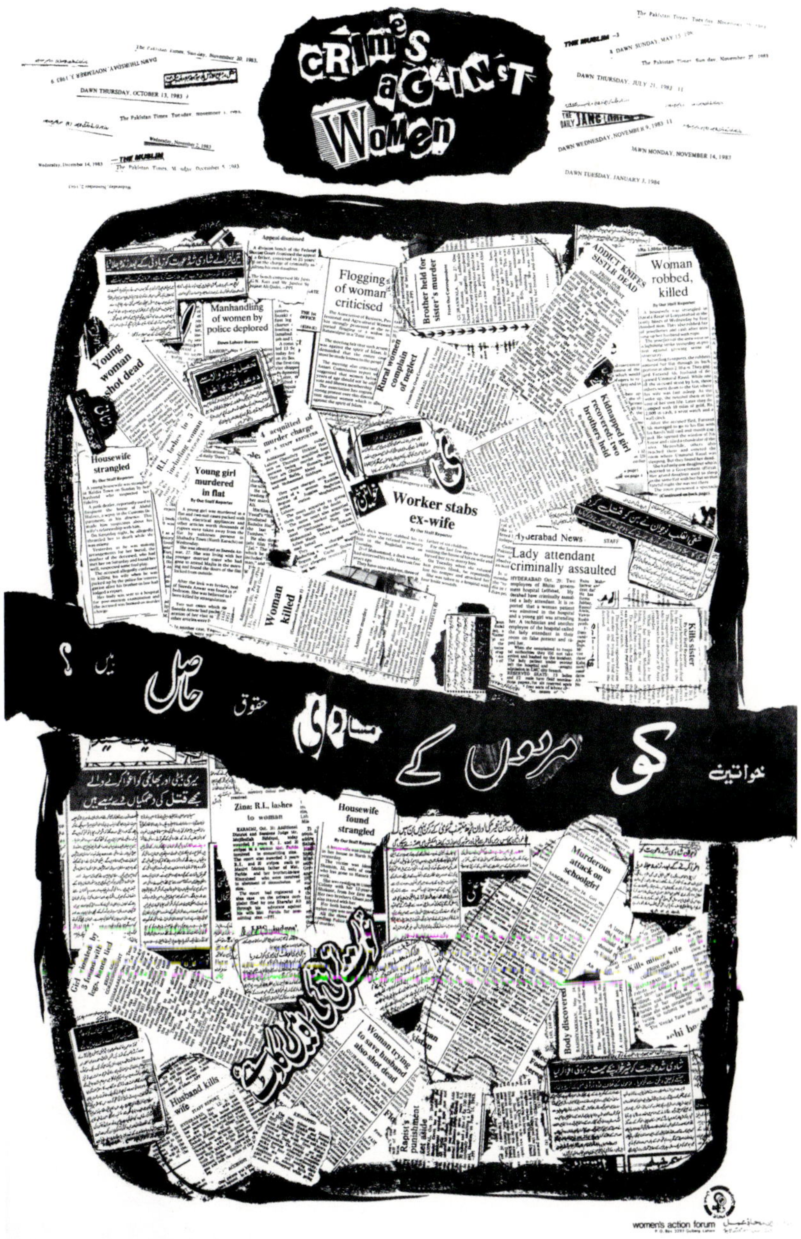

Art-World Activism

by Rachel Warriner

By the end of the 1960s, women artists had begun to interrogate their exclusion from the art world. With the benefit of shared stories and mutual support, artists exposed sexism and racism as systemic, and organized against them. Several groups staged protests and took direct action in a bid to redress the balance.

In October 1971, at the height of the early feminist arts activism emerging in New York, American artist Nancy Spero sent an angry, but succinct, letter to the critic and activist Lucy R. Lippard. In her letter, Spero signed a decree condemning those "enemies" that threatened "women's liberation in the arts," presenting their defeat as an inevitability, not worthy of dissection, but a done deal.

The text, composed on a bulletin typewriter, looks bureaucratic. Typewritten text was, at this time, a formal device in Spero's work. She had adopted it in her *Codex Artaud* (1971–72), interjecting the hysterical subjectivity of the eponymous playwright with fractured and fragmented transcriptions seeking to highlight her own experience of exclusion under patriarchy. In her letter to Lippard, Spero's text is free of mistakes and clearly typed, concisely declaring its message. The sign-off, which proclaims "love," stands in marked contrast to the imagined vanquishing of the foes that are the focus of the letter, suggesting a context in which emotions are heightened and hard lines are drawn between adversaries and allies. Spero's letter offers an insight into the mood in New York among feminist arts activists campaigning to overthrow what they saw as the exclusive and oppressive patriarchal structures of the art world.

When Spero took to her typewriter to compose this letter, the sense that feminism was becoming a real force for change was being felt by many artists involved in the movement. Besides her letter to Lippard, Spero wrote a number of manifestos—similarly angry declarations that proclaimed the end of men's domination of the art world, and in which she talked of "increasingly angry and militant women artists" as those who will bring about change. Those same enraged women artists represent the force that underpins her letter to Lippard. In these short few lines of violent threat and expressions of love, we can see Spero's understanding of this feminist community as being a powerful and united force for change, capable of defeating the old, masculine order. The violence, ambition, and bombast of Spero's letter is symptomatic of the angry optimism of feminists working during the turbulent moment of the late 1960s and early 1970s and is suggestive of the lively activist network from which this challenge to patriarchy was mounted.

". . . art is always viewed in the aggressive histories of male dominance."

Nancy Spero, writing in her *Feminist Manifesto* (1970–71)

Lippard and Spero became friendly through their respective feminist arts-activist commitments, initially coming into contact through meetings of the Art Workers' Coalition. Their first joint action was in the Ad Hoc Women Artists' Committee, formed in 1970, in response to the bias of the 1969 Whitney Annual, in which only eight out of 143 artists represented were women. Using tactics of direct action, including sit-ins, leafleting exhibitions, lobbying curators and museum directors, and protesting the Annual's launch by projecting images of work by women artists onto the Whitney's exterior walls, the Ad Hoc Committee mounted a determined campaign against the art world's bias. It built on the work of the earlier Women Artists in Revolution (formed 1969), of which Spero had been a member. Considering women's experience of the art world, the group worked to forge solidarity between women artists and examined the problem of their exclusion.

Among the many other groups looking to challenge the misogyny of the art world, two—the Women Students and Artists for Black Art Liberation and Where We At: Black Women Artists—sought to address the double exclusion experienced by black women artists.

Other groups, including Women in the Arts and West-East Bag, attempted to raise visibility for women artists by providing spaces for their work to be developed and discussed. The A.I.R. Gallery and SoHo 20 were established as venues for displaying and promoting women's practice. Women working together created new networks and support structures that facilitated feminist art's development and sustained women artists in their pursuit of their careers.

N Y OCT 29

DEAR LUCY

THE ENEMIES OF WOMEN'S LIBERATION IN THE ARTS WILL BE CRUSHED.

LOVE

Nancy

Right: **Nancy Spero's Letter to Lucy R. Lippard, October 1971**

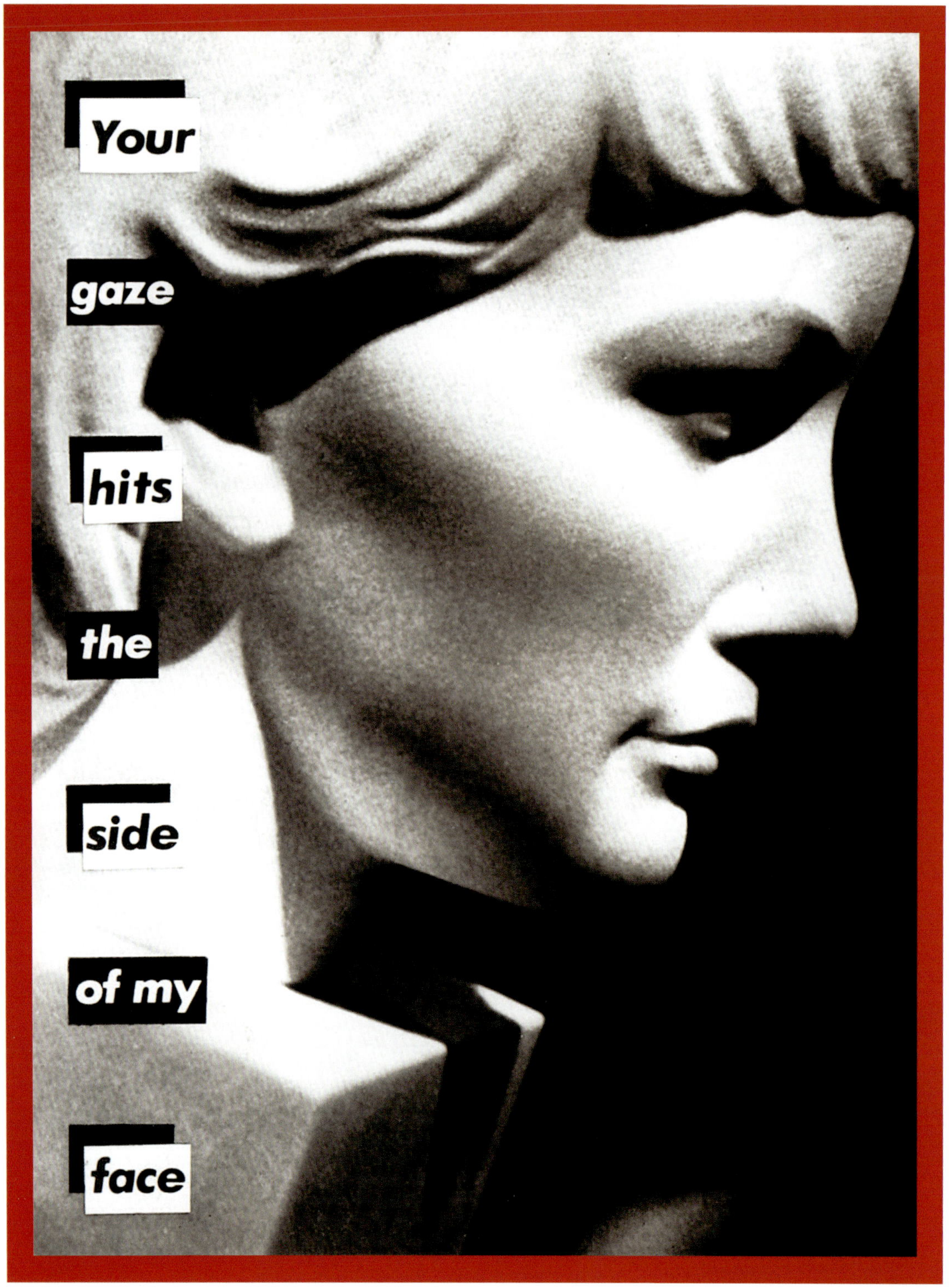

Above: **Barbara Kruger, *Untitled (Your gaze hits the side of my face)*, 1981**

This early photo-collage by the American artist Barbara Kruger incorporates a found image of an unknown portrait bust in raking light with overlaid text: "Your gaze hits the side of my face." The image is strikingly graphic, alluding to the visual languages of advertising and agitprop. However, there is no particular product or cause advertised. Instead, the text seems to speak to the viewer looking at the work, perhaps voicing the feelings of the sculpture. Kruger's use of the word "gaze" relates to contemporary debates around the gendered dynamics of looking and being looked at. The phrase confronts the masculine, probing gaze, which is deflected by the side of the face, here—ironically—made of stone.

Below: Jenny Holzer, *Untitled (Because There is No God)* from Inflammatory Essays, 1983

Inflammatory Essays was a series of street posters, each comprising a number of hundred-word, twenty-line texts on square, colored paper. The essays draw on theoretical texts and arguments from a broad spectrum of extreme views. They are aggressive in tone and were made to be encountered in the streets of Manhattan, New York. Since their original installation, the posters have been shown in museums and galleries, usually pasted directly onto the wall, running from ceiling to floor in a grid. The texts are meant to prompt urgent reactions in their readers, pushing them to act.

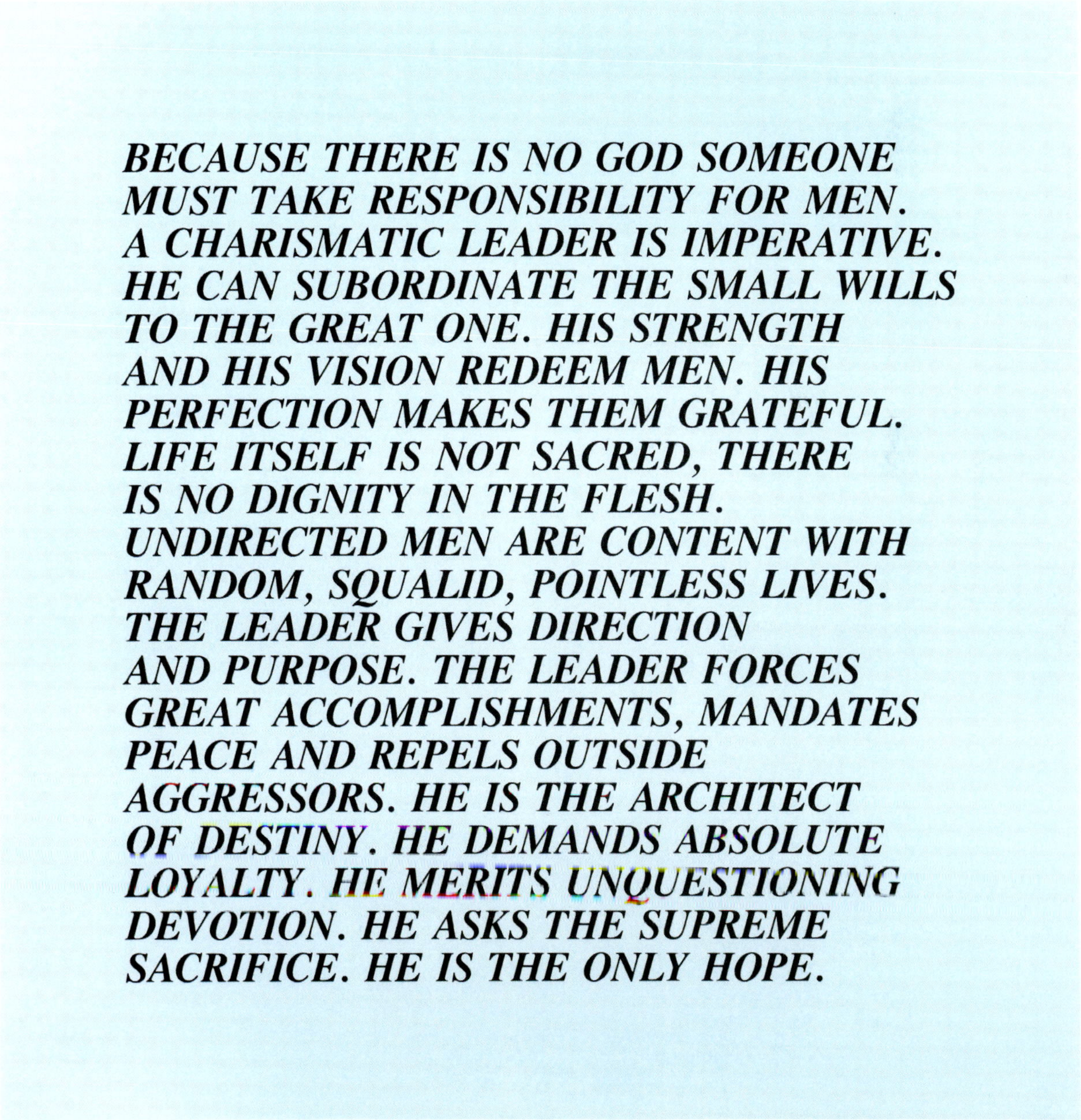

Muses Having Fun

The general strike, student demonstrations, and occupations that swept across France in the summer of 1968 were a public manifestation of a social unrest that had been mounting for years. They provided a platform from which various social groups, not least women activists, could voice their grievances. Out of various feminist activities rose a burgeoning visual culture.

Delphine Seyrig may seem an unlikely entry point into French feminist visual culture. Born in Lebanon and raised in the United States and France, she was a highly acclaimed actress who starred in films by Alain Resnais, Marguerite Duras, and François Truffaut. But alongside this celebrated career in front of the camera—including the title role in Belgian director Chantal Akerman's *Jeanne Dielmann*—Seyrig was also a director, an activist, and an organizer. She was a public feminist in the 1970s and—like prominent theorists that included Simone de Beauvoir and Christine Delphy in France, Kate Millett in the United States, and Germaine Greer in the United Kingdom—she used her status to spread a message. Seyrig did not just speak or write a feminist message, she was also successfully engaged in cultural production and distribution. This activism was important because, by making her own films and videos as well as organizing distribution channels and protesting, Seyrig could shift the representational terrain of women's lives and defiantly establish her own political identity.

Alongside Ioana Wieder and Carole Roussopoulos, Delphine Seyrig was a member of the women's video collective *Les Insoumuses* that later became *Les muses s'amusent*, which translates as "the muses are having fun." The group used a Sony Portapack camera to film protests, as well as to make incendiary and anarchic, issue-based documentaries and experimental videos. In contrast to film cameras that required more stock and processing, the Sony Portapack, which was light and easy to carry and operate, allowed footage to be shot, played back, and erased. It was also associated with the avant-garde cinema of France's leading director, Jean Luc Godard.

As Ros Murray has argued, the collective's reference to "muses" is a reversal of the passive role played by the figure of the muse in the mythical understanding of the creative process, and a troubling of the roles directors like Godard gave to actresses. No longer solely the inspiration, the collective's name suggested a break with, and the subversion of, tradition. This dissidence paralleled the mood of social unrest evident in the *Mouvement de libération des femmes* (MLF) and throughout France after May 1968. The political events of that summer were not only organized in protest of poor working conditions and pay, but more generally, as a critique of broader social conditions under President Charles de Gaulle. Although the uprisings had largely been quashed by late summer, the social critique of the movement had prompted women activists to protest their social status—particularly their access to contraception and abortion—as well as legal autonomy. Between May 1971 and June 1973 the MLF journal *Torchon Brûle!* was published at the School of Fine Arts, Paris, every Wednesday. With a print run in the thousands, it was a useful tool of consciousness-raising and communication. In August 1970, MLF activists, including Christine Delphy, participated in a particularly spectacular action, in which they processed through Paris streets to lay a floral tribute to the "unknown wife of the unknown soldier" at the Tomb of the Unknown Soldier. As an act of feminist *détournement*, the action paid tribute to women's lives lost to history, as well as lives curtailed by the conservative social arrangement of the family. Beyond this act of symbolic civic disobedience, Delphy also theorized the housewife as an economic subject in her influential book *Main Enemy: A Materialist Analysis of Women's Oppression*, published in English in 1977. In 1981 she also founded the journal *Nouvelles questions féministes* with Simone de Beauvoir.

In 1971 the *Gouines rouge* (Red Dykes) was formed by lesbian feminists including Delphy and the writer Monique Wittig. The group was part of the MLF and the *Front homosexuel d'action révolutionnaire* (FHAR). While FHAR had provided a space for gay and lesbian activism and political organizing against bourgeois heterosexuality, and had close affiliation with the MLF, *Gouines rouge* was organized in response to the "double movement of revolt of women and homosexuals," and guarded against the disappearance of lesbians within FHAR as the organization swelled. *Gouines rouges* continued under the rubric of the MLF until 1973, when it dissolved. Other groups took up the debate, most notably the *Groupe Lesbiennes de Jussieu* who argued for lesbian separatism. Their 1979 poster shows a city suburb ruptured by a stream of tightly looped text, spelling "*lesbiennes*."

The Argentine-French artist Lea Lublin enacted her own protest actions. In May 1968, while unrest raged, she participated in the annual May Salon at the Musée d'Art Moderne, Paris. Rather than submit work, she occupied the gallery with her son. *Mon Fils* saw her perform the various tasks of parental care in the museum as an exhibit. After making this work, Lublin moved beyond the museum, asking provocative questions to passersby and recording the interactions via closed-circuit cameras. In *Dissolution dans l'eau* (1978), Lublin printed some of these questions on a large banner-like white sheet, which she then waved through the streets like a flag, before dropping it from the Pont Marie in Paris, where it floated on the surface of the water and then sank. As the questions disappear from view, their stereotypical accusations were laid to rest.

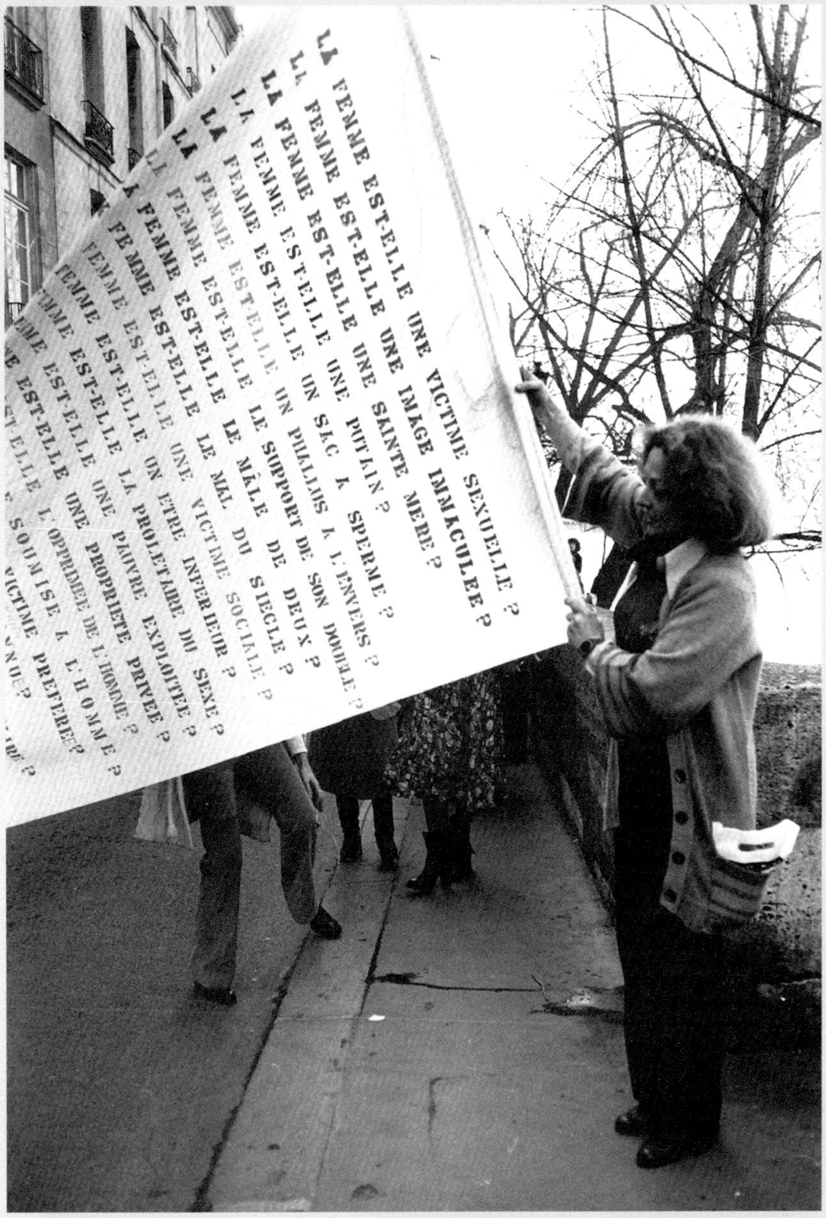

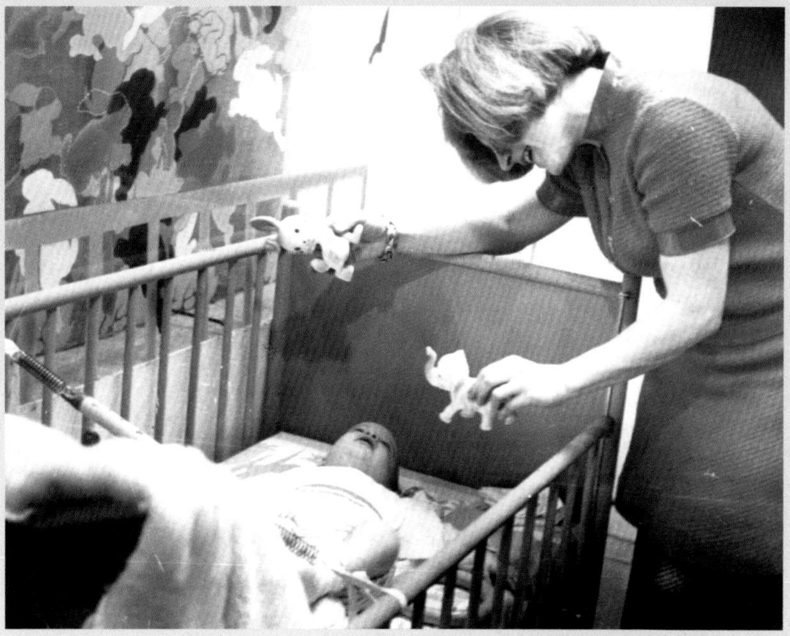

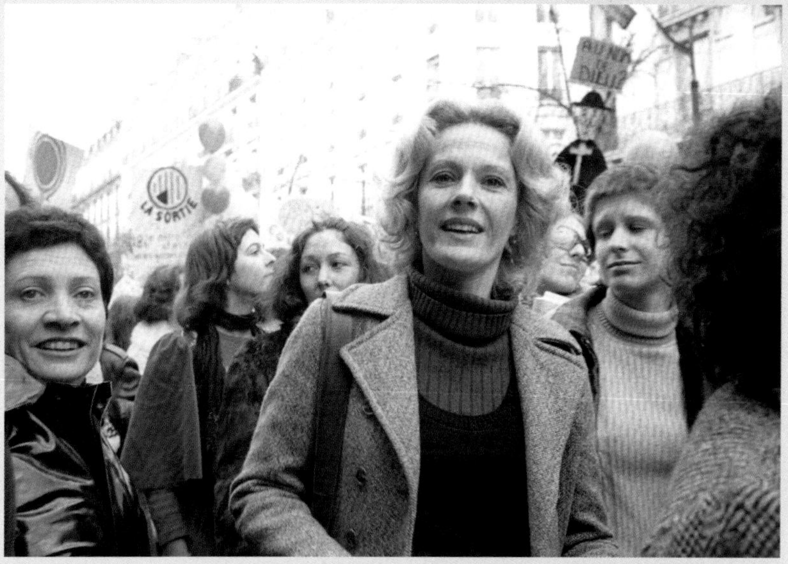

"The woman is she a sexual victim?"
"The woman is she a saintly mother?"
"The woman is she stupid?"

Some of the questions posed by Lea Lublin's *Dissolution dans l'eau*, 1978

Left: **Lea Lublin, *Dissolution dans l'eau*, 1978**

Top right: **Lea Lublin, *Mon Fils*, 1968**

Bottom right: Delphine Seyrig participates in a women's demonstration.

Below left: **Thalia Campbell, postcard of Greenham Common Women's Peace Camp banner, 1984**

In September 1981 a group of women began a protest against the siting of nuclear weapons on RAF Greenham Common in Berkshire, England. After a march to Greenham a number of women chained themselves to the fences of the RAF base and established a camp there. By February 1982 the camp had been designated for women only. Despite many violent evictions, it lasted until 2000. The women of the Greenham Common Peace Camp not only protested against the presence of nuclear weapons and the political games that threatened nuclear war, but also against the use of common land, which is protected from private ownership and enclosure in English law. This banner was designed by one of the peace camp members Thalia Campbell. Campbell made banners to communicate the demands of the peace activists and displayed them on the fence of the RAF base.

Below right: **Lotta Femminista poster (Feminist Struggle), 1973**

This poster advertises the cause of the Lotta Femminista, or Feminist Struggle, a group of women activists connected to the Wages for Housework campaign in Italy in the early 1970s. It depicts a woman trapped within the shape of a house. The Italian text below this declares, "Against domestic work that sustains the world but suffocates and limits women." The International Wages for Housework movement was founded in Padua, Italy, in 1972, by Selma James, Brigitte Galtier, Mariarosa Dalla Costa, and Silvia Federici. A feminist economic movement, informed by the Marxism of both the Italian "Workerists" (*operaismo*) and the American and Trindadian decolonialist and Black Power movements, Wages for Housework asserted that domestic labor was a massive, invisible part of the economy. They argued that women should receive a wage for their housework, and as such be involved in the larger struggle for fair working conditions.

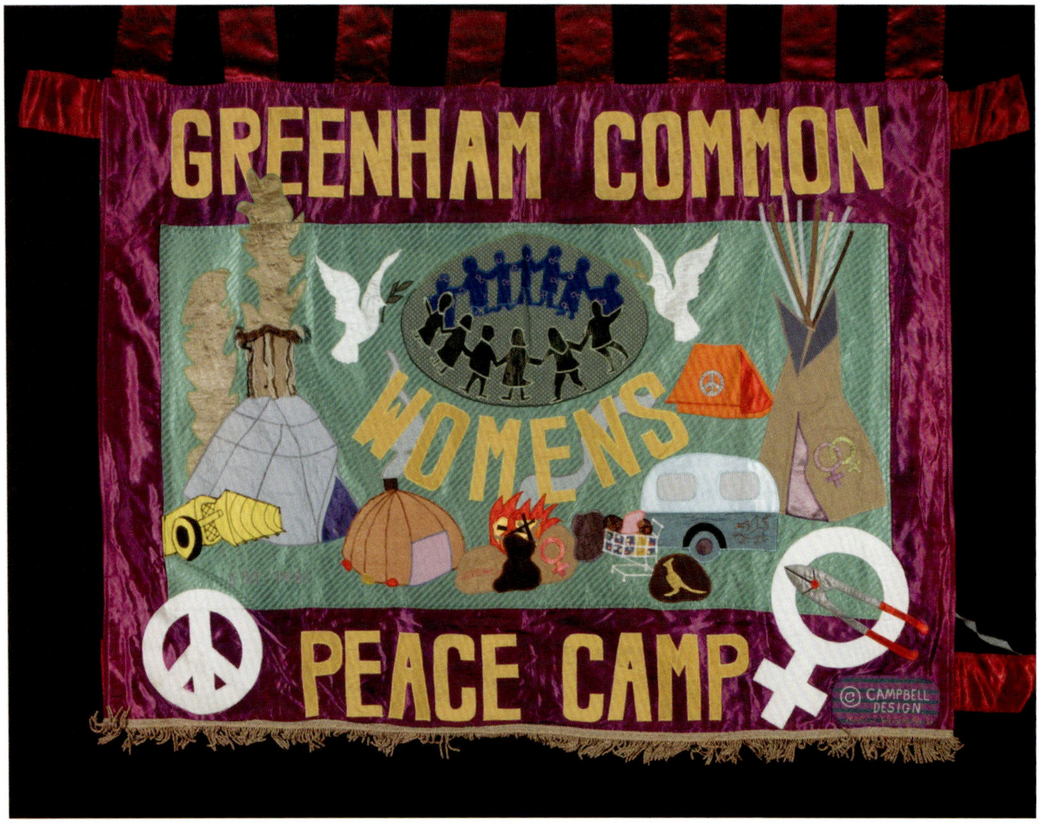

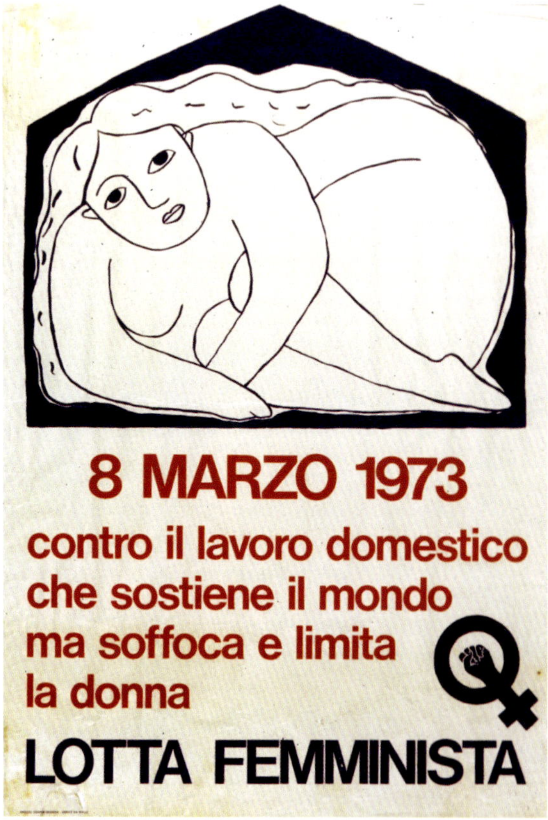

Top: **Hengameh Golestan, Women's Unity protest, 1979**

Hengameh Golestan is an Iranian photographer. Born in 1952, between 1974 and 1984 she worked documenting everyday life in Iran, before moving to London. Her work focused on the lives of women and children, and in 1979 she photographed scenes of the Iranian Revolution. This photograph was taken during the Women's Unity protest on March 8, 1979, which saw 100,000 women occupy public space against legislature to make the hijab compulsory.

Bottom: Swiss women demonstrate to have the vote, on January 27, 1971.

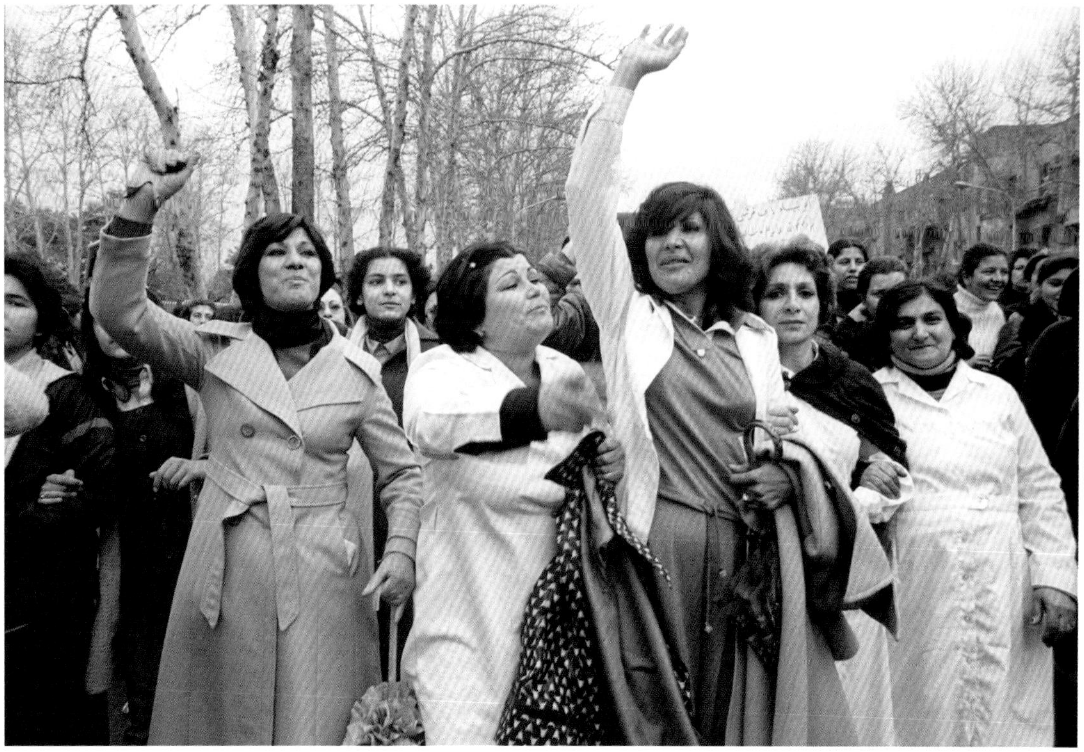

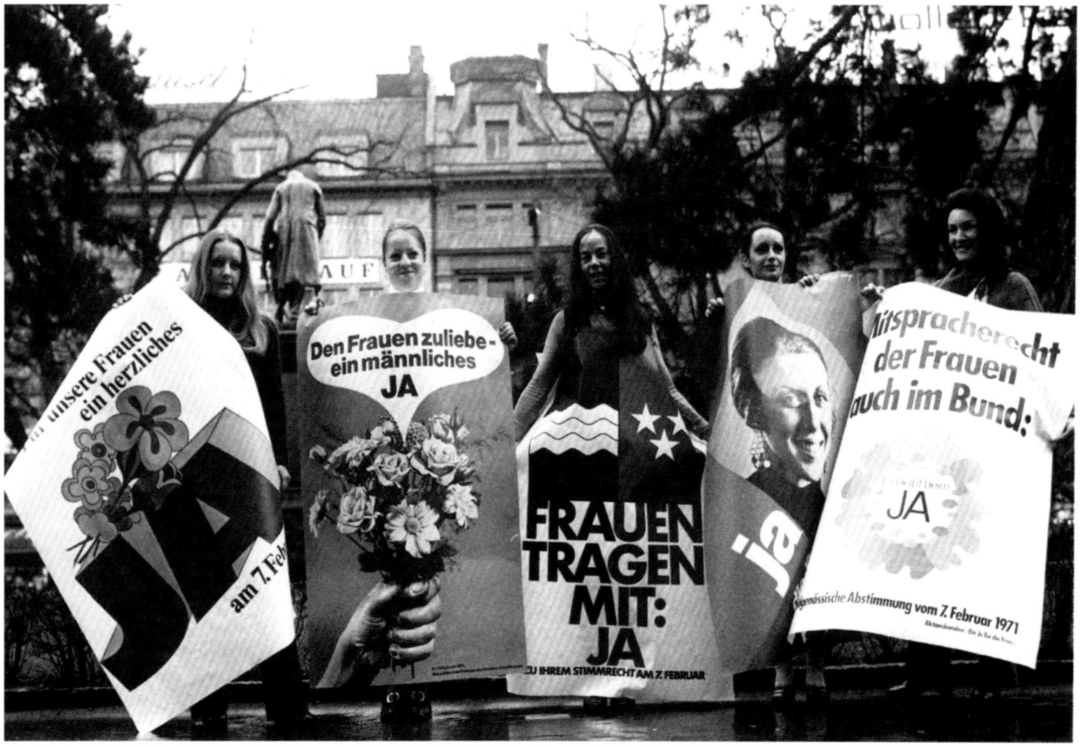

Defiant Confrontation

by Alice Correia

In 1988, *Along the Lines of Resistance: An Exhibition of Contemporary Feminist Art* opened at the Cooper Art Gallery in Barnsley, England. While the exhibiting artists voiced different concerns and addressed different oppressions, the exhibition sought to highlight a single shared expression: that of defiant confrontation.

Curated by Sutapa Biswas, Sarah Edge, and Claire Slattery, the exhibition showcased the work of twenty young women artists, including Chila Kumari Burman, Sonia Boyce, Mona Hatoum, and Monica Ross. By selecting artists from a variety of social, political, and cultural backgrounds, the curators recognized the plurality of feminist voices in a genre that had previously been dominated by the white middle classes. More significantly, perhaps, the exhibition highlighted the necessity for diverse feminist art practices in the face of Thatcherite politics, which sought to shut down opposition and protest, and made institutional attempts to curtail and historicize the feminist movement itself. The curators noted that, by the late 1980s, feminist art was regarded as "yet another category or movement to be named, contained, and passed over."

Central to the exhibition was a concern with "public and private violence," whether in the form of war, colonial oppression, or everyday racism. As such, work detailing the experiences of women during the Northern Irish "Troubles," including Anne Tallentire's performance *Altered Tracks* (1988) and Trisha Ferguson's etchings *Ireland 1, 2, 3* (undated), occupied a shared space of resistance with Maud Sulter and Lubaina Himid's joint installation, *A Room for MaShulan* (1988), addressing the legacies of colonialism within the African diaspora. One of the most notable works in this exhibition was Chila Kumari Burman's mixed-media diptych *Convenience Not Love* (1986–87), which focused on the treatment of South Asian women by U.K. immigration officials and the forms of control exerted over their bodies by the state.

The two parts of Burman's work engage in a dialogue about the nature of Britishness and female agency. The left-hand panel is divided into two sections, respectively dominated by an old-style, navy-blue British passport, and the photo-silk-screened figure of then prime minister, Margaret Thatcher, standing in front of a Union flag, on a golden ground. A vivid green speech bubble expands from her mouth, repeating a statement she made in 1978: "That if there's any fear that it might be SWAMPED people are going to react and be rather HOSTILE"; in her comment Thatcher was referring to the apparent fears of ordinary—that is, white—British people that their country might be swamped with foreigners if immigration was not rigorously controlled.

If the left-hand panel contains imagery of "Britishness," the right-hand panel is a visually excessive rendering of "South Asia," comprising hand-drawn vignettes recounting the tribulations of migration, family photographs, and a mass of found media imagery presenting historic and contemporaneous South Asian figures, circulating around a row of passports from Sri Lanka, Pakistan, India, and Bangladesh. Burman has utilized the diptych format to establish not only a visual conversation between the two geographic spaces, but to make explicit the racism and inequalities faced by the South Asian diaspora in Britain. Asian migrants are kept at a distance from Britain's golden lands by Thatcher's protective stance, a skein of barbed wire, and—if required—a swarm of riot police located on the far left.

Art historian Lynda Nead asserted in 1995 that *Convenience, Not Love* "deals with immigration laws and the virginity tests that determined the entry of Asian women into Britain." This interpretation is supported by the inclusion, in the right-hand panel, of a hand-drawn cartoon strip that narrates the demeaning and humiliating treatment of South Asian women seeking to join their husbands or fiancés already living in the United Kingdom. Burman recounts the practice of "virginity testing," controversially exposed on February 1, 1979, by *The Guardian* newspaper: On January 24, a 35-year-old Indian woman arriving at Heathrow Airport had been subjected to an internal medical examination, to determine whether or not she had previously had children. On the basis of this information, it was believed possible to determine whether or not she was still a virgin, and on the basis of this so-called virginity test, her application to enter the United Kingdom to marry her fiancé was deemed legitimate. That Asian women were treated with suspicion is made explicit in the title of the work: It was believed that women would marry and come to the United Kingdom on the basis of convenience, not love—that they would do anything to get a British passport. And even if citizenship were granted, the reception of new migrants to Britain was hostile.

In the right-hand panel of Burman's work, alongside the more prosaic images of women washing clothes, cooking, and laughing together, Burman included images of Lakshmibai, the Rani of Jhansi, pictured on horseback. In 1857, Lakshmibai led an Indian rebellion against the British in imperial India. There is also a hand-tinted press photograph of a picket line of striking female workers at the Grunwick Film Processing Laboratory, North London, from 1976–78. In their unambiguous affirmation of female agency, Burman's aggregated community of women challenges stereotypical assumptions of South Asian womanhood as meek and passive. The multiplicity of collaged images is disruptive and dynamic: Harnessing the material and formal qualities of her assemblage technique, Burman illustrates the impossibility of pinning down South Asian femininity.

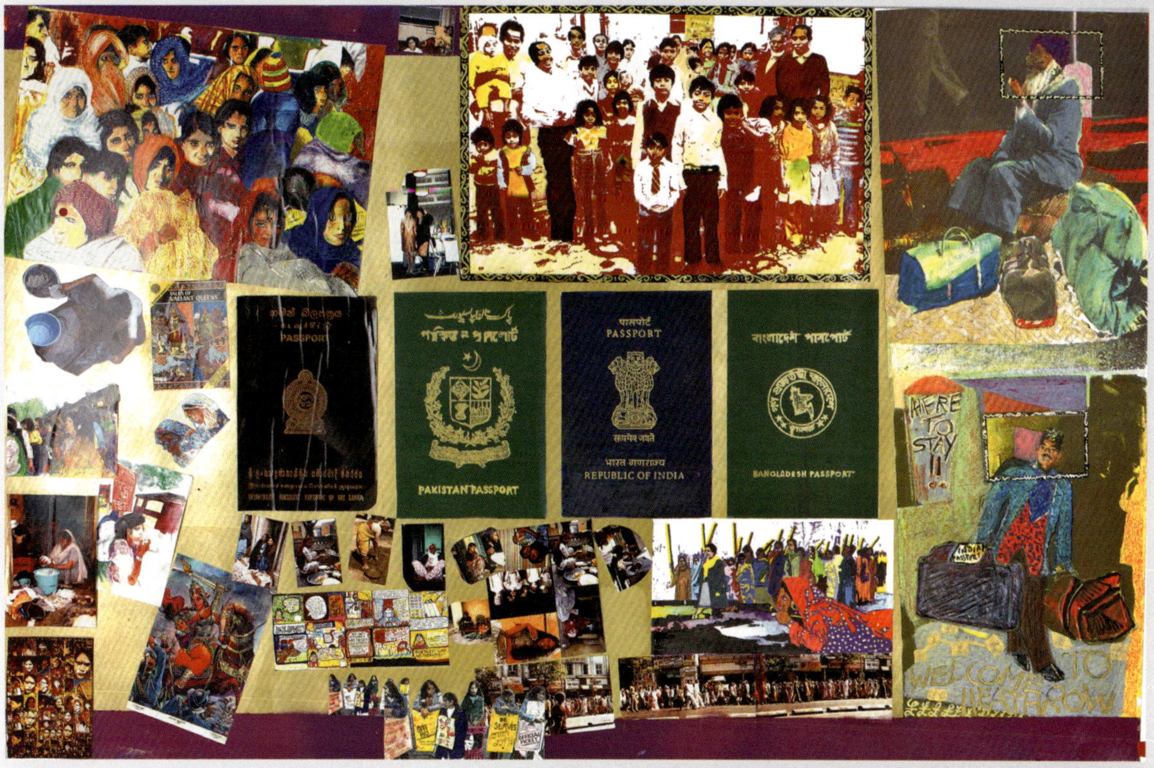

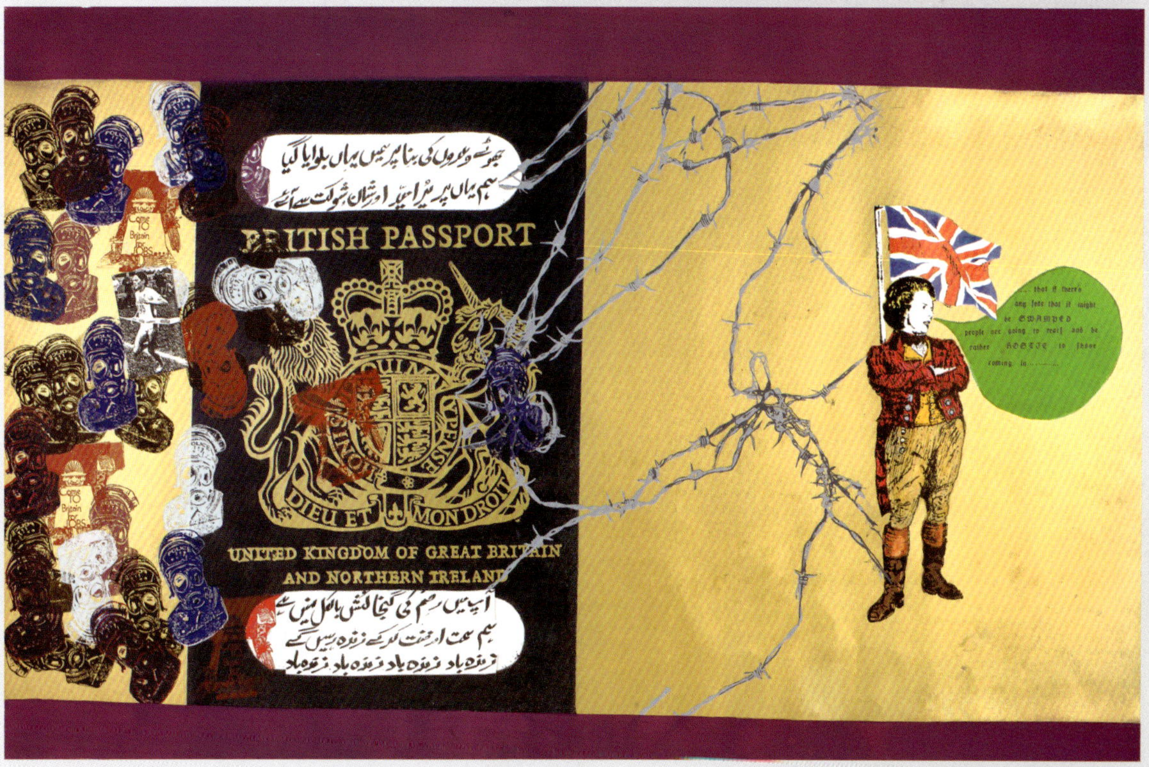

"You allow us to come here on false promises. We come here full of hope and destiny. You have no mercy. We will struggle and survive. Long live. Long live. Long live."

Translation of the Urdu text that features in the windows of the British passport in Burman's *Convenience, Not Love*

This page: **Chila Kumari Burman, *Convenience Not Love*, 1986–87**

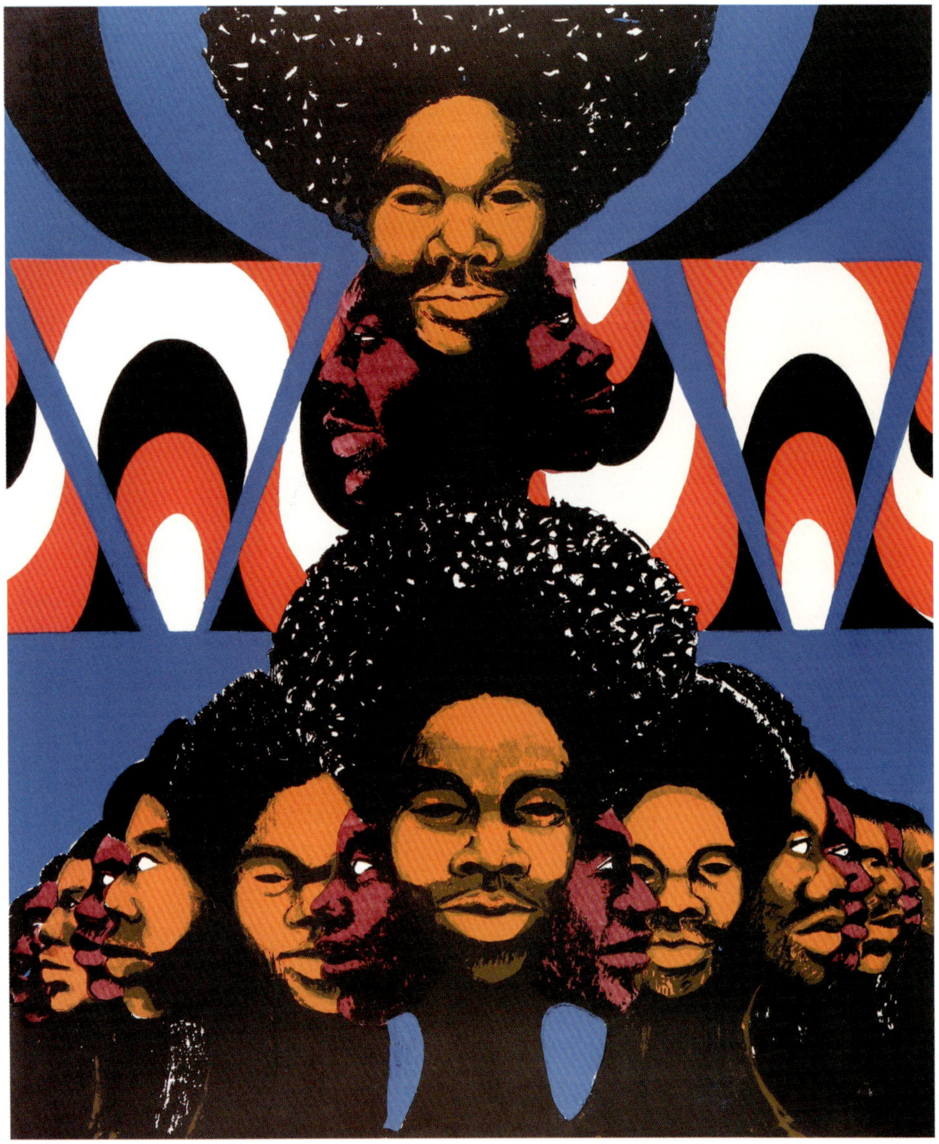

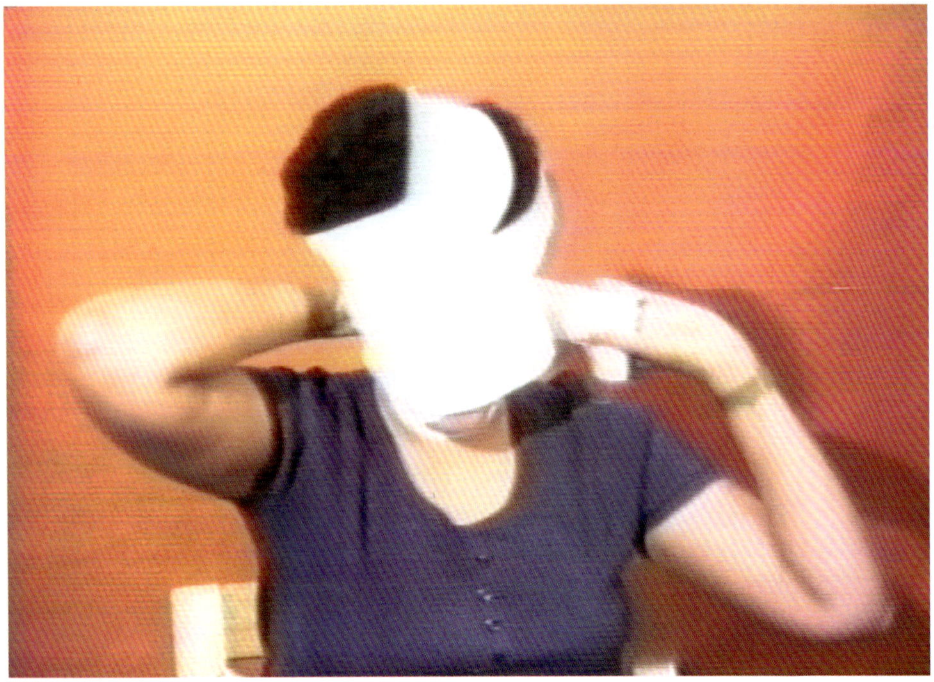

Top left: **Barbara Jones-Hogu, *High Priestess*, 1971**

Barbara Jones-Hogu studied painting, drawing, and printmaking at the School of the Art Institute of Chicago in 1964, and an MSc in printmaking at the Institute of Design, Illinois Institute of Technology in 1970. This silk-screen print was made in the studio at the Institute of Design, at which time Jones-Hogu cofounded the African Commune of Bad Relevant Artists, known as AfriCOBRA, and began making prints as part of that collective. *High Priestess* celebrates powerful black women and speaks to contemporary black feminism. The central, elevated face is supported by two figures in profile, and by a series of faces in the lower row. Although these faces fit into a pattern—they are alternately orange and purple in color—their features are all different and seem to represent both men and women. The blue, red, white, and black background relates to the United States flag, and to Jones-Hogu's prints, *Nation Time* and *Unite* (both 1971).

Bottom left: **Howardena Pindell, *Free, White and 21*, 1980, still**

Free, White and 21 is a sixteen-minute video, and Pindell's first work in this medium. During the 1970s Pindell had lived in New York, working at the Museum of Modern Art (MoMA), and making abstract canvases at night. Pindell made this work during a time of reflection following a serious car accident. Pindell appears as both herself and made up as a white woman. When she appears on screen, she recounts instances of racism that either she or her mother had experienced while living in the still-segregated American South in the 1940s and 1950s. She also recounts racism in the art world and the women's movement. The white woman character responds to her stories, at first showing false sympathy, and increasingly becoming more hostile. The video was first shown at the all-women collective gallery A.I.R.

Below right: **Elizabeth Catlett, *Phillis Wheatley*, 1973**

Elizabeth Catlett studied at Howard University, Washington, D.C., graduating in 1937. In the 1940s she lived between Harlem and Chicago, participating in the movements for black art and culture in both cities. In 1946 she moved to Mexico, where she lived and worked for the rest of her life. Catlett worked in both printmaking and sculpture. Her work focused on social and political issues, and particularly on the histories of race and gender oppression in the United States. Phillis Wheatley (1753–84) was the first African-American woman to have her poetry published.

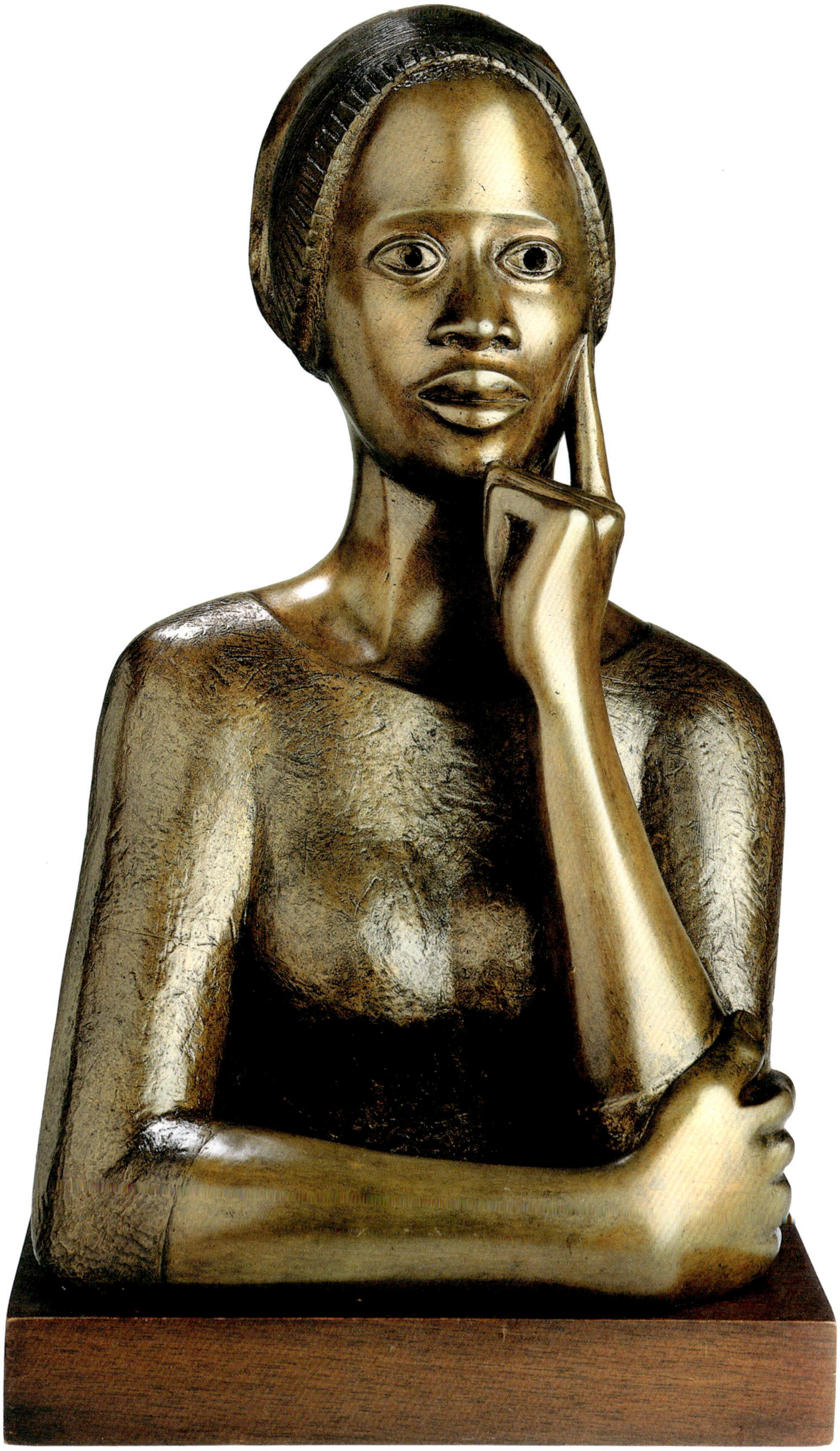

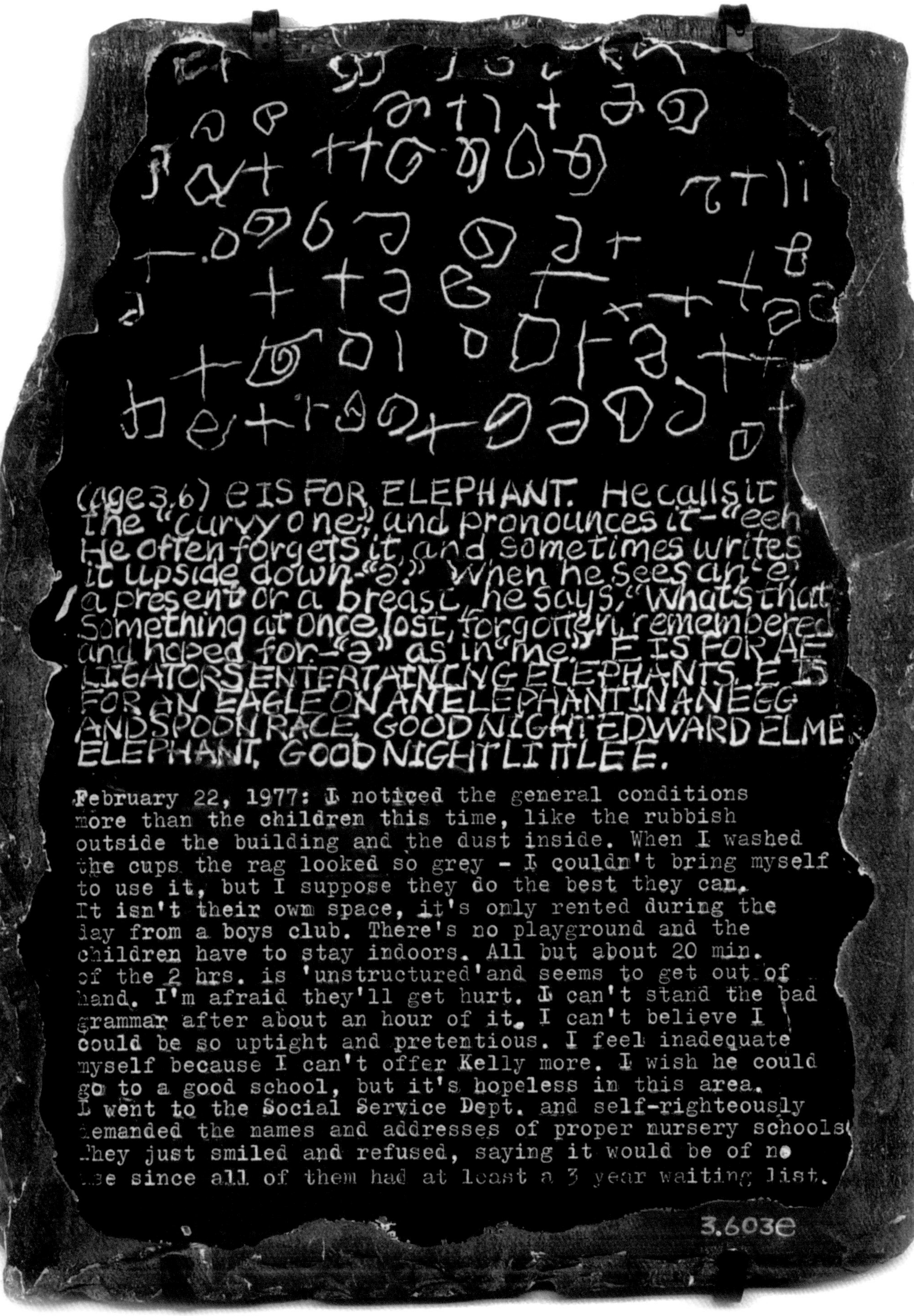
(age 3.6) e IS FOR ELEPHANT. He calls it the "curvy one", and pronounces it – "eeh He often forgets it, and sometimes writes it upside down – "ə". When he sees an "e", a present or a breast, he says, "What's that Something at once lost, forgotten, remembered and hoped for – "ə" as in "me". E IS FOR AL LIGATORS ENTERTAINING ELEPHANTS. E IS FOR AN EAGLE ON AN ELEPHANT IN AN EGG AND SPOON RACE. GOOD NIGHT EDWARD ELME ELEPHANT. GOOD NIGHT LITTLE E.
February 22, 1977: I noticed the general conditions more than the children this time, like the rubbish outside the building and the dust inside. When I washed the cups the rag looked so grey – I couldn't bring myself to use it, but I suppose they do the best they can. It isn't their own space, it's only rented during the day from a boys club. There's no playground and the children have to stay indoors. All but about 20 min. of the 2 hrs. is 'unstructured' and seems to get out of hand. I'm afraid they'll get hurt. I can't stand the bad grammar after about an hour of it. I can't believe I could be so uptight and pretentious. I feel inadequate myself because I can't offer Kelly more. I wish he could go to a good school, but it's hopeless in this area. I went to the Social Service Dept. and self-righteously demanded the names and addresses of proper nursery schools. They just smiled and refused, saying it would be of no use since all of them had at least a 3 year waiting list.
3.603e

Finding Feminist History

Refiguring the Past

7

". . . woman must write her self: must write about women and bring women to writing, from which they have been driven away as violently as from their bodies."

French philosopher, Hélène Cixous, in her essay "*Le Rire de la Meduse*" ("The Laugh of the Medusa"), 1975

Alongside the personal stories shared in the consciousness-raising (CR) group, the early years of women's liberation saw women embark on research to retrace lives lost to history. One of the first women's liberation events in Britain was organized by the historian Sally Alexander with Arielle Aberson at Ruskin College in Oxford, and one of the most influential reading groups of the British movement was called the History Group. As group member Sally Alexander has recalled, it set out to ask, "What was the source of women's oppression?" Over the decade, feminist politics transformed the scholarly field of history. Research was also taken up by amateurs anxious to find voices silenced by the patriarchal concerns of canonical history. And so, along with refuges, campaigns for wages for housework, for nurseries, and for abortion legislation, women formed research groups, established new courses at colleges and universities, and set up archives. Just as CR provided the means for women to recognize one another's oppression and humanity, so feminist history provided precedent and context. Historical research was made political in this moment, because it showed the erasure of women's lives, and reclaimed those stories for the present.

Such research was important for artists and art historians, particularly after the publication of Linda Nochlin's 1971 article, "Why Have There Been No Great Women Artists?". Nochlin's essay explored the social, cultural, and economic conditions that had kept women from accessing artistic "greatness." The article discussed the impossibility of a woman training as a painter in a Renaissance studio or of completing life-drawing experience in the age of the academy. It was more difficult for a woman to travel and, as Griselda Pollock argued in her book *Vision and Difference* (1988), to experience the city in the ideal mode of the *flâneur*—a prerequisite for the great impressionists. These analytic unpackings of the conditions of "greatness" were paralleled with extensive research into women artists. Nochlin worked alongside students in her groundbreaking class at Vassar College, New York, finding the names of, and researching the lives of, historic women artists. At the same time, Pollock was a member of the Feminist Art History Group in London, with scholars, writers, and artists Denise Cale, Pat Kahn, Tina Keane, Rozsika Parker, Alene Straussberg, Lisa Tickner, and Anne de Winter. The group supported research into women artists, organized syllabuses, and taught.

Historical research supported exhibitions of women's art, including Nochlin and Ann Sutherland Harris's iconic *Women Artists 1500–1955* (1976), which originated at Los Angeles County Museum of Art and toured to Austin, Pittsburgh, Philadelphia, and Brooklyn, New York. This ambitious historical display was conceived as a starting point for more focused exhibitions on particular periods, themes, and artists. It foreshadowed many other exhibitions, including those of contemporary artists' work, such as *Women of Sweetgrass, Cedar and Sage* (1985), curated by artists Harmony Hammond and Jaune Quick-to-See Smith, which focused on work by contemporary Native American feminist artists. The art in this exhibition presented a different relationship to history and tradition, as the critic Nancy Luomala wrote in her review of the show: "This is not formula art . . . but a deeply rooted, knowing art that comes from centuries of women working with images from a collective Native North American knowledge."

Many artists brought historical awareness into their artworks, articulating the trauma of loss and the pleasure of reclamation. In *Litany for Women Artists* (1977), British-Irish artist Hannah O'Shea collated the names of women artists, ordered them alphabetically, and sang their names to the lilt of a Catholic litany during one-hour shows. O'Shea's performance powerfully evidenced the sheer number of women artists, many of whom had been all but lost from the art-historical record. By singing their names, drawing them out across the long notes of the litany, she also invoked their presence, as if calling them to the present. In this way her performance registered as both loss and celebration.

An examination of the representation of women in art paralleled that of their isolation from the means of its production. Many artists sought to describe the violent limits of iconographies such as the female nude, the Mary Magdelene, and the Madonna. In her 1975 video *Glauben Sie nicht, dass ich eine Amazone bin* (*Do Not Think I am an Amazon*), the German artist Ulrike Rosenbach performed the violence of images. The video shows a close-up view of a reproduction of a virgin, eventually the image appears to move and we see an image of the artist's face superimposed onto the haloed head. Then arrows begin to hit the virgin, and we see the Amazon-like artist load and aim her bow. Of course, as the arrows pierce the virgin, they also pierce the artist, suggesting that both figures—the virgin and the Amazon—are destructive.

Perhaps the best-known attack on artistic representations of women is the Guerrilla Girls' poster, *Do women have to be naked to get into the Met. Museum?* (1989). The anonymous

Page 136: **Mary Kelly, *Post-Partum Document: Documentation VI Pre-Writing Alphabet, Exergue and Diary*, 1978**

This is one element of a multipart installation in six sections titled *Post-Partum Document*, made between 1973 and 1979. Mary Kelly made this piece while she was living and working in London, after the birth of her son. The work is a nonfigurative exploration of the mother-child relationship, focusing on important moments in a child's development and analyzed through psychoanalytic theory. Earlier parts of the work—including baby clothes and soiled diapers—caused outrage in the British tabloid press when they were shown at the Institute of Contemporary Arts (ICA) in London in 1976. This part of the work comprises a slate mounted on white card and displayed in a plexiglass box. The three bands of text show Kelly's son's attempts to write the letter "e," Kelly's description of this process in her handwriting, and an apparently typewritten diary entry. Together the texts document the child's emergence into language.

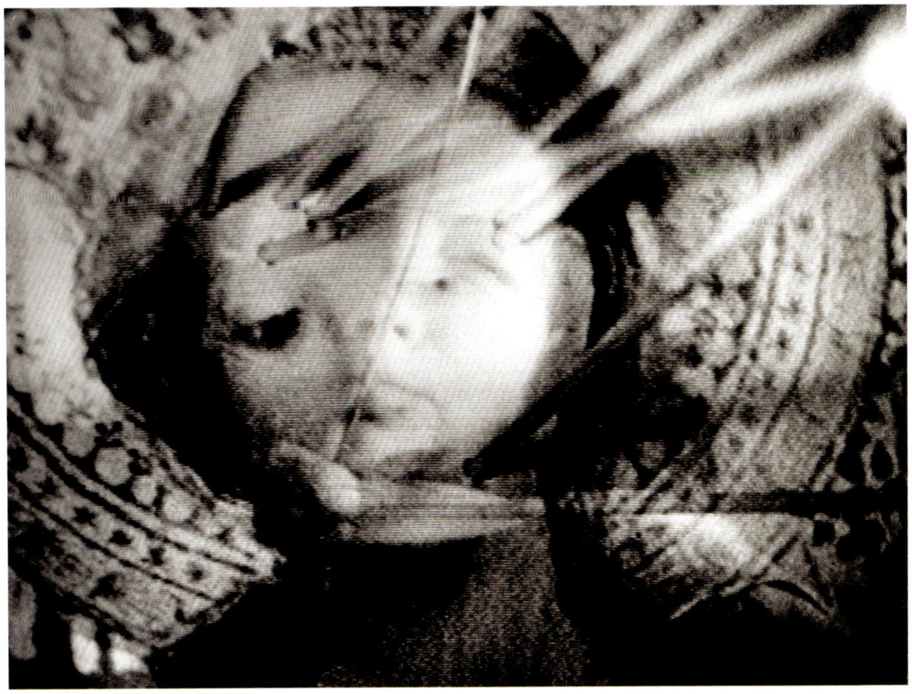

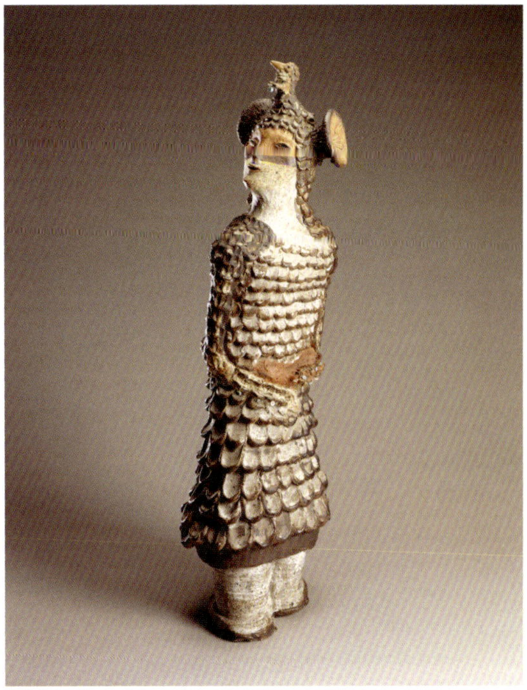

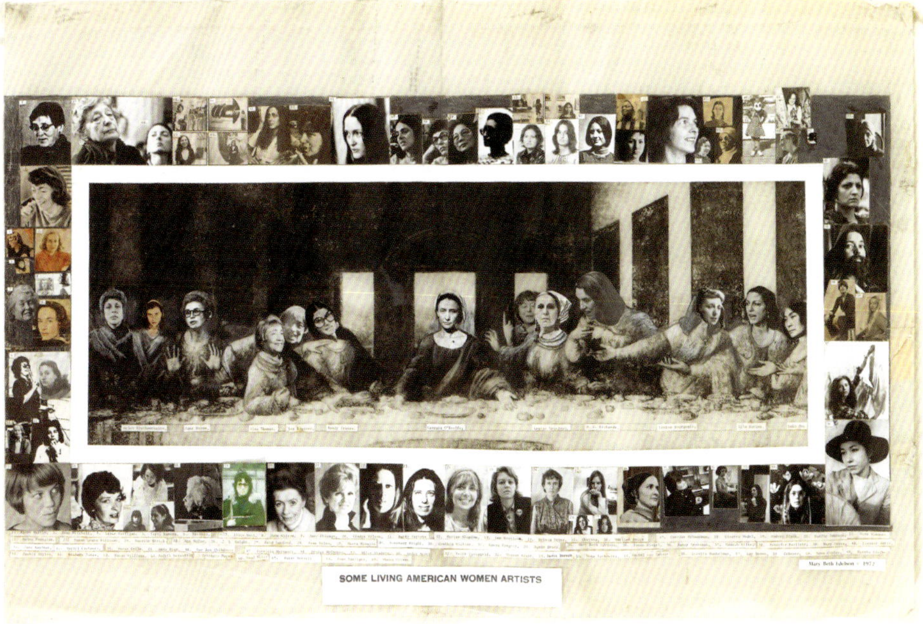

Top left: Ulrike Rosenbach, *Glauben Sie nicht, dass ich eine Amazone bin* (*Do Not Think I am an Amazon*), 1975, still

Glauben Sie nicht, dass ich eine Amazone bin was a live video performance in which Rosenbach performed, while two cameras recorded and relayed the action on a video screen. The performance comprised Rosenbach as an Amazon shooting arrows into an image of the *Madonna im Rosenhag* (1451) by Stefan Lochner. The camera recorded Rosenbach's face, and the face of the Madonna, and the two images were superimposed on a single monitor so that the artist's face merged with the holy Virgin. When the arrows hit, they hit both the face of the artist and the painting. The artist has said that this work is part of the analysis of the "cultural image of the woman in history."

Top right: Otellie Loloma, *Bird Woman*, 1962

Bird Woman is a clay sculpture of a woman attired in symbols associated with action in the Hopi tradition. The figure has traditional moccasins, a bird headdress with turquoise and shell *heishi*, and butterfly hair whorls that signify a maiden status. The bird and the butterfly were both important symbols that could represent movement and magic for the Hopi. Otellie Loloma was born in 1921 and trained in ceramics at Alfred University, New York, in 1945. In the late 1950s she established the Kiva Craft Center with her husband Charles Loloma, and then joined the Institute of American Indian Arts, Santa Fe, New Mexico, in 1962.

Bottom: Mary Beth Edelson, *Some Living American Women Artists*, 1971

This photo-collage by the American artist Mary Beth Edelson is part of a series of iconoclastic works on paper dating from the early 1970s. The image juxtaposed a reproduction of Leonardo's *The Last Supper* with portraits of North American women artists. Each of the thirteen figures is transformed, with a new identity, with a further seventy portraits framing the edge. This work is one of a number of collages including one featuring the members of A.I.R. gallery, titled *Death of the Patriarchy/A.I.R. Anatomy Lesson* (1976). *Some Living American Women Artists* was included in an exhibition called *22 Others* at the Henri Gallery, Washington, D.C., in 1973, which comprised work prompted by other artists' suggestions.

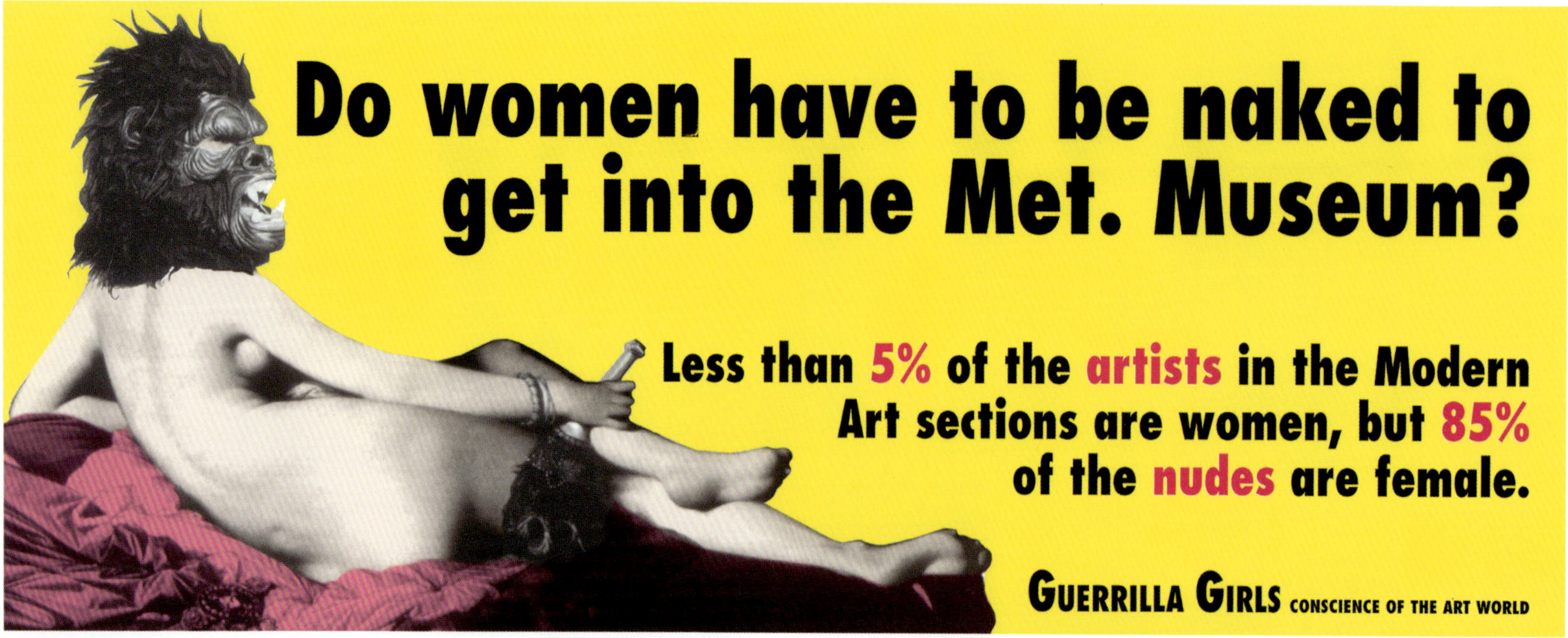

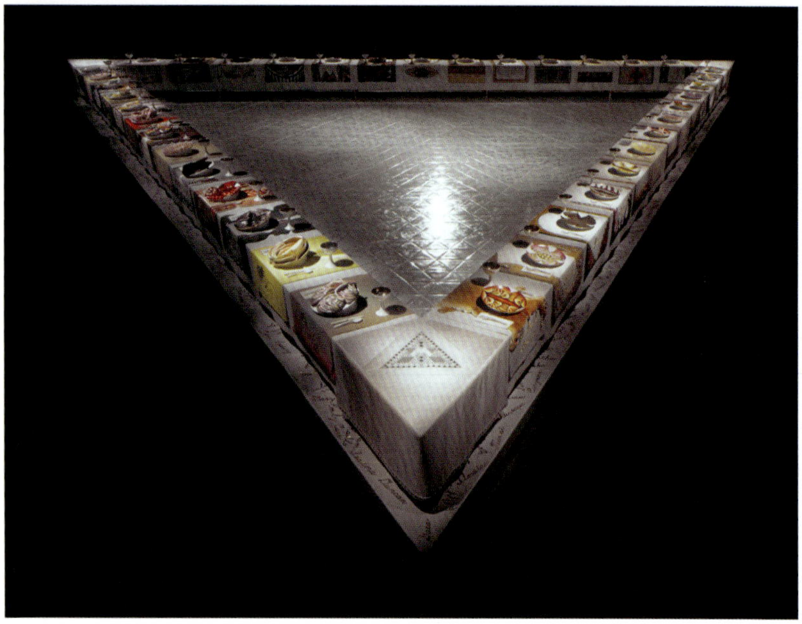

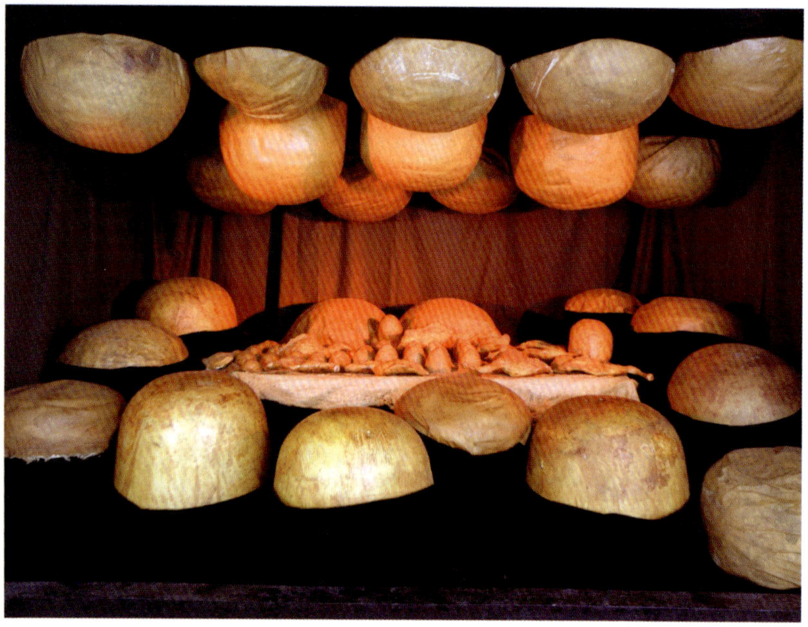

Top: **Guerrilla Girls, *Do women have to be naked to get into the Met. Museum?*, 1989**

The Met poster, which reimagines Jean-Auguste-Dominique Ingres's *Odalisque and Slave* (1842), was originally commissioned by the Public Art Fund but was rejected, so the Guerrilla Girls rented space on New York City buses to broadcast their message.

Bottom left: **Judy Chicago, *The Dinner Party*, 1979**

Chicago's installation comprised four parts: a triangular table with place settings for ninety-nine women, a ceramic-tile floor with 999 more names, heritage panels that situate those names on timelines, and a sequence of tapestry banners.

Bottom right: **Louise Bourgeois, *Destruction of my Father*, 1974**

Bourgeois describes the dinner table setting in the installation as the invocation of a dream in which she bit off the head of her father.

group of women artists, who wear gorilla masks in public to conceal their identities, formed in 1984 in response to the Museum of Modern Art's *International Survey of Painting and Sculpture*, which included fewer than 10 percent women artists.

The Guerrilla Girls' poster is just one example of women artists' interventions in cultural institutions, acts, and actions that provided precursors to the institutional critique of the 1990s. Contemporary to the Guerrilla Girls were New York artists Jenny Holzer and Barbara Kruger, who, among others, found new ways to disseminate their art, often using supposedly poor materials such as posters, matchbooks, and prints. Holzer's *Truisms* and Kruger's graphic works circulated through public spaces in the city and in galleries. These displays challenged how art is valued in an art-world system that was increasingly populated by commercial galleries. Kruger's intervention in the viewing encounter and Holzer's democratic aesthetic offer two approaches to using art to provoke patriarchal institutions.

Of equal importance to interventions in the physical spaces of the museum were critical, analytic approaches to master narratives and, particularly, the power wielded through language. The interrogation of language was an important aspect of feminism in France, with the works of philosophers including Hélène Cixous (the first to use the term *écriture féminine*), Catherine Clement, Julia Kristeva, and Luce Irigaray. Each of these women described woman's difficult outside, or "othered," position in language, with Irigaray arguing that feminine pleasure could only ever lie beyond language in the prelinguistic experience between mother and child. Artists have engaged with these complex theories in a number of ways, but perhaps French artist Annette Messager's *Ma Collection de Proverbes* (*My Collection of Proverbs*, 1974) provides a provocative parallel. This work comprises a collection of misogynist phrases embroidered onto white cloth. It is Messager's combination of homely technique and appropriated crude, vernacular speech that articulates defiance without uttering a word of her own.

Judy Chicago's *The Dinner Party* (1973–79) is, perhaps, the most ambitious attempt at monumentalizing great women. If Chicago's work depended on tracing a long history of women's cultural importance, other artists found empowerment in myth, spirituality, and fiction. For instance, Mary Beth Edelson performed ceremonies to summon ancient goddesses, documented in her series *Woman Rising* (1973–74), and Ana Mendieta performed rituals such as her 1974 *Untitled (Blood and Feathers #2)*. Informed by Afro-Cuban culture and Santería religion, Mendieta's work marked her connection to Cuba following her exile to the United States as a child. In 1981, Mendieta carved a series of figures titled *Esculturas rupestres* (*Rupestrian Sculptures*) at Escaleras de Jaruco and Varadero Beach, outside Havana. These relief sculptures—documented by photographs—are named after the goddesses of the indigenous Taíno and Ciboney people. They not only stand for a culture almost lost, but also mark the artist's first return to Cuba since 1961.

Other artists found that historical research was connected with personal history. The British artist Rose Garrard entwined investigations into the history of women artists with representations of them from both art history and popular media. Much of her work engaged with artifacts taken from her family home, gifted by her mother, who was an antiques dealer. The objects and images used in her performances often had multiple meanings, raising memories of childhood struggle as well as cultural misrepresentation. Louise Bourgeois also often foregrounded the personal and the psychic: Her *Destruction of the Father* is an important instance of the feminist act of rewriting master narratives.

Critical approaches to history were important to the artists Lubaina Himid and Maud Sulter. Himid's *A Fashionable Marriage* (1986) remade a scene from William Hogarth's eighteenth-century series *A Rake's Progress* as an installation. Himid appropriates Hogarth's satirical language for a critical take on her contemporary art world. The critic sits on the fence, while the white, feminist artist-bride—comprising panels evoking Judy Chicago and Susan Hiller—comforts herself that the white dress is a plot to escape, rather than a symbol of entry into bourgeois security. The connection to Hogarth also evidences the colonial legacy of British culture, and its continuity in Himid's remake. Sulter, who was a photographer and a poet, embarked on her own historic retelling in a series of portraits titled Zabat, a name that derives from a ritual dance performed by women. Made for Rochdale Art Gallery in 1989, Zabat comprised a series of portraits of black women. Each figure was given a second name as a title—among them, Himid, Sulter, the poet Dorothea Smart, the singer Dr. Ysaye Maria Barnwell, the artists Delta Streete and Dionne Sparks, the musician Pat Agana, and the writers Alice Walker and Abiola Agana. Walker's portrait is titled *Phalia*, after the muse of comedy.

Between 1960 and 1988 a number of repositories for women's history were set up, and even a new woman-centered language emerged to describe the approach. These two things came together in the Herstory Archives, established by Sahli Cavallaro, Deborah Edel, Valerie Intyre, Joan Nestle, Pamela Oline, and Julia Stanley in New York. Exchanging "his" for "her," the name of the archive was part of a larger movement to create a decentered language. Nestle described her commitment to the Herstory Archives as creating a "healing place," rooted in "silenced voices, the love letters destroyed, the pronouns changed, the diaries carefully edited, the pictures never taken, the euphemized distortions that patriarchy would let pass." The archive was made up of collections amassed by the archivists, but also included donations from lesbian women, providing markers of their relationships. The Herstory Archives, which are still open, are indicative of the shared sense of responsibility for writing and caring for histories that emerged in the women's liberation movement. But they also indicate how different histories, particularly those structured by secrecy and illegality, are more precarious than others.

Below: **Paz Errázuriz, *Evelyn, La Palmera, Santiago*, from La Manzana de Adán (Adam's Apple), 1983**

Errázuriz is a Chilean photographer who began working in the 1970s under Augusto Pinochet's dictatorship. Errázuriz began using photography to document life in Pinochet's Chile, and particularly to make visible the lives of those who were marginalized and oppressed under the regime. Her series La Manzana de Adán comprises portraits of transsexual sex workers in Santiago. This series was made after Errázuriz cofounded the Independent Photographers' Association, and it was in the context of this group that she developed a politically committed photography. Errázuriz worked with the sitters in La Manzana de Adán for four years, becoming friends with her subjects—her portraits not only represent her subjects, but also invoke the communities they belong to and their relationship to the photographer.

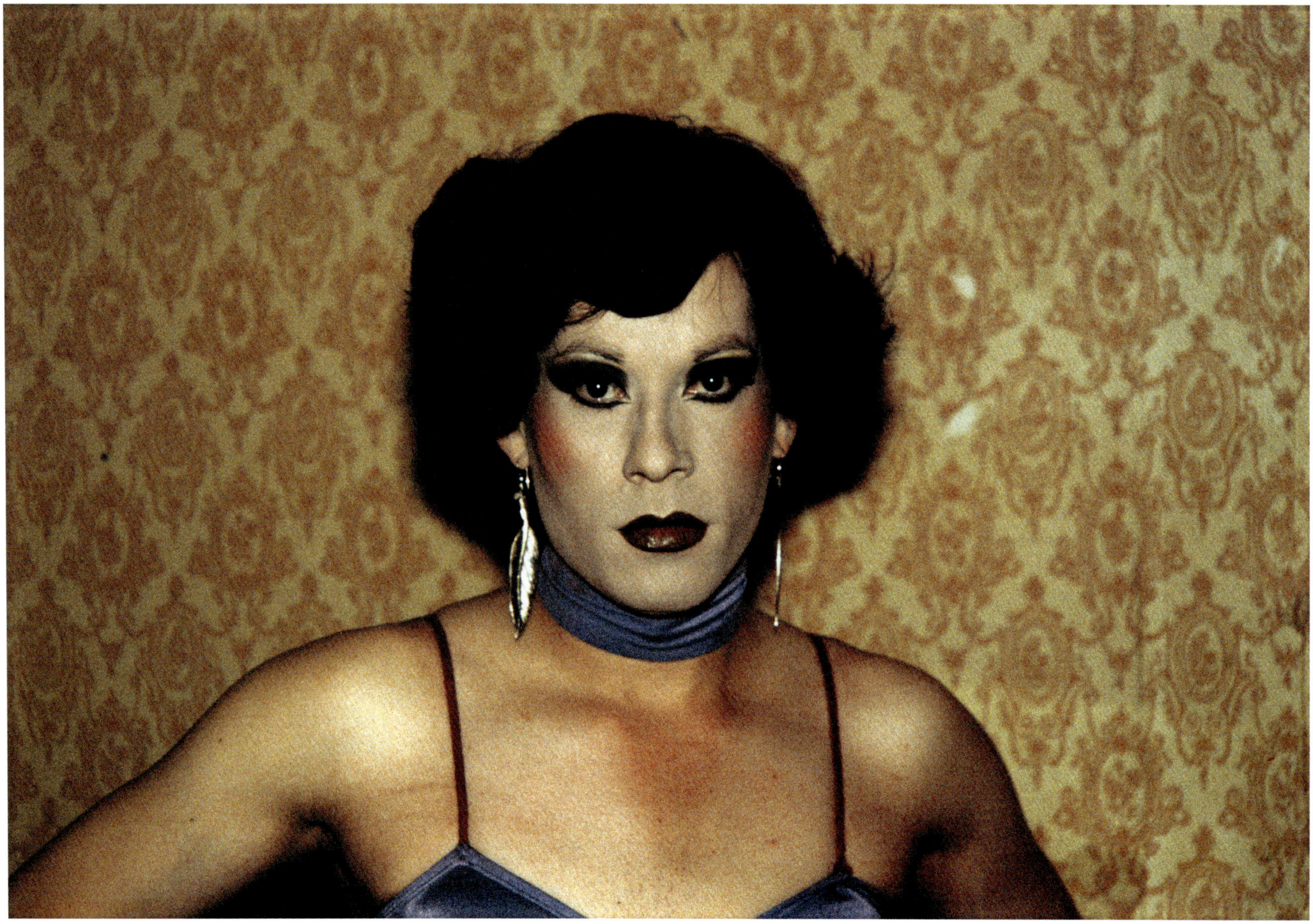

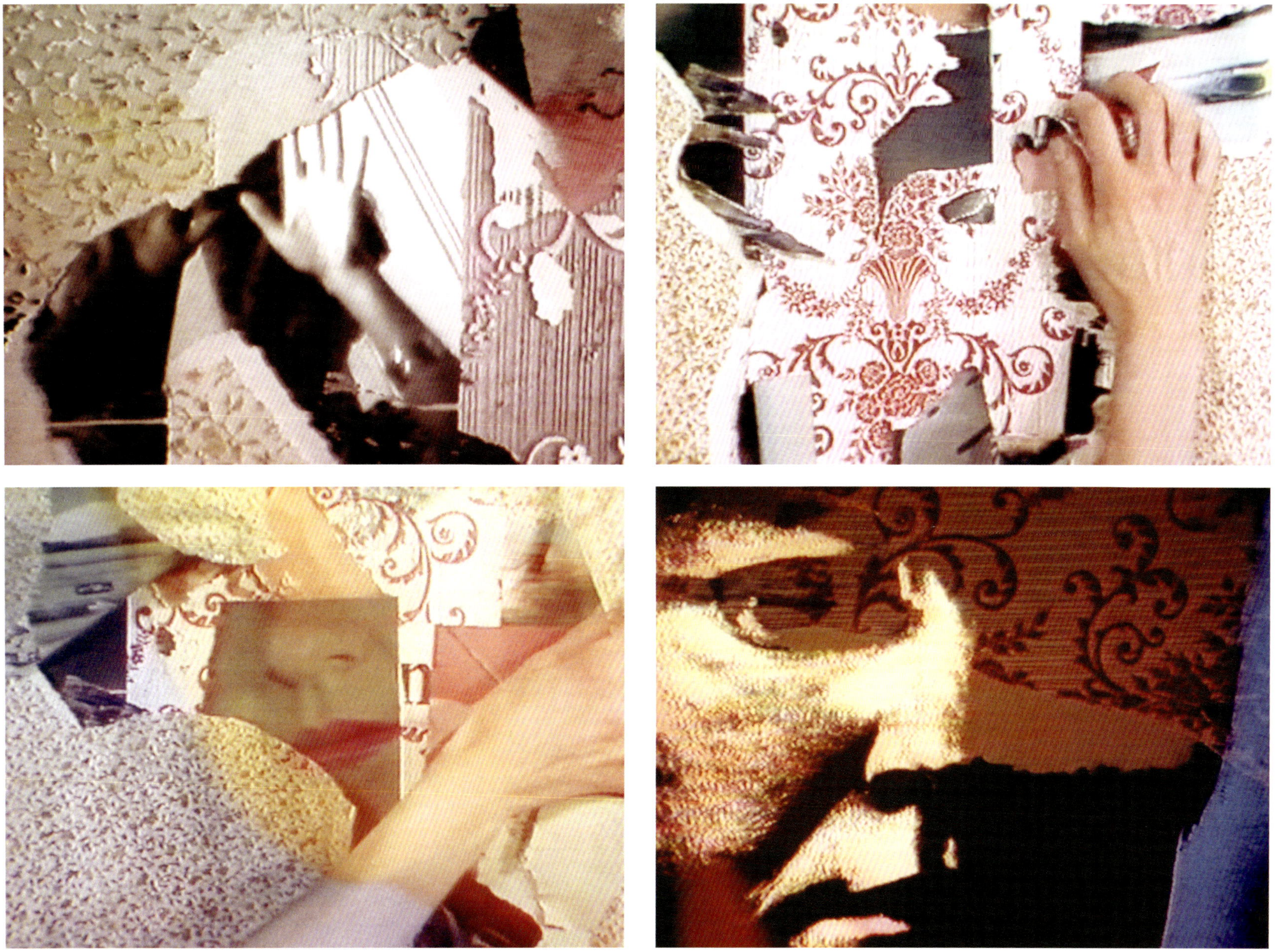

This page: Tina Keane, *Faded Wallpaper*, 1988, stills

Tina Keane took Charlotte Perkins Gilman's 1890 novella *The Yellow Wallpaper* as the inspiration for *Faded Wallpaper*. The novella, which had been republished by the all-woman press Virago, told a story of a woman's domestic suffocation, and her refuge in the pattern of her bedroom wallpaper. The eighteen-minute video loosely tells this story, while images of the woman protagonist are overlaid with wallpaper patterns that mutate in form. Hands tear at the wallpaper, as if to get to the truth, but instead of resolution, images and sounds become more intense. The video was made after two live video performances at Tate Gallery in 1984 and the Serpentine Gallery in 1985, both in London.

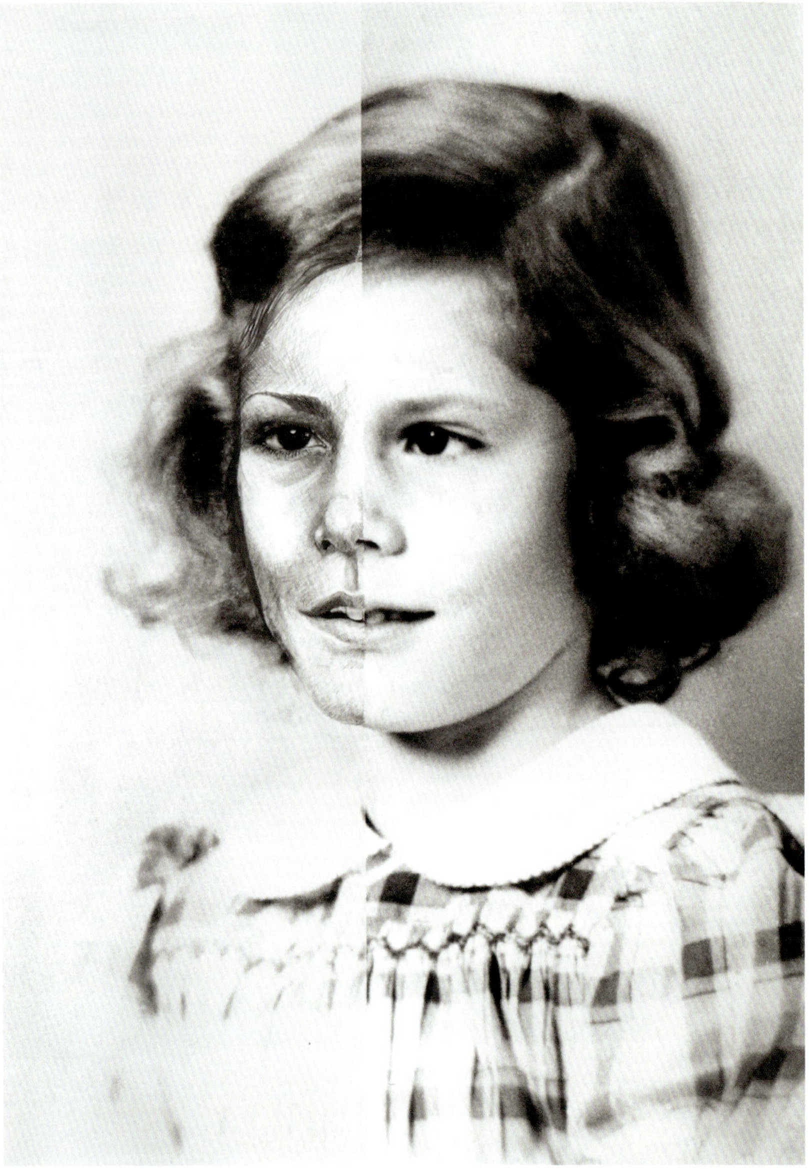

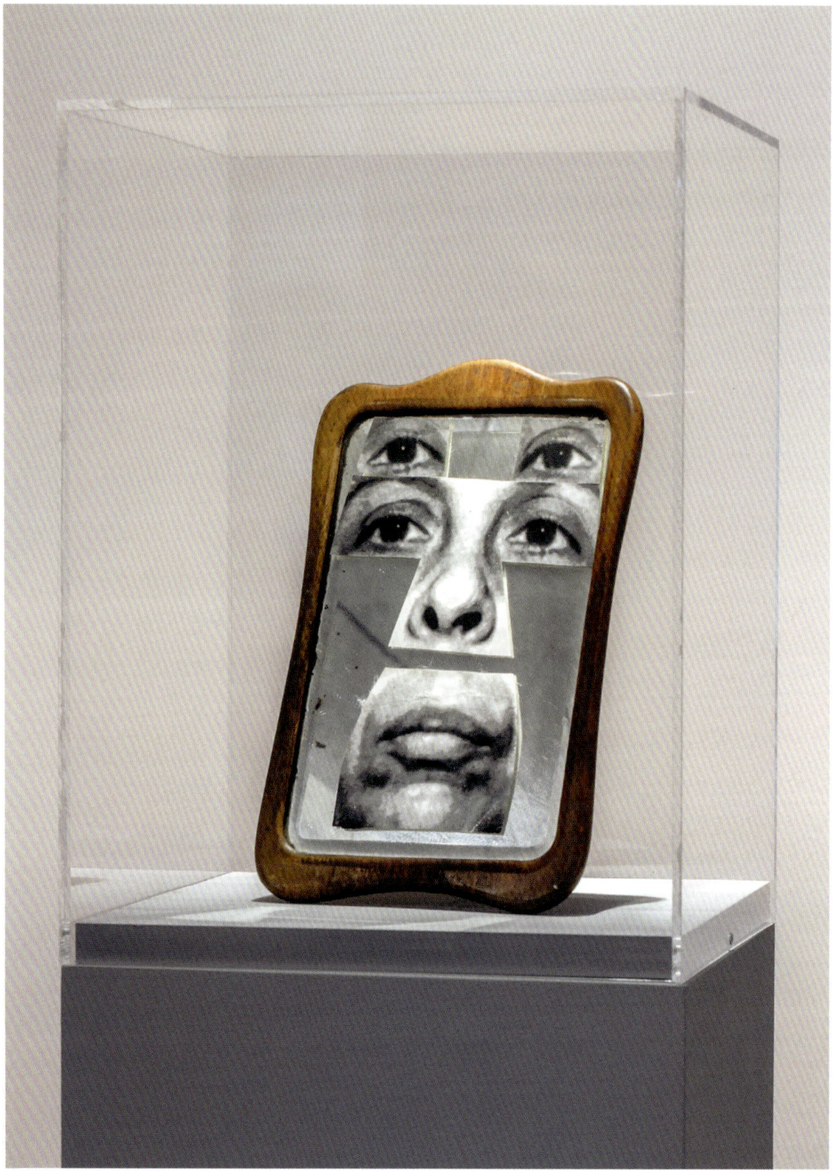

Above left: Suzy Lake, *6 over 28*, 1975

This is one work from Lake's Over 28 series. For this series Lake combined a studio portrait photograph of herself at various stages of life, with a graphite drawing of the artist at age twenty-eight. These images see the artist engage with her personal history, perhaps suggesting how identity both shifts and stays the same. With its focus on the artist's identity and past life, this series departs from other series, such as Transformations, in which the artist's face merges with those of other people, investigating gender identity, aging, and the performance of self. In other works, such as *Choreographed Puppets* (1976) and *ImPositions* (1977), Lake powerfully explores social control through binding or restraining her body in constructed situations. Lake began her career in Detroit, Michigan, before moving to Canada in 1968. In 1971 she cofounded Véhicule Art Inc. in Montréal.

Above right: Geta Brătescu, *Self-Portrait in the Mirror*, 2001

Brătescu is a Romanian artist, who works across drawing, installation, sculpture, and moving image. Living in socialist Romania, Brătescu was not an official sanctioned artist; however, after the thaw in Nicolae Ceausescu's relations with the West in the late 1960s, she was able to continue her studies and eventually find a studio through the Romanian Artists' Union. Through the 1970s and 1980s she made works that explored her identity and her place in the world. *Self-Portrait in the Mirror*, is a playful manifestation of this. While a viewer may recognize the representation of her portrait overlaid in fragments on the mirror, to see it clearly the viewer has to bring their own face to meet the artist's.

Top right: Sutapa Biswas, *Housewives with Steak-Knives*, 1985

Biswas made this monumental painting-collage in 1985 for her final-year degree show at the University of Leeds, U.K. The work invokes the Hindu goddess Kali—the creator and the destroyer—who appears here in the guise of an Asian woman. In three of her four hands, Kali holds a flag and a flower, the knife of the title, and a severed head; she raises her fourth, red-painted hand, palm out. The figure wears a necklace of severed heads—representing white, patriarchal power—while her flag features a reproduction of Artemisia Gentileschi's *Judith Slaying Holofernes* (ca.1620) *Housewives with Steak-Knives*, with its invocation of domestic care, brings love and anger into close proximity, in particular it contends with the characterization of women, and especially women of Asian heritage with docility. This work marked the end of Biswas's studies at Leeds, during which she entered into a sustained dialogue with her teacher—the feminist art historian Griselda Pollock—concerning the presence of imperialism in the institution. Their interaction shaped both Biswas's work and Pollock's teaching.

Bottom right: Rose Garrard, *Beyond Still Life*, 1980

Beyond Still Life is a performance piece by the British artist Rose Garrard. She made the work for the exhibition *About Time*, which she cocurated with Catherine Elwes, and which took place at the ICA, in London, as part of a trilogy of exhibitions of women artists. *Beyond Still Life* comprised four sculptural assemblages, a video camera, and monitor. The sculptures included three plaster figures, each resembling the artist and holding another cast object—either a vase, a book, or a bird. Garrard moved a video camera around the set focusing on each of the benches in turn, while the footage was relayed on the screen. She took a seat next to each plaster figure, finally coming to the final figure-less bench, which held the original versions of the other cast objects. In this work Garrard exposed the composition of an image, punning on the still-life painting genre and the stilled representations of the artist. The vase, book, and bird were objects from the artist's family home and had particular personal resonance for Garrard. Their arrangement and rearrangement in *Beyond Still Life* replayed her time spent composing, drawing, and painting as a child.

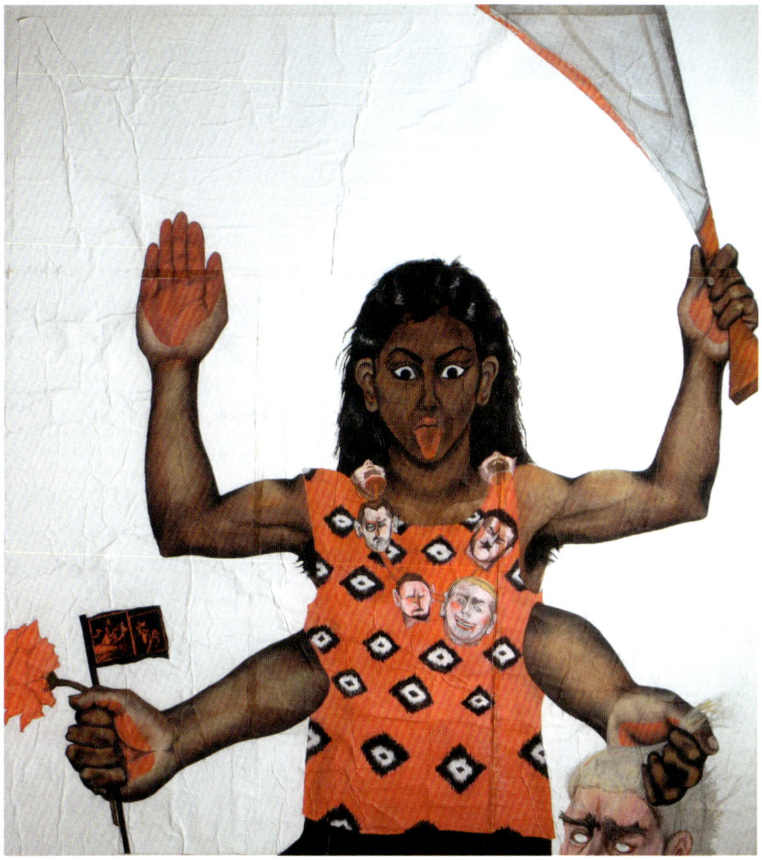

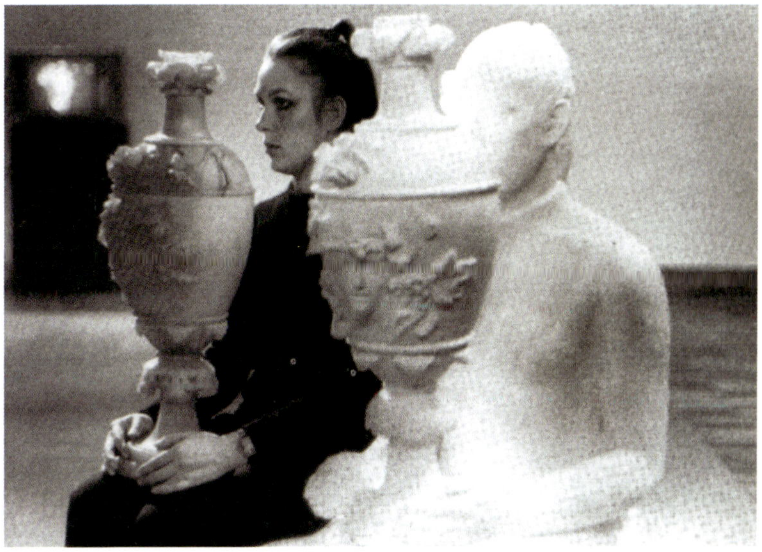

Reimagining Los Angeles

From the early 1960s, the city of Los Angeles grew rapidly from a collection of small neighborhoods into a sprawling urban jungle. While philosophers and architects celebrated the transformation, many communities suffered. Nonetheless, the women's liberation, anti-racist struggle, and Chicano/a activism sought to reimagine the city and revise the erasure of its complex histories.

In 1961, communities in Chavez Ravine, Los Angeles, were cleared to make way for Dodgers Stadium—just one of a number of clearances to build new infrastructure. The inauguration of this future-oriented landscape depended on the destruction of something else, which also meant the imposition of a singular idea for the city onto the diverse groups that inhabited it. The people hit the hardest by this new vision were African Americans and Mexican Americans living in the suburbs.

Many feminist-influenced artists troubled the status quo of the larger Californian art world. Joyce Kozloff headed up protests at the Los Angeles County Museum of Art in 1971, while Judy Chicago's Feminist Art Program—first at Fresno, then at the California Institute of Art—saw the development of a feminist pedagogy and the production of significant performances. The latter included Suzanne Lacy and Aviva Rahmani's *Ablutions* and Faith Wilding's *Waiting*, as well as the important group exhibition *Womanhouse*. By 1973, the Woman's Building opened in downtown Los Angeles, established by Judy Chicago with her colleagues from the California Institute of the Arts (Cal Arts), Arlene Raven and Shelia Levrant de Bretteville. The building hosted a revamped Feminist Art Program renamed the Feminist Studio Workshop, alongside art galleries, a café, graphic design studio, bookshop, and travel agent: all directed toward women. The Woman's Building played host to reimaginings of women's history, from its precedent in Sophia Hayden's structure for the 1893 Columbian Exposition in Chicago, to Terry Wolverton's *Oral History of Lesbianism*, performed there in 1979.

The artist Senga Nengudi made the freeways the subject of her work, *Ceremony for Freeway Fets* (1978), which comprised an installation beneath the freeway overpass at Pico Boulevard. It featured an improvised dance performance by the artists David Hammons and Marion Hassinger to the accompaniment of musicians, who, like Hammons, Hassinger, and Nengudi, were members of the group Studio Z. Nengudi transforms this liminal place into a site for a mystical ritual, and the concrete columns of the freeway into a grand architecture augmented by nylon-stocking objects, characteristic of her work. *Ceremony for Freeway Fets* is important because it sought solidarity and unity, particularly between men and women. Hammons and Hassinger played masculine and feminine spirits, unified by a masked Nengudi—who played the neutral role of the spirit—representing the need for mutual respect within the African-American community in the struggle against racism. The ritualistic quality of the performance also spoke to an act of looking back, retrieving, and reperforming a set of historical actions for the present.

The question of solidarity was also important for the Mexican-American women who were part of the Chicano/a movement. At the time, the "woman question" was not prioritized within the broader struggle for Mexican-American rights. In response, Chicanas organized together, within, and between the Chicano *movimento* and the women's movement. Artists were an important part of this activism. A number of groups and artists experimented with, and transformed, the mural tradition. In her book *Walls of Empowerment*, Guisela Latorre writes of the mural as something on the border, between "urban life and Mexican traditions." This form connected contemporary activists with the grand tradition of Mexican muralism, but it also set a clear message of claiming space in the midst of the city's development. A mural on the exterior of a building might mark it as belonging to a particular local group, but the content of these murals also described life inside the buildings, and illustrated the Chicano/a indigeneity to the Americas.

One of the most ambitious murals in this Californian movement—extending from Los Angeles to the San Francisco Bay Area to San Diego—was Judy Baca's *Great Wall of Los Angeles*. The mural was described by the artist as a depiction of the history of the city from the perspective of its oppressed populations. Located on the wall of a drainage canal called the Tujunga Wash, it rewound to a Paleolithic origin scene, spooling out across 2,754 ft (839 m) to the 1940s, like an elongated filmstrip. The mural engaged with multiple histories of oppression in the city and was a means of connecting divided communities.

The *Great Wall of Los Angeles* was not solely Baca's vision. The scale of its ambition and the labor required could only be matched by the work of many. Baca produced the mural over four summers with a team of designers and artists, as well as a group of young workers from a juvenile correction program, each paid $3.10 per hour. These young participants received training and learned to translate images from sketches onto the large plane of the wall; they were taught how to paint, how to use gradient, and how to create shadow. Moreover, the process of working on the mural introduced them to, and informed them about, the history of the Chicano/a community. In this way, artists in Los Angeles found spaces from the Woman's Building, to the shelter provided by freeway overpasses, to the empty walls of a drainage canal to rewrite the history and, therefore, the future of their city.

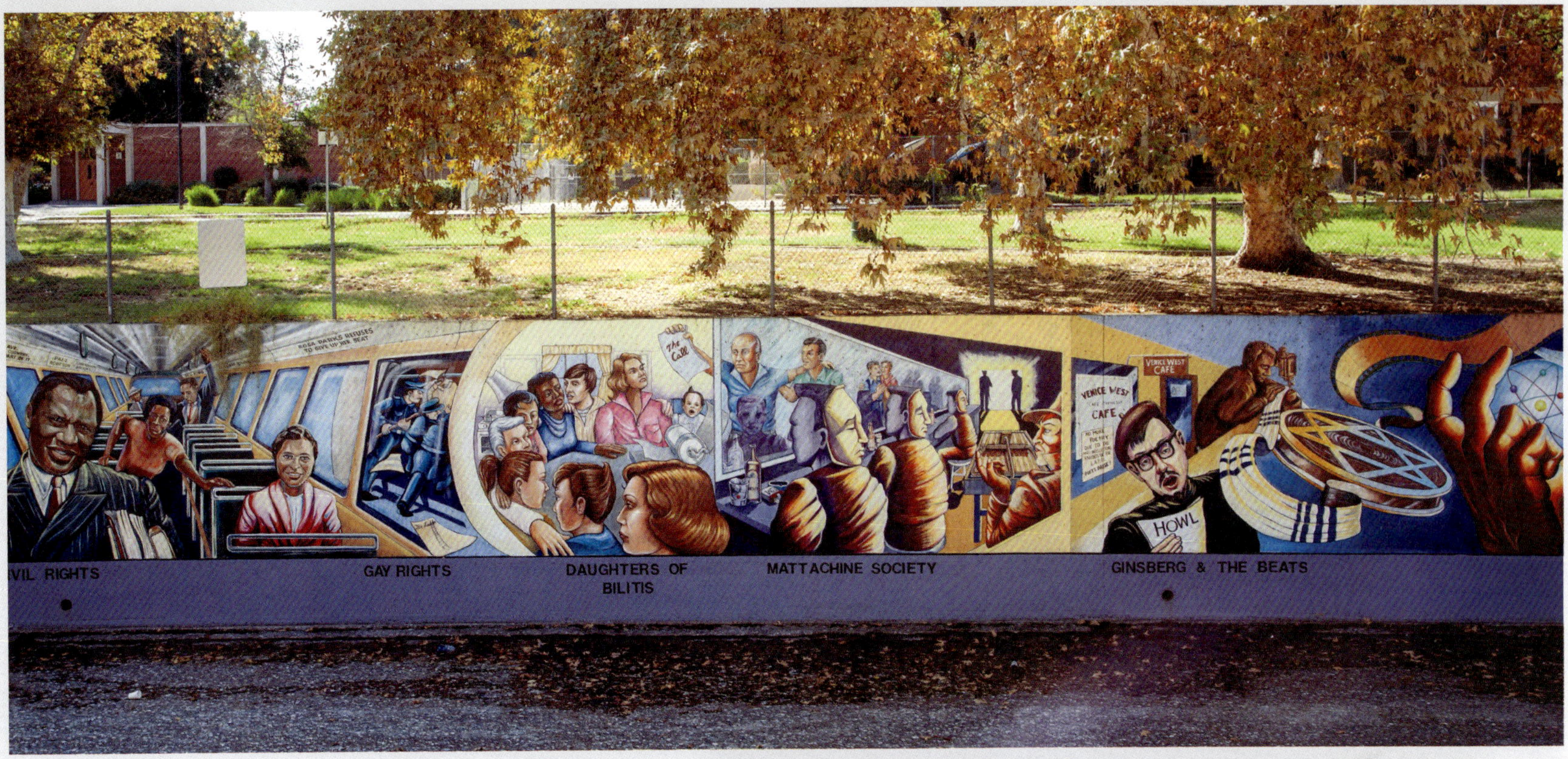

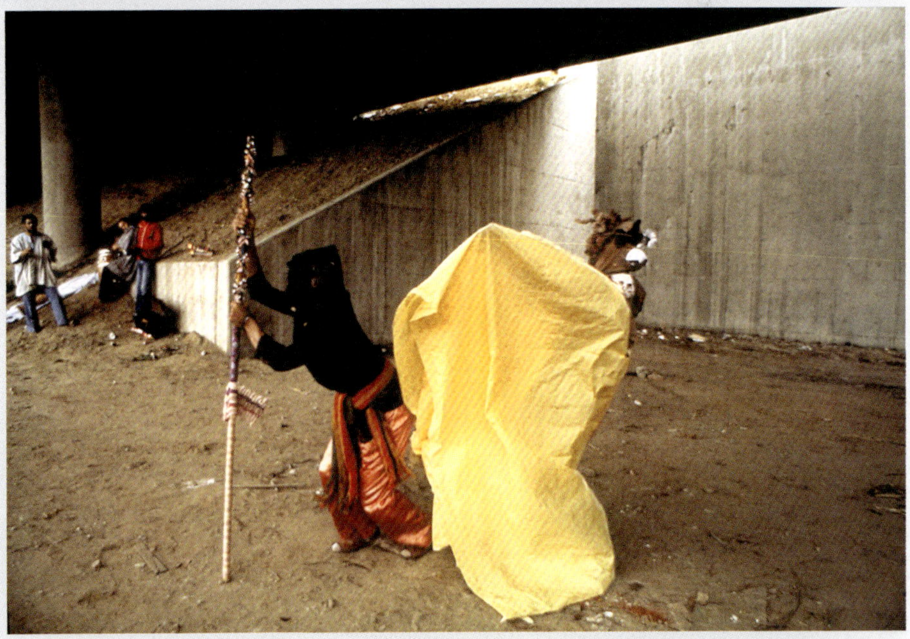

"The Indian of the Americas emerged within these murals as a timeless ideal and a fluid allegory of cultural affirmation that reconstructed Chicanas/os' fragmented past while providing entire communities with a vocabulary that celebrated their contemporary cultural practices."

Art historian Guisela Latorre, in *Walls of Empowerment* (2008)

Top: **Judy Baca, *Great Wall of Los Angeles*, 1983**

Baca's alternate view of Los Angeles included images of its indigenous inhabitants walking across a bridge connecting the north and south continents of America, as well as being split apart by development clearances, making way for freeways and the Dodgers' Baseball stadium. It also included an image of a World War II Rosie-Riveter-type worker being sucked back into the home at the end of the conflict.

Bottom: **Roderick "Quaku" Young, Senga Nengudi's *Ceremony for Freeway Fets*, 1978**

Nengudi's work offers an important counter perspective to the Los Angeles celebrated by postmodern theorists. Rather than pay attention to the freeway, she looked to the arid wasteland beneath it.

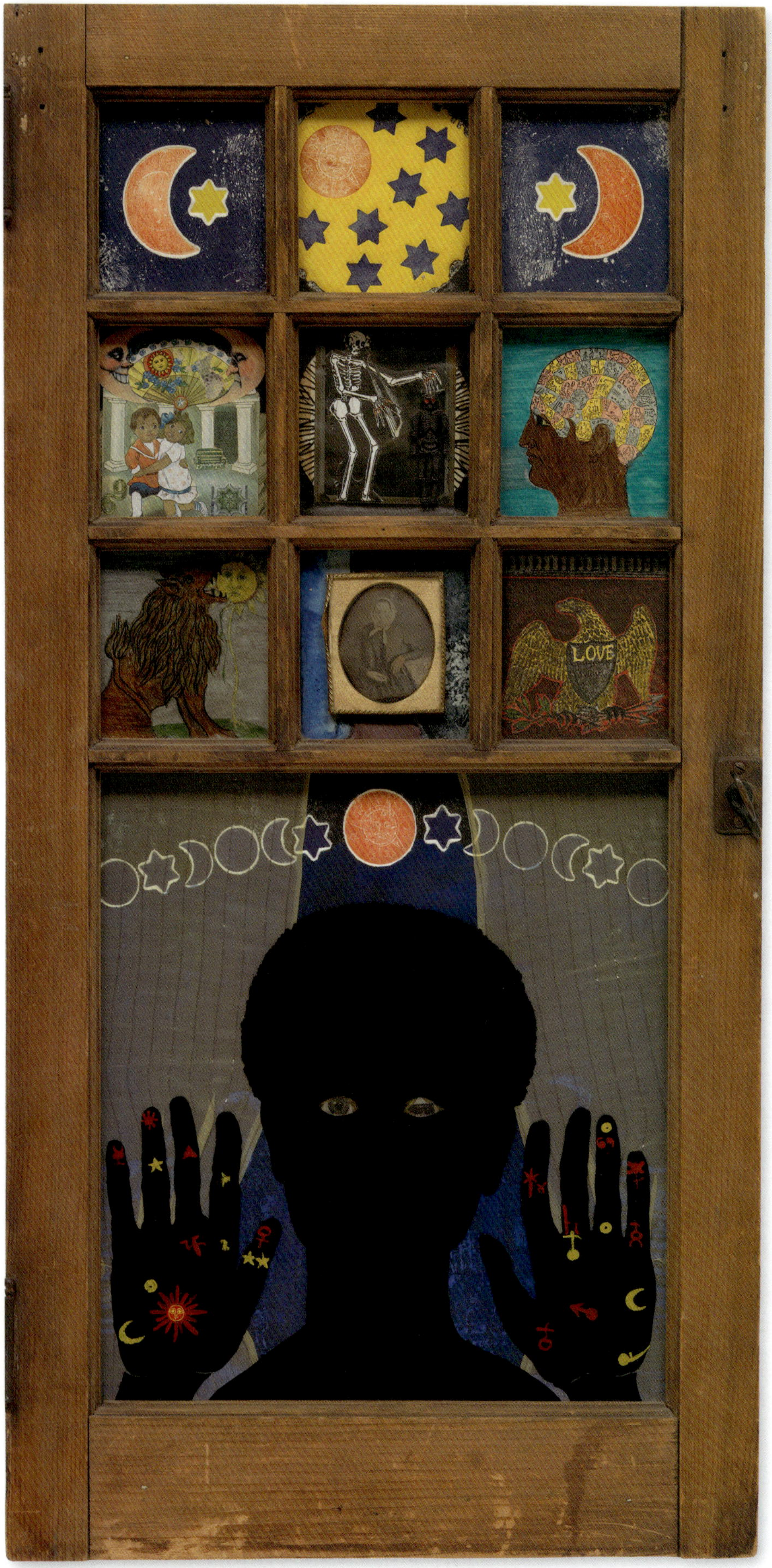

Left: Betye Saar, *Black Girl's Window*, 1969

Black Girl's Window is one of Saar's most famous assemblages—works that incorporate materials found in flea markets or junk stores, and that are often of symbolic or iconographic interest to the artist. Saar, who was a member of the Black Arts Movement (BAM) in the 1970s, has made a number of works that subvert stereotypes of African Americans presented in popular culture and commercial advertising. The most famous of these is the rifle-and-grenade-toting figure in *The Liberation of Aunt Jemima* (1972). *Black Girl's Window* is an exploration of the artist's heritage and biography. The window shows a woman in silhouette, with hands up as if pressed against the glass. In the frames above appear her astrological sign, the lion, as well as references to love, death, childhood, and even the study of phrenology. In the middle segment on the bottom row, Saar has included a photograph of her grandmother, referencing her Irish heritage.

Below left: **Ana Mendieta, *La Vivificación de la Carne, El Laberinto de Venus* series, (*The Vivification of the Flesh*, Labyrinth of Venus series), 1982**

Ana Mendieta lived and worked in the United States for most of her life, having arrived in Iowa as an exile from Fidel Castro's Cuba. Mendieta was an important contributor to, and critic of, the women's art movement in New York. She joined the all-women gallery A.I.R. in the late 1970s, but was critical of the dominance of white, middle-class women there and in the broader movement. Mendieta made her Labyrinth of Venus series in Iowa. She described her actions in the landscape as "earth-body" works, making outlines in the earth and photographing them. The forms of the sculptures were informed by various cultures, such as African, Afro-Cuban, ancient European, and indigenous Taíno traditions.

Below right: **Betsy Damon, *7,000 Year Old Woman*, 1977; Photographed by Su Friedrich**

Damon performed *7,000 Year Old Woman* as part of the first lesbian art show at 112 Green Street gallery, New York. She performed again numerous times, including in 1978 at the De Appel center in Amsterdam, the Netherlands. Damon described invoking the figure of an ancient woman, who could be "me, the 'I' about which I know very little." Her manifestation invoked the many-breasted form of ancient fertility goddesses, through bags of colored flour tied to her body, and the clown, with white face paint. Damon wrote: "I have some skill and discipline, but she has enchantments of her own. I get to know her through the performances; this means I learn to exist through her."

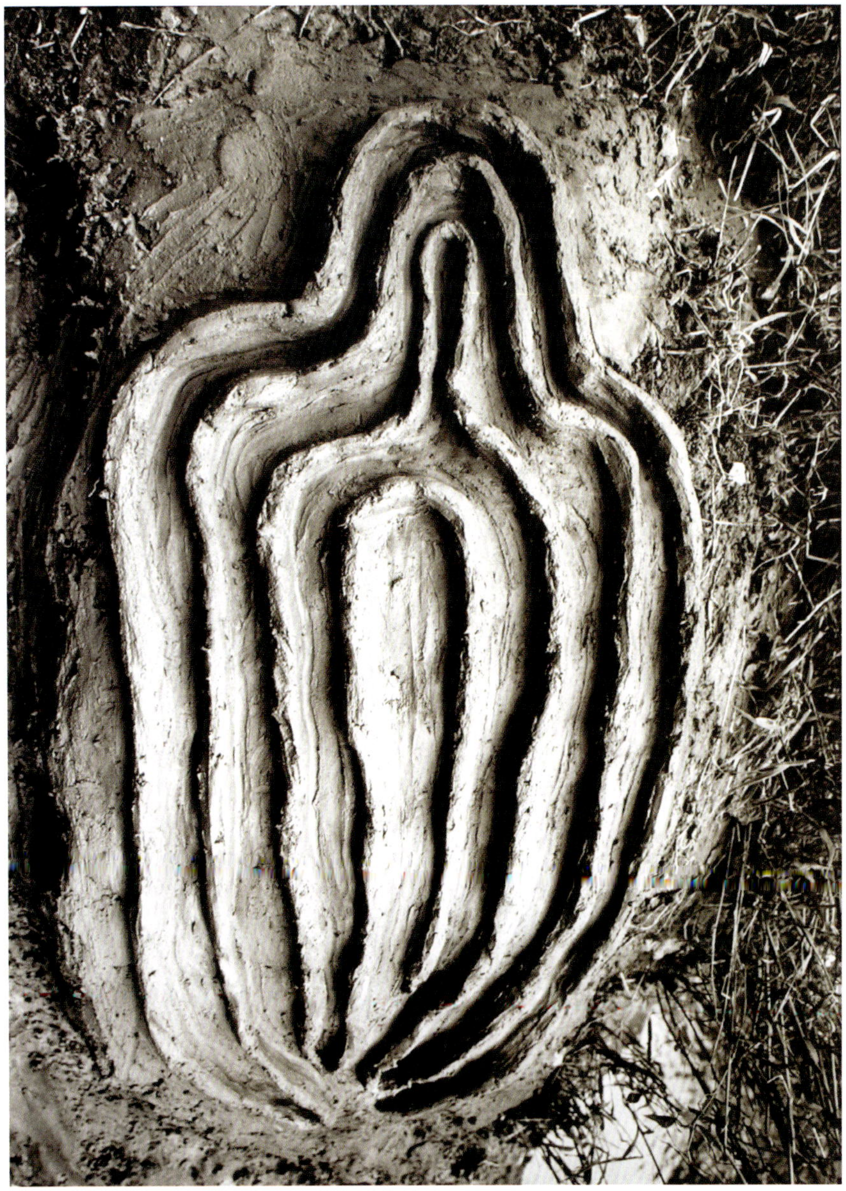

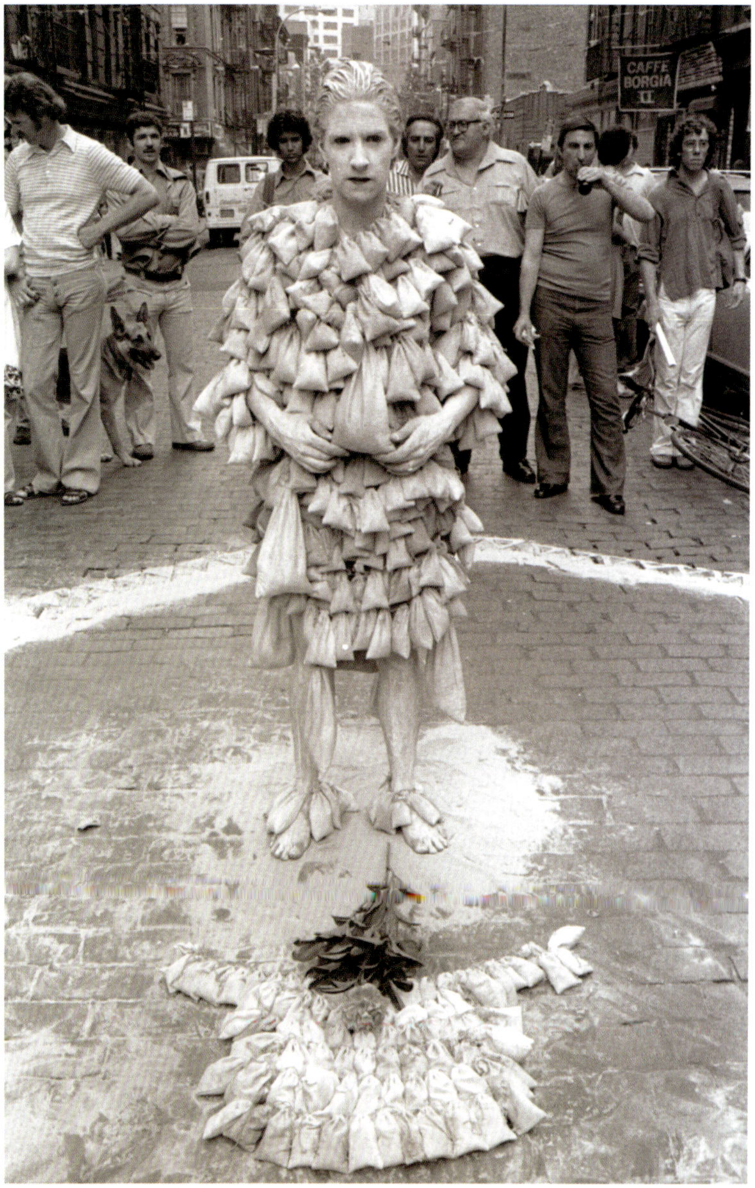

Kunst Mit Eigen-Sinn

In 1985, an exhibition at the Museum of Modern Art and the Museum of the 20th Century in Vienna, Austria, sought to raise awareness of women artists' ongoing—and pioneering—attempts to transform art and culture.

Entitled *Kunst Mit Eigen-Sinn*, the exhibition was curated by Austrian artist VALIE EXPORT along with Sylvia Eiblmayr, Heidi Grundmann, Cathrin Pichler, and Monika Prisch-Maier. It was conceived as a corrective to international exhibitions such as *Documenta* and *Zeitgeist*, which had under-represented women artists in the 1980s. The imperative for *Kunst Mit Eigen-Sinn* was to parallel earlier group exhibitions that had been organized as a testament to, and exploration of, women's art, but also to mark a departure from such events by describing women artists' current contribution to the arts scene.

The exhibition title made use of German wordplay to announce the desire of the curators to represent the art (*Kunst*) of the individual artists—their own sense (*eigen Sinn*)—in the larger context of women's new—willful (*eigensinnig*)—presence in the art world. As such the title communicated the ongoing necessity of collaboration and communal support between women, which had characterized women's liberation, but also working without the limits of dictates or didacticism. The imperative for *Kunst Mit Eigen-Sinn* was to parallel earlier group exhibitions that were organized as a testament to, and an exploration of, women's art, but also to mark a departure from them in describing women artists' attempts to transform art and culture. Whereas those exhibitions provided women artists with the opportunity to come together and to share their work—with an ethic not too dissimilar to consciousness-raising—this exhibition sought to address the complexity of art-making within patriarchal culture. Scheduled to take place during Frauen '84, a year of women in Vienna, it was postponed owing to conflicts in the museums' schedules.

The delayed opening, in 1985, meant that the exhibition came after the 1984 Venice Biennale, *Arte Allo Speccio* (Art in the Mirror), which had seen a number of artists returning to classical themes. As such, *Kunst Mit Eigen-Sinn* intervened even more pointedly in an art world increasingly dominated by a return to more traditional media and retromania. This "return of the good old days," as the English critic William Feaver put it, represented an art world in ruins, returning to traditional values that made for an uneasy parallel to the political retrenchment in the governments of both Thatcher and Reagan in Britain and the United States respectively. EXPORT and her coorganizers were particularly committed to "counter-balanc[ing]" these "restorative trends," and made space for a "wide variety of art media," including "the field of new technologies" that was already central to EXPORT's own art practice. Along with plastic art—art that is physical, visual, and three-dimensional—the curators organized film and video screenings, a performance program, symposiums, and concerts. A series of live events brought many of the exhibiting artists to Vienna, prompting an unofficial congress of women artists and providing an important site of discussion, debate, and celebration between women working in different countries. Given the climate of artistic retrenchment, *Kunst Mit Eigen-Sinn* pioneered artists at the forefront of experimental practice, with the implicit suggestion that it was the gender of the artists that supported this new perspective. While there was little interest in defining coherent aesthetic traits between women by 1985—an idea that was deemed both reductive and essentialist—women artists were seen to be at the cutting edge of art, both in their use of new technology and in the content of their work.

The show ran for six weeks from March 29 to May 12 and featured over one hundred artists and filmmakers. The conference catalog notes that exhibitors hailed from Austria, Australia, Canada, former Czechoslovakia, former Federal Republic of Germany, France, Great Britain, Hungary, Iceland, Italy, Japan, the Netherlands, Poland, Portugal, Spain, Switzerland, the United States, and former Yugoslavia. In most of the European countries, as well as in the United States, the curators invited resident artists to aid their selection, evidencing a substantial attempt at collaborative organization. However, this collaboration only extended so far. The list tellingly excludes work from South America, Africa, much of Asia, and New Zealand, while geographic areas somewhat closer, but ideologically separated, are also not represented. In this way the exhibition repeated many of the exclusions of the decade before.

Writing later, in 1988, EXPORT revisited the title of the exhibition, translating it as "Art with a Sense of One's Own," a variation that acknowledges a debt to Virginia Woolf's classic text, *A Room of One's Own*, and to the continuing theme of self-determination throughout feminist discourse. This was particularly pointed in *Kunst Mit Eigen-Sinn*, as much of the work exhibited engaged with the body: either the body in fragments—more than a sum of its parts—or the body as hyperaware and a cipher for engaging with the surrounding environment.

The exhibition received mixed critical response. The critic Jürgen Hohmeyer, writing in *Der Spiegel*, described it as a "ghetto" exhibition and an "anti-emancipatory exercise." Unable to read the work on its own terms, he lamented the necessity of a women's show and returned the debate to the question of a "feminist aesthetic." By contrast, German artist Barbara Hammann described the exhibition as "vivid," commenting that, "without priorities being set, a self-assured panorama has emerged of the media and themes that women artists deal with today."

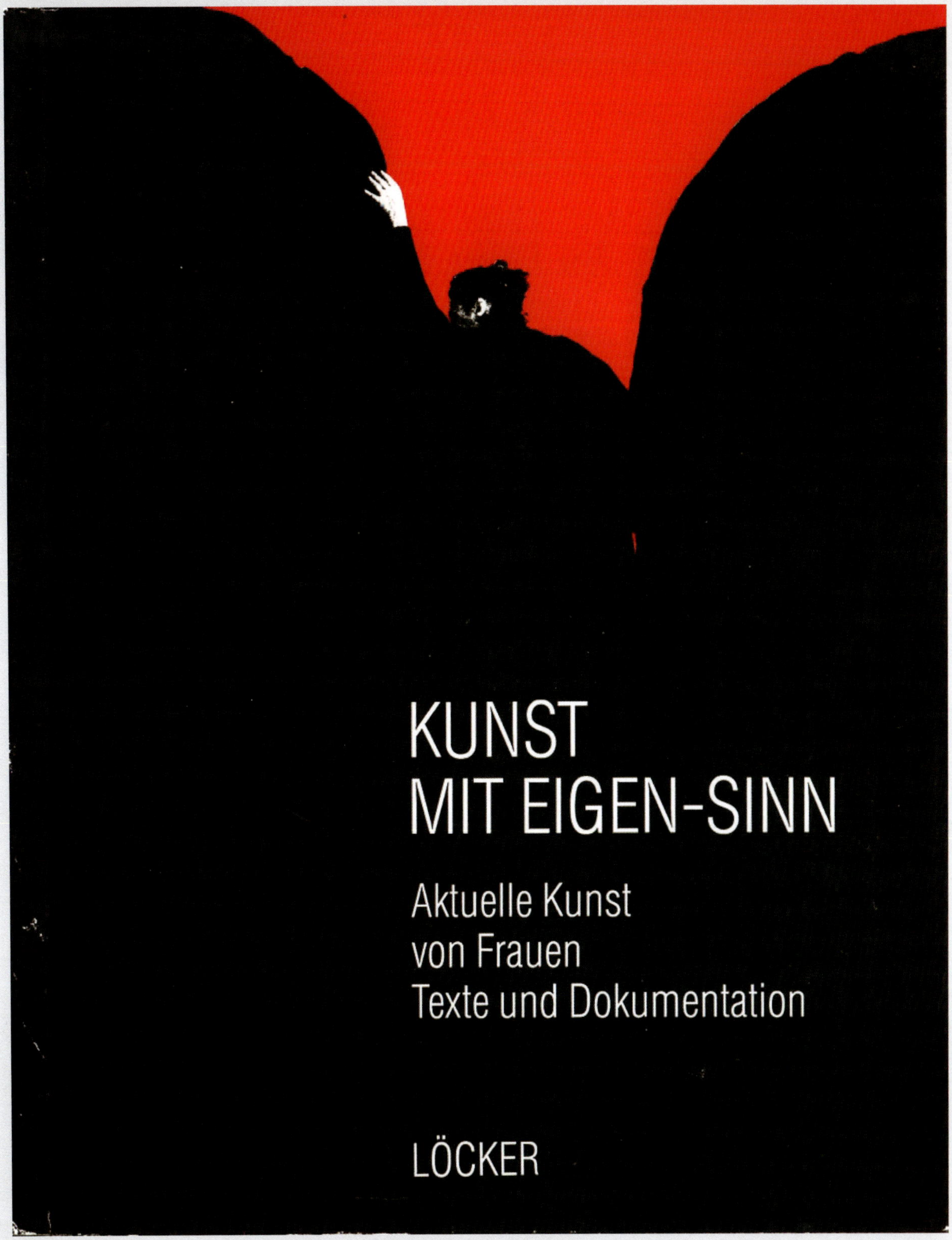

Above: **Helena Almeida, *Kunst Mit Eigen-Sinn*, exhibition catalog cover, 1985**

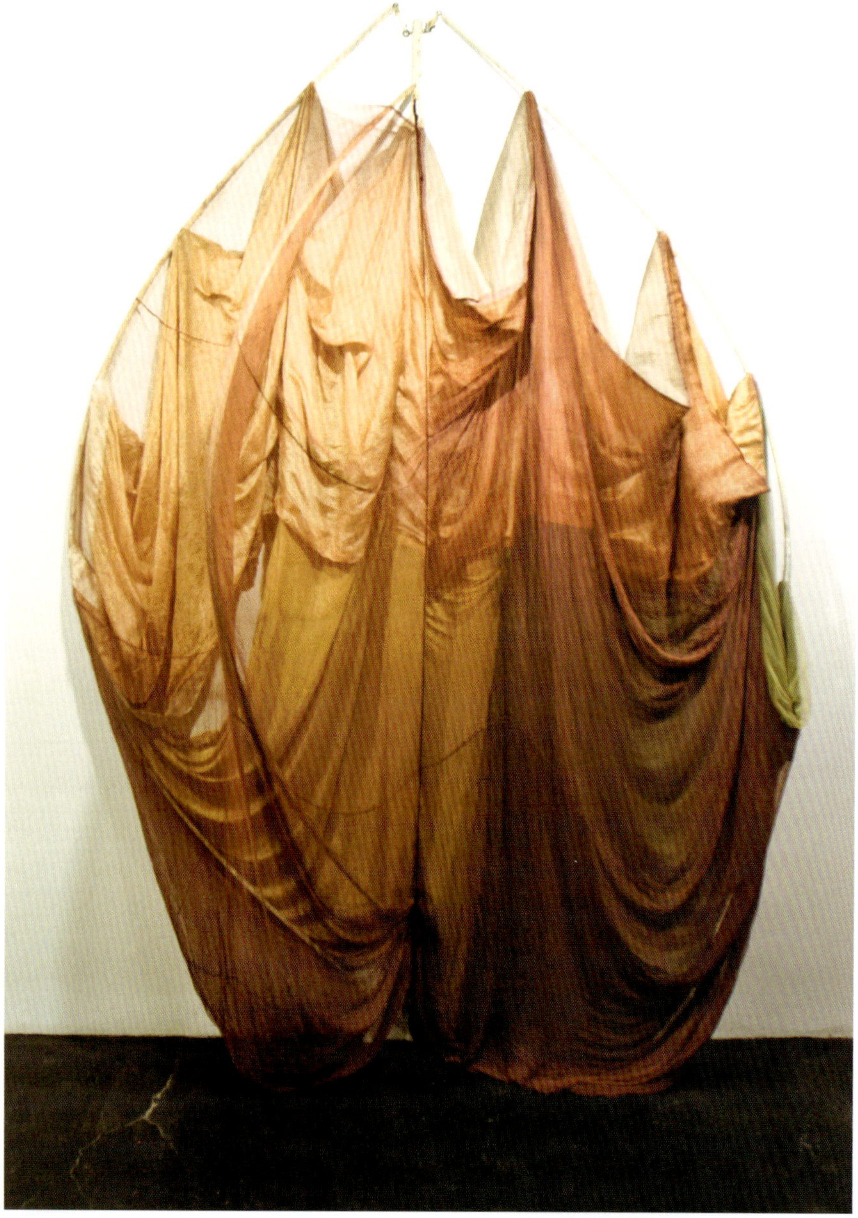

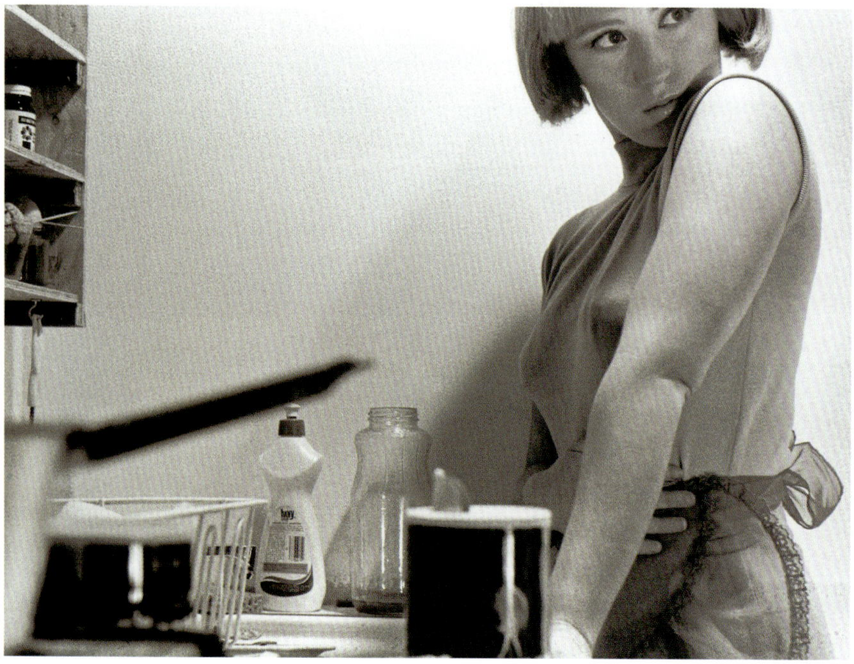

Top left: Rosemary Mayer, *The Catherines*, 1972–73

Based in New York, Mayer was an active participant in the emerging women's movement in the city. She attended consciousness-raising sessions, and was a cofounder of the cooperative A.I.R. gallery. Mayer's work often cites women from literature, history, and myth. The title of this work refers to Catherine the Great, the Russian empress; Caterina Sforza, an Italian noblewoman; and Catherine of Siena, the theologian. The three figures parallel the three supports—two flush to the wall, one extending forward—from which colored fabric hangs. Mayer used fabric in a number of works, investigating the possibilities of color saturation. The works are often fleshy or bodily in palette, extending from pinks through purples to peaches. Nonetheless she was reluctant to see the works as analogues for the body alone. Mayer was also interested in sixteenth-century painting, and her folding and draping fabric might be compared with the depiction of clothing and furnishing in art history.

Bottom left: Cindy Sherman, *Untitled Film Still #3*, 1977

Cindy Sherman began making her *Untitled Film Stills* in 1977, and the series grew to comprise seventy images by 1980. In each black-and-white photograph, Sherman posed as a different personification including the femme fatale, the housewife, the girl, and the prostitute. Each figure is captured as if in a scene from a Hollywood film, yet the characters invoked in Sherman's work are not taken from actually existing films. Instead, the staged images mimic the dramatic, posed shots of different genres. In this suite of images, Sherman creates a catalog of popular culture stereotypes of women, and shows that each role is a construction that can be exchanged with any other, like changing clothes.

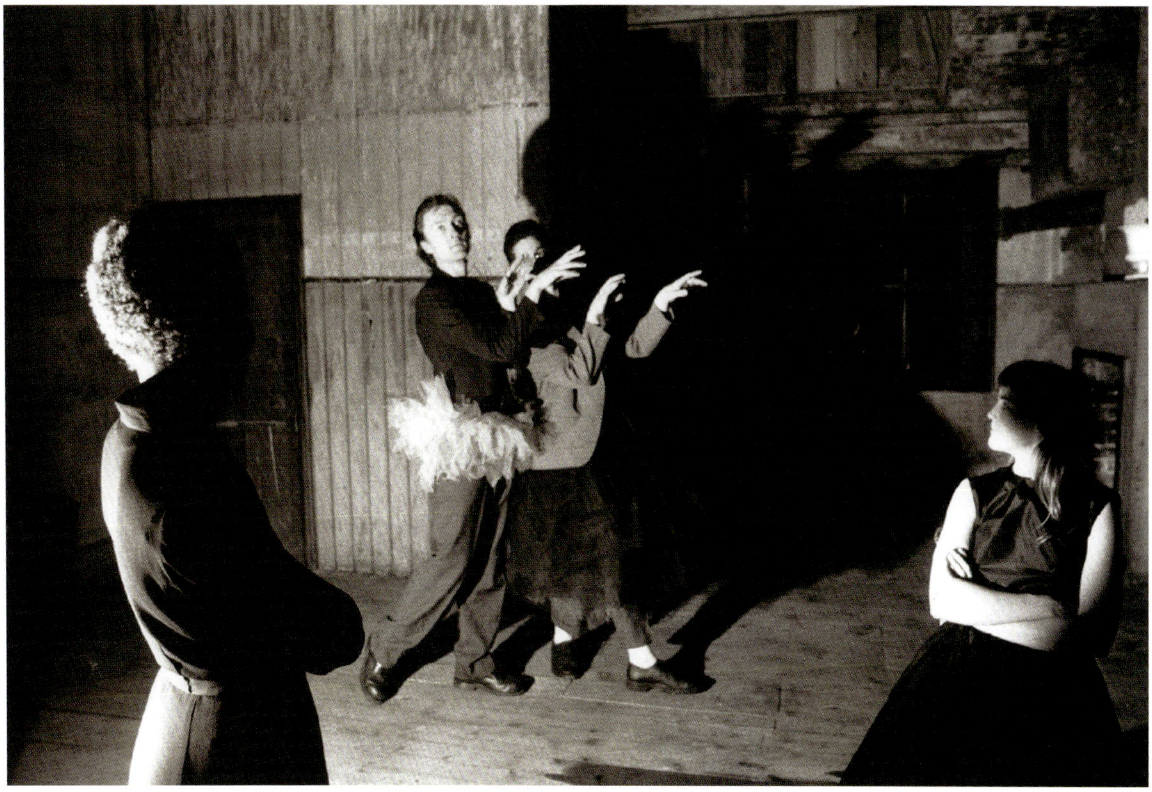

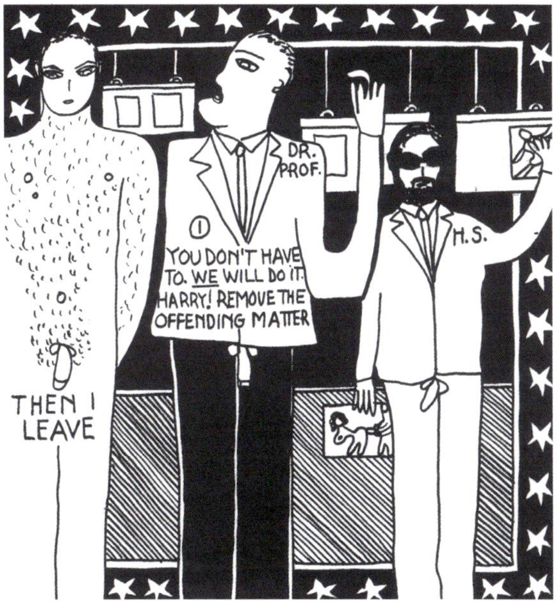

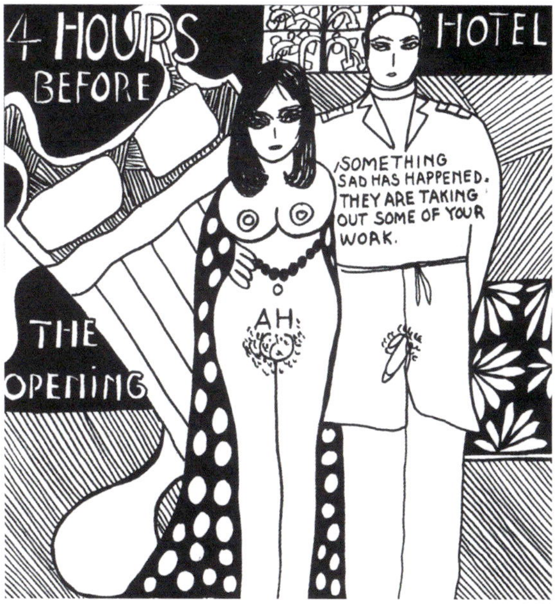

Top: **Sally Potter, *Thriller*, 1979**

Thriller is Potter's critical reimagining of Puccini's opera *La bohème*. In this feminist retelling, the good girl Mimi and the bad girl Musetta—both from Puccini's narrative—are recast as heroines and friends. Potter's Mimi knows she must die before the end of the film, and spends the film investigating the reasons for her death, and her relationship to Musetta. This work transforms the original into a genre-bending short film. The film stars Colette Laffont as Mimi and Rose English as Musetta. Both worked with Potter again in her next film, *The Gold Diggers* (1983), with the visual artist English also serving as artistic director for both films. English and Potter's collaboration during this period extended to live performances, which sometimes took place in their shared, squatter accommodation in London.

Bottom left & right: **Dorothy Iannone, *The Story of Bern*, 1970**

The Story of Bern (Or) Showing Colors is an artist book by the North American artist Dorothy Iannone. Iannone made this work in response to the attempted censorship of her work in 1969, during the exhibition *Freunde* at the Kunsthalle Bern, Germany. The gallery wanted to cover up the genitals of her figurative images. Iannone's partner, the Swiss artist Dieter Roth, removed his work from the exhibition in protest, and the curator, Harald Szeemann, also resigned. *The Story of Bern* represents Iannone's perspective on the incident. In retelling the event through her own narrative, illustrated by the artist, she reclaims the events. The figurative style used throughout the book is characteristic of Iannone's work and her celebration of spirituality and sexuality.

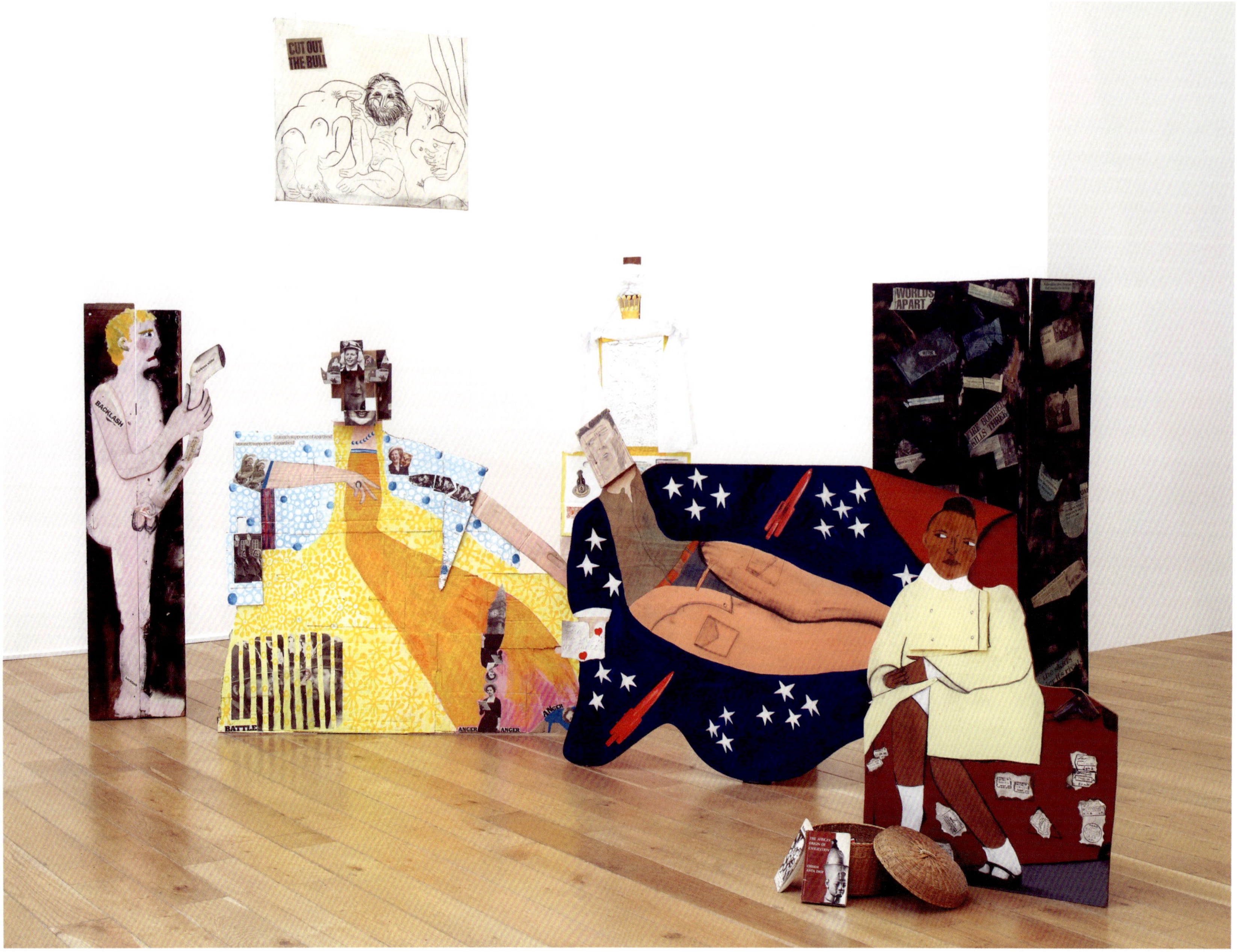

Above: Lubaina Himid, *A Fashionable Marriage*, 1986

A Fashionable Marriage is a multipart installation based on the British eighteenth-century artist William Hogarth's satirical print *The Countess's Morning Levee*, part of his Marriage A-la-Mode. Hogarth's characters are remade for the 1980s, and include Prime Minister Margaret Thatcher as the countess and the U.S. President Ronald Reagan as her lover. Hogarth's ambassador becomes an art critic sitting on the fence, while an envoy becomes the personification of an arts funding body. *A Fashionable Marriage* both updated and subverted Hogarth's original. In particular, this work subverts Hogarth's invocation of deviance and social ill through the figure of the black person. In *A Fashionable Marriage* the black woman artist—Himid—takes the center stage, in a grand dress and with articulated limbs, amid, but also anchoring, the chaos. She is accompanied by a black girl—the photographer and poet Maud Sulter—with a basket of books at her feet, who knowingly surveys the scene.

Opposite: Maud Sulter, *Phalia* (Portrait of Alice Walker), from the Zabat series, 1989

This photograph is from Maud Sulter's Zabat series, which includes nine images of creative women, each titled for one of the nine Greek muses. The series was originally produced for Rochdale Art Gallery, England, in 1989, in celebration of 150 years of photography. Sulter's celebration of black women was an important intervention in the anniversary. Her use of conventional motifs—such as the background, frame, and props—hints at the history of the medium, and black women's almost-invisibility from the portrait tradition. This image is of the feminist activist and author Alice Walker; she is represented as the muse of comedy and the bringer of flowers, Phalia. Zabat reverses the usual idea of the muse as the inspiration of the male poet and instead instills power in the woman creator.

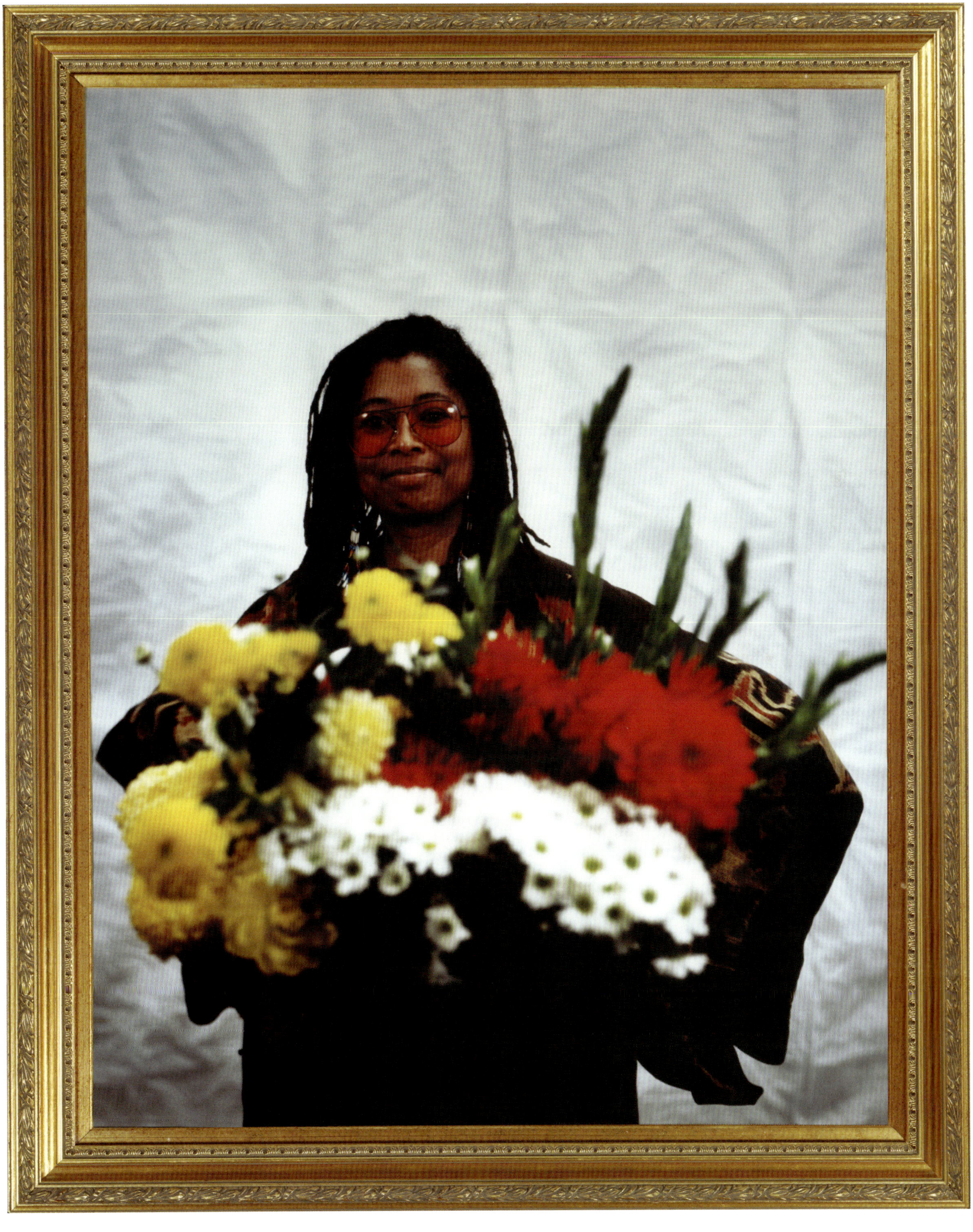

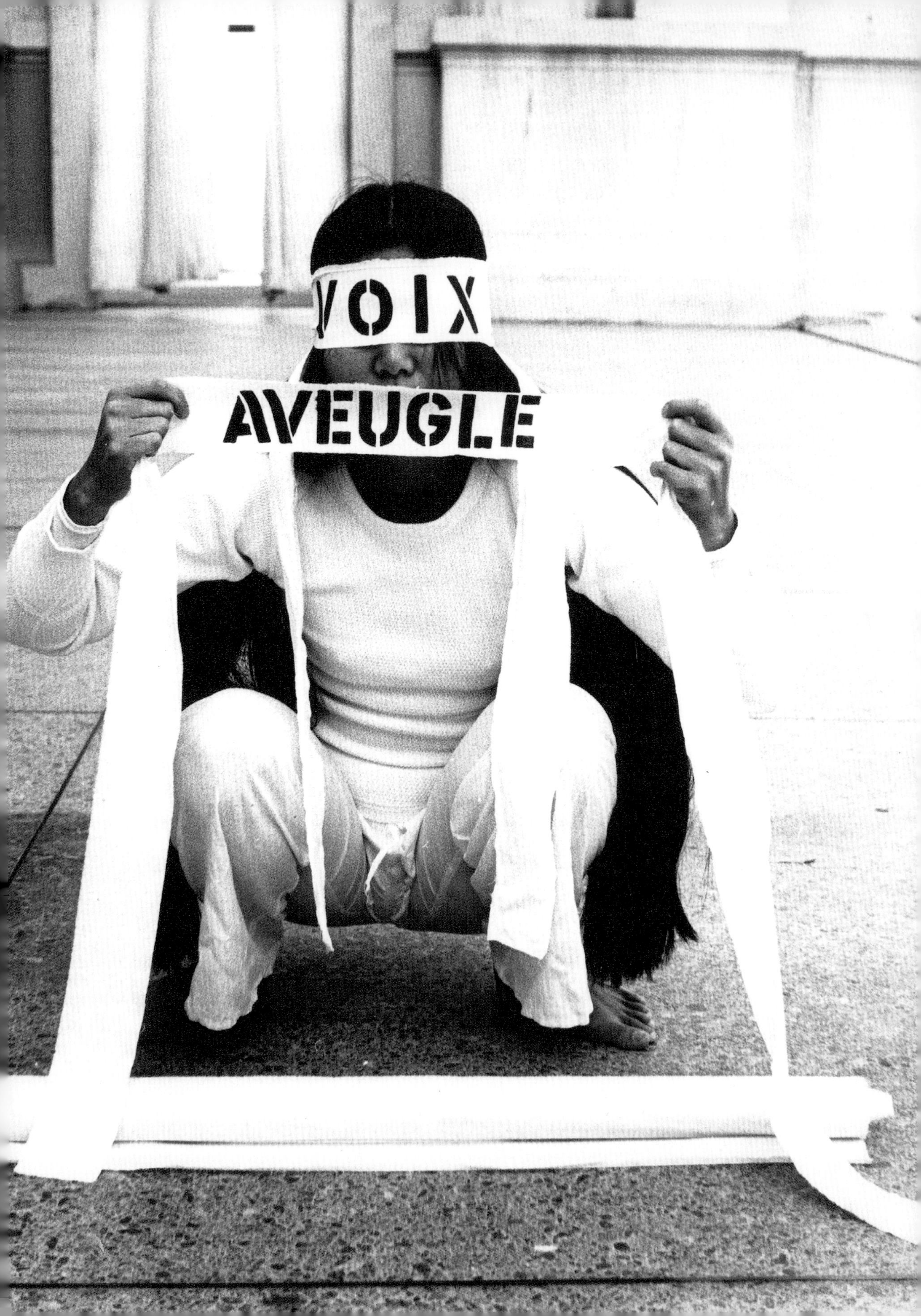
VOIX
AVEUGLE

Sense and Sensibility

8

Touching/Seeing/Hearing/Feeling

"Will we search for that which makes the whole? Searching, searching, searching—what a sad search! Will the desire to seek the whole work against women's multiplicity and become a reductionist exercise, building up to a neat, well secured whole, all the diverse and particular parts which women are and make?"

Yve Lomax, 1982

Alongside Linda Nochlin's rhetorical question, "Why Have There Been No Great Women Artists?" the women's liberation movement prompted another question: "Is there such a thing as definably feminine aesthetic?" Although most critics and artists could find no singular approach, Judy Chicago and Miriam Schapiro proposed that women's art was characterized by "central core" iconography. Chicago suggested that many women artists used a "central image" in their work, "sometimes surrounded by folds or undulations, as in the structure of the vagina," and that this iconography was a "framework for an imagery that allows for the complete reversal of the ways in which women are seen in the culture." In their 1973 article, "Female Imagery," in *Womanspace* journal, Chicago and Schapiro illustrated their argument with reproductions of their own art, as well as those of Lee Bontecou and Eva Hesse. Although their desire to pinpoint common aesthetic traits between women artists past and present rings of gender essentialism, and has been much interrogated and maligned as a result, Chicago and Schapiro's argument responds to a larger desire to articulate different ways of making and thinking about art that accompanied the interrogation of the history of art, as well as the means of production and display facing women artists. From the 1960s through the 1980s, artists experimented with new senses and sensibilities to communicate difference.

In 1982, the Midland Group in Nottingham, England, hosted an exhibition titled *Sense and Sensibility in Feminist Art Practice*, curated by Carol Jones. Taking its title from Jane Austen's 1811 novel, the exhibition reinscribed the difference implied between sense and sensibility in Austen's book, connecting sense and sensibility as a process of coming to know through attentiveness to one's environment. The exhibition was also concerned with proposing other modes of engaging with the world than through sight. So although women's art could not be strictly defined, exhibitions such as *Sense and Sensibility* evidenced a feminist art practice that saw and felt the world differently. The exhibition catalog included Griselda Pollock's essay "Screening the Seventies," which argued for new approaches to tackling the "politics of representation." Pollock's essay might be read against Chicago and Schapiro's desire for central core imagery, in that she describes a break with "alternative imagery valorizing 'real women.'" Pollock writes: "We are not seeking a new meaning for Woman but rather a total dissolution of the system by which sex/gender is organised to function as the criterion upon which differential and degrading treatment is assigned and naturalised."

One way to achieve this dissolution was by leaving behind a fixed idea of womanhood and femininity, one that circulated in art and visual culture and that reproduced stereotypes and ideals. For some artists—particularly Yve Lomax and Marie Yates, who featured in Mary Kelly's 1983 exhibition *Beyond the Purloined Image*—this meant removing or fragmenting images of women in their artwork, often juxtaposing these works with text. The effect was to prompt a different reaction in the viewer; one that departed from the eroticized looking described by Laura Mulvey in her influential 1974 article "Visual Pleasure and Narrative Cinema," and that, instead, encouraged a more engaged process of looking. In Yates's *The Missing Woman* (1982–84), the viewer is invited to become a detective, searching out a woman from the fragments of letters and images brought together in her multilayered re-photographed images. The parts do not add up to a whole, but allow for multiple potential stories to be told. Lomax's *Open Rings and Partial Lines* (1983–84) also comprise text and images that refuse to be united, sustaining, as Pollock has argued, "difference and heterogeneity."

The turn toward the sensate in art and feminism marked a break with the association of thought with rationality and disembodiment. The false division between mind and body was comically unpacked in British artist Kate Walker's "Feministo," published in the small magazine *MAMA: Women Artists Together* (ca. 1977). The poster separates thought from emotion, woman from man. This dichotomy was also exploited in the work of the *écriture féminine* writers, particularly in Luce Irigaray's *The Speculum of the Other Women*. Irigaray's book was published in France in 1975 and resulted in her expulsion from the École freudienne de Paris, which was directed by her mentor Jacques Lacan. Irigaray's expulsion from this prestigious institution parallels the argument in her book—namely, that Western philosophy is based on a male perspective that excludes women. Throughout the book, Irigaray strategically occupies the position of the feminine other, revealing the

Page 156: Theresa Hak Kyung Cha, *Aveugle Voix*, 1975

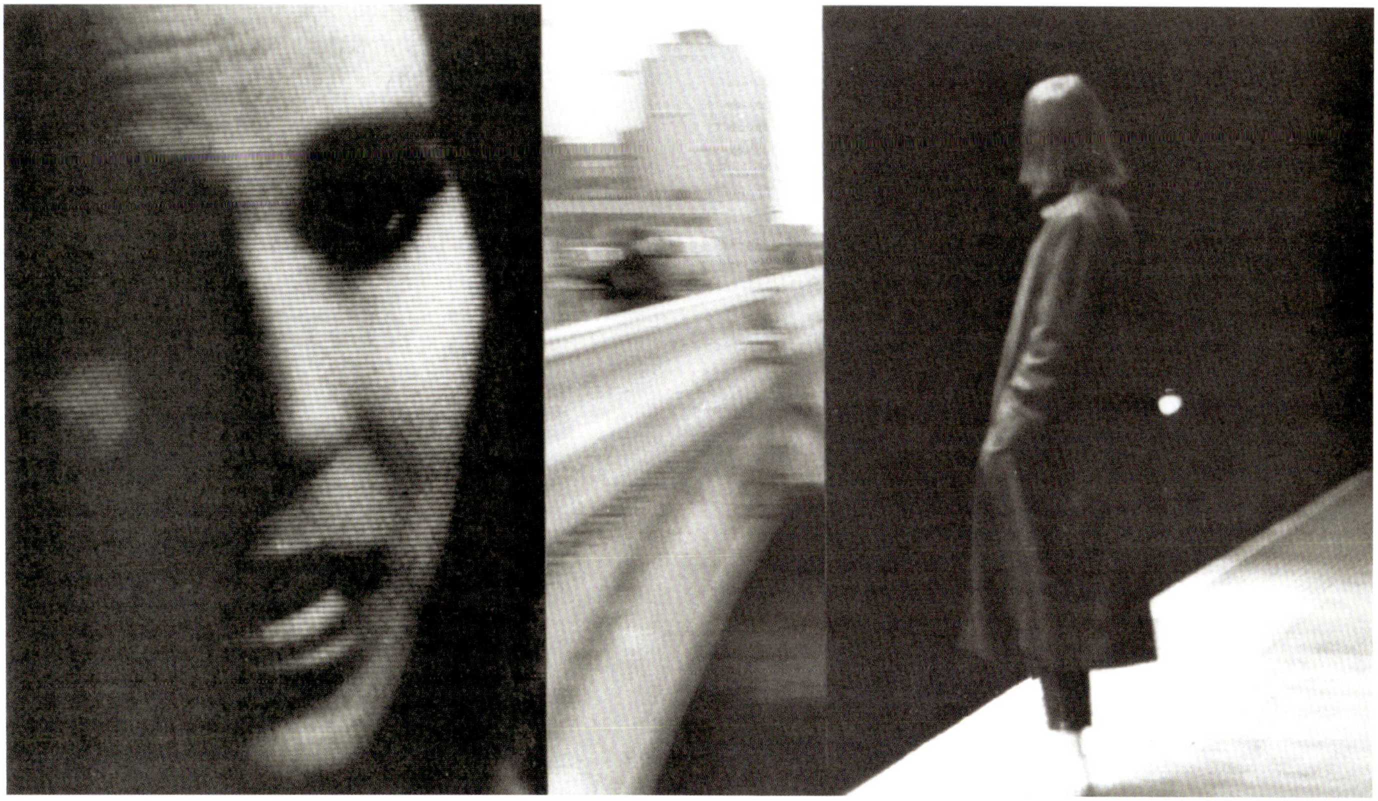

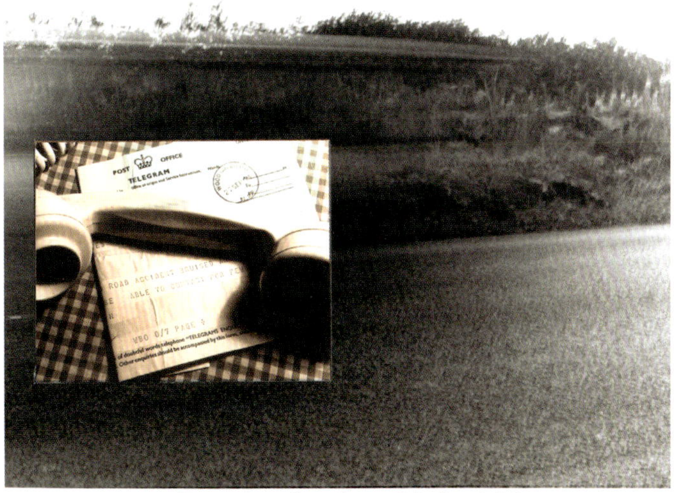

Somewhere there is a point of certainty

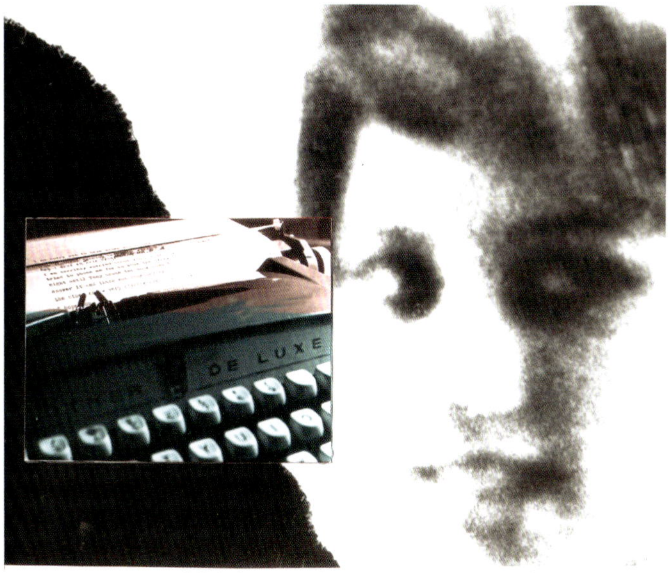

Affair between image and self image

Top: Yve Lomax, *Open Rings and Partial Lines*, 1984

Open Rings and Partial Lines is a multipart work. The images in each panel seem to both interact, in their representations of women and transit, and to disconnect, as they are each of a different angle and quality. The work asks the viewer to make connections and perhaps to create a narrative between the images, but does not specify what story should be told. Lomax made the work during a period when the truth-value of images was being decisively interrogated, and this work purposefully tries to resist a simple interpretation and to open up the representation of women in popular culture from the constraint of stereotype. Lomax wrote of the series: "There is nothing whole or essential regarding sexuality. Sexuality is a construction which concerns many parts."

Bottom left & right: Marie Yates, *The Missing Woman*, Phase II, 1983

These two panels form part of Yates's multipanel installation *The Missing Woman*. Each panel comprises a series of overlaid images and text. Sometimes these texts act as captions to images, and sometimes they appear within the images as letters, or official documentation. While the former give a loose sense of place, the latter offer clues to the missing woman of the title. Like Lomax's *Open Rings and Partial Lines*, *The Missing Woman* was made in a context of critical acuity, particularly in relation to the representation of women. Yates presents the viewer with a mystery, asking us to find the missing woman. Yet after reading the work, the viewer may come to realize that the woman is impossible to find, because she is impossible to represent fully and, therefore, always missing from the picture.

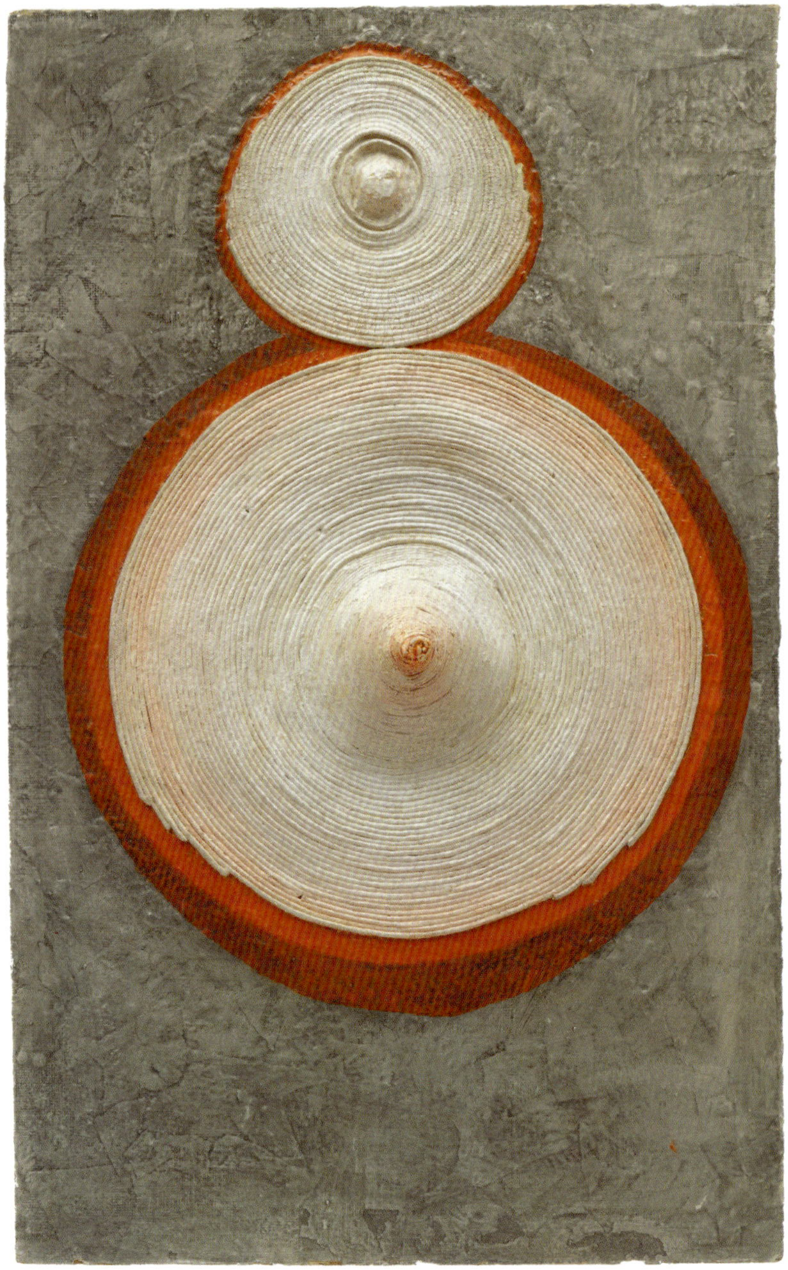

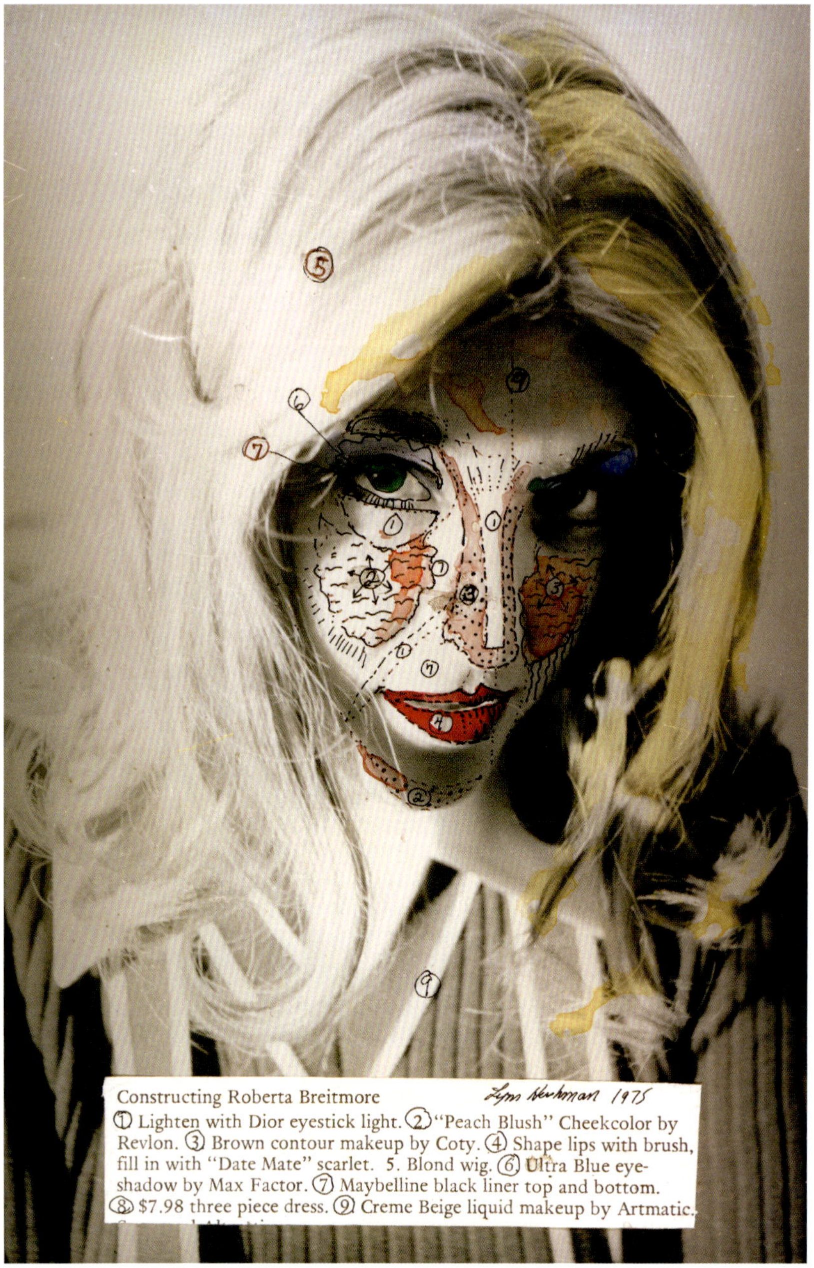

Above left: **Eva Hesse, *Ringaround Arosie*, 1965**

This relief work comprises two circular forms of pale, cloth-covered wire wound in spirals that end in a raised mound like a nipple. The circles are edged in red and the teat-like tips are white and pink. The surface was built up from a Masonite base with plaster, papier-mâché, and paint, resulting in a densely textured effect. *Ringaround Arosie* is suggestive of body parts and Hesse described it as "both breast and penis" in a letter to her friend Sol LeWitt. The title puns the process of making work—the roundabout action of constructing the spirals—with the children's nursery rhyme. The work was made while Hesse was working in Germany for a year; this period was one of transition that resulted in her self-designation as sculptor on her return to the United States.

Above right: **Lynn Hershman Leeson, *Roberta's Construction Chart 1*, 1975**

In 1973, the artist Lynn Hershman Leeson invented the character Roberta Breitmore. She then transformed herself into Breitmore, complete with costume, gestures, handwriting, and demeanors. She not only played the role for the camera, or for art gallery performances, she performed it in real life. Hershman Leeson opened a bank account, rented an apartment, and had psychoanalysis as Breitmore. The performance was documented in a series of drawings and "surveillance photographs" that capture Breitmore's activity. This work is a map or "construction chart" for Breitmore's signature makeup. Hershman Leeson ended the performance in 1978 with an exorcism ritual in the Palazzo dei Diamanti in Ferrara, Italy.

association of women with silence to be little more than fabrication. These occupations situate writing and speech in the body, as a means of disrupting the dichotomies of Western thought, and as a starting point for the redefinition of femininity.

Irigaray's use of language troubled the logic of argument, using metaphors, homonyms, and anecdotes. These experiments in sensible and embodied language, as well as Irigaray's analysis of representation, relate to the work of many artists, including Theresa Hak Kyung Cha. In her performance *Aveugle Voix* (1975) Hak Kyung Cha engages with the difficulty of communication across language. For this work, the artist, writer, and filmmaker, while dressed in white, covers her mouth with a white band stenciled with the word "*Aveugle*." Using another white band, this time stenciled with the word "*Voix*," she covers her eyes. *Aveugle voix* literally translates from French as "blind voice," without sight and speech. Hak Kyung Cha then unfurls a banner printed with the text "Words – fail – me – *sans* – *mot* – *sans* – *voix* – *aveugle* – gesture" and moves across its surface, performing different gestures. The combination of English and French, and of idioms and their mistranslations (*aveugle voix* also means "blind sight") relates the difficulty and particularity of moving between languages and cultures, as well as the expediency of silence.

Ketty La Roca is another artist who uses language as material in her work. Beginning in 1970, the Italian artist embarked on a focused investigation of the gesture and expression of the hand. For La Roca the hand represented a mode of communication freed from semiotics. Her series *My Words, and You?* (*Le mie parole, et tu?*) comprises monochrome photographs of hands gesturing; counting, pointing, making a fist, and pairs of entwined hands—one feminine, one masculine—holding, catching, and containing one another. The surfaces of the photographs are marked with the handwritten word "you." Scrawled on both hands, this text appears to refer to both bodies, playing with identity and identification. La Roca's use of pronouns inscribes an exchange in which one verifies the other's existence. While this relationship may sometimes be read as a confrontation between man and woman, it could also refer to the Italian feminist process of *autocoscienza* and, as such, the new relationships formed in the context of feminism. In this way La Roca's work may be read in parallel with the Italian feminist theorists Carla Lonzi and Adriana Cavarero, who both interrogated and articulated a mode of feminine and feminist speech.

Cavarero's later work on the voice is especially pertinent to many women artists' experiments with sound. In her 2005 book, *For More Than One Voice: A Philosophy of Vocal Expression*, Cavarero reconsiders the relationship between speech and voice as gendered and politicized. Rather than emphasize the content of what is being said, Cavarero is interested in the speaking voice. Like Irigaray and Julia Kristeva before her, Cavarero considers the denigration of the embodied subject in philosophy and instead retrieves the deviant or unruly speaking body from its subordinate relationship to language. Although indirectly, this sense of disruption and breakdown parallels a number of artists working with the oral and the aural. Anne Bean's performances, recordings, and musical collaborations seem particularly attuned to Cavarero's interest in the discordant. Through the 1970s Bean experimented with transforming her voice, both in performance and through recorded distortions. Bean was involved in different groups from 1975 to 1979 including The Moodies, Bongo Fury, and Absolutely Furious, all of which involved costume, projection, and performance, as well as music. As she has noted, Bean also became her own group called Anne Archy, by recording Super 8 sound films of herself playing instruments and projecting them while performing. Both an act of splitting and proliferation, Bean's performances transgressed medium and autonomous subjectivity.

The American artist Lynda Benglis experimented with splitting and attachment in her *Female Sensibility* (1973). In this video, two heavily made-up women—Benglis and her friend Marilyn Lenkowsky—emphatically kiss and caress each other, with a soundtrack of a radio show and a telephone call. On one level, the video is a spoof of contemporary attempts to define women's art. Each woman provides the other with a malleable body, to be touched and moved in place—even these affectionate, delicate gestures seem to constrict the women on screen. The tender relationship between the two women seems to parody the association of women with softness, and perhaps also alludes to Betty Freidan's homophobic description of a "lavender menace" in the women's liberation movement.

Many artists were experimenting with other senses and sensibilities before the context of the women's liberation movement asked if there was a feminine aesthetic. Carolee Schneemann experimented with imaging sex and sexual desire from a woman's perspective. Her film *Fuses* (1965) documented the artist and her male partner having sex in front of a bright window. Their shadowy silhouettes move together, between cuts and lengths of overpainted and scratched film. At one point Schneemann's cat moves into the frame, becoming another erotic interlocutor. The film was censored both outside and in feminist contexts, despite Schneemann's interest in investigating the possibilities of erotic representation. In *Kitch's Last Meal* (1973–78), Schneemann documents her daily life with her cat, Kitch, ending with the elderly cat's death. This work is both a document of the artist's life and of her close relationship with the cat. Schneemann's work evidences the artist's resistance to taking the position of filmmaker I/eye, instead understanding her creative production drawn out across lived relationships and her tactile working with the material. It stands in for a broader negotiation of the possibility of the body to be an intelligent and sensate instrument, which both differences and differentiates itself from the Western, patriarchal tradition of disembodied rationality.

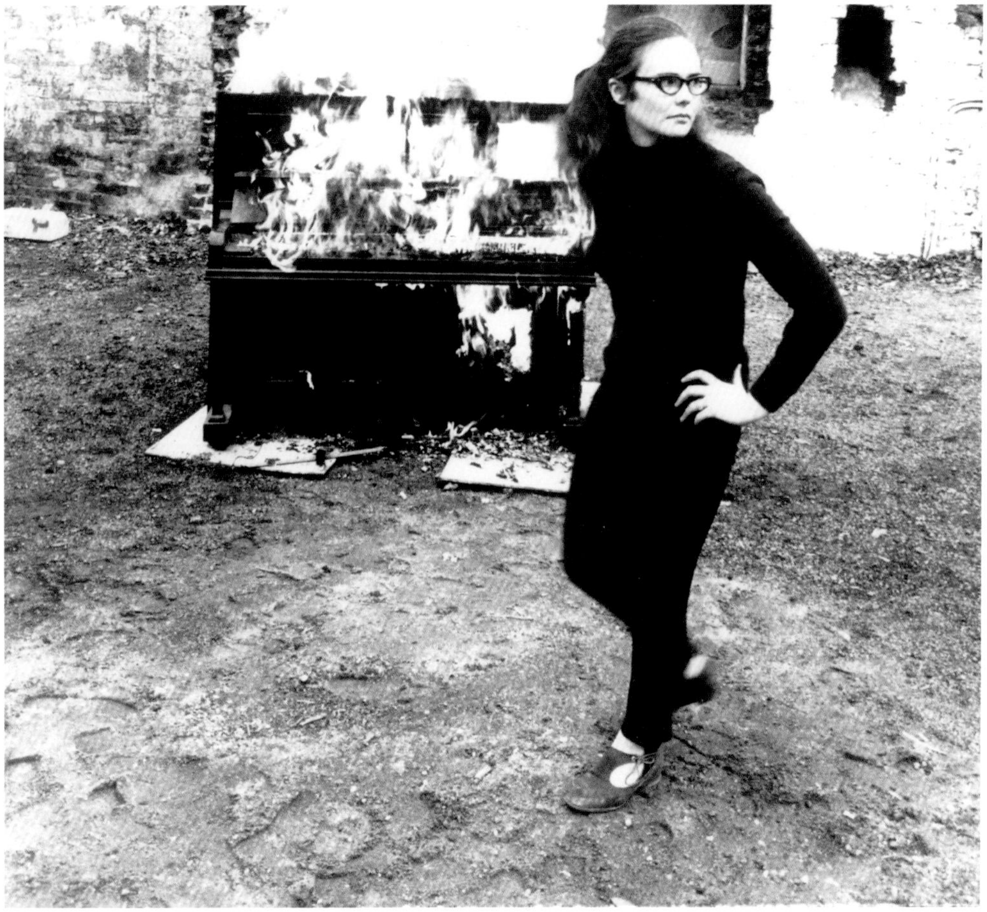

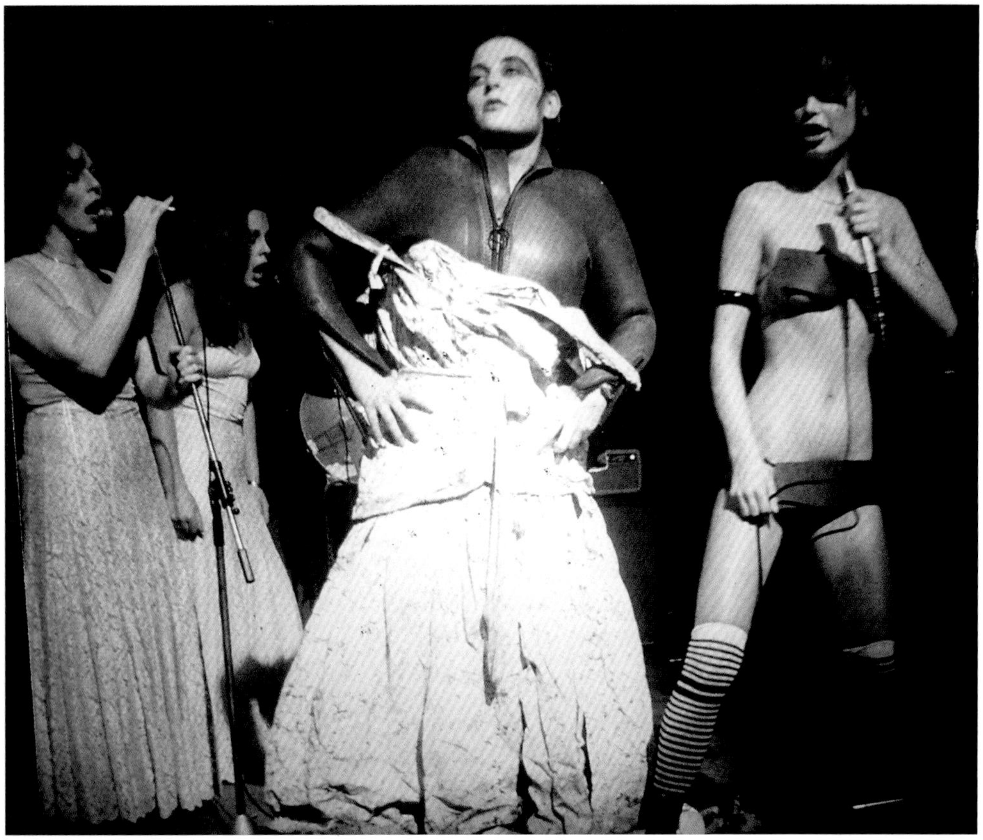

Top left: **Annea Lockwood, *Piano Burning, London*, Piano Transplants, 1968**

Lockwood is a composer who works with unconventional instruments and found sounds. Her series of Piano Transplants (1969–82)—performed throughout the United Kingdom and the United States—involved playing a broken piano while it was buried, drowned, or burned. Each photograph was accompanied by a score or set of instructions—the latter in this case: *Set upright piano (not a grand) in an / open space with the lid closed. / Spill a little lighter fluid on a twist of paper and / place inside, / near the pedals. / Light it. / Balloons may be stapled to the piano.* In the 1960s and 1970s Lockwood experimented with the form of the score, collaborating with the composer Pauline Oliveros and the artist Alison Knowles, who also used scores in her FLUXUS works. Lockwood moved to New York to teach in 1973, where she became more involved in women's liberation. Between 1975 and 1976 Lockwood and Knowles edited and self-published *Women's Work*, which gathered together scores by twenty-four women artists, composers, and writers including Mieko Shiomi, Simone Forti, Oliveros, Carolee Schneemann, and Carol Law, among others.

Bottom left: **Anne Bean in Bongo Fury, ca. 1975–79**

This photograph documents a live performance by the London-based artist Anne Bean at Garage Gallery, London, in 1974. Bean was a pioneer of live art in the 1970s and has continued to make genre-defying performances and installations. In this performance, Bean performs with the band Moody and the Menstruators, which ran from 1971–74 and comprised Bean's fellow students from Reading School of Art. The band transcended boundaries between art and music, and played with gender identity; they wore elaborate costumes styled on pantomime, Kabuki theater, and bands such as Roxy Music, while their performances took from dada and futurist precedents, as well as pop and post-punk music. This band later developed into Moodier, and then into Bongo Fury, in which Bean collaborated with a number of London-based avant-gardists. During this time Bean also embarked on a solo project called Anne Archy, for which she performed with a recorded version of herself playing instruments.

Below left: **Gee Vaucher, Collage for *International Anthem*, Number 2, *Domestic Violence*, 1979**

International Anthem was a publication described as the "nihilist newspaper for the living," produced between 1977 and 1980 by Gee Vaucher. Vaucher is an artist and former member of the anarcho-pacifist punk band Crass, the members of which lived communally on an Essex farm. Vaucher designed much of the band's art and participated in its political actions, including a 1982 hoax in which Crass circulated a constructed, taped conversation between Margaret Thatcher and Ronald Reagan. Vaucher's early works date from the 1960s, and include many collages, such as this image for the cover of *International Anthem*. The collages were influenced by the work of John Heartfield and dada and surrealism more broadly, but are firmly rooted in Vaucher's anarchism, as well as gender politics. Vaucher started *International Anthem* as a space to circulate her work, along with that by her fellow Crass members, Eve Libertine and Penny Rimbaud.

Below right: **Linder, *What I Do to Please You I Do*, 1981**

This is an early photomontage by Linder, the British artist who is also well known for her album cover designs for the punk band, the Buzzcocks. She, herself, was a front woman for the Manchester-based band Ludus. Linder's early works juxtaposed images culled from print magazines. These works, including *What I Do to Please You I Do*, present a critique of gender roles, and particularly those played out in the bourgeois family. This work is part of a series titled She/She, originally published as a booklet, *Pickpocket: SheShe*, to accompany the release of Ludus's 1981 six-track *Pickpocket*. The series comprises fourteen panels, featuring nine photographs of Linder and five short texts. The texts are taken from songs on the album. In the images Linder appears to perform a photomontage on her own image, obscuring—as in this work—part of her face with a fragment from a fashion magazine. Like others in the series, the image is seductive and glamorous, but also hints at suffocation, gagging, and masking, suggesting the double-sided appeal of feminine beauty.

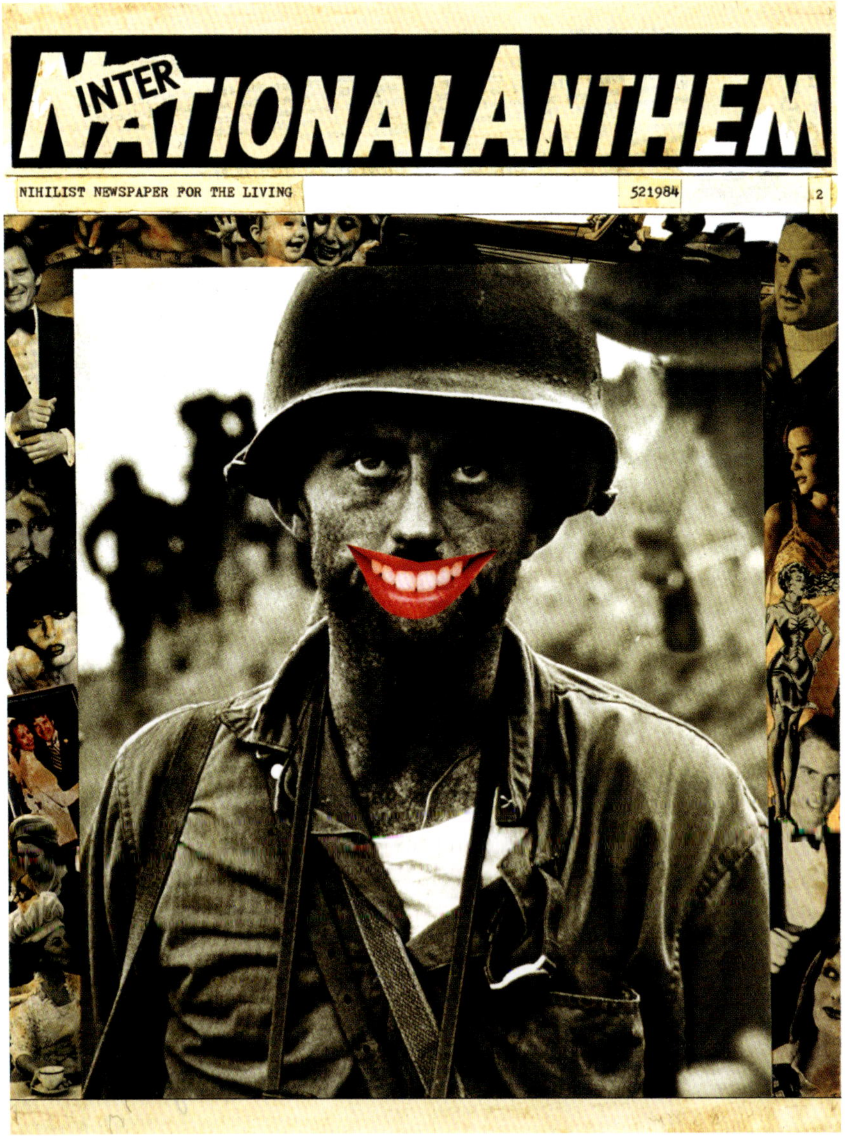

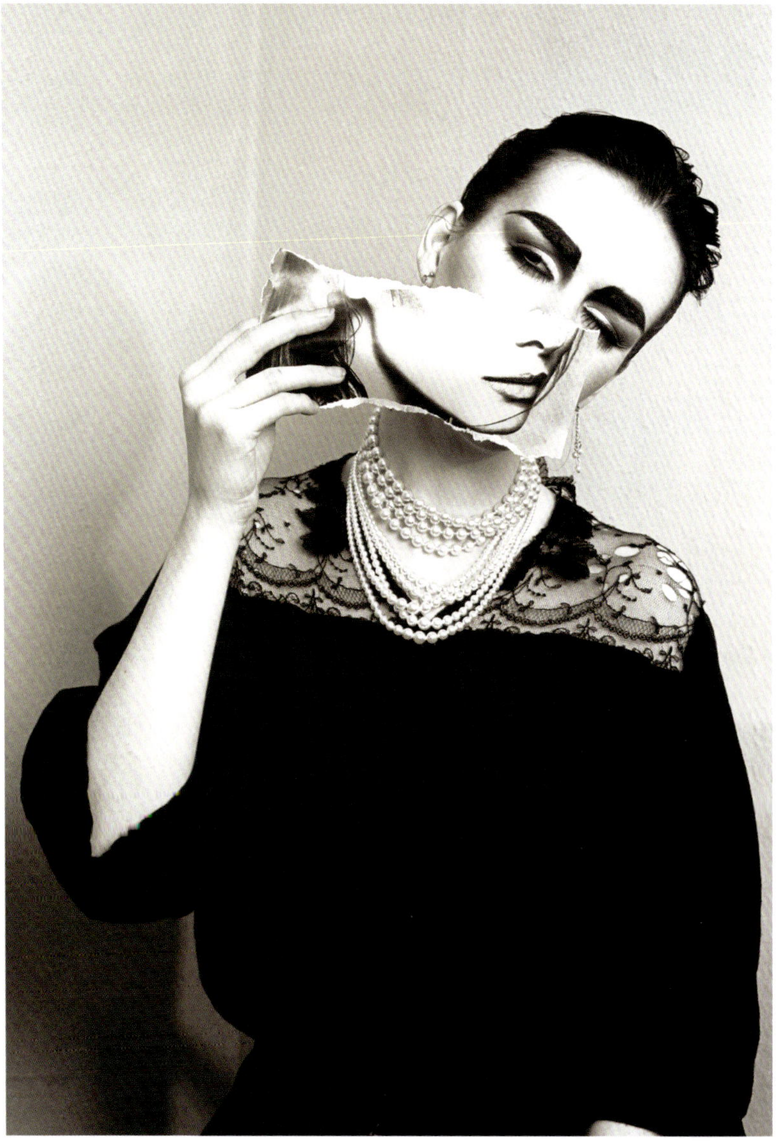

Listening to Others

by Irene Revell

During the 1970s, American composer Pauline Oliveros explored a number of engagements with feminism, the first of which was entitled *To Valerie Solanas and Marilyn Monroe, In Recognition of Their Desperation - - - -* (1970), a work that encouraged its musicians to listen to, and be influenced by, those performing alongside them.

Pauline Oliveros (1932–2016) was a composer perhaps best known for her philosophy of what she called Deep Listening®—that is, "listening in every possible way to everything possible to hear no matter what one is doing." Essential to her work was an exploration of involuntary hearing compared to the act of selective listening. Working prolifically over seven decades, Oliveros made her first major impact in 1962, when she cofounded the San Francisco Tape Music Center, an initially self-organized studio of immense influence on the twentieth-century development of electronic music. There, she would pioneer tape work, experimenting with delay(s), collapsing moments of the past, present, and future, which she further explored with her ongoing "Expanded Instrument System."

During the 1960s, Oliveros was drawn to working with the long tones and drone-like forms that provide the basic materials in her 1970 score, *To Valerie Solanas and Marilyn Monroe, In Recognition of Their Desperation - - - -*. Toward the end of the 1960s, Oliveros also started more actively to explore meditation and improvisation, while encountering the nascent women's movement: "[S]hortly after it was published in 1968 the *S.C.U.M. Manifesto* by Valerie Solanas fell into my hands. Intrigued by the egalitarian feminist principles set forth in the manifesto, I wanted to incorporate them in the structure of a new piece that I was composing. . . . Marilyn Monroe had taken her own life. Valerie Solanas had attempted to take the life of Andy Warhol. Both women seemed to be desperate and caught in the traps of inequality: Monroe needed to be recognized for her talent as an actress. Solanas wished to be supported for her own creative work."

To Valerie Solanas and Marilyn Monroe, In Recognition of Their Desperation - - - -, is a composition for six or more musicians on any instrument(s) and has three parts of equal length, indicated by red, yellow, and blue lighting respectively, either thirty, forty-five, or sixty minutes in total. The work was commissioned by the New Music Ensemble of the San Francisco Conservatory of Music and premiered at Hope College, Michigan, in September 1970. The score's three pages of text instruction specify certain aspects in detail, while others are left entirely to the determination of those staging the performance. All players follow the same parts with no hierarchy.

The piece draws specifically on Valerie Solanas's insistence on the need for the autonomy of the individual within any group or collective process, outlined in Solanas's *S.C.U.M. Manifesto*—a work that presents the world as having been ruined by men and that was down to women to fix. In Oliveros's piece, each player independently chooses five tones and certain forms of "modulation" in advance of the performance and without prior discussion. In the first part, the players introduce their own tones, and in the second the players can begin to "steal" elements from the other players, while the third part mirrors the first. Although the complex instructions call on a degree of competence in any given instrument, the emphasis of the piece is on intensive listening to others rather than traditional musical virtuosity. And "if any player starts to dominate the musical texture, the community that is created by the piece absorbs the outstanding sounds back into the collective." The long, discordant tones create a serene, contemplative underpinning that befits the dedication in the work's title; while the dynamism of the ongoing play between the individual performances and the sound of the group as a whole act as a potent metaphor for the political and artistic practices emerging in the contemporaneous women's movement.

There have been numerous iterations of the work over the subsequent decades. In 1977, the score itself was published by Smith Publishing, and a vinyl recording was released in 2011 consisting of the work's premier at Hope College and a later 1977 performance at Wesleyan University. The score was exhibited as part of the exhibition project *WACK! Art and the Feminist Revolution* (2007–09). Diverse recent performances include one in the Turbine Hall at Tate Modern, London (2012); an opera by Opera Povera, Redcat, Los Angeles (2012); at the Gardiner Museum, Toronto (2017); and a filmed version made in Berlin by artists Pauline Boudry / Renate Lorenz (2013).

To Valerie Solanas and Marilyn Monroe, In Recognition of Their Desperation - - - - is the first in a number of explicit engagements Oliveros would make with feminism, while she consistently championed the work of other women throughout her career. In 1971 she formed the Women's Ensemble at the University of California San Diego, in which she developed her Sonic Mediations, a series of short text instructions that "question dominant notions of music, talent, sound, ability, and musical authority," as Martha Mockus explains in her book *Sounding Out: Pauline Oliveros and Lesbian Musicality*. Oliveros collaborated with a number of artists, including Linda Montano and Alison Knowles, on works that address feminist themes, and also wrote texts, starting with her 1970 *New York Times* article, "And Don't Call Them 'Lady' Composers."

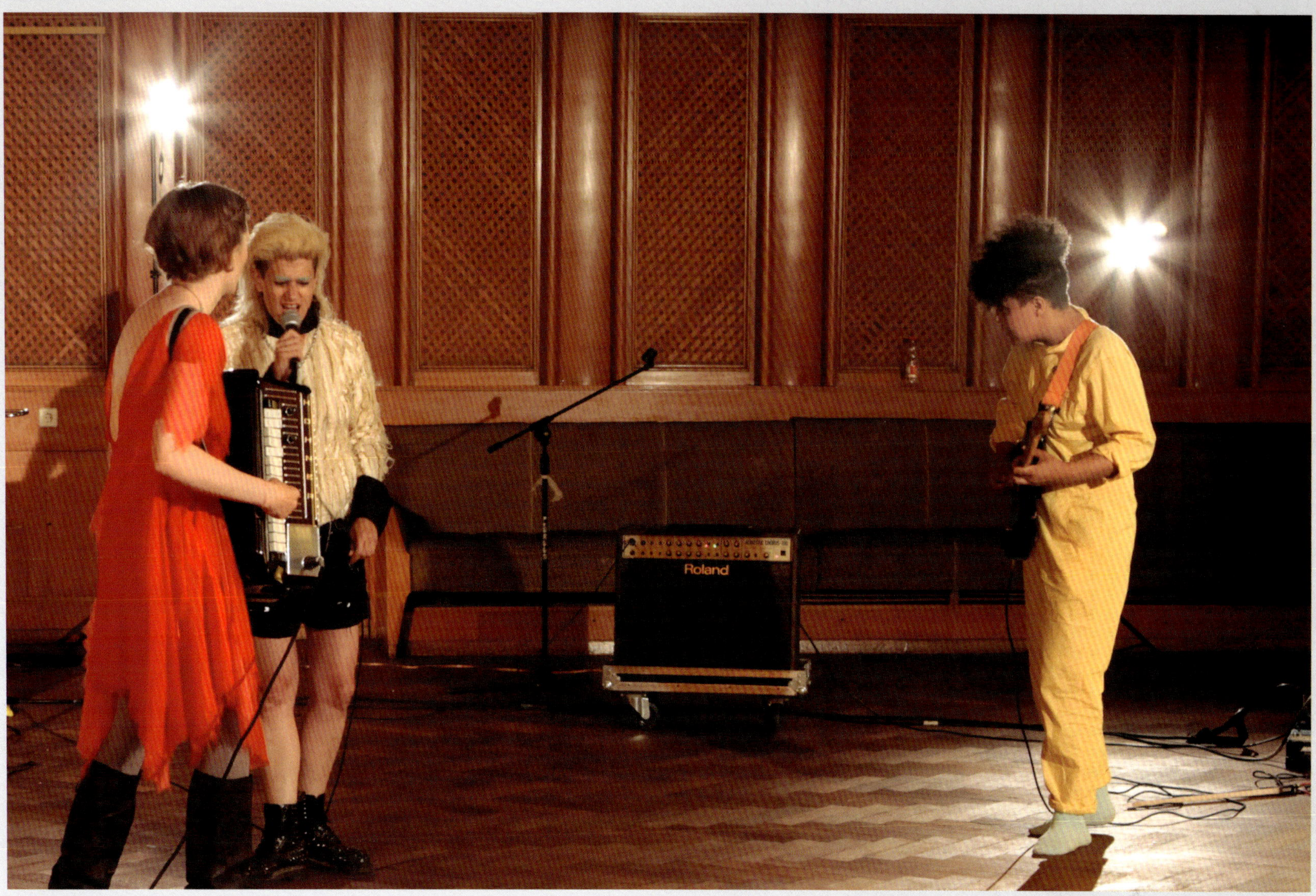

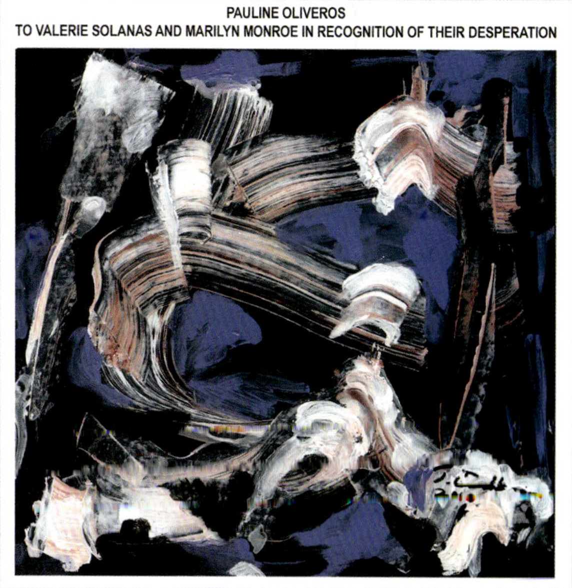

"The women's movement was surfacing and I felt the need to express my resonance with this energy."

Pauline Oliveros, writing in 2010

Top: Pauline Boudry/Renate Lorenz, *To Valerie Solanas and Marilyn Monroe In Recognition of Their Desperation - - - -*, 2013, still

A still from the film version of *To Valerie Solanas and Marilyn Monroe In Recognition of Their Desperation - - - -*, made by Boudry and Lorenz in Berlin, 2013. Performing in the film were Rachel Aggs, Peaches, Catriona Shaw, Verity Susman, Ginger Brooks Takahashi, and William Wheeler.

Bottom: *To Valerie Solanas and Marilyn Monroe In Recognition of Their Desperation - - - -*, 2010, record cover

Featuring artwork by Judith Lindbloom on the cover, a recording of *To Valerie Solanas and Marilyn Monroe In Recognition of Their Desperation - - - -* was released on vinyl by Roaratorio Records.

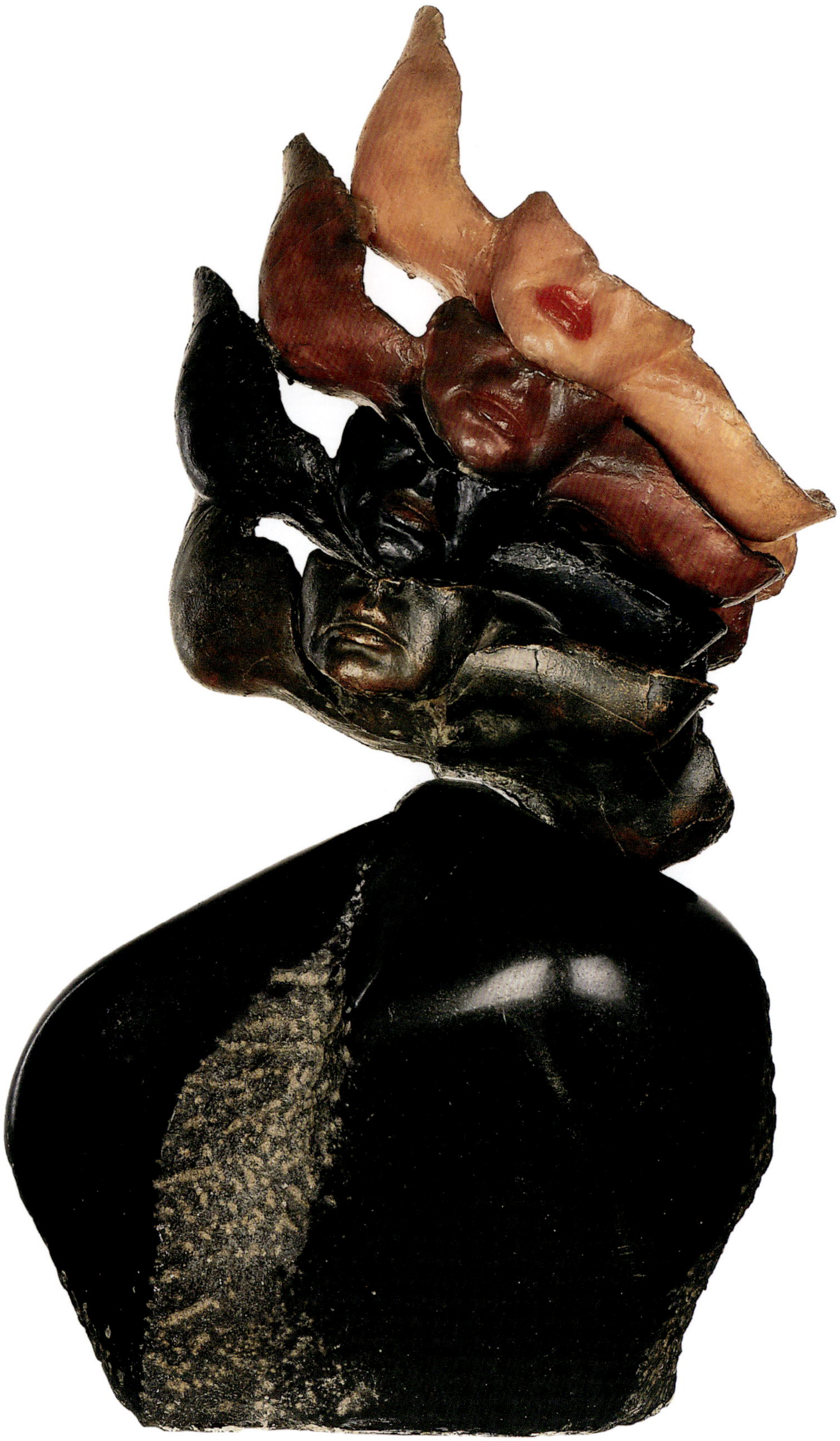

Left: **Alina Szapocznikow, *Multiple Portrait*, 1967**

Multiple Portrait comprises a marble base and four polyester-resin casts of the lower face and shoulders of the Polish artist Alina Szapocznikow. The work plays on, and subverts, the form of a traditional portrait bust, transforming it into an anatomically incorrect semiabstract form. Both casting from the body and the repetition of forms that casting allows, are characteristic of Szapocznikow's work from the 1960s. More particularly this work relates to the artist's experiments with self-portraiture in 1966 and 1967. In two self-portraits, from 1966, the artist's face and body are fragmented and remade. Lips appear prominently in both works, and also in *Multiple Portrait (Double)* from 1967, perhaps suggesting the importance of sensuality to her work, as well as punctuating her sculptures with an element of kitsch.

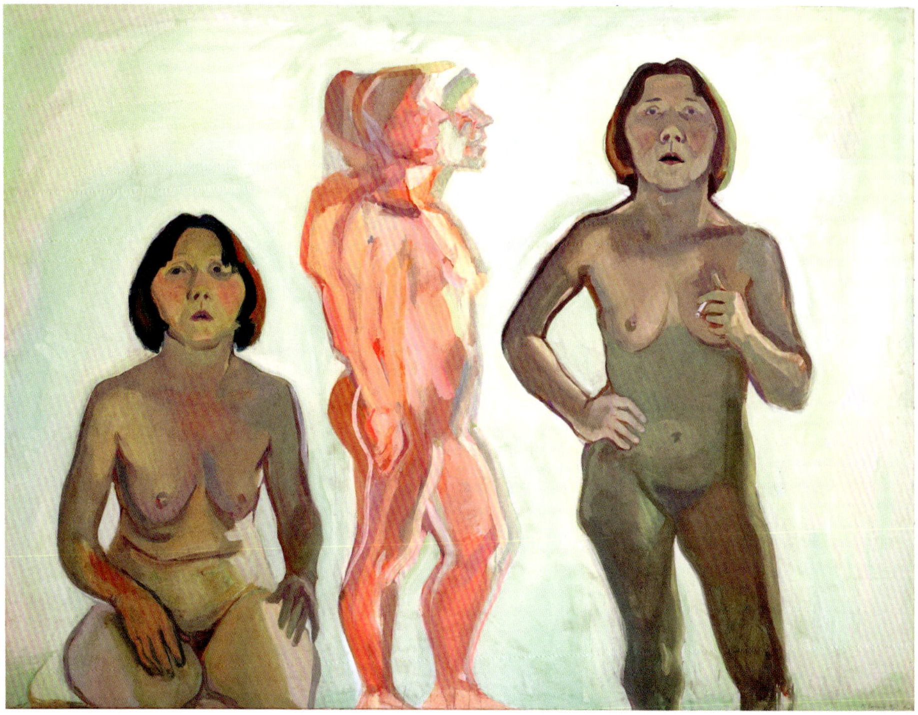

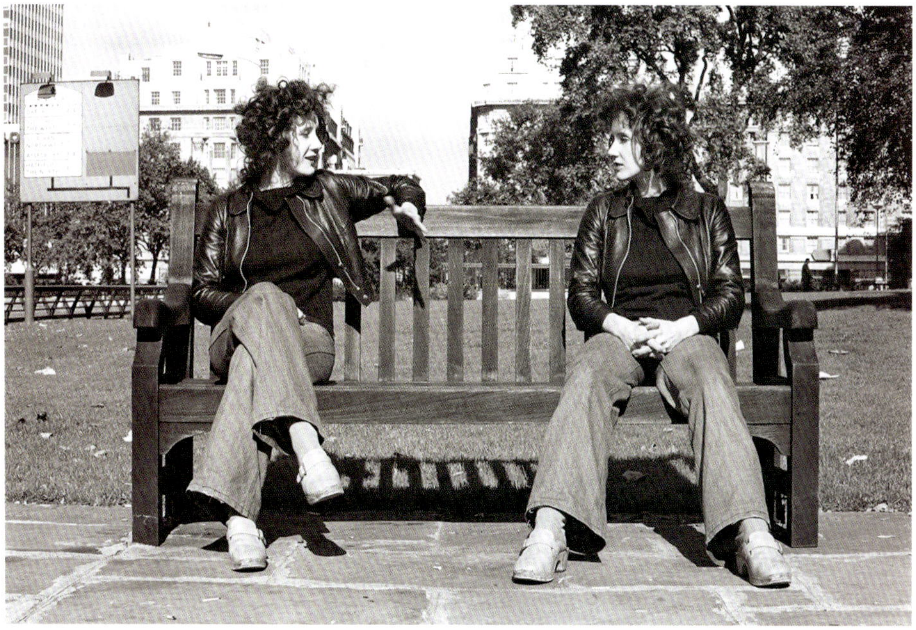

Top: Maria Lassnig, *Dreifaches Selbtsporträt / New Self, (Triple Self-Portrait / New Self)*, 1972

Maria Lassnig was an Austrian painter, who experimented throughout her career with self-portraiture and the representation of subjective experience. Lassnig grew up in Nazi-controlled Vienna, where she went to art school and continued to work until 1968, when she moved to New York to study filmmaking and animation. Lassnig worked in many different ways, sometimes painting herself as she might appear in a mirror, sometimes working on the canvas while kneeling or lying on it, sometimes painting abstract portraits, and sometimes painting a feeling or emotion through the transformation of the face or body. In New York Lassnig engaged with feminist politics, and her work from this period, especially her films, interrogate gender and romantic relationships. This work, which features three self-portraits of the artist—seated, in profile, and standing—perhaps shows Lassnig as she looks for her new self in the midst of activism, her studying, and her work in New York.

Bottom: Rose Finn-Kelcey, *Divided Self*, 1974

This work by the British artist Rose Finn-Kelcey is a double-photographic self-portrait, comprised of two photographs collaged onto a single plane. The effect is to show Finn-Kelcey in conversation with herself—perhaps two opposing parts of herself, as the title *Divided Self* implies. The setting is close to Speaker's Corner in London's Hyde Park, a site famous for free, political speech. Rather than appear standing speaking to a public audience, in *Divided Self*, political speech is reconfigured as an intimate conversation, even an interrogation of the self. Finn-Kelcey's work from the 1970s often engaged with speech and voice. For instance in her performance *One for Sorrow, Two for Joy* (1976) she occupied the window of London's Acme Gallery with two magpies attempting to find an alternate language, "to talk," as Finn-Kelcey commented, "about a potential for women having a voice."

Below: **Eunice Golden, *Wrappings #1*, 1976**

Eunice Golden is a New York artist who is best known for her experiments representing the male nude. This aspect of Golden's work was rooted in feminism and women's liberation activism. She was a member of the Ad Hoc Women Artists' Committee, the cooperative gallery SoHo 20, and The Fight Censorship Group, whose members included Hannah Wilke, Louise Bourgeois, Judith Bernstein, Martha Edelheit, Juanita McNeely, Barbara Nessim, Anne Sharpe, and Anita Steckel. With The Fight Censorship Group, Golden argued for women's right to create phallic imagery and to exhibit it, paralleling the many representations of the female nude. Golden described her interest in the male nude as both political and erotic; she was aware that she was both "a product of male-oriented culture" and that she had "erotic fantasies and needs." Her work sought an empowered, interrogative, and erotic female gaze. Alongside her paintings, Golden worked in photography, of which *Wrappings #1* is a part. In this work, both men and women were wrapped in sheets of opaque plastic that variously obscure and reveal their bodies, as well as eliciting a haptic response in the viewer.

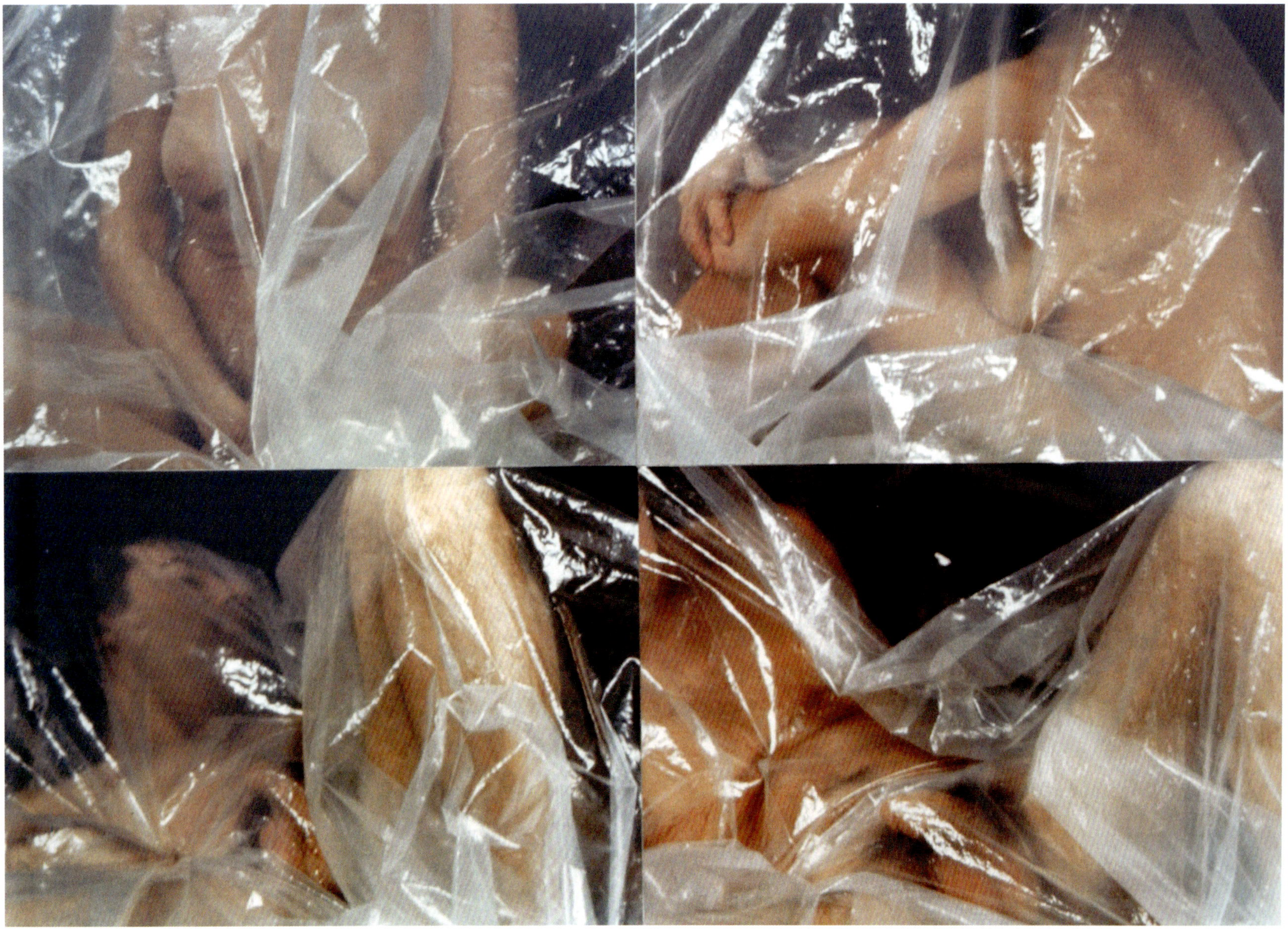

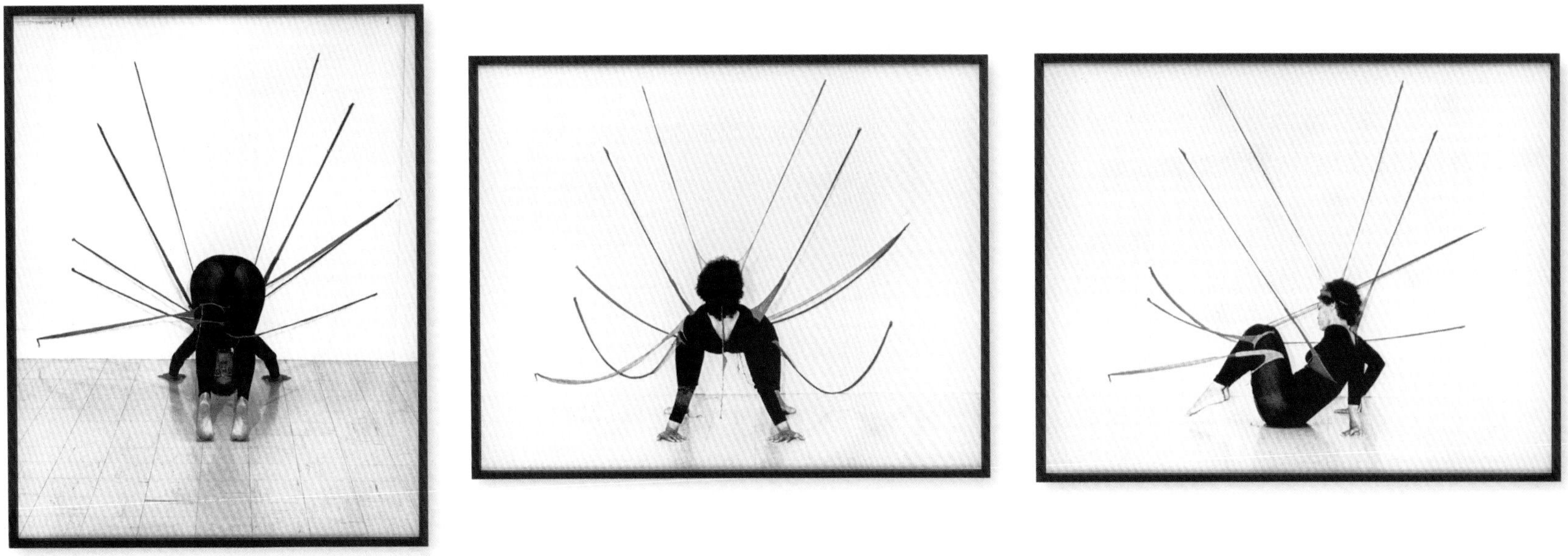

Above: **Senga Nengudi, *Performance Piece*, 1978**

This triptych of silver gelatin photographs shows nylon stocking sculptures activated by the dancer and choreographer Maren Hassinger. Hassinger and Nengudi collaborated on a number of works through the 1970s, via the Los Angeles group Studio Z. *Performance Piece* comprises staged photographs that relate to Nengudi's important sculptural series R.S.V.P., which comprises configurations of stockings knotted, stretched, and filled to create abstracted, bodily forms and musical notations. Nengudi began working with nylon stockings after her son was born in 1974, and the material has a number of resonances. It is easily available and economical, but also directly relates to femininity, and through Nengudi's work, to both malleability and constraint, strength, and vulnerability.

Containers and Capsules

by Catherine Spencer

For the British sculptor Veronica Ryan, history and memory were entwined. In her important work *Relics in the Pillow of Dreams*, she explored the intransigence of places left behind, and new environments in the context of the diaspora. For Ryan, sculpture was a container, or capsule, resonant with personal and social history.

Veronica Ryan grew up in Britain, where she had lived since moving from the Caribbean island of Montserrat as a child, and where she had studied at the Bath Academy of Art, The Slade, and the School of Oriental and African Studies. She later moved to New York and continues to live in both the U.K. and the U.S. today. Across the sculptural production that she created while in the United Kingdom and the United States, the concept of the container or capsule has proved a rich one, conveying both constraint and potential, manifested, in particular, by her engagement with plant forms and organic imagery, which can in turn be linked to histories of colonization, diaspora, and cultural exchange.

Ryan's *Relics in the Pillow of Dreams* (1985) is a cast-bronze sculpture that lies supine on the floor, rather than sitting on a plinth, and is shaped like a square pillow dented by the bodily impressions of a restless sleeper. Into several of these declivities, Ryan has secreted small, ambiguous items suggestive of seedpods dropped from flowering plants. The pillow acts as a reliquary for part-objects charged with memory, shared associations, and, as the title explicitly states, dreams and subconscious desires: "I consciously experimented with organic forms in earlier work. It was one way of addressing and identifying objects which belong to the place I came from. With these shapes I responded to the memories of Montserrat. Memories of growth, the landscape, taste and colours which were intrinsically bound up with 'my place'; which was also the unfamiliar place."

Ryan has discussed the importance that the philosopher Gaston Bachelard's book *The Poetics of Space* (1958) holds for her practice, describing her excitement at encountering a text that "deals with a number of concepts that are important for my work, especially for the notion of interior and exterior spaces, boxes, corners, houses, shells, etc." In his phenomenological account of interiors and exteriors, Bachelard traces the psychic resonances that imbue the everyday architecture of the home, as well as exploring the wider dynamics of enclosure, containment, and encirclement. The shell is a particularly important example of these operations for Bachelard, and he devotes a whole chapter of his study to its form, which he also links to the structure of the nest. Bachelard treats the shell and the nest as sites of refuge for thoughts, ideas, and dreams, and yet also as liminal phenomena from which life might emerge as well as retreat.

The items embedded into the surface of *Relics in the Pillow of Dreams*, while reminiscent of plant forms, also have interstices and openings that suggest shells and insect life, particularly insect pupae and larvae. While the use of the word "relics," and their memorialization through the bronze-casting processes (which also results in a sculpture redolent of artifacts recovered from an archaeological site), suggests that, although these containers have been cast aside, they still retain the possibility traced by Bachelard to operate as receptacles for memory, dreams, and desires and, by extension, to catalyze new ideas and even actions. Like Bachelard's ideas, Ryan's sculpture delights in contradictory dynamics of containment, oscillating between protection and nurture, and confinement and claustrophobia.

The objects housed in the pillow reliquary are at once part of the subject but also markers of this difference and dislocation. The undulating surface of the pillow is evocative of the sea as well as the dream-state; the organic matter carried on its surface offers a historical analogy between the migration of plants through floating seeds and pods, and multiple diasporic histories, including the forced relocation of the slave trade and the post-World War II movement of people from the Caribbean to Britain. *Relics in the Pillow of Dreams* acts as a container for this specific art history too, as well as for the fusion of the highly subjective with the socio-historical that Ryan achieves through her sculptural capsules, shells, and pods.

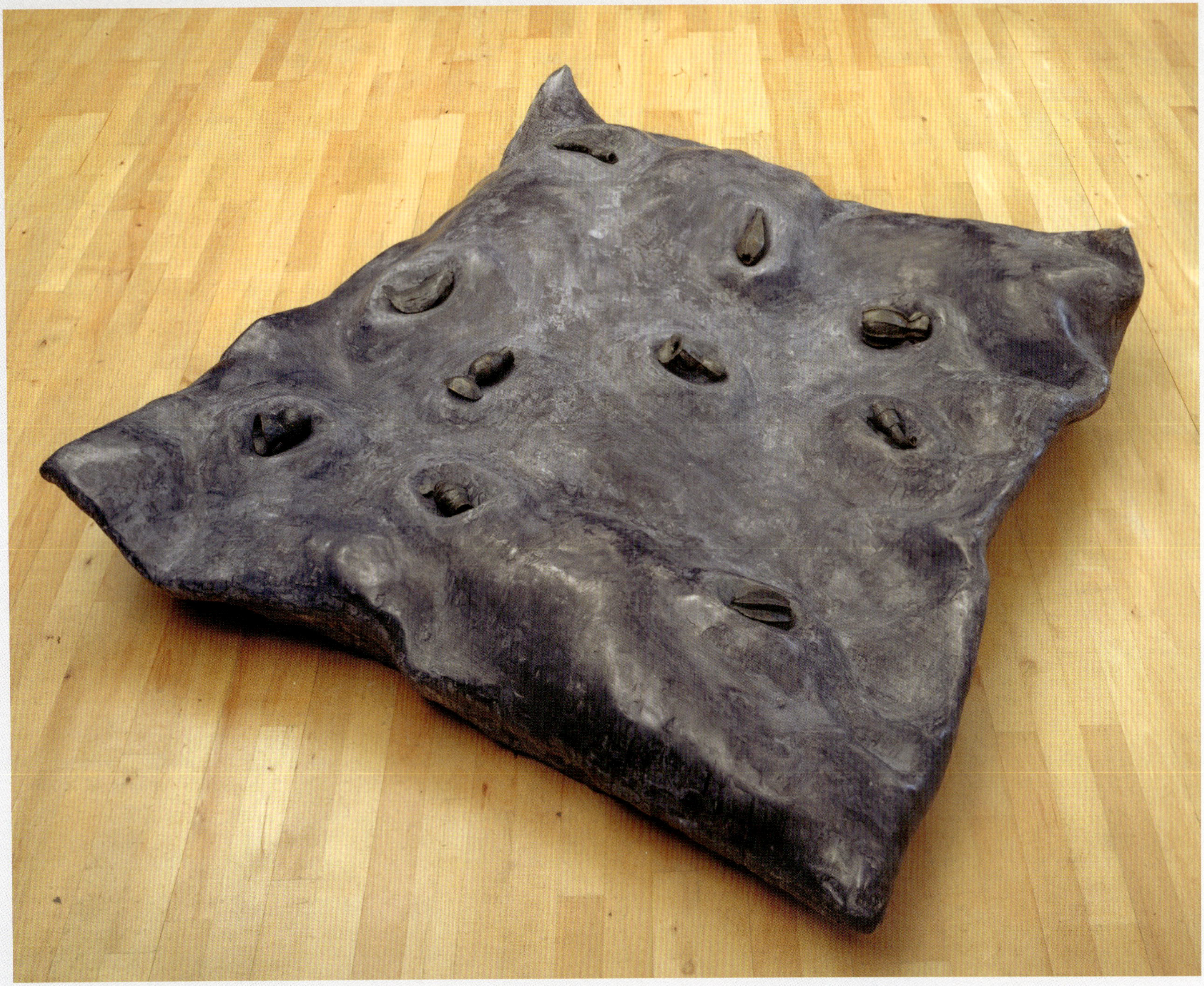

"... capsules, divisions, compartments, are all metaphors for the wider issues of dissociation, fracture, displacement, alienation and so on."

Veronica Ryan emphasizes the importance of vessel motifs and the concomitant act of containment for her work in the catalog for her 1995 exhibition, titled *Compartments/Apart-ments*, at the Camden Arts Centre, London

Above: **Veronica Ryan: *Relics in the Pillow of Dreams*, 1985**

Below: **Kazuko Miyamoto, Yoshiko Chuma inside *Trail Dinosaur*, 1978**

Miyamoto grew up and studied in Tokyo, before moving to New York in 1964. During her early years in New York, Miyamoto's practice shifted toward minimalism and postminimalism, eventually migrating from gridlike arrangements on gallery walls to three-dimensional installations with string. These works marked, measured, and transformed space, alerting the viewer to their place in the world. In her *String around a Cylinder of my Height* (1977), Miyamoto created a relationship between space, sculpture, and the artist's body, resulting in a kind of abstracted self-portrait. In 1972 Miyamoto took part in the exhibition *13 Women* alongside a number of artists including Louise Bourgeois and Mary Miss. In 1974 she joined the cooperative gallery A.I.R., and exhibited her string constructions numerous times. This image documents a performance by Yoshiko Chuma in Miyamoto's solo exhibition at A.I.R. (*New Work*, 1979), further developing the relationship between her work and the body. In 1980 she coorganized the *Dialectics of Isolation: An Exhibition of Third World Women Artists of the United States* with Ana Mendieta and Zarina.

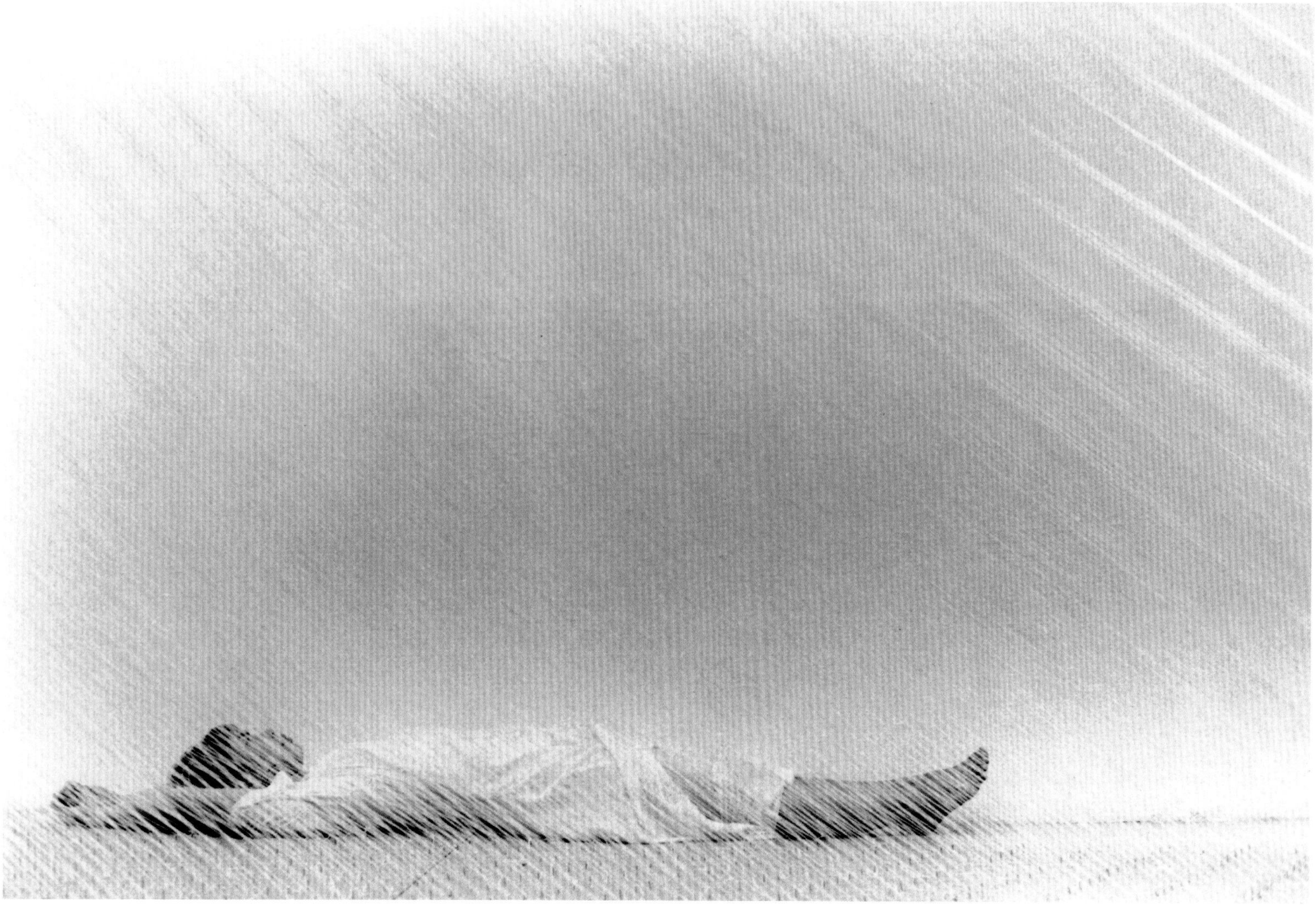

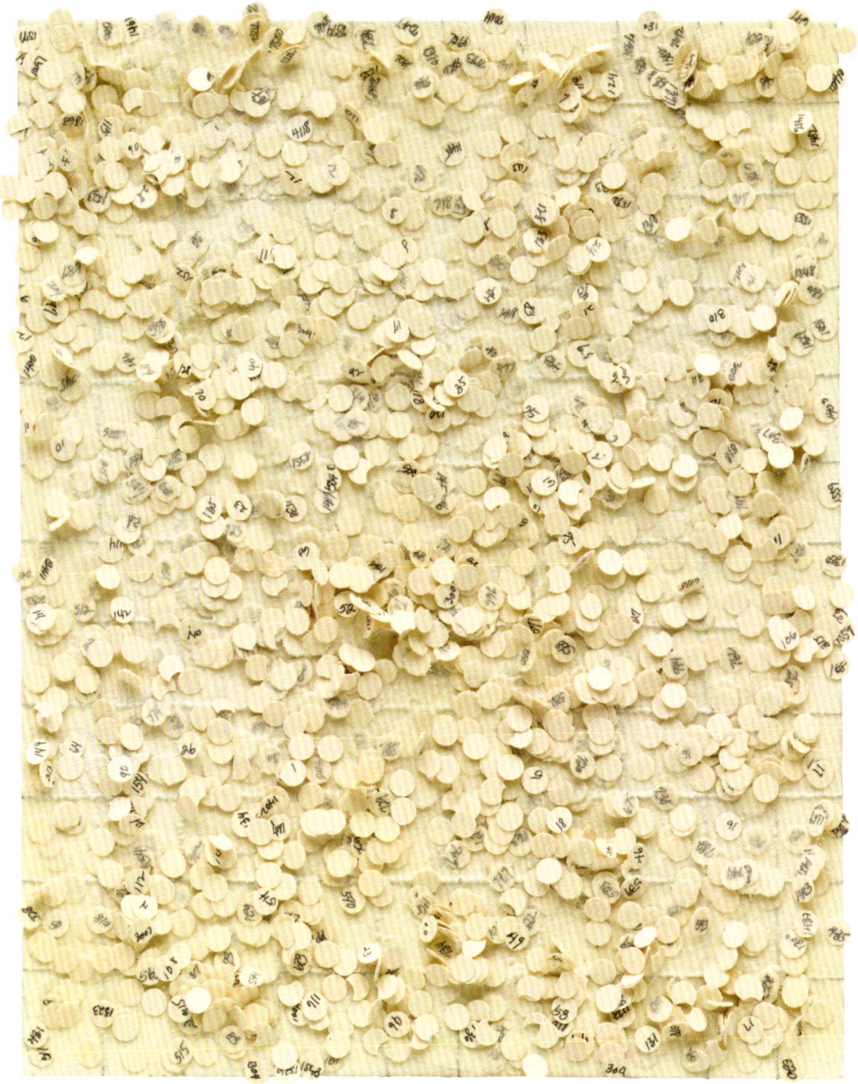

Above left: Zarina, *Untitled*, 1979

Zarina was born in Aligarh, India, and lived in Thailand, Japan, France, and Germany before settling in the United States in 1975. Zarina originally studied mathematics, and intended to become an architect before beginning her study of printmaking. Geometry and architecture suffuse much of her work, as does the theme of home. This was explored in depth in her seminal series of thirty-six woodcuts, *Home is a Foreign Place*. While she was much influenced by New York minimalism, her work is also attentive to texture and touch. This is evident in her preference for printmaking rather than drawing, as well as specifically in this untitled work, which comprises a paper surface punctured with sewing needles. In 1980 Zarina designed the catalog that accompanied the exhibition *Dialectics of Isolation: An Exhibition of Third World Women Artists of the United States* organized by Ana Mendieta and Yoshiko Miyamoto.

Above right: Howardena Pindell, *Untitled (#7)*, 1973

This work comprises layers of punched paper, a by-product from a hole punch, pasted on to a translucent paper surface. Some of the small circular paper confetti are marked in ink from their original surfaces, while a talcum-powder layer and a sewing-thread grid add to the depth and texture. This intricate work was made while the artist was living in New York and working at the Museum of Modern Art (MoMA). Pindell often worked at night in her small apartment. This context shaped her work; she used cheap, easily accessible materials such as paper confetti. When she made large-scale canvases, she worked with them unstretched, often cutting and stitching them back together. The labor of her night work registers on the dense surfaces of many of her pieces, although this one is remarkably light and delicate. Pindell studied for an MFA at Yale University in the 1960s, and was a member of A.I.R. gallery from 1972–73. Subsequently she has fought racial discrimination. In 1987 she presented the findings on equality, diversity, and exclusion garnered through her Art World Surveys, in a paper titled: "Statistics, Testimony, and Supporting Documentation."

Sexual Revolution

by Flora Dunster

The 1980s saw an escalation of debates regarding the representation of women, debates that intensified in relation to understandings of lesbian sexuality. These "Sex Wars" unfolded as a sexual revolution under feminism's own roof, a rift in opinion that has been historicized as the division between revolutionary feminists and "sex radicals."

Lightning rods of the Sex Wars debate included pornography, BDSM (bondage, discipline, sadism, and masochism), and butch/femme role-play. In some feminist and lesbian circles, such practices were seen as repressive in their mimicking of masculinity, exploitation, and violence. In others, they were considered liberating in their capacity to loosen expectations of what a woman, or a lesbian, did and how her desires manifested.

Photography became a crucial medium in testing the limits and possibilities for representations of women. Working as a form of activism, it drew on contemporaneous critical theory (a focus at the Birmingham Centre for Contemporary Cultural Studies at the time), and was supported by the United Kingdom's independent photography scene and attendant publications, such as *Creative Camera* and *TEN.8*.

The work of Tessa Boffin emerged from this context and dovetails with the "queer moment" of the early 1990s and the tail end of the Sex Wars, a period marked by the ongoing AIDS crisis, the British parliament's passing of Section 28 (the 1988 law that prohibited the "promotion" of homosexuality by local authorities), and homophobia in the tabloid press. Themes of sexuality and sexual health—guided by Simon Watney, Boffin's mentor at the Polytechnic of Central London where she studied—permeate her interests as a photographer, writer, curator, and educator.

Boffin's series *The Knight's Move* was published alongside an accompanying essay in the multiauthored volume *Stolen Glances: Lesbians Take Photographs* (1991), which Boffin coedited with collaborator Jean Fraser, and which toured as an exhibition of the same name in England and Scotland. *The Knight's Move* invests in the imaginative potential of photography, over and above fantasies. Responding to the paucity of historical lesbian imagery, Boffin invents a lesbian past. Citing Stuart Hall's essay "Cultural Identity and Diaspora" (1990), she recaps two methods for engaging with marginal narratives. The first is to rediscover figures who have been "lost," and who align with a coherent identity in the present. The second is to produce identities, not through proof of past existence, but by a willful and inventive relationship to history that augments contemporary notions of, for instance, the lesbian. This is the knight's move—a sideways step that surpasses what is known in favor of what could be.

Drawing from Hall's second strategy, *The Knight's Move* unfolds as a sequence of black-and-white studio portraits book-ended by two photographs taken in London's Abney Park cemetery. The portraits, arranged as diptychs, portray four historical types as lesbians: knight, knave, Casanova, and lady-in-waiting—two of whom hold plaques listing the names of "real" lesbians from the past. Between these pairings is a fifth, lone figure, an androgynous angel with densely feathered wings, nude but for a loincloth and bondage-esque harness, indicative of Boffin's queer and sex radical politics. These five women are united in the final image, a composite that sees the four "fantasy" lesbians arranged under the angel's wings, the angel herself standing with her fist raised defiantly in the air. As they emerge from the cemetery's shadows, and Boffin's substantiated role models are led by the queer angel into the present of the viewer, "the gap between reality and fantasy" is bridged.

Boffin's stake in the possibilities of fantasy speaks to debates around images of women, particularly insofar as her images might generate desire, or pose their subjects as desirable. This is central to Boffin's purpose, in that she offers photographs that trigger the desire of women for women by inciting her viewer's imagination. However, as *Stolen Glances'* introduction explains, its participating photographers steal and invert heterosexual representations. *The Knight's Move* is not a mimicking of patriarchal narratives—the chauvinism of the Casanova, the violence of the knight—but the fantasy of these figures as lesbians, a maneuver that lifts and reinterprets them as erotically charged sites of identification, a knight's move to mobilize new avenues for rethinking lesbian histories.

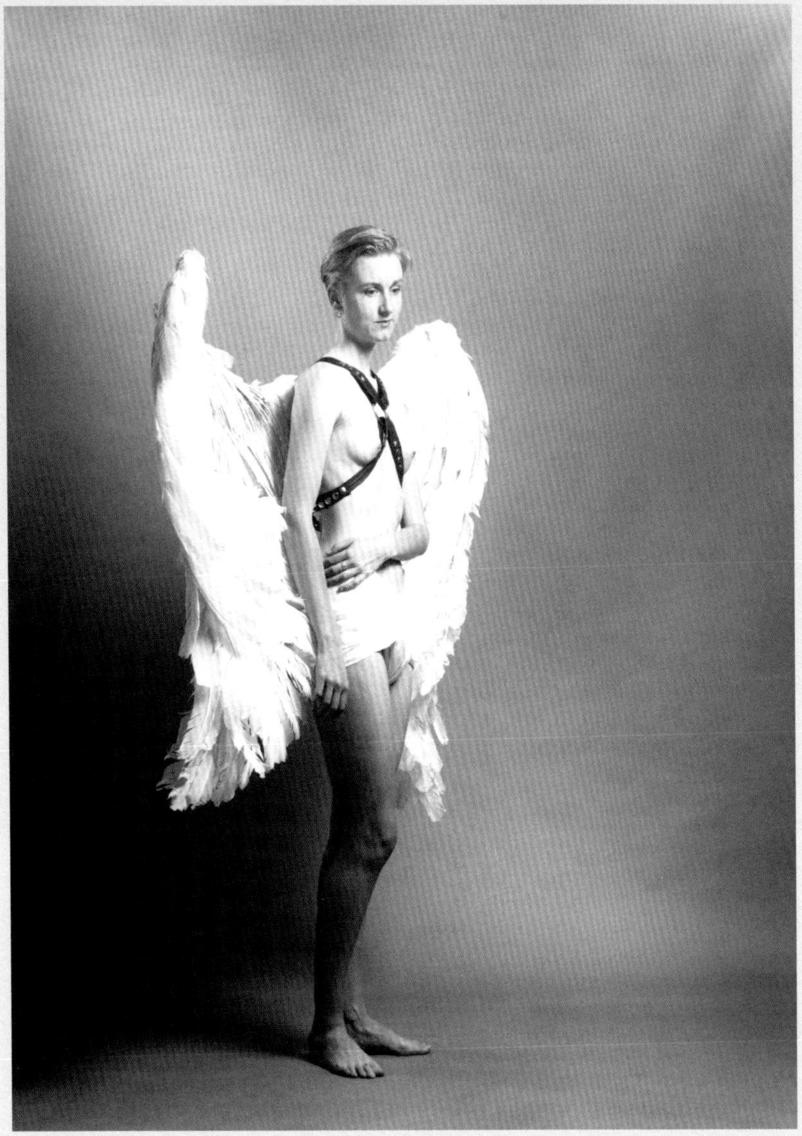

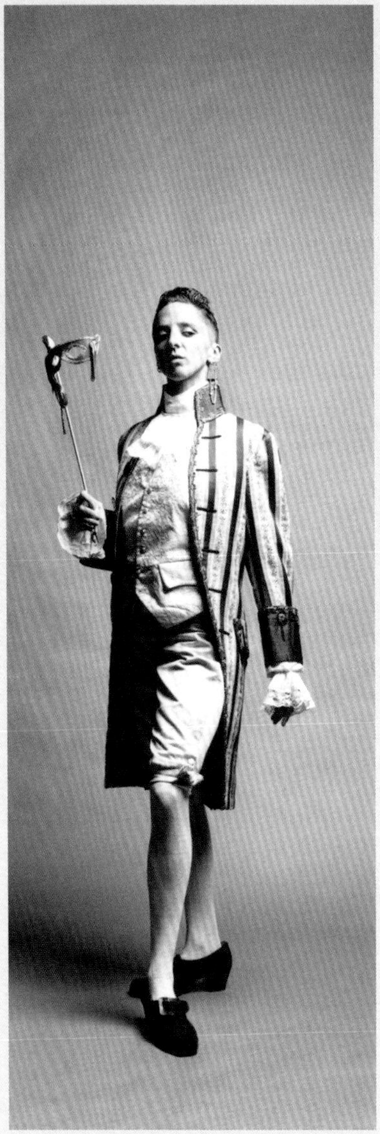

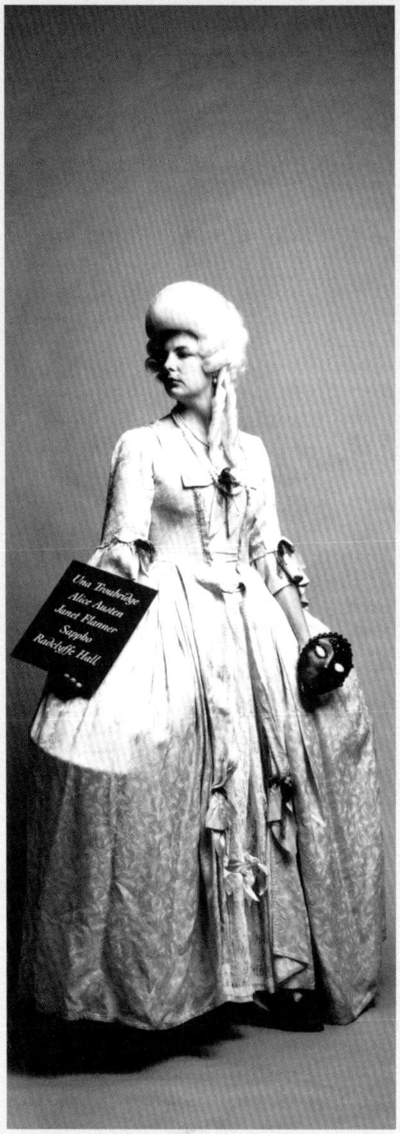

Top left to right: **Tessa Boffin, The Knight's Move:**
***The Angel; Casanova; Lady-in-waiting*, 1990**

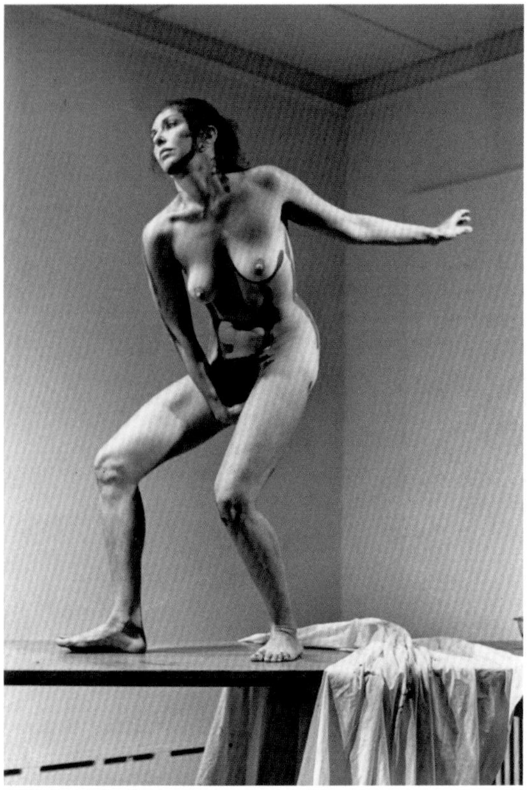

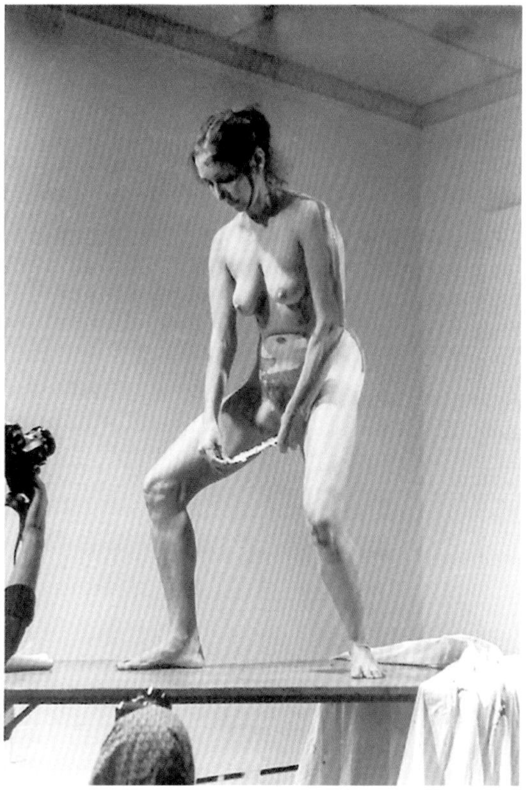

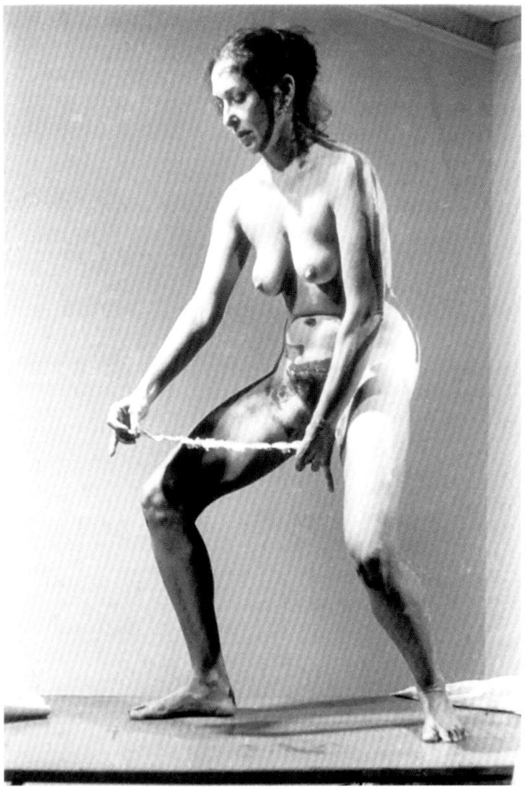

This page: **Carolee Schneemann, *Interior Scroll*, 1975**

For this work Schneemann entered and approached a table where she undressed and draped herself in a sheet. She then told the audience she would read from her book *Cezanne, She was a Great Painter*, before dropping the sheet to reveal her naked body semicovered by an apron, and painting her face and body. She read from the book, while moving into a variety of life-model poses. After some time Schneemann removed the apron and extracted a long paper scroll from her vagina, which she then read. The text was partially a script from her 1973 film, *Kitch's Last Meal*. *Interior Scroll* was first performed in a women-only exhibition titled *Women Here and Now*, which took place in East Hampton, New York.

Right: Renate Bertlmann, Zärtliche Pantomimen, (Tender Pantomimes), 1976

Renate Bertlmann is an Austrian artist, who explored the social role of women, as well as eroticism, sex, and religion in her works from the 1970s. This image derives from Bertlmann's Zärtliche Pantomimen (Tender Pantomimes) series, which in turn relates to several photographic series such as Zärtliche Berührungen (Tender Touches) and Zärtlicher Christus (Tender Christ). While earlier works in these series focus on condoms and latex teats, or objects adorned with condoms and teats, the Zärtliche Pantomimen show the artist performing in a series of costumes and masks comprising household objects, including the teats. These prostheses make her body strange, although still anthropomorphic. While she is covered in metal addenda and latex, the photographs are remarkably haptic. As Magdalena Felice has written of these works, the connotations of the materials used are both "sexual and infantile" and evoke "associations of sexuality, contraception, motherhood, and childhood experiences."

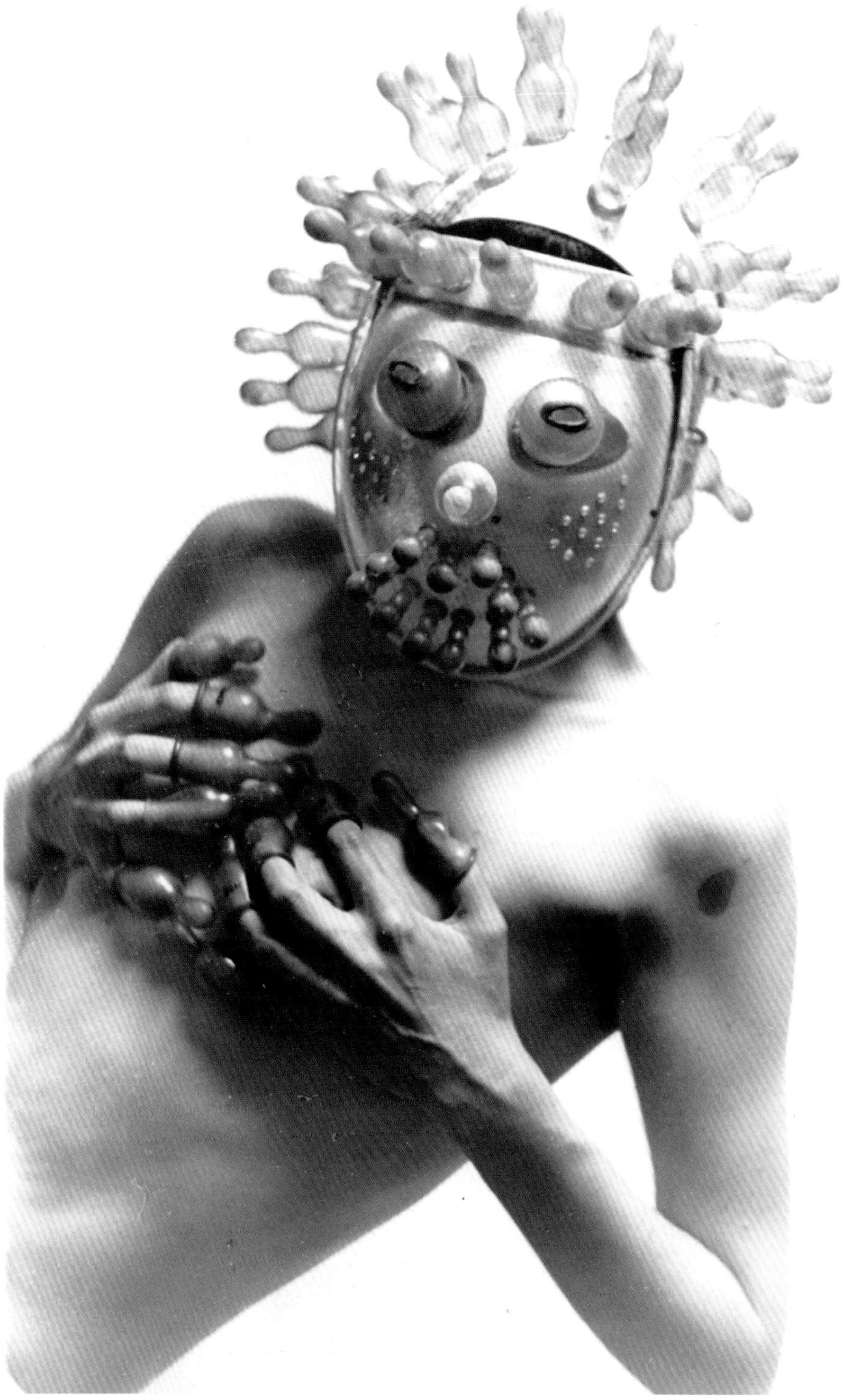

Redefining Feminism

1989–present

Part 3

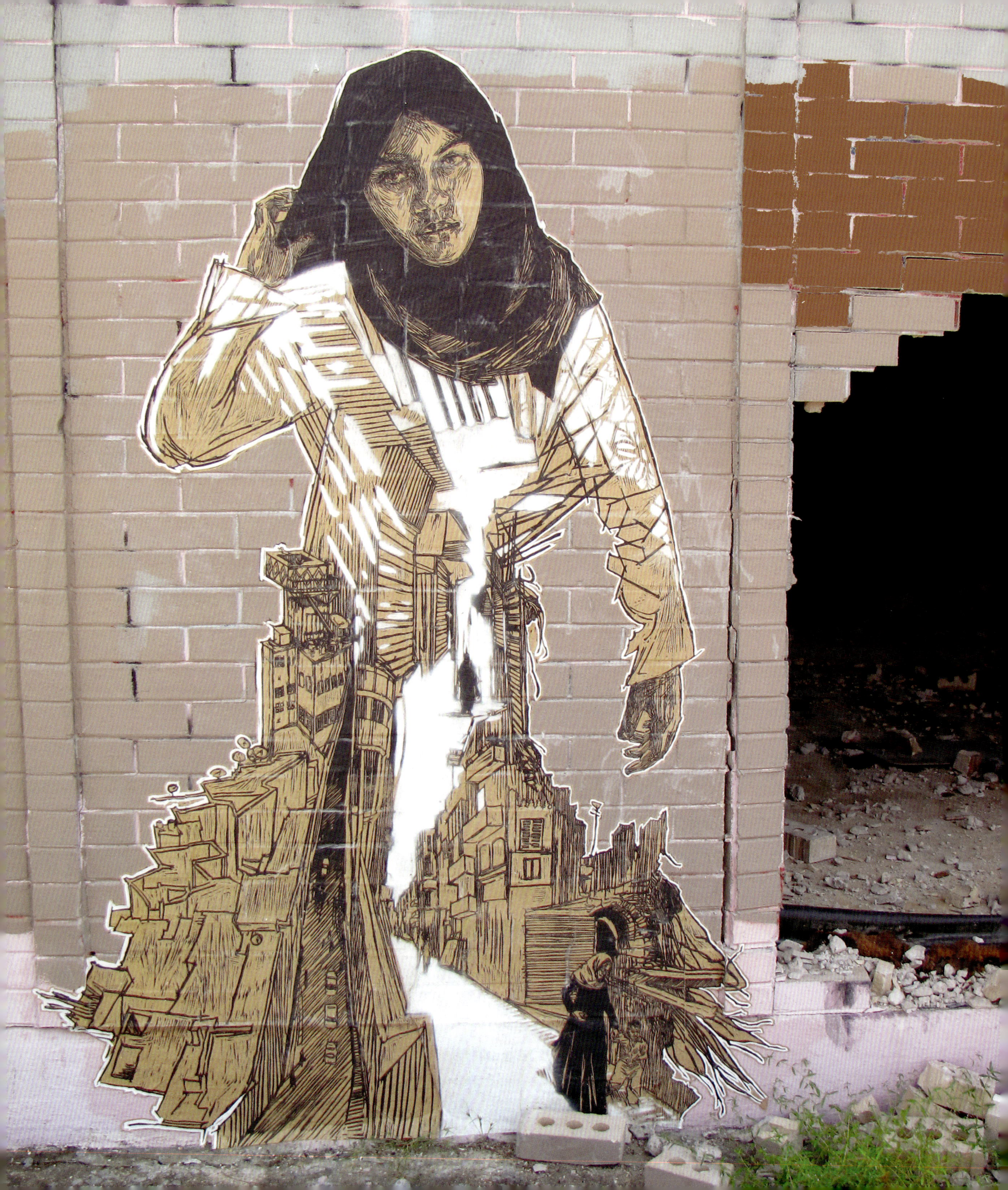

9

The Public Feminist

Engaging Audiences Beyond the Art World

"We have to be more reflective about what power is, what it is for, and how it is measured. To put it another way, if women are not perceived to be fully within the structures of power, surely it is power that we need to redefine rather than women?"

Mary Beard, *Women and Power: A Manifesto*, 2017

A basic tenet of the women's liberation movement during the 1960s and 1970s, "the personal is political," summarized highly complex experiences and ideas in a simple manner. From 1989 onward, these complexities became ever more apparent. The realms of the personal, the private, the public, and the political became increasingly difficult to navigate, with the distinctions between them becoming increasingly porous.

It is worth recalling how volatile and fast-moving global events have been since 1989, and how they have affected women in particular. To start with, 1989 saw the fall of the Berlin Wall, giving rise to new global categories of "post-Soviet," "former East," and "former West." Internet servers became publicly available in 1991, the first text message was sent in 1992, email subsequently grew exponentially as a communication medium through the 1990s; Facebook was founded in 2004, and opened to anyone with a valid email address in 2006. In 2001, four aircraft were hijacked in the skies over the United States, and three flown with devastating effect into the Pentagon and the twin towers of the World Trade Center in New York, leading to the U.S.-led invasion of Iraq in 2003 and the "war on terror," the reverberations of which are still being felt. In 2008, the financial systems around the world entered crisis, with billions wiped off the stock exchanges, and the values of the U.S. dollar, the British pound, and the euro being plunged into free fall; neoliberal governing systems responded with a prolonged period (still in place a decade later) of austerity politics, which shifted the responsibility for social care predominantly onto the shoulders of women and feminized subjects. The following year, 2009, was the first year in which more people in the world lived in cities than in rural environments, according to the United Nations (UN). In 2011, the "Arab spring" saw revolutionary movements in Arabic and west Asian countries; the following years saw the internal overthrow of some autocratic leaders such as Hosni Mubarak in Egypt, the consolidation of others such as Recep Tayyip Erdoğan in Turkey, and the growth of organizations like Islamic State (otherwise known as Daesh, ISIS, or ISIL). At the end of 2011, Occupy Wall Street sparked Occupy events and movements around the world, aimed at highlighting social inequality and the "failings" of democracy. Refugees, those fleeing conflict such as the protracted civil war in Syria—and those forced from their homes due to the effects of climate change—moved around the world in unprecedented numbers. In 2013, three queer black women founded Black Lives Matter in the United States. While 1998 had seen the first transgender competitor in the Eurovision song contest, in 2014, Conchita Wurst, who self-identifies as a gay drag queen, won the competition. Various countries have had female presidents or prime ministers (early examples include Mongolia, 1953; Ceylon, 1960; India, 1966; and Israel, 1969) but in 2016, for the first time in the United States, a woman, Hillary Clinton, was on the final slate for a major party. Despite winning the popular vote, she lost the electoral college, and 2017 started with the inauguration of President Donald Trump, who has been recorded on tape describing his own acts of lewd behavior. That year ended with the #MeToo movement, in which women from all walks of life made public that they had been subjected to assaults by men, and 2018 saw #Time'sUp solidarity movement, and Oprah Winfrey use her immense power when accepting an award at the Golden Globes ceremony to speak to a mass audience about the matter of systemic sexual harassment. That year also saw, at last, women in Saudi Arabia being allowed to drive on public streets.

Feminist artists responded to these events in a variety of ways, in order to engage with a growing and diverse range of audiences. Frequently they explored personal concerns, political identities, and events as part of an increase in feminist visual activism. Much of this activism has clearly been created with the public domain in mind—and indeed to create publicly visible solidarity movements—and reflects the differing meanings of the word "public": people in general (the public); done on behalf of, or in the name of, the people (a public organization); open or accessible (in public); or an audience (an artist's public following).

One key area of activist concern for feminist artists over the recent decades has been the working world. Much of women's labor remains unrecognized by both state and corporate mechanisms, as it is unpaid and attached to the home. In 2017, the gender pay gap in the United States was a whopping 18 percent, according to the Bureau of Labor Statistics, and was 9.1 percent in the United Kingdom, according to the Office for National Statistics. In 2017 The Pew Research Center found that black American women earned on average $35,000 a year, while white American men earned $53,000. Women are more likely to be self-employed, or to work part-time or in precarious jobs. Statutory maternity leave in the United Kingdom is up to fifty-two weeks, including a percentage of pay up to thirty-nine weeks; while in the United States it is a mere twelve weeks, which is unpaid. Sex work is predominantly undertaken by women; while many enter the profession voluntarily, sometimes arguing that they are just being paid for doing what other women are expected to provide within

Page 180: **Swoon, *Cairo*, pasted on different surfaces in urban streets, including Brooklyn (2009), Paris (2010), Melbourne (2011), and on wood for gallery exhibition (2015)**

"This portrait is a celebration of the cultural diversity of the city of Berlin, and specifically of its large and vibrant Turkish community," says Swoon; she thinks of this series of work as "a long-distance love letter to the city that informed so much of my early work, and which inspired and embraced the creative evolution of art on the streets like few other places in the world."

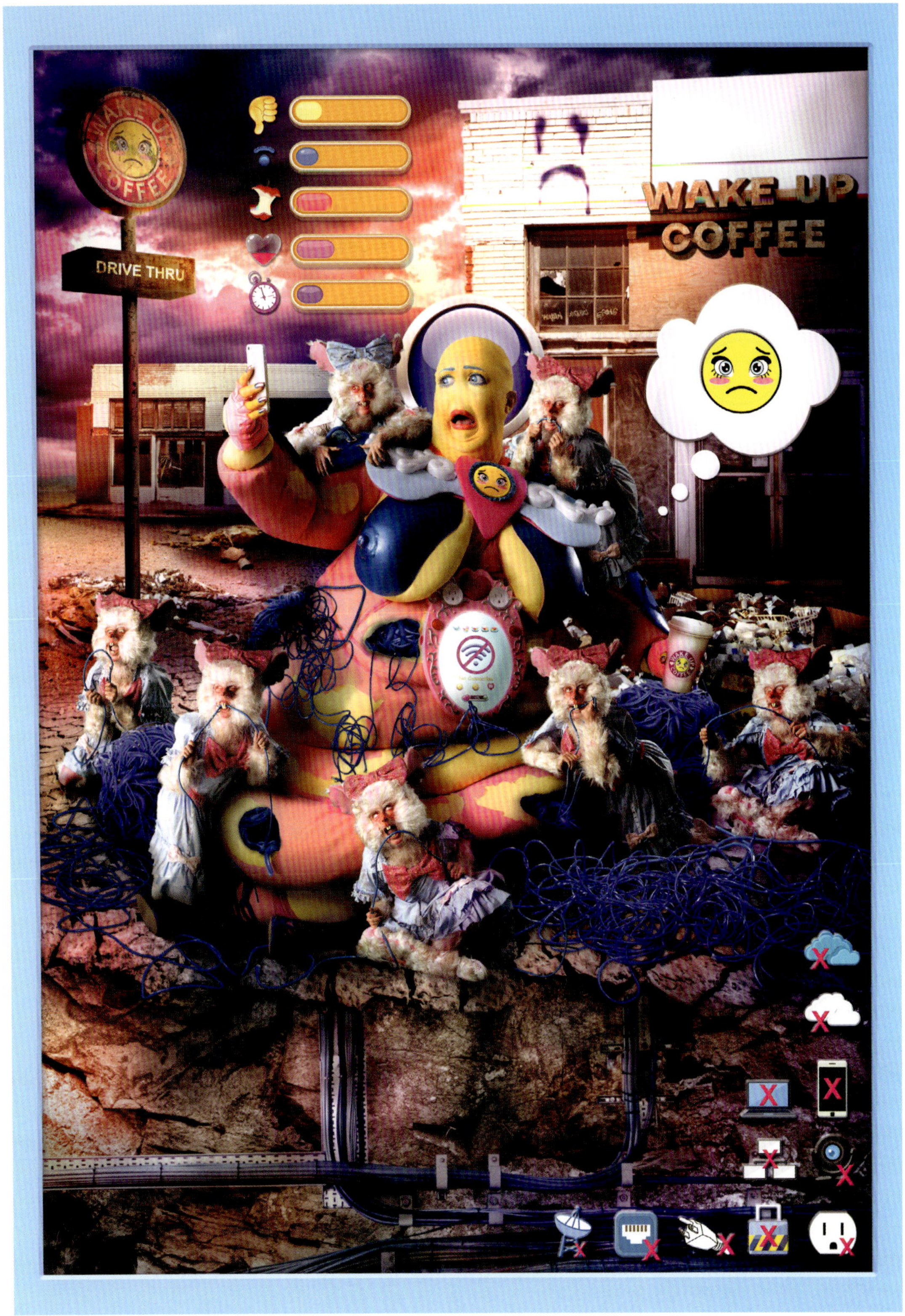

Above: **Rachel Maclean, *We Want Data!* from *Wot u ☺ about?*, 2016**

Maclean's films are all software-based and use her own manipulated and morphed image as the basis for all the characters depicted. *Wot u ☺ about?* moves from the sickly sweet alternative realities created for social media to the monstrous nature of what people can feel their lives to be in contrast. The focus is on the transition from being a child to being an adult.

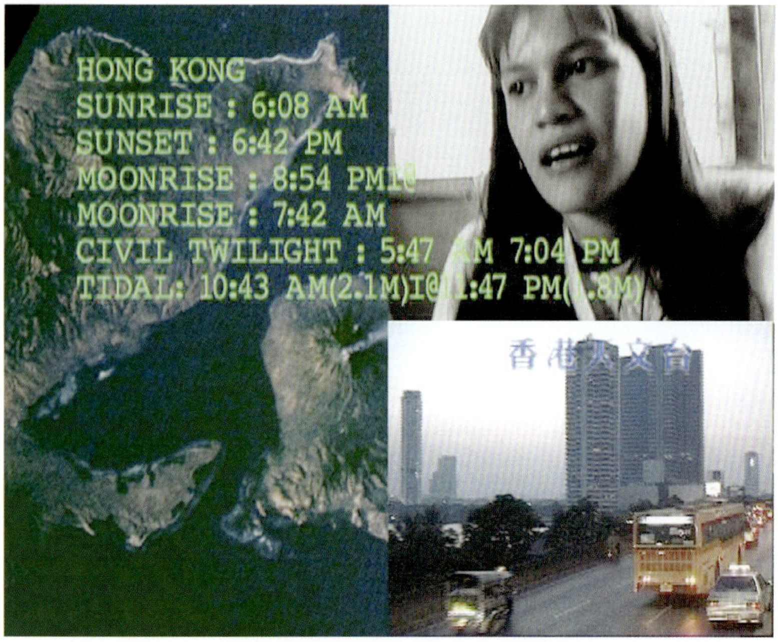

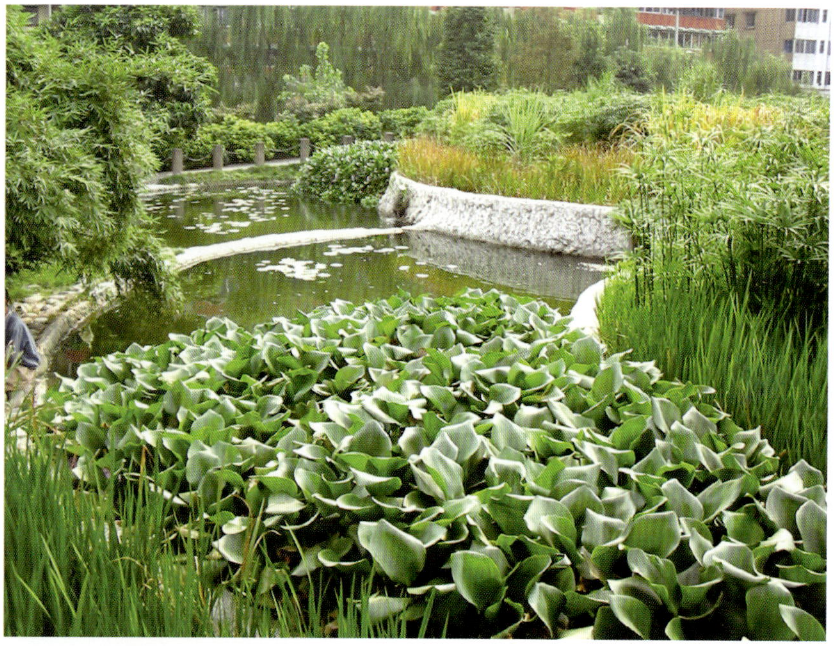

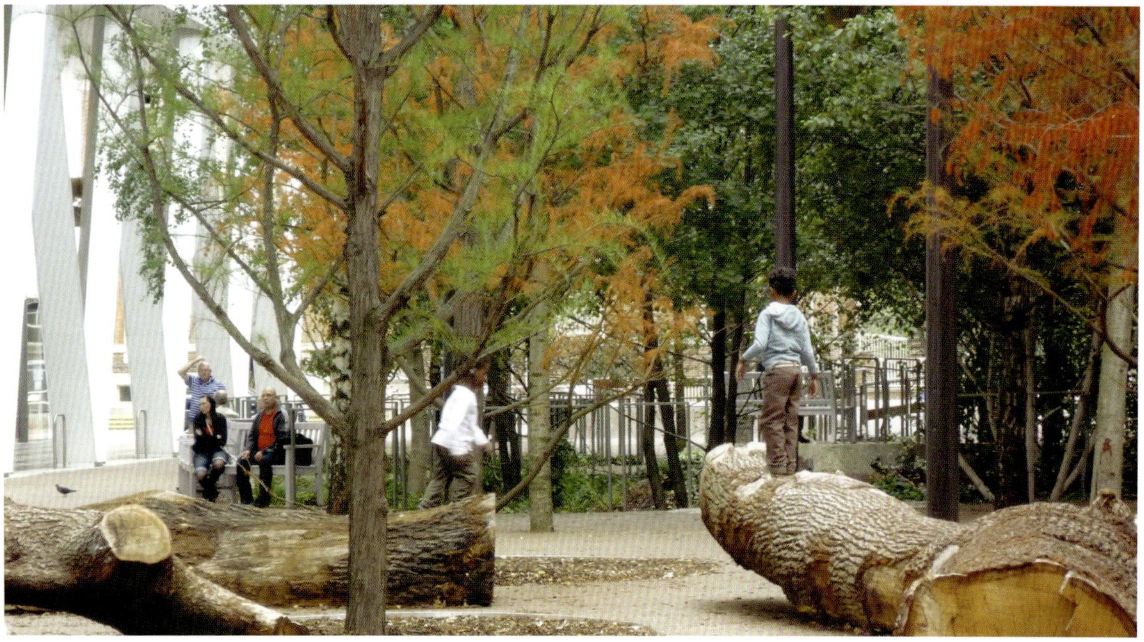

Top left: **Ursula Biemann, *Remote Sensing*, 2001**

Swiss artist Ursula Biemann focuses on the conditions of labor of migrant workers and the specificities of gender within this. She visited free-trade zones, resorts for sex tourists, and the towns that grow up around military bases. The video incorporates images from NASA satellites and other geo-technologies. Geography and location are demonstrated as complex and often beyond the scope of national governance, and the development of new technology makes them more so. This work records the journeys of women and their reasons for engaging in the sex trade. It represents women's bodies as being the location for their work and for their subjectivity, and as goods that are trafficked between men. The work speaks of the displacement of women within hidden capitalist exchange.

Top right: **Betsy Damon, *Chengdu Living Water Garden*, 1996–98**

As a veteran of the 1970s women's movement, Damon's approach to caring for the water we all need is deeply informed by feminist politics of how to be in the world, with respect for all its resources. This area of Chengdu in China was badly polluted. Damon's garden, designed to look like a fish from above, uses flowforms to reoxygenate the water, plants that can purify it, and sand and gravel-based pools to filter it. It results in water that is clean enough to play in.

Bottom left: **muf, Barking Town Square, 2010**

The architecture firm muf formed in 1994 as a collaboration between Juliet Bidgood and Liza Fior (both architects), Katherine Clarke (artist), and Kath Shonfeld (urban theorist), and has remained mainly female in its staff. muf won awards for their work to create a communal and usable central environment in Barking, London. It includes a 23-ft-high (7 m) false "ruin" made from recycled bricks from local demolition, built by students at a local bricklayers' college—a quirky, unique addition to a modern city-center development.

a personal relationship, it is often the last option for women who are impoverished through having lost work elsewhere (as a result of austerity measures, or fleeing war or ecological disasters). Girls, trans women, and refugees are particularly vulnerable in this respect.

Swiss artist Ursula Biemann's work explores the sexualization of U.S./Mexico border areas in *Performing the Border* (1999), both in the form of sex workers who cater to border workers, to the military, and to travelers, and in the form of the entertainment industries on the border and the representation and experience of sexualized violence. Claire Fontaine, a Paris-based feminist collective of two artists founded in 2004, concerns itself with global movements and with labor, with a focus on capital and capitalism, work relations, and exploitations.

The shaping of the physical environment is a prominent focus for feminist artists. "Mega-cities" of more than ten million people increased from ten in 1990 to twenty-eight in 2014 and are projected to rise to forty-one by 2030. This is due to increases in population, internal migration from rural areas to cities, and, to a lesser extent, by international migration. Women clearly have a major stake in how urban landscapes are formed, as many of them retain the primary responsibility for family and domestic, home-based life. Yet, to date, women have not played an equitable part in the physical shaping of urban environments. Although figures have improved in the last decades, this century sees women as only 31 percent of architects in Europe (according to the Architects' Council of Europe, 2010), 20 percent in the United States (American Institute of Architects, 2004), and approximately 25 percent in Australia (2013 analysis of Australian Institute of Architects membership). One example of an architectural firm founded and run by women architects and artists is muf. They have won international awards for their work, which specializes in building inclusive and accessible urban environments—children's play parks, housing project common areas, and town streets and squares—that enable people to feel a sense of ownership of their public surroundings through the ways in which they can be used.

As the urban footprint of the world increases, the crisis facing the wider global environment deepens. In many cultures, women have been represented as being closer to nature than men because of their childbearing capacity. This is a characterization that many feminist writers from Simone de Beauvoir onward have argued against, proposing that in Western cultures the cultural and philosophical binary oppositions of nature/culture, emotion/rationality, mind/body have also mapped to dominant constructions of femininity/masculinity. Culturally, this has consigned women to the realm of the nonrational—or even of the animal—in religion and philosophy. A number of artists have sought to address this in very differing ways. Betsy Damon uses analysis of water flow to create flowforms that purify and reoxygenate water, while also creating city gardens in which to socialize and relax. Patricia Piccinini imagines the hybrid life-forms of a post-human genetic future. Artist, sex educator, and former sex worker Annie Sprinkle, with her wife—artist and activist professor Beth Stephens—pioneers the exuberant eco-sexual movement.

A number of feminist works express a sense of disconnect between the home and the public realm. This is reflected in, and exacerbated by, the amount of time we spend not in the physical environment, but in the digital one. Our use of social and digital media has increased exponentially from a standing start in the 1990s, to the point that many people spend more time in virtual and online communication than face to face. Argentinian artist Amalia Ulman and Scottish artist Rachel McLean, in different ways, explore the dislocation and psychic disturbance that can result from selfie culture. Ulman created a teenage character through Instagram posts, whose life of erratic and extreme makeover was played out in five months worth of posts and gained many followers who advised her, abused her, and propositioned her. Micol Hebron in the United States comments on, campaigns about, and works through social media, its use of algorithms, and its policing of representations. In particular, following Facebook's banning of naked female nipples, she made digital templates of men's nipples to stick over images of women's nipples. At the same time, performing artists use new technologies to reach audiences in mind-boggling numbers. Beyoncé is one example of this: Her 2014 performance with the word "feminist" in giant letters behind her; her use of spectacular events, such as a 2016 performance in the interval show of the American Football Super Bowl final; and the release of her 2016 video album *Lemonade* all carried political messages to vast markets, thanks to new technologies.

Since around 2005, curating has come increasingly to the fore in relation to the art and visual culture of the feminist movement. Those who have engaged in exhibiting feminist art have done so from a variety of standpoints and with differing strategies to make the work public and to engage with wider communities. Taking on board feminist perspectives on authorship, collectivity, and social change, curators have developed feminist methodologies, frameworks, and institutions. Their efforts sit within the context of a historically vastly male-dominated realm of art history and museum direction (according to the U.S. National Museum of Women in the Arts, work by women artists makes up only 3–5 percent of major permanent collections in the United States and Europe). One feminist curator who has forged this path is Xabier Arakistain, who has produced not only a series of major feminist exhibitions, but also a series of annual conferences and related publications on feminist art. Other curators who dedicate themselves to championing feminist art hail from Nigeria, Thailand, the United Kingdom, and the United States, among other places. These curators play a vital part in bringing to light feminist work that is so often concerned with the intimate connection in modern-day society between our personal lives and our public lives and the pressures under which many of us now live.

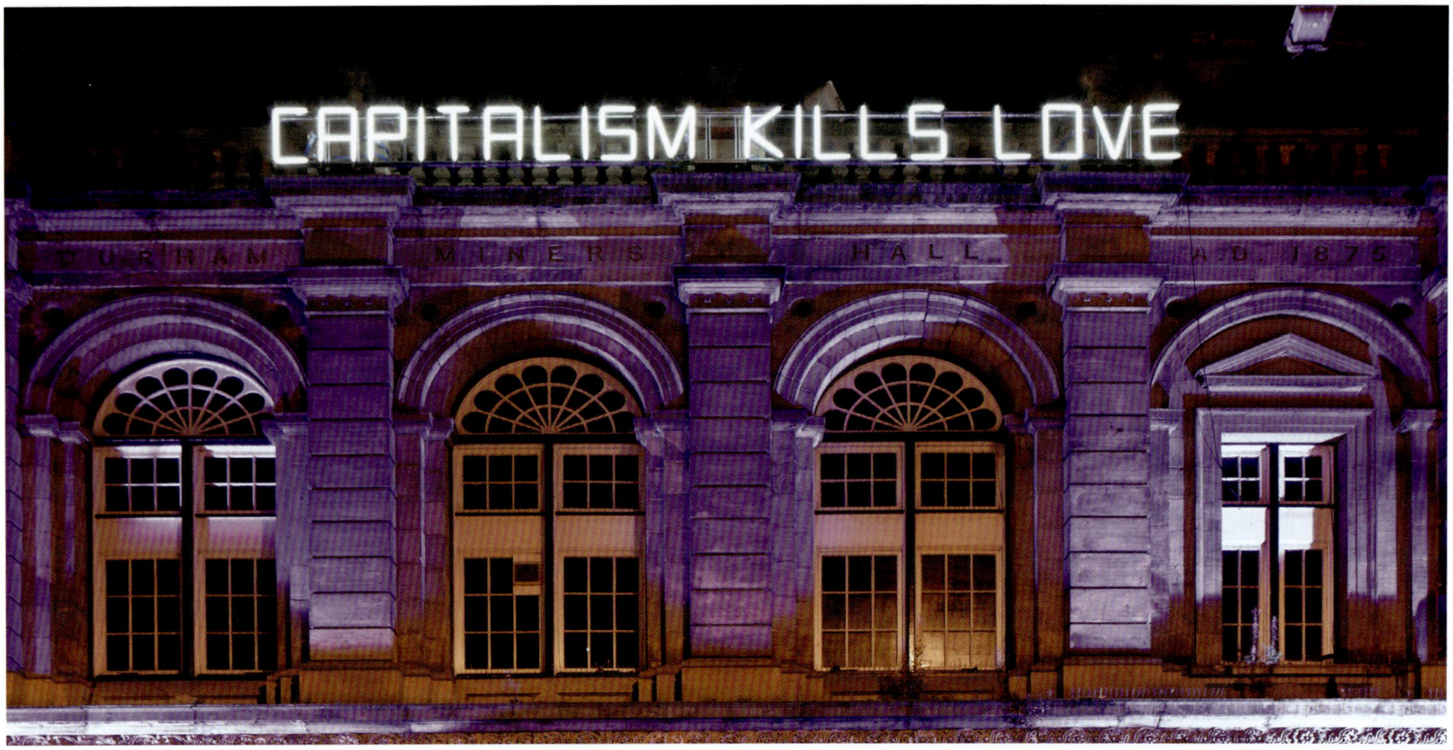

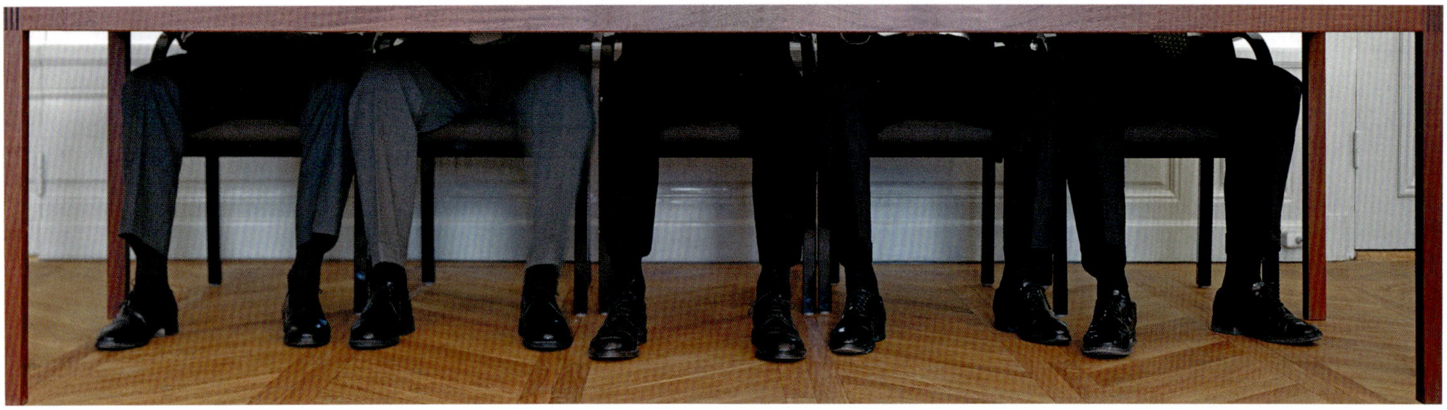

Top: **Claire Fontaine, *Capitalism Kills (Love)*, 2008. Installation view at the Durham Miners' Hall, Lumiere Light Festival, Durham, England, November 17–21, 2011**

This work was installed on the front of the old Miners' Hall in Durham, northeast England. The word "LOVE" flashes on and off, so the words can be read in at least three different ways: Capitalism is killing us; capitalism kills the love we have for each other; and "capitalism kills, love"—said not as a slogan, but colloquially—"love" being a common working-class term of address in the northeast.

Bottom: **Maria Friberg, *Somewhere Else*, 1998, still**

Much of Swedish artist Maria Friberg's work has focused upon masculinity—men in suits, in their public and professional roles in vulnerable or compromised situations. This is the female gaze returned to men in a way that does not speak of sexual desire, but of the desire to analyze the superficial trappings of power and authority, and to expose them as insubstantial covers for the human beings underneath. Friberg's video *Somewhere Else* is typical of this. We see under an office table the gray-suited, black-shod bodies of five men seated next to each other. In attitudes of "man-spreading," each man's knees come into contact with those of the man sitting next to him; they shift and move, in a manner that could suggest aggression, eroticism, embarrassed awkwardness, or absurdity. The power struggles of the male-dominated office are exposed.

Below: Vanessa Beecroft, *VB46* and Toxic Titties, *VB46-TT (Beecroft Intervention)*, 2002

Vanessa Beecroft is an Italian artist whose works involve models (selected to tight bodily specifications) standing naked in 4-in-high (10 cm) heels. Toxic Titties (a collective of queer feminist artists Cassils, Julia Steinmetz, and Clover Leary) infiltrated Beecroft's work *VB46*, as their own artwork, *VB46-TT (Beecroft Intervention)*. They unionized the models, which forced up the cost of their labor: Cassils included in *Beecroft Intervention* a scanned check for $2,900—up from $1,500—for five days' work: one full day of body-hair waxing, bleaching, and cutting; three days (including one fifteen-hour day) of photography; and a four-hour gallery performance.

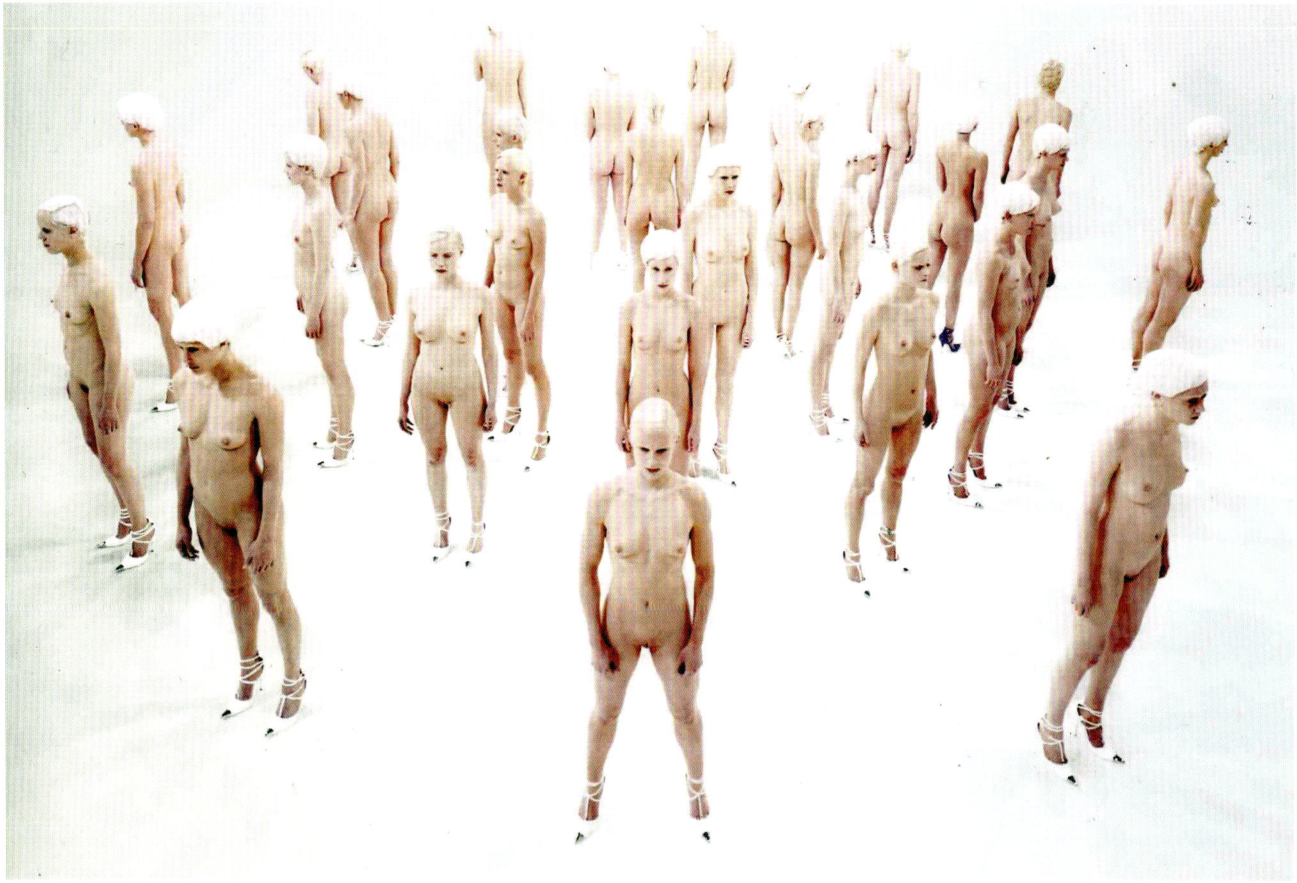

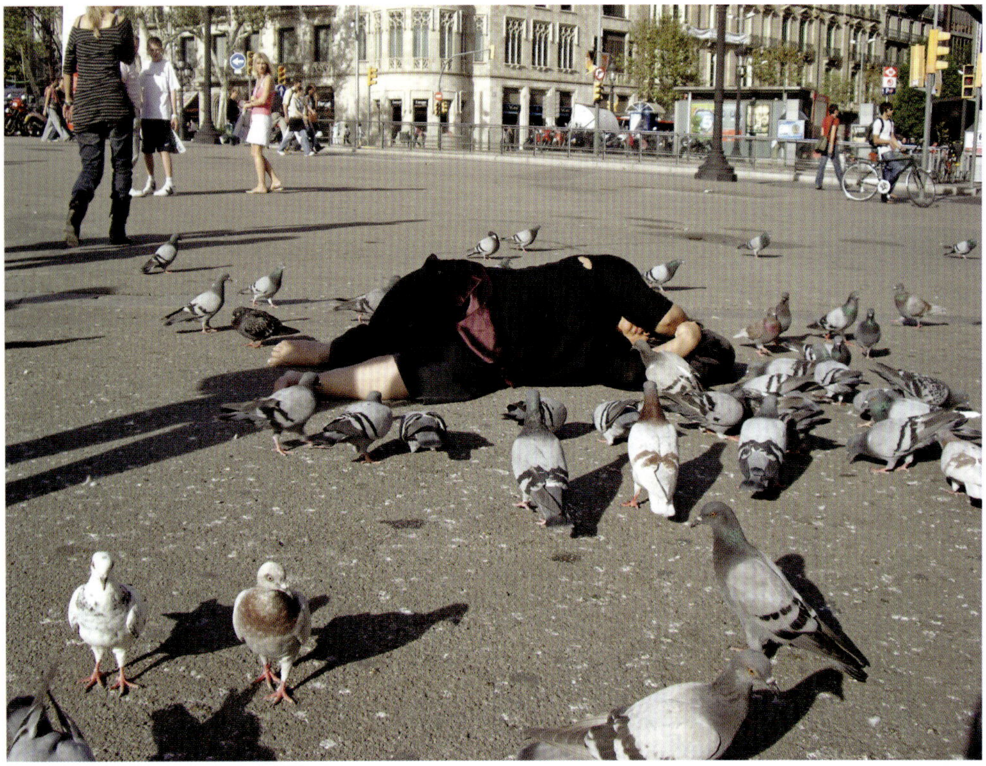

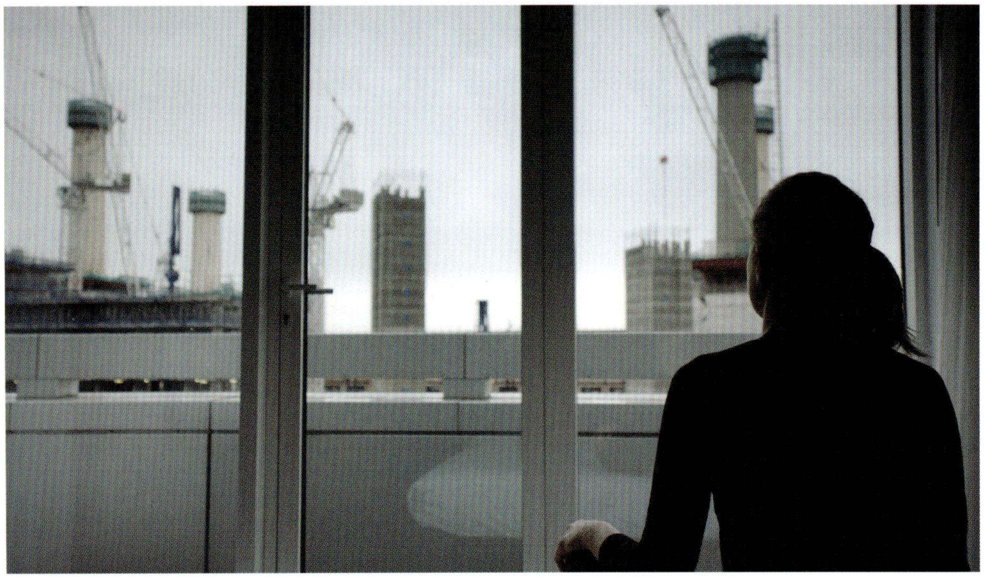

Top: **Sonia Khurana, *Logic of Birds*, 2006, still**

Indian artist Sonia Khurana explores the possibility of occupying space in a body that is raced as South Asian and gendered as female. In the video *Bird* (1999), she stands on a plinth, naked, flapping her arms and legs in a vain attempt to take off. In *Logic of Birds*, she occupies urban spaces in the opposite way to that of the upright, white, colonizing male: abject, vulnerable, grounded, alienated, other, she lies in an anonymous European public space as pigeons peck the ground around her.

Bottom: **Alice May Williams, *Dream City—More, Better, Sooner*, 2016, still**

The site where Battersea Power Station stands was, in 1908, planned to be an amusement park called Dream City for what was then a working-class area of London. Instead, the Power Station employed local people as workers. Following its decommission (1983) it stood empty, and it is now being converted into luxury living accommodation. Williams's film about the site is a meditation upon work and mental health, capital, class, and imagined futures.

Below: **Suzanne van Rossenberg, drawing from A Room with a Lesbian View, 2003–2014; 2007**

Suzanne van Rossenberg is an artist and an LGBTI rights worker and activist. Her cartoon series often feature her alter-ego, Patricia Cornflake. The series A Room with a Lesbian View took one impulse from Virginia Woolf's essay "A Room of One's Own." Drawn from her window in Leiden, the Netherlands, with its view of the Gothic church, van Rossenberg's drawings individually and collectively interrogate what it is to claim lesbian space in urban and cultural environments that historically have denied it, and to rewrite those stories.

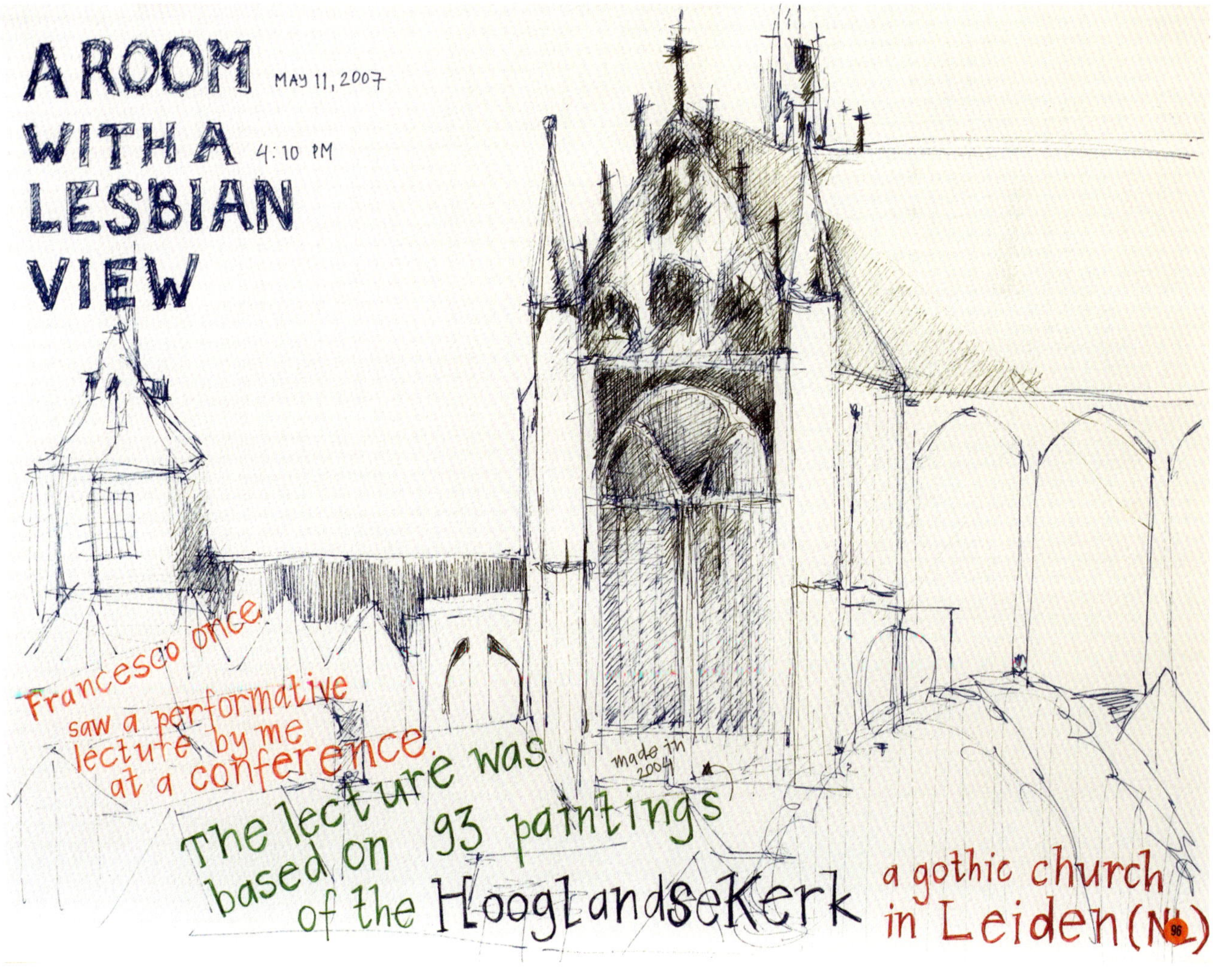

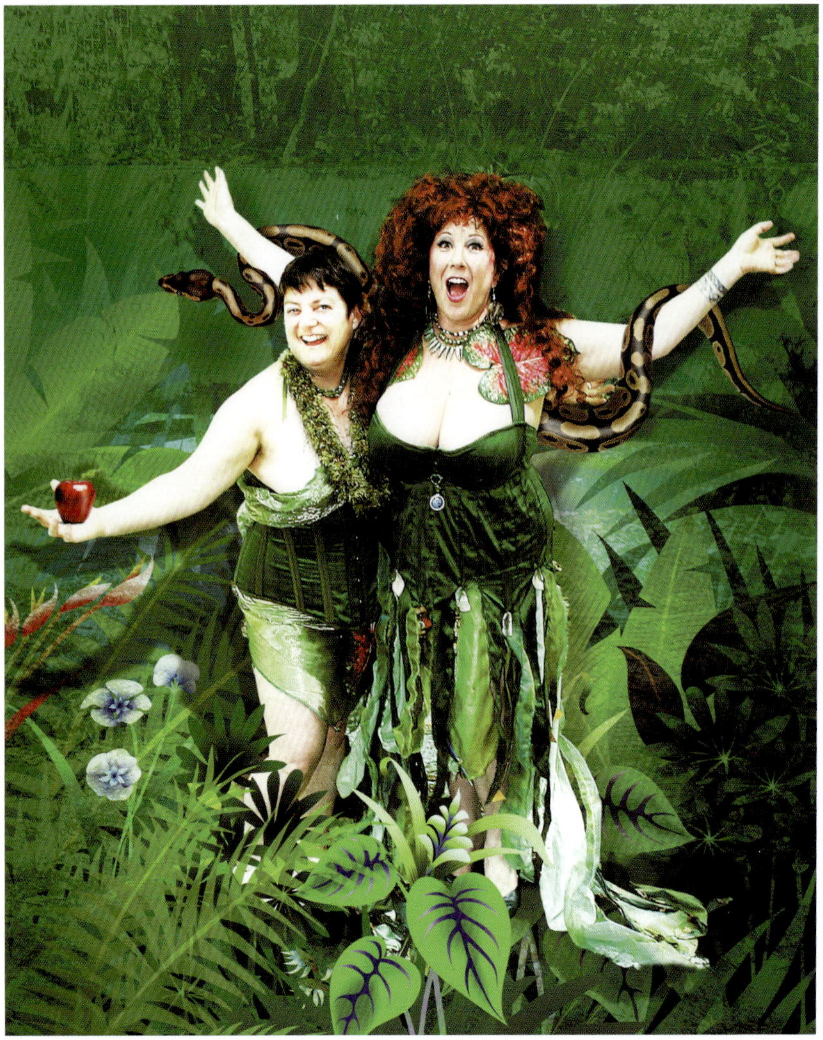

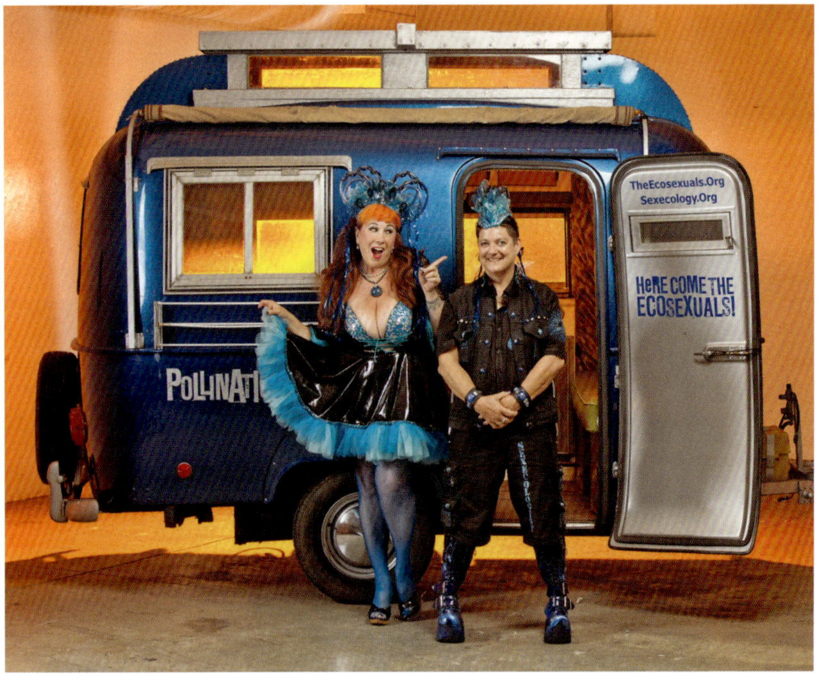

This page: **Annie Sprinkle and Beth Stephens, *Madam and Eve*, photo: Greg Archer, 2008 (top); *Pollination Pod*, 2015 (bottom)**

Artist, sex educator, and former sex worker Annie Sprinkle, with her wife—artist and activist professor Beth Stephens— pioneers the exuberant eco-sexual movement. This not only queers any notions of women being closer to nature (both of them marrying Mother Earth is joyously queer in their performances), but also is militantly activist about care for the planet. "Nature is your lover, not your mother," says Sprinkle. The pair have had weddings with Coal, Rocks, Snow, the Appalachian Mountains, and more.

Below: **Patricia Piccinini, *The Young Family*, 2002**

In a world where animals have been cloned and human ears have been grown on the backs of mice, Piccinini's hyperreal, hypersurreal, believably fleshy sculptures imagine part-human life-forms that may not be far in the future. She says of this work: "On one hand we need organs to help people in need, on the other hand we are looking at an animal that wants to exist for the sake of itself. I can't help but feel an enormous empathy for this creature."

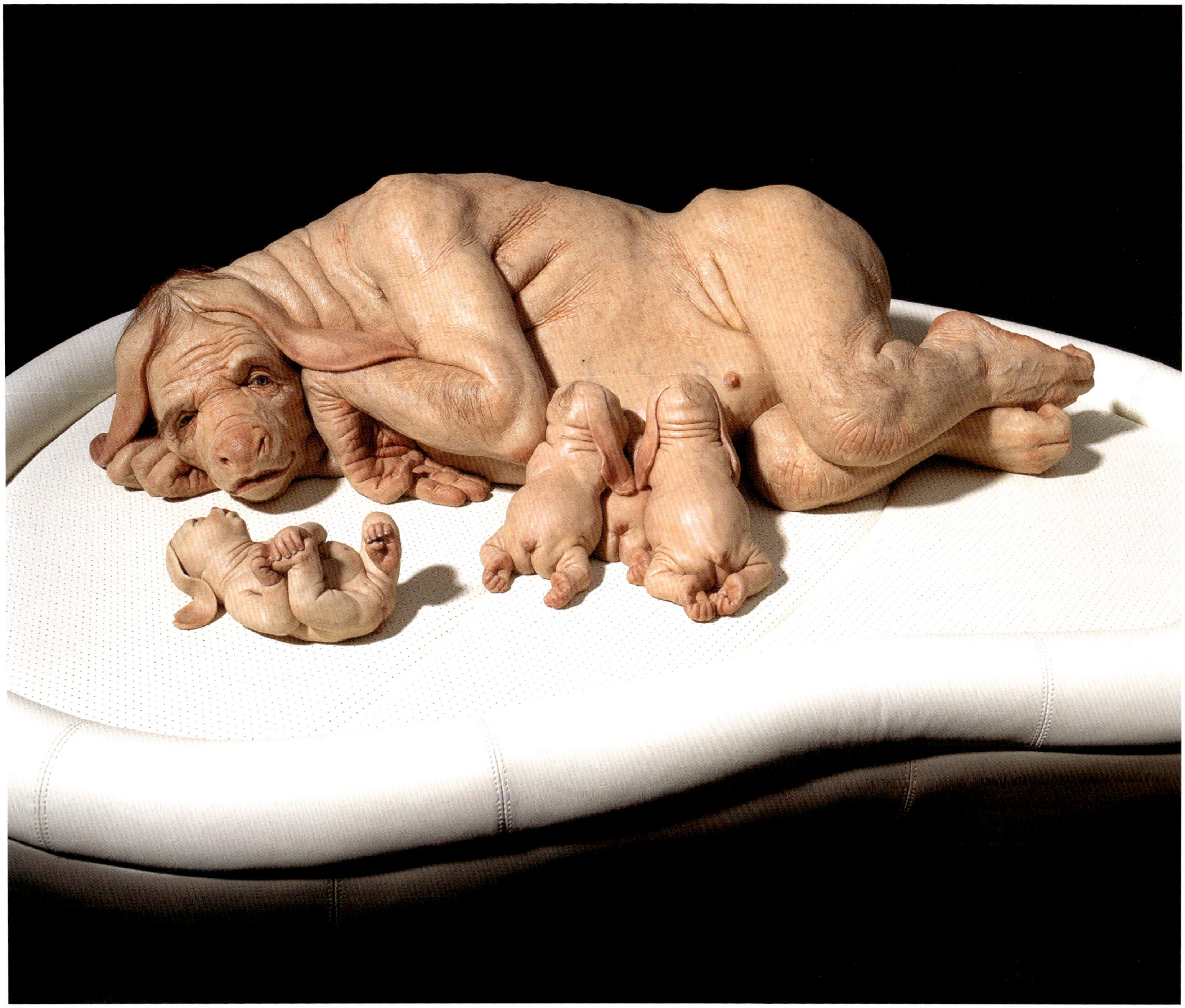

Bringing the Message to the Masses: Beyoncé

Beyoncé is one of several artists to have found ways of using mass media, social media, and online formats to bring her message to audiences in vast numbers.

In 2014, Beyoncé was the closing act at the Video Music Awards (VMAs), watched by 12.4 million Americans. In her medley performance, she sampled a substantial audio section of Nigerian author Chimamanda Ngozi Adichie's 2012 TEDx Talk, "We should all be feminists." It starts: "We teach girls to shrink themselves, to make themselves smaller. We say to girls 'You can have ambition, but not too much. You should aim to be successful, but not too successful, otherwise you will threaten the man,'" and it ends with the definition: "Feminist: the person who believes in the social, political, and economic equality of the sexes." This was projected in vast letters to the sound of Ngozi Adichie's voice, while Beyoncé and her dancers gathered on stage to transition into a performance of "Flawless" with the single word FEMINIST projected.

"Flawless" was released in 2013—the year a poll found that 82 percent of Americans believed women and men should be equal, but only 20 percent identified as feminists. The song is in three parts: The first part has many repeats of the line "bow down bitches"; the second part has the same sample of Ngozi Adichie's voice and words; and the third part talks of beauty, repeating: "I woke up like this/We flawless, ladies tell 'em." The video evokes a British punk mosh pit of the 1970s and 1980s. Some of the dancers are contemporary London Rudeboys (skinheads) with Ben Sherman shirts and fourteen-hole Doc Martens, connoting both racism and the 1980s Rock Against Racism movement. The song's narrative arcs from what can be read either as the unsisterly and nonfeminist command to bow down or, alternatively, as a demand that she, as a successful black woman, is given her due for her hard work and success; it then moves through the powerful words of the Nigerian feminist, to a communal affirmation of female physical self-esteem. The video suggests resolution of possible racist antagonism through dance.

Two years later, Beyoncé performed again at the VMAs, this time watched mainly through video streaming, with over sixty-two million streams. She performed a medley of songs from her video album *Lemonade*, ending with "Formation" and the dancers moving into formation of ♀, the female gender symbol. "Formation" was released as a video on February 6, 2016, the day after what would have been the twenty-first birthday of Trayvon Martin (the seventeen-year-old African American shot by a neighborhood watch member in 2012). The next day saw the first public performance of "Formation," during the halftime show of the fiftieth Superbowl, when 115.5 million Americans tuned in. Beyoncé performed with a group of female backing dancers, all wearing black. Her own costume included bandoleers; the dancers wore afros and black berets. The immediate visual reference was to the Black Panther Party for Self-Defense: The venue for the game was in the San Francisco Bay Area, where the Black Panthers had formed fifty years earlier. At one point, the dancers lined up to form an "X"—a reference to Malcolm X. The song's words and the video version reinforced this affirmation of racial identity, black pride, and political affiliation with lines such as "I like my baby heir with baby hair and afros/I like my negro nose with Jackson Five nostrils," and visual references to Trayvon Martin, Hurricane Katrina, and Black Lives Matter.

Ambivalences about sexual politics within Beyoncé's work are long-standing. "All the Single Ladies" (2008) included the repeated line "If you liked it, then you should have put a ring on it"—a possibly heteronormative approach equating a woman's value to her marriage potential, but which also has a tradition within songs by African American women, fighting for familial stability against the legacy from slavery and generations of social upheaval. For example, in "Love Child" (1968), Diana Ross sings lyrics written from the point of view of a woman recalling her experiences as a child born outside marriage, in order to justify to her partner why she does not want to risk a pregnancy. Beyoncé's narrative in the video concept album *Lemonade* starts with her rage at the infidelity of her husband Jay Z and moves to their eventual reconciliation. As such, this could also be seen as continuing on a well-worn path in popular culture of women's anger eventually giving way to forgiveness of adulterous husbands. While it is clear that Beyoncé does this on her terms—showing dignity and strength in the face of hurt—it is not a particularly radical feminist message, suggesting no matter the hurt caused, men can "get away" with causing such hurt and will be forgiven. While supporting Beyoncé's honoring of black women, African American feminist writer bell hooks has criticized *Lemonade* for its representations of the black female body as a sexualized commodity in a hyper-capitalist context. However, *Lemonade* represents black female strength, resilience, and determination in the character of Beyoncé and others who appear in the film. It also visualizes sisterhood: We see generations of Beyoncé's female extended family; cameos from black celebrities that include Serena Williams, Zendaya, and Quvenzhané Wallis; there is political solidarity with the mothers of Trayvon Martin, Michael Brown, and Eric Garner, holding photographs of their murdered sons; and she visualizes a creative community, through homage to many women artists—most prominently, the poems of Warsan Shire; Julie Dash's film *Daughters of the Dust*; Pipilotti Rist's video *Ever is Over All*; and the photographs of Carrie Mae Weems. While some have seen this as plagiarism, again, it can be placed in the context of black American music sampling and borrowing—as seen in Childish Gambino's *This is America* (2018). "Sampling" exists in art history: To take a famous example, Manet's *Olympia* (1863) was "borrowed" from Titian's Venus of Urbino (ca. 1538), which in turn was "borrowed" from Giorgione's *Sleeping Venus* (ca. 1510). Cumulatively, Beyoncé's expression of political, artistic, solidarity, and sisterhood is the strongest feminist message from the album, which sold 485,000 copies in its first week.

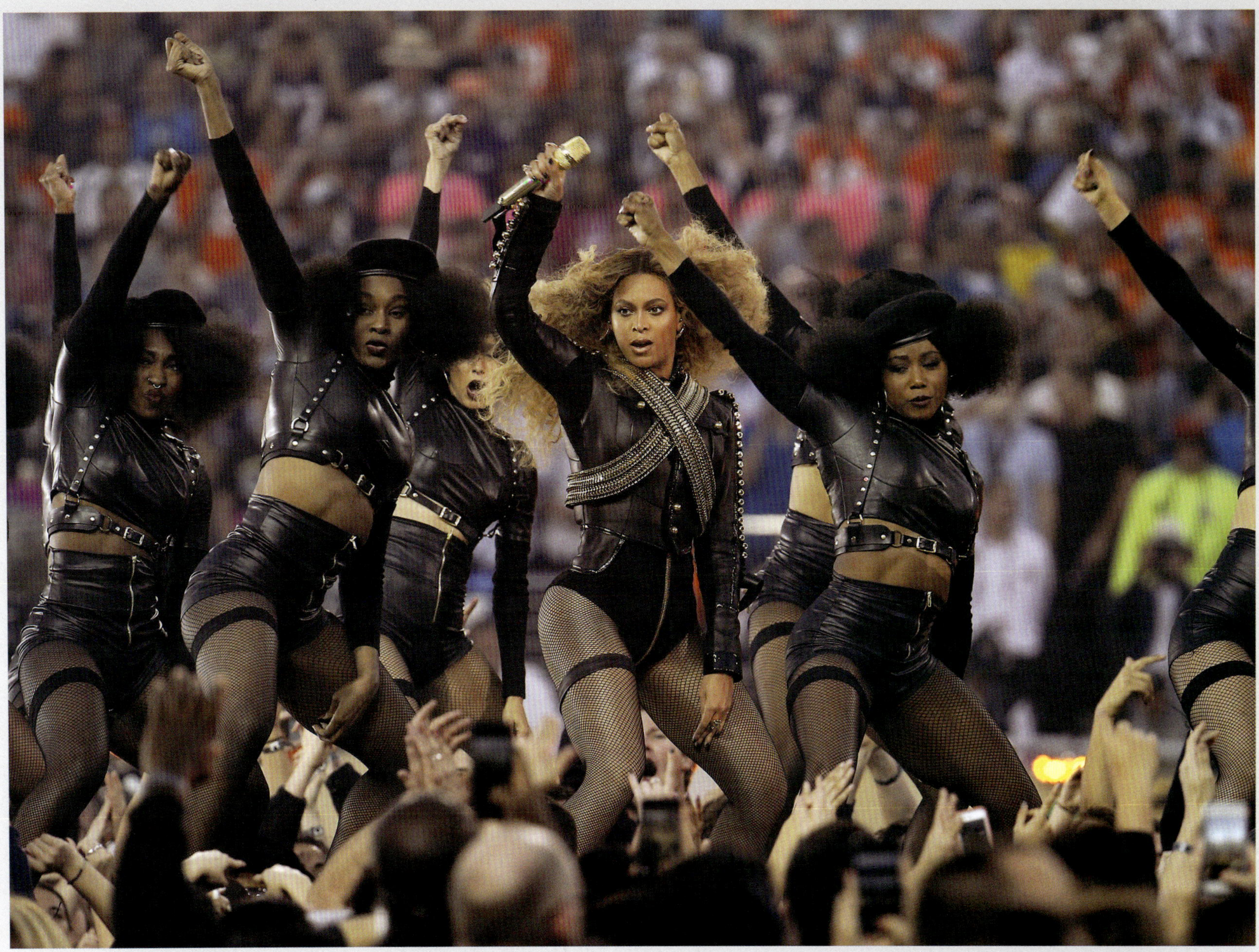

"I put the definition of feminist in my song and on my tour, not for propaganda or to proclaim to the world that I'm a feminist, but to give clarity to the true meaning. I'm not really sure people know or understand what a feminist is, but it's very simple. It's someone who believes in equal rights for men and women [. . .] When we talk about equal rights, there are issues that face women disproportionately."

Beyoncé, in Tamar Gottesman, "Beyoncé? On Feminism, Motherhood, and the Real Message in Formation," *Elle* magazine, May 2016

Top: **Beyoncé performing *Formation*, Super Bowl halftime show, San Francisco, 2016**

The afros and berets of Beyoncé's dancers immediately evoke the women associated with the Black Panther Party for Self-Defense, while the song lyrics reference Beyoncé's own success as a black woman, her hard work and her money, ending with the line: "Always stay gracious, best revenge is your paper."

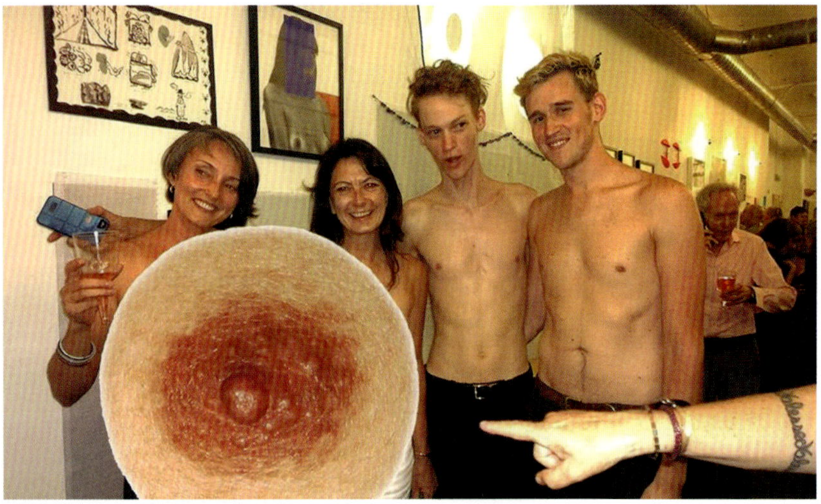

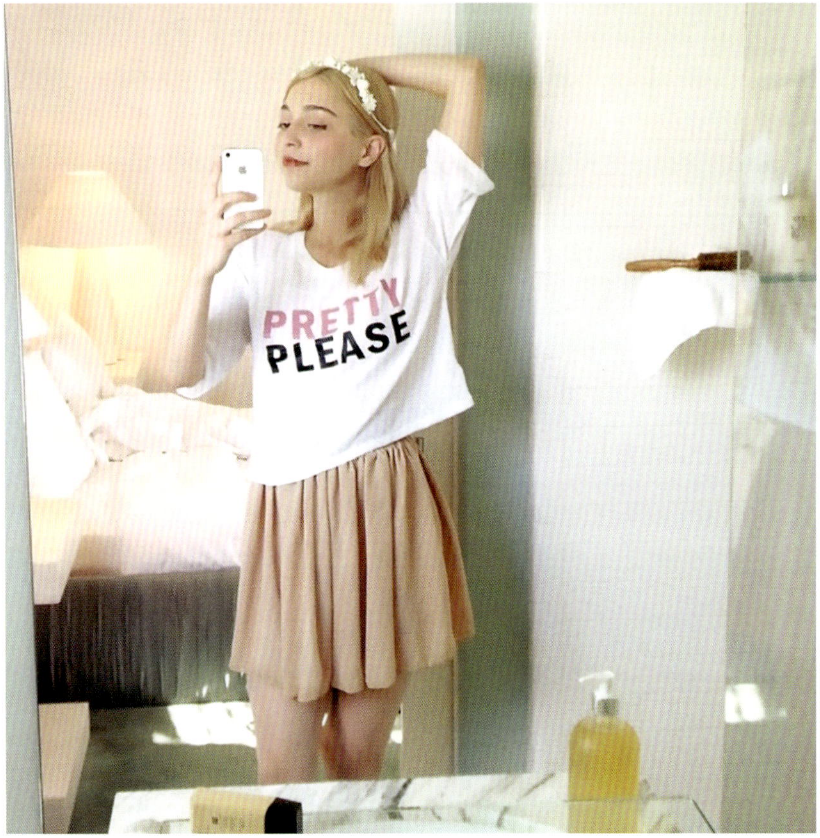

Top: Micol Hebron, Digital Nipple Pasty, 2014

Micol Hebron is an American interdisciplinary artist and activist. Her projects include Gallery Tally, which counts the number of male and female artists represented by commercial galleries. Her Digital Nipple Pasty was a humorous response to the censorship of female-identified nipples on Facebook and elsewhere—a response that included the artist and three friends arriving topless at the opening of a breast cancer awareness exhibition. Googling "male nipple," Hebron found only images of nipples from cis, white, young men. She took one of these privileged nipples to make a digital template to place on photos of naked female-identified nipples. Posted on Facebook Hebron's template became a meme and was re-tweeted by Paris Hilton and Sarah Silverman among others. It highlighted social media's double standards, and questioned who determines gender identity, and how.

Bottom: Amalia Ulman, *Excellences & Perfections*, 2014

On April 19, 2014, Argentinian artist Amalia Ulman announced *Excellences and Perfections* on her Instagram account and started posting selfies and other photographs of her life: not in itself unusual. Between then and September 19, 2014, a story unfolded—she is recruited as a model by a photographer; splits up with her boyfriend; becomes a sugar baby; buys clothes, drugs, and body-transforming surgery with the money; and is herself consumed by this life of consumption. This was a carefully scripted performance, exposing the narcissistic femininity in contemporary Western online culture—and the complicity of online strangers. "The sadder the girl, the happier the troll," says Ulman.

Below: VNS Matrix, *The Cyberfeminist Manifesto for the 21st Century*, 1991

VNS Matrix were an Australian group of techno-futurist utopian activists and thinkers. Formed in 1991, they were among the first to use the word "cyberfeminist" (along with British cultural theorist Sadie Plant); they split up in 1997, the same year as the First Cyberfeminist International event in Germany. For them, cyberspace was a place to dissolve gender and form a feminist sexual and cultural environment and non-patriarchal worlds. They developed the game All New Gen, where "All New Gen and her DNA Sluts […] battle against Big Daddy Mainframe and his technobimbo sidekicks."

Bottom: Hito Steyerl, *How Not To Be Seen: A Fucking Didactic Educational .MOV File*, 2013, still

This film got the first part of its title from a Monty Python sketch of the same name: a spoof British government public-service film. Steyerl's film also uses absurdity—suggestions for invisibility include self-camouflage; being smaller than a pixel; or being a woman over fifty. But the absurdity is based on something more sinister than the fact that older women disappear: Some sequences are filmed on black-and-white-painted squares on a runway in the American desert, once used for testing the resolution of military cameras. Being smaller than a pixel is sound advice.

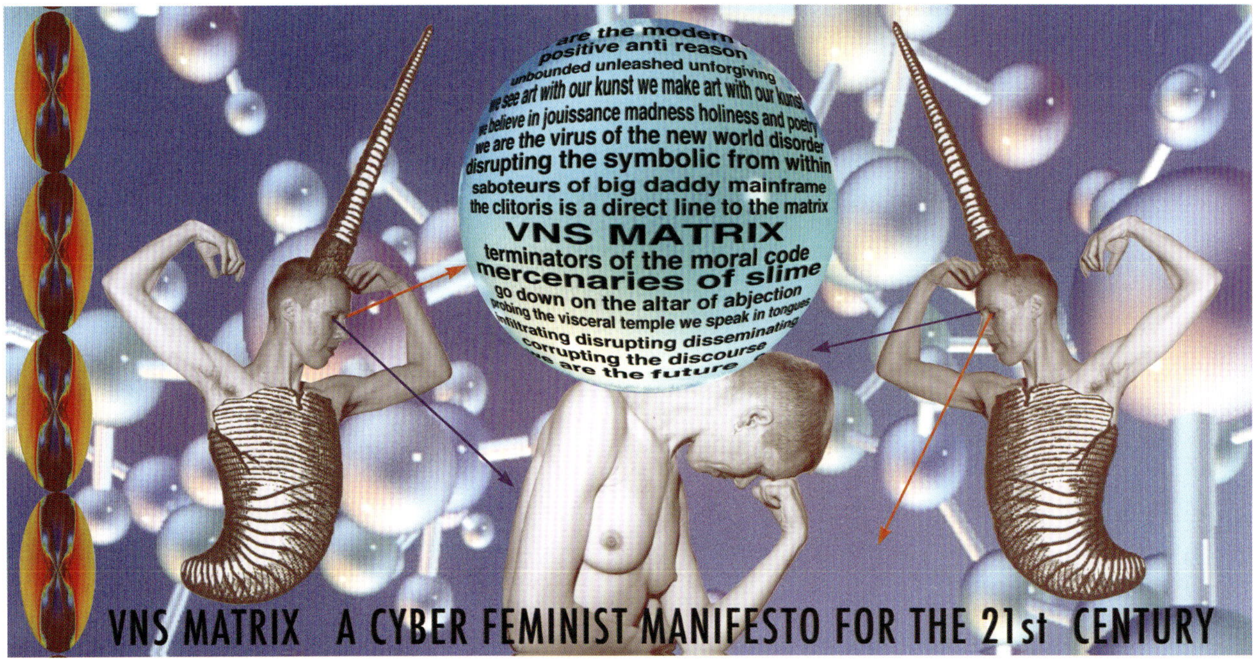

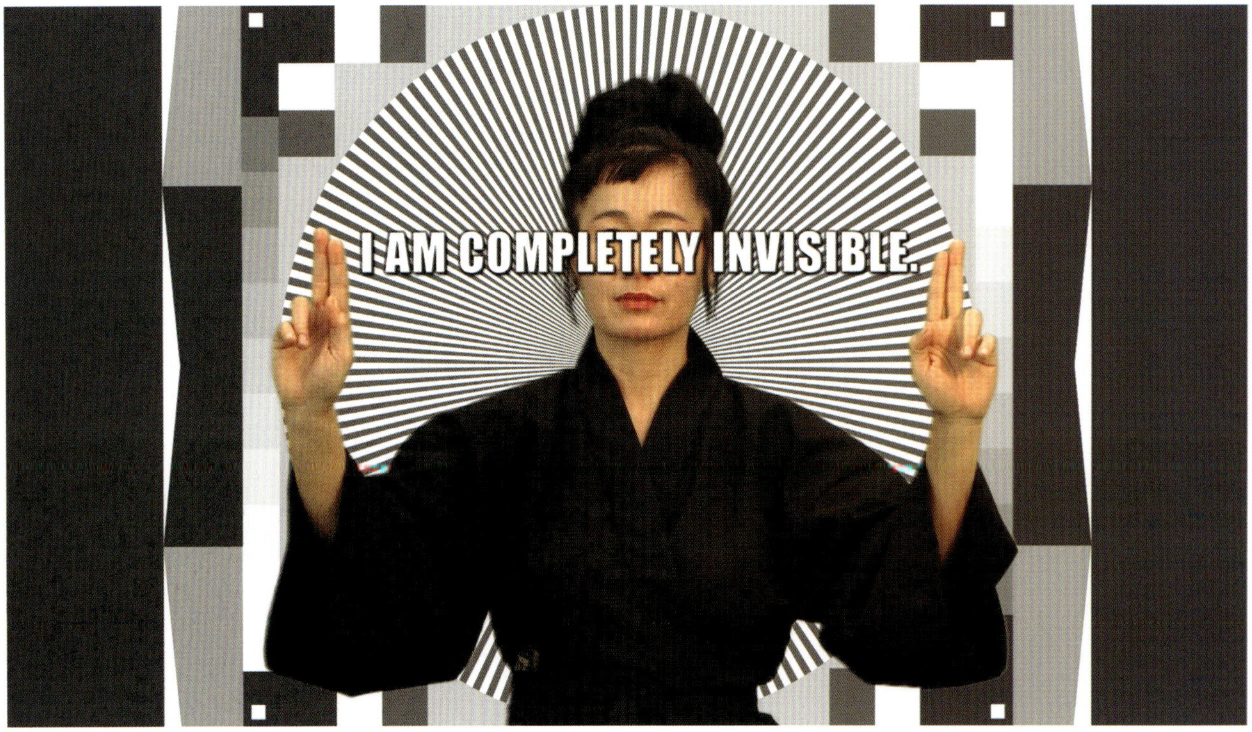

Making Feminist Art Public: Xabier Arakistain

Since the start of the twenty-first century, there has been a rise in major museum exhibitions across the globe dedicated to subjects relating to feminism, women artists, and/or sexuality and gendered identity. However, these are not always straightforwardly feminist, which raises the question: How can a curator be feminist in all aspects of their work?

In 2005, The Museum of Contemporary Art in Tokyo, the Centro Atlántico de Arte Moderno, Gran Canaria, and the Dunkers Kuturhus, Helsingborg, Sweden, all mounted survey exhibitions of contemporary women artists. These were followed, in 2007, by exhibitions of women artists, feminist artists, and art focused upon gendered and sexual identities, in Los Angeles, New York; Bilbao, Spain; and Santiago de Compostela, also Spain. Since then, over twenty major museums around the world have spent considerable time, space, and resources in mounting survey exhibitions of feminist art—sometimes pertaining to the particular country, and sometimes to particular time spans. Mostly, however, the curators were guest curators and we often have to look outside big museums for the most radical feminist curating practices.

Xabier Arakistain is a curator who lives in Bilbao, in the Basque Country, northern Spain. The first exhibition he curated, *Trans Sexual Express* (1999) included 50 percent male and 50 percent female-identifying artists. While the exhibition was touring Barcelona, Budapest, and La Coruña, Arakistain began working for the Bilbao Art Foundation, where he also introduced fifty/fifty parity of male/female artists to the exhibition program. From these beginnings he has curated, organized, and advocated to an explicitly feminist agenda.

In February 2005, Arakistain brought together an international and cross-generational group of feminist artists, curators, and scholars at the ARCO annual art fair in Madrid. He had been appointed in 2003 to lead conversations on feminism and art in conjunction with ARCO; the first one took place in February 2004. In 2005, however, he set an ambitious aim to go beyond amassing statistics about the omission of women artists or art-historical evidence about their existence. The title of the three-day meeting was "Equality Policies Between Men and Women Within the Art World: Designing strategies." As the title implies, Arakistain wanted to have real-world impact. The eventual outcome of the meeting was a manifesto that called for 50 percent inclusion of women artists in all state-funded exhibitions. Five days later, a Basque Law of Equality was passed, which included a few lines recommending equitable representation of women. The Spanish Socialist Party also received the manifesto and drew up a law for equality between men and women, which was passed by the Spanish government in 2007. It included a comprehensive article on "Equality in Artistic and Intellectual Creation and Production," which drew from the ARCO manifesto. As it states that public authorities "will endeavor" to ensure equal treatment, and that public bodies will "adopt initiatives" and "implement policies" rather than achieve results, it resides as a recommendation rather than enforceable law. However, it remains on the public statutes as a goal to be aimed for and as a form of legal structures that could be adopted and extended elsewhere.

In 2007, Arakistain was appointed director of the Cultural Center of Montehermoso in the town of Vitoria-Gasteiz, near Bilbao. It was set up following the definition of "culture" established by UNESCO: "That culture is a site for reflection upon ourselves and society; it is a means of producing new understandings, and for changing things; and it should be open to all and encourage equality." With his colleagues, Arakistain established a program that worked toward equality, using quotas in both the programming and the budgeting. It also produced new knowledge and aimed to effect structural change through specific feminist programming. This meant that he examined the entirety of the budget, including staff salaries, and the amount of money spent on exhibitions, to ensure equality of distribution of resources; he also examined and planned the programming to ensure fifty/fifty dedication of time and space to exhibiting and promoting male and female artists. Further, he had an explicitly feminist mission—to increase feminist knowledge and promote feminist thought, including the deconstruction of sexual stereotypes. Arakistain also worked with feminist anthropologist Professor Lourdes Méndez and the University of the Basque Country, to establish an annual interdisciplinary course "Artistic Production and the Feminist Theory of Art: New Debates." This brought feminist artists and scholars from around the world together with Spanish and Basque feminist scholars in a conference format, with proceedings that published the papers in full in three languages. In 2012, the course moved to Azkuna Zentroa, Bilbao, where it continues as "Feminist Perspectives in Art Production and Theories of Art."

Throughout this time, Arakistain developed his practice of curating major feminist exhibitions. In 2007, he was the curator of *Kiss Kiss Bang Bang: 86 Steps in 45 Years of Art and Feminism* (Museum of Fine Arts, Bilbao), an international survey of art made with feminist politics at its heart. At Montehermoso, among other feminist exhibitions, he curated (with Maura Reilly) *The Furious Gaze*—an exhibition that addressed the mirage of equality in the art world; and *Kick in the Eye: Eight Feminist Strategies to Interrupt the Male Gaze*. Since leaving Montehermoso, Arakistain has worked as an independent curator, with a focus upon retrospective exhibitions in museums of major feminist artists. This has included retrospectives of the American feminist artist Judy Chicago and the British feminist artist Margaret Harrison, neither of whom had been granted retrospectives before.

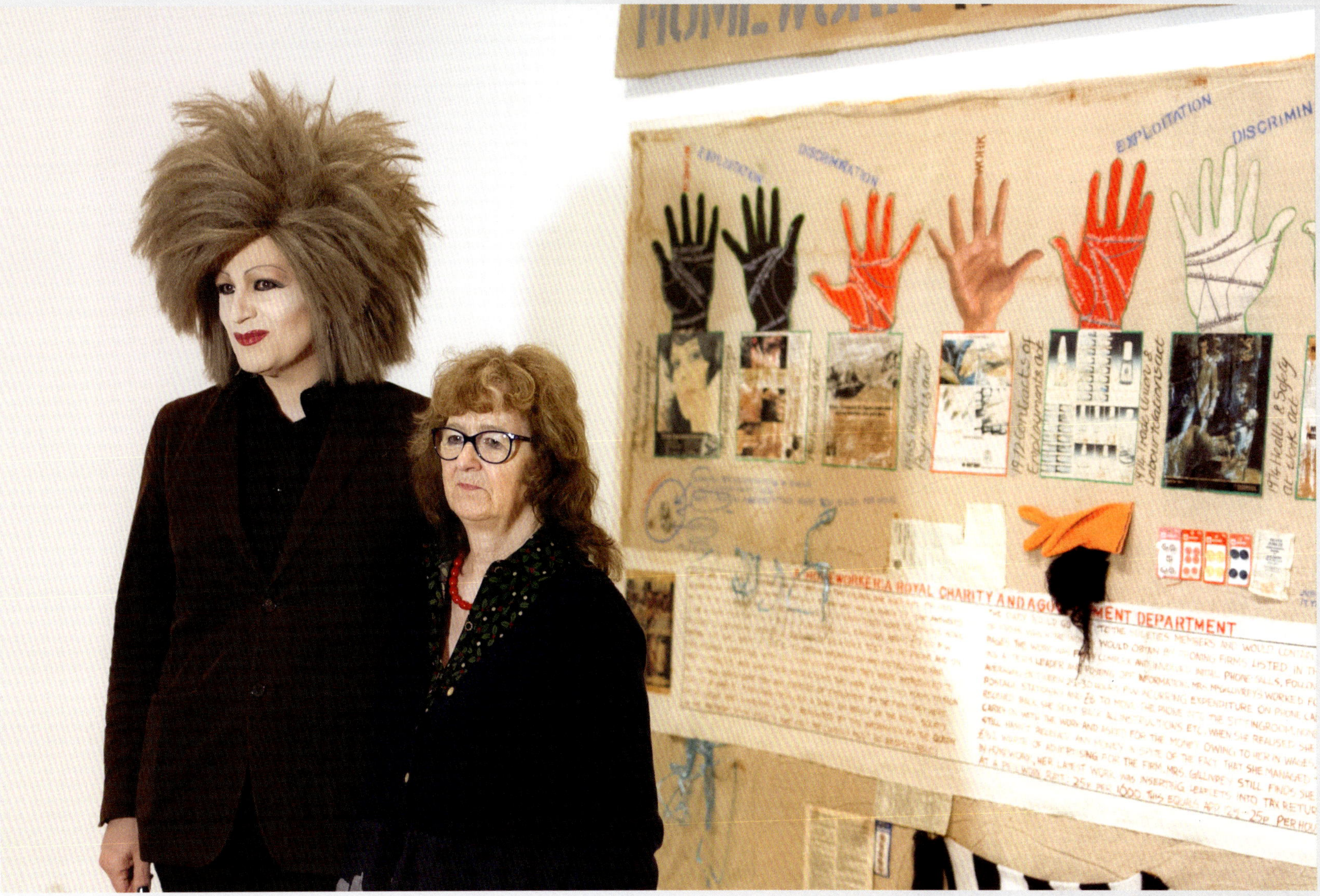

"The symbolic impact of the laws facilitated my winning a public competition for the launching of a cultural center whose programs would ensure the inclusion of women on equal terms to men."

Xabier Arakistain, 2015

Above: Curator Xabier Arakistain and English artist Margaret Harrison at the opening of the retrospective exhibition of her work that he curated, Azkuna Zentroa, Bilbao, Spain. October 20, 2017 to January 14, 2018.

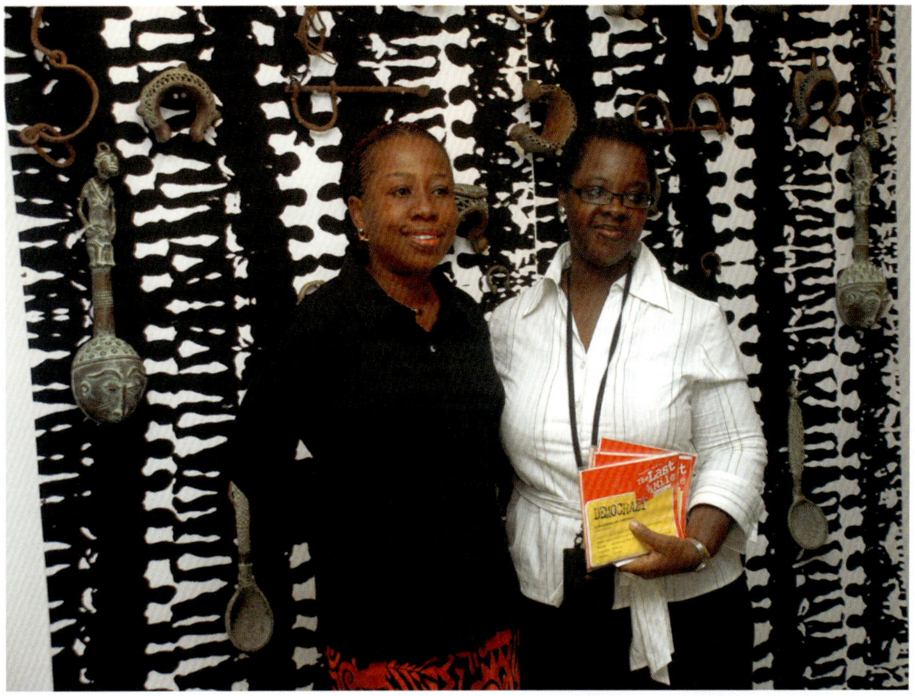

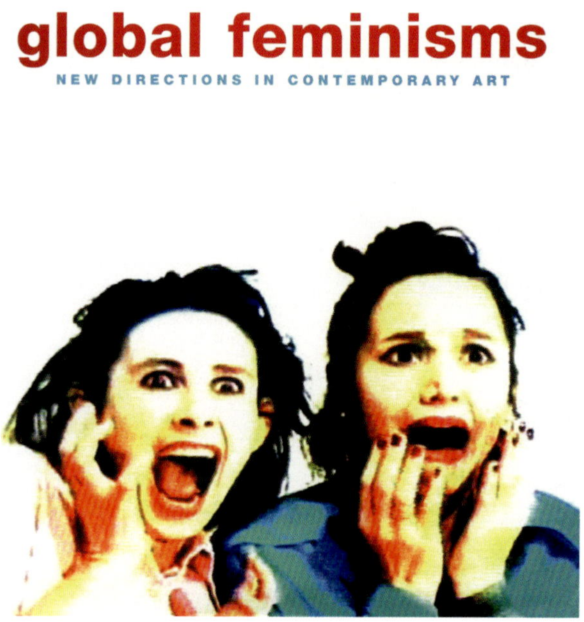

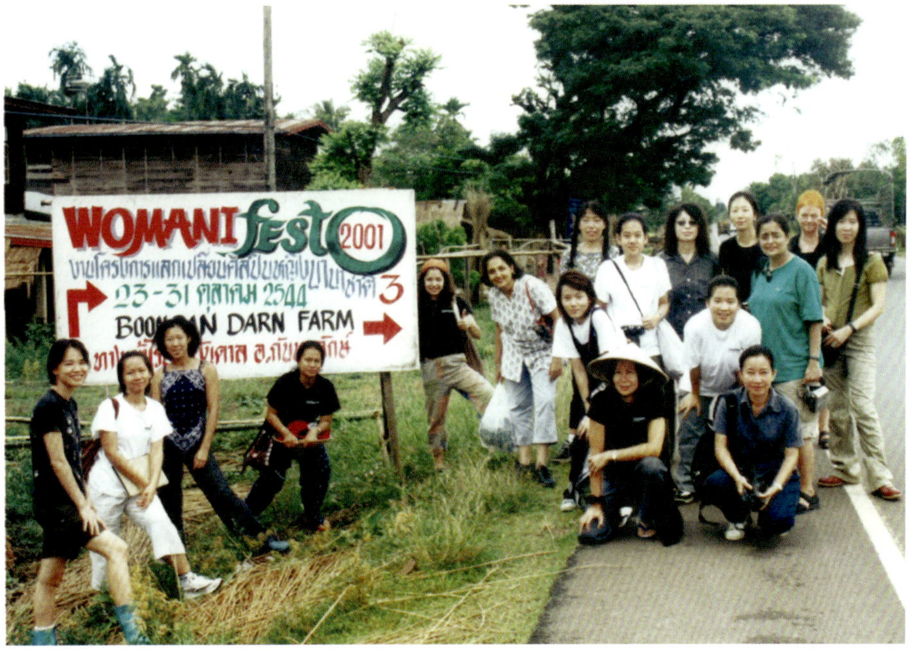

Top left: **Bisi Silva (right), pictured with visual artist Ndidi Dike**

Bisi Silva founded the Centre for Contemporary Art (CCA) in Lagos, Nigeria, in 2007. It is a key exhibition venue and research archive on contemporary African art. Silva was a cocurator of the *Dak'Art*, Senegal (2006), *Thessaloniki Biennale* (2009), and *Bamako Encounters* (2015), and is on the editorial board of *n.paradoxa: International Feminist Art Journal*. *The Progress of Love* (2012) was a CCA collaboration with the Menil Collection, Houston, Texas, with work from Africa, Europe, and the United States exploring "the changing modes and meanings of love in today's global society."

Top right: **Front cover for *Global Feminisms: New Directions in Contemporary Art*, cocurated by Maura Reilly, 2007**

Maura Reilly is presently the director of the National Academy of Design, New York. In 2007 she became the founding director of the Sackler Center for Feminist Art at the Brooklyn Museum, New York, which was also the first permanent home for Judy Chicago's *The Dinner Party* (1979). An influential writer and curator, in 2009 Reilly cocurated, with Linda Nochlin, *Global Feminisms*, an exhibition of work by artists born since 1960.

Bottom left: **Womanifesto, 2001**

Varsha Nair is a curator, artist, and writer. Born in Uganda, educated in India, she has been living in Bangkok since 1995. In 1997 she launched Womanifesto, a biannual series of international exchanges. That year, and again in 1999, it was an exhibition of contemporary feminist artists from throughout Asia. In 2001, it was a workshop; in 2003, a publication, *Procreation/Postcreation*; in 2005–2006, *No Man's Land*, a web project; and its final iteration was a residency program in 2008. *Womanifesto I* and *II* remain the most comprehensive exhibitions of Asian women artists.

Below: **Varsha Nair, from Promise of Transience, 2007**

Promise of Transience was a series of private performances using henna, made in India and Thailand. This photograph is from a performance in Baroda, India. Photo by Meeta Patel.

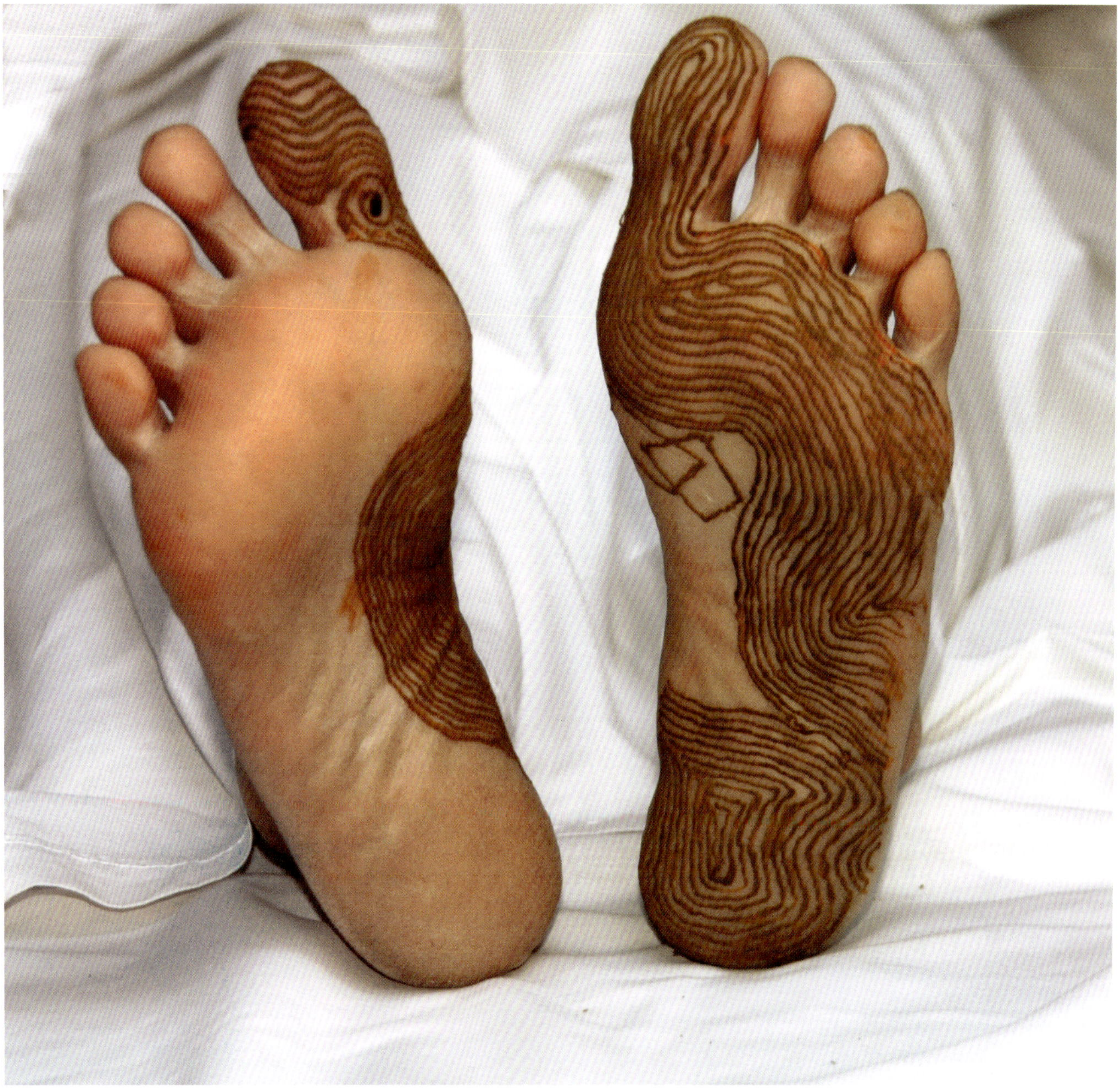

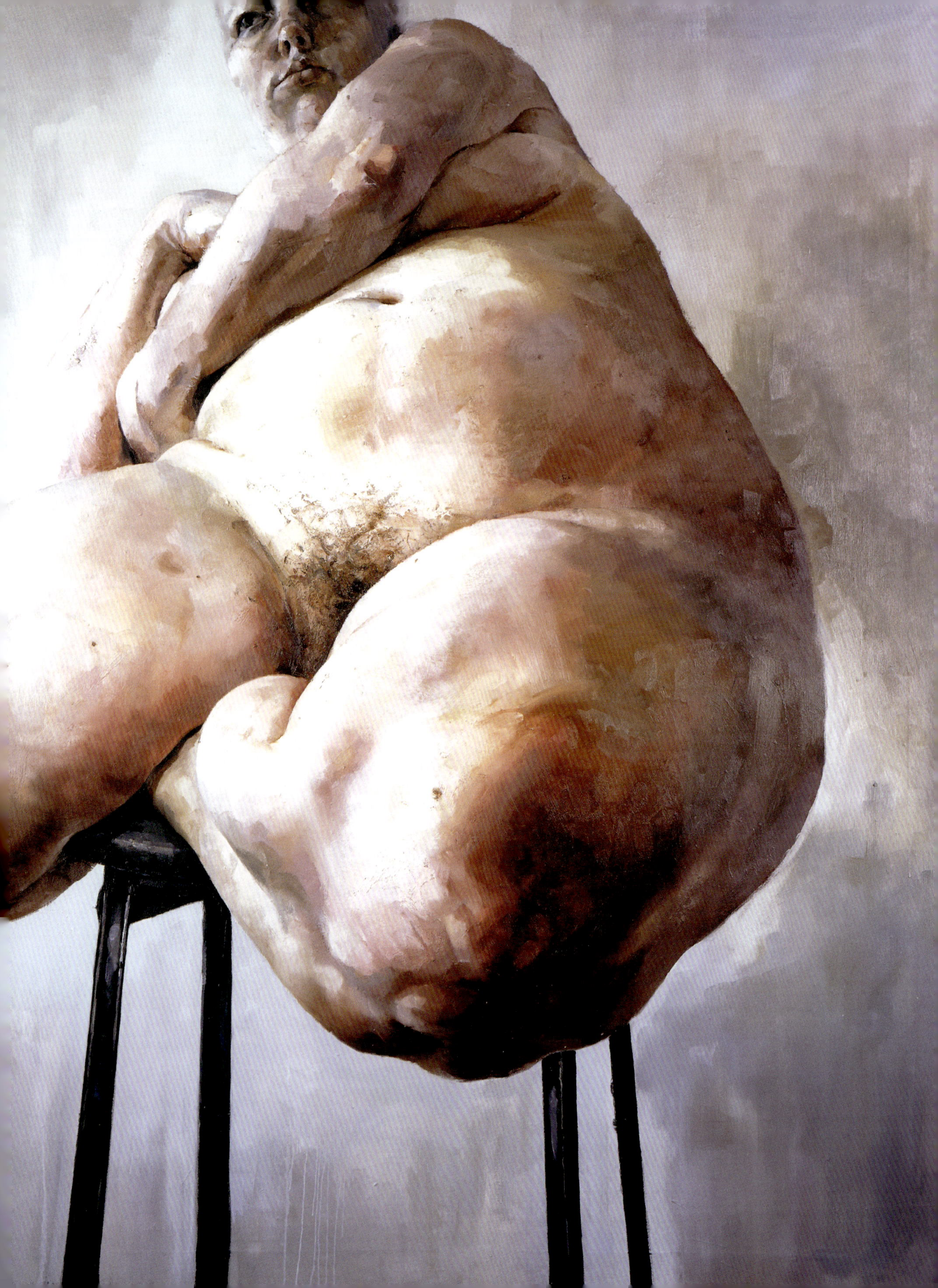

The Personal Feminist

Making the Personal Political

"The real question is—how are we to live our lives?"

Feminist activist and academic, Lynne Segal, *Out of Time*, 2013

The concept of "the personal" has always been of importance to feminist theory and activism. One of the key intended outcomes of feminist activism and related processes in the 1970s and 1980s—such as consciousness-raising—was that a woman could come to understand that things she thought pertained only to herself may in fact reflect a pattern that affected many women. Such a realization would then lead to the idea that, collectively, through sharing personal stories, political deductions could be drawn, strategies worked out, group action taken, and the feeling of being alone or powerless dispelled. In the twenty-first century, the rise of social media has increased the blurring of the categories of personal and private. The "personal" (which pertains to your own person, your emotional life, or something that attaches only to you) and the "private" (which designates something restricted to particular individuals) become hard to differentiate when individuals put details of emotional or medical traumas, or intimate or family photographs, on social media, where they can be read and seen by strangers.

The challenge for feminists—including artists—has often been one of retaining a sense of collective engagement with the challenges of structural sexism and the misogyny of individuals. This was particularly hard around the turn of the century, when feminism appeared to be reduced to issues of individual empowerment or assimilation and achievement in existing structures. It is, therefore, understandable that many modern-day feminist artists are responding to similar personal issues that affected artists of earlier decades—including the body, mothering, sexuality, and the home—but frequently demonstrating that, if the personal is political, then institutional politics also help shape the personal. The ways in which feminist politics developed its concerns and the issues it was involved with were mediated through analyzing personal issues.

One key area of this analysis has seen artists reflect on the most intimate arena of the personal: the body. The socialization of girls and women to have bodies that look certain ways and behave in a certain manner has always been a crucial area of contention for feminism, and can be traced back to the dress reform movements of the nineteenth century. English artist Jenny Saville explores the discomfort that women have been made to feel about the substance of their own bodies—of themselves—being excess, too much, and hateful; and she does so with a method of painting that suggests tenderness and love for that flesh. Being made to feel too big is just one issue in the personal politics of the body. Others include being too old, too different in physical and mental abilities, not white enough. The ability to love the body that is deemed to be unlovable by dominant cultural expectations is of particular urgency for women of color in white-dominated societies. For the black American/South African photographic artist Ayana Velissa Jackson, the high aesthetic of traditional oil painting is the field to engage with. It is one that has historically exoticized, brutalized, or marginalized black women. Jackson inserts the bodies of black women into poses that recall individual paintings or generic painting styles, creating new beauty and a black aesthetic in a predominantly white aesthetic tradition. French artist ORLAN has spent much of her career also engaging with, and exposing, the impossible requirements for female beauty within that same tradition. Working with surgeons, and staging the events as performances, she underwent a series of nine plastic-surgery operations between 1990 and 1995 to give her attributes that were regarded as the pinnacles of female beauty in painting at different times and places. They include the chin of Botticelli's *Venus*, the forehead of Leonardo's *Mona Lisa*, and the mouth of Boucher's *Europa*. In taking on these attributes as her physical reality, the representations of female beauty in art are laid bare as being contingent upon passing aesthetic fashions, and far removed from the bodies of actual women. Martha Wilson is another artist who has been concerned with the dominant concept of femininity as a construct—including what is desirable femininity—since the 1970s, with her recent work focusing on the aging body. Much of Joanna Frueh's past work has focused on the erotics and power of her own body, seeking modes of representation that gain from investment in mythological figures such as Aphrodite. In one work, she presents her own body following a double mastectomy, seeking the same aesthetic and beauty.

Key to the development of feminist thinking in recent decades has been its intersection with queer theory and trans* theory. Queer theory argues that all identities, including gender identities and sexual identities, are fluid, not fixed, challenging sexual politics based upon clearly labeled identities such as gay, lesbian, straight, male, female, etc. Trans* activism advocates for the rights and visibility of all gender-non-conforming people—transgender, genderqueer, intersex, and others who don't fit into conventional binary gender categories. In Toronto, Canada, an example of work that is part of such queer thinking can be found with Allyson Mitchell and Deirdre Logue. They have done much to insist upon a thoroughly radical approach to all that they do, not only as artists, but also as the founders of Feminist Art Gallery, or FAG. They have

Page 200: **Jenny Saville, *Prop*, 1993**

English artist Jenny Saville first became known for the paintings she presented as her BA degree exhibition at Glasgow School of Art, all of which were bought by art collector and advertising company director Charles Saatchi. *Prop* is one of them. Her paintings were often 6–7 ft (1.8–2.1 m) tall portraits of naked women (usually herself). They were "women who've been made to think they're big and disgusting," said Saville; but she painted them with tiny brushes, as though lovingly, minutely, stroking the flesh into being.

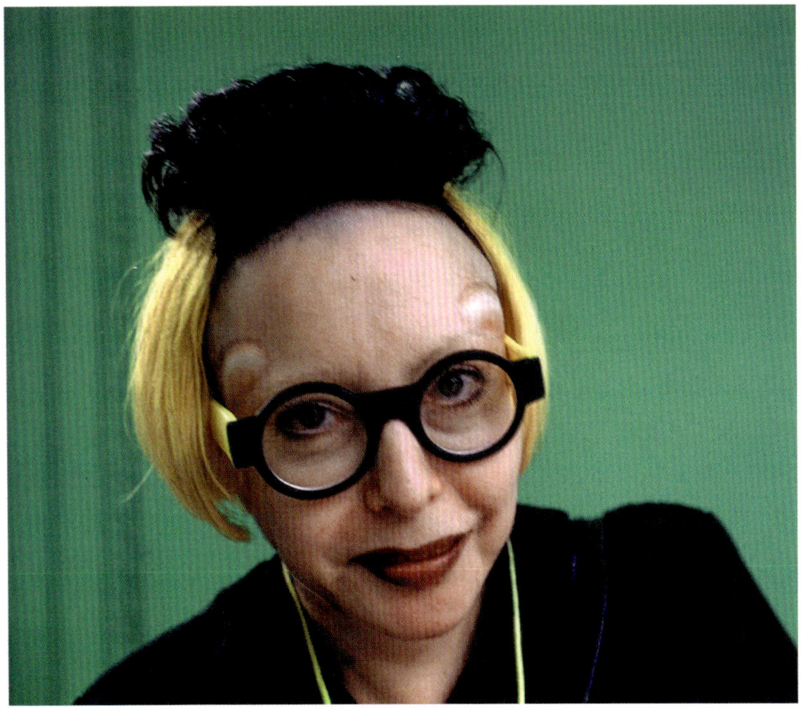

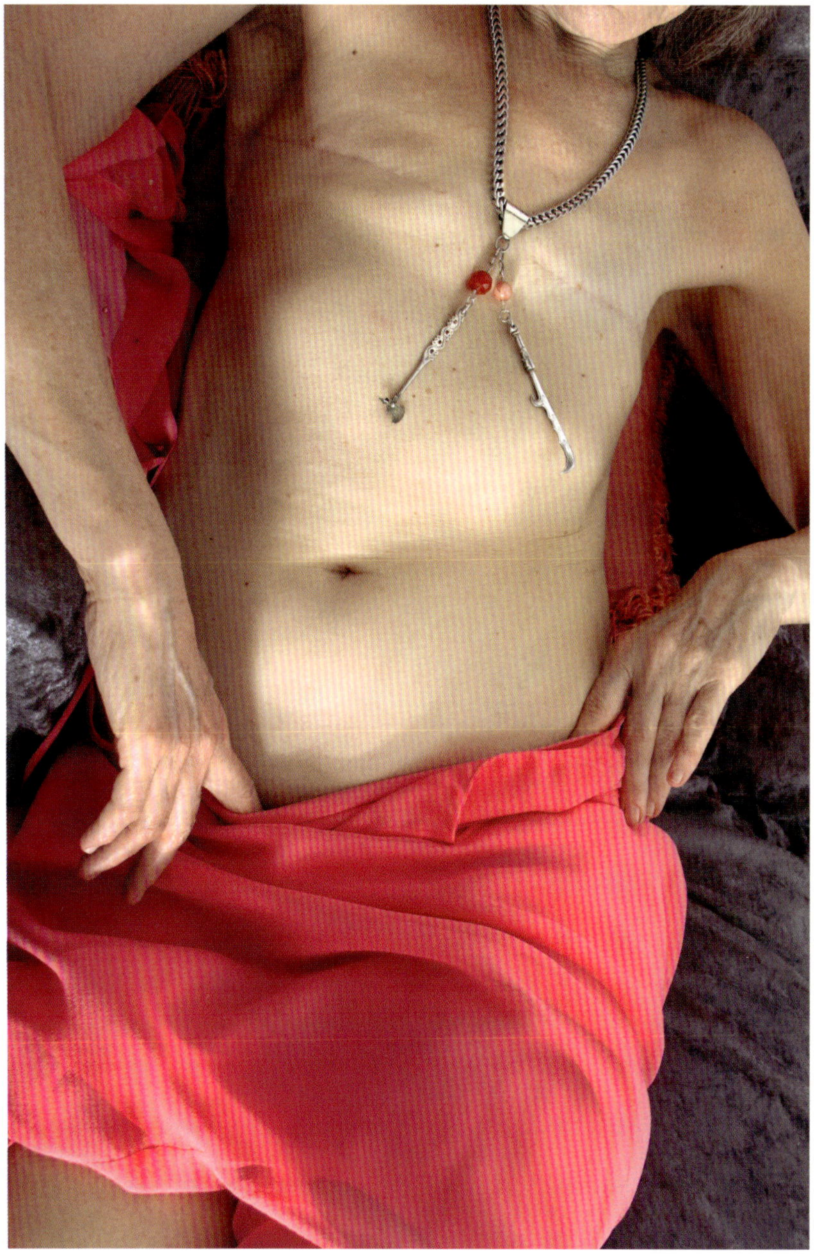

Above left: **ORLAN**

In 1978 performance artist ORLAN had emergency surgery. Remaining conscious throughout, she was fascinated by the role of the surgeon. The experience led her to think about the uses of surgery and art to create aesthetic standards for women's bodies, and prompted her to undergo such surgery herself. "My goal was [. . .] to sculpt my own body to reinvent the self. [. . .] I tried to use surgery not to better myself or become a younger version of myself, but to work on the concept of image and surgery the other way around." In recent work, ORLAN uses digital rather than surgical manipulation to increase the modifications.

Above right: **Frances Murray with Joanna Frueh, *Sword* and *Ax* from the series Self-Evidence, 2013**

Joanna Frueh's work has always been grounded in her body and in words. In her "lectures" the viewer soon realizes that every detail is worked out in her performance of being a desiring female subject: her clothing, the pauses, and her interactions with the audience. The erotics present in human exchanges are brought to the fore, based upon long-standing studies of yoga and psychoanalysis. The series of photographs Self-Evidence, in collaboration with Frances Murray, were taken after Frueh's recovery from a double mastectomy following a breast cancer diagnosis.

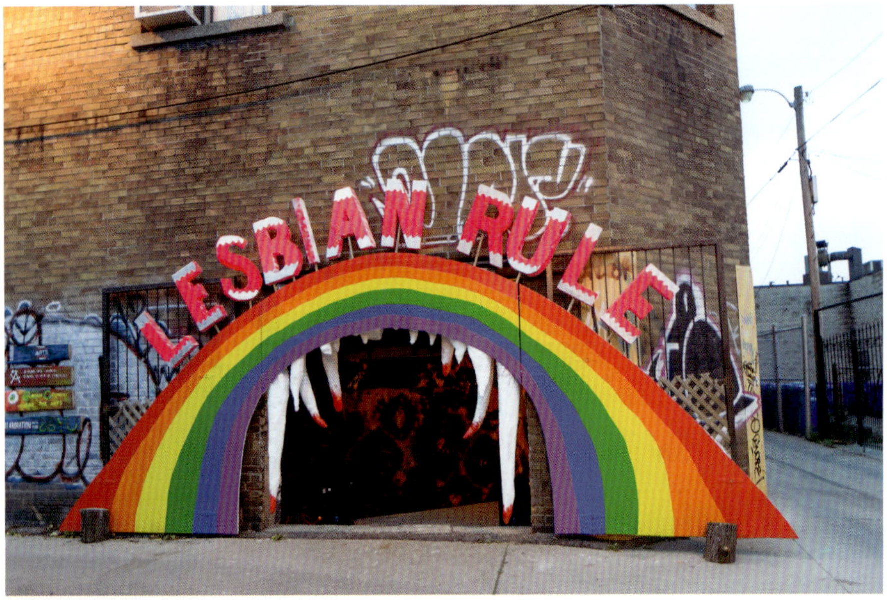

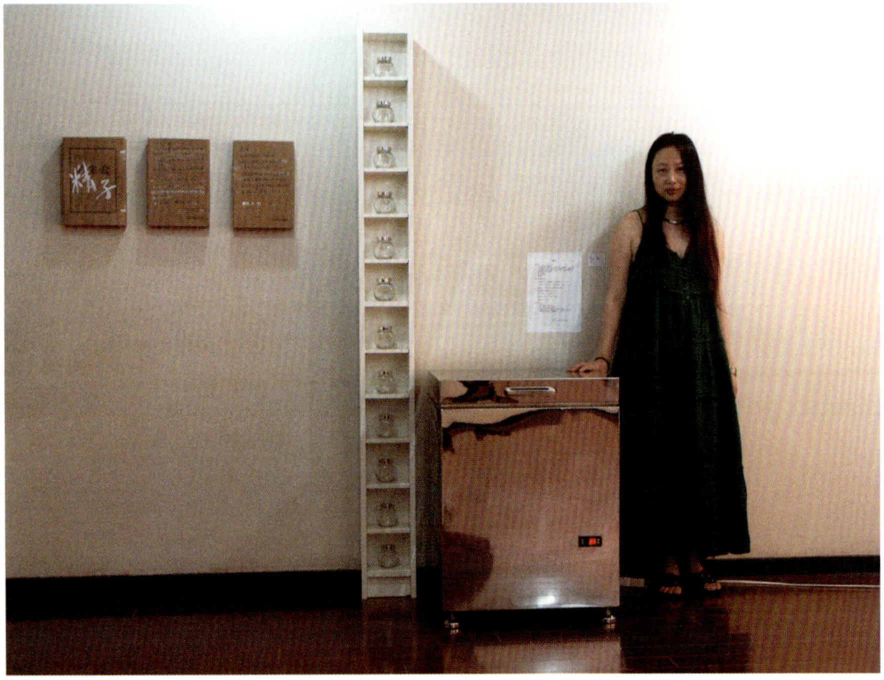

Top: Allyson Mitchell and Deirdre Logue, *Killjoy's Kastle: A Lesbian Feminist Haunted House*, 2013–14

This work was created in Toronto, then London, and finally Los Angeles by Allyson Mitchell and Deirdre Logue, who describe themselves as maximalist artists. Mitchell was baffled when four Canadian galleries touring her *Ladies Sasquatch* exhibition (2006–10) put parental advisories in the rooms containing the sculptures. Concluding that these works were too feral and unassimilated for societies that would accept queer relationships that conformed to heteronormative standards, Mitchell decided to push what boundaries she could. Her subsequent collaboration with Logue, *Killjoy's Kastle*, had two main influences: the cultural theorist Sara Ahmed, whose blog is called feministkilljoys—an idea both artists embraced—and Christian evangelical "hell houses." Mitchell and Logue questioned their fearful representation of what they called sin. *Killjoy's Kastle* contained lesbian zombies sniffing out feminist brains, riot ghouls, bearded clams, polyamorous vampire grannies, and many other frights. Criticism about lack of access, and over the inclusion of trans* bodies, led to deep discussion about the politics of inclusion and the playful criticism of pervasive stereotypes.

Bottom: Xiao Lu, *Sperm*, 2006

On February 5, 1989, Xiao Lu stood in front of her work *Dialogue* at the opening of *China Avant Garde*, in Beijing, China. She drew out a gun, and shot life-size photographs of a male/female couple. The exhibition was closed immediately, and she was detained. Later, critics described this work in light of the Tiananmen Square protests of June that year; but Xiao Lu addresses the personal politics of it. Her partner self-aggrandized and betrayed her by claiming the shooting for himself; after they split, a key theme in works by Xiao Lu is a rejection of heteronormative structures. Working with a Western doctor because Chinese women can only get IVF if they are married, she made the performance/installation and video *Sperm*. She set up a gallery space with clinical refrigeration units, and asked for men to donate sperm for her IVF, making it clear that she wanted no emotional, social, sexual, or other relationship. No one donated sperm. In 2009 she married herself in a performance, *Wedding*.

worked with the local community to position FAG not as a sign of gentrification of the neighborhood, but as an integral part of the community. They have deliberately not wanted FAG to become an institution with a rigid identity, nor to do what many not-for-profits do, to grow bigger and become part of the recognized establishment. Instead, FAG has purposefully remained a critical and intersectional site, working with the arts community, the local neighborhood community, and the LGBTQ community equally—perhaps the most queer position that can be taken up these days. Their artwork inevitably has the same stance, and includes *Killjoy's Kastle: A Lesbian Feminist Haunted House*. In its different iterations over three years, this project has taken on critique that it was exclusionary or insensitive to some trans* or racial identities from earlier presentations. Logue and Mitchell have faced those discussions, engaging with them to ensure that the gallery's radical politics and sense of queer community are current and responsive. A similar constant questioning can be found in the work of Del LaGrace Volcano, who holds that "disobedience, disruption, and defiance of gender norms and ALL norms are the cornerstone of queer cultural production." Volcano was born intersex, raised female, and became known within queer communities for pioneering documentary and staged photographic work, exploring lesbian communities from within. The book *Love Bites* ensured a wide distribution for the work, helping to build communities. Since the 1990s, Volcano has been living as both male and female with the aim of building intersex communities through face-to-face meetings and identities and experiences mediated through photographic projects.

In her long-term friendship with, and work about, Mona Ahmed, Indian photojournalist Dayanita Singh has also made visible a particular trans* community—this time, the "eunuchs" or "hijras" of India. About half of them are indeed thought to be people who have been castrated; and about half (one million) are intersex. Revered for their ability to bless, feared for their ability to curse, they are both granted a certain social role and utterly marginalized in a caste-riven culture. Singh was initially commissioned to make a photo spread for the U.K.'s *The Times* newspaper in 1989, which is when she met Mona Ahmed. When she discovered what the photos were to be used for, Mona Ahmed asked Singh to destroy them, which Singh did. This act led to the photographer questioning her role in the exoticization of Indian subjects by the West, and won the complete trust of her subject. Their working relationship, in turn, produced one of the most remarkable long-term representations of gender-diverse lives anywhere. What emerges most strongly is the difficulty Mona Ahmed had in establishing a home and a domestic environment.

The home has been considered a "woman's realm" in modern thought since the ideological development of the "separate spheres" for men and women at the time of the Industrial Revolution. Then, for the first time in modern Western culture, vast numbers of men left the home to go to work, rather than working in home-based workshops or agricultural production, where both sexes had a role. Consequently, the home became a private sphere, separate from work, and lost its visible economic role in the means of production. Enlightenment philosophy explored this separation, often supporting it, but also producing early feminist writers such as England's Mary Wollstonecraft and Olympe de Gouges from France. In the 1970s, feminism produced the Wages for Housework movement and worked in cooperatives and collectives. Since the 1990s, feminism has had divergent economic strategies. On the one hand, there is the assimilationist strategy promoted by American Sheryl Sandberg with her 2013 book *Lean In*, and related courses encouraging women to excel within the existing capitalist structures. On the other hand are the strategies promoted by many of the artists in this section, resisting both capitalist insistence on the separate work and economic spheres of men and women, as well as neoliberal economic ideology—which, as it is based upon benefit to the individual rather than on collective economic and cultural good, most feminist and other liberatory or social justice movements reject. Dutch artist Melanie Bonajo's documentary trilogy *Night Soil* shows this resistance, examining in turn psychedelic-using communities, an activist women sex-workers group, and a radical farming and land-use movement. Other artists who explore resistance in neighborhood or home environments include examples such as FAG, mentioned earlier, Julita Wojcik, and Shadi Ghadirian's series of works reflecting the domestic impact of living with militarization in Iran, *Like Every Day and Nil Nil*.

Mothering is a key site of contention in this resistance, as is the reconfiguring of the sphere of home. While in postcommunist Poland, Elżbieta Jabłońska exposes the impossibility of being the perfect mother with the help of American superhero costumes; in the Chinese model of communism even becoming a mother could at times be impossible. Xiao Lu makes this public in her poignant, desperate installation *Sperm*, where she sought donors for artificial insemination before she was too old for it according to the laws at the time in China. In the United States, Marni Kotak resists the hyper-medicalization of giving birth, and Catherine Opie queers motherhood, while artists such as Lenka Clayton persistently and consistently, project after project, dissect the separate spheres of motherhood, work, and the art world.

In all of these works, we can see that the tenet "the personal is political," while it is perhaps more nuanced in the light of fifty years of feminist experience, nonetheless still resonates. Lynne Segal's question, "How are we to live our lives?" challenges us, as feminists, to incorporate our politics into a set of ethics for our everyday ways of being: Where do we sleep? What do we eat? What do we expect of—and give to—those we share spaces and intimacies with? How do we use languages? And how do we choose to represent ourselves and others?

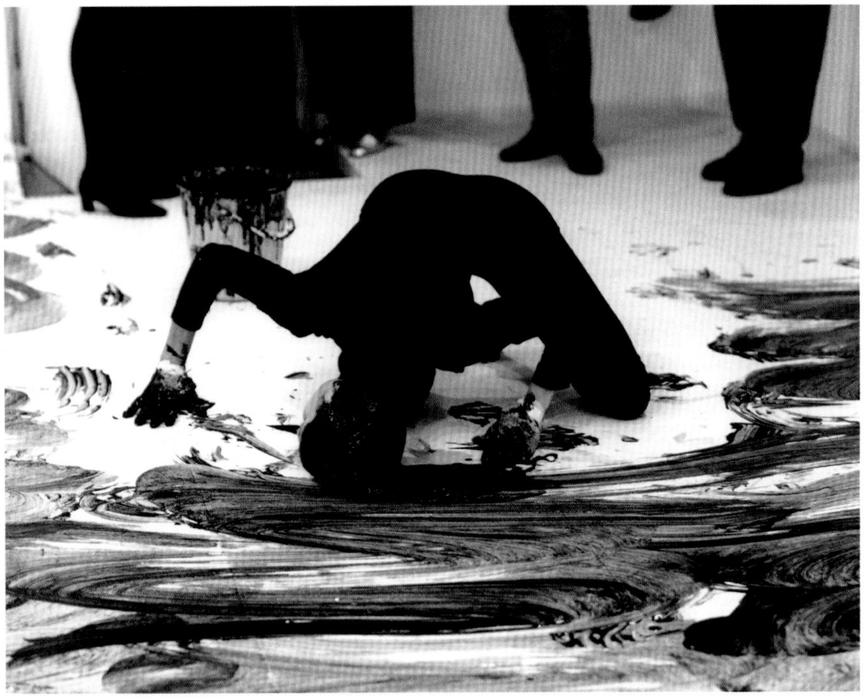

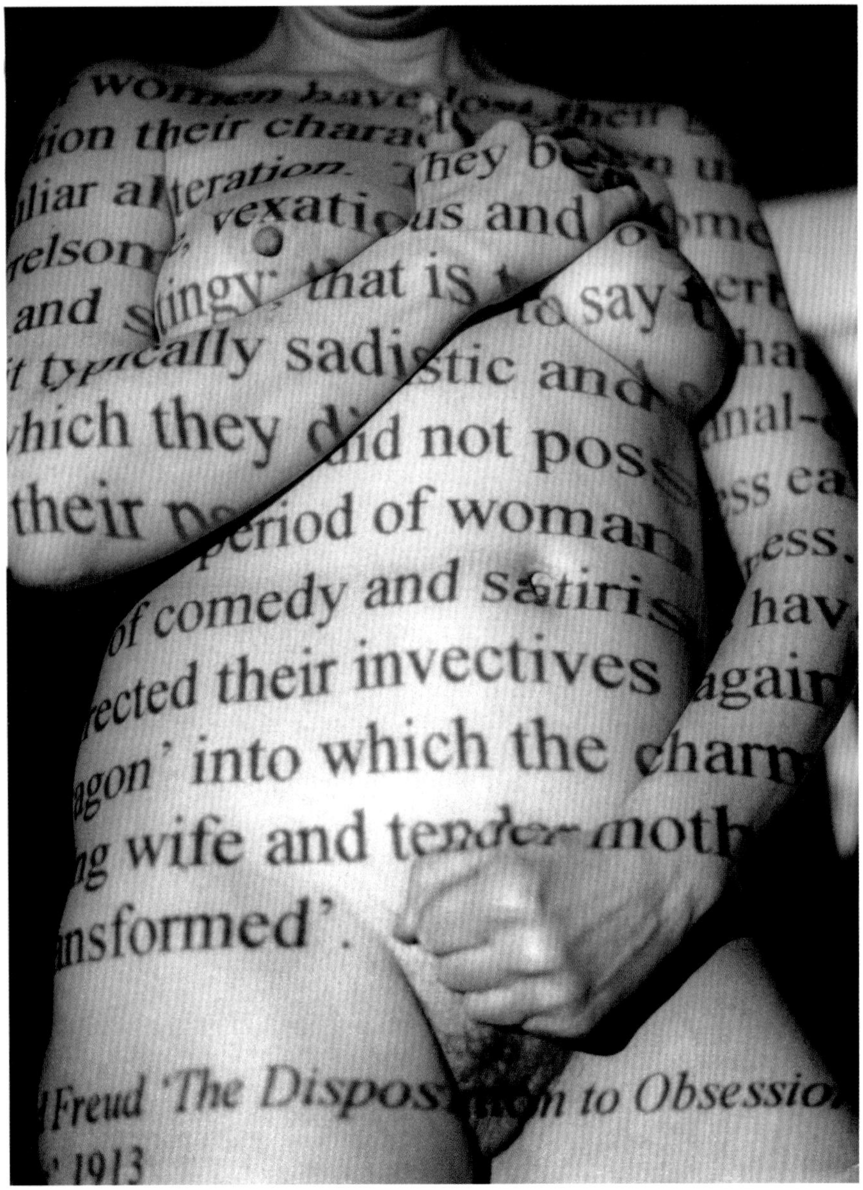

Top: **Janine Antoni, *Loving Care*, 1993**

Janine Antoni is a Bahamian artist who works mainly in sculpture and performance. *Loving Care* was a performance repeated in different venues (1992–94). Antoni dressed in simple black, placed a bucket of hair dye on the white gallery floor, knelt next to it, and dipped her long hair into it. Using repetitive, rhythmic movements, she "mopped" the floor with her dye-laden hair, leaving swirls showing where she had been and redipping her hair in the dye when it needed replenishing. In this, she is literally making visible the invisible work of cleaning—work that is generally seen only when it has not been done, and is usually women's work: the "loving care" expected within families. In addition, *Loving Care* was a popular brand of hair dye, marketed to women to preserve a semblance of youthful looks.

Bottom: **Rosy Martin & Kay Goodridge, *"After women have lost their genital function . . . ," Sigmund Freud, The Disposition to Obsessional Neurosis, 1913*; from Outrageous Agers, 2001**

In 1983, Rosy Martin developed "re-enactment phototherapy" with Jo Spence: having deconstructed their visual representations as white, working-class, middle-aged women, the phototherapy reconstructed their experiences. Outrageous Agers was a series made with Kay Goodridge, with defining theoretical texts projected upon the resistant, real bodies, to make visible the cultural, medical, and psychoanalytic shaping of women's aging.

This page: **Katarzyna Kozyra, *Bathhouse*, 1997, still; *Men's Bathhouse*, 1999, still**

Bathhouse is a five-channel video projection of footage secretly filmed by Kozyra in the Gellért Baths in Budapest, Hungary. We see women at ease with themselves, unidealized, not judged, caring for themselves. Every so often, a Rembrandt painting of a woman is juxtaposed with the images that has evoked it. *Men's Bathhouse*, 1999, similarly to *Bathhouse*, is filmed secretly. This time, however, Kozyra had to adopt a disguise: The artist performed a male body to capture the images, complete with a prosthetic penis, false body hair, and a towel over her shoulders to disguise her breasts. We see young men naked, older men with modesty aprons, and a homosociality that is normally hidden to women. Overladen is the tension of knowing that the artist's disguise could be discovered, and (for women viewers) that this is forbidden territory.

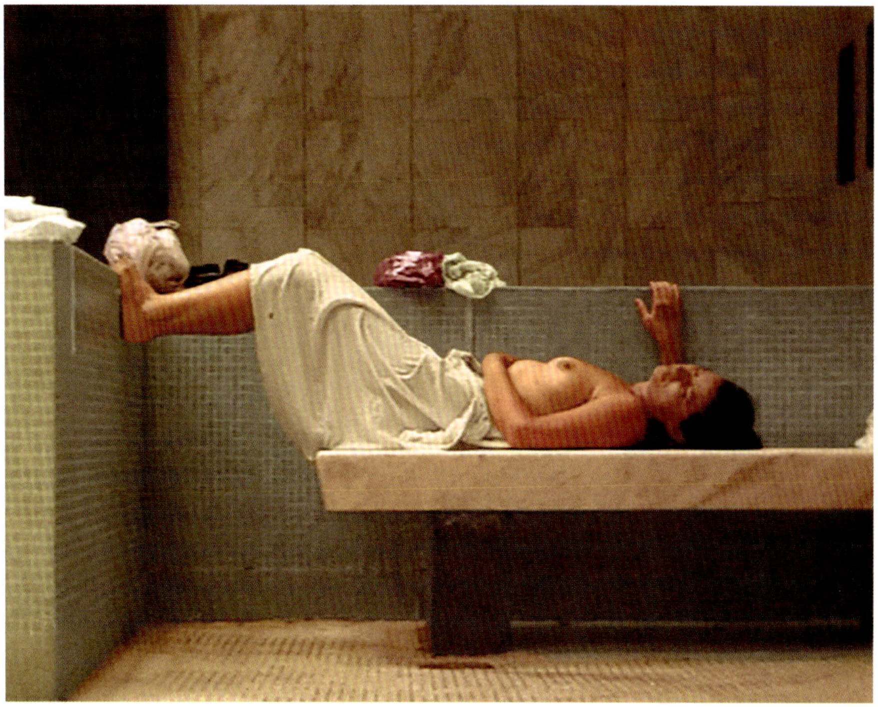

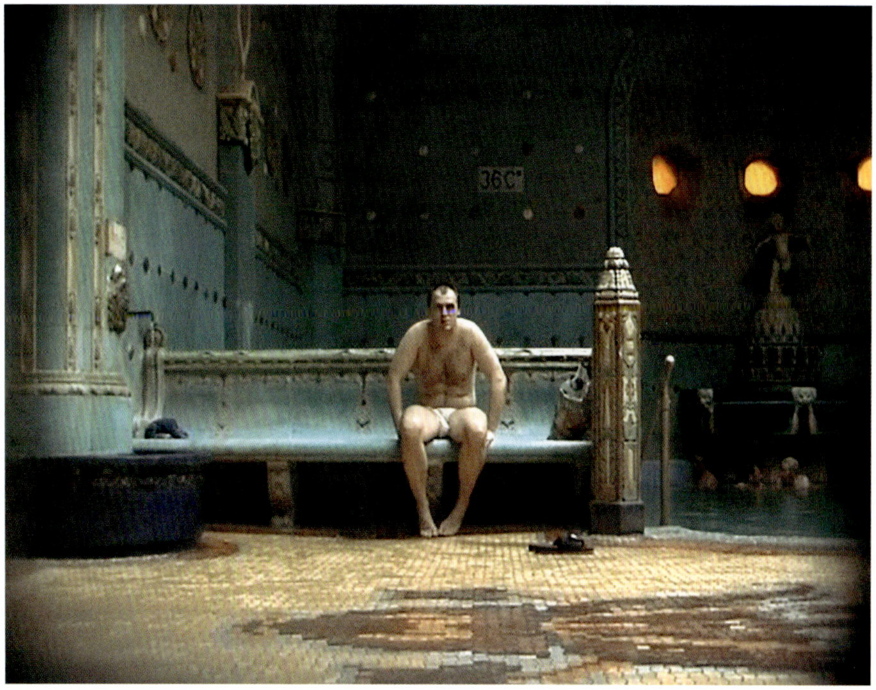

Aging: Martha Wilson

Martha Wilson's recent work frequently juxtaposes photographs taken for her 1970s projects with similarly posed recent photographs, exposing the arbitrariness of assigning beauty to a young woman's body, but not to the aging body of the same woman with her wisdom and experience.

"I have one or two more decades to complete my mission from God: To make the world safe for avant-garde art."

Martha Wilson, in her essay "The Personal becomes Political in Time," 2000

The gallerygoer who walked into New York's P.P.O.W. gallery in September 2011, to see the exhibition of Martha Wilson's new work, was immediately confronted by a challenge. The first work visible, on a wall that shielded other works from view, was a black-and-white photograph measuring some 7 x 4 ft (2.1 x 1.2 m), of Wilson's face: a self-portrait, taken when the artist was in her early sixties. Slightly turned to look over the viewer's right shoulder, Wilson smiles broadly, as if about to chuckle; her eyes are kindly and amused. Her eyelashes are almost invisible and she appears to wear no makeup. Her skin is soft, with deep lines around her eyes and mouth, and many little creases. Her face is shiny in the flat light. Her teeth are bared, uneven, and a couple appear discolored. Her lips have uneven tones, and there appear to be a few broken blood vessels on her chin. She is jowly, double-chinned, her neck almost as wide as her face. Her hair is cut short; from a central part, it is greased down flat against her skull. In small black letters across the bottom of the photograph is the title of the work: *I have become my own worst fear*.

Walking toward this large image, the space to the left came into view. It contained a video projection, also of Wilson's face, black-and-white, and large; but this was from 1974, when she was twenty-seven. We watch as she applies makeup in two sequences: first as expected; and then to produce the opposite effect of what is deemed desirable. There, we see the younger woman projecting into the future what she fears she will look like: The makeup emphasizes blemishes, creases, greasy shine, and her hair has a center part and is combed flat. Turning back to the first, oversize, photograph, we see that fear made manifest. Two photographs resulting from the early performance are called, respectively: *I Make up the Image of my Perfection* and *I Make up the Image of my Deformity*.

This is bold and subversive work. As can be seen in the earlier video, Wilson has always maintained a fearless approach to using representations of herself. The image that the younger Wilson feared did not use any more makeup than did the image that she desired; the new photograph appears to use none—apart, perhaps, from something oily to make the skin shine and to slick the hair down—this is not "costume" or even "dressing up" in any real sense of the word. The charade of female beauty, as enhanced by cosmetics and appropriate expressions and poses, is exposed as being utterly flimsy; and the fear of postmenopausal age—becoming the opposite of what our culture wants for female beauty—is something that most of us, with the luck of an expected lifetime, will have to confront as we age.

This was Wilson's first major exhibition of new work for some years. Elsewhere in the exhibition, a further subtlety to this mix of older and younger images emerged: not only the emotional fear of becoming that image of "undesirability"—the postmenopausal woman—but also the potentiality that every young woman's body has to become that older woman's body. Two head-and-shoulder self-portraits titled *Beauty and Beastly* (1974/2009) look at each other in profile, each seeming to be slightly startled by the image of the other: evidently the same woman, Wilson, in mirror image.

In *Before and After* (1974/2008) two square color photographs show Wilson standing frontally before the camera, naked, seen from her pubic area to just below the shoulders. We are invited to explore the biographical journey of her body, and its visible signs of experience and aging; but also, as an artwork, to contrast the formal elements—the changes in shapes and relationships between the different parts of the torso. We are also invited again to confront the collapse of time—this is, after all, the same body, the same photographic truth. Wilson's genius is not only in her lack of pity for, or judgment upon, her woman's body at any stage of its story, but in her compassionate and dispassionate eye, which enable the gallerygoer also to confront their own fears about aging with the same generosity and love.

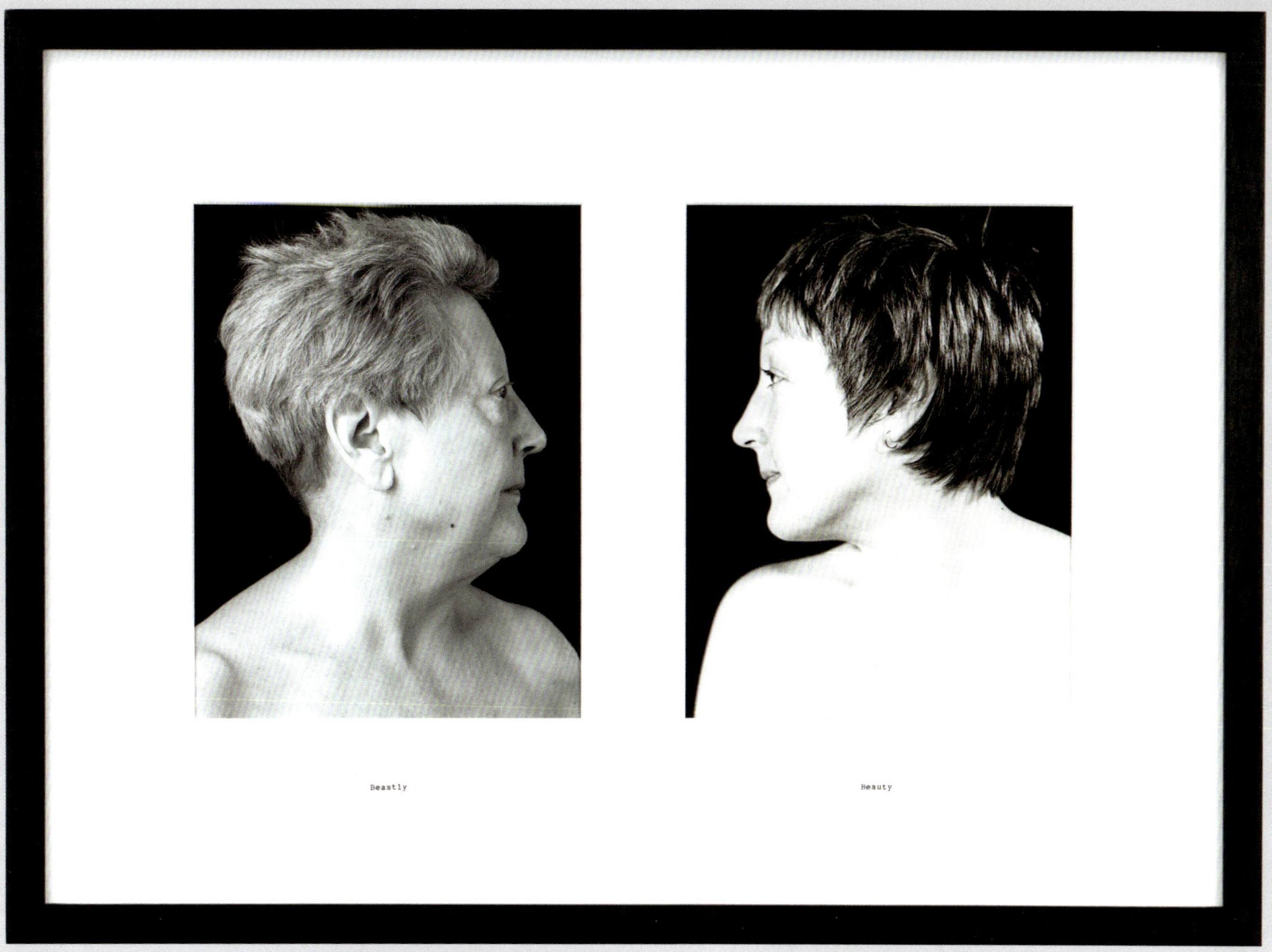

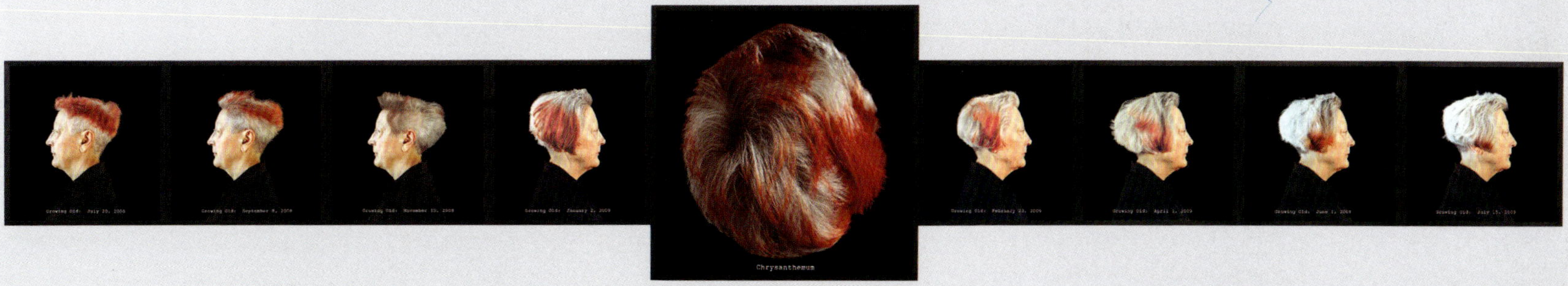

Top left and right: Martha Wilson, *Beauty and Beastly*, 1974/2009

In both *Beauty and Beastly* and *Before and After*, Martha Wilson is juxtaposing a photograph she took of herself in 1974, aged twenty-seven, with another taken thirty-four or thirty-five years later. The results prompt the viewer to consider what it means to age, where social concepts of female beauty reside, and the relationship between the self and the body.

Bottom: Martha Wilson, *Growing Old*, 2008–09

Women are encouraged socially to dye their hair as they grow older—to "cover the gray" and to continue with a "natural, younger" look. Wilson was known for having dyed her hair a bright orange-pink and then, later, for having blocks of white in her asymmetric cut. In this series of photographs, Wilson charts the time it took to grow the color out of her cut, thus literally "growing old" during the process of the hair growing out, but also culturally being seen as older as her gray emerges.

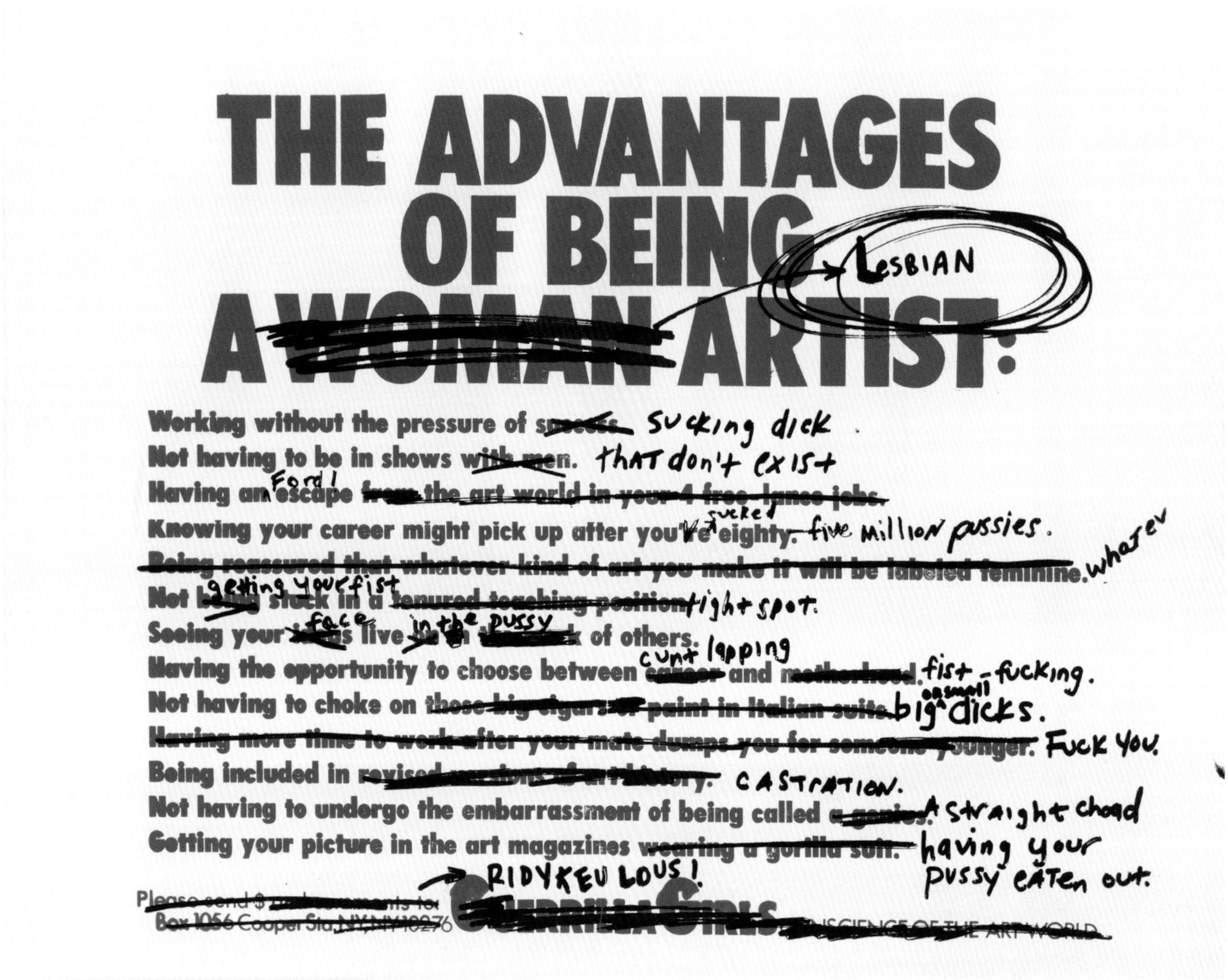

Above: **Ridykeulous, *The Advantages of Being a ~~Woman~~ Lesbian Artist*, 2006**

Ridykeulous is a collaborative queer and feminist curatorial partnership established in the United States in 2005 between painter Nicole Eisenman and multimedia artist A.L. Steiner, dedicated to producing exhibitions, events, and writing that uses humor and irony to critique the art world. In this image, they take the famous 1988 poster *The Advantages of Being A Woman Artist* by the Guerrilla Girls and edited it so that a queer feminist could identify with it. In the first line, for example, "Working without the pressure of success," the word "success" is crossed out, and "sucking dick" written in. The Guerrilla Girls did not respond to this edit; but they did later ask if they could feature it in one of their exhibitions, indicating their acceptance and embracing of the critique.

Below left: **Vaginal Davis**

Vaginal Davis is a performer, painter, writer, and filmmaker living in Germany. Born intersex in Los Angeles, she adopted a stage name that pays homage to Angela Davis, has self-identified as being a "sexual repulsive," and says she is too gay for the punk scene and too punk for the gay scene. In performance, she has been a practitioner of "terrorist drag": drag that does not try to alter the body or conform to gender stereotypes, but rather dresses for pleasure and show. She has performed regularly as Bricktop, the stage name of Ada Smith, a 1920s black bisexual performer in Paris. Davis does not aim to be Bricktop, but uses elements of dress that act as signs for a particular history, and through which modes of being and representation can be reinvented for a new generation. The approach has been hugely influential for queer, feminist, and black artists and performers.

Below right: **Del LaGrace Volcano, Self-portrait collaboration with Gérard Rancinan I, Paris, 2004**

Del LaGrace Volcano is a queer feminist intersex photographer. Raised as a girl, and living as a woman until aged thirty-seven, Volcano has since lived as gender variant who is both male and female, and uses the pronoun herm. Herm's early work explores lesbian life and masculine lesbian identities through self-portraiture, portraiture, and narratives. Herm holds that "disobedience, disruption, and defiance of gender norms and ALL norms are the cornerstone of queer cultural production."

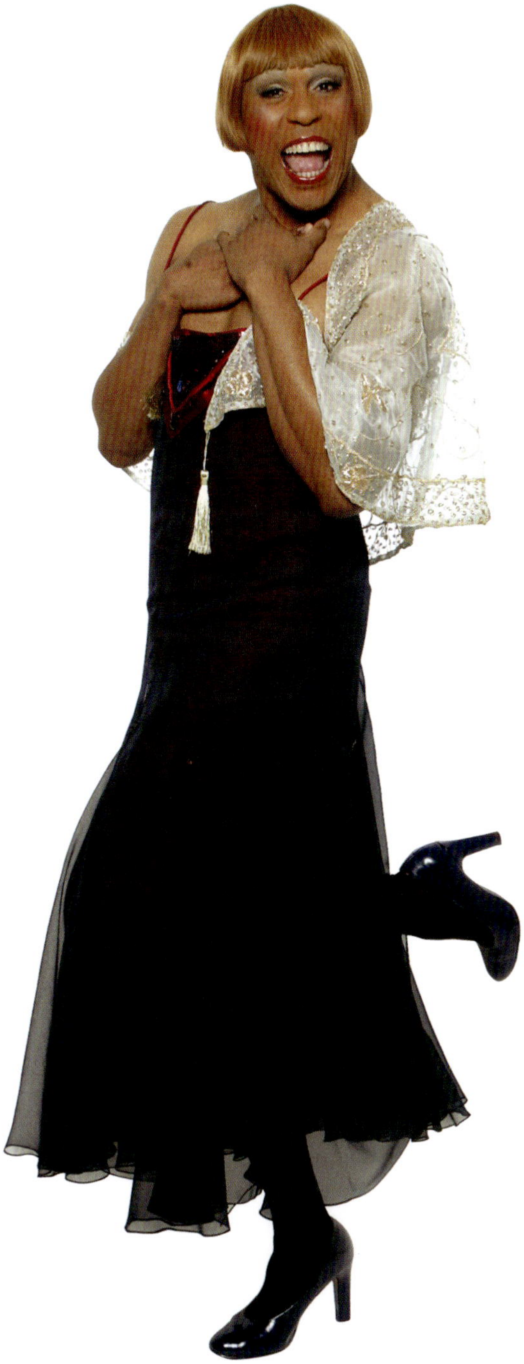

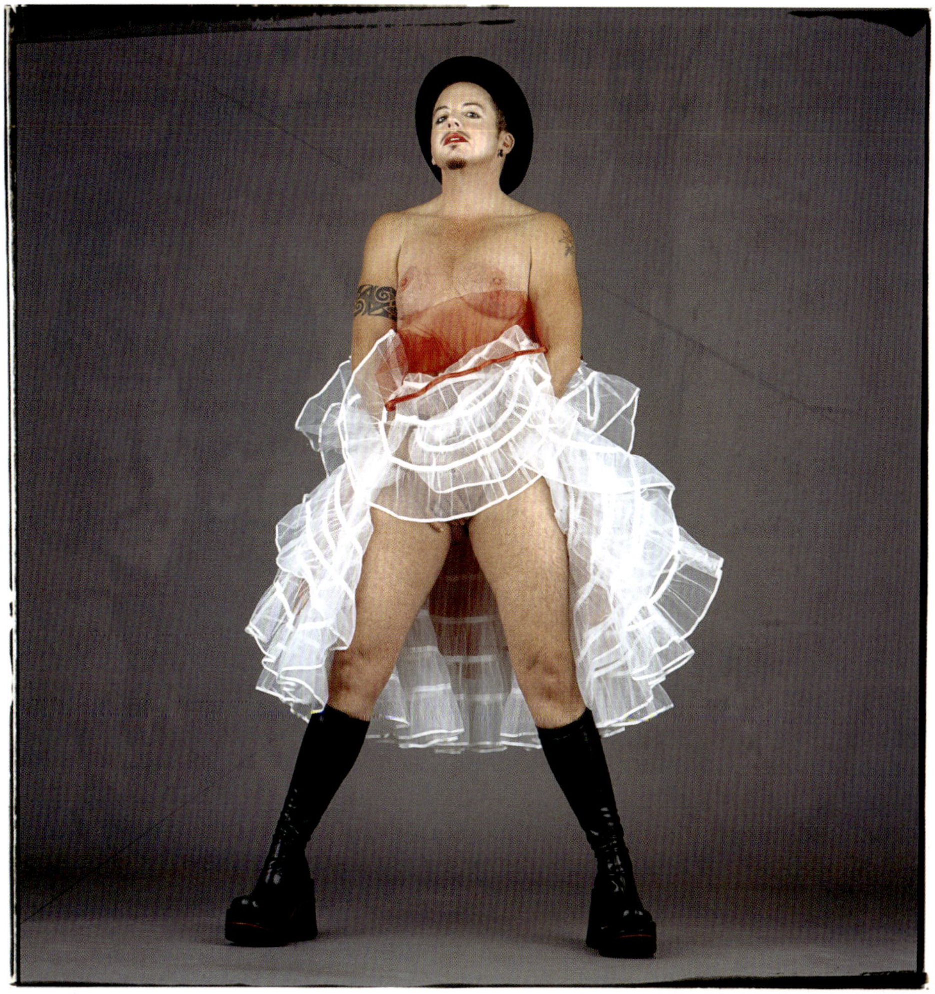

Mothering: Lenka Clayton

Mothering has been a key site of tension and struggle, as well as joy, in the relations between the sexes and in forming how we understand gender identities.

Mothering is not just the biological fact of reproduction, but the representation of what it means to be a particular gender: female. Women are often defined and judged by their relationship to mothering. In recent years British prime minister Theresa May has been subject to questions about her emotions and her "womanliness" as someone who has not had children.

Male and female artists have had a great part to play in this, and cannot always be assumed to take particular views. We can look from the saccharine sweetness of Elizabeth Vigée LeBrun's self-portraits with her daughter, to the romanticized images of Auguste Renoir, the empathy in Suzanne Valadon's painting *Puberty*, to the shocking, clinical brutality of Damian Hirst's *Mother and Child Divided*. There are many artists throughout the generations who have addressed mothering from a feminist viewpoint. They have analyzed the sexual politics of mothering, the emotional as well as physical labor, and the social expectations. They have also touched on the hyper-medicalization of the process with attendant commercialization through IVF, elective cesarean sections, the fraught politics and economics of surrogacy, and the nature of the economic exchanges and familial expectations that are involved in being a mother.

One such artist is Lenka Clayton, an English artist who has settled in the United States. She was invited to exhibit in the Carnegie Museum in Pittsburgh at the same time that she became pregnant for the first time; the exhibition was scheduled to open at the time that the baby would be a few weeks old. Clayton's work for the exhibition was *Maternity Leave* (2011). In this work, Clayton refused to differentiate between creation (which is usually seen as a cultural and social activity) and procreation (which is often understood as being "natural," even in countries where conception, pregnancy monitoring, and birthing increasingly engage with medical and other technologies). Museum visitors looking at *Maternity Leave* saw two physical elements placed in the gallery: a plinth in the center of the gallery with a Fisher Price baby monitor on it, and a framed document on the wall. The unseen, but audible part of the work, could be heard though the monitor. For three months, it transmitted a live audio broadcast of the domestic world of the tiny baby and his parents.

"In America where I live there is no government regulated maternity or paternity leave, and no public subsidy for new parents. For each week of the exhibition the Carnegie Museum paid me a maternity benefit, exactly equivalent to the 'Maternity Allowance' I am eligible for were I living in England where I am from."

Clayton, on the agreement between Clayton and the Carnegie Museum —the framed document that featured as part of her exhibition

Clayton described the work as "a private, durational performance that took place in our home" and the monitor in the Carnegie Museum as its means of broadcast. The framed document was her contract with the Carnegie, committing the museum to paying the artist a maternity benefit. The work raises issues of the relationship between the personal and the public, the state and individual citizens and families, public institutions and artists, audiences and artists, being an artist and being a parent, as well as, of course, of the relationship between mother and son.

The questions are raised in Clayton's subsequent series of works: 63 Objects Taken from my Son's Mouth (2011–12) is exactly that—items from cigarette butts and random scraps of plastic to stones and buttons are laid out in a grid formation, giving a minimalist sculptural presence. Documented also in list form, the level of constant need for alertness in the work of a caring relationship is evoked. In 2013, with the baby now a two-year-old toddler, Clayton made three video works called *The Distance I Can Be From My Son*, each work supplemented with an indication of a particular environment: park, alley, and supermarket. In each case, we see the little boy testing his legs and his boundaries by running away from his mother; then at a particular point, she has to run after him.

Following her Carnegie Museum exhibition, Clayton established the "Artists' Residency in Motherhood" in 2012, initially as a framework for her own professional life as a mother of first one, then two small children; and from 2016 as an open residency for artists who are mothers to self-direct in their own homes. The manifesto encourages mothers to allow parenting to shape their work, "rather than try to work 'despite' it," and the project includes a mentoring program. Today, nearly four hundred artists who are mothers from around the world have registered on the website ArtistResidencyInMotherhood.com.

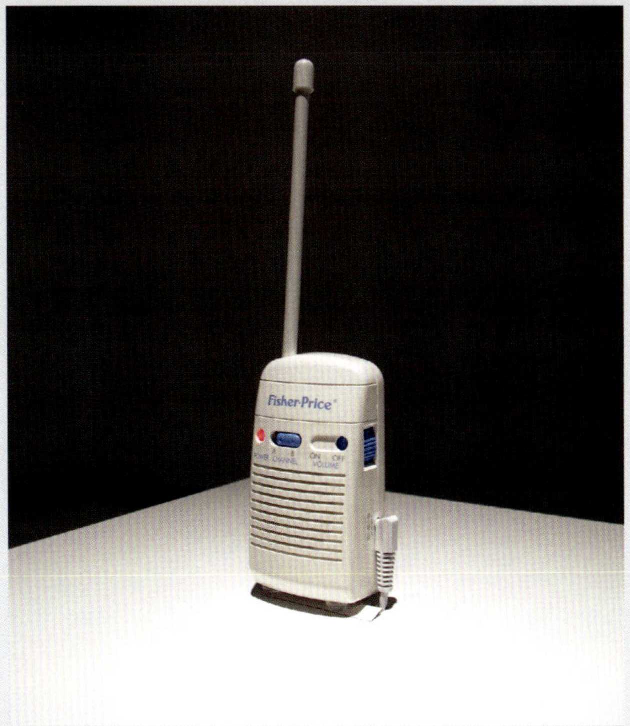

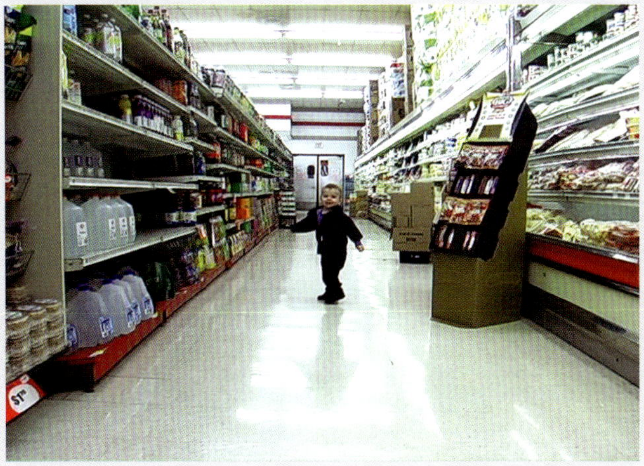

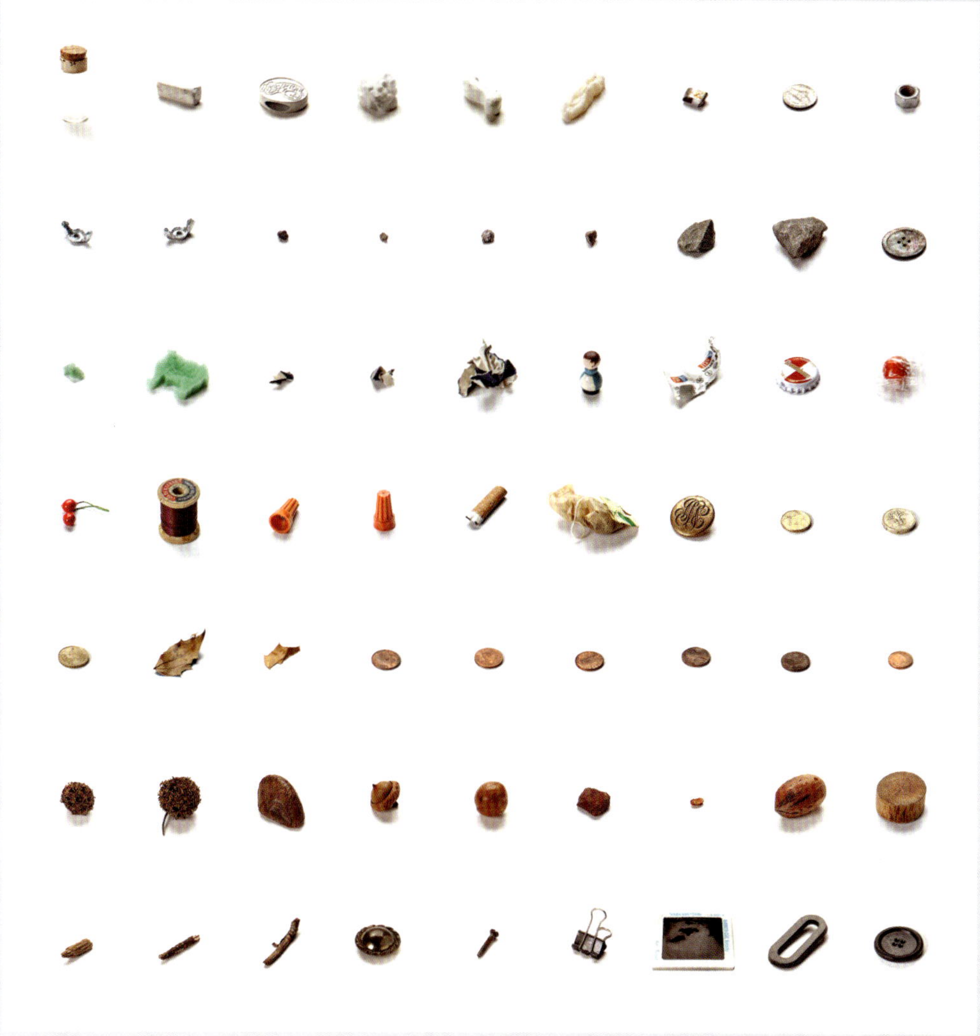

Top left: **Lenka Clayton, *Maternity Leave,* 2011**

In *Maternity Leave*, Clayton claimed from the museum as her artist's fee the benefits she would be due as a mother in her homeland, the United Kingdom. She placed in the gallery a baby monitor that listened into her home constantly during the exhibition—the means through which visitors could appreciate the emotional and physical labor of mothering that usually goes unacknowledged. Maternity leave is demonstrated to be not "leave" as in "vacation," but a period taken off work to undertake other labor.

Bottom left: **Lenka Clayton, *The Distance I Can Be From My Son (Supermarket)*, 2013, still**

This still is taken from one of three short videos in which both Clayton and her two-year-old son appear to be testing their interdependence. We see the little boy walk and run away from the static camera, sometimes stopping to look back, or to examine something he finds. Eventually the artist/mother runs after him from behind the camera. The distances vary, but the tipping point appears to be connected to the artist/mother's ability to have visual surveillance of what the son is exploring.

Above right: **Lenka Clayton, *63 Objects Taken from my Son's Mouth*, 2011–12**

In the introduction to the 2014 book version of this, Clayton describes arriving after an overnight flight with her fifteen-month-old son in Paris. He starts exploring the floor and puts something in his mouth; the artist/mother retrieves it and, horrified, finds it is a sachet of rat poison. She flushes it down the toilet; hence it becomes the only item that she removes from his mouth between eleven and eighteen months old that is represented by words rather than a photograph in the book and that is also absent from the sculpture.

Below: **Elżbieta Jablońska, *Supermother*, 2002**

Since the birth of her son, Polish artist Elżbieta Jablońska has incorporated aspects of mothering, caring, and Polish cultural and social expectations of women into her work. She regards the moment of becoming a mother as the culturally regarded major life-changer, where things that happened before are regarded as trivial. Following the physical and emotional drama of giving birth, a woman's life is deemed to have started. Jablońska's work includes explorations of the tension between mothering, helping, and serving. Her 2002 project *Supermother* was a multiformat exhibition with events for children, installations, and diagrams that expose the functions of the mother. In a series of photographs that were also presented as billboards throughout Warsaw, she dressed in the costume of various American male superheroes: Batman, Superman, and Spider-Man. Sitting with her son on her lap, she drew upon the *polska matka* (the mythical archetype Polish mother), as well as Catholic iconography of the Virgin Mary.

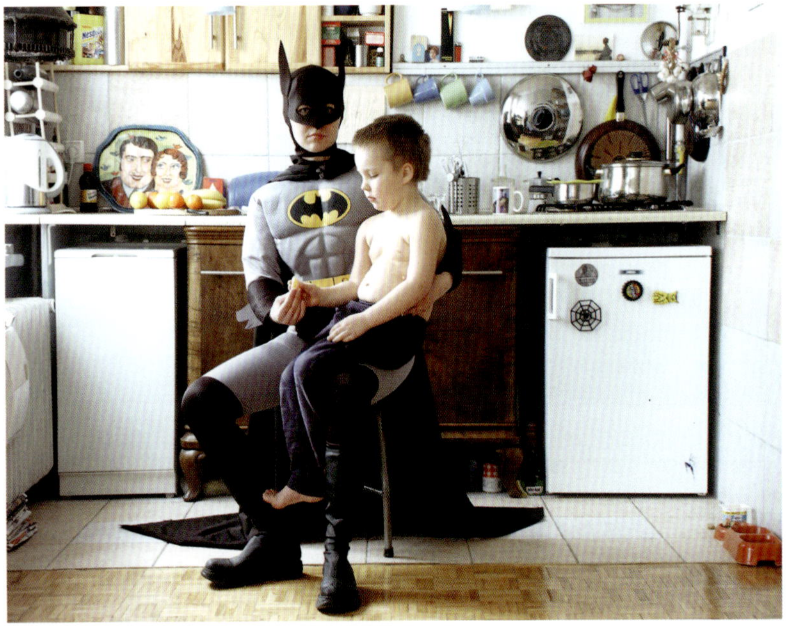

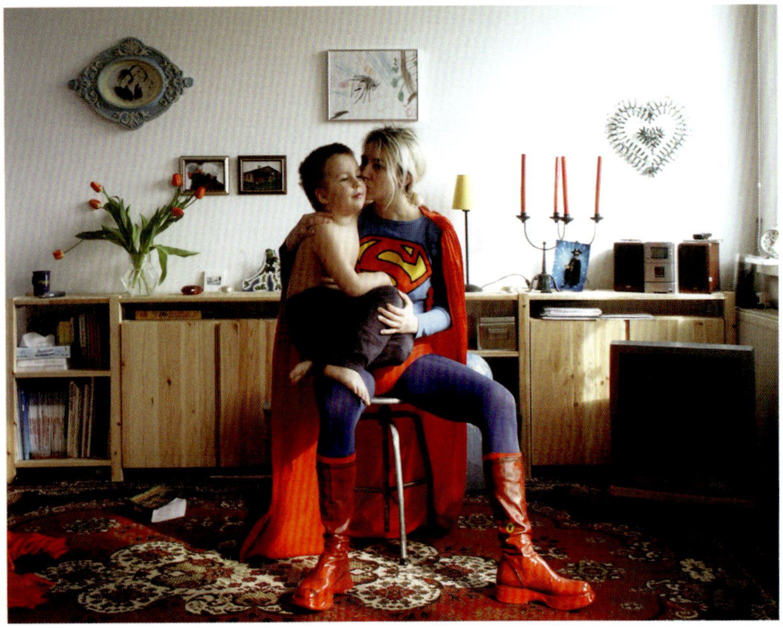

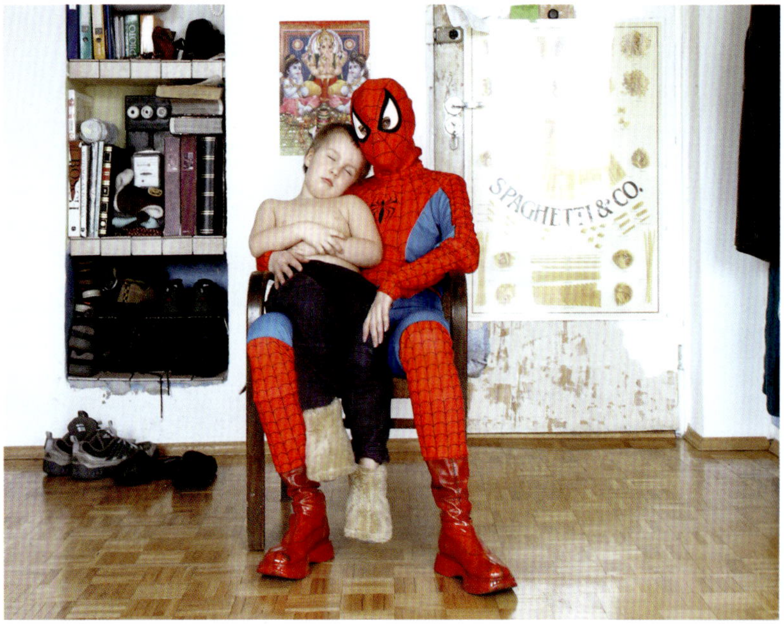

Top: Marni Kotak, *The Birth of Baby X*, 2011, performance/installation

Marni Kotak's month-long exhibition *The Birth of Baby X* was at Microscope Gallery, Brooklyn; during it, she gave birth to her son as a live performance on October 25, 2011. Kotak's work turns her everyday life into art, echoing the happening and durational performance artists of the 1960s–1970s, such as Allan Kaprow's attention to the aesthetics of the everyday, or Tehching Hsieh's year-long physical challenges. Thus, this exhibition was a logical extension of Kotak's practice. Working with a midwife and a doula, she built a serene room in the gallery, equipped with kitchen, her grandmother's bed, and a birthing bath. About twenty people were invited to witness the birth itself, which was completely natural. Kotak points out that in the United States 30–40 percent of births are by cesarean section, while assisted home births are illegal in several states, making a natural birth increasingly rare. The witnesses spoke of the joy of the event and the calmness of the baby himself.

Bottom: Catherine Opie, *Self-Portrait/ Nursing*, 2004

Self-Portrait/Nursing shows the artist naked from the waist up, striking the pose of a Bellini madonna as she looks down at her son while he feeds from her. On her chest, she bears the scars from an earlier work entitled *Self-Portrait/Pervert* (1994). In that piece, Opie was frontally and formally posed as a Holbein portrait, also naked from the waist up, hands loosely clasped in her lap, with pins neatly piercing her arms, a black bondage hood, and the word "pervert" scratched into the skin of her chest in decorative, archaic script. It was a defiant moment in the so-called "Culture Wars" of the United States, where bi, gay, and lesbian artists in particular were censored and even prosecuted —for example, the prosecution of Cincinnati Contemporary Arts Center for exhibiting Robert Mapplethorpe's work. The fact that the scars remain visible in Opie's *Self-Portrait/Nursing* ten years later carries Opie's history into the image and queers the concept of the mothering body.

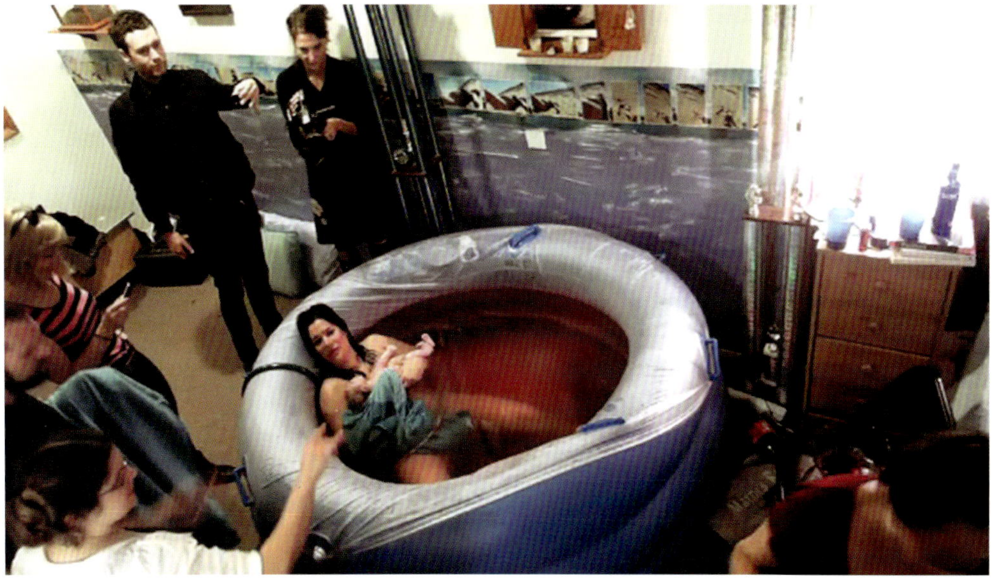

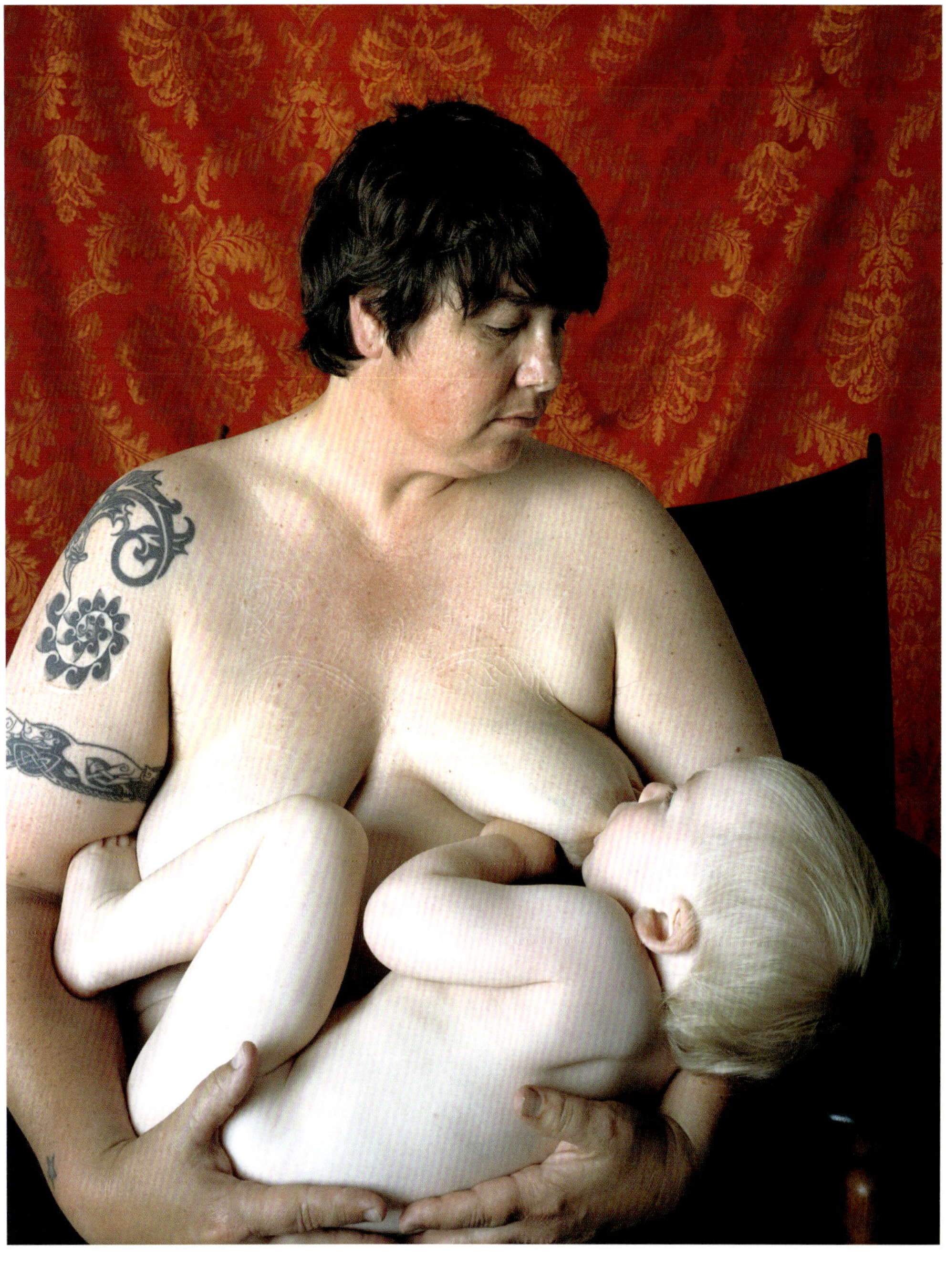

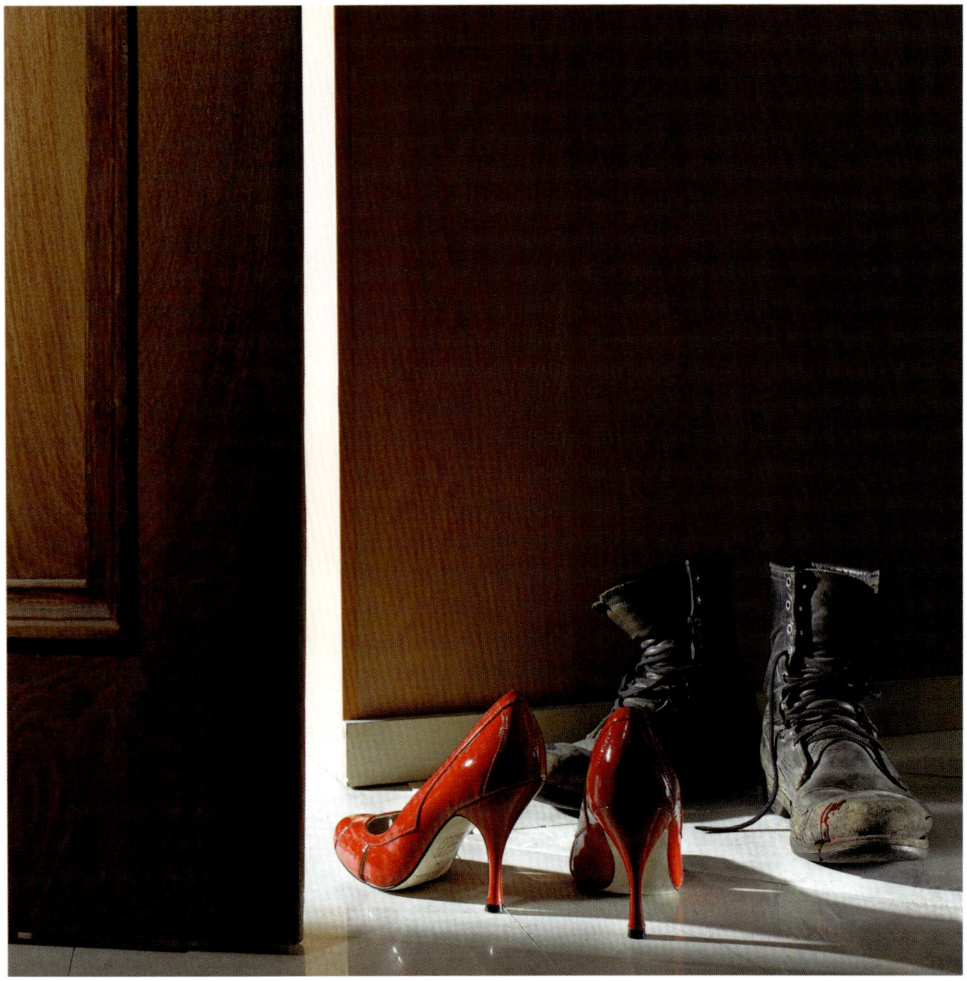

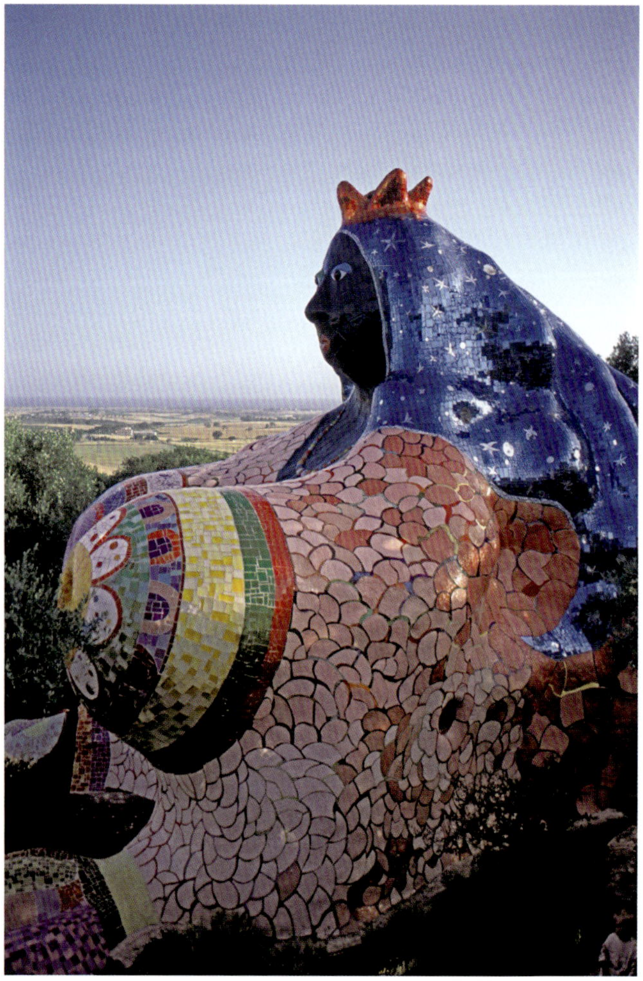

Above left: **Shadi Ghadirian, Nil Nil series, 2008**

Shadi Ghadirian is an Iranian artist who works in series of photographs. From ages four to twelve, she lived through the Islamic Revolution and the overthrow of the Shah; her work provides analysis of women's domestic lives in Tehran since then. The series Like Every Day (2001–02) shows women draped with colorful, patterned fabrics like a chador, and where we should see their faces there are instead domestic objects—a meat cleaver, an iron, a teapot, and so on. These were made in response to the wedding presents she was given. Nil Nil (2008) visualizes the presence of a soldier in the house: a hand grenade nestled among apples and oranges in a fruit bowl; an army identification dog tag among necklaces in a jewelry box; a gas mask in a bag of children's toys. In one image, two pairs of shoes are next to an open door: one pair of red high-heeled pumps, and a pair of army boots, splashed with blood.

Above right: **Niki de Saint Phalle, *The Empress***

Following years of dreaming and planning, work on Niki de Saint Phalle's *Giardino dei Tarocchi* (*Tarot Garden*) in Tuscany, Italy, began in 1978; it opened to the public in 1998 and development of it ended in accordance with her wishes upon her death in 2002. The tarot arcana elements in *Giardino dei Tarocchi* built upon Saint Phalle's sculptural works. Her massive 1966 work *Hon–En Kotedrol* (*She–A Cathedral*) was a female figure made from a metal armature and card, painted in bright colors, that people could walk into. They entered through her vagina; there was a milk bar in one breast. Saint Phalle subsequently made many sculptures she called *Nanas*—large, colorful, joyous female figures. The sphinx-like empress in the *Giardino dei Tarocchi* went further: Saint Phalle designed her as her home. One breast is a kitchen; the other a bedroom; her mirror-mosaic belly is a living space; the shower is a serpent; and her back supports a terraced garden.

Below: **Melanie Bonajo, Night Soil, 2015**

Night Soil is a series of three half-hour documentaries by Dutch artist Melanie Bonajo. Each looks at different movements that attempt to counter patriarchal and capitalist systems by setting up profoundly different ways of working. *Fake Paradise* looks at women in the communities that use ayahuasca, a psychedelic Amazonian plant; *Nocturnal Gardening* focuses on communities creating farming methods that are off-grid, ethical toward animals, address racism in the food system, or engaging with indigenous land rights. *Economy of Love* focuses on a women's activist sex-work group in Brooklyn, that aims to educate women and men about the power of the female orgasm, to shift the ways in which sex work is structured and understood, and to raise awareness of the language that it uses. The women develop an interdependent feminist unit, based on radical practices of respect, and where the bodily and the spiritual are treated as one.

Bottom: **Dayanita Singh, from *Myself, Mona Ahmed*, 2001**

Mona Ahmed was one of India's third-sex community, estimated at anything between one million and two million strong, of intersex and castrated people. In 1989 photographer Dayanita Singh met her to take some photographs, and a friendship began that only came to an end with Mona's death in 2017. Singh works mainly in series and book format: Her book, *Myself, Mona Ahmed* (2001), tells Mona Ahmed's story in visual form. Rejected by her birth family, she changed her name —Mona being a female name, Ahmed being male—and spent the rest of her life attempting to build family, build community, and build homes. Her home for the last decades of her life was one she built herself among the graves of her ancestors. Singh's photographs are intimate, loving, and show us Mona Ahmed's desire for family building, along with the passages in her life where she is successful at that and her grieving when it is denied her.

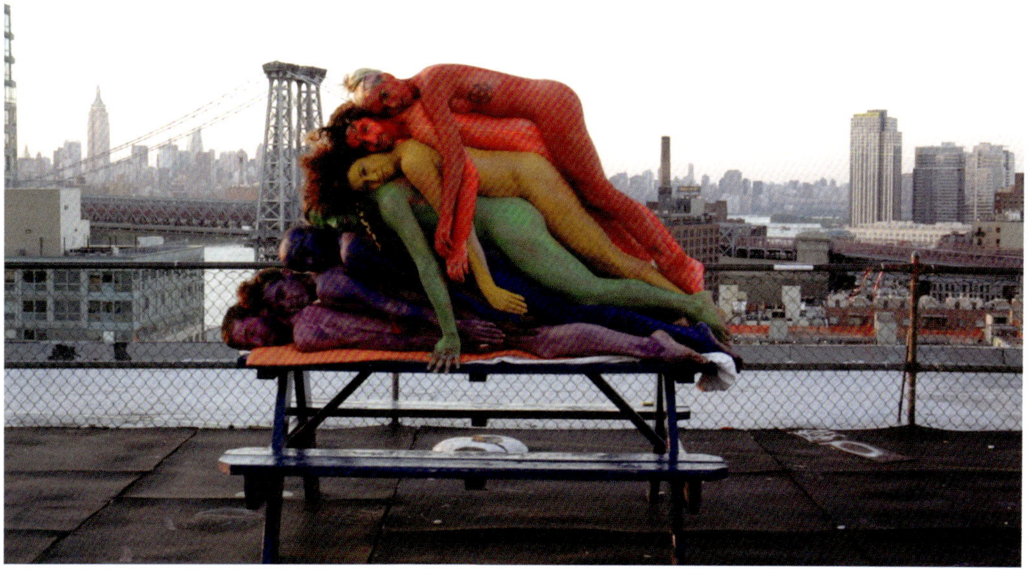

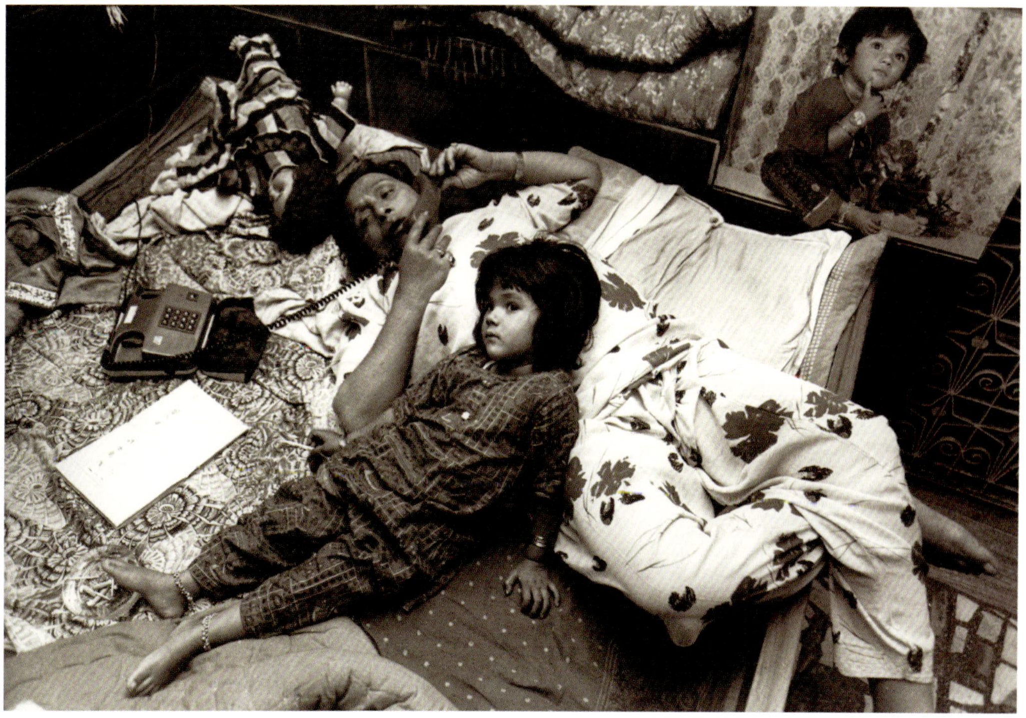

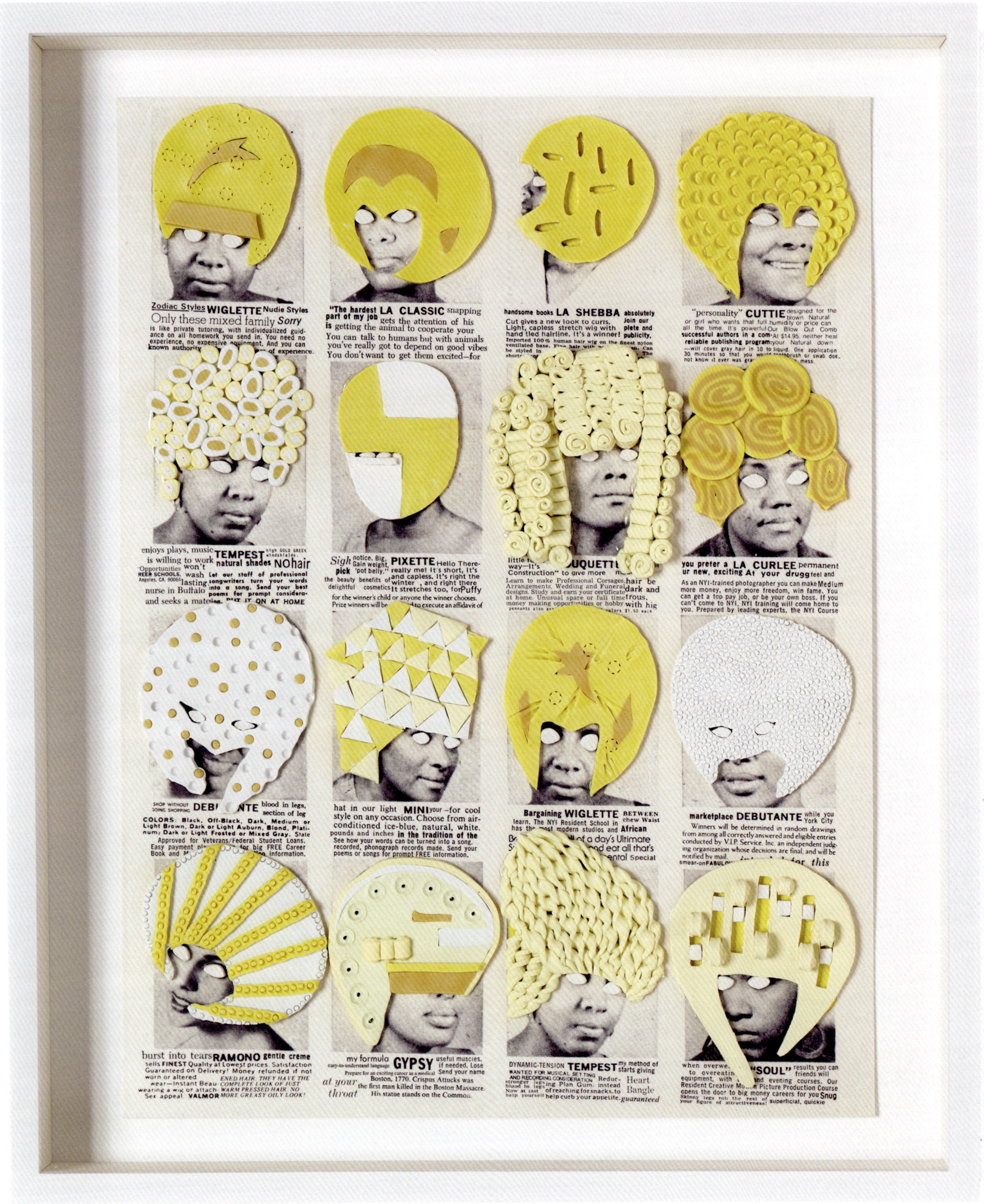
WIGLETTE
LA CLASSIC
LA SHEBBA
CUTTIE
TEMPEST
PIXETTE
LA CURLEE
MINI
WIGLETTE
DEBUTANTE
RAMONO
GYPSY
TEMPEST
"SOUL"

11

The Citizen Feminist

Citizenship and Politics

"Political art is the one that is made when it is unfashionable and when it is uncomfortable, legally uncomfortable, civically uncomfortable, humanely uncomfortable. It affects us. Political art is uncomfortable knowledge."

Tania Bruguera, from "Political Art Statement," 2010

Feminist artists respond to changes in world politics and the events that shape all our lives. The events of 1989—the year that saw the fall of the Berlin Wall and the biggest shift in global politics since the start of the Cold War in the late 1940s—also instigated a time of reconsideration for feminism and global feminist analysis. In much of the former Eastern bloc (the countries that were aligned with the Soviet Union), feminist art and writing from Western Europe had not been encountered. Additionally, any feminist art and analysis that happened in the former Eastern bloc occurred within a very different framework than that of the West, and also did not travel in any meaningful way into Western Europe.

The first major exploration of sexual politics in the art of the twenty-seven European Eastern bloc countries before and after 1989 was an exhibition entitled *Gender Check: Masculinity and Femininity in the Art of Eastern Europe*, which was shown in Vienna and in Warsaw from 2009 to 2010. The exhibition explored art from the postwar period up to 2009. It showed clearly that many of the issues that feminist and LGBT artists in Western Europe had addressed were also under scrutiny in the former Eastern bloc: body, sexuality, desire, economics, religion, home, work, and so forth. So, too, were many of the aesthetic and material modes, including figuration, conceptualism, performance, and photography. It was, however, within a very different set of political and cultural references: Soviet Socialist realism had long promoted images in art that showed "strong" women, women workers, and women who were politically active. The stereotype was of the woman tractor driver, as much as it was of the idealized maternalism of "Mother Russia"; and in the secular Soviet period, the image of the Madonna was much less prevalent than it was in the predominantly Christian West. Three works by former Eastern bloc artists in this chapter explicitly address the changing circumstances for women as the East opened up: the racism directed at the first woman to give birth to quintuplets in the Czech Republic, who was Roma; the racism directed at Bosnian women by a Dutch member of the UN peacekeeping army; and the brutal effect of war upon all women in the search for national identity.

The tensions between national, racial, and gendered identities have long been present as a subject for feminist artists. In 1989, and of great importance for feminism, African-American legal scholar Kimberlé Crenshaw named these struggles between different kinds of identities as "intersectionality." Through studying legal casework in the United States she had realized that it was possible for someone to sue for discrimination as a black person, or as a woman, but it was not possible to sue for discrimination as a black woman—even though black women were subject to experiences (in salaries and work conditions, for example) that black men, white men, and white women were not.

Intersectionality was a term that emerged from the rarefied pages of the academic journal in which Crenshaw published, and became a watchword for progressive feminist politics. Intersectionality challenged the assumption that either predominant school of feminist thought—the white, middle-class Second Wave of American feminism, or the mainly white, socialist-influenced school of British feminism—spoke for all women alike. For feminist artists working to make cultural and political change, how identity is represented has always been crucial. Once intersectionality had been identified and defined, artists continued to explore how their national identities, their racial identities, and their gendered identities intersected: what it was to be a citizen of a time and place, inhabiting the body they inhabited. What had shifted was that this could now be named and therefore explored more clearly.

Citizenship is perhaps the most taken for granted of identities, yet at the same time we can probably all recognize that national identity is subjected to oversimplification and stereotyping. The representation of what it is to be a citizen in countries where cultural and

Page 218: **Detail from Ellen Gallagher, *DeLuxe*, 2004–2005, see opposite.**

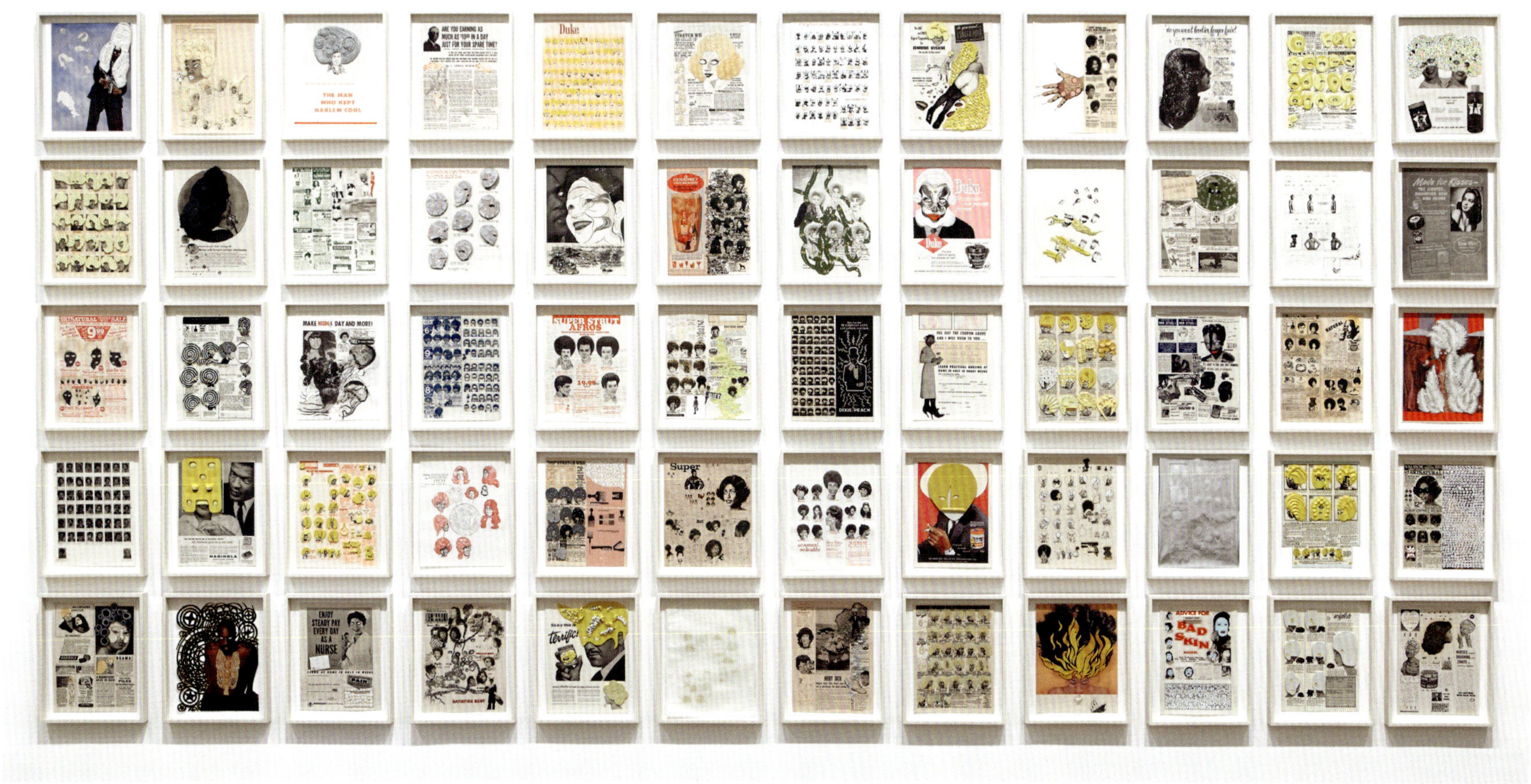

Above: **Ellen Gallagher, *DeLuxe*, 2004–2005**

Ellen Gallagher's *DeLuxe* addresses the complex identities of African Americans as they have been represented in popular culture. A grid of sixty pages that is a tour de force of printing technology, which includes photogravure, spit bite, and silk screen, *DeLuxe* is further augmented with paint, plasticine, toy eyeballs, and coconut oil. The transformed pages that comprise *DeLuxe* have been unpicked from the spines of mid-century "race magazines." For Gallagher, the specificity of the ad copy is important: that these were individual young women (mainly) who were advertising products aimed at making African Americans aspire to notions of beauty that are delineated by industrial capitalism. *DeLuxe* revels in that absurdity as it presents an afro-aerial view, oscillating between optimism and pessimism.

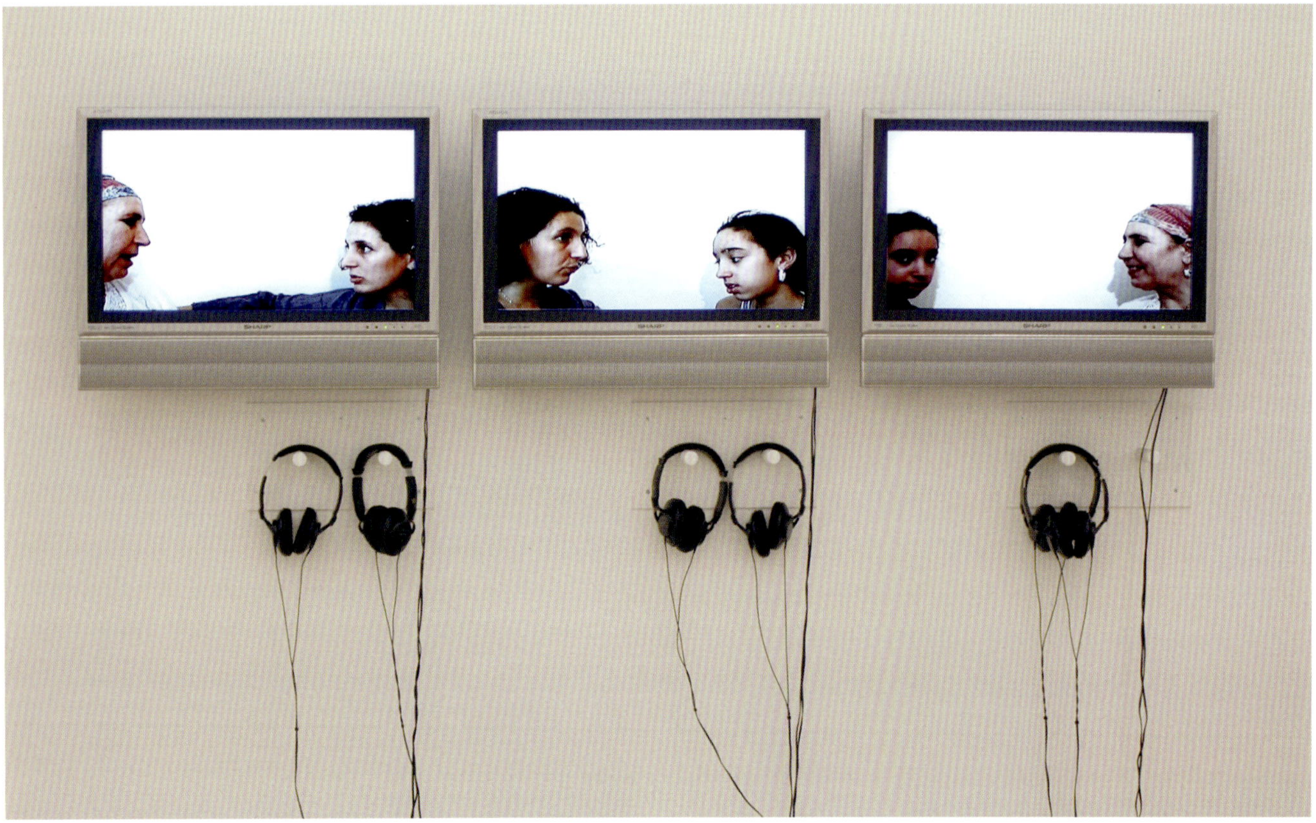

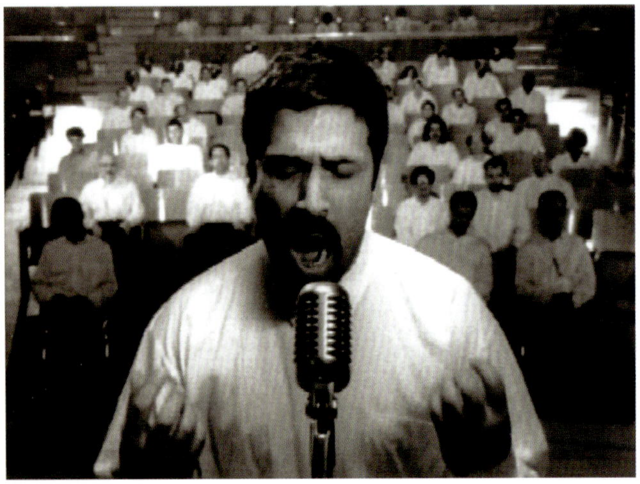

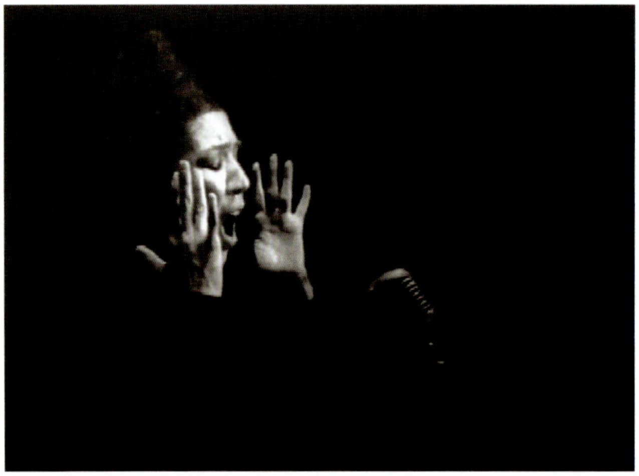

Top: Zineb Sedira, *Mother Tongue*, 2002

Zineb Sedira considers herself to be Algerian, French, and British. Her parents, born and raised in Algeria, left after the brutal War of Independence (1954–62) and Sedira was born in Paris, France. She moved to London in the 1980s, where her daughter was born. In the first section of her video *Mother Tongue* (2002), we see Sedira asking her mother a series of questions in French about her childhood; her mother answers in Arabic, but both women understand each other fluently. In the second video, Sedira is asked the same questions by her daughter in English, and answers in French—again, with fluent understanding. In the final video, the granddaughter asks her grandmother the questions in English, and there is incomprehension, silence, embarrassment; the grandmother ventures some comments in Arabic, and is likewise met with incomprehension. The longing for communication is suffused with loneliness and the realization of loss of history and culture.

Bottom left & right: **Shirin Neshat, *Turbulent*, 1998, stills**

Shirin Neshat is an Iranian artist who moved to the United States to study. Her art practice found its focus after she returned to Iran in 1990 and was shocked at its change from a relatively secular (women could wear what they wished) and modernizing society to one that was increasingly hard-line Islamic (with girls and women legally required to wear the veil from the age of nine). *Turbulent* is an installation of two screens facing each other. On one, a man stands on a stage; behind him are rows of men in the audience. On the other is a woman with rows of empty seats behind her. The man sings a beautiful old love song by the mystic Farsi poet Jalal al-Din Rumi; his audience applauds. He turns to leave, but stops as the woman begins to make noises. Forbidden to sing in public, her "song" is wordless, tuneless: moans, deep breaths, cries, and ecstatic noises. The camera's movement circles the woman. The men are silenced, awestruck.

political focus is on the good of the state and the community is very different from that of countries in which the political benefit is focused on individuals. The work of Tania Bruguera, a Cuban artist who lives in New York as well as Havana, often pinpoints places of antagonism between individual political wishes and those of a communist state, as well as exploring the identity and lives of migrants in hostile host countries. Another example of feminist art exploring the nature of citizenship and identity is Keep It Complex—a collective, feminist, intersectional "remain" project centered on the Brexit referendum of 2016 in the United Kingdom. The aim of the project is to allow citizens to enact their full democratic rights of voting with as much information as they need, through the medium of art.

A wide variety of artists in our highly complex and boundaried world explore the legacy of national identity, its cultural heritage, and political complexities. Sigalit Landau, for example, uses a shocking but simple visual metaphor for the experience of Jewish life in Israel, playing on the concept that those who build barriers against others simply fence themselves in. Some of these artists occupy an intersectional position in their work. Jeannette Ehlers, as a black Danish-Trinidadian woman who lives in Denmark, explores the legacy of Danish colonial history and confronts her audiences with it. Fiona Foley, who is of Australian Aboriginal heritage, and Tracey Rose, from South Africa, similarly attempt to unpack very complex and very specific histories and present-day realities in their work. Few artists have done this to greater impact than Vanessa German, whose sculptural and spoken-word art speaks of a legacy of historical, racialized disempowerment, and of her constant love for her community.

The second global historical event in recent decades to profoundly shape thinking about national identity was 9/11—the terrorist attack on New York's World Trade Center. The events of that day, demonstrating the willingness of Islamic extremists to use unconventional weapons (including suicide), not only resulted from a long history of bungled international relationships, but also set in motion further wars and conflicts, and indeed the Arab Spring of 2011, with its uprisings and related ongoing conflicts.

In the West, following 9/11, increased racism toward Muslim citizens and noncitizens alike, and foreign policies that focused aggression upon Muslim-majority countries, went hand in hand with the art world's increased interest in artists from those same countries—many of whom were transnational. Shirin Neshat is one of the best known of these artists; she says that now she can no longer speak for her birth country of Iran, but at the same time, does not feel she can speak for America, as she is not of that country and needs also to critique her new home. French/Algerian artist Zineb Sedira makes work that speaks poignantly about loss of cultural identity through three female generations: her mother, herself, and her daughter.

Another such event of the early twenty-first century was the financial crisis of 2008–09 and the politics of austerity that most Western countries embraced subsequently. The Occupy Wall Street movement started as a demonstration of resistance to austerity in New York in 2011 and spread as Occupy movements in other countries. One of the attractions of Occupy was the involvement of artists and writers on art and visual culture from the start, which meant that there was a strong awareness of how the movement would represent itself in the media. There were also attempts to build participatory and inclusive modes of demonstrating. While many women and people of color reported instances of abuse during the Wall Street encampment, the attempts to make demonstrations look and feel more inclusive were well grounded: Occupy (in its various incarnations) provided an important testing ground for new and evolving strategies of organized resistance and demonstration, including attempts to ensure that usually marginalized voices were heard and abusive behavior in the movement was confronted. Some of the strategies developed traveled around the world, and others that had been forged elsewhere arrived on Wall Street. The terminology used in the Occupy movement, such as talking about "the 1 percent" and "the 99 percent," even entered mainstream media usage.

In very different ways, several artists show how Occupy entered the consciousness of the art world. American illustrator Molly Crabapple documented the events on Wall Street, and also painted in an entertaining manner her imaginings of how and why Occupy was happening. Fellow American Andrea Fraser also attempted to draw her audience into the economics and politics of the movement, through refusing to make art, and instead writing analysis of how the financial crash actually helped bolster the high-end art market as people invested more in artworks, while making the lives of most artists increasingly precarious. Her willingness, as a "blue-chip" gallery artist, to confront and expose her own complicity and entanglement with art-world privilege accounts, in large part, for the power of her work. In the United Kingdom, Rachael House convened celebratory events to "smash" patriarchy, the monarchy, and heteronormativity. In embracing the joy of collective action, House also shows the power of intersectional feminist thinking and the legacy of decades of feminist, queer, and radical activism, reaching back to Greenham Common and forward to Occupy.

What we see in this chapter is how artists from South Africa to Afghanistan, America to India, Australia to Northern Ireland, respond to the political structures, identities, and events that shape and impact upon their lives. Extraordinarily diverse in the ways they produce their work, as they are in their nationalities, faiths, cultures, and classes, nonetheless for each of them their gendered identity informs how they are positioned in those political contexts, and how and why they make their art.

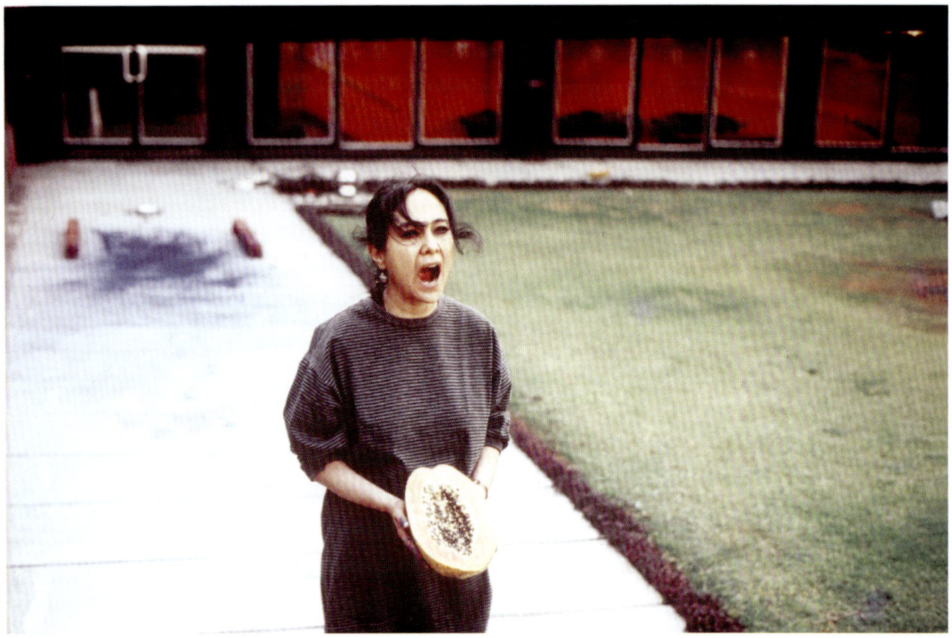

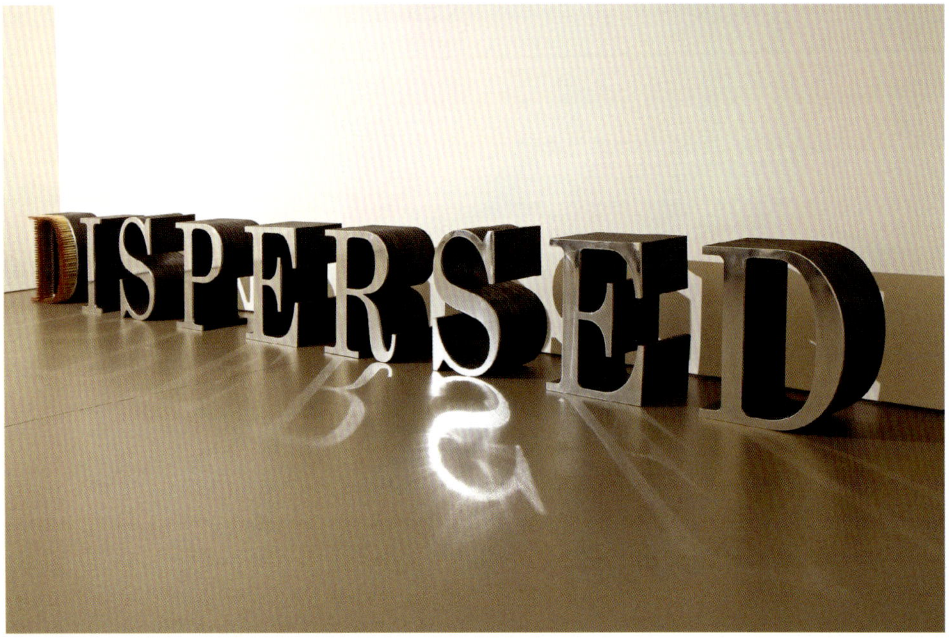

Top: Rummana Hussain, *Living on the Margins*, 1995, still

In 1992, the Babri Masjid in Bombay was destroyed by Hindu fundamentalists, causing riots and the deaths of over two thousand people. It left Muslim Indians feeling attacked and vulnerable. Prior to this Rummana Hussain, who was Muslim, had made paintings addressing social issues in an allegorical form. After this time, she began to use performance, conceptual, and installation methods to understand and explore anew her cultural and political identity. *Living on the Margins* was one of the first contemporary art performances in India. Hussain invited a small handful of women to witness the work, which took place in the courtyard of the National Centre for Performing Arts, Mumbai. She walked slowly around it, holding half of a large papaya in front of her belly, its central seed cavity evoking genitals, and her mouth open in a silent scream as she walked for thirty minutes until exhausted. She placed the papaya with small candles and invited the audience to scatter blue powdered laundry bleach.

Bottom: Fiona Foley, *Dispersed*, 2008

Fiona Foley is a mixed-media indigenous Australian artist of the Badtjala people, Fraser Island, Queensland, who has a commitment to supporting indigenous Australian cultural practices both traditional and contemporary—particularly those that are remote from the mainstream arts environment of (white) Australia. She was a founding member of the Boomali Aboriginal Artist Co-operative, Sydney, to help support the independence of indigenous culture. She regards herself more as an educator than a political artist. Her artwork lays out facts—the actual cheap items, for example, that were given to the Wurundjeri people in exchange for the land where Melbourne now stands, or using very direct and legible ways of conveying her message. The sculpture *Dispersed* refers to the euphemism used for the mass killing of indigenous people in the nineteenth century by the police in order to remove them from land that was desired by the white colonists. The letters are made of charred wood and metal; the initial letter D is filled with casings of .303-caliber bullets.

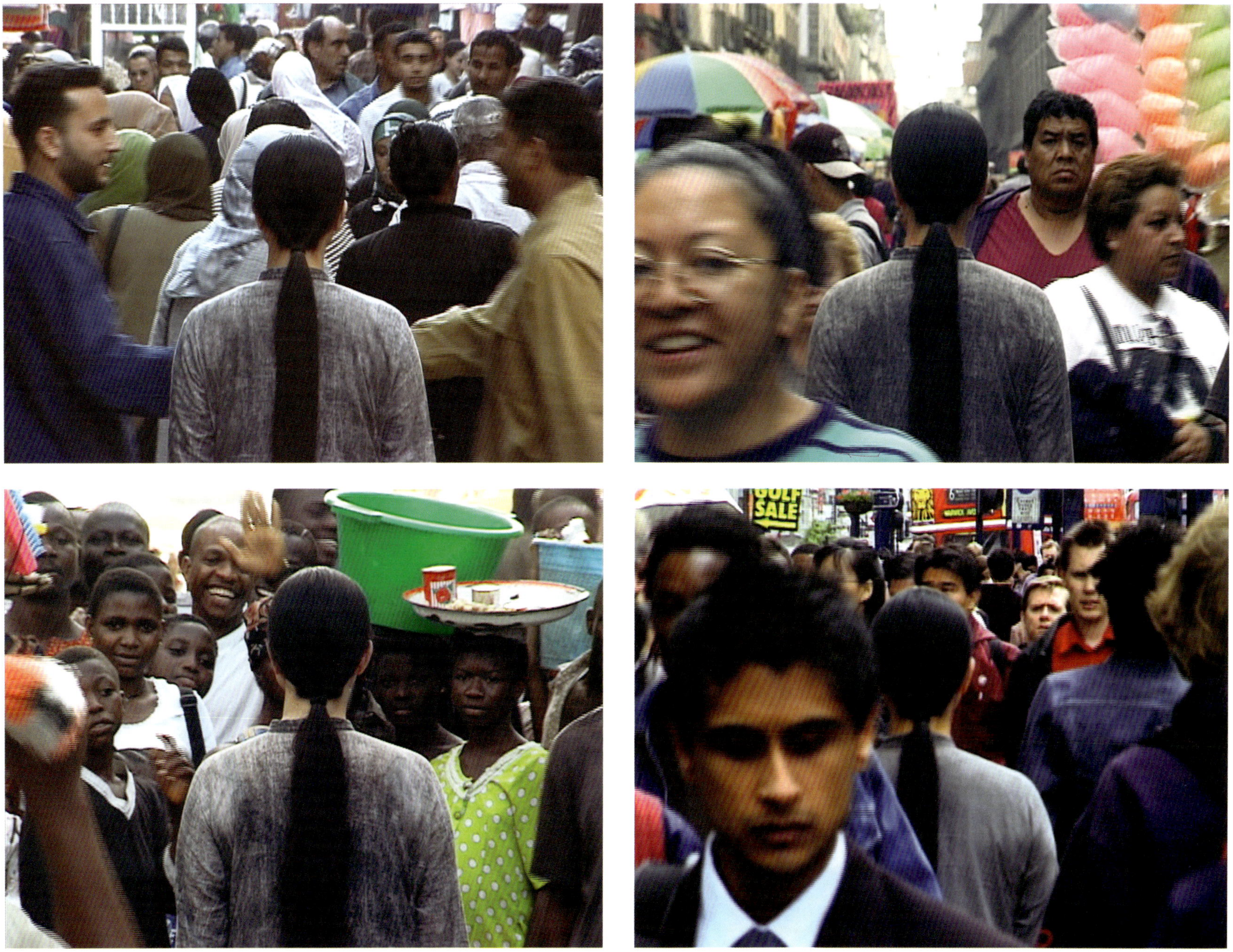

This page: **Kimsooja, A Needle Woman, 1999–2001, stills from Cairo (top left), Mexico City (top right), Lagos (bottom left), and London (bottom right)**

Artist Kim Soo-Ja changed her name when she needed to pick a name for a domain site in 2000. In what she designated as an artwork, *A One-Word Name Is An Anarchist's Name*, she became Kimsooja, a name that would not indicate her marital status, gender, or cultural identity. A Needle Woman is a series of performance videos showing Kimsooja from behind, seen centrally in the image, wearing the same clothes, and hair tied the same way. She appears at the same scale in different crowded urban environments, projected in such a way that the viewer feels complicit with the crowd. Her later videos were performed in response to the histories of violence and unresolved conflict within cities that included Patan, Jerusalem, Havana, and Sana'a, among others. Kimsooja stands still and appears to be a constant in the seven-minute videos, linking the cities together, as a needle can be used to join cloth, or stitch wounds in order to allow healing.

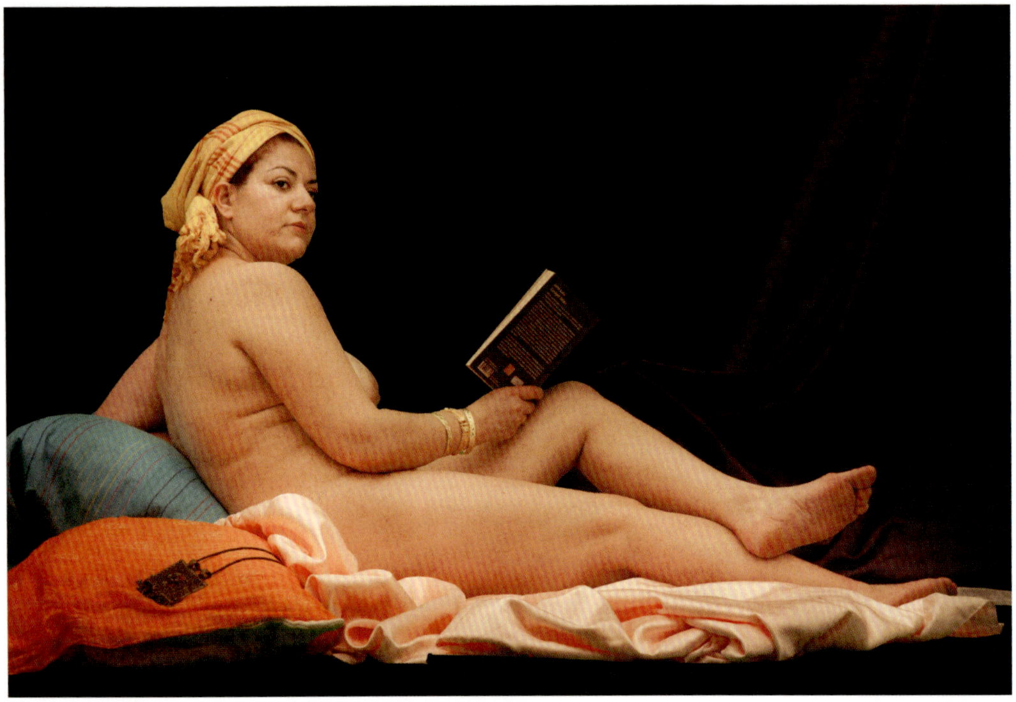

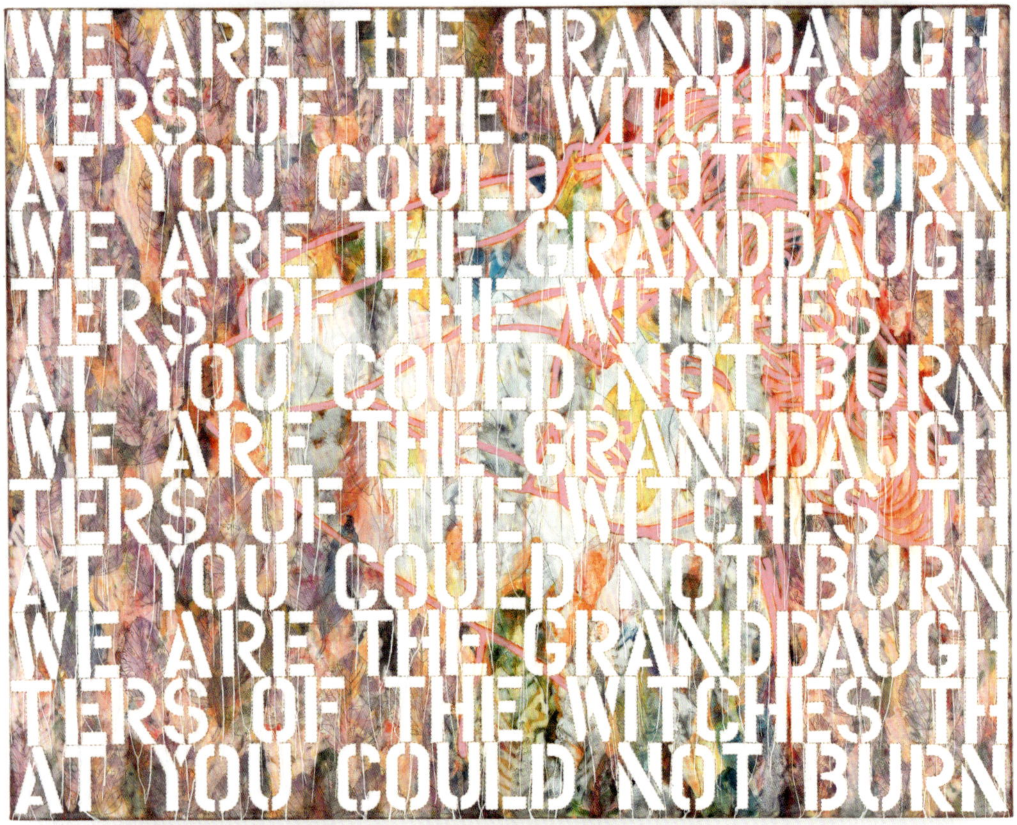

Top: **CANAN, *Turkish Delight Series I*, 2011**

CANAN was born Canan Sahin; her name changed upon marriage to Canan Senol. Turkish law states that upon divorce, women can only keep their married names with permission from their ex-husbands. As she was known as Canan Senol professionally, she did not want to revert to Sahin, so instead announced she would be known as CANAN. In Turkish, her name is the feminine version of "spirit." When Turkey was modernized in 1928–29, it moved from using Arabic script to using Latin script. In effect, this has involved a loss of access to recorded history. CANAN's work for many years has evoked Ottoman art history, particularly miniatures and ceramics. In the details, viewers can see a new version of storytelling about women's lives, a negation of the controlling representations and narrative provided by the male gaze and visualization. Similarly in the Turkish Delight Series, she enters into orientalist European art history: Looking back at the viewer, she resists the controlling, romanticizing, exoticizing gaze of the colonialist.

Bottom: **Ghada Amer, *Sindy in Pink-RFGA*, 2015**

Ghada Amer is an Egyptian artist now living in the United States. Her work engages with the realm of abstract painting, which is laden with male "greats," and with masculine terminologies. Amer, however, subverts this by using—in combination with paint and brush—needle and thread, with their connotations of feminine skills. Further, the imagery that emerges from the tangle of threads on her canvases is frequently that of female bodies, taken from pornography—women twisting toward the viewer, adopting sexual poses, kissing other women, or masturbating. Then, further, these images are often overlaid with repetitive texts. Strong images are evoked through delicate and vulnerable materials. In this way, there are many ambiguous or contradictory messages about the realms of the masculine and the feminine, about the expression of sensuality and sexuality, the place of female pleasure and who can represent it, and how this is coded in art.

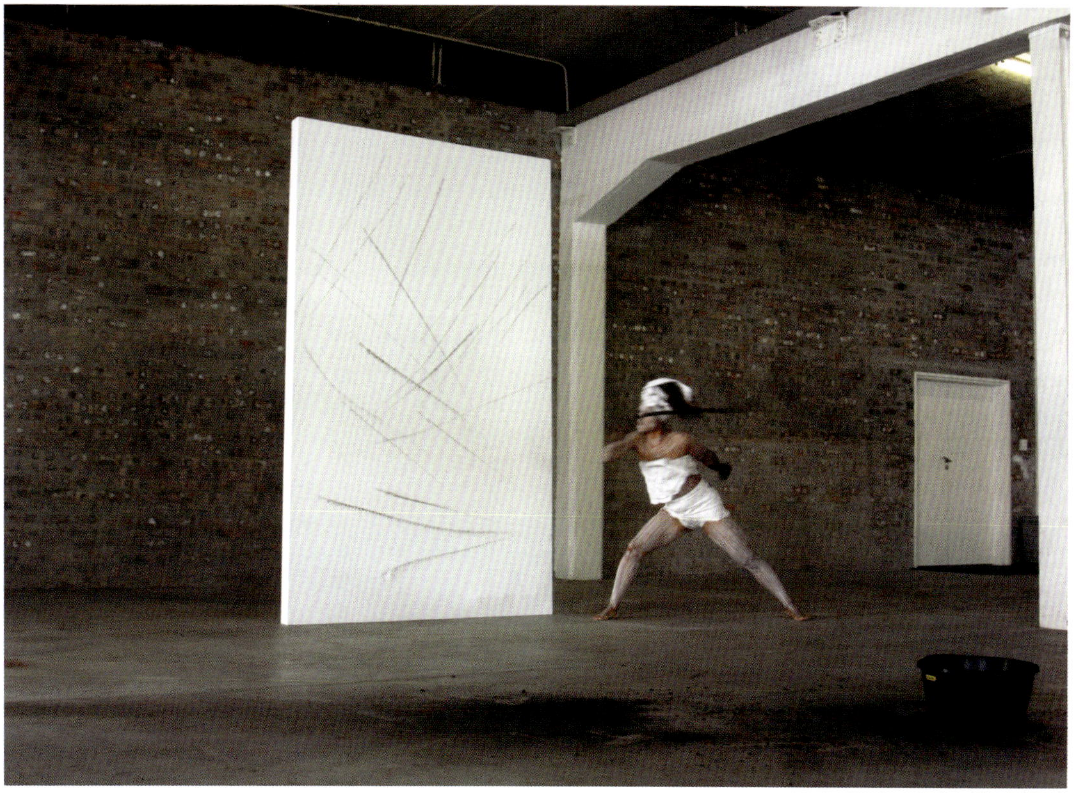

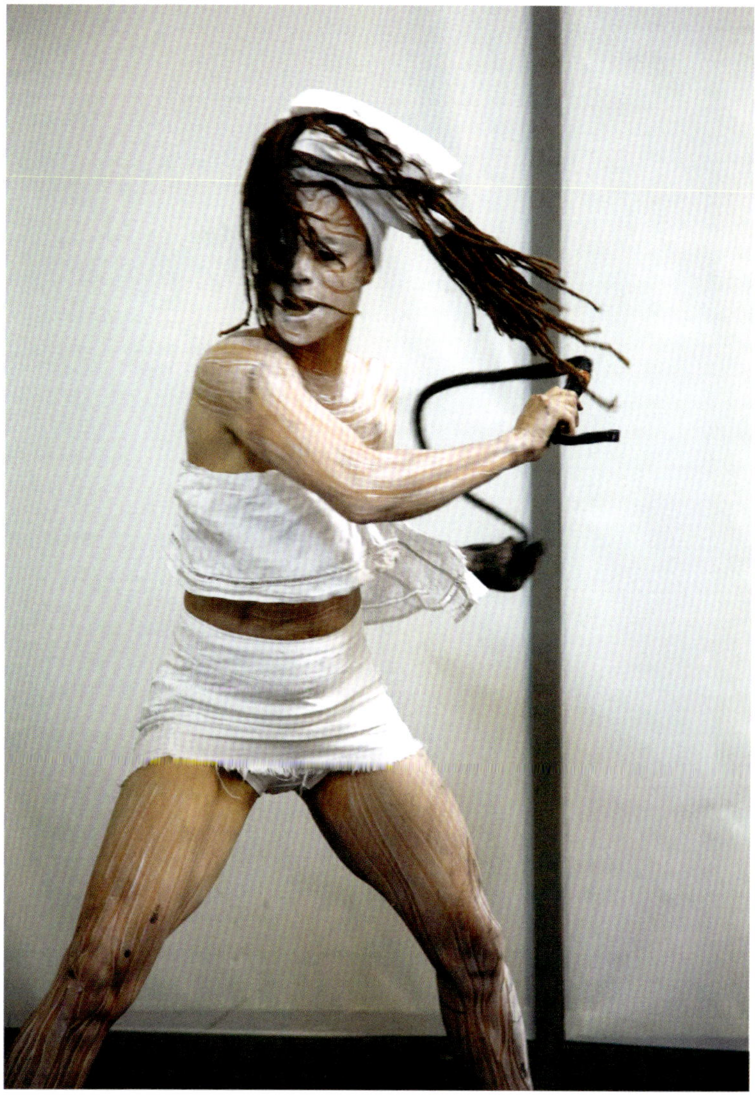

This page: **Jeannette Ehlers, *Whip It Good*, 2013**

Jeannette Ehlers is a Danish-Trinidadian artist. The history of people of color in Denmark and Scandinavia is often overlooked, but Denmark has a long colonialist history. Ehler's performance and related exhibitions under the title *Whip It Good* asks people to confront racist history in a visceral way. A large, white-painted canvas is prepared. Ehlers approaches it with a long whip that has been dipped in charcoal dust. As she whips the canvas, black scars are left. When she stops, she asks people in the audience to come forward to whip the canvas. There is palpable tension as individuals decide whether to do this or not; in the performance in South Africa, no white people would take the whip, while in Denmark, they were keen to do so. The canvases are subsequently exhibited. In a related photograph, Ehlers with her whip evokes a famous 1967 portrait of Black Panther cofounder, Huey Newton, sitting in a wicker-back chair with a gun and a spear.

Individuals and the State: Tania Bruguera

Tania Bruguera is a Cuban artist who resides variously in Havana and in New York, in the United States. Much of her mature artwork is a critique of governments through exercising active citizenship. While the Cuban government is the main object of her attention, her work criticizes America's attitude toward migrants—some of whom are fleeing totalitarian regimes, war, or disaster—and she explores state power in the countries in which she exhibits. While making her work she has been arrested and detained a number of times.

Bruguera's father was a diplomat for the Cuban revolutionary government whose family traveled with him for his postings overseas; her mother (who had been an activist against the prerevolutionary regime) eventually divorced him because of their political differences and took eleven-year-old Tania back to Cuba. Usually, such biographical detail can distract from the artwork, or prejudice assessment of it; but here it is an interesting backdrop, showing the absolute seriousness and commitment to political thought and engagement within Bruguera's family.

During the Havana Biennial of 2009, Bruguera showcased *Tatlin's Whisper #6* (Havana Version). The title refers to the Russian architect Vladimir Tatlin, whose utopian tower to house the Bolshevik Comintern was never built. Bruguera set up a formal podium, where citizens of Cuba were invited to speak on any aspect of the Cuban government for one minute. The first person who spoke had a white dove placed on their shoulder—alluding to Fidel Castro's first speech following the 1959 revolution, when a white dove landed on his shoulder and two others circled the stage. *Tatlin's Whisper #5* (2008) had been presented at Tate Modern, London. It involved two mounted Metropolitan police officers using crowd-control techniques to corral and manipulate the visitors in the Turbine Hall. In 2015, Bruguera announced that she would restage *Tatlin's Whisper #6* (Havana Version), this time in Revolution Square, beneath the commemorative image of Che Guevara that is on a building there. Refused permission to do so, she said she would do it anyway, and was then detained for three days and had her passport taken away.

Upon her release, Bruguera decided to establish INSTAR: the Hannah Arendt Institute of Artivism, in her home in Havana. Its first act was to gather people together to read the whole of political theorist Arendt's 1951 book *The Origins of Totalitarianism*, broadcast through speakers to the street at the volume of a domestic television; the event took one hundred hours and involved fifty people. During this time, electrical supply workers who were working nearby were instructed by the state to use jackhammers to dig up the road outside the house.

The message of such works—and others, such as Bruguera's 2016 video performance announcing that she would run for president in the 2018 elections (an impossibility, as only those born in the country and members of the national assembly can become president)—are aimed more at people outside Cuba than inside, even though they focus upon the Cuban political system. In 2014 President Obama had eased relations with Cuba and America's economic blockade; Bruguera's words were testing the rhetoric of that moment.

Bruguera has also practiced what she calls her "artivism" from her New York home. Her long-term project *Immigrant Movement International* (2010–15) used what she called *"Arte Útil"* (often translated as "useful art"), which echoes the movement of the same name founded in 1969 by Argentinian Artist Eduardo Costa and is related to twenty-first century Social Practice and Institutional Critique movements. These movements have engaged with the structures of institutions that housed them, expanded the notions of art audiences to work collaboratively with communities, and established methods of working with others in a way that can make a difference. Bruguera established a storefront as a drop-in center where immigrants could get help and that could be a focus for workshops and partnerships with social service organizations. As part of her work, she drew up a Contract of Moral Commitment to Promote Immigrant Rights in the Public and Private Sphere on an Everyday Basis, whereby people could pledge to an ethical code in their relationship with all immigrants. An Awareness Ribbon for Immigrant Respect was also created, in the form of a badge that people could wear. In July 2015, the City of New York announced that Bruguera would be the first artist-in-residence for the Mayor's Office of Immigrant Affairs, a position that would last a year, and where she would engage with the office's new municipal ID-card program, aimed at giving ID papers to people who have none.

Bruguera's work adheres to the prime tenet of feminism that the personal is political, as can be seen in all of the works mentioned here. Her main target is the use and abuse of power, as manifested through the state and its various institutions and subsidiaries (government, police, and so forth), and as implemented by men. Cumulatively, her work evokes the state as embodied by patriarchy, enacted by men. Once again, the importance of intersectional critique—here, of gender, race, and citizenship in the ways in which state power is deployed—is demonstrated.

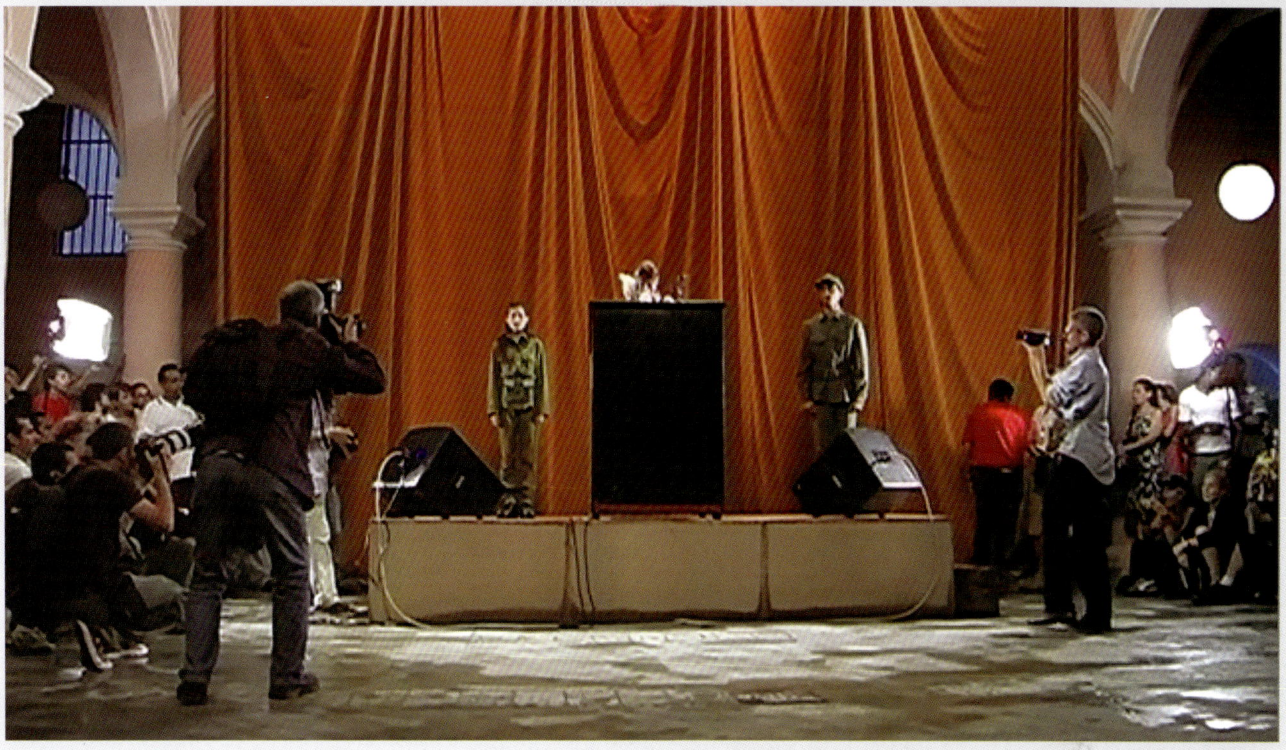

"Being a political artist is functioning in the political timing of things . . . Working with what is political has to do with understanding what the future is."

Tania Bruguera, from "Political Timing," Immigrant Movement International Blog, published on June 29, 2011

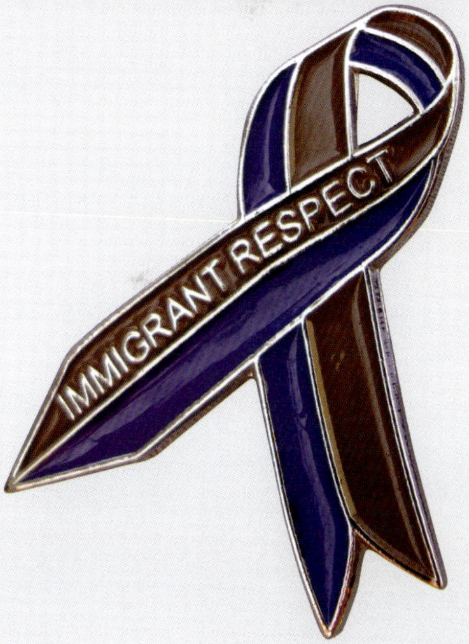

Top: **Tania Bruguera, *Tatlin's Whisper #6* (Havana Version), 2009**

This performance took place at the Havana Biennial. People were invited to speak about whatever they wished for sixty seconds, after which the two performers dressed as soldiers led them away. The contrast of this with the placing of a white dove on the speaker's shoulder makes for a complex work—the symbol of peace and of hope after the success of the popular Cuban revolution, juxtaposed with state mechanisms of control.

Bottom: **Tania Bruguera, Awareness Ribbon for Immigrant Respect, 2011**

Many campaigns use loops of colored ribbon as identification markers and badges. Bruguera made this badge through her Immigrant Movement International project, which found that there was no such form of displaying solidarity for migrant rights campaigns. It was named the "Immigrant Respect" ribbon to bring home the human beings deserving of respect who are at the heart of such campaigns.

Below: **Roma Kale Panthera Groupe: Tamara Moyzes and Vera Duždová, *SuperMom*, 2014, ephemera**

Tamara Moyzes practices what she calls "artivism"—art with activist intent intersectional interventions—in which she collaborates with other individuals and groups. When the first-ever quintuplets were born to a woman in the Czech Republic, the mother experienced such extreme threats and actual abuse that she had to be given protection. The cause of this aggression was racism: She was Roma. It was said she was getting benefits that no "real Czech" woman would get. Moyzes, working with Vera Duždová as the Roma Kale Panthera Groupe, made a video, installation, and objects. The video showed a pregnant woman being gifted, in daytime-TV style, the "Prenatal Luxury Box," containing six gifts that no Czech woman had received before: dog poop; threatening letters; safety-window films to protect against Molotov cocktails; a fire extinguisher; patrol officers; and a police escort—all things that the Roma woman had received in actual life.

Below: **Šejla Kameric, *Bosnian Girl*, 2003**

Bosnian Girl is a black-and-white photograph of the artist herself from the waist up. Across the lower half of the photograph is handwriting with many errors: "NO TEETH...? A MUSTACHE...? SMEL LikE SHiT...? BOSNiAN GiRL!." In small print below is the artist's name and the explanation: "Graffiti written by an unknown Dutch soldier on the wall of the army barracks in Potocari, Srebrenica 1994/95. Royal Netherlands Army troops, as a part of the UN Protection Forces (UNPROFOR) in Bosnia and Herzegovina 1992–95, were responsible for protecting the Srebrenica safe area. Photography by Tarik Samarah." Kameric made the work for public distribution; it was plastered on walls, turned into cards, appeared in newspapers, and many girls used it as their profile photograph on social media even ten years later. She says that the U.S. Embassy in Sarajevo ordered the posters to be removed from the streets around the embassy, and that half the professors at a Dutch art school, the Rijksacademie, interpreted it as an attack on them.

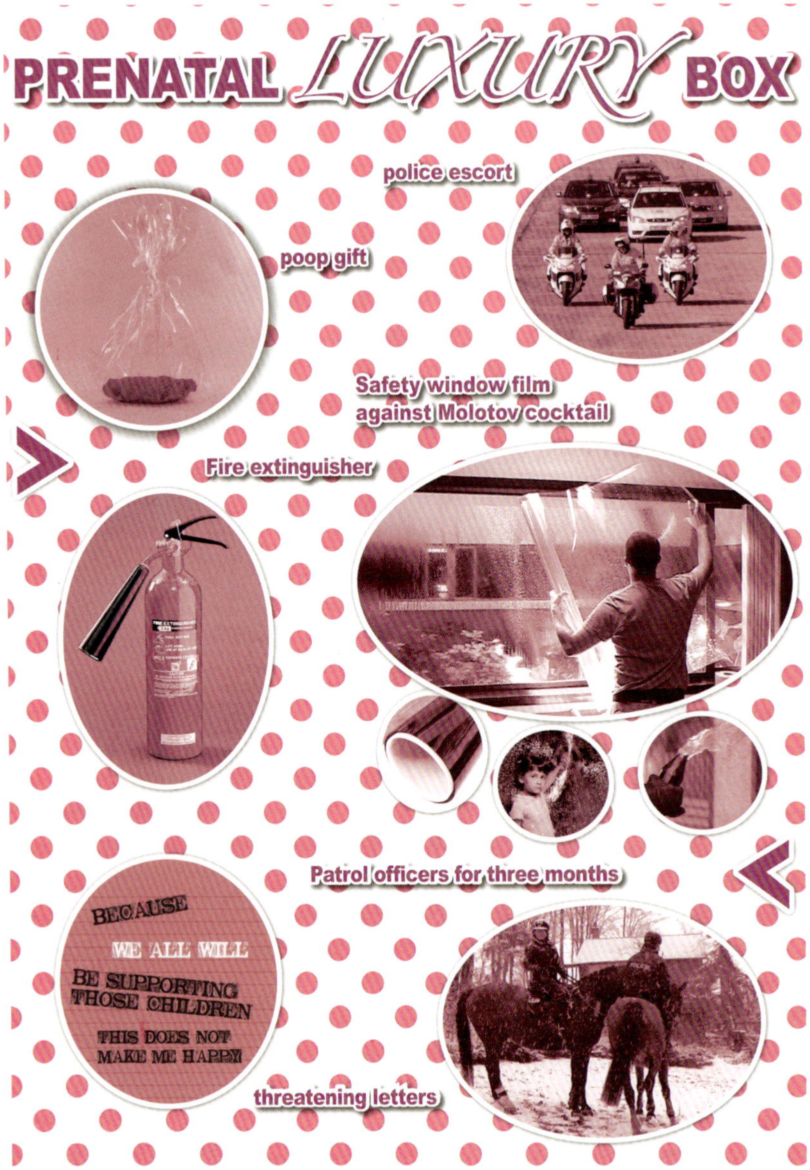

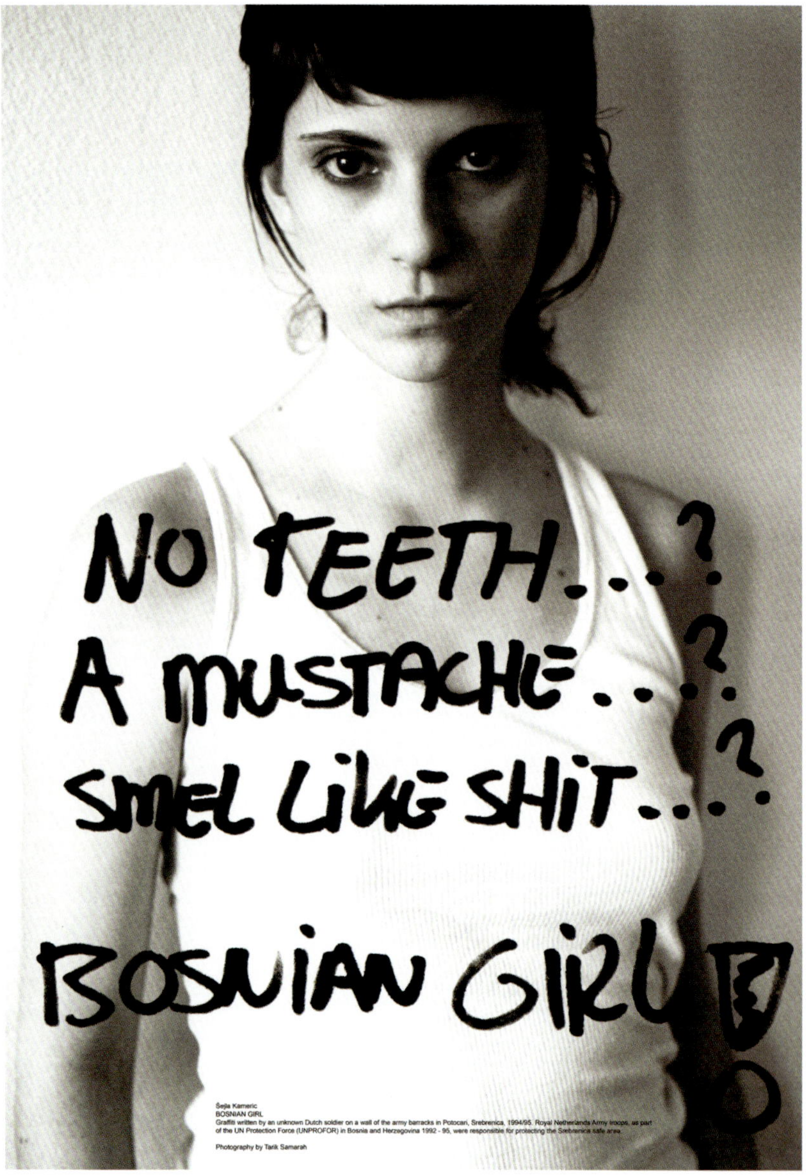

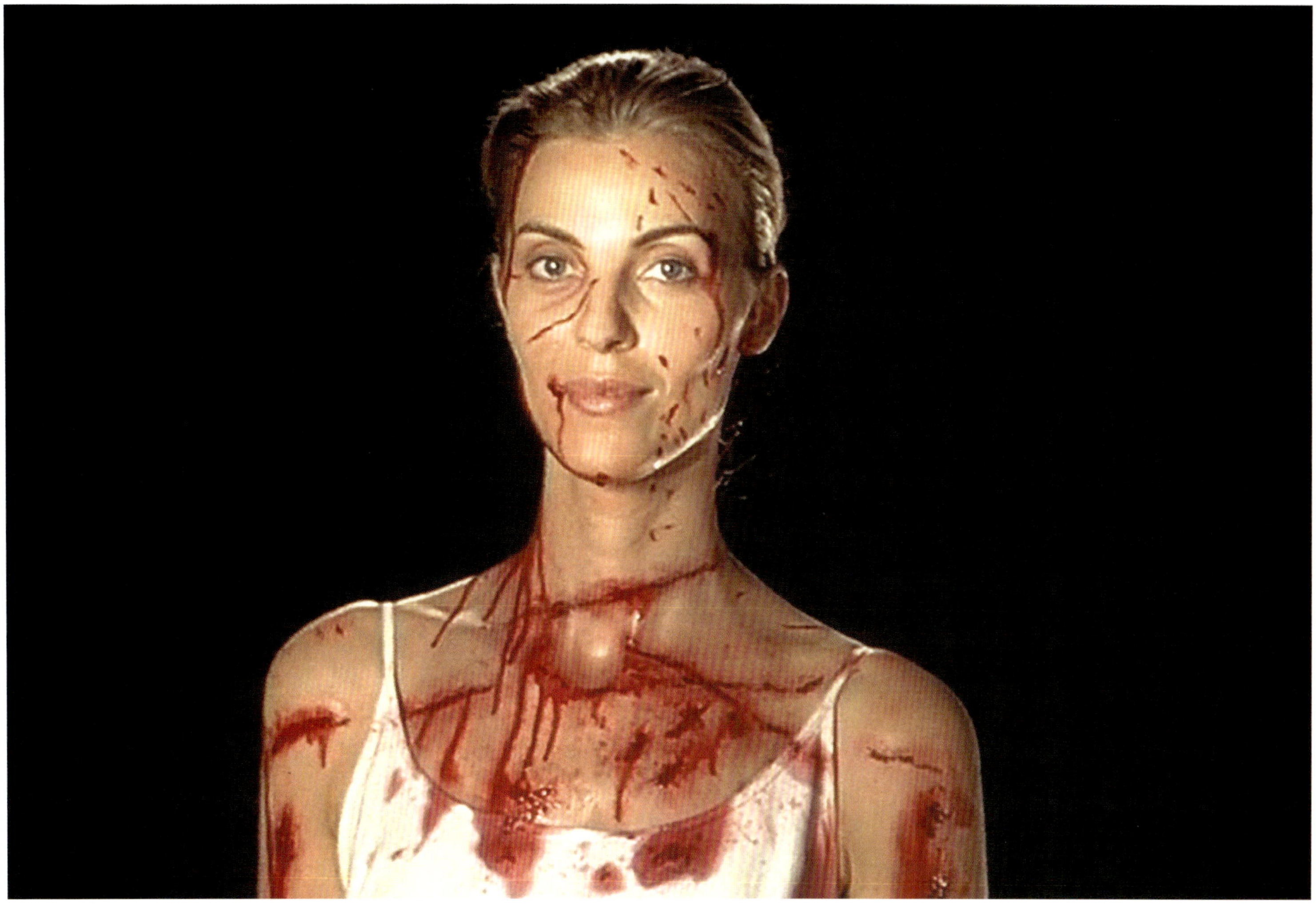

Above: **Milica Tomić, *I am Milica Tomić*, 1998–99**

Milica Tomić was born in Belgrade, in the former Yugoslavia, which, beginning in 1991 divided into seven independent states through a series of wars. She is a member of the artists' group Grupa Spomenik (Monument Group), which questions issues of state memorializing and representation of wars, and addresses the politics of memory. Her own work addresses the politics of identity and hidden histories. Tomić's video work *I am Milica Tomić* gets to the heart of native and collective identities. Dressed in a simple white petticoat, Tomić looks straight ahead as the camera circles her. She says her name and national identity in sixty-four languages: "I am Milica Tomić; I am English," "sono Milica Tomić; sono Italiano," and so on. As she speaks, wounds appear on her body, like whipmarks, which bleed and slowly cover her skin. Her face shows no sign of pain and remains impassive as she continues giving her name and identity in the different languages, and we see the wounds gathering. The video repeats seamlessly.

This page: **Ghazel, *Boxing* (top), *Feminist* (bottom left), *Moto* (bottom right), Me series, 1997–2000, stills**

Ghazel was born in Tehran, Iran, in 1966. In 1979 the Shah (who had secularized and modernized the country) was overthrown by Ayatollah Khomeini and, in 1983, women and girls over the age of nine were legally required to cover their hair. Experiencing this implementation of the veil as a teenager was to shape Ghazel's future artwork. From 1997 onward she has produced the Me series—short videos, and photographs with texts, all in black-and-white, showing the artist doing everyday actions while wearing her chador. The work does not focus on the veil as such, but rather on the actions that the woman is trying to make, and how she is restricted or prevented. She rides a motorbike; she does karate; she swims; she sunbathes; she climbs ladders; all wearing the chador. Some of the images are absurd, some humorous, and some simply sad, when we sense the displacement of the woman's energy and desire by the chador in scenes where she seems to want to disappear into corners or walls.

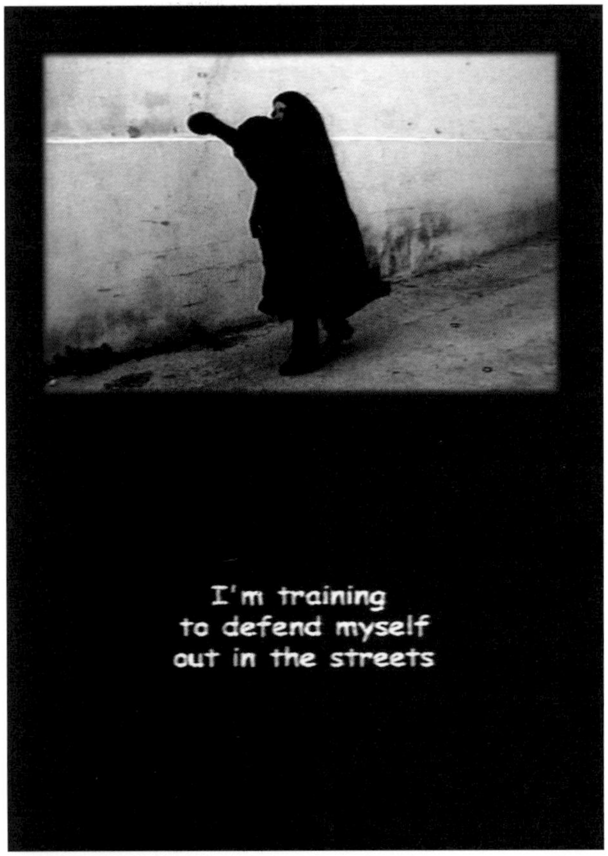

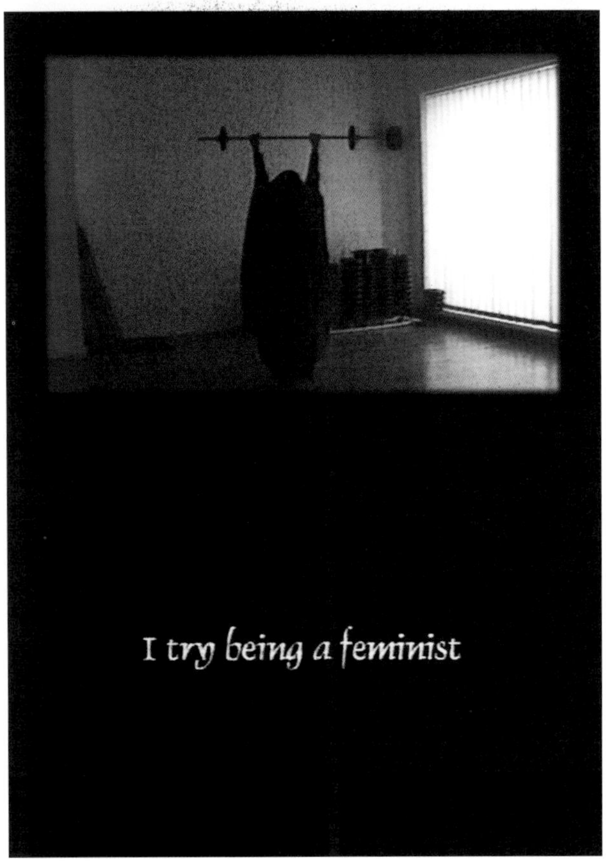

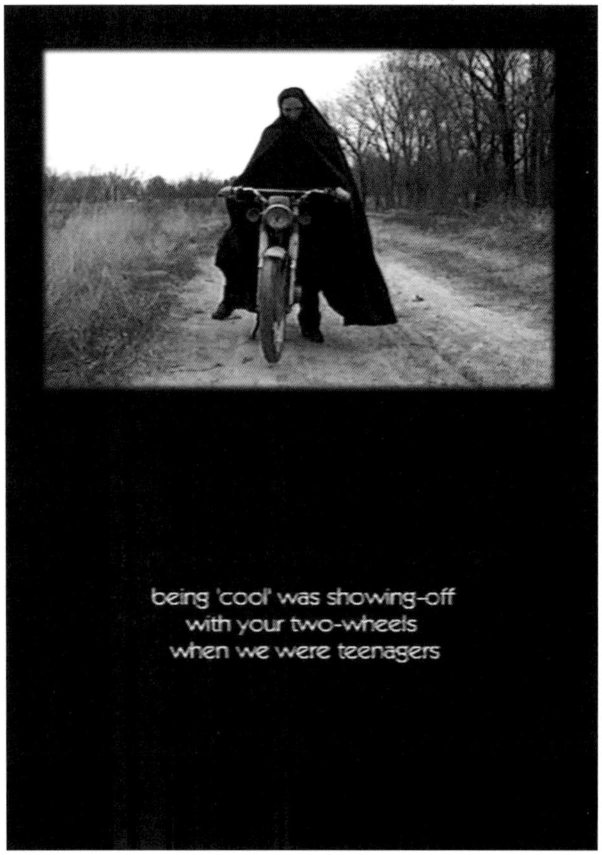

This page: Parastou Forouhar, *Written Rooms*, 2017–18

Parastou Forouhar says: "I see a fundamental difference between politics and art. One is committed to find answers as the other explores existential questions and doubts." She has more reason than many to explore existential questions: Born in Iran, she had a father who was a political prisoner during her childhood; aged sixteen, a bomb exploded in their house; twenty-six years later, after Forouhar had moved to Germany, her parents were both murdered at home, and the Iranian Ministry of Information later admitted culpability. Forouhar's work aims not to dwell upon the politics of her homeland, but to address more existential, cross-cultural issues. It resists the orientalizing and romanticizing gaze of the "Western" viewer upon both ancient Persian culture and more recent resistance movements. Her series of Written Rooms appear to non-Farsi readers to be covered in waves of Farsi script, indecipherable, but decorative, ripe for romantic projections; yet to Farsi speakers the rooms are equally indecipherable, a silent cacophony of lettering.

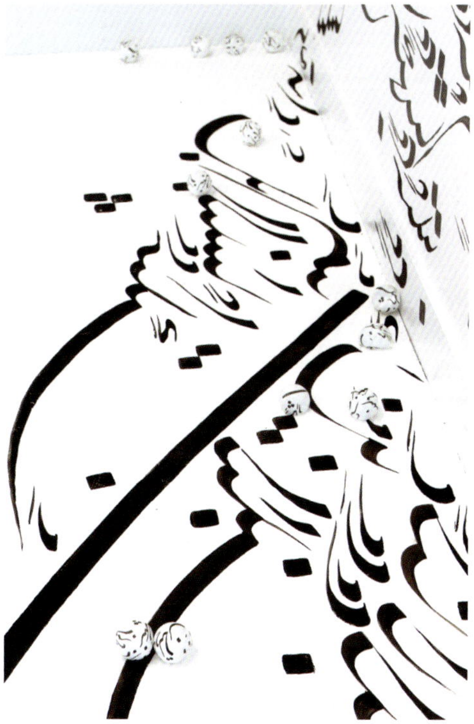

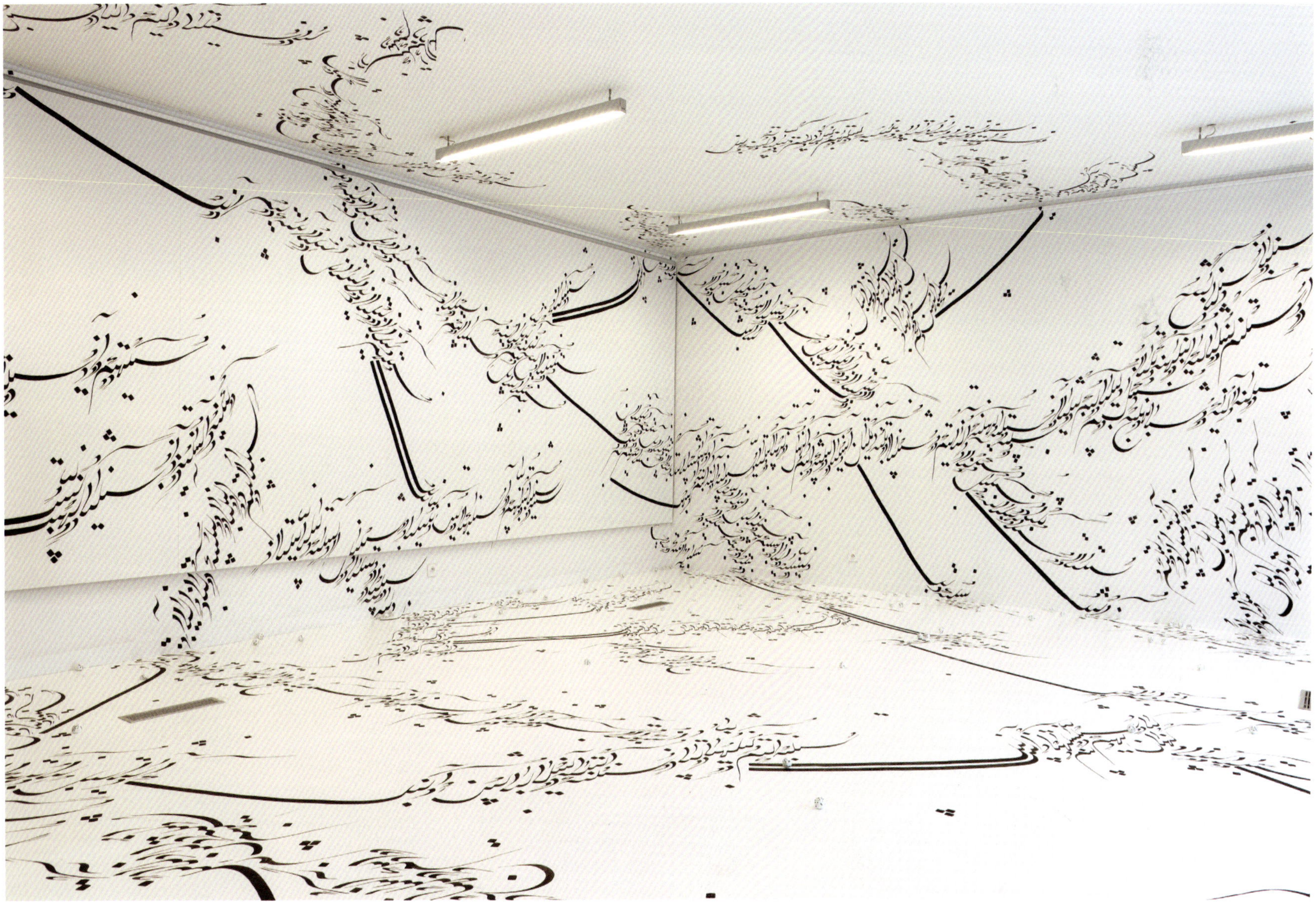

Local Community: Vanessa German

Vanessa German describes herself as "a citizen artist." She lives as a black lesbian woman in her adopted hometown of Pittsburgh, Pennsylvania, where her home is in one of the most deprived neighborhoods in the richest nation on Earth. Her extension of her art into engagement with her local neighborhood and community has changed lives. She embodies the hope and change that are possible through engaged citizenship.

If you go along Hamilton Avenue in the Homewood neighborhood of Pittsburgh, Pennsylvania, one house stands out from the rest. Homewood has many family homes, in conditions from neat and proudly cared for, through states of disrepair or abandonment. The sense of spaciousness in parts of the neighborhood comes from derelict and ruined houses being demolished and the lots grassed over. This is the place that Rachel Maddow of MSNBC television network called "America's most dangerous neighborhood," where shootings are a regular occurrence. It is also one of America's poorest neighborhoods. On Hamilton Avenue, amidst the red brick, is a bright-blue house, covered with mosaics of figures, flowers, hands, eyes; this is the ARThouse, created for local children by artist Vanessa German.

Vanessa German is a mixed-media artist, a sculptor, writer, and spoken-word performer, who spent her childhood in the Mid-City area of Los Angeles. This was also a violent area, where German witnessed a shooting as a child. She moved to Pittsburgh in 2000, in her twenties, and began to establish herself as a spoken-word poet and as an artist. Living in Homewood, she was all too aware of the neighborhood's problems; but it was her home, and she came to love it.

In 2011 a local man was shot and killed in German's neighborhood. That same year, her artwork outgrew the spaces in her house, so she began making her work on her porch. Local kids coming home from school would ask her what she was doing and would ask to help. Rather than have them work on her sculptures, German gathered boards and materials from the demolished houses and leftover paints and brushes from friends' theater projects, and would tell the children: "You need to make a decision. You need to choose a color and a purpose. What do you want to make today?" While she got back to her work, the children would start making things—and then call their friends to join them, repeating the same challenge. It became a regular after-school activity for some, an alternative to impersonating gang members, or to burying the trauma of violence within. German named it *Love Front Porch*.

"I grieve and I create. I reach out to my family and I make it my business to FEEL, to HEAR, to WITNESS, and to continue on in my life and in my creativity, as I find that the truest love and the truest healing in the act of Making Art and being with Art and Seeing and being inspired. I believe in the power of art, and I believe in the power of Love, and I do not necessarily have to distinguish between the two."

"Vanessa German: I am armed. I am an army." Pavel Zoubok Gallery, October 2016

One afternoon in 2011, at 3pm—the time that the school buses were bringing the children home—German heard twenty-one shots fired. Fearful and angered, she made signs that read: "Stop shooting—we love you" and stuck them in her front yard in the style of American political placards. People asked for signs for their own homes, and with the help of the children over 2,500 were eventually distributed across the neighborhood.

Following a tenant's eviction, the house opposite German's home lay empty. German negotiated with the public housing office to use the building on a temporary basis, to extend the Love Front Porch activity. This became the first ARThouse. She provided a regular place for the children to make things, to learn about their own creativity and their own potential. For the children, and for German, experiencing the power of making art as unconditional love was life changing. Knowing that the time in the house was limited, German began raising funds, including through sales of her sculpture and from crowdsourcing, to purchase a foreclosed house a few doors down the road: a permanent home for the ARThouse that was launched in 2015. On the risers of the steps leading up to the porch are the words, written by the poet and artist RB Mertz: "The ARThouse Poem: Being at the ARThouse / Where You Realize / You Had Wings / The Whole Time."

Meanwhile, German has continued with her work as a sculptor and performer. She makes figures from old dolls, vintage figurines, crockery and cutlery, beads, shells, knickknacks, and electric plugs, which she names "power figures." Drawing upon African and African-American traditions of assemblage, the figures speak of the legacy of brutal history and of resilience in the face of loss. They recall the central African tradition of *nkisi nkondi* or *minkisi* figures, Italian renaissance *pietás*, and, when arranged together, the terra-cotta warriors of Emperor Qin Shi Huang.

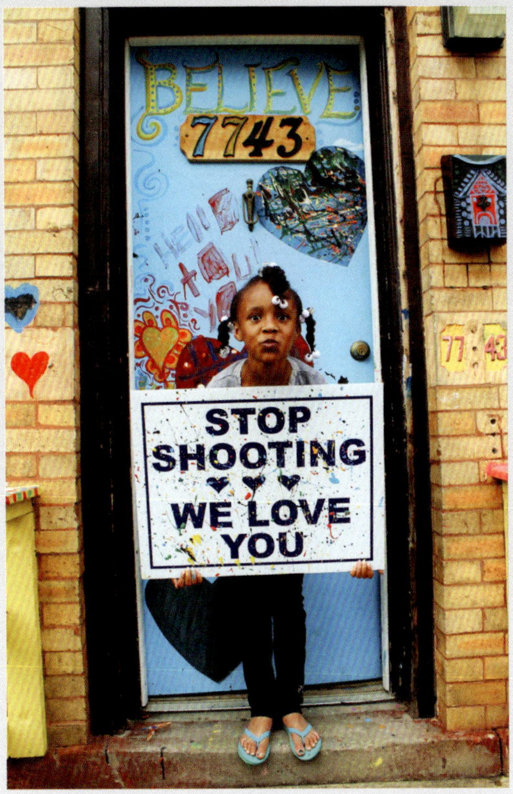

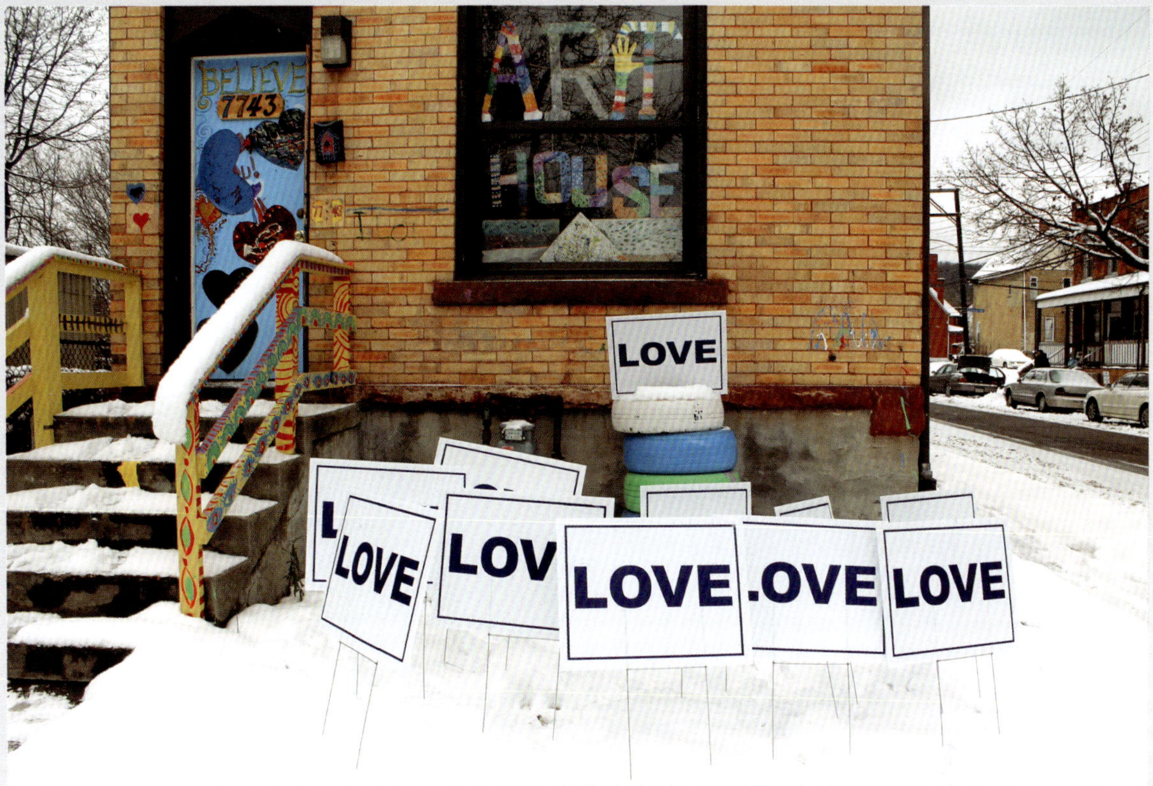

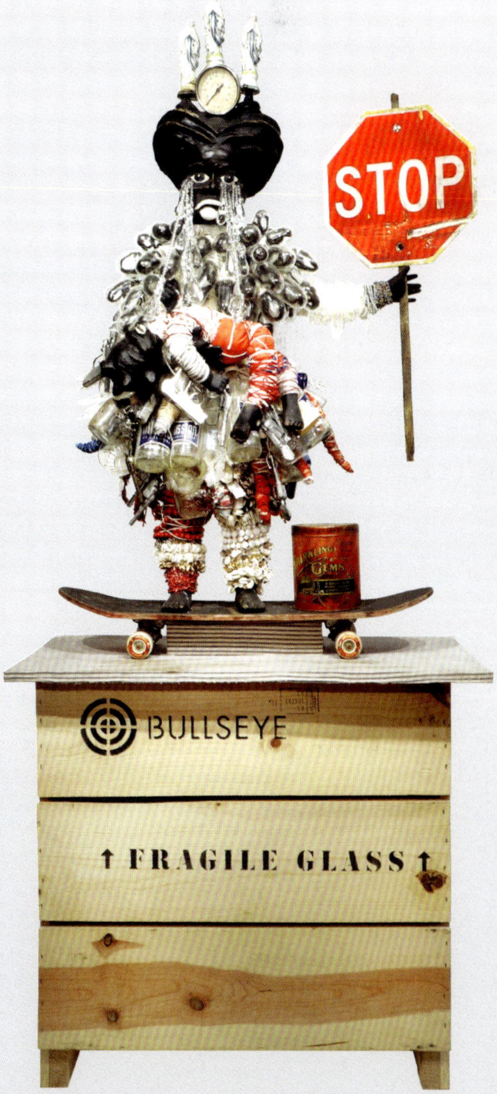

Top left: Zoe, aged nine, stands in front of the ARThouse, Homewood, PA holding a STOP SHOOTING sign.

Top right: Vanessa German, *A lawn filled with Love*

Bottom right: Vanessa German, *So many many dead black bodies, or, the why niggas always gotta be shootin' when they get mad, or take your beef outside, or, the trauma stays and stays and stays, or once again, the derivative____makes a mockable, public spectacle of her grief*, 2014

This work is one of German's series of Power Figures, which speak directly to the anguish and rage at the loss of young black lives to guns. Both spiritual and political, it makes reference to African *nkisi nkondi* sculptures, to European Catholic *pietá* images, and to contemporary American culture with the traffic stop sign, the skateboard, and the elements that speak of structural racism. The mother figure weeps glass tears. German describes it as made from "Old baby doll parts, skate board, found STOP sign, bullseye glass cr0 pigment, sorrow, the way i had to lay out for ra-ra that there are so very many ways to die – that he need not get shot, pain from the funeral, hand blown glass vessels with my rare friend's hair in them, he is a black, gay, male, therapist, a healer – and his hair is like a universal prayer for strength and clarity and hope, that girl on the street who threw herself on to the police car."

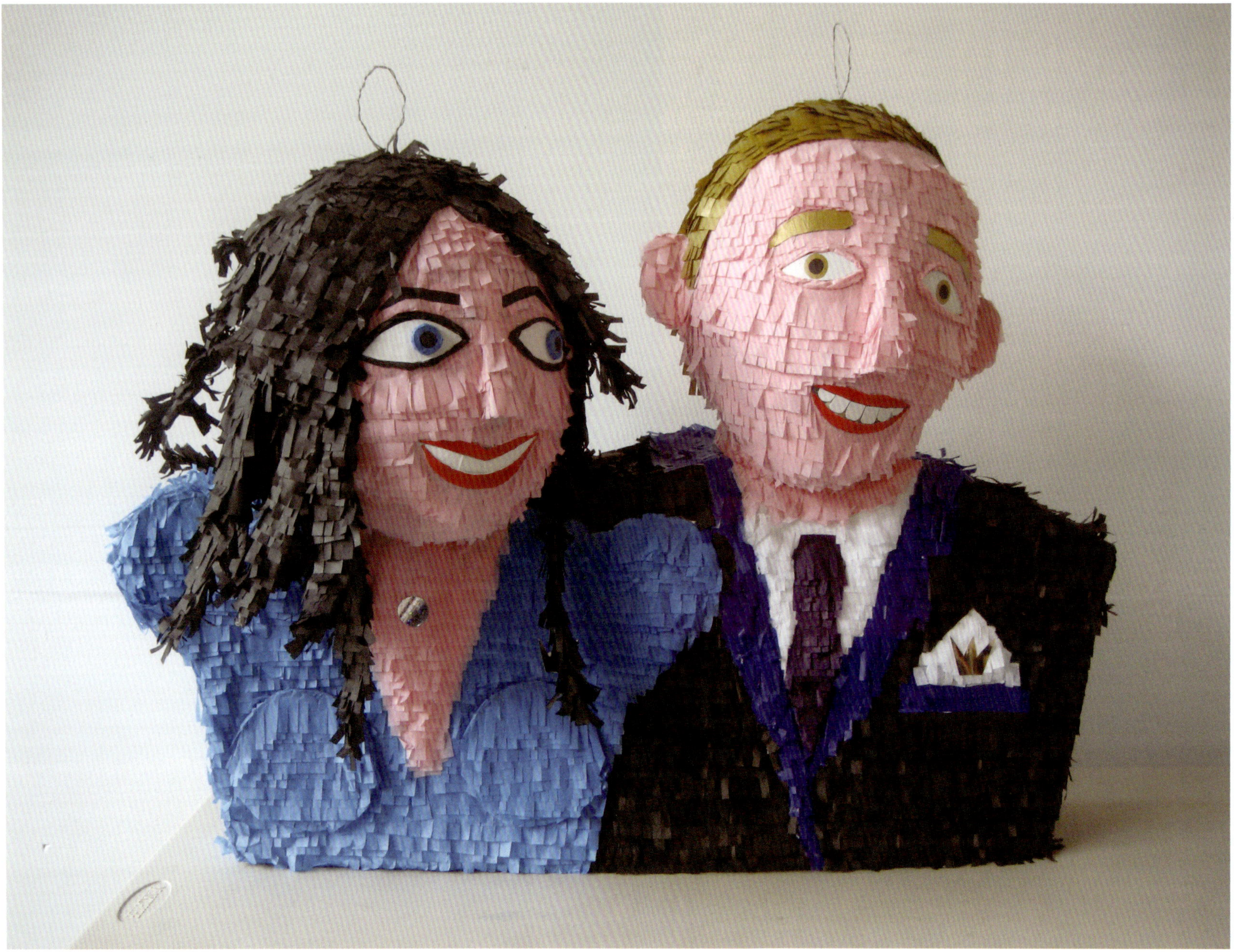

Above: Rachael House, *Kate 'n' Wills*, 2011

Rachael House is a multidisciplinary artist in London, whose work focuses on feminist and queer politics and resistant history, aimed to reach as many like-minded people as possible, and draw in as many people who are not like-minded, through humor, personal engagement, and events. In the 1990s she was part of the queer "zine-scene," with a zine titled *Red Hanky Panky*. Other projects have ranged from *Translab Residency, Singapore* (2010) to an ongoing series of feminist discos and making piñatas to be gleefully smashed with glittery sticks; one reading "Challenge Heteronormativity" was featured at the Victoria & Albert Museum, London, and at the New Hall Collection, Cambridge University (2016). In 2012, coinciding with the wedding of Prince William and Kate Middleton, House hosted *My Big Fat Royal Wedding*, complete with disco—as the invitation read, "dancing can be a revolutionary act"—and a piñata to allow participants to "smash the monarchy and the patriarchal shackles of wedlock."

Below left: Andrea Fraser: *There's No Place Like Home*, 2012

When she was invited to participate in the 2012 Whitney Museum's Biennial Exhibition of contemporary American art, Andrea Fraser submitted an essay that was reproduced in the catalog. Fraser is known for her work in the field of "institutional critique"—art that examines and exposes the workings of institutions. She focuses upon the art world itself, on the power relations, erotics, and non-art-related structures that underpin museums and galleries of contemporary art. For example, she held performances as the "docent," or volunteer workers, in major U.S. museums. Her essay for the Biennial examined the economic realities of the contemporary art world. Using theories from the social sciences and economics, as well as economic and art auction data from before and after the 2008–09 financial crash, she demonstrated that not only do art prices rise the more unequal a society is, but also that economic turbulence is harmful for artists, who have economically precarious lives, but of benefit to those who could afford to collect art as the value of their collections rises further.

Below right: Molly Crabapple, *We Are All in this Together*, 2011

When Wall Street was Occupied on September 17, 2011, artist, illustrator, and journalist Molly Crabapple was living in her studio nearby. She saw it immediately as not only a movement that she supported, but also as an opportunity for her work and her politics to come together in a meaningful way. Instead of simply signing petitions or donating money, she could dedicate her art to serving the movement. Visiting the site daily she noted the diversity and collective nature of the growing community was not being recorded by the media, so started making protest posters that could be plastered around the city.

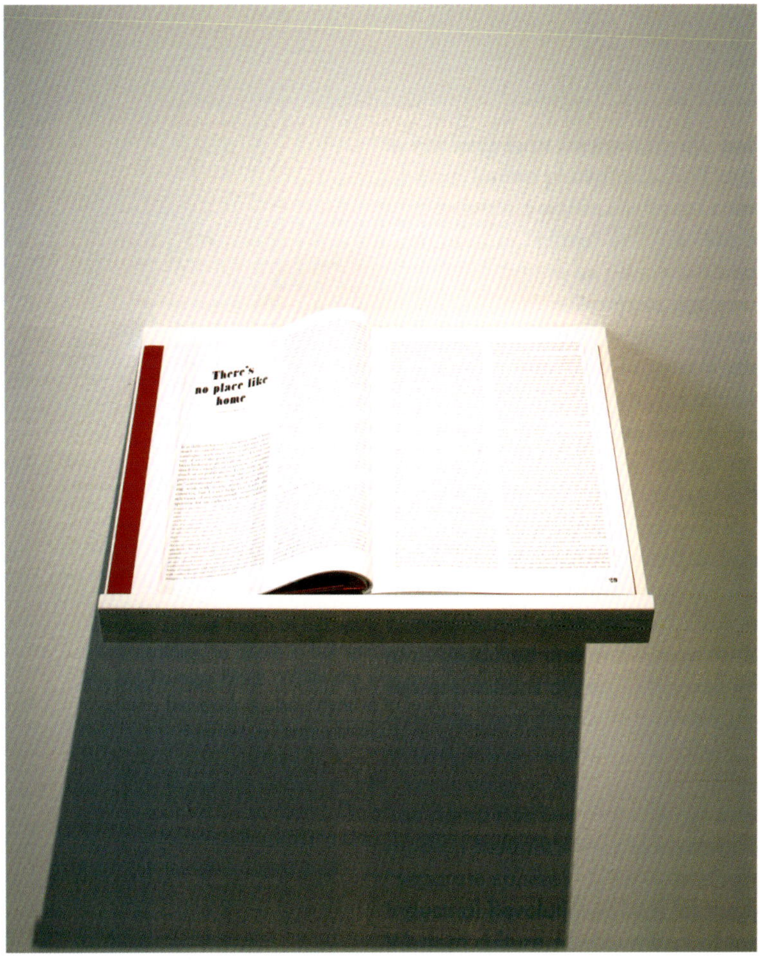

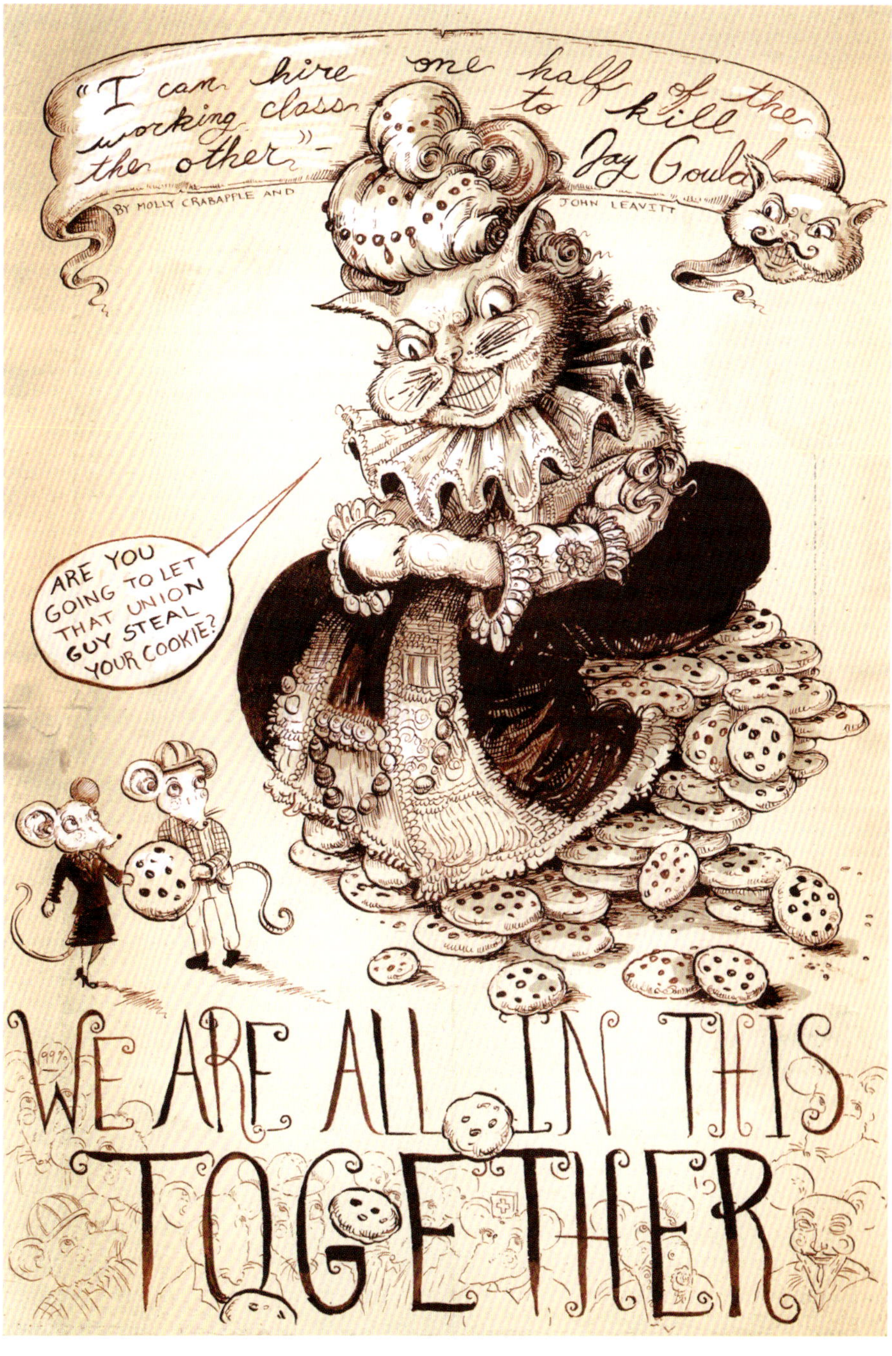

Politics: Keep It Complex

The prime act of citizenship in a democracy is voting, and the prime indicator of citizenship is a passport. The U.K. referendum on European Union membership, June 23, 2016, allowed British, Commonwealth, and Irish citizens who lived in the United Kingdom, and U.K. passport holders who had lived outside the United Kingdom for less than fifteen years, a chance to vote on leaving or remaining in the EU.

"We start conversations between people who disagree with each other. We use art to make politics. #keepitcomplex #makeitclear"

From the collective's twitter bio, MakeItClear also being the name of its website

Keep It Complex is a collective of women artists, designers, and arts administrators who began to organize together in the run-up to the referendum to equip voters with the information necessary to make a decision, and since then, on resisting the decision and processes of Brexit. The members of the collective describe themselves as "a self-organized and mostly self-funded group who try to make political action possible for ourselves and others." They use their collective skills as artists and art workers to have open conversations about politics through various activities. They aim to engage people who are not the usual audiences for art activities, in places that are not always the most comfortable, while keeping clear what they want: "a peaceful, caring, angry, anti-austerity, factual, DIY, transnational, struggling, messy, family-friendly, queer, inclusive, intergenerational, generous, diverse society."

During the referendum the collective networked with the organization EU-UK, which was started by artists and designers to make sure discussion about the arts and culture were included in the debate. The campaign was run largely through social media—Facebook, Twitter, and Instagram—and through a network of events held around the country. EU-UK posted posters and reading material on its website; the site is still live, and campaigning on Brexit and related issues is continuing through Keep It Complex.

Keep It Complex has a mouse-face logo, inspired by Zella in the feminist sci-fi movie, *Born in Flames*: "But I always say, if you were the army and the school and the head of the health institution and the head of the government, and all of you had guns, which would you rather see come through the door: one lion, unified, or five hundred mice? My answer is that five hundred mice can do a lot of damage." This sense of a network of many people collectively building strength runs through all of the collective's work.

The feminist and intersectional politics informing Keep It Complex's position and its organizational processes are made clear on the website. Various pages provide resources on how to organize locally, invitations to Keep It Complex's own events and records of its previous events, resources to replicate and adapt events, and reading lists. For example, the page "Host a meeting" includes a short resource list with downloadable links. Besides a link to radical Brexit resources, the list takes visitors through initial meetings, to organizing more formally, and to publishing. A pamphlet on how to "huddle" or start local organizing in groups of ten to fifteen people, produced by the Women's March on London, is a clear and positive guide. Also included is a leaflet from Global Justice on running meetings at the next level of community organizing; a manual from Malmö Free University for Women (founded by artists in 2006) on radical ways of educating; and the Salvage collective's forum on working together as cis, trans, and intersex women survivors and activists on care, abuse, and oppression. Further documents provide foundational feminist thinking about how to have discussions across differences of identity and experience, and how to organize without replicating oppressive structures.

Keep It Complex has included practical ideas in the information that it wishes to share, and in its creative processes. The Make Your Own Material page includes instructions to make badges, T-shirts, and posters, including another resource list linking to instructions on how to knit sweaters with slogans and logos, Tania Bruguera's "slogan library" on immigration from her Immigrant Movement International website for use at home, and the See Red Women's Workshop feminist posters of 1974–90 to print out. In order to raise funds, Keep It Complex produced three sweaters with slogans, which are for sale. Keep It Complex member Kathrin Böhm designed a series of spoof "vote conservative" posters to fight the 2016 election, all of which were freely downloadable.

Keep It Complex events include performative and visual elements. The series Digesting Politics—discussions over lunch that have taken place in the U.K. cities of Birmingham, Edinburgh, Margate, Middlesborough, and Barking—can be replicated at home with the collective's downloadable placemats and posters. The aim is to focus on different Brexit-related issues, and they conclude with decisions about calls to action for further campaigning. Fun events include a live-action role play (LARP) of *Prime Minister's Question Time*, where participants can assume roles of differing British politicians (with dressing-up clothes and political rosettes provided), after which there is time to discuss the experience and what kind of parliament the group would actually like to have.

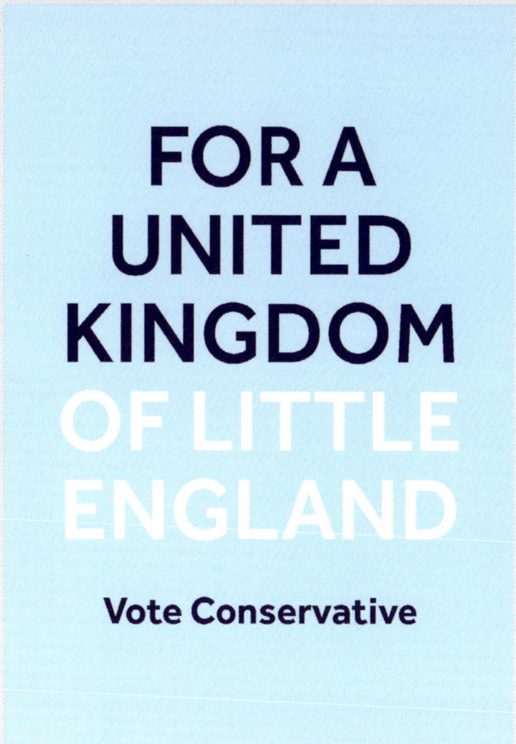

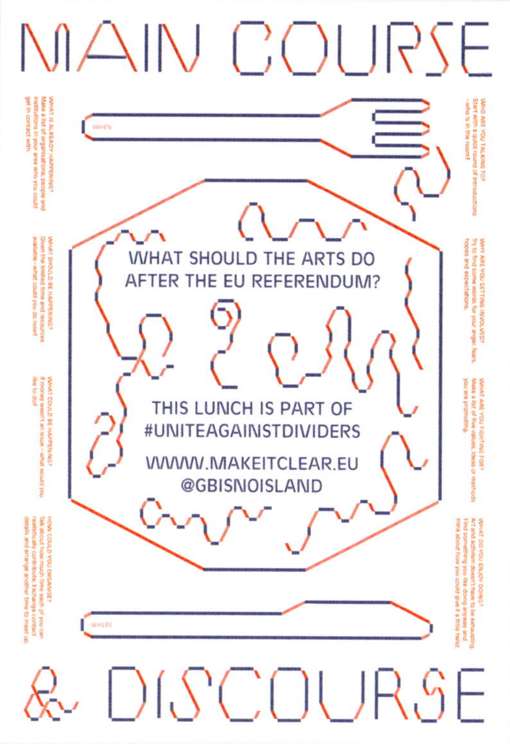

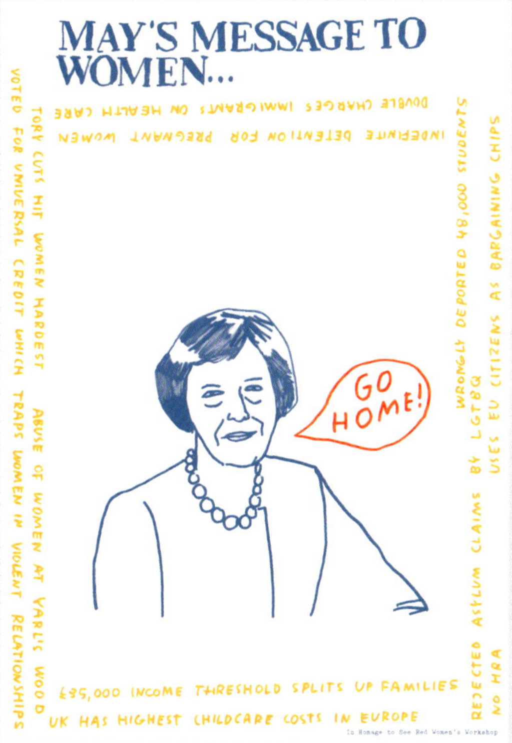

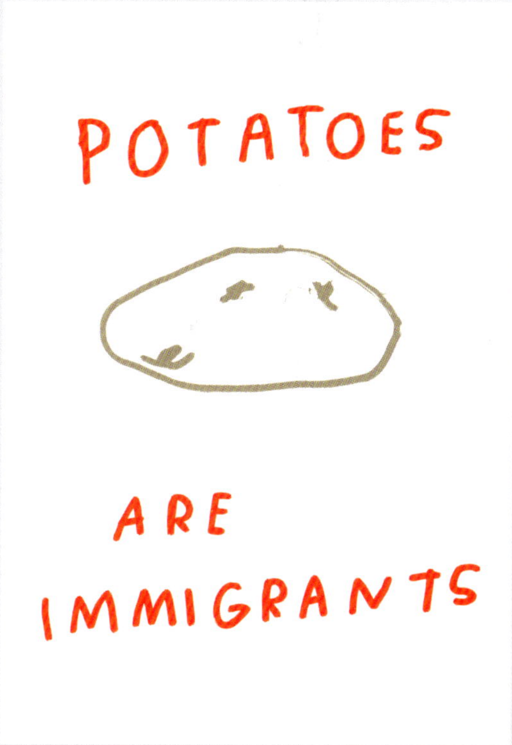

This page: **Keep It Complex**

The politics of gender are not always at the fore in discussions around Brexit. Keep It Complex address this, as a collective of radical, intersectional feminists. They use their skills as artists to produce posters that can be downloaded, including spoof Conservative Party posters for the General Election of June 8, 2017, and runners for lunch and dinner tables with conversation prompts on them.

Top left: **Keep It Complex with Laura Gordon, *Vote Conservative*, 2017, stickers**

Top right: **Keep It Complex with Europa/Mia Frostner, *Main Course and Discourse*, 2016, placemat**

Bottom left: **Keep It Complex with Europa/Mia Frostner, *In homage to See Red Women's Workshop, May's Message to Women*, 2016**

Bottom right: **Keep It Complex with Europa/Mia Frostner, *Potatoes are Immigrants*, 2016**

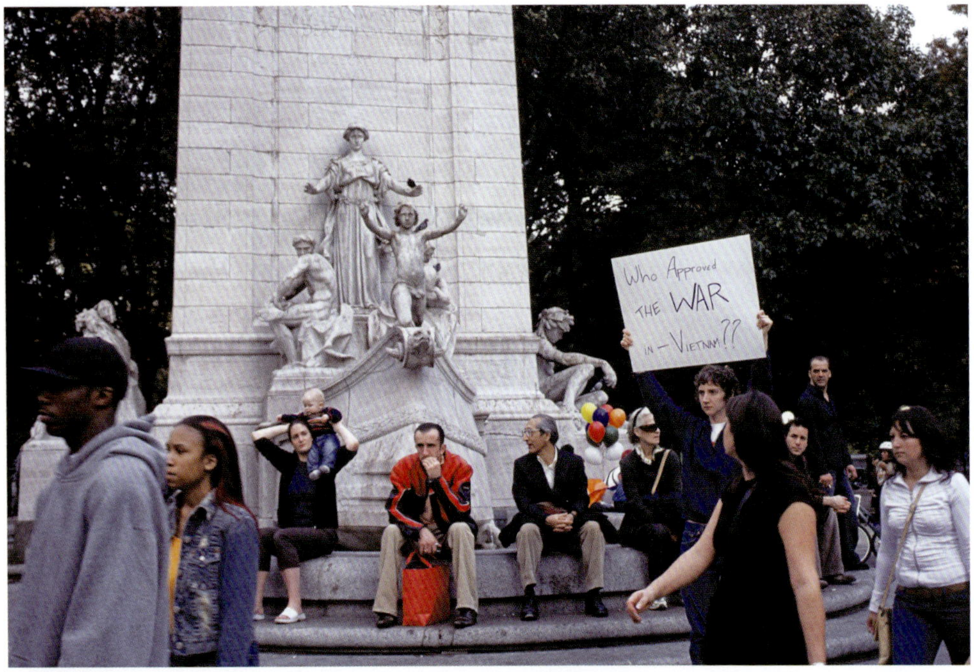

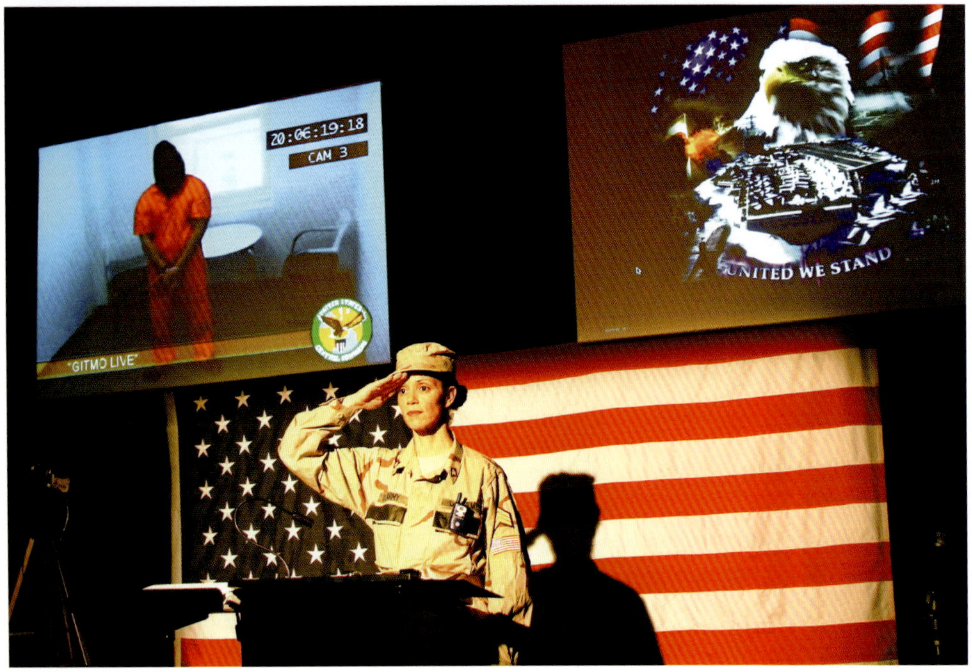

Top: Sharon Hayes, In the Near Future, 2005–2009

In the Near Future by U.S. artist Sharon Hayes takes two forms: a series of unannounced street performances that took place from 2005 to 2009; and 354 photographs of those performances, taken by people she engaged with on the street, typically shown as slide projections in gallery spaces. There was an increase in mass demonstrations that took place in many countries in the early twenty-first century, against the invasion of Iraq. In contrast, Hayes carried out her street performances in different countries around the world, standing alone, holding a placard with a slogan written on it that either repeated or evoked slogans used by protesters in events that still resonated with the present sites. For example, she carried a sign demanding "Ratify the E.R.A." on Wall Street in New York; and in Warsaw, Poland, she carried one that said: "There was, there is, there will be"—a slogan of the Solidarity movement in the 1980s, with the word "solidarity" removed. Sometimes cryptic, the signs provoked discussions with passersby.

Bottom: Coco Fusco, *A Room of One's Own: Women and Power in the New America*

This is a photograph taken at a performance lecture by Cuban-American artist Coco Fusco, in which she plays an experienced female military interrogator. She makes a presentation about American women's expanding role in the military. First, she acknowledges Virginia Woolf's extended essay, *A Room of One's Own* (1929), which argued that a woman needed an income and a room of her own in which to work as a writer. She then argues that the War on Terror allows women support and a room of their own for interrogating Islamic fundamentalist prisoners, using sexual mockery to humiliate them: true emancipation where women are no longer victims. The irony of this is that Woolf was a committed pacifist who argued in *Three Guineas* (1938) that women should reject the combative, militaristic masculinity that led to war. Fusco's performance references the torture of prisoners in Abu Ghraib prison, Baghdad, by women soldiers under a woman commander and a woman secretary of state.

Below: **Regina José Galindo, *Who Can Erase the Traces, 2003***

Regina José Galindo is an artist from Guatemala City. When it was announced in 2003 that Efraín Ríos Montt had been given permission to stand as a presidential candidate, she was enraged. Montt had been a military dictator in 1982–83, a period that saw large-scale, bloody abuses of human rights, the worst in the country's history. Gallindo purchased some human blood, and walked from Palacio Nacional de la Cultura to the Corte de Constitucionalidad. Taking the blood in a white bowl, she dipped her bare feet in it to leave bloody footprints. At the Corte de Constitucionalidad, a line of armed police stood between her and the entrance. She ended the forty-five minute performance with two final red footprints, placed the bowl next to them and went back to work, washing her feet in a fountain. This performance, *Who Can Erase the Traces*, was documented by photographs, which were distributed widely with texts about the unsuitability of Montt to be president; and Galindo produced the video documentation in 2003. Montt lost the 2003 election.

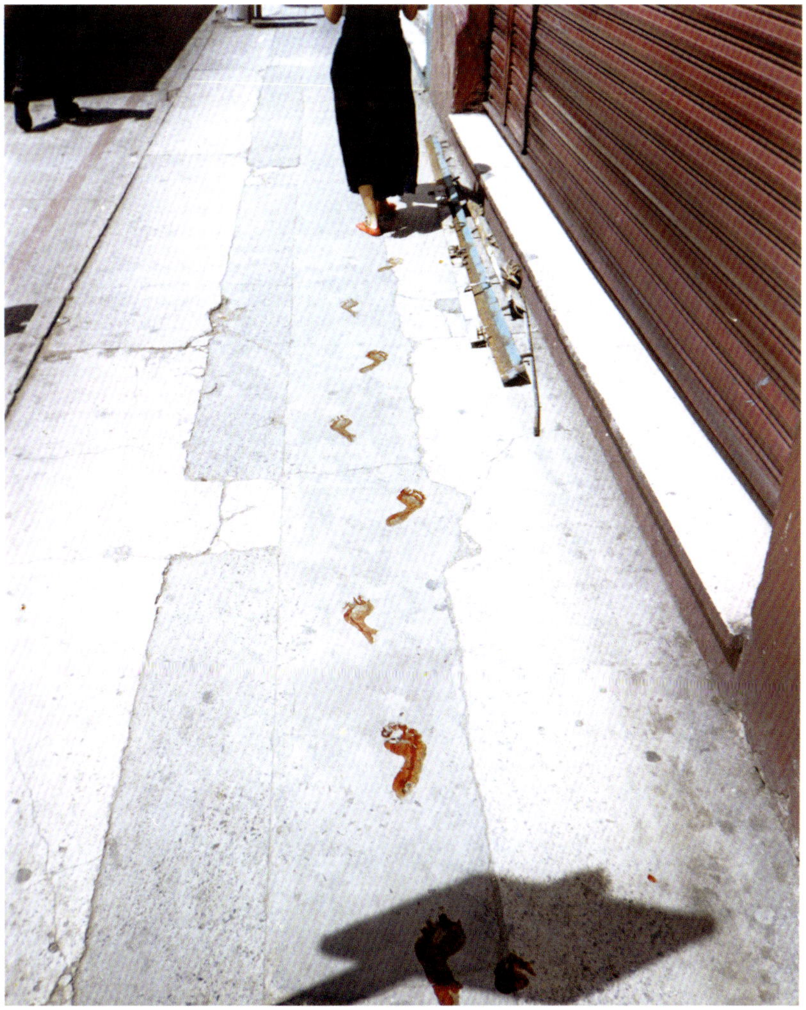

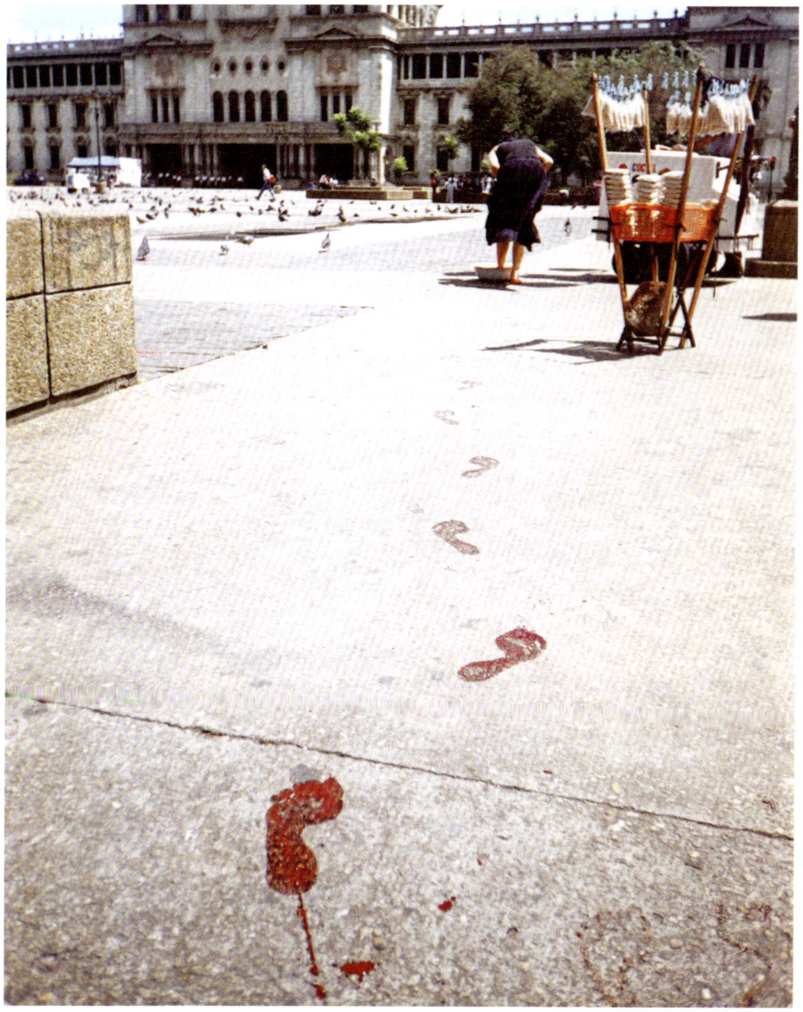

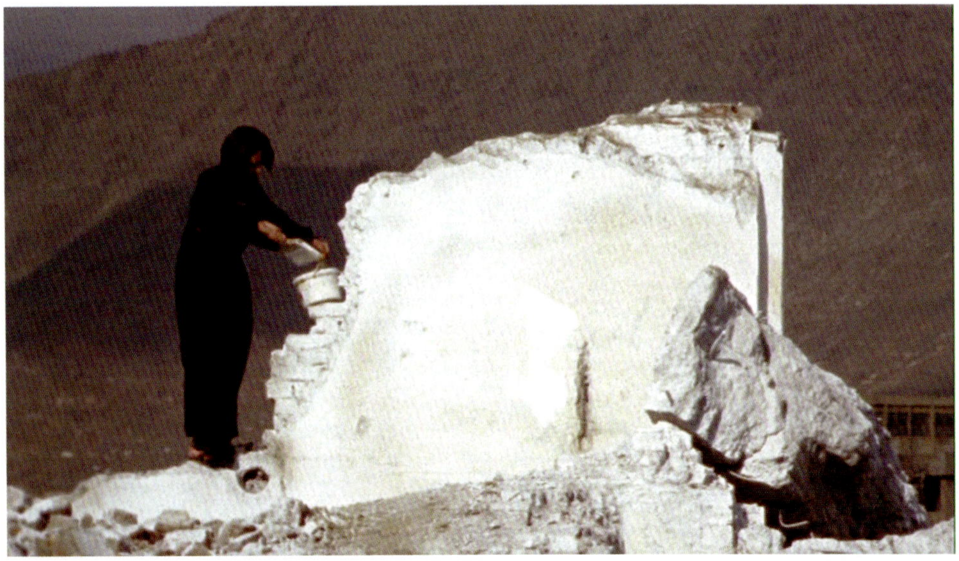

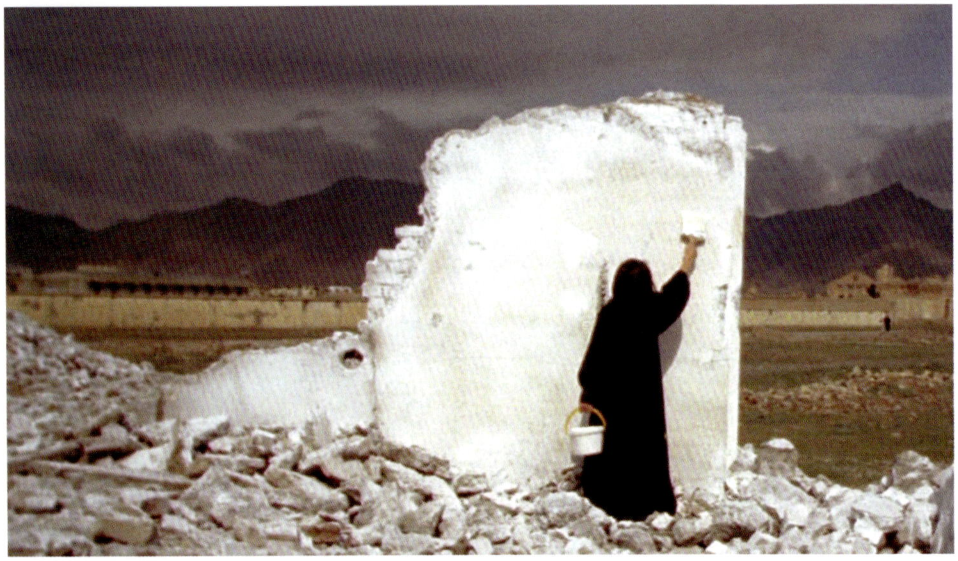

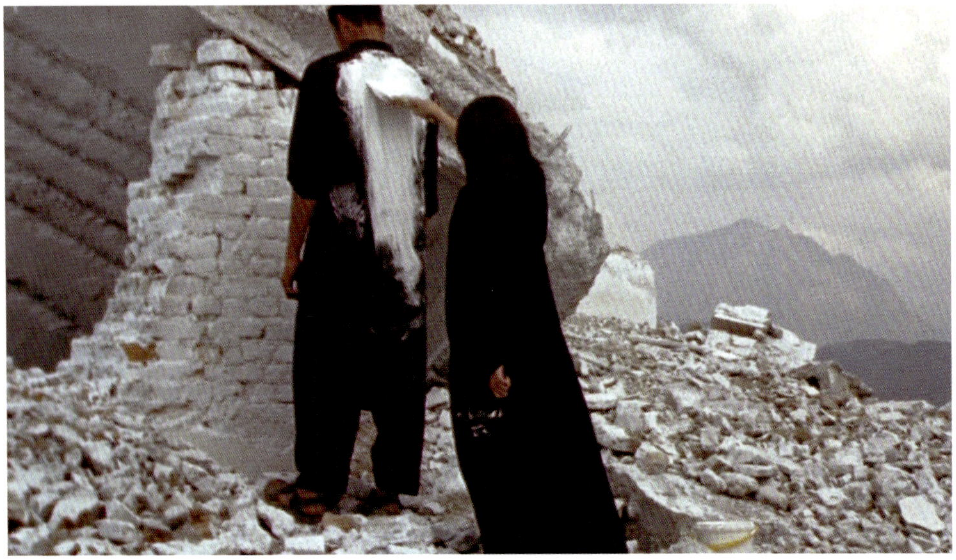

Left: Lida Abdul, *White House*, 2005, stills

Lida Abdul considers herself a nomadic artist. Born in Kabul, she became a child refugee in India and Germany following the Russian invasion of Afghanistan in 1979, and was unable to return until after the fall of the Taliban in 2001. Her video *White House* (2005), intended for viewing on a loop as an installation, shows her at the bombed-out ruin of the former Presidential Palace on the outskirts of Kabul. Dressed in black, with rhythmic movements she paints the ruins white—including the rubble and the clothing of a man who wanders through the scene. At the end, a group of goats clambers through the ruins. The painting took over two days, distilled here to five minutes of film. The intent of the video is layered: Clearly, the title *White House* alludes to Washington, D.C., and the ruination of U.S. foreign policy in Afghanistan. History is whitewashed. Further, she has turned these ruins into a monument in their own right: a commemoration of all the deaths that have occurred in Afghanistan.

Below left and right: Sandra Johnston, *To Kill An Impulse*, 1996

The "Troubles" of Northern Ireland ran from the civil rights movement of the late 1960s—with its focus upon the rights of Catholics to be considered full citizens, to vote, and to own property—through to the effects of the Good Friday Agreement in 1998, which were felt in the early twenty-first century. Sandra Johnston's work demonstrates the vulnerabilities and precariousness of the (woman's) body. Her video work *To Kill An Impulse* interweaves two sets of imagery. One is constructed from found footage of women (some Protestant, some Catholic) at "political" funerals of the men in their families who have been killed by the opposite side. It is expected of the women to be seen at the funeral, but the suppression of their emotions in front of the cameras is visible in their gestures. The other is of Johnston performing openly to the camera in a private performance in an abandoned dumpster. The site of the performance evokes the murder of Margaret Wright, a thirty-one-year-old Protestant women who, in a Belfast bar one night in 1994, was believed to be Catholic by a Protestant Loyalist gang. She was stripped, tortured, crushed, shot four times in the head, and dumped still alive in a trash bin, where she died. Johnston herself had been attacked by a gang a few days before this event.

Bottom: Jenny Holzer, *COLIN POWELL GREEN WHITE*, 2006

Jenny Holzer's series of works called War Paintings (2005 onward) are based on redacted documents and other confidential material from the U.S. government that have emerged from the War on Terror that followed the attacks on the United States on September 11, 2001, and from U.S. military operations in Afghanistan and Iraq. These documents include notes, interrogation records, autopsy reports, and accounts from prisoners. All were heavily censored before being disclosed. Holzer has painted hugely enlarged reproductions of them. Holzer is best known for works with text that are mechanically produced, through printing or neon, for example. Here however, she wanted the works to carry human contact, and the consideration of every gesture that can come from oil painting. The contrast between the shocking content of the words, the heavy black blocks of redacted text, and the painstaking brushwork, slows down the viewer, encouraging them to reconsider the context leading to the production of the documents.

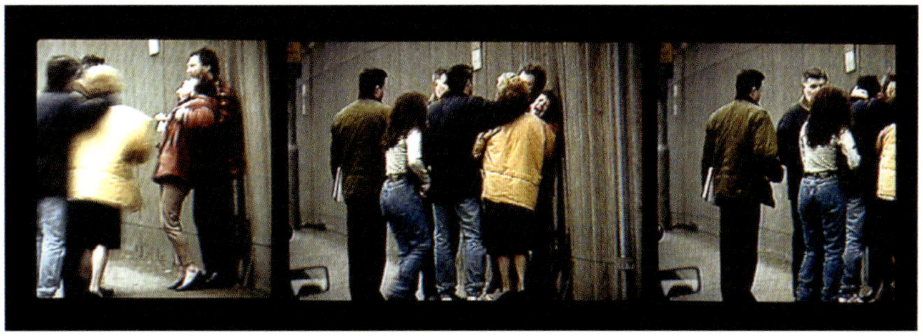

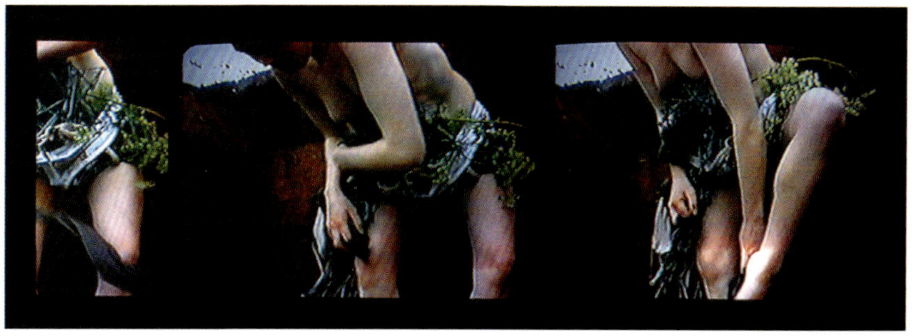

CONFIDENTIAL
THE CHAIRMAN, JOINT CHIEFS OF STAFF
WASHINGTON, D.C. 20318

CM-671-90
3 December 1990

MEMORANDUM FOR THE SECRETARY OF DEFENSE

SUBJECT: DIA Reorganization Proposal (U)

1. (U) I appreciate the opportunity to comment on Duane Andrews' proposal to strengthen Defense intelligence and to reorganize the Defense Intelligence Agency.

2. (U) [redacted]

3. (U) [redacted]

4. [redacted]

a. [redacted]

DECLASSIFIED BY VICE DIRECTOR, JS

Classified by: CJCS

CONFIDENTIAL

b. [redacted]

c. [redacted]

d. [redacted]

e. [redacted]

2

CONFIDENTIAL

f. [redacted]

5. [redacted]

6. [redacted]

3

CONFIDENTIAL

7. (U) [redacted]

COLIN L. POWELL
Chairman
Joint Chiefs of Staff

Copy to:
Deputy Secretary of Defense
ASD (C3I)

4

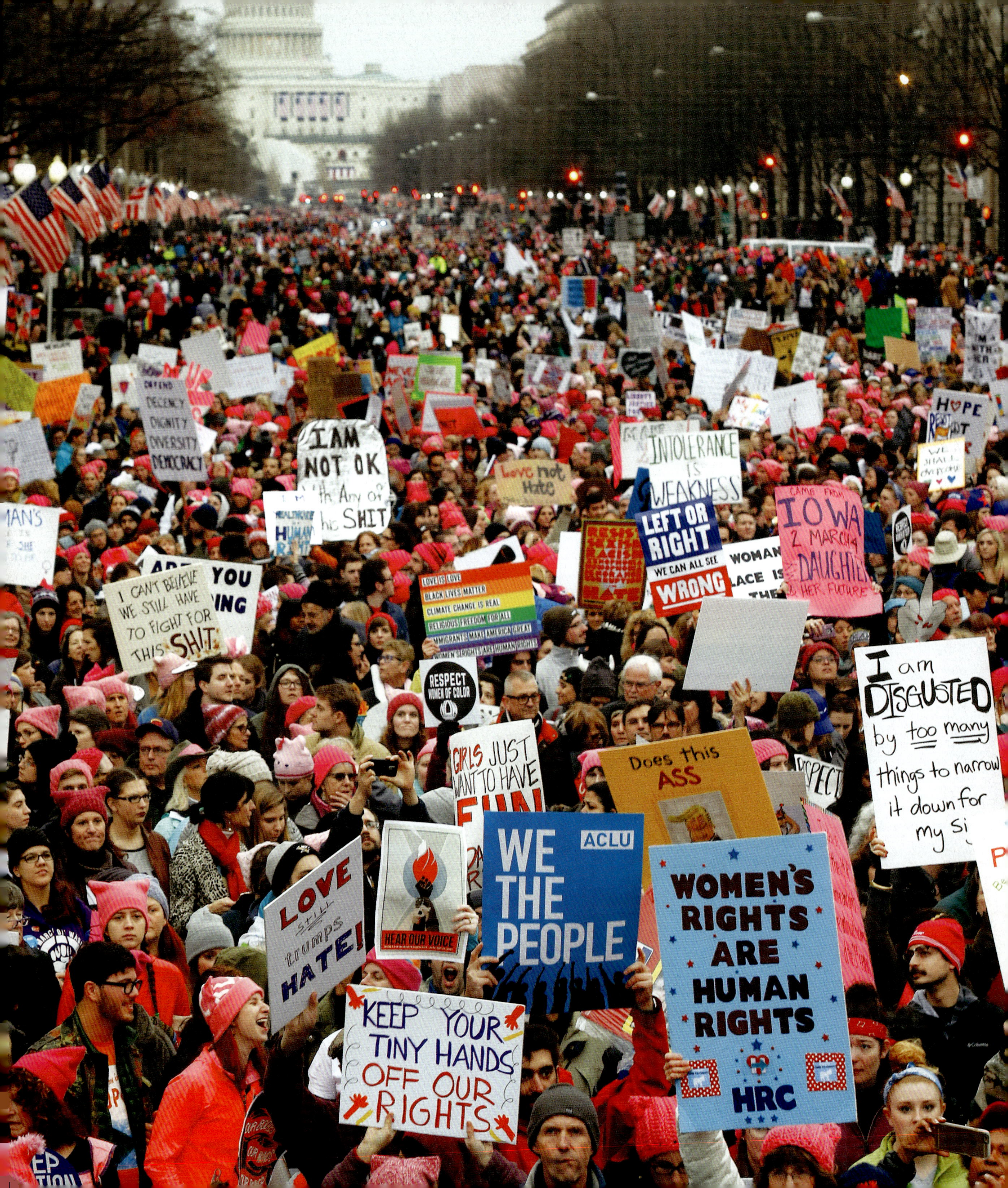
I AM NOT OK With Any of This SHIT
INTOLERANCE IS WEAKNESS
Love not Hate
LEFT OR RIGHT WE CAN ALL SEE WRONG
I CAN'T BELIEVE WE STILL HAVE TO FIGHT FOR THIS SHIT
LOVE IS LOVE
BLACK LIVES MATTER
CLIMATE CHANGE IS REAL
RELIGIOUS FREEDOM FOR ALL
IMMIGRANTS MAKE AMERICA GREAT
WOMEN'S RIGHTS ARE HUMAN RIGHTS
RESPECT WOMEN OF COLOR
GIRLS JUST WANT TO HAVE FUN
Does this ASS
I am DISGUSTED by too many things to narrow it down for my sign
WE THE PEOPLE
ACLU
LOVE still trumps HATE!
HEAR OUR VOICE
KEEP YOUR TINY HANDS OFF OUR RIGHTS
WOMEN'S RIGHTS ARE HUMAN RIGHTS
HRC
HOPE
IOWA 2 MARCH 4 DAUGHTER HER FUTURE

The Activist Feminist

Making Interventions

12

"Our struggle calls for the liberation of Black people. This means we continually fight against the denigration of our human rights and our dignity as Black people. In four years, we have built a Black queer, women, and youth-led movement. However, we have many more struggles to overcome and victories to win. We work to manifest a world where Black people are not constantly fighting to survive, but can thrive in safe and sustainable environments."

Patrisse Khan-Cullors, artist and cofounder of Black Lives Matter, in *Black Lives Matter: Celebrating 4 Years* (2017)

What is feminist activist art? Clearly, if feminism aims to change systems of oppression, inequality, and disadvantage for women, and to change cultures of sexism and patriarchal dominance, then people need to organize actively to make change. This can happen when groups get together, or it can happen when one person has the goal of making a difference; it can happen through bold public actions or more subtle interventions; but it all has to happen within the broad framework of feminist thinking, in order to fit within this definition. Many artists have explored, or engaged with, the politics of feminism, and the use of art and aesthetics intentionally as feminist activism. Of course, if feminism is a political position, then all the art that we address in this book will, to some extent, be political, and much of it will be activist. But how can we see these different categories more clearly, and distinguish between commenting on inequity or discrimination, and actively demanding systemic change? How can we understand the political and aesthetic effectiveness of a work of art? What is the relationship between the choices that artists make concerning aesthetics and materials, and their feminist, activist, intentions for the work?

There may of course be a fine line between simply bringing attention to something, and aiming to change it. In 1984, American art critic and feminist Lucy Lippard made a distinction between activist art and political art when she wrote in her essay "Trojan Horses: Activist Art and Power": "Although 'political' and 'activist' artists are often the same people, 'political' art tends to be socially concerned and 'activist' art tends to be socially involved—not a value judgment so much as a political choice. The former's work is a commentary or analysis, while the latter's art works within its context, with its audience." This is very helpful. "Political art," for Lippard, probably includes most of the art in this book. It is work that is concerned with the inequalities and discriminations that can arise in different cultures from being a particular sex or gender. Much of it is also intersectional, attending to discrimination and realities experienced as a result of being identified with a particular race, nationality, sexual orientation, class, ability, or age. It will often work within the wider art world of galleries and art events, even though the audience may come from well beyond that world. Lippard is using the word "activism" to mean something distinct. Activism, for her, is a set of actions intended to make a difference socially, culturally, or politically, beyond the artwork itself: The artist is acting to increase equality, lessen discrimination, and address issues that primarily affect women.

How does this activism and political analysis relate to the art world, with its more usual discussions of aesthetics and skills? There are two key types of art to explore. The first involves art that feminists have engaged with as activists, and artworks where the very process of making and/or distributing the work has been intended as something that will intervene to make a discernible difference in people's lives, that will transgress current laws or social practices, or that will rally protest beyond the art world. These works often fall within the genres of "social practice" or "institutional critique"—modes of art that, in turn, owe much to feminist thinking. The second type of art explores actions and organizations whose prime intent is activist rather than artistic, but which draw upon feminist art practices. These are activist events that have made great use of the impact of visual images in what they do, that have used visual signifiers from false beards to pink saris, to point out discrimination, or to provide identity and build solidarity.

To give an example of the distinctions to be made around just one feminist concern: While access to safe abortion has been an issue about which feminists have campaigned,

Page 244: **Women's march, Washington, D.C., January 21, 2017**

In 2017, the Victoria & Albert Museum, London, added a pink knitted "pussy hat" to its Rapid Response Collection of items that demonstrate evidence of social, political, and economic change. The pussy hat project began after the election of Donald Trump to be president of the United States, to protest his sexism and other regressive views, alongside plans for a women's march in Washington, D.C., on January 21, 2017, the day after his inauguration. The aim was "to make a unique collective visual statement which will help activists be better heard" and that people elsewhere could show solidarity by wearing the hat. The hat was simple to knit: a pink rectangle which, when folded and with side seams stitched, formed "ears" —a riposte to Trump who had been caught on video boasting about "grabbing women by the pussy." As well as in Washington, D.C., pussy hats were seen in 673 marches around the world, from Iceland to Antarctica, Guam to the Azores.

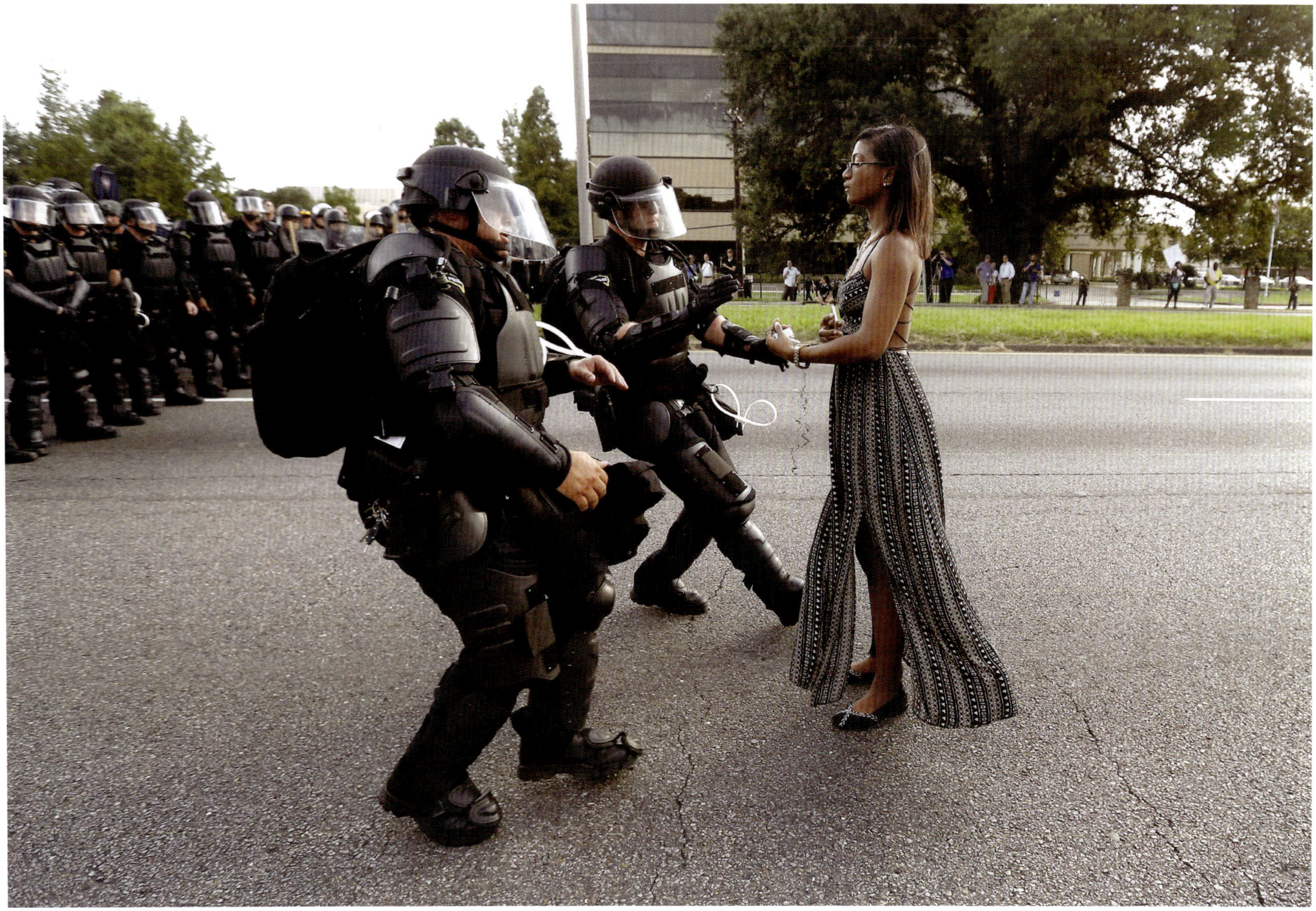

Above: **Jonathan Bachman, Ieshia Evans being arrested at a #BlackLivesMatter rally protesting the shooting death of Alton Stirling, Baton Rouge, LA, July 9, 2016**

#BlackLivesMatter was set up as a movement by three black queer women—Alicia Garza, Patrisse Cullors, and Opal Tometi—in response to the acquittal of George Martin who had killed seventeen-year-old Trayvon Martin in 2012. It grew exponentially as people responded to a series of acquittals of people, including police, who had killed African Americans, and is now a worldwide movement. #BlackLivesMatter has been highly visual in three ways. It has used visuals in its activities and protests, from wearables to images to performative gestures, promoting unity and focus. There have been striking images that have emerged from these protests, often in the form of photojournalism, which have then spread virally. Artists have joined with #BlackLivesMatter to make videos and other works. For example, *The Provocateurs*, a series of twelve-minute videos featuring radical Black artists, was filmed at the California African American Museum in 2017 in the context of the exhibition *We Wanted a Revolution: Black Radical Women, 1965–85.*

I want a dyke for president. I want a person with aids for president and I want a fag for vice president and I want someone with no health insurance and I want someone who grew up in a place where the earth is so saturated with toxic waste that they didn't have a choice about getting leukemia. I want a president that had an abortion at sixteen and I want a candidate who isn't the lesser of two evils and I want a president who lost their last lover to aids, who still sees that in their eyes every time they lay down torest, who held their lover in their arms and knew they were dying. I want a president with no airconditioning, a president who has stood on line at the clinic, at the dmv, at the welfare office and has been unemployed and layed off and sexually harrassed and gaybashed and deported. I want someone who has spent the night in the tombs and had a cross burned on their lawn and survived rape. I want someone who has been in love and been hurt, who respects sex, who has made mistakes and learned from them. I want a Black woman for president. I want someone with bad teeth ~~and an attitude~~, someone who has eaten ~~that nasty~~ hospital food, someone who crossdresses and has done drugs and been in therapy. I want someone who has committed civil disobedience. And I want to know why this isn't possible. I want to know why we started learning somewhere down the line that a president is always a clown: always a john and never a hooker. Always a boss and never a worker, always a liar, always a thief and never caught.

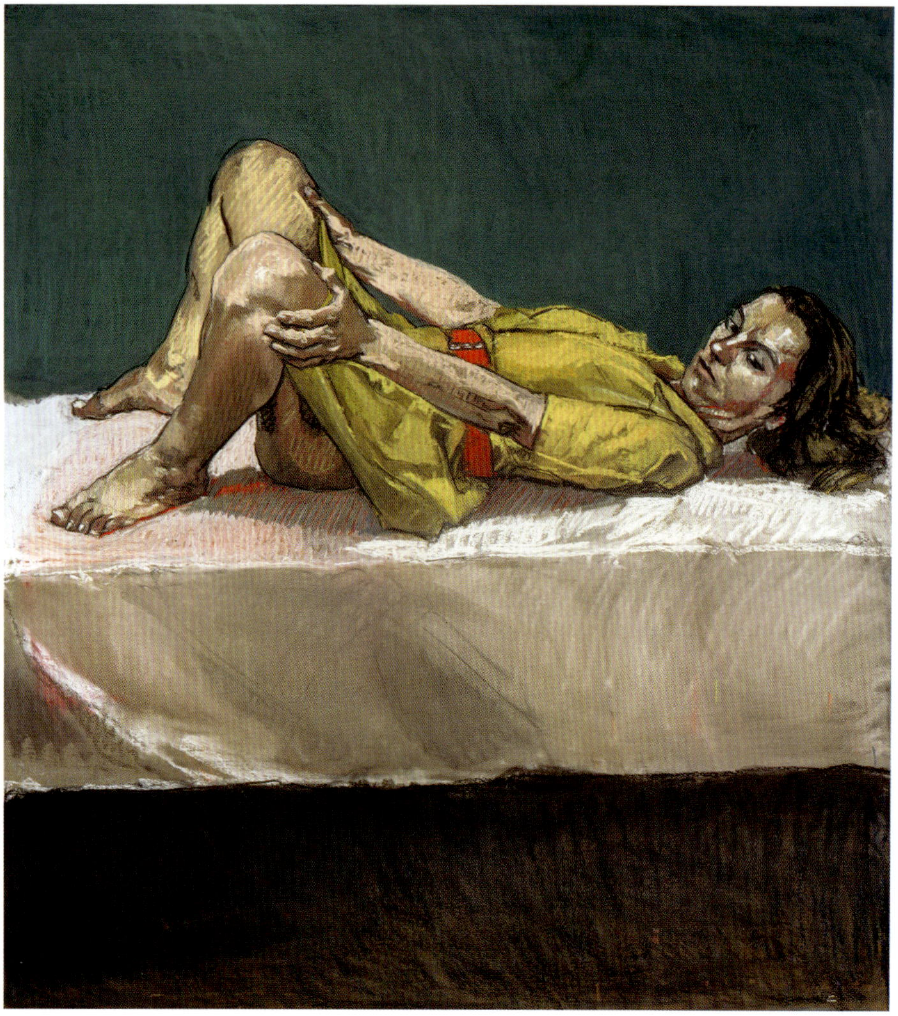

Above left: Zoe Leonard, *I Want a President*, 1992

I Want a President is a statement by artist Zoe Leonard, written in 1992, when George H.W. Bush, Bill Clinton, and Ross Perot were running to be president of the United States. Its hard-hitting comments about the forms of disempowerment that collectively affect a majority of U.S. citizens emphasizes the privileged positions that these three men came from. The statement was to have been published in an LGBT journal, but circulated as an anonymous text before finally being published by the feminist and queer arts collective *LTTR* in 2006. In 2008 it was distributed as a handout and in other formats at a queer film festival in Sweden. Before their general election in 2010, a group of Swedish feminist artists and activists worked with Zoe Leonard on edits to suit the Swedish situation, and arranged a mass reading of the text. Similar readings have taken place in many countries before general elections, including Lithuania (2011), Denmark (2011), Spain (2011), Finland (2012), France (2012), U.K. (2015), and again in the United States in 2016.

Above right Paula Rego, *Triptych*, 1998

Paula Rego is not known for being an activist artist: Her paintings allude more to personal and familial dramas, folk and religious mythologies, often drawn from her Portuguese background. When a referendum on liberalizing highly restrictive abortion laws was held in Portugal in 1998, under 32 percent of the population voted and the proposal was defeated by 51 percent to 49 percent of voters. Rego was angered by the hypocrisy of those who did not vote. She described the devastating effect of backstreet abortions on women, causing mutilation and sometimes death—after which women's bodies would be dumped in the sea. She painted *Triptych* (of which the central panel is shown) and made associated prints out of anger, showing very young women, some in school uniform, alone after an abortion had been performed, clearly in distress, in pain, and isolated. Following the exhibition of her works in Portugal, Rego was willing for them to be used in campaigns for access to safe abortions. A second referendum was held in 2007, with 44 percent turnout, and 59 percent of those, in favor of liberalization.

Paula Rego's paintings on the subject are not intended to impact legislation or medical care directly. Rather, Rego is using her skills as a narrative painter to draw the gallerygoer into considering something more than figurative painting and the disinterested representation of the human condition. Specifically, she presents us with a nonjudgmental representation of the experience of schoolgirls getting backstreet abortions—something that was common in Rego's home country of Portugal. As a skilled painter, Rego works to affect the gallerygoer in all her work; here, the paintings are unlikely to change the point of view of the viewer, but they will certainly challenge them to confront what such an experience might be like and shake them out of apathy. This happened in Portugal: The paintings were made in response to a referendum on the subject in which fewer than one-third of people voted. The response to the paintings helped build concern so that, at the time of a second referendum, there was a larger turnout, with a clear majority in favor of legal changes. In contrast, at a far remove from Rego's work, Women on Waves engage directly with providing information about and drugs (not surgery) for early abortion. This is not an art project, but it started off as a design problem: How to design a process where medically sound information about safe and early abortion could legally be given to women in countries where abortion is illegal? The answer brought together legal expertise, clinic design, graphic design, service design, and marine design, to produce a robust boat that could stay in international waters, beyond the legal jurisdiction of any one country, and a process whereby women could access the information.

Another approach to feminist art is to address political and cultural issues that are not specifically feminist issues or issues that primarily affect women, but that are given feminist analysis. Zoe Leonard's text work, *I Want a President* was made for an LGBT arts magazine in 1992, but the journal closed before it could be published. It is written on behalf of the dispossessed: women, trans people, queer people, the sick, the poor, the unwanted. The text was distributed as photocopies and was eventually published by *LTTR* in 2006. Some Swedish artists—Malin Arnell, Kajsa Dahlberg, Johanna Gustavsson, and Fia-Stina Sandlund—who saw it wanted to perform a public reading at the time of their General Election in 2010, and worked with Leonard to adapt it for the Swedish circumstances. They were followed by public readings at general election times by groups in Estonia, Denmark, and Spain (2011), Finland, France, and Puerto Rico (2012), the United Kingdom (2015) and the United States (2016). Thus it has entered the political arena organically, although that was not the original intention of the artist.

In contrast, the organization Black Lives Matter was founded with political intent, and has engaged artists and visual practices to make its messaging, interventions, and campaigns stronger. It was founded in response to the acquittal of the murderer of black teen Trayvon Martin, by three women who thought that black liberation movements too often marginalized women, queer, and transgender people. Thus, it includes radical gender politics throughout its ways of working. It is also acutely aware of the power of visibility, visual signals, and of looking. As a result it works with artists such as Tatyana Fazlalizadeh (famous for setting up the project Stop Telling Women To Smile) in developing the annual Black Futures Month, in February 2017. Also, Black Lives Matter incorporates powerful performative visual signals into its demonstrations, such as the gesture of demonstrators lifting both hands in the air while chanting "hands up don't shoot," which results in many memorable documentary photographs and carries the message of presence and resistance into newspapers, TV news, and social media platforms.

Artists who address politics from within the art world, and activist artists who intend to have impact beyond it, can be the same person at different times. This is true of both Tanja Ostojić, from former Yugoslavia, and South African artist Zanele Muholi. Both could be described as "political" or as "activist" at different times or in relation to different projects. Ostojić has dealt overtly with political issues, political and legal structures, and public interventions in her work. Muholi has instigated activist projects directly, and has used her abilities as an artist not only in gallery spaces, but as a means through which activism can be practiced.

When we think of activism, we often think of street demonstrations. What the artists and the collective groups in this chapter can teach us is the effectiveness of thinking strategically about visual activism, and what they show is how effective the right strategy can be in the right place at the right time.

Below and bottom left: **Women on Waves, Portugal 2004 (top), Ireland 2001 (bottom)**

Each year, it is estimated that two million women worldwide have illegal, unsafe abortions, and 47,000 die from the consequences: one every nine minutes. While abortions are very safe medical procedures when carried out in clinics, illegal abortions are highly risky. Rebecca Gomperts, a Dutch woman who trained as an artist and as a doctor, helps women who cannot access safe abortions, by interweaving design, medicine, and the law. The design issue was to create a portable clinic of high medical standards and robust enough to travel on a boat; the legal issues are to work within Dutch medical laws and international shipping laws. In 1999 Gomperts designed a clinic in a shipping container. On a boat, she travels legally to offer women who are under six weeks pregnant medical abortifacient drugs while in international waters. Women on Waves was presented at the 2001 Venice Biennale as an art project, and has worked with artists and designers on exhibitions about abortion and spoof ads for Deisel fashion to bring attention to the abuse of women's rights in the fashion industry.

Below right: ***Barbara Kruger, Untitled (Pro-Life for the Unborn/ Pro-Death for the Born), 2000–04***

In her early twenties, Kruger worked as a graphic designer for women's magazines, but stopped in 1969 in order to work as an artist. Her graphic design skills are at the fore in all her work, where she uses easily understandable graphics and slogans to address complex issues. Here, she points out the contradictions inherent in President George W. Bush calling himself "pro-life" (that is, anti-abortion), while waging a war that killed anything between 151,000 (Iraq Family Health Survey) and 601,000 (*The Lancet*) on the Iraqi side; 190 media workers; and 4,400 U.S. troops (U.S. Dept. of Defense), and approximately 300 other nationality coalition troops.

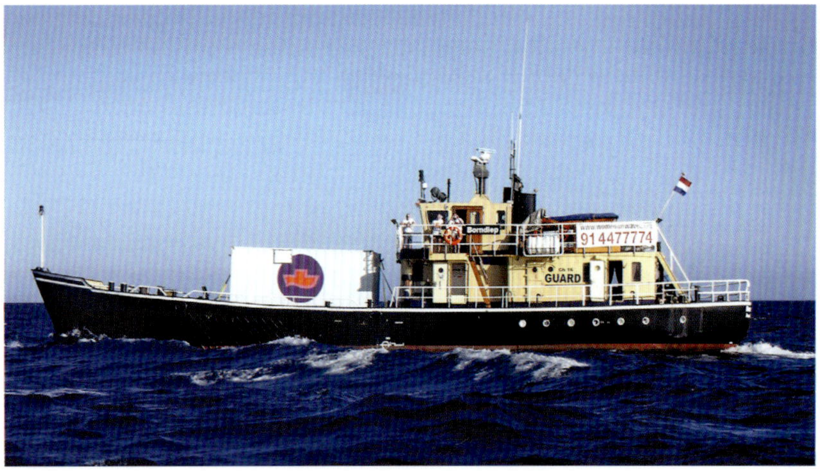

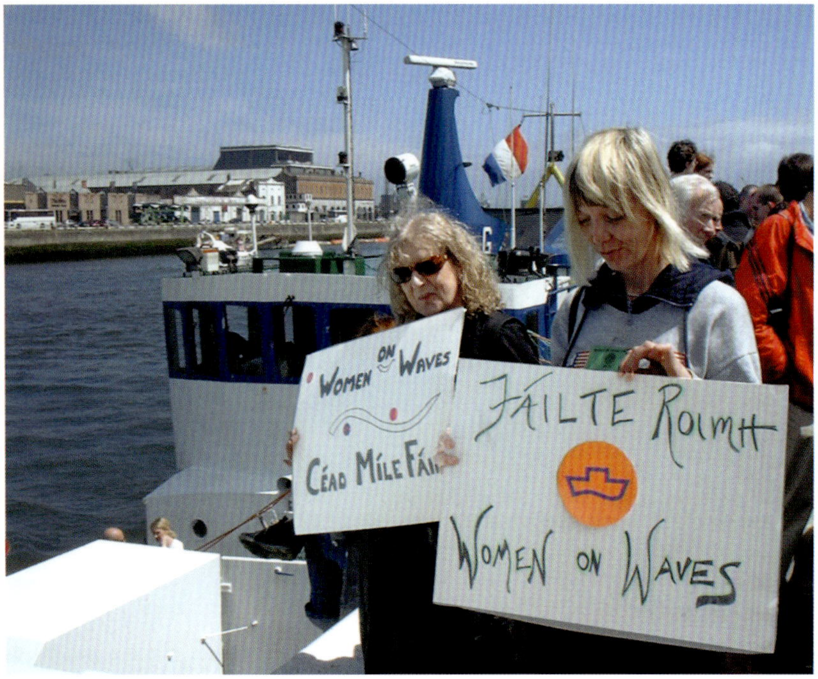

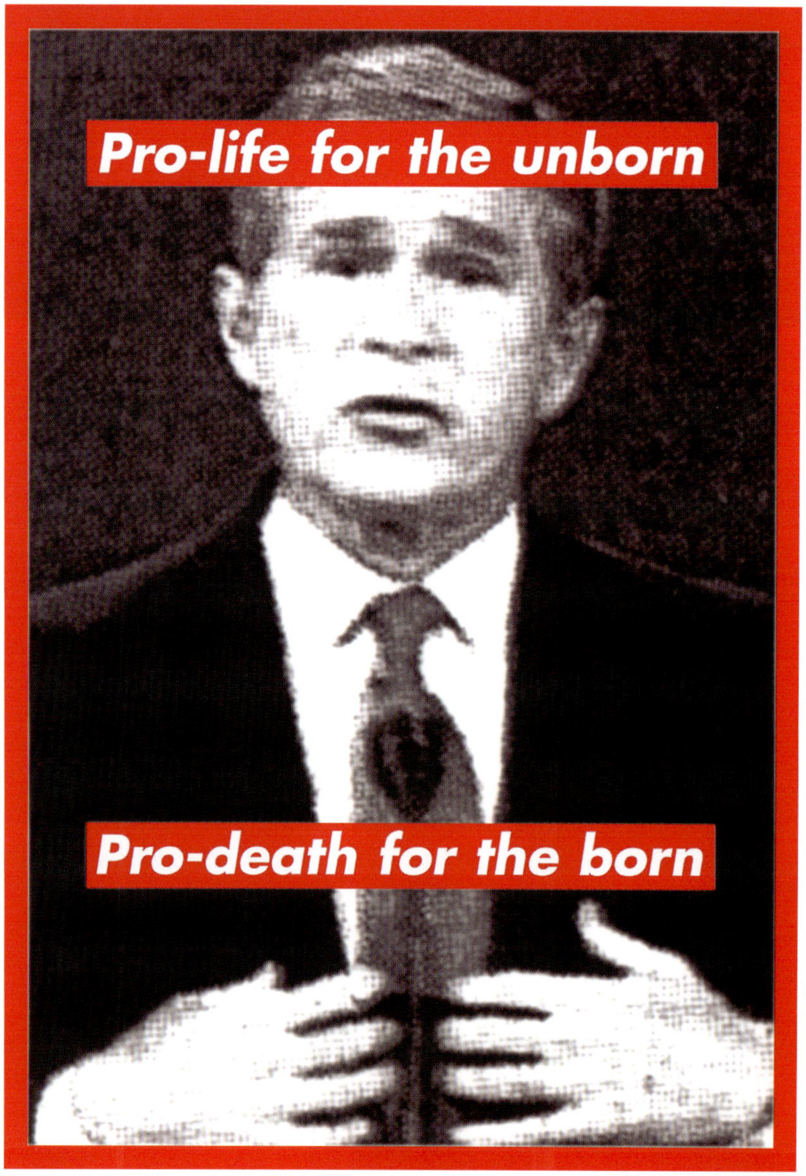

Right: **Andrea Bowers, *Trans Liberation: Building a Movement (Cece McDonald)*, 2016**

Andrea Bowers is an American artist whose art is entwined with her activism and whose engagement with different issues, communities, and individuals informs her work. She addresses the problem of how to represent issues in their full complexity rather than reduce them to visual slogans, and how to remedy the absence of particular communities without reductively pointing at them. Bowers has collected an archive of revolutionary graphic art from the late nineteenth century onward that features activist women. She observed the lack of representation of trans women in such imagery and addressed this in her 2016 exhibition *Whose Feminism is it Anyway?* in New York. This focused on three activist trans women of color: Jennicet Gutierrez, Cece McDonald, and Johanna Saavedra. In her photograph of Cece McDonald, Bowers echoes nineteenth-century English socialist artist Walter Crane's *In Memory of the Paris Commune* (1891): a central angel figure, with spread wings and a hammer tucked in her belt, and a city at her feet in the background. Using such elements from left-radical graphics, Bowers reinserts trans women into the tradition of resistant political representation.

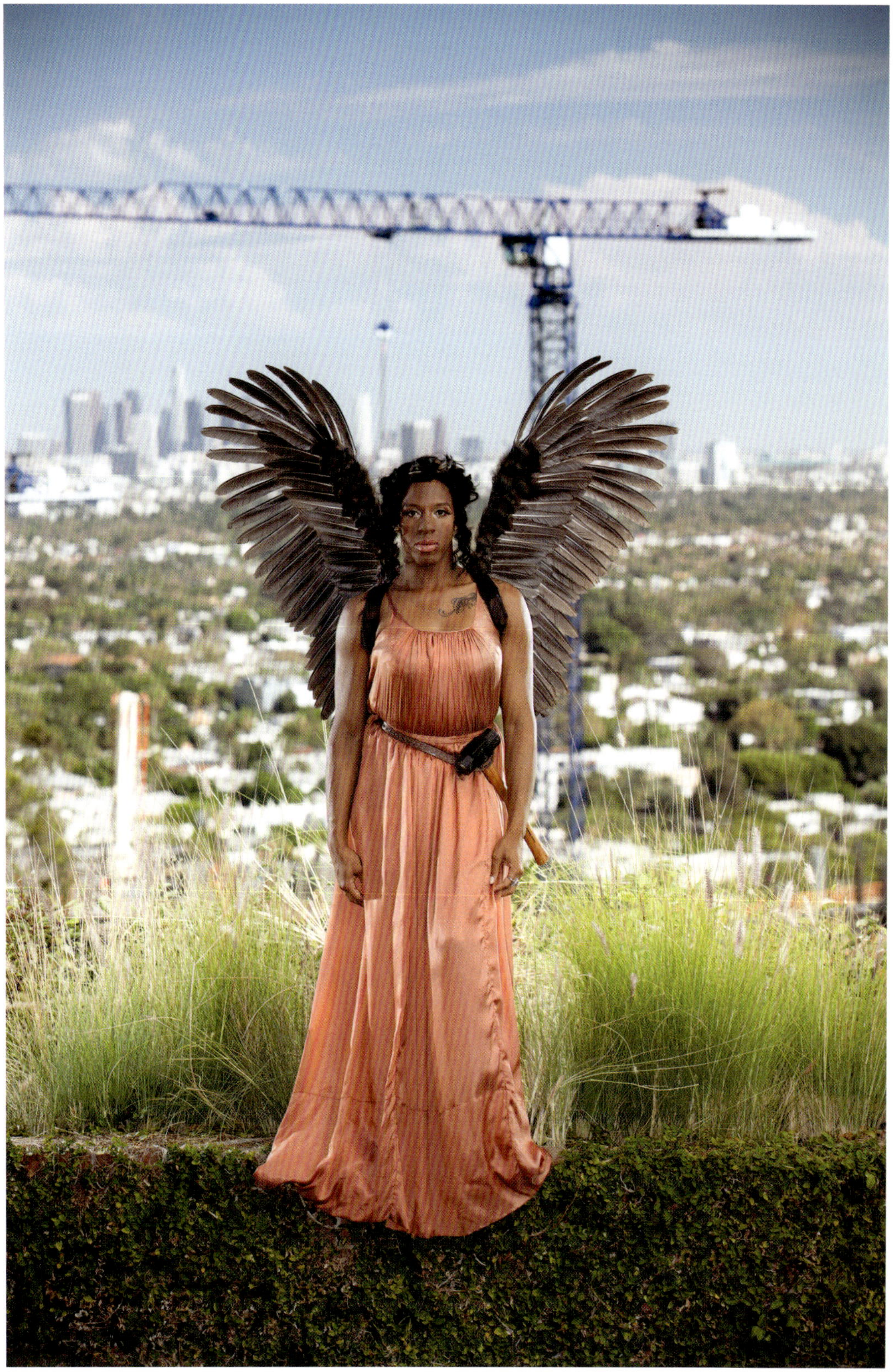

Migration: Tanja Ostojić

The work of Tanja Ostojić focuses on the rights of women to be in particular places and to travel across borders. Beyond this, her work addresses the economic precariousness that women have to endure and their strategies of resilience, and the monitoring of identities in law and at boundaries.

The spur for Ostojić's work is not hard to find: She was born in former Yugoslavia. In World War II, the fascist Axis countries had invaded Yugoslavia, led by Germany, Italy, and Hungary; between 1941 and 1945 over one million people of the population of 15.4 million were killed. Following the war, Yugoslavia became a socialist federal republic, respecting the plurality of national identities, but did not align itself with the Soviet Union. However, ethnic and religious tensions grew in the 1980s and, following the collapse of the USSR, a series of bloody wars from 1991–2001 saw ethnic cleansing, the use of rape as a weapon of war, and over 130,000 deaths. Yugoslavia broke up into seven independent states. Ostojić now claims no national allegiance.

During the late 1990s, while the Yugoslav wars were continuing, Ostojić noted the increasing number of websites where women from Eastern European countries would advertise themselves as available for marriage to men from the EU countries. These women were desperate to leave the situations they were in and were highly vulnerable, often traumatized. By marrying EU nationals, they hoped to gain freedom; however, many were trapped into unlooked-for sex work or domestic slavery. For those who were not given papers by the traffickers or their new EU husbands, having left everything in their former homes—and sometimes also facing racist and nationalist abuse from their new EU neighbors—they were now living in appalling situations.

These websites functioned as shadowy versions of the dating websites that were growing: The women would dress up for their photographs and generally make themselves attractive for potential husbands. In 2000, Ostojić produced a photograph that exposed what was actually going on with these sites: a frontal image of herself naked, expressionless, all her body hair shaved off, and the slogan "Looking for a husband with a EU passport" up one side. She posted it online with the invitation to contact her at hottanja@hotmail.com. The nature of the exchange on these sites was revealed: nothing to do with love, but the need of women to leave war-torn former Yugoslavia, appealing to the desire of random men to have access to their bodies and control over their futures.

Ostojić exchanged over five hundred emails with people—mainly men in the EU—and entered a six-month correspondence with a German media artist, Klemens Golf. She made it clear from the start that this was an art project, and that there would be no sex and no romance involved. They met as a sixty-minute, live-streamed performance in front of the Museum of Contemporary Art, Belgrade, in November 2001, and then married in January 2002, having agreed that either could divorce the other whenever they wished, and there would be no financial or property implications. The wedding, in a registry office, was also presented by Ostojić as an artwork, in the medium of law: There were only two witnesses at the actual event, other than the participants, and it exists now only as documentation. Ostojić then obtained a three-year visa followed by a two-year visa to stay in Germany. In 2005, she and Golf divorced, also celebrated as a performance party in a German gallery.

"Migrants are constantly abstracted by the media and discriminatory laws, and often treated as a single alienated group. The aspect of personal and direct speech, as opposed to abstract speech, is an important element throughout my work. I showed myself in that position, with my own story, as well as later collecting the individual stories of others whom I met, so that the audience would get a chance to understand the variety and depth of the matter, and identify with me, with them, with us."

Tanja Ostojić, from "Crossing Borders: Development of Different Artistic Strategies" in *Integration Impossible? The Politics of Migration in the Artwork of Tanja Ostojić*, 2009

While undertaking this work, Ostojić made other related pieces. The Integration Project was a multiyear archival research effort on the politics of exclusion in the EU. For the accompanying *Dinner Discussion* (2004) immigrants, artists, philosphers, and legal political scholars met to discuss themes of diversity of people in the EU without citizen status. The photograph *After Courbet: L'Origine du Monde* (2005) depicted a woman lying in the exact same position as that of the model in Courbet's notorious painting. The only difference in the pose is that, rather than being naked, the woman wears blue panties with the stars of the EU flag on them. The woman is Ostojić herself, a non-EU citizen. Installed as a public billboard project in Vienna, the work was taken down after two days, following public protests. The image, with its message of the sexual politics informing EU identity, was too provocative for Viennese tastes—though it was later presented at the Forum Stadtpark, Graz, Austria—an arts center that was prepared to stand up for this important work.

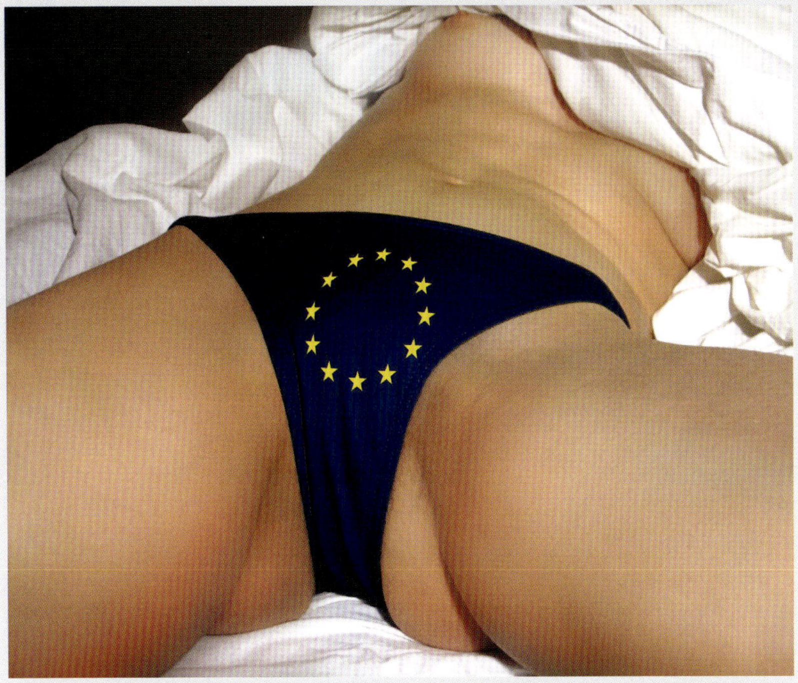

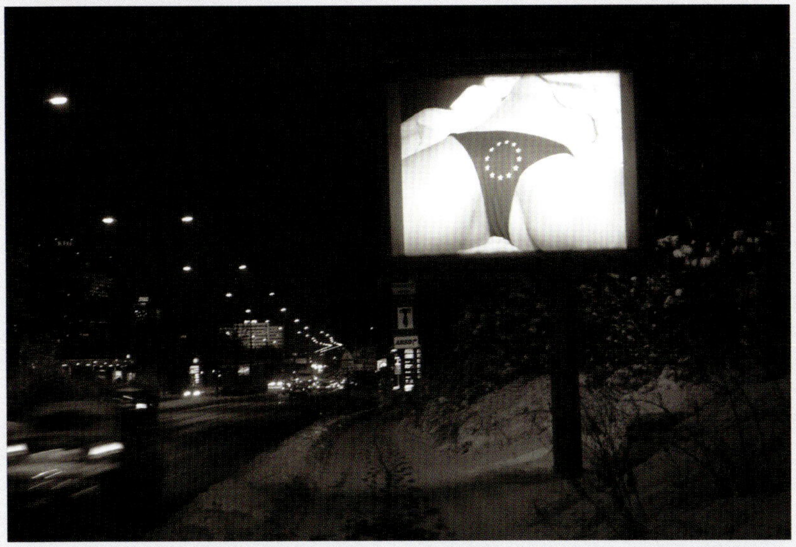

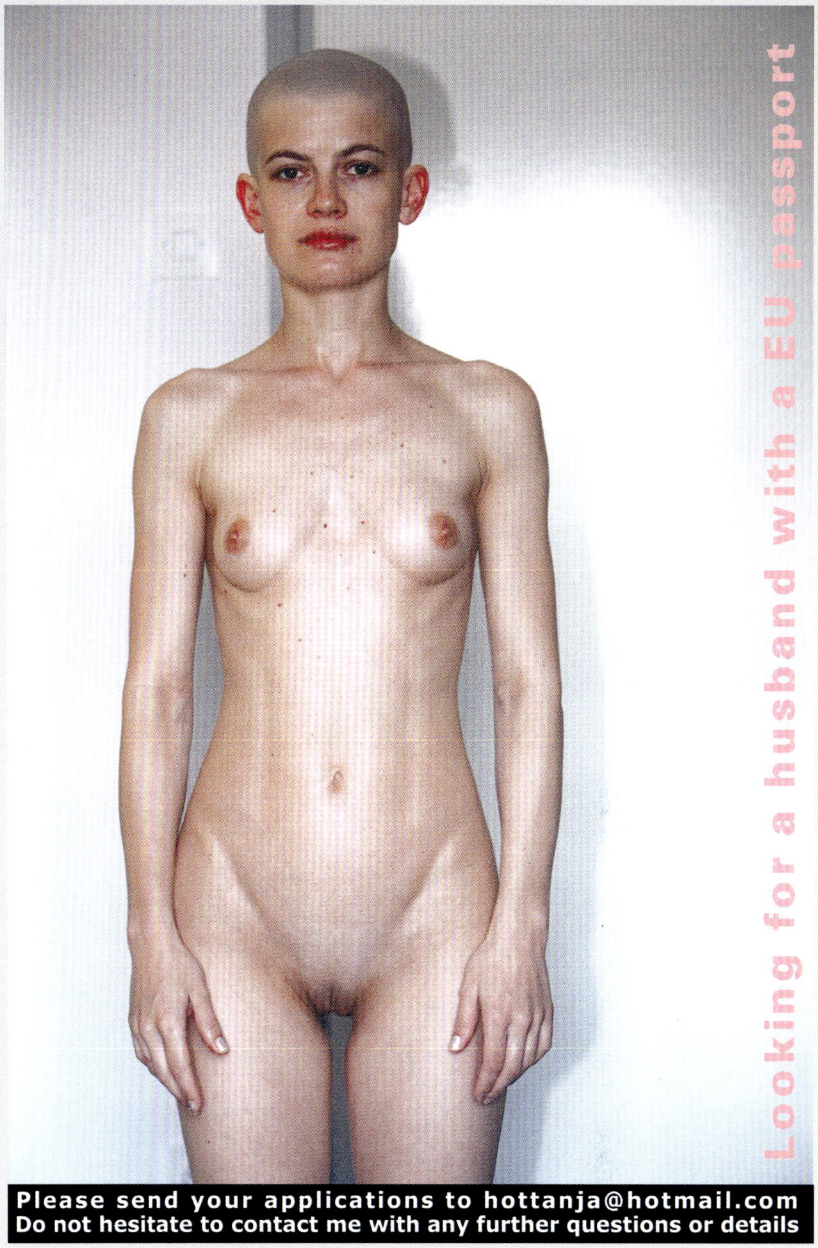

Top and bottom left: **Tanja Ostojić, *Untitled/After Courbet*, photograph and billboard, 2004**

Ostojić used Courbet's *L'Origine du Monde* (1866) as the inspiration for this work, in part because of his engagement with class politics and his belief in the role of art for emancipation through action. The image, however, is clearly located in modern political realities—in particular, the sexual politics of migration across the EU border. This critical message was clear to the Austrian authorities, as they removed the image from a billboard at a public art festival, EuroPart, in Vienna, where it had been posted at the time that the Austrian prime minister was about to start his term as president of the EU.

Above right: **Tanja Ostojić, *Looking for a Husband with a EU Passport*, 2000–05, detail.**

Ostojić posted this image online to expose the nature of the websites on which women were advertising themselves for marriage in order to leave the region of the former Yugoslavia, which was beset with civil wars. Her four-year marriage as an art project incorporated attempts to gain permanent visas, and coincided with other works that exposed the economic, sexual, and social realities of migration for women, including minority Roma women.

Below: **Pussy Riot, "Mother of God, Drive Putin Away," 2012**

On February 21, 2012, Moscow feminist punk band Pussy Riot staged an unannounced performance in the Cathedral of Christ the Savior. Founded in 2011, and instantly recognizable by their brightly colored balaclavas (to maintain anonymity), dresses, and tights, Pussy Riot would film their guerrilla public performances and post them online. In the cathedral they performed "A Punk Prayer" on a raised platform reserved for pronouncements by the clergy or for giving communion. The song included lines like "Virgin Mary, Mother of God, banish Putin," "KGB's chief saint descends to guide the punks to prison vans," and "Virgin Mary, Mother of God, be a feminist, we pray thee." This was to protest against the Orthodox church's support for the increasingly autocratic Putin. After cathedral workers broke up the performance, Nadezhda Tolokonnikova, Maria Alyokhina, and Yekaterina Samutsevich were arrested, convicted of "hooliganism motivated by religious hatred," and imprisoned. Samutsevich was released on probation in October 2012; Tolokonnikova and Alyokhina were released in 2014 after twenty-one months in prison.

Opposite top: **Teresa Margolles, *Muro Baleado (Culiacán)*, 2009**

Mexican artist Teresa Margolles has made two scuptures called *Shot Wall (Muro Baleado)*. They appear at first to conform to some aspects of minimalist sculpture: uncompromising rectangles of brick. Then the viewer realizes that the pockmarks in the walls are bullet holes, and that these walls have been transported to the gallery from scenes of shootings. *Muro Baleado (Ciuad Juárez)* is the wall from a primary school where four people aged fifteen to twenty-five were killed; *Muro Baleado (Culiacán)* was a garden wall with bullet holes from gunfire between a drug gang and police, where two police officers were killed. Margolles removed the walls (building new ones in their place), and reconstructed them as sculptures. She draws attention to the high rates of violent deaths in Mexico not by showing graphic images, but by showing the actual traces left by the violence. She says: "Between 2006 and 2012 there have been more than 50,000 murders. They have names and surnames, there are people who are going to cry, there is a broken family with a gap. Mexico is a hurt society."

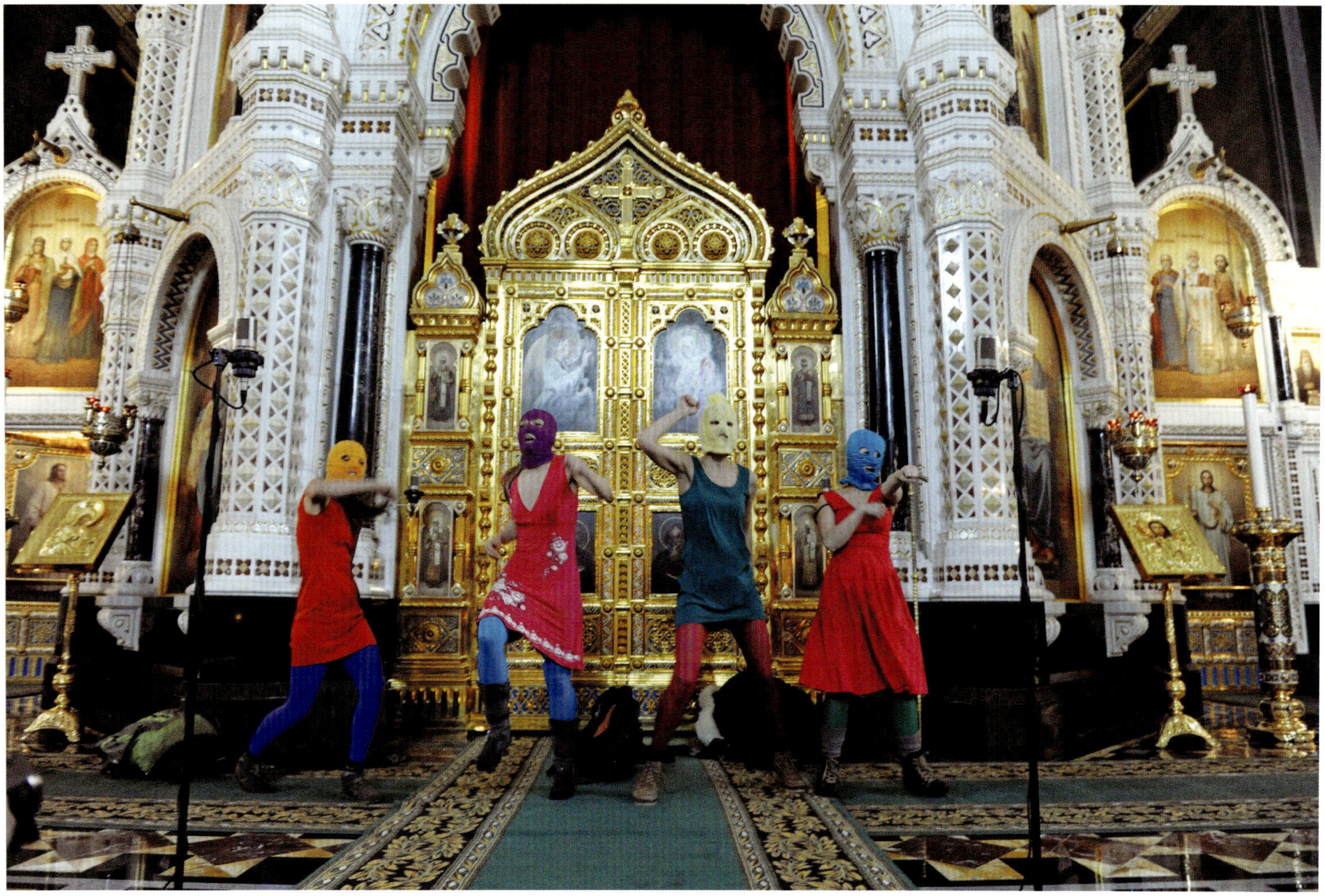

Bottom: **Sethembile Msezane, *Chapungu—The Day Rhodes Fell*, 2015**

On April 9, 2015, the large statue of British colonialist Cecil Rhodes (1853–1902) was removed from its site in the University of Cape Town grounds, in South Africa. Students and others had been protesting its presence as a symbol of white rule and of the slowness of the university to respond educationally to the changes in South Africa since the end of apartheid. On the day it was removed, MFA student Sethembile Msezane stood on a plinth with her back to the statue. She wore a veil of Zulu beadwork over her face, and wings made of wood and hair attached to her arms. At the point the statue was lifted, Msezane lifted her arms. The four-hour performance was titled *Chapungu—The Day Rhodes Fell*, after the bird that appears in sculptures at the eleventh- to fourteenth-century sacred site of the Great Zimbabwe. White explorers plundered these sculptures in the nineteenth century, and the only one that has not been returned is the one that was sold to Rhodes; it remains in the library of his house in Cape Town.

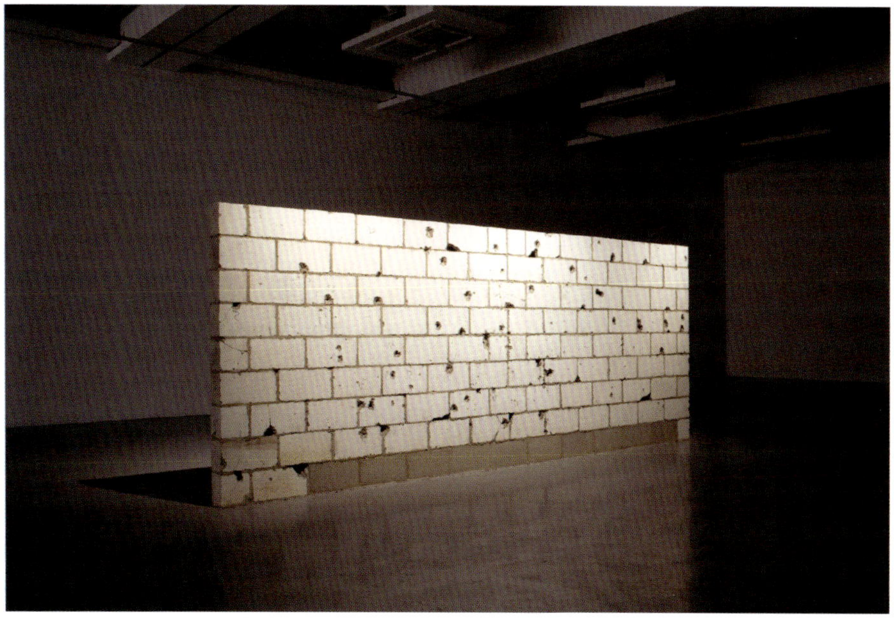

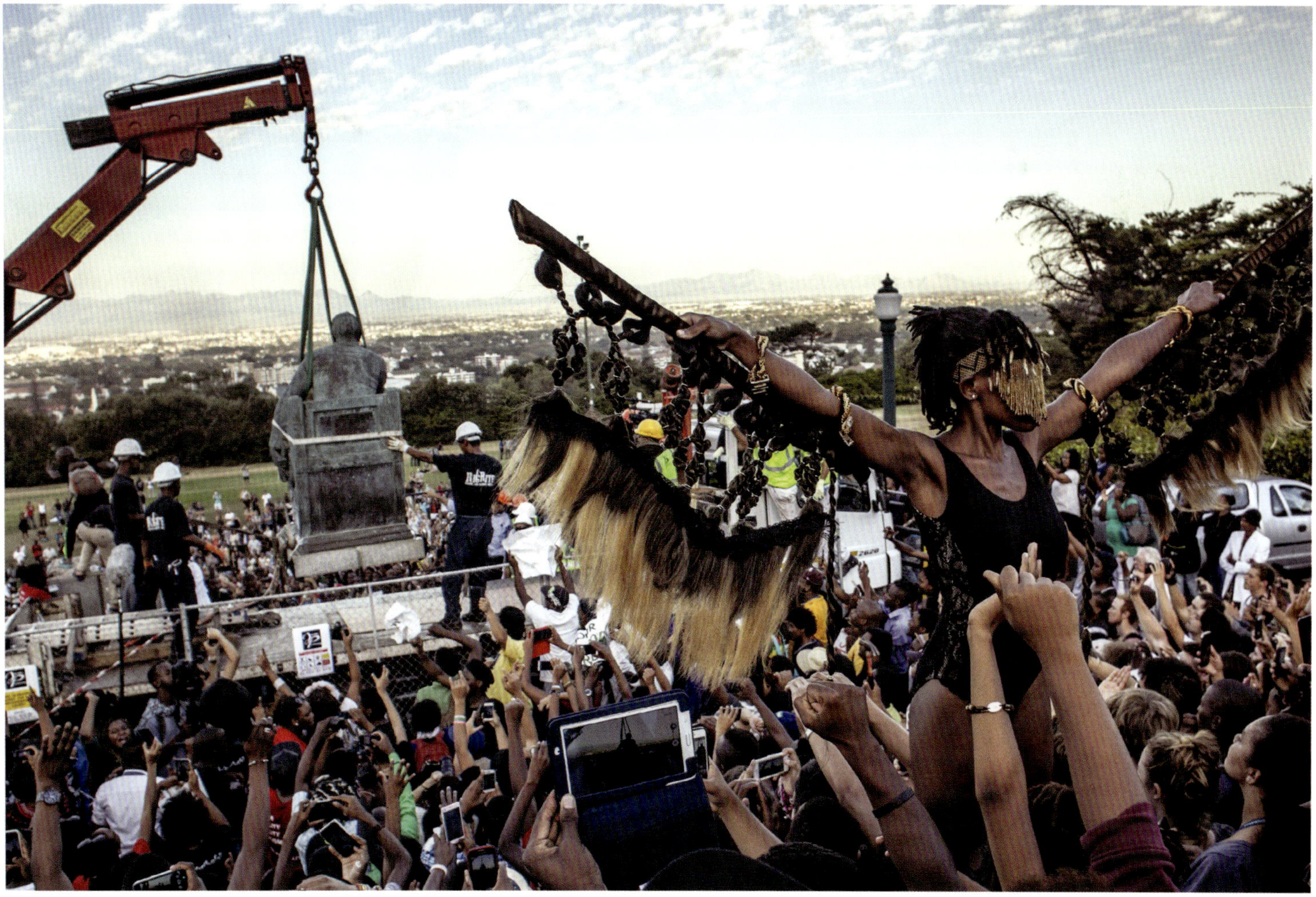

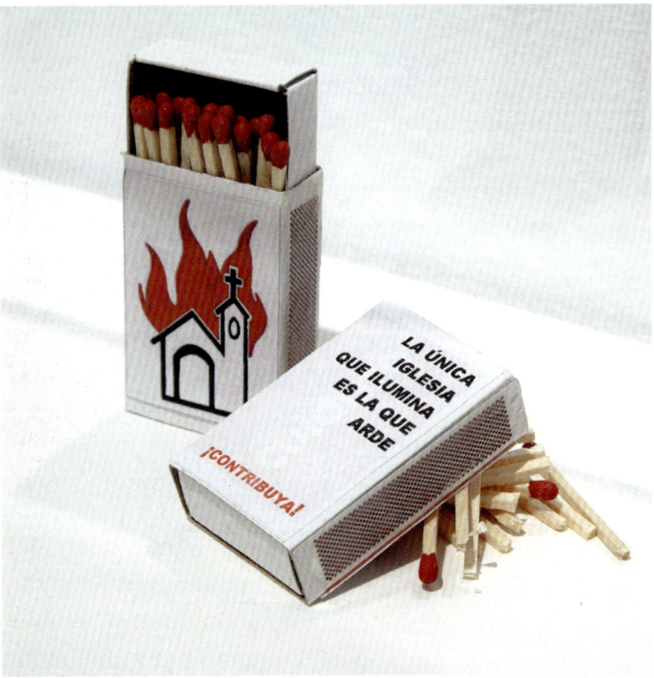

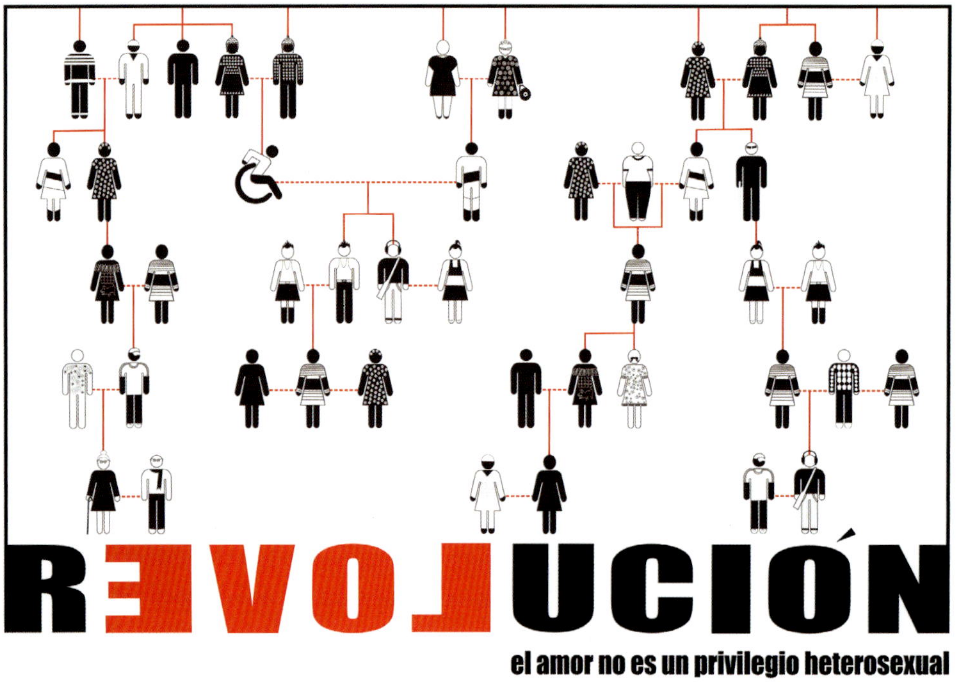

Above left: **Mujeres Públicas, *Cajita de fósforos* (*Matchbox*), 2005**

The Argentinan collective Mujeres Públicas began its work in 2003, using public spaces as a stage where their messages can be transmitted, amended, taken into schools and homes. For their *Matchbox* project (*Cajita de fósforos*), Mujeres Públicas affixed the graphic of a burning house onto the lids of regular boxes of matches, and on the reverse the statement of late-nineteenth-century anarchist theorist Piotr Kropotkin: "The only church that illuminates is a burning church" (quoted many times by Spanish anarchist Buenaventura Durruti). Mujeres Públicas added the word: "contribute." The matchboxes were distributed in many public places and in 2014 were exhibited in Madrid, Spain, in the exhibition *Useful Knowledge*. Later projects include feminist mapping of women's histories in Buenos Aires, which involved public walks and performances.

Above right: **Mujeres Públicas, *Revolución, el amor no es un privilegio heterosexual* (*Revolution, love is not a heterosexual privilege*)**

This is one of the poster projects of Mujeres Públicas, which was carried out in Buenos Aires, Argentina. The image plays on family trees, or networks of relationships, and the insertion of "love" into the heart of "revolution." The posters were wheat-pasted on all manner of surfaces, covering existing posters, public benches, walls, vans, and other unusual places. The aim, as with all of this collective's urban projects, is to create an alternative environment, intervening in the dominant one, that is inclusive and welcoming of all genders and sexualities.

Opposite top & bottom: Sisters Uncut protesting against cuts to support for victims of domestic violence occupy the red carpet at the premier of the film *Suffragette*, London October 7, 2015 (top). Sisters Uncut occupy Holloway Prison visitors center, London, demanding its reuse for domestic violence services, May 27, 2017 (bottom). Sisters Uncut is an intersectional feminist direct-action collective with a focus on domestic violence and protesting against the cuts in services that leave those trying to escape and survive domestic violence with no routes out. Their methods are highly visual and are designed to capture media attention. The intervention at the London premier of *Suffragette* brought a lot of attention, new members, and a small shift in government funding. As Sisters Uncut said at the time: "The suffragettes took direct action because they couldn't wait any longer for the right to vote. We are taking direct action because we can't wait any longer for survivors' safety . . . as long as violence against women continues, the battle for women's liberation has not yet been won." The occupation of the recently closed Holloway Prison visitors center was to demand its reuse as a center for survivors.

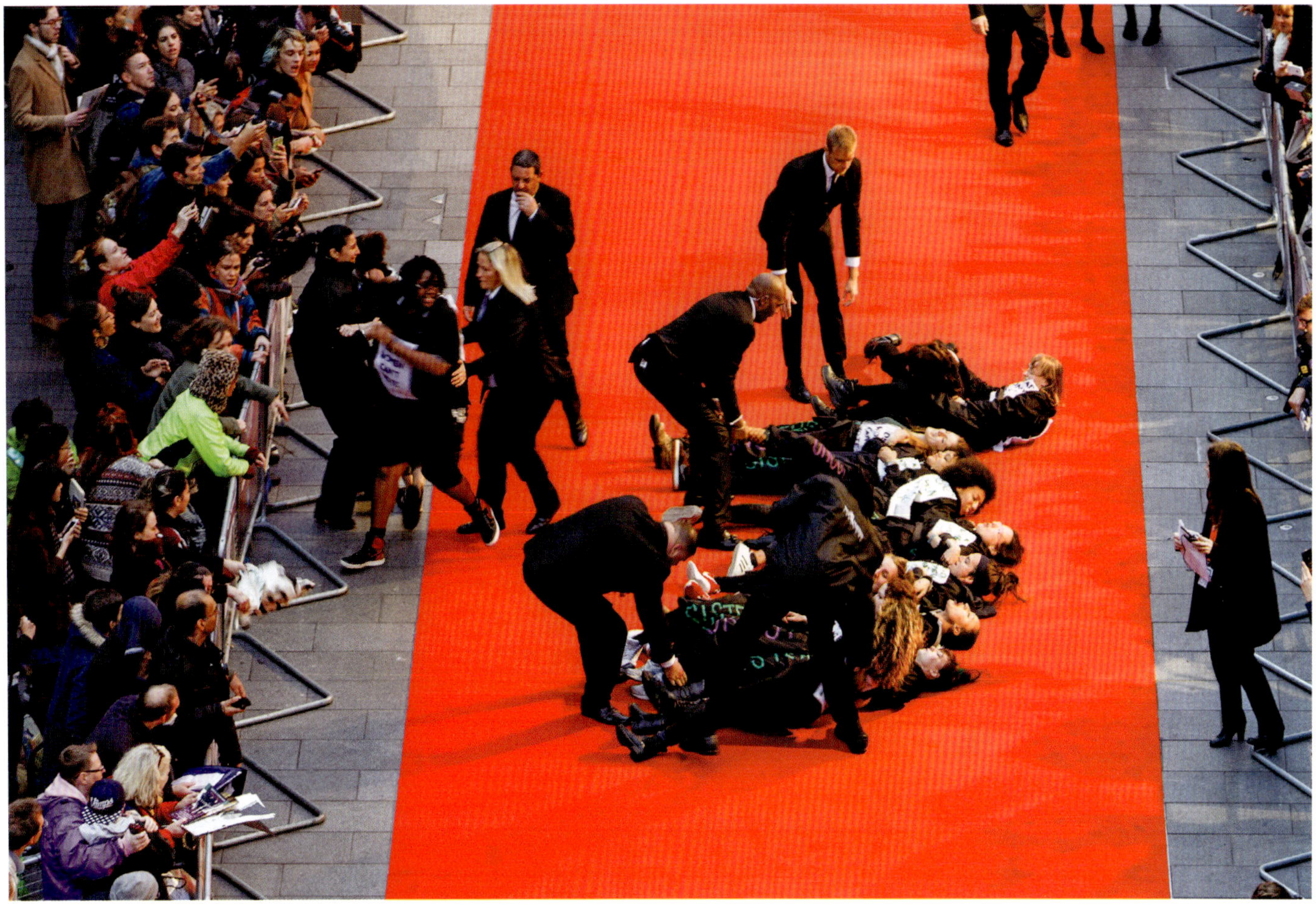

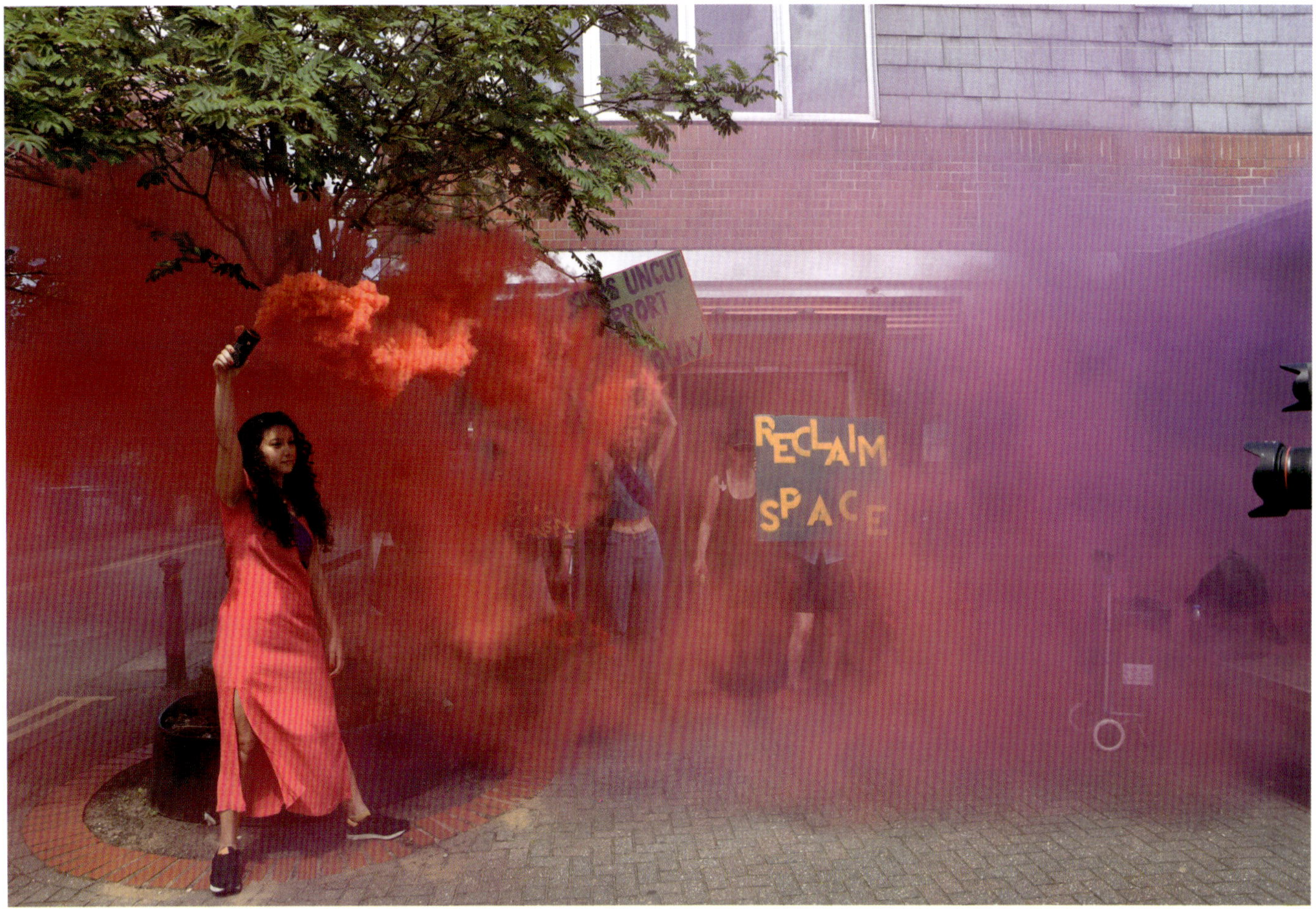
RECLAIM
SPACE

Queer, Black, and Proud: Zanele Muholi

Living and working in South Africa, Zanele Muholi is a visual activist who uses her work to support LGBTQI+ communities. In documenting and making public the queer-, trans-, and gyno-phobic atrocities perpetrated against black lesbians and trans men, she seeks to find ways of making their lives and dignity visible.

On April 20, 2012, Zanele Muholi's flat in Vredehoek, Cape Town, South Africa, was broken into, rooms trashed and items stolen. Muholi was out of the country at the time; her partner Liesl Theron had returned home late evening to find the devastation. This was no ordinary burglary, however: Theron's belongings were untouched, as was the kitchen; the TV, a printer, some camera equipment, a projector, and other items were left. The only items taken were a laptop and over twenty hard drives holding five years' worth of Muholi's photographic and video work, including her backup copies. Thousands of images and hours of film were lost. It was clear that the theft targeted Muholi's work.

Muholi calls herself not an artist or a photographer, but a visual activist. It is an important distinction. Her background is in activism: She cofounded the Forum for Empowerment of Women (FEW) in 2002, and in 2009 she founded Inkanyiso, a collective forum for visual activism and documentation of queer black lives. She describes her photographic practice as self-care, an alternative to psychotherapy; but it is also a political act. Muholi had no art training until, in her late twenties, and as South Africa freed itself from apartheid, she attended Market Photo Workshop, run by white anti-apartheid photographer David Goldblatt. She then went to Canada for an MFA, graduating 2009. By then, however, her aesthetic and her mission as a photographer were already formed: "To rewrite a black queer and trans visual history of South Africa for the world to know of our resistance and existence at the height of hate crimes." This project needed not only intimate understanding of, and acceptance by, the community—her own community; Muholi also needed to develop the right aesthetic to carry out this task.

Muholi's longest-standing project, *Faces and Phases*, was started in 2006. It is a series of portraits of black lesbians and trans men. The images show them looking at the camera, in solemn black-and-white, mainly from about the waist upward. The backgrounds are generally flat and out of focus: Instead we focus on the person in the photograph, who is creating the image with Muholi. The expressions are vastly different from those in most portrait photographs: There are no posed smiles, no laughs, none of the acting up to the camera often associated with portrait photography. What the faces do express, though, is the intensity of interaction with the photographer in the moment: trust, confidence in the connection, intimacy, and tenderness. The bravery of the moment is also often discernible.

"I dare us to ask why queer bodies remain on the outside of an unquestioned heteronormative sociality. I am inspired by the black, African, diasporic, queer ancestors who came before us, and by those who are living today. I credit all the participants who made this work possible as an act of creative and visual documentation aimed at profiling our queer spirits, and imagining new languages and possibilities for future generations."

Zanele Muholi, from "Ngibonile—I have seen . . ." in *African Women Photographers No. 1: Zanele Muholi*, 2011

South Africa has written into its post-apartheid constitution some of the most progressive legislation in the world regarding diversity, equality, and LGBT rights. In practice, this is not only routinely ignored, but South Africa also witnesses some of the most brutal treatment of black lesbian women anywhere. Many believe that lesbianism is unnatural, un-Godly, and un-African, and that there is a cure for it: rape. Muholi has dedicated *Faces and Phases* to a close friend. "She was a so-called 'curative' rape survivor," says Muholi, and had been subjected to three attacks, which left her with HIV. She died in 2007 aged twenty-five. Such "curative" rapes are often protracted, may involve multiple men, and are mixed with other violent acts. Sometimes the women die. The police are generally not interested in those who go to them to register a rape, especially if the woman is lesbian. The people in the book presentation of *Faces and Phases 2006–14* sometimes speak of their experiences of rape, their fears of violence, and of not knowing at any time who might be watching them; Muholi has only photographed people who are adult, and who are prepared to be recognized with their queer identity.

In 2015 Muholi began a series of self-portraits, *Somnyamma Ngonyama* (*Hail, the Dark Lioness*). In them she uses found objects—often discarded household objects—to adorn herself in surprising ways: ways that frequently echo the insistence of white colonialists that black Africans should wear tribal artifacts in photographs, no matter how inappropriate; or that recall particular figures and images in black cultural history. In these images, Muholi's skin appears extraordinarily black, with a matte, light-absorbing quality. She does not darken her skin, but rather uses manipulation in the printing process to produce the effect. This series is as poetic as the other is documentary, and with the same intensity and purpose: to provide a visual history from within a community that, until now, has not had one.

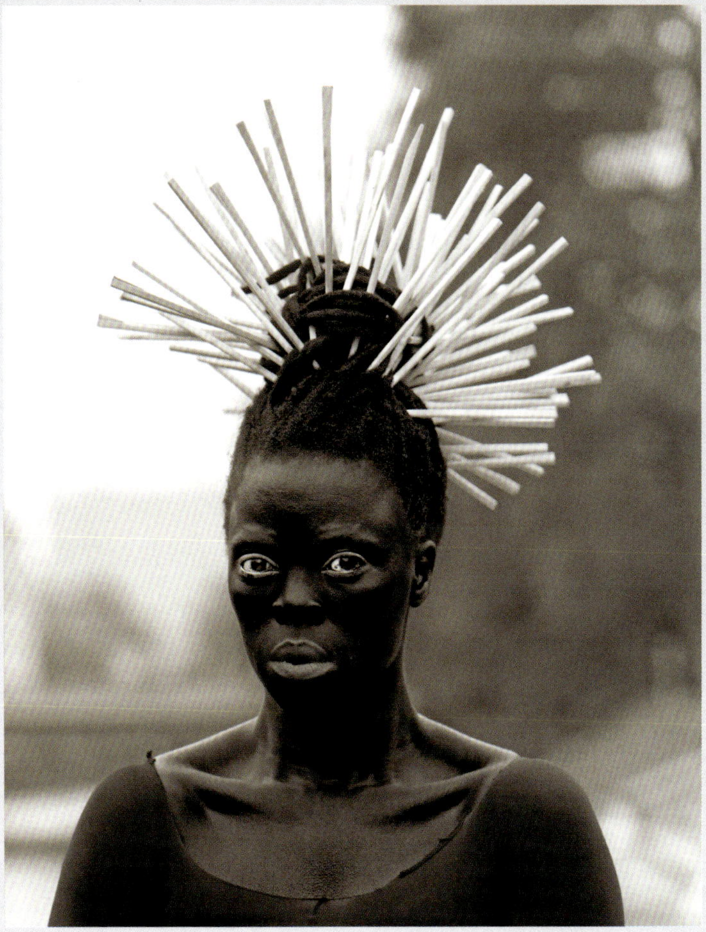

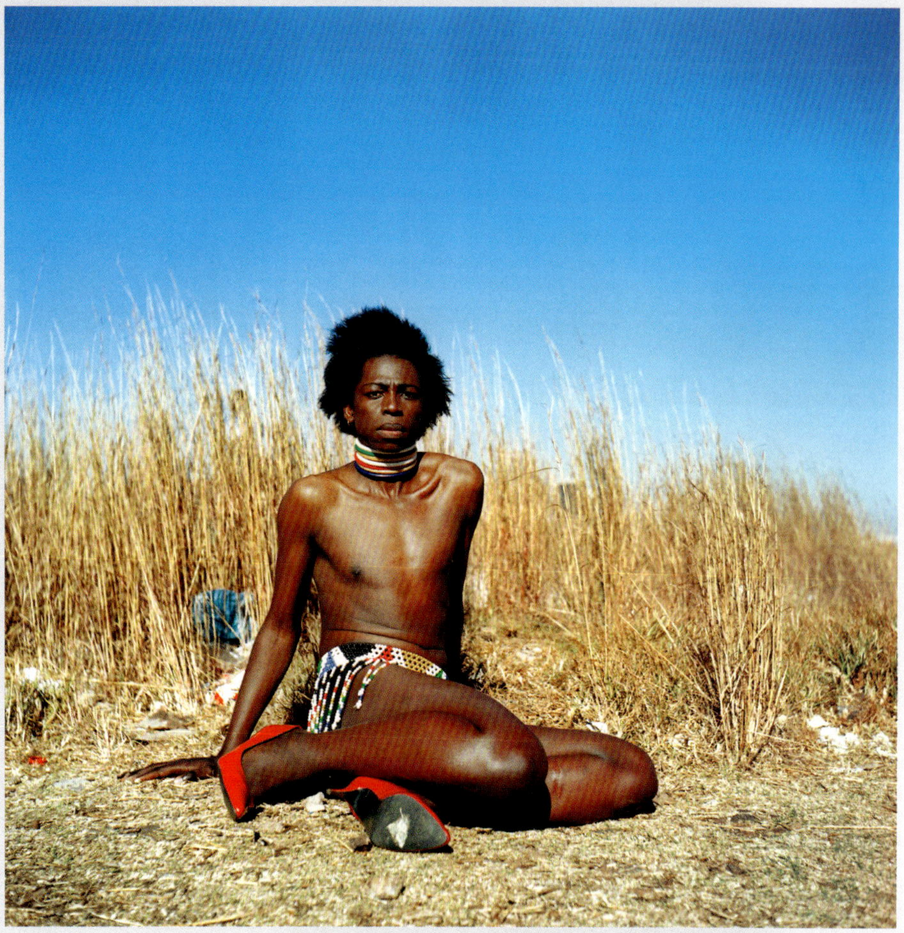

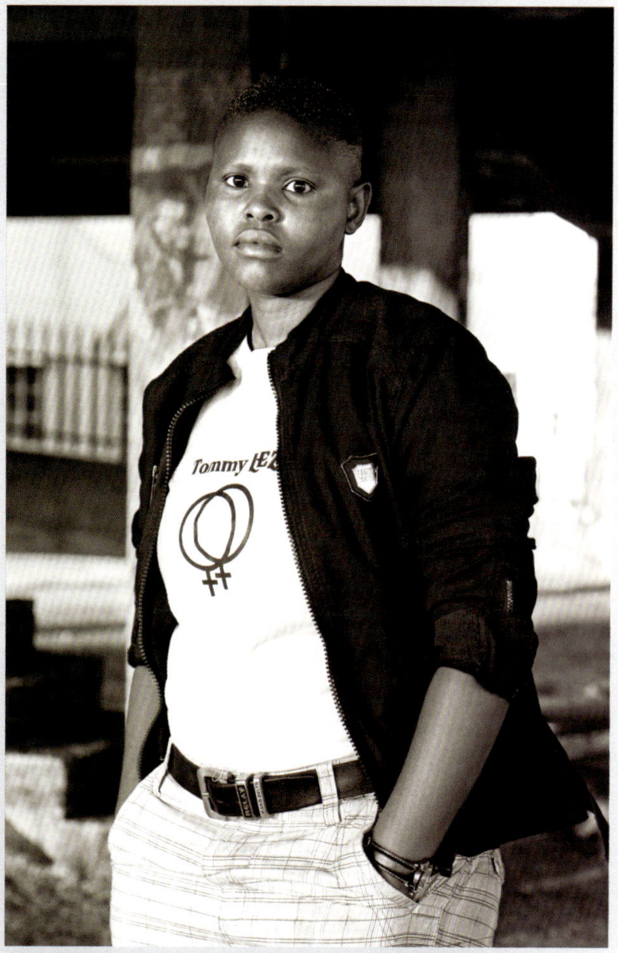

Top left: **Zanele Muholi, from: *Somnyamma Ngonyama (Hail, the Dark Lioness), Ndivile II, Malmo*, 2015**

"I'm only enhancing the contrast in postproduction. I'm speaking of the contrast in a literal sense. What does it mean, contrasting? That confusion, that mix, that fix . . . That's what I'm trying to say, with the heightening of the contrast. Contrast is based on confusion, on confusing. Contrast is when two opposing forces clash. Contrast is about difference. What does the use of high contrast mean in relation to black skin? I get a lot of questions, and comments such as 'I like how she paints her face.' Why would I have to paint my face? [...] I am black 365 days. I don't need to mimic being black."

Top right: **Zanele Muholi, *Miss D'Vine 1*, 2007**

In this photograph, drag queen Miss D'Vine wears traditional South African items, in a subversion of traditional expectations of gender roles and performance.

Bottom right: **Zanele Muholi, from: *Faces and Phases: Noluntu Makalima, Yeoville, Johannesburg*, 2013**

Noluntu Makalima, Yeoville, Johannesburg.

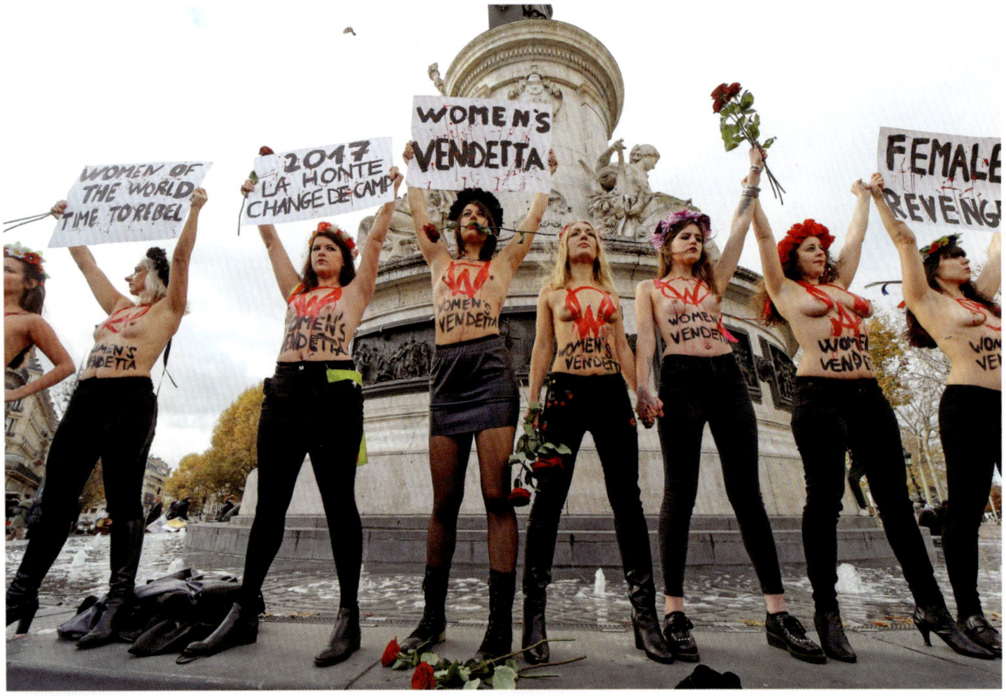

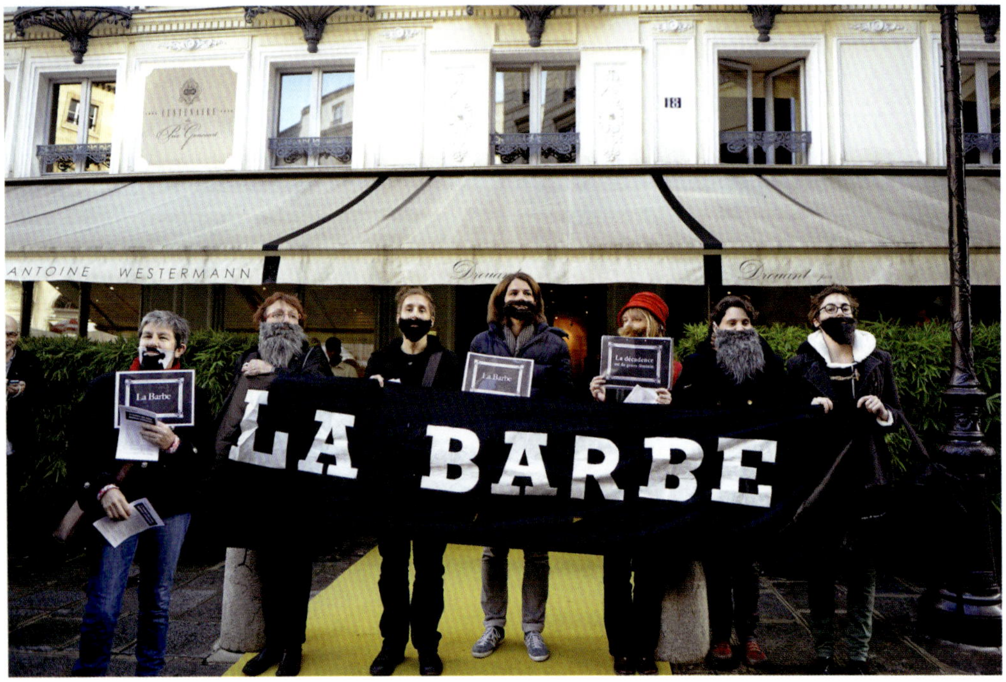

Top: **Femen protest against violence against women, Place de la République, Paris, November 25, 2017**

Femen was formed in the Ukraine in 2008 in order to fight on the three fronts: sexual exploitation of women; dictatorship; and religion. The group discovered that going topless for protests guaranteed media coverage, and so members incorporated this into their protests, usually with slogans written onto their bodies and garlands of flowers on their heads. Increasingly subjected to death threats, the Ukraine office was closed in 2012 and some members moved to Paris, establishing a new office. While its opposition to what they call "political Islam" and its requirement that women wear veils has led to conflict with some Muslim feminists like Chitra Nagarahan, they have worked with others, like artist Aliaa Elmahdy, and some Iranian women have used Femen's topless strategies to protest the hijab. Femen describes its activists as "sextremists" who use their bodies as feminist political instruments.

Bottom: **Members of La Barbe protest in front of the Drouant restaurant in Paris, November 4, 2013**

In French, "la barbe" means not only "the beard," but also "boring," or "this has gone on too long!" French feminist group La Barbe was formed in 2008, following rampant sexism among politicians fighting the first woman candidate for the French presidency. Mary Cenival, a cofounder, was a member of ActUp-Paris: like ActUp's activism around AIDS, so, too, La Barbe uses visual methods and media engagement to make its point. It is simple: The women don false beards and infiltrate all-male or male-dominated political or cultural organizations. They read out ironic texts complementing them on preserving male environments. Here, they protest at the venue of a major literary award ceremony that only recognized men.

Below: Gulabi Gang, rally against violence against woman, November 5, 2009

In 2002 when a friend of Sampat Pal Devi was beaten by her alcoholic husband and the police ignored what had happened, Devi gathered some other women around her and went to their house, where they beat the husband in public view, telling him he should mend his ways. Following this, Devi called upon women to join her in a recognizable group to fight such injustices. The Gulabi Gang was born. Gulabi is Hindi for pink: The women affiliated with the Gang (now said to have anything from 240,000 to 400,000 members) wear pink saris and carry pink-painted sticks. As well as beating abusive men, they campaign peacefully for social justice. They have much to protest: most are poor, of the Dalit caste. Uttar Pradesh has India's highest rates of sexual violence; the disproportionately low number of women in the population speaks to practices of infanticide and femicide. Devi herself was married at the age of nine and sent to live with her husband at twelve. The massed pink saris are a powerful visual signifier of resistance, solidarity, and action in a dispossessed population.

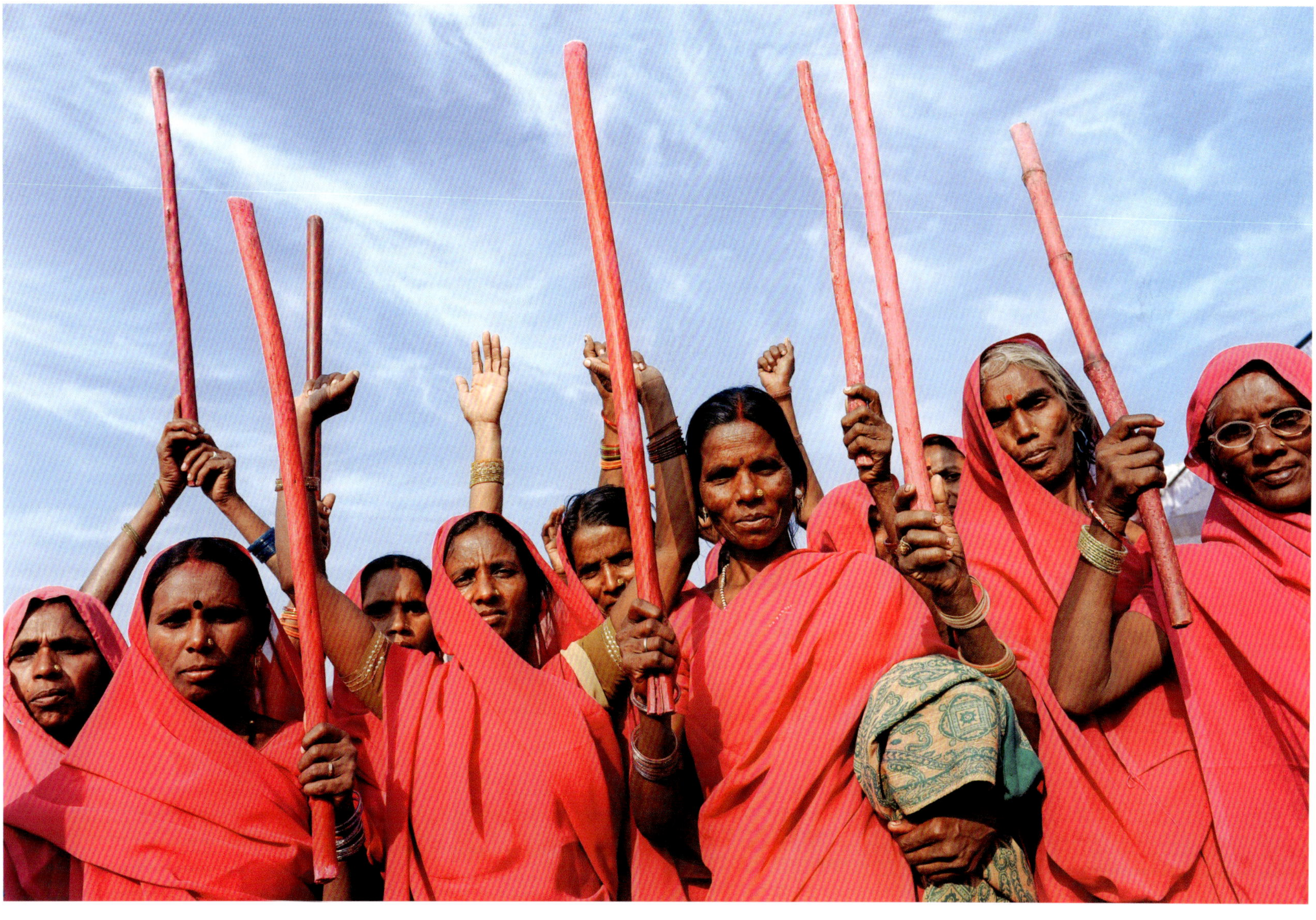

Selected Bibliography

Introduction

Choi, Binna, and Maiko Tanaka, eds. *Grand Domestic Revolution Handbook*. Utrecht: Valiz/Casco, 2014.

Cixous, Hélène, Keith Cohen, and Paula Cohen. "The Laugh of the Medusa," *Signs: Journal of Women in Culture and Society*, Vol. 1, no. 4 (Summer, 1976): 875–893.

Downie, Louise. *"Sans Nom: Claude Cahun and Marcel Moore," Heritage* magazine (2005): 8–14. jerseyheritage.org/media/PDF-Heritage-Mag/Sans%20Nom%20Claude%20Cahun%20%20Marcel%20Moore.pdf, 2005.

Francois-Cerrah, Myrian. "Feminism has been hijacked by white middle-class women," *New Statesman*, 2014. newstatesman.com/politics/2015/02/feminism-has-been-hijacked-white-middle-class-women

Grant, Catherine. "Fans of Feminism: Re-writing Histories of Second-wave Feminism in Contemporary Art," *Oxford Art Journal*, Vol. 34, no. 2 (June 1, 2011): 265–286.

Kokoli, Alexandra M. *The Feminist Uncanny in Theory and Art Practice*. London: Bloomsbury Academic, 2016.

Krasny, Elke, Lara Perry, and Dorothee Richter, eds. "Curating in Feminist Thought," *ONCURATING*, no. 29 (May 2016). on-curating.org/files/oc/dateiverwaltung/issue-29/PDF_to_Download/OnCurating_Issue29_DINA4.pdf

Mulvey, Laura. "Visual Pleasure and Narrative Cinema," *Screen*, Vol. 16, no. 3 (October 1, 1975): 6–18.

Pollock, Grisdela. *Vision and Difference: Feminism, Femininity and Histories of Art*. London: Routledge, 2003.

Preciado, Beatriz. *Testo Junkie: Sex, Drugs, and Biopolitics in the Pharmacopornographic Era*. New York: The Feminist Press, City University of New York, 2013.

Reilly, Maura. *Curatorial Activism: Towards an Ethics of Curating*. London: Thames & Hudson, 2018.

Scourti, Erica. *The Outage: Her Story*. London: Banner Repeater, 2014.

Part 1

Adams, Katherine H., and Michael L. Keene. *Women, Art & the New Deal*. Jefferson: McFarland & Co., 2016.

Allen, Raye Virginia. *Gordon Conway, Fashioning a New Woman*. Austin: University of Texas Press, 1997.

Atkinson, Diane. *Funny Girls, Cartooning for Equality*. London: Penguin Books, 1997.

Aulich, James. *War Posters, Weapons of Mass Communication*. London: Thames & Hudson, 2011.

Borzello, Frances. *A World of Our Own, Women as Artists*. London: Thames & Hudson, 2000.

Calloway, Stephen. *The Cult of Beauty, The Aesthetic Movement 1860–1900*. London: V&A Publishing, 2011.

Campbell Orr, Clarissa. *Women in the Victorian Art World*. Manchester: Manchester University Press, 1995.

Chadwick, Whitney. *Women, Art and Society*. London: Thames & Hudson, 2012.

Cherry, Deborah. *Beyond the Frame, Feminism and Visual Culture, Britain 1850–1900*. London: Routledge, 2000.

Cherry, Deborah. *Painting Women, Victorian Women Artists*. London: Routledge, 1993.

Claridge, Laura. *Tamara Lempicka, A Life of Deco and Decadence*. London: Bloomsbury Publishing, 2000.

Crawford, Elizabeth. *Art and Suffrage, A Biographical Dictionary of Suffrage Artists*. London: Francis Boutle Publishers, 2018.

Deepwell, Katy. *Women Artists between the Wars*. Manchester: Manchester University Press, 2010.

Farrington, Lisa E. *Creating Their Own Image: The History of African-American Women Artists*. Oxford: Oxford University Press, 2013.

Florey, Kenneth. *Women's Suffrage Memorabilia, An Illustrated Historical Study*. Jefferson: McFarland & Co., 2013.

Friedewald, Boris. *Women Photographers from Julia Margaret Cameron to Cindy Sherman*. New York: Prestel Publishing, 2014.

Heller, Nancy G. *Women Artists, An Illustrated History*. New York: Abbeville Press, 1987 (1997 edition).

Howgate, Sarah. *Gillian Wearing and Claude Cahun, Behind the Mask, another Mask*. London: National Portrait Gallery, 2017.

Library of Congress: loc.gov/collections/national-american-woman-suffrage-association/about-this-collection/

Mancoff, Debra N. *Danger! Women Artists at Work*. London: Merrell Publishers, 2012.

National Museum of Women in the Arts: nmwa.org

Nunn, Pamela Gerrish. *Canvassing, Recollections of Six Victorian Women Artists*. London: Camden Press, 1986.

Nunn, Pamela Gerrish. *Victorian Women Artists*. London: Women's Press, 1987.

Palmer, Kathleen. *Women War Artists*. London: Tate Publishing, 2011.

Pankhurst, Richard. *Sylvia Pankhurst, Artist and Crusader*. London: Paddington Press, 1973.

Parker, Rozsika and Griselda Pollock. *Old Mistresses, Women, Art, and Ideology*. New York: I.B. Tauris, 2013.

Peterson, Karen & J.J. Wilson. *Women Artists, Recognition and Reappraisal from the Early Middle Ages to the Twentieth Century*. London: The Women's Press, 1976.

Phillips, Melanie. *The Ascent of Woman, A History of Suffragette Movement and the Ideas Behind It*. London: Little, Brown, 2003.

Rideal, Liz. *Mirror, Mirror, Self-portraits by Women Artists*. London: National Portrait Gallery, 2001.

Rose, Lucy Ella. *Suffragist Artists in Partnership: Gender, Word & Image*. Edinburgh: Edinburgh University Press, 2017.

Sellars, Jane. *Women's Works, Paintings, Drawings, Prints and Sculptures by Women Artists in the Permanent Collection of Museums and Galleries of Liverpool*. Liverpool: National Museums & Galleries on Merseyside, 1988.

Sparham, Anna. *Soldiers and Suffragettes – The Photography of Christina Broom*. London: Philip Wilson Publishers, 2015.

Speck, Catherine. *Beyond the Battlefield, Women Artists of Two World Wars*. London: Reaktion Books, 2014.

Tickner, Lisa. *The Spectacle of Women, Imagery of the Suffrage Campaign 1907–14*. London: Chatto & Windus, 1987.

Tufts, Eleanor. *Our Hidden Heritage, Five centuries of women artists*. New York: Paddington Press, 1974.

Williams, Val. *The Other Observers, Women Photographers in Britain 1900 to Present*. London: Virago Press, 1986.

Woman & her Sphere: womanandhersphere.com/

Part 2

Applin, Jo. *Lee Lozano: Not Working*. New Haven: Yale University Press, 2018.

Bryan Wilson, Julia. *Fray: Art and Textile Politics*. Chicago: University of Chicago Press, 2017.

Butler, Cornelia, and Lisa Gabrielle Mark, eds. *Wack!: Art and the Feminist Revolution*. Cambridge: MIT Press, 2007.

Giunta, Andrea, and Cecilia Jajardo-Hill, eds. *Radical Women: Latin American Art, 1960–1985*. Munich and Los Angeles: Del Monico Press and the Hammer Museum, 2017.

Hak Kyung Cha, Theresa. *Dictee*. Los Angeles: University of California Press, 2009 (Reprint).

Hockley, Rujeko, and Catherine Morris, eds. *We Wanted a Revolution: A Sourcebook*. Durham: Duke University Press, 2017.

Irigaray, Luce. *Speculum of the Other Woman*, translated by Gillian C. Gill. Ithaca: Cornell University Press, 1985.

Jakubowska, Agata, and Katy Deepwell, eds. "All-women art spaces in Europe in the long 1970s," *Value-Art-Politics*. Liverpool: Liverpool University Press, 2018.

Jones, Amelia. *Body Art/Performing the Subject*. Minneapolis: University of Minnesota Press, 1998.

Kelly, Mary. *Imaging Desire*. Cambridge: MIT Press, 1997.

Kerman, Monique. *Contemporary British Artists of African Descent and the Unburdening of a Generation*. Sweden: Springer, 2017.

Knaup, Bettina, and Beatrice Ellen Stammer, eds. *Re.Act.Feminism: A Performing Archive*. reactfeminism.org

Lippard, Lucy R. *From the Center: Essays on Art and Feminism*. New York: E.P. Dutton, 1976.

Lippard, Lucy R. *The Pink Glass Swan: Selected Feminist Essays on Art*. New York: The New Press, 1995.

Lonzi, Carla, and Vai Pure. *Dialogo con Pietro Consagra*. Milan: Scritti di Rivolta Femminile, 1980.

Macmillan, Uri. *Embodied Avatars: Genealogies of Black Feminist Art and Performance*. New York: New York University Press, 2015.

Minh Ha, Trin T. *When the Moon Waxes Red: Representation, Gender and Cultural Politics*. London: Routledge, London, 1991.

Mulvey, Laura. "Visual Pleasure and Narrative Cinema," *Screen*, Vol. 16, no. 3 (October 1, 1975): 6–18.

Murray, Ros. "Raised Fists: Politics, Technology, and Embodiment in 1970s French Feminist Video Collectives," *Camera Obscura*, Vol. 31, no.1 (2016): 93–121.

Parker, Rozsika, and Grisdelda Pollock, eds. *Framing Feminism: Art and the Women's Movement, 1970–1985*. London and New York: Pandora Press, 1995.

Piper, Adrian. "The Triple Negation of Colored Women Artists," *The Feminism and Visual Culture Reader* (2003): 239–248.

Raven, Arlene. *Crossing Over: Feminism and Art of Social Concern*. Ann Arbor: University of Michigan, 1988.

Reckitt, Helena, ed., Peggy Phelan (survey). *Art and Feminism*. London: Phaidon Press, 2001.

Rosler, Martha. *Decoys and Disruptions: Selected Writings 1975–2001*. Cambridge: MIT Press, 2004.

Schor, Gabriele. *Feminist Avant-Garde of the 1970s: Works from the Sammlung Verbund Collection*. Munich: Prestel, 2016.

Schor, Mira. *Wet: Essays on Painting, Feminism and Art Culture*. Durham: Duke University Press, 1997.

Sulter, Maud, ed. *Passion: Discourses on Black Women's Creativity*. Chatham: Urban Fox Press, 1990.

Vergine, Lea. *Body Art and Performance: The Body as Language*. Milan: Skira, 1974 (2nd edition, 2000).

Wilson, Siona. *Art, Labour, Sex Politics: Feminist Effects in 1970s British Art and Performance*. Minneapolis: University of Minnesota Press, 2014.

Wolverton, Terry. *Insurgent Muse: Life and Art at the Woman's Building*. San Francisco: CityLights, 2002.

Ziherl, Vivian, ed. *The Lip Anthology: An Australian Feminist Arts Journal, 1976–1984*. London: Macmillan, 2013.

Part 3

Arakistan, Xabier (ed). *Kiss Kiss Bang Bang: 45 Years of Art and Feminism*. Bilbao: Museo de Belles Artes de Bilbao, 2007.

Berktay, Fatmagül, et.al. eds. *Dream and Reality: Modern and Contemporary Women Artists from Turkey*. Istanbul: Istanbul Modern, 2011.

Blessing, Jennifer. *Catherine Opie: American Photographer*. New York: Guggenheim Museum, 2008.

Burton, Johanna (ed). *Trigger: Gender as a Tool and a Weapon*. New York: New Museum, 2017.

Dimitrakaki, Angela. *Gender, artWork and the Global Imperative: A Materialist Feminist Critique*. Manchester: Manchester University Press, 2013.

Dimitrakaki, Angela, and Lara Perry, eds. *Politics in a Glass Case: Feminism, Exhibition Cultures and Curatorial Transgressions*. Liverpool: Liverpool University Press, 2013.

Ewington, Julie, ed, *Contemporary Australia: Women*. Queensland: Queensland Art Gallery/Gallery of Modern Art, 2012.

Eyene, Christine, ed. *Where We're At! Other Voices on Gender*. Milan: Silvana Editoriale & Bozar Books, 2014.

Fernandez, Maria, Faith Wilding, and Michelle M. Wright. *Domain Errors! Cyberfeminist Practices*. New York: Autonomedia and subRosa, 2002.

Fontaine, Claire. *The Human Strike Has Already Begun & Other Writings, Mute* magazine and Post-Media Lab, 2013.

Frueh, Joanna. *Monster Beauty: Building the Body of Love*. Berkeley: University of California Press, 2001.

Gaspar de Alba, Alicia, and Alma López. *Our Lady of Controversy: Alma López's Irreverent Apparition*. Austin: University of Texas Press, 2012.

Gržinić, Marina, ed. *Integration Impossible? The Politics of Migration in the Artwork of Tanja Ostojić*. Berlin: Argobooks, 2009.

Horne, Victoria, and Lara Perry, eds. *Feminism and Art History Now: Radical Critiques of Theory and Practice*. New York: I.B. Tauris, 2017.

Huangfu, Binghui, ed. *Text and Subtext: International Contemporary Asian Artists Exhibition and Text and Subtext: Contemporary Art and Asian Women*. Singapore: Earl Lu Gallery, 2000.

Jacir, Emily, and Omar Kholeif, eds. *Emily Jacir: Europa*. London: Whitechapel Art Gallery, 2015.

Jones, Amelia, and Erin Silver, eds. *Otherwise: Imagining Queer Feminist Art Histories*. Manchester: Manchester University Press, 2016.

Knaup, Bettina, and Beatrice Ellen Stammer, eds. *Re-Act Feminism: A Performing Archive*, Verlag für Moderne Kunst and Live Art Development Agency, 2014.

Lu, Xiao. *Dialogue*, Hong Kong: Hong Kong University Press, 2010.

Melandri, Lisa. *Mickalene Thomas: Origin of the Universe*. Santa Monica: Santa Monica Museum of Art, 2012

Morineau, Camille, ed. elles@centrepompidou/*Women Artists in the Collection of the Musée National d'Art Moderne Centre de Création Industrielle*. Paris: Centre Pompidou, 2009.

Morineau, Camille. *Niki de Saint Phalle 1930–2002*. Bilbao: La Fábrica and Guggenheim Bilbao, 2014.

Muholi, Zanele. *Faces and Phases 2006–2014*. Göttingen: Steidl Verlag, 2014.

Oehler, Alison Brand, ed. *Vanessa German: The Incredibly True Sometimes Horrific Often Humorous Adventures of a Wacky Black Girl, or, A Visual Ritual Into the Power of the Black Imagination*. Pittsburgh: Concept Gallery, 2018.

Pejić, Bojana. *Gender Check: Femininity and Masculinity in the Art of Eastern Europe*. Vienna: Museum Moderner Kunst Stiftung Ludwig Wien, 2009.

Reilly, Maura, and Linda Nochlin, eds. *Global Feminisms: New Directions in Contemporary Art*. London: Merrell Publishers, 2009.

Richardson, John. *Jenny Saville: Continuum*. Rizzoli International Publications and the Gagosian Gallery, 2012.

Robinson, Hilary, ed. *Feminism-Art-Theory 1968–2014*, Hoboken: Wiley-Blackwell, 2015.

Silva, Bisi, and Kristina van Dyke, eds. *The Progress of Love*. Houston and Lagos: The Menil Collection and Centre for Contemporary Arts, 2012.

Singh, Dayanita. *Myself, Mona Ahmed*. Zürich: Scalo Publishers, 2001.

Steinmetz, Julia, Heather Cassils, and Clover Leary. "Behind Enemy Lines: Toxic Titties Infiltrate Vanessa Beecroft," *Signs: Journal of Women in Culture and Society*, Vol. 31, no.3 (2006).

Taylor, Meg, ed. *I'm Not Myself At All: Deirdre Logue and Allyson Mitchell*. Kingston: Agnes Etherington Art Centre, 2015.

Westen, Mirjam, ed. *Rebelle: Art & Feminism, 1969–2009*. Arnhem: Musem voor Moderne Kunst, 2009–10.

Wilson, Martha. "The Personal Becomes Political in Time," *n.paradoxa: International Feminist Art Journal*, Vol. 5 (2000).

Picture Credits

Every effort has been made to trace the copyright holders of the artworks in this book. In order for any errors or omissions to be corrected in future editions, please contact The Elephant Book Company Ltd.

P9: *EAT HERE*, installation view at Schirn Kunsthalle Frankfurt, 2015–16; photographer credit: Norbert Miguletz; image courtesy Heather Phillipson; **P10T:** Candice Lin & Patrick Staff, *Hormonal Fog* (study), 2016, hacked fog machine, dried herbs, herbal tincture, wood, plastic, and miscellaneous hardware. Dimensions variable. Courtesy the artists, from the installation at Witchy Methodologies, ICA, 2017. Photo by Nicholas Tudor; **P10B:** Sondra Perry, *Resident Evil*, 2016. Installation view at The Kitchen, New York. Photo: Jason Mandella. Courtesy of The Kitchen, New York; **P14:** Mary Evans Picture Library; **P17T:** National Gallery of Art Washington; Gift of Mrs. Charles S. Carstairs; **P17B:** Metropolitan Museum of Art, New York; Gift of Cornelius Vanderbilt, 1887; **P18T:** Bridgeman Images/Royal Collection Trust © Her Majesty Queen Elizabeth II, 2018; **P18B:** Bridgeman Images/Philadelphia Museum of Art, Pennsylvania, PA, USA / Purchased with the Director's Discretionary Fund, 1976; **P20:** Getty Images/VCG Wilson/Corbis; **P21:** Metropolitan Museum of Art, New York; Gift of Max N. Berry, 2015; **P22L:** Bridgeman Images/Manchester Art Gallery, UK; **P22R:** Bridgeman Images/Musée d'Orsay, Paris, France; **P23L:** Alamy/Paul Fearn; **P23R:** Library of Congress, Prints & Photographs Division, LC-USZC4-1542; **P25:** AKG Images; **P26:** chrisdorney/Shutterstock.com; **P27L:** Smithsonian American Art Museum, Gift of Joseph S. Sinclair; **P27R:** Bridgeman Art Library/Saint Louis Art Museum, Missouri, USA / American Art Purchase Fund; **P29TL:** Metropolitan Museum of Art, New York; Gilman Collection, Purchase, Harriette and Noel Levine Gift, 2005; **P29TC:** The J. Paul Getty Museum; **P29TR:** The J. Paul Getty Museum; **P29BL:** Library of Congress, Prints & Photographs Division, LC-DIG-ppmsca-38981; **P29BC:** Library of Congress, Prints & Photographs Division, LC-USZ62-83111; **P29BR:** Library of Congress, Prints & Photographs Division, LC-DIG-ppmsca-38271; **P30:** Bibliothèque Nationale de France; **P31TL:** Library of Congress, Prints & Photographs Division, LC-DIG-ppmsca-38276; **P31TC:** Library of Congress, Prints & Photographs Division, LC-DIG-ppmsca-38282; **P31TR:** Library of Congress, Prints & Photographs Division, LC-DIG-ppmsca-43194; **P31BL:** University of Southampton 1894: https://archive.org/details/krl00000763; **P31BC:** Heidelberg University Library, supporting images from Mary Evans; **P31BR:** Heidelberg University Library, supporting images from Mary Evans; **P33TL:** Mary Evans Picture Library/Everett Collection; **P33TR:** National Portrait Gallery, Smithsonian Institution; **P33BL:** Bridgeman Images/Royal Collection Trust © Her Majesty Queen Elizabeth II, 2018; **P33BR:** Bridgeman Images/National Museum in Cracow, Poland; **P34T:** Heidelberg University Library; **P34BL:** Mary Evans Picture Library; **P34BR:** LSE Women's Library; **P35:** Victoria & Albert Museum, London, Prints, Drawings & Paintings Collection; **P36:** Getty Images/Ken Florey Suffrage Collection/Gado; **P39TL:** Library of Congress, Prints & Photographs Division, LC-DIG-ppmsca-12512; **P39BL:** LSE Women's Library; **P39R:** Alamy/Pictorial Press Ltd; **P40T:** LSE Women's Library; **P40BL:** LSE Women's Library; **P40BR:** LSE Women's Library; **P42L:** Harvard University, Schlesinger Library on the History of Women in America, W602279_1; **P42R:** Mary Evans Picture Library; **P43:** Alamy/Everett Collection; **P44:** Getty Images/Museum of London/Heritage Images; **P45TL:** LSE Women's Library; **P45TR:** LSE Women's Library; **P45B:** LSE Women's Library; **P47:** LSE Women's Library; **P48L:** Getty Images/Museum of London/Heritage Images; **P48R:** Harvard University, Schlesinger Library on the History of Women in America, W602277_1; **P49:** Library of Congress, Prints & Photographs Division, LC-USZC4-5806; **P51TL:** Library of Congress: https://lccn.loc.gov/05028628; **P51TR:** Archive.org; **P51CR:** Alamy/Heritage Image Partnership Ltd; **P51B:** Mary Evans Picture Library/(c) The March of the Women Collection; **P52TL:** Mary Evans Picture Library/Everett Collection; **P52TR:** Archive.org; **P52BL:** National Womans Party/Nina Allender; **P52BR:** Virginia Commonwealth University (VCU) Libraries; **P53:** Alamy/ClassicStock; **P54:** Mary Evans Picture Library/(c) The March of the Women Collection; **P55L:** Bibliothèque Nationale de France; **P55R:** Mary Evans Picture Library; **P57L:** © Museum of London; **P57R:** © Museum of London; **P58:** Getty Images/K.J. Historical/Corbis; **P61:** © Imperial War Museum (Art.IWM ART 2850); **P62T:** National Archives and Records Administration; **P62BL:** Mary Evans Picture Library/© The March of the Women Collection; **P62BR:** Mary Evans Picture Library/© *Illustrated London News Ltd*; **P64L:** © Imperial War Museum (Art. IWM ART 3051); **P64R:** Georgia O'Keeffe (American, 1887–1986) *The Flag*, 1918 Watercolor on paper Sheet: 11 15/16 x 8 13/16 in. (30.32 x 22.38 cm) Framed: 23 x 17 x 1 ½ in. (58.42 x 43.18 x 3.81 cm) Milwaukee Art Museum, Gift of Mrs Harry Lynde Bradley, M1977.132 Photographer credit: Larry Sanders, © Georgia O'Keeffe Museum/Artists Rights Society (ARS), New York; **P65:** courtesy Australian War Memorial Archive and the estate of Hilda Rix Nicholas; **P66:** Mary Evans Picture Library/© The March of the Women Collection; **P67:** Molly Lamb Bobak, *Private Roy*, Canadian Women's Army Corps; CWM 19710261-1626, Beaverbrook collection of War Art, Canadian War Museum; **P69L:** Library of Congress, Prints & Photographs Division, LC-USZC4-11361; **P69R:** Library of Congress, Prints & Photographs Division, LC-DIG-ppmsca-40985; **P70:** Mary Evans Picture Library/Onslow Auctions Limited; **P71TL:** Library of Congress, Prints & Photographs Division, LC-USZC4-3357; **P71TC:** Mary Evans Picture Library/Courtesy of The Land of Lost Content Collection; **P71TR:** Library of Congress, Prints & Photographs Division, LC-USZC4-11192; **P71B:** Getty Images/Photo 12/UIG; **P73TL:** Getty Images/Bettmann; **P73TR:** © Imperial War Museum (Q98431); **P73BL:** © Imperial War Museum (Q66153); **P73BR:** Library of Congress, Prints & Photographs Division, LC-DIG-ppmsca-50596; **P74:** Mary Evans Picture Library; **P77TL:** Library of Congress, Prints & Photographs Division, LC-USZC2-904; **P77TR:** Mary Evans Picture Library/© *Illustrated London News Ltd*; **P77B:** Getty Images/Bettmann; **P78TL:** Getty Images/Bettmann; **P78BL:** Bridgeman Images/Jersey Heritage Collections; **P78R:** Lois Mailou Jones Pierre-Noel Trust and Bequest of the Artist Smithsonian American Art Museum, Washington, D.C./ Art Resource, NY/Scala, Florence; **P80L:** © Tate, London 2018; **P80R:** Isabel Bishop, *Tidying Up*, 1941 Oil on Masonite 15 x 11 ½ inches © Estate of Isabel Bishop. Courtesy of DC Moore Gallery, New York/Bridgeman Images/Indianapolis Museum of Art at Newfields, USA /Delavan Smith Fund; **P81:** Metropolitan Museum of Art, New York; Robert Lehman Collection, 1975; **P82:** Bridgeman Images/© DACS 2018; **P83:** Popova, Liubov Sergeievna (1889–1924): *Painterly Architectonic*, Digitale (1) 1917. New York, Museum of Modern Art (MoMA). Oil on canvas, 31½ x 38 ⅝' (80 x 98 cm). Philip Johnson Fund. Acc. n.: 14.1958.© 2018. Digital image, The Museum of Modern Art, New York/Scala, Florence; **P85L:** Mary Evans Picture Library/Imagno; **P85R:** © Tamara Art Heritage / ADAGP, Paris and DACS London 2018. Photo: AKG Images/MPortfolio / Electa; **P86:** Bridgeman Images/Private Collection / Photo © Christie's Images; **P87:** © Banco de México Diego Rivera Frida Kahlo Museums Trust, Mexico, D.F. / DACS 2018. Photo: Bridgeman Images/Museo de Arte Moderno, Mexico City, Mexico / De Agostini Picture Library / G. Dagli Orti; **P89TL:** Getty Images/A.H. Fish/Condé Nast; **P89TR:** Mary Evans Picture Library / Peter & Dawn Cope Collection; **P89BL:** Mary Evans Picture Library/*Harper's Bazaar*/Hearst; **P89BR:** Getty Images/Helen Dryden/Condé Nast; **P90 x4:** Mary Evans Picture Library/© *Illustrated London News Ltd*; **P91:** Topfoto/Ullstein Bild; **P94:** © DACS 2018. courtesy MACBA Collection. MACBA Consortium, © Eulàlia Grau, VEGAP, Barcelona, 2018, Photographer: Tony Coll; **P97:** Courtesy Mierle Laderman Ukeles and Ronald Feldman Gallery, New York; **P98L:** Courtesy of Barbara T. Smith and The Box, LA.; **P98TR:** Courtesy Ann Hamilton Studio. Photo: Wayne McCall; **P98BR:** Photo © Andrew Whittuck. Courtesy Daily Life Ltd.; **P100:** © Sonia Boyce. All Rights Reserved, DACS/Artimage 2018. Image: © Arts Council Collection, Southbank Centre; **P101T:** Courtesy © Moongift Films; **P101B:** © Carrie Mae Weems. Courtesy of the artist and Jack Shainman Gallery, New York; **P102L:** Su Richardson; **P102R:** National Museum in Wrocław, Photo: Marek Gardulski © Bettina Bere ; **P103:** Ree Morton (1936–1977), *Signs of Love*, 1976. Acrylic, oil, colored pencil, watercolor, and pastel on nitrocellulose-impregnated canvas, wood, and canvas with felt, dimensions variable. Whitney Museum of American Art, New York; gift of the Ree Morton Estate 90.2a-n. © Estate of Ree Morton. Courtesy Alexander and Bonin, New York Photo: Sheldan C. Collins; **P105:** Courtesy of Marta Minujín and Henrique Faria, New York & Buenos Aires; **P106T:** Alamy/Everett Collection; **P106B:** Courtesy of the Harvard Film Archive; **P107T:** Courtesy of the California Institute of the Arts Institute Archives; **P107B:** © Martha Rosler, courtesy LUX Distribution; **P108-9:** Courtesy Joyce Kozloff and DC Moore Gallery, New York; **P111L:** Courtesy Faith Ringgold; **P111R:** ©1971 Faith Ringgold / ARS, NY and DACS, London 2018. Collection Rose M Singer Center, Rikers Island, NY. Courtesy Faith Ringgold; **P112T:** Copyright Penny Slinger; **P112B:** *Triplice Tenda*, 1969–1971 AM2005-281 Accardi Carla (1924–2014) © DACS 2018. © ADAGP, Paris Localisation: Paris, Centre Pompidou – Musée national d'art moderne – Centre de création industrielle. Photo (C) Centre Pompidou, MNAM-CCI, Dist. RMN-Grand Palais / Georges Meguerditchian; **P113:** © ARS, NY and DACS, London 2018. © Tate, London 2018; **P114:** Wadsworth Atheneum Museum of Art, Hartford, CT, Alexander A. Goldfarb Contemporary Art Acquisition Fund © The Estate of Lee Lozano. Courtesy Hauser & Wirth; **P117TL:** Courtesy Suzanne Lacy and Leslie Labowitz. Photo Maria Karras; **P117BL:** © Sheila Levrant de Bretteville; **P117R:** Hackney Flashers Collective; **P118TL:** © Yoko Ono. Courtesy Galerie Lelong & Co., New York; **P118TR:** © Mona Hatoum. Courtesy Kunstmuseum St. Gallen (Photo: Stefan Rohner); **P118BL&R:** © Sanja Iveković Courtesy: Kontakt. The Art Collection of Erste Group and ERSTE Foundation; **P120:** British Library Images; **P121TL:** Private Collection; **P121TR:** Private Collection; **P121BL:** LSE Women's Library; **P121BR:** Courtesy archivesautonomies.org; **P122L&R:** © See Red Women's Workshop; **P123L:** *Masawi Huqooq* (1983–84), poster for Women's Action Forum, offset print, 68.6 × 48.3 cm © Lala Rukh Courtesy the estate of Lala Rukh; **P123R:** *Crimes Against Women* (1985), poster for Women's Action Forum, offset print, 67.3 × 44.5 cm © Lala Rukh Courtesy the estate of Lala Rukh; **P125:** Nancy Spero *Letter to Lucy R. Lippard*, 1971 October 29. Lucy R. Lippard papers, 1930s–2010, bulk 1960s–1990. © The Nancy Spero and Leon Golub Foundation for the Arts/DACS, London/VAGA, NY 2018. Courtesy Archives of American Art, Smithsonian Institution.; **P126:** COPYRIGHT: BARBARA KRUGER. COURTESY: MARY BOONE GALLERY, NEW YORK; **P127:** Holzer, Jenny (b. 1950): *Untitled (Because There is No God)*, from digitale (3)(A) Inflammatory Essays, 1979/82. Offset lithograph in black on pale blue wove paper, 542 x 542 mm. Gift of David C. and Sarajean Ruttenberg, 1998.914.9.. Chicago (IL), Art Institute of Chicago. © 2018. The Art Institute of Chicago / Art Resource, NY/ Scala, Florence © Jenny Holzer. ARS, NY, and DACS, London 2018; **P129L:** © Lea Lublin; **P129TR:** © Lea Lublin; **P129BR:** Photo by Aimé Dartus / INA via Getty Images; **P130L:** © Thalia Campbell, *Greenham*

Common Women's Peace Camp on loan from The Peace Museum; **P130R**: Private Collection. © 2018. White Images/Scala, Florence; **P131T**: Hengameh Golestan, *Untitled* (Witness '79 series), photograph, 1979, Tehran © Hengameh Golestan, courtesy of the artist and Archaeology of the Final Decade; **P131B**: Getty Images/Hulton-Deutsch Collection/CORBIS; **P133**: © Chila Kumari Burman. Private Collection. Photo: Andrew Barklem; **P134T**: Barbara Jones-Hogu, *High Priestess*, 1970, screenprint on paper, 37 x 26 in. © Estate of Barbara Jones-Hogu, courtesy of Lusenhop Fine Art; **P134B**: Courtesy Howardena Pindell and Garth Greenan Gallery, New York; **P135**: © Catlett Mora Family Trust/DACS, London/VAGA, NY 2018; **P136**: Collection: Arts Council, UK. Courtesy of Mary Kelly and Pippy Houldsworth Gallery, London; **P139TL**: © Ulrike Rosenbach VG Bildkunst; **P139TR**: H-371; BIA Collection Property Transfer, 1971; Courtesy of the Museum of Contemporary Native Arts, Santa Fe, NM; **P139B**: Edelson, Mary Beth (b. 1933): *Some Living American Women Artists* Digitale (1)(A)1972. Cut-and-pasted gelatin silver prints with crayon and transfer type on printed paper with typewriting on cut-and-taped paper, 28¼ x 43" (71.8 x 109.2 cm). Purchased with funds provided by Agnes Gund, and gift of John Berggruen (by exchange).Inv. n.: 4.2010. New York, Museum of Modern Art (MoMA). © 2018. Digital image, The Museum of Modern Art, New York/Scala, Florence Courtesy David Lewis, New York; **P140T**: © Guerrilla Girls, courtesy guerrillagirls.com; **P140BL**: © Judy Chicago. ARS, NY and DACS/Artimage, London 2018. Photo: © Donald Woodman; **P140BR**: Louise Bourgeois *THE DESTRUCTION OF THE FATHER*, 1974 Latex, plaster, wood, fabric, and red light 237.8 x 362.3 x 248.6 cm. Collection Glenstone © The Easton Foundation/DACS, London/VAGA, NY 2018. Photo: Rafael Lobato; **P142**: © Paz Errazuriz; **P143** x4: © Tina Keane, courtesy LUX Distribution; **P144L**: Courtesy Georgia Scherman Projects and Suzy Lake; **P144R**: © Geta Brătescu. Courtesy Hamburger Kunsthalle, Hamburg, 2016 and Hauser & Wirt. Photo: Kay Reichers.; **P145T**: From the Rose Garrard Archive; **P145B**: Bridgeman Images/ Bradford Museums and Galleries; **P147T**: Getty Images/Citizens of the Planet/UIG; **P147B**: Photo by Tom Powel Imaging. Courtesy Lévy Gorvy and Thomas Erben Gallery. © Senga Nengudi; **P148**: Saar, Betye (b. 1926): *Black Girl's Window*. 1969. New York, Museum digitale (1)(A) of Modern Art (MoMA). Wooden window frame with painted pasted paper, lenticular print, framed photograph, and plastic figurine, 35¾ x 18 x 1½" (90.8 x 45.7 x 3.8 cm). The Modern Women's Fund and Committee on Painting and Sculpture Funds. Inv. nr.: 549.2013© 2018. Digital image, The Museum of Modern Art, New York/Scala, Florence Courtesy of the artist and Roberts Projects, Los Angeles, California.; **P149L**: © The Estate of Ana Mendieta Collection, LLC. Courtesy Galerie Lelong & Co.; **P149R**: Courtesy Betsy Damon. Photo: Su Friedrich; **P151**: Courtesy of Helena Almeida. Image courtesy Galerie Hubert Winter; **P152T**: Rosemary Mayer: *The Catherines*, 1973, Nylon, cheesecloth, pellon, fiberglass rayon, ribbon, dyes, wood, and acrylic paint 116 x 48 x 48 inches. © The Estate of Rosemary Mayer Photo credit: Shireen Abrishamian; **P152B**: Courtesy of Cindy Sherman and Metro Pictures, New York; **P153T**: © Adventure Pictures Ltd; **P153B**: © Dorothy Iannone, Courtesy of Dorothy Iannone and Air de Paris, Paris; **P154**: Courtesy of Lubaina Himid, Nottingham Contemporary and Hollybush Gardens. Photo: Andy Keate; **P155**: Copyright Maud Sulter, courtesy of V&A Prints, Drawings & Paintings Collection; **P156**: Theresa Hak Kyung Cha: *Aveugle Voix*, 1975; performance, 63 Bluxome St., San Francisco (rehearsal: UC Berkeley Greek Theater); University of California, Berkeley Art Museum and Pacific Film Archive; gift of the Theresa Hak Kyung Cha Memorial Foundation. Photo: Trip Callaghan; **P159T**: Courtesy Yve Lomax; **P159BL&R**: Courtesy Marie Yates; **P160L**: Hesse, Eva (1936-1970): *Ringaround Arosie*, 1965. New York, Museum Digitale (1)(A) of Modern Art (MoMA). Pencil, acetone, varnish, enamel paint, ink, and cloth covered electrical wire on papier-mache and masonite, 26⅜ x 16½ x 4½" (67 x 41.9 x 11.4 cm). Fractional and promised gift of Kathy and Richard S. Fuld, Jr. Acc. n.:240.2005.© 2018. Digital image, The Museum of Modern Art, NewYork/Scala, Florence © The Estate of Eva Hesse. Courtesy Hauser & Wirth Photo: Abby Robinson, New York; **P160R**: Lynn Hershman Leeson; **P162T**: Courtesy Annea Lockwood. Photo by Geoff Adams; **P162B**: Courtesy Anne Bean; **P163L**: Courtesy Gee Vaucher; **P163R**: © Linder Courtesy of the artist and Blum & Poe, Los Angeles/New York/Tokyo and Stuart Shave/Modern Art, London; **P165T**: Pauline Boudry/Renate Lorenz, *To Valerie Solanas and Marilyn Monroe, In Recognition of Their Desperation - - - -*, 2013 (film still, courtesy of the artists); **P165B**: Courtesy Roaratorio Records. Artwork by Judith Lindbloom ; **P166**: © Alina Szapocznikow, courtesy of Piotr Stanislawski and Museum of Art in Łódź; **P167T**: © Maria Lassnig Foundation; **P167B**: Copyright The Estate of Rose Finn-Kelcey and Courtesy The Estate of Rose Finn-Kelcey; **P168**: © 1976 Eunice Golden; **P169**: Photo by Tom Powel Imaging. Courtesy Lévy Gorvy and Thomas Erben Gallery. © Senga Nengudi; **P171**: © Veronica Ryan © Tate, London 2018; **P172**: Artwork Courtesy Kazuko Miyamoto and EXILE; **P173L**: © Zarina; Courtesy of the artist and Luhring Augustine, New York. Photo: Lamay Photo; **P173R**: Courtesy Howardena Pindell and Garth Greenan Gallery, New York.; **P175** x3: © Courtesy of the Gupta + Singh Archive; **P176** x3: Courtesy of Carolee Schneemann, Galerie Lelong & Co., and P•P•O•W, New York © Carolee Schneemann. Photo: Anthony McCall; **P177**: Copyright Renate Bertlmann. Courtesy of Richard Saltoun Gallery; **P180**: Rex Dingler, Flickr/Creative Commons; **P183**: *It's What's Inside That Counts* 2017, (Film stills) 30 min Digital Video Rachel Maclean; Commissioned HOME, University of Salford Art Collection, Tate, Zabludowicz Collection, Frieze Film and Channel 4; **P184TL**: Courtesy of Ursula Biemann; **P184TR**: Courtesy Betsy Damon; **P184B**: muf architecture / art; **P186T**: © Studio Claire Fontaine. Courtesy of Claire Fontaine and Lisson Gallery. Photo credit: Matthew Andrews; **P186B**: Copyright Maria Friberg Courtesy Connersmith, Washington DC; **P187**: Courtesy Vanessa Beecroft and Ronald Feldman Gallery, New York; **P188T**: © Sonia Khurana; Photo by Katerina Valdiva Bruch.; **P188B**: *Dream City—More, Better, Sooner*, (video still) Alice May Williams, 2016. Commissioned for the Jerwood/FVU Awards 2016: Borrowed Time, a collaboration between Jerwood Charitable Foundation and Film and Video Umbrella. In association with CCA: Centre for Contemporary Arts, Glasgow and University of East London. FVU is supported by Arts Council England; **P189**: © Suzanne van Rossenberg, courtesy the artist.; **P190T**: © Elizabeth Stephens and Annie Sprinkle; *Madam and Eve* 2008, sexecology.org Photo: Greg Archer; **P190B**: © Elizabeth Stephens and Annie Sprinkle; *Pollination Pod* 2015–16, theecosexuals.org ; **P191**: © Patricia Piccinini, *The Young Family* 2002; courtesy of the artist and Roslyn Oxley9 Gallery, Sydney.; **P193**: Alamy/ EduStarts / Splash News; **P194T** & inset: Courtesy Micol Hebron; **P194B**: Amalia Ulman, *Excellences & Perfections* (Instagram Update, 1st June 2014), 2015. Courtesy the Artist and Arcadia Missa; **P195T**: Courtesy VNS Matrix; **P195B**: Image courtesy of Hito Steyerl and Andrew Kreps Gallery, New York; **P197**: © Maite Arberas. Azkuna Zentroa. Courtesy Xabier Arakistain; **P198TL**: Courtesy of Bisi Silva and Centre for Contemporary Art (CCA), Lagos; **P198TR**: Private Collection; **P198B**: © Varsha Nair; **P199**: © Varsha Nair; **P200**: Prop, 1993 (oil on canvas), Saville, Jenny (b.1970) © Jenny Saville. All rights reserved, DACS 2018/ Private Collection / Photo © Christie's Images / Bridgeman Images; **P203L**: ORLAN / Photo © Marcello Mencarini / Bridgeman Images; **P203R**: © Frances Murray; **P204T**: Photo Credit: Michael Miranda AGYU, Image Courtesy Allyson Mitchell and Deirdre Logue ©; **P204B**: Courtesy Xiao Lu; **P206T**: Photographed by Prudence Cumming Associates at Anthony d'Offay Gallery, London, 1993 © Janine Antoni; Courtesy of the artist and Luhring Augustine, New York.; **P206B**: Courtesy Rosy Martin; **P207T&B**: Courtesy of Katarzyna Kozyra Foundation; **P209T**: 1974 photograph by Victor Hayes 2008 photograph by Michael Katchen, Courtesy of the artist and P.P.O.W.; **P209B**: Compositing Artist Kathy Grove Courtesy of the artist and P.P.O.W.; **P210**: Courtesy the artist and Anton Kern Gallery, New York; **P211L**: Photo by Ken Hively/*Los Angeles Times* via Getty Images; **P211R**: © Del LaGrace Volcano, Self-Portrait Collaboration with Gérard Rancinan I, Paris, 2004, 24 x 24 in., digital c-print, photography courtesy Del LaGrace Volcano and Gérard Rancinan; **P213TL**: © Lenka Clayton; **P213BL**: © Lenka Clayton; **P213R**: © Lenka Clayton. Photo: Tom Little; **P214** x3: © Elżbieta Jablońska; **P215T**: Image courtesy of Marni Kotak and Microscope Gallery; **P215B**: © Catherine Opie, Courtesy Regen Projects, Los Angeles; **P216L**: Courtesy of Shadi Ghadirian and Yavuz Gallery; **P216R**: Alamy/Birgit Koch/Fotosonline; **P217T**: Courtesy Melanie Bonajo & AKINCI; **P217B**: Courtesy Dayanita Singh and Frith Street Gallery, London; **P218**: © Ellen Gallagher Courtesy the artist and Hauser & Wirth; **P221**: © Ellen Gallagher Courtesy the artist and Hauser & Wirth; **P222T**: © Zineb Sedira. All Rights Reserved, DACS 2018; **P222BL**: Copyright Shirin Neshat Courtesy the artist and Gladstone Gallery, New York and Brussels; **P222BR**: Copyright Shirin Neshat Courtesy the artist and Gladstone Gallery, New York and Brussels; **P224T**: Courtesy of Talwar Gallery © Estate of Rummana Hussain; **P224B**: © Fiona Foley, courtesy the artist; **P225** x4: Courtesy of Kimsooja Studio; **P226T**: © CANAN; **P226B**: © Ghada Amer. Courtesy Cheim & Read, New York; **P227T&B**: © Jeannette Ehlers; **P229T&B**: © Tania Bruguera; **P230L**: Courtesy of the artist Tamara Moyzes © Tamara Moyzes; **P230R**: © Šejla Kamerić. Courtesy Galerie Tanja Wagner, Berlin. (Photo: Tarik Samarah); **P231**: © Milica Tomić; **P232** x3: © Ghazel & ADAGP Courtesy of Ghazel; **P233T&B**: Parastou Forouhar/ Pi Artworks London; **P235TL&R**: Courtesy of Vanessa German; **P235B**: Courtesy of Vanessa German and Pavel Zoubok Gallery, New York; **P236**: Courtesy Rachael House; **P237L**: Courtesy Andrea Fraser; **P237R**: © Molly Crabapple 2011; **P239** x4: Keep It Complex; **P240T**: Sharon Hayes, In the Near Future, 2009, detail. Courtesy of the artist and Tanya Leighton Gallery; **P240B**: ©Photo: Eduardo Aparicio; **P241** x2: © Regina José Galindo; **P242** x 3: Courtesy of Lida Abdul and Giorgio Persano Gallery; **P243T**: Photographic credit Sandra Johnston; **P243B**: © Jenny Holzer. ARS, NY and DACS, London 2018; **P244**: Getty Images/Jessica Rinaldi/*The Boston Globe*; **P247**: Reuters/Jonathan Bachman; **P248L**: Courtesy Zoe Leonard, Hauser & Wirth, New York and Galerie Gisela Capitain, Cologne; **P248R**: © Paula Rego, *Triptych*, 1998 (pastel on paper mounted on aluminum), Rego, Paula (b.1935) / Private Collection / Bridgeman Images; **P250TL**: Women on Waves; **P250BL**: Women on Waves; **P250R**: COPYRIGHT: BARBARA KRUGER. COURTESY: MARY BOONE GALLERY, NEW YORK; **P251**: Image courtesy of Andrea Bowers and Andrew Kreps Gallery, New York; **P253TL**: Photo: David Rych Copyright: Ostojić / Rych; **P253BL**: Photo: Ursula Mayer Courtesy: Tanja Ostojić; **P253R**: Photo: Borut Krajnc Courtesy: Tanja Ostojić; **P254**: Alamy/ITAR-TASS News Agency; **P255T**: Courtesy Teresa Margolles and Galerie Peter Kilchmann, Zurich; **P255B**: Getty Images/ Charlie Shoemaker; **P256L&R**: Courtesy Mujeres Públicas; **P257T**: Getty Images/Tristan Fewings; **P257B**: Getty Images/Matthew Chattle/Barcroft Images / Barcroft Media; **P259** x3: © Zanele Muholi. Courtesy of Stevenson, Cape Town/Johannesburg and Yancey Richardson, New York; **P260T**: Getty Images/ Photo by Michel Stoupak/NurPhoto; **P260B**: Getty Images/ ERIC FEFERBERG/AFP; **P261**: Alamy/Joerg Boethling.

Index

Note: Page numbers in *italics* refer to the captions to illustrations.

Biographies and acknowledgments

Consulting Editor: Helena Reckitt is a curator, lecturer, and cultural organizer with broad international experience in the field of contemporary visual art. She is currently Reader in Curating in the Art Department at Goldsmiths, University of London, United Kingdom, having previously taught at institutions including Atlanta College of Art and Emory University, Georgia, United States, and York University, Toronto, Canada. In 2011 Helena was the Clark Collection Critic and Curator in Residence at the University of Victoria in Wellington, New Zealand. Other previous roles include Senior Curator of Programmes, the Power Plant, Toronto (2006–10); Senior Director of Exhibitions and Education, Atlanta Contemporary Art Center, Atlanta, Georgia (2002–05); Head of Talks/Deputy Director of Talks, Institute of Contemporary Arts, London (1990–98); and Associate Commissioning Editor, Film and Performance Studies, Routledge, London (1988–90). Reckitt has edited the books *Art and Feminism* (Phaidon Press, 2001), *Acting on AIDS* (Serpent's Tail, 1998, with Joshua Oppenheimer), and *Sanja Iveković: Unknown Heroine, A Reader* (Calvert 22, 2013).

Consultant, Part 1: Maria Elena Buszek is Associate Professor of Art History at the University of Colorado, Denver, United States. She was previously Assistant Professor of Art History, School of Liberal Arts, Kansas City Art Institute and Curatorial Assistant at the Los Angeles County Museum of Contemporary Art, California. She is coeditor of *A Companion to Feminist Art Practice and Theory* (Blackwell-Wiley) and the author of *Pin-Up Grrrls: Feminism, Sexuality, Popular Culture* (Duke University Press). She also won the Lo Presti Prize: Best Essay Collection for her *Extra/Ordinary: Craft and Contemporary Art*.

Author Part 1: Lucinda Gosling is Head of Sales and Research at the Mary Evans Picture Library, London, United Kingdom. She has more than two decades of experience in curating, managing, and developing historical and international archives. She has written widely on the visual arts of the nineteenth and early twentieth centuries, including on the impact the two world wars had on women's roles.

Author Part 2: Amy Tobin is Faculty Lecturer in the History of Art, University of Cambridge, and Curator at Kettle's Yard, Cambridge, United Kingdom. Her research looks at the history of feminist-influenced art and the possibilities of feminist futures. She completed her PhD at the University of York in 2017 with a thesis titled "Working Together, Working Apart: Feminism, Art and Collaboration in Britain and North America, 1970–1981." She has taught Modern and Contemporary Art and Theory at the Universities of York and Birmingham and Goldsmiths College, London, United Kingdom.

Author Part 3: Professor Hilary Robinson is Professor of Feminism, Art, and Theory at Loughborough University, United Kingdom. Her teaching and research focuses on feminist art theory, and publications include *Visibly Female: Women and Art Today* (1987); *Reading Art, Reading Irigaray: The Politics of Art by Women* (2006); *Feminism-Art-Theory 1968–2014* (2015), and (with Maria Buszek) *The Companion to Feminist Art* (2019). Hilary's academic career has unfolded in Belfast, Northern Ireland; Pittsburgh, Pennsylvania, United States; and London, United Kingdom. At the University of Ulster (1992–2005) she taught art theory to studio students. She became Professor of the Politics of Art and subsequently Head of School for Art & Design. In 2005 Hilary was appointed Dean of the College of Fine Arts and Professor of Art Theory and Criticism at Carnegie Mellon University, Pittsburgh, Pennsylvania. While in Pittsburgh she also served as a board member for The Andy Warhol Museum and The Mattress Factory Museum for Contemporary Art. She moved back to the United Kingdom in 2012 to become Dean, School of Art and Design, Middlesex University, before taking up her present position in 2017.

Author acknowledgments
Lucinda Gosling would like to thank editor Anna Southgate for her patience and vigilance and Helena Reckitt and Joanna de Vries for their advice and suggestions.

Amy Tobin would like to thank the following for their contributions: Alice Correia, a Research Fellow in Art History at the University of Salford, U.K. Dr. Correia specializes in modern and contemporary British art, with a particular interest in feminist and postcolonial practice; Flora Dunster, a PhD candidate in drama, theater, and performance studies, at the University of Sussex, U.K. Dunster considers the development and impact of the "Sex Wars," with a focus on lesbian lens-based media in the United Kingdom, and its influence on queer theory and feelings; Irene Revell, a curator whose work across contemporary art, sound, performance, and moving image seeks out new contexts and connections for practices with challenging social and political implications (Irene would like to thank the Pauline Oliveros Trust); Catherine Spencer, a Lecturer in Modern and Contemporary Art in the School of Art History at the University of St Andrews. Spencer's essays have appeared in *Art History, Tate Papers, British Art Studies, and Oxford Art Journal*; Rachel Warriner, a teacher of Art History at City and Guilds of London Art School, U.K. Dr. Warriner completed her PhD at University College Cork on feminist art and politics in 1970s New York.

Hilary Robinson would like to thank her coworkers on this book; the members of Write-Read-Write, a feminist art writers group; all those who identify as feminists; and all the artists whose work help keep her sane and focused on the issues.